ROUTLEDGE HANDBOOK OF SUSTAINABLE DESIGN

Routledge Handbook of Sustainable Design considers the design, not only of artifacts, but of structures, systems, and interactions that bear our decisions and identities in the context of sustaining our shared planet. In addressing issues of design for global impact, behavior change, systems and strategy, ethics and values, this handbook presents a unique and powerful design perspective.

Just as there are multiple definitions of design, so there are several definitions of sustainability, making it difficult to find unity. The term can sometimes be seen as a goal to achieve, or a characteristic to check off on a list of criteria. In actuality, we will never finish being sustainable. We must instead always strive to design, work, and live sustainably. The voices throughout this handbook present many different characteristics, layers, approaches, and perspectives in this journey of sustaining.

This handbook is divided into five sections, which together present a holistic approach to understanding the many facets of sustainable design:

- Part 1: Systems and design
- Part 2: Global impact
- Part 3: Values, ethics, and identity
- Part 4: Design for behaviour change
- Part 5: Moving forward

This handbook will be invaluable to those wishing to broaden their understanding of sustainable design and to students and practitioners of environmental studies, architecture, product design and the visual arts.

Rachel Beth Egenhoefer is a designer, artist, writer, and professor whose work integrates technology, craft and design. Her work focuses on sustainability and systems thinking in the context of behaviour change. As an educator, she is involved in several initiatives to promote sustainability in both the design field and across higher education curricula. Egenhoefer is an associate professor of design in the Department of Art + Architecture at the University of San Francisco.

"A timely book that (finally) situates design within a systems context. Diverse articles examine the social and environmental implications of designed images, artifacts, systems and structures in a globally inter-connected and interdependent world as well as the ethics and values that underpin them. Essential reading for designing responsibly in the 21st century."

— **Terry Irwin**, Head, School of Design, Carnegie Mellon University

"This compelling collection is an outstanding resource for people who see design as a tool that can be used to create a better civilization, whether they be practitioners, students, researchers, or enthusiasts. Egenhoefer reminds us of our responsibility to use our professional skills and opportunities to not just do good design, but to do good!"

— **David Berman**, RGD, FGDC, Sustainability Chair, Icograda/ico-D

"The comprehensive and anticipatory nature of this book is profoundly informative and operationally useful in ways that previous books have not been. It is by being so comprehensive on the front end that we designers can mitigate the Law of Unintended Consequences that has so often plagued the practice of design.

While this book is aimed at designers, it would also be useful for political leaders, policy makers and theoretical thinkers in any field. As a society, we are woefully silo-ed by profession, nationality and paradigm. This condition does not accrue to our collective benefit. Any approach that seeks to dismantle this myopic state of affairs will persevere. This book seeks to do just that."

— **Peter Dean**, Co-Founder and Concentration Coordinator, Nature Culture Sustainability Studies Concentration, Rhode Island School of Design (RISD)

"We are only beginning to explore how design can create the conditions for net positive change throughout society. This handbook shows how design thinking is breaking out of its past boundaries to have a positive influence on all aspects of theory, practice and being."

— **Janis Birkeland**, Professor, University of Melbourne, author of Design for Sustainability and Positive Development

"Sustainability does not have meaning independent from what needs to be sustained, and this need is an object of environmental, economic, political and philosophical contestation. It follows that the concept, and its associated practices begs vigorous debate. This book makes a contribution to the substance of such a debate."

— **Tony Fry**, The Studio at the Edge of the World and University of Tasmania

"This is essential reading for those beginning to explore sustainable design. Rachel Beth Egenhoefer has taken a unique approach to illustrating both the breadth and depth of the field. The structure around five themes provides very different perspectives and enables the reader to understand how the approach of design and sustainability together can begin to make real change in the world."

— **Tracy Bhamra**, Pro Vice-Chancellor and Professor of Sustainable Design, Loughborough University, UK

"*Routledge Handbook of Sustainable Design* pushes design beyond artifacts, common definitions and methodologies. Instead, it advances the discourse to a more impactful, holistic and systemic level, incorporating a much-needed variety of voices, perspectives, and ideas that challenge the designer's ever-changing role and responsibility in a complex, interconnected and uncertain world."

— **Mike Weikert**, Director, Center for Social Design + Master of Arts in Social Design, Maryland Institute College of Art

ROUTLEDGE HANDBOOK OF SUSTAINABLE DESIGN

Edited by Rachel Beth Egenhoefer

Routledge
Taylor & Francis Group

LONDON AND NEW YORK

First published 2018
by Routledge
2 Park Square, Milton Park, Abingdon, Oxon OX14 4RN

and by Routledge
711 Third Avenue, New York, NY 10017

Routledge is an imprint of the Taylor & Francis Group, an informa business

British Library Cataloguing-in-Publication Data
A catalogue record for this book is available from the British Library

Library of Congress Cataloging-in-Publication Data
Names: Egenhoefer, Rachel Beth, editor.
Title: Routledge handbook of sustainable design / edited by Rachel Beth Egenhoefer.
Other titles: Handbook of sustainable design
Description: Abingdon, Oxon ; New York, NY : Routledge, 2017.
Identifiers: LCCN 2017006575 | ISBN 9781138650176 (hbk) | ISBN 9781315625508 (ebk)
Subjects: LCSH: Sustainable design
Classification: LCC NK1520 .R683 2017 | DDC 745.4—dc23
LC record available at https://lccn.loc.gov/2017006575

ISBN: 978-1-138-65017-6 (hbk)
ISBN: 978-1-315-62550-8 (ebk)

Typeset in Bembo
by Apex CoVantage, LLC

Printed and bound in Great Britain by
TJ International Ltd, Padstow, Cornwall

CONTENTS

Acknowledgements   *ix*

List of contributors   *x*

Introduction   1
Rachel Beth Egenhoefer

1 The political economy of design in a hotter time   3
David W. Orr

PART 1

Systems and design   **11**
(Section introduction, Rachel Beth Egenhoefer)

2 Systems thinking for design   13
Diana Wright and Marta Ceroni

3 Design strategies for impact   27
John Bruce

4 Applied sustainability   40
*Wendy Jedlička, Jeremy Faludi, Pete Markiewicz, Tim Frick
and Mark McCahill*

5 Sustainable design for scale   55
Andrea Steves and Rebecca Silver

6 Systems and service design and the circular economy 73
Rhoda Trimingham, Ksenija Kuzmina and Yaone Rapitsenyane

7 Ecological theory in design: participant designers in an age of entanglement 86
Joanna Boehnert

PART 2
Global impact 99
(Section introduction, Rachel Beth Egenhoefer)

8 Global perspectives for sustainable design 101
Douglas Bourn

9 Politics and sustainability 115
Harold Wilhite

10 Design for localization 125
Helena Norberg-Hodge

11 Intercultural collaborations in sustainable design education 135
Denielle Emans and Kelly M. Murdoch-Kitt

12 Life-cycle thinking and sustainable design for emerging consumer electronic
product systems 148
Erinn G. Ryen, Callie W. Babbitt and Alex Lobos

13 Data clouds and the environment 170
Arman Shehabi

14 Increasing urban sustainability using GIS 179
*Luiz Felipe Guanaes Rego, Maria Fernanda Campos Lemos and
Luís Carlos Soares Madeira Domingues*

PART 3
Values, ethics, and identity 191
(Section introduction, Rachel Beth Egenhoefer)

15 Empathy, values, and situated action: sustaining people and planet
through human centered design 193
Bruce Hanington

16 Practicing empathy to connect people and the environment 206
Theresa J. Edmonds

17 Surrendering to the ocean: practices of mindfulness and
    presence in designing   219
    Yoko Akama

18 Confronting the five paradoxes of humanitarian design   231
    Brita Fladvad Nielsen

19 Codesigning for development   250
    Maria Rogal and Raúl Sánchez

20 The Internet of life: changing lifestyles and sustainable values in
    fast-developing China and India   263
    Benny Ding Leong and Brian Lee

21 Fashion, the city, and the spectacle   281
    Dilys Williams

22 Designing individual careers and work environments for sustainable value   295
    Cynthia Scott

PART 4
Design for behaviour change   **313**
(Section introduction, Rachel Beth Egenhoefer)

23 An introduction to design for sustainable behaviour   315
    Casper Boks

24 How design influences habits   328
    Tang Tang and Seahwa Won

25 The temporal fallacy: design and emotional obsolescence   348
    Jonathan Chapman and Giovanni Marmont

26 Discourse design: the art of rhetoric and the science of persuasion   357
    Marilyn DeLaure

27 Using data visualization to shift behaviors   372
    Adam Nieman

28 Securing sustainability: culture and emotions as barriers to
    environmental change   387
    Allison Ford and Kari Marie Norgaard

29 Nature-based design for health and well-being in cities 399
    Angela Reeve, Cheryl Desha and Omniya El Baghdadi

PART 5
Moving forward   **415**
(Section introduction, Rachel Beth Egenhoefer)

30 How many ways to design for sustainability? 417
    Fabrizio Ceschin and Idil Gaziulusoy

31 The structure of structural change: making a habit of being alienated
    as a designer 433
    Cameron Tonkinwise

32 Empowering citizens through design 446
    Diamond James

33 Biomimicry: nature inspiring design 459
    Denise K. DeLuca

34 The value of the sharing economy 470
    Brhmie Balaram

35 Going from STEM to STEAM 483
    Sara Kapadia

36 Design for the circular economy 498
    Ruud Balkenende, Nancy Bocken and Conny Bakker

Index *515*

ACKNOWLEDGEMENTS

In the course of editing this book many profound changes occurred, from the personal to the global. I am incredibly thankful for the hard work, dedication, innovation, and patience from the many contributors to this publication. Throughout this process, a team of individuals worked passionately on their contributions while also giving birth, tending to sick family members, battling illness, moving across continents, campaigning for or protesting against elections, and working tirelessly on a plethora of other projects. The experience of working with so many individuals across our shared planet has constantly reminded me that we are all human, filled not only with our research but also with compassion.

I am grateful to Khanam Virjee, Rebecca Brennan, Kelly Watkins and everyone at Routledge for their assistance and patience in this project and for their eagerness to continue to promote *Sustainable Design*. Special thanks also to Rhoda Trimingham and Kristin Hughes who provided additional editorial support.

I am thankful to the University of San Francisco for their financial and academic support of this project, as well as for promoting sustainability and social justice in higher education. I am fortunate to be surrounded by colleagues who encourage holistic understandings of the design practice, and who advance my knowledge of sustainability across many disciplines. My students continually challenge me to extend my teaching and research efforts in the field.

Most importantly, this book would not have been possible without my husband, Kyle Jennings, who encouraged me and supported me through every step of this process from the first idea to the final word. And lastly, to our daughters, Henrietta and Willamina; every day you give me more reason to work toward a sustainable future.

CONTRIBUTORS

Yoko Akama is a Japanese design researcher and associate professor in the School of Media and Communication, RMIT University, Melbourne, Australia. She is the recipient of several major research grants in Australia and the United Kingdom and winner of the prestigious Good Design Australia Award in 2014.

Callie W. Babbitt is an associate professor in the Golisano Institute for Sustainability at Rochester Institute of Technology, where she conducts research to proactively quantify and minimize environmental impacts of emerging technologies. Callie's research group creates new methods and models in the field of industrial ecology that are inspired by the study of ecological systems in nature. They apply these models to study sustainability challenges and solutions for food waste management, consumer electronics, lithium-ion batteries, electric vehicles, and nanomaterials. Callie holds an MS and PhD in Environmental Engineering from the University of Florida and a BS in Chemical Engineering from Georgia Institute of Technology.

Omniya El Baghdadi, PhD, is a faculty member in the Science and Engineering Department and the Institute for Future Environments at the Queensland University of Technology.

Conny Bakker is an associate professor of circular product design in the Industrial Design Engineering department of Delft University of Technology. Her research areas include Design for the Circular Economy; developing design methods and strategies for product life-extension, reuse, remanufacturing and recycling; as well as the business models that enable these strategies.

Brhmie Balaram is Senior Researcher at the Royal Society for the Encouragement of Arts, Manufactures and Commerce (RSA).

Ruud Balkenende is Professor of Circular Product Design in the Industrial Design Engineering department of Delft University of Technology. His research focuses on methodical and technological aspects of design for circular economy.

Nancy Bocken is Associate Professor of Sustainable Business Model Development in the Industrial Design Engineering department of Delft University of Technology. Her research areas include sustainable business models, systems change, and closing the idea–action gap in sustainability.

Joanna Boehnert, PhD, is a research fellow in design at CREAM (Centre for Research and Education in Arts and Media) at the University of Westminster and the founder of EcoLabs. Her research focuses on how design communicates complex ecological and socioeconomic issues and facilitates transitions to sustainable ways of living. She established EcoLabs in 2006 to work at the interface of social movements and design practice. She is a Canadian who works in London and lives by the sea in Margate.

Casper Boks is a professor of design for sustainability in the Department of Design of NTNU Norwegian University of Science and Technology. Casper's research areas include design for sustainable behaviour and practices, and implementation of design for sustainability in industry. Casper has recently published in journals such as *Journal of Cleaner Production, Journal of Design Research, International Journal of Sustainable Engineering*, and *International Journal of Design*.

Douglas Bourn is Director of the Development Education Research Centre at University College London – Institute of Education. His research areas are global learning within formal education, global perspectives and global citizenship with higher education, and global skills. He has published widely on the theme of learning about global issues within formal education and global skills in vocational and higher education.

John Bruce is a professor of strategic design at Parsons School of Design, The New School. John's research areas include end of life, media, and collaboration. John has recently directed the film *End of Life*.

Marta Ceroni, PhD, is the director of programs at the Academy for Systems Change in Norwich, Vermont. She earned a PhD in ecology from the University of Parma, Italy. Marta focuses on cultivating system leadership for deep social change.

Fabrizio Ceschin is a senior lecturer in the Department of Design at Brunel University London, with ten years of research and teaching experience in the area of design for sustainability, with a particular focus on sustainable product-service systems, distributed economies, and sustainability transitions. His last book is *Sustainable Product-Service Systems: Between Strategic Design and Transition Studies*.

Jonathan Chapman is a Professor and Director of the Doctoral Program at Carnegie Mellon University's School of Design. His sustainable design teaching, research, and consultancy has advanced thinking in a range of settings, from Sony, Puma, and Philips to the House of Lords and the UN. He is the author of several books, including: *Emotionally Durable Design* and *Routledge Handbook of Sustainable Product Design*.

Marilyn DeLaure is an associate professor of communication studies and environmental studies at the University of San Francisco. Her research investigates how people effect social change; she has published essays on dance, civil rights rhetoric, and environmental activism. She is coeditor of *Culture Jamming: Activism and the Art of Cultural Resistance*, and coproducer of a documentary film about cargo cycling titled *Motherload*.

Denise K. DeLuca, PE, is an independent consultant and educator in the field of biomimicry, teaches biomimetic design in the Masters of Sustainable Design program for the Minneapolis College of Art & Design, is the education director at the International Living Future Institute, and is author of the book *Re-Aligning with Nature: Ecological Thinking for Radical Innovation*. DeLuca earned her bachelor's degree from the University of Wisconsin-Madison College of Engineering, and her master's from the Montana State University College of Engineering.

Cheryl Desha is Associate Professor at Sciences Group and Cities Research Institute, Griffith University, and Adjunct Professor at Science and Engineering Faculty and Institute for Future Environments at the Queensland University of Technology.

Luís Carlos Soares Madeira Domingues is a researcher in the field of urban ecology at the Oswaldo Cruz Foundation and a professor of urban design in the Department of Architecture and Urbanism, Pontifical Catholic University of Rio de Janeiro – PUC.

Theresa J. Edmonds is an independent researcher and facilitator in the field of sustainable design. She has a BS in mechanical engineering from Olin College, and an MA from Creighton University.

Rachel Beth Egenhoefer is the design program director and an associate professor at the University of San Francisco. Her work as an artist, designer, writer, and professor explores sustainability and systems thinking in relation to interaction design and behavior change.

Denielle Emans is a professor of graphic design at Virginia Commonwealth University in Qatar and a PhD candidate within the Centre for Communication and Social Change at the University of Queensland in Brisbane, Australia. She holds a master's degree in graphic design from North Carolina State University's School of Design and a bachelor of arts in communications from the University of North Carolina, Chapel Hill.

Jeremy Faludi, LEED AP BD+C, is a sustainable design strategist and researcher, and Assistant Professor of Sustainable Design Engineering at Dartmouth College.

Allison Ford is a doctoral candidate in the sociology department of the University of Oregon; she also holds an MA in international environmental policy from the Middlebury Institute of International Studies. Her research areas include environment, culture, emotions, and gender.

Tim Frick is CEO of Mightybytes, speaker, and author of four books, including *Designing for Sustainability: A Guide to Building Greener Digital Products and Services*.

Idil Gaziulusoy is a design researcher and a sustainability scientist. She is Assistant Professor of Sustainable Design in the Department of Design at Aalto University. İdil's research areas include design and sustainability transitions, urban futures, and frontiers of design for sustainability field.

Bruce Hanington is Associate Professor and Director of Graduate Studies in the School of Design at Carnegie Mellon University. He is coauthor of *Universal Methods of Design: 100 Ways to Research Complex Problems, Develop Innovative Ideas, and Design Effective Solutions*.

Diamond James is an independent researcher in the field of social design. She has a master of arts in social design from the Maryland Institute College of Art. Her design practice explores the intersection of race, class, and design in American cities.

Wendy Jedlička, IoPP–CPP, ISSP–SA, is principal of Jedlička Design, and lecturer on design, business, and sustainability at Minneapolis College of Art & Design and University of Wisconsin – Stout.

Sara Kapadia is an independent researcher in the field of educaton, STEAM, and early childhood development. Sara earned bachelor's degree from the University of Cambridge, her master's degree from University of London, and her PhD from Claremont Graduate University where she founded and runs the open–access, art–science, peer reviewed publication *The STEAM Journal*: scholarship.claremont.edu/steam

Ksenija Kuzmina, PhD, is a lecturer in design innovation and management at Loughborough University in London. Her research interests cover service design methodologies, social innovation, systems thinking, and circular economy thinking.

Brian Lee is an assistant professor in the School of Design, Hong Kong Polytechnic University. Lee's research areas include co-creation, sustainable product design, design for elderly, and user interaction in public space. Lee has recently published "A Reflection on Designing Participatory Design Workshop – Case Study of Elderly Product Development Workshop with Multidisciplinary Collaboration" and "Park Furniture Design in Hong Kong: A Case Study of Inclusive Design and Its Relation to User Interaction."

Maria Fernanda Campos Lemos is a professor of urban design and planning in the Architecture and Urbanism Department of Pontifical Catholic University of Rio de Janeiro. Lemos's research areas include urban sustainability and resilience and cities' adaptation for climate change.

Benny Ding Leong is an assistant professor of the School of Design, Hong Kong Polytechnic University. His research areas include lifestyle design research, design for sustainability (DfS) and people-centered design. He has recently published "Learning the Unlearned: Product Design for Sustainability" and "Future Shade of Green: Introduction to the Practice of Product Design for Sustainability."

Alex Lobos is Associate Professor and Graduate Director of Industrial Design, as well as extended faculty at Golisano Institute for Sustainability, all at Rochester Institute of Technology, NY. His work focuses on sustainability, emotional attachment, and user-centered design. Alex holds an MFA from the University of Notre Dame and a BID from Universidad Rafael Landivar.

Pete Markiewicz, PhD, is an instructor at The Art Institutes in Santa Monica, CA specializing in development for games, software, and the Web. In addition to teaching, he is a WebVR UX developer, and author on a variety of topics including US generations.

Giovanni Marmont is a PhD researcher and lecturer at the University of Brighton, whose research lies at the intersection of material culture studies, philosophy of technology, and political theory. His most recent work explored the politics of acts of improvised use through Heidegger, Agamben, and the Situationist International (publication forthcoming, 6th STS Italia Conference).

Mark McCahill is one of the Internet's pioneers (Internet Gopher, POPmail, Croquet Project). He currently works at Duke University's Office of Information Technology as an architect of 3D learning and collaborative systems.

Kelly M. Murdoch-Kitt is an Assistant Professor in the Penny W. Stamps School of Art & Design at the University of Michigan, Ann Arbor. Her recent pedagogic research collaborations explore methods, tools, and benefits of effective intercultural design collaboration. She is also exploring the impacts of integrating sustainability challenges into project-based design courses.

Brita Fladvad Nielsen, PhD, is a post-doctoral researcher of design thinking at the Department of Urban Planning at the Norwegian University of Science and Technology (NTNU). Her research areas include design thinking as a research approach, particularly focusing on the area of humanitarian design around the area of sustainable energy.

Adam Nieman is one of the founders of Real World Visuals, a data visualisation company that specialises in engaging new audiences. His PhD research focused on the visual culture of science.

Helena Norberg-Hodge is the director of Local Futures. A pioneer of the "new economy" movement, she is a recipient of both the Goi Peace prize and the Right Livelihood Award, or "Alternative Nobel Prize." She is the producer of the award-winning *The Economics of Happiness* and author of *Ancient Futures*.

Kari Marie Norgaard is an associate professor of sociology and environmental studies at the University of Oregon. Her work explores the social organization of denial, and environmental justice for Native American tribes on the Klamath River. Her book, *Living in Denial: Climate Change, Emotions and Everyday Life*, documents the importance of emotions in environmental and social change.

David W. Orr is Paul Sears Distinguished Professor Emeritus, Counselor to the President, Oberlin College.

Yaone Rapitsenyane, PhD, is a sustainable design researcher and educator in the Department of Industrial Design and Technology, Faculty of Engineering and Technology at the University of Botswana.

Angela Reeve, PhD, is a faculty member in the Science and Engineering Department and the Institute for Future Environments at the Queensland University of Technology.

Luiz Felipe Guanaes Rego is a professor in the Department of Geography and is the director of The Interdisciplinary Center for the Environment of the Catholic University of Rio de Janeiro (NIMA/PUC-RIO). His research interests include models of the geographic space in GIS to support the analyses, activities, and monitoring of sustainable land use at the local level.

Maria Rogal is Professor of Design in the School of Art + Art History at the University of Florida. Her research areas include social design, design theory, and intercultural design. Her publications include "Decolonizing Graphic Design" in the *11th European Academy of Design Conference Proceedings* and "Identity and Representation: (Yucatec) Maya in the Visual Culture of Tourism" in the *Latin American and Caribbean Ethnic Studies Journal*. She is the founder of Design for Development, a design research initiative with projects in the United States and México.

Erinn G. Ryen, PhD, is a visiting assistant professor at Rochester Institute of Technology Department of Public Policy. Erinn's research areas focus on adapting models and concepts from natural ecological systems to find new ways to evaluate the life-cycle impacts of our industrial systems, as well as design policies, business models, and technologies to encourage sustainable practices and behaviors. Erinn holds a PhD in sustainability from the Golisano Institute of Sustainability at Rochester Institute of Technology, MPA in environmental policy and administration from Syracuse University, MS in environmental resource engineering from SUNY College of Environmental Science and Forestry, and a BS in applied economics and business management from Cornell University.

Raúl Sánchez is Associate Professor of English at the University of Florida. His research interests include composition studies, rhetorical theory, cultural studies, and decolonial theory. With Iris D. Ruiz, he recently coedited *Decolonizing Rhetoric and Composition Studies: New Latinx Keywords for Theory and Pedagogy*. He is the author of *The Function of Theory in Composition Studies* and *Inside the Subject: A Theory of Identity for the Study of Writing*.

Cynthia Scott, PhD, MPH, is a professor of sustainable leadership at the Presidio Graduate School. Cynthia's research areas include stress prevention, change leadership, and social entrepreneurs. Cynthia has recently published *Leadership for Sustainability and Change*.

Arman Shehabi, PhD, is a research scientist in the Energy Analysis and Environmental Impacts Division at Lawrence Berkeley National Laboratory. He has over 15 years' experience measuring and modeling the energy and air quality implications of building design, with extensive research focused on the information and communication technology (ICT) sector.

Rebecca Silver serves as the assistant director of the NYU Entrepreneurial Institute, where she leads operations and major programs, and supports entrepreneurs focused on socio-environmental challenges. Rebecca is also adjunct faculty at both the School of Visual Arts and Parsons School for Design, teaching entrepreneurship, design, and sustainability.

Andrea Steves is an independent artist and researcher based in Oakland, California. She has an MBA in nonprofit management/sustainability from the University of Michigan and an MFA from University of California–Santa Cruz in digital arts and new media.

Tang Tang, PhD, is a lecturer in sustainable design in the School of Design at the University of Leeds, UK. She specialises in user-centred design for sustainable behaviour. Her current research interests include design for emotion and well-being, participatory and codesign for social sustainability, and transformation design. Tang has recently published a book chapter "Design Interventions for Sustainable Behaviour," and a research paper "Design Research Collaboration Workshops: A Methodology for Research Collaboration and Activity Planning."

Cameron Tonkinwise is Professor of Design at UNSW Art and Design. Cameron's research areas include service design, social design, and sharing economies. Cameron has recently published a number of articles mapping the practice of transition design.

Rhoda Trimingham, PhD, is a senior lecturer in the Design School at Loughborough University. Her research interests are in sustainable design, including product service systems, packaging, and global human development.

Harold Wilhite is Professor Emeritus at the University of Oslo, Center for Development and the Environment.

Dilys Williams is a professor of fashion design for sustainability at London College of Fashion, University of the Arts, London. Dilys established and is director of the Research Centre for Sustainable Fashion, where she explores social and ecological design in fashion's personal, industrial, and educational spheres.

Seahwa Won completed her PhD on color information in design, and worked on a project that explored packaging design opportunities for healthy eating at the University of Leeds, UK. She is currently an independent researcher in the field of design and consumer behavior.

Diana Wright, MS, is an independent researcher and technical editor in the fields of systems and sustainability. She earned a master of science in natural resources from the University of Michigan. Diana focuses on how we understand and talk about the systems around us through research and analysis as well as editing and publications development.

INTRODUCTION

Rachel Beth Egenhoefer

Designing sustainably

"Sustainability is a cultural problem; it is about how we live in the world," writes Dilys Williams in her chapter *Fashion, the city, and the spectacle*. As designers, we are the ones creating this world. Design is not limited to images and objects, but also includes the systems and structures that surround them. It is not just product, fashion, graphic, web, or architectural design, but also the cultural and personal associations with objects and interactions, the politics and economies that give rise to global industries; it is the connections to and within these larger systems. It is what we value, how we choose to spend our time, money, and energy. And all of these things have been designed.

Design is a creative tool, an active process, an ever-changing end result. Today's designer must embrace a holistic practice that goes beyond any distinct medium, for the products, systems, and services that we create exist and interact within a larger world. Therefore, an array of disciplines informs and encompasses design, and design also enlightens the areas around it.

It is essential to view design as a problem-solving tool, and humanity's effect on the planet is perhaps the most significant trial at stake. The *Routledge Handbook of Sustainable Design* considers the design, not only of artifacts, but also of structures, systems, and interactions that bear our decisions and identities in the context of sustaining our shared planet. In addressing issues of design for global impact, behavior change, systems and strategy, ethics and values, this handbook presents a unique and powerful design perspective.

Just as there are multiple definitions of design, so there are many definitions of sustainability, making it difficult to find unity in this diversity. In fact, one thing that many contributors to this book have in common is their reluctance to use the word 'sustainability.' The term can sometimes be seen as a goal to achieve, or a characteristic to check off on a list of criteria. In actuality, we will never finish being sustainable. We must instead always strive to design, work, and live sustainably. We must do this in a way that not only replenishes the resources we use, but also nourishes the world around us physically, emotionally, and culturally. The voices throughout this handbook present many different characteristics, layers, approaches, and perspectives in this journey of sustaining.

The *Routledge Handbook of Sustainable Design* is divided into five sections:

Part 1: Systems and design
Part 2: Global impact
Part 3: Values, ethics, and identity
Part 4: Design for behaviour change
Part 5: Moving forward

Together these themes present a holistic approach to understanding the many facets of sustainable design. *Systems and design* introduces the reader to systems thinking – understanding the many connections between the components of a design and the design process. Understanding how to identify, work with, and leverage these connections is key to understanding the greater impact of design and sustainability. *Global impact* focuses on the effects design has on local and global scales. From broad overviews to specific product systems, this section presents considerations of how design decisions affect every individual who touches a product, from design and extraction, to use, and disposal. *Values, ethics and identity* considers how design relates to individual and collective values. It challenges us to slow down and contemplate how to align meaning and doing. *Design for behavior change* looks at different components that affect our actions as both designers and consumers. Understanding these nuances allows us to design smarter and more meaningful outcomes. Finally, *Moving forward* presents ideas and philosophies for the future as we continue to live, design, and interact with finite resources on our shared planet.

Throughout the process of compiling this book, I was often reminded of the humanistic aspects of research. Just as design is a holistic process, we are holistic people. The researchers and practitioners who contributed to this book are also parents, siblings, spouses, companions, friends, teachers, and students. They are gardeners, painters, bakers, hikers, swimmers, musicians, and more. They are introverts and extroverts, living in urban and rural areas, from cultures near and far to them. These relationships, passions, characteristics and customs define who we are in conjunction with our professional selves. No discussion of sustainability would be complete if it didn't include this personal aspect, for we need to sustain ourselves in order to sustain others. We need to laugh and cry, hear and be heard. I hope that you, the reader, consider this as you interact with this book and your practice of sustainable design.

We know, at present, that our global society is depleting natural resources at an unprecedented rate. Temperatures are rising, ice is melting, storms are coming. The future remains unclear. Just as the design process can be, it is scary and exciting, daunting and inspiring. Now, more than ever, we must embrace the wild ride before us and design sustainably.

1

THE POLITICAL ECONOMY OF DESIGN IN A HOTTER TIME

David W. Orr

Design is all the rage. We wear designer jeans; some of us live in designer houses; a few drive cars with designer interiors. Buyers of luxury houses and buildings pay "starchitects" sizeable fees to design buildings that defy gravity, conventional geometry, and human scale. Some propose to redesign our genes by means liberated from sexual selection unhindered by philosophy or the piddling constraints of convention. The goal is super-human perfection, but the more likely result would be the geneticists' version of an arms race. Others are designing the means to further expedite consumption by tailoring our electronically tracked proclivities to the expanding bazaar of commercial opportunities. The goal is higher profits. Whatever you want someone will design it for you but at a price high enough to exclude the great majority of humanity and without any thought for those who will follow us and will find their grasp on life, liberty, and happiness made more tenuous by previous design decisions.

Missing in the buzz about design are flesh and blood people and the long-term effects of the design choices being made. The poor and disadvantaged are conspicuously absent from the articles and advertisements in airbrushed architectural and design magazines. Missing, too, is a thoughtful analysis of the fine print of the deal where, it is said, the devil resides. What are the social, ecological, and spiritual implications of various design choices? How might these affect the prospects of other species and future generations? And nowhere in the high-tech fluff and puffery do human fallibility, ignorance, and our propensity for goof ups raise their not-so-perfect heads.

The ironies stack up like cordwood. For one, we pay lots of money to visit the historic cities of Europe precisely because their cramped old towns with crooked, narrow streets and ancient buildings retained much of their charm and attraction because they grew, imperfections and all, much as Jane Jacobs once explained, by trial and error. They grew incrementally to meet particular needs in specific places, not as the result of the grand design schemes of logical and linear minds of men like Robert Moses and le Corbusier with their straight lines, motorized transport, and efficiencies tailored to the needs of the hurried class.

No reasonable person can deny the need for intelligent design, particularly as it reduces material, water, and energy use, and therefore pollution. But since World War II we discarded much of that kind of older design intelligence and infrastructure. I recall, for example, the light-rail system of Pittsburgh that was once an efficient, dependable, and cheap way to move around the city. My present home, Oberlin, Ohio, was once part of an interurban system that connected many of the cities and towns between Toledo and Cleveland. Light-rail systems like these were dismantled all over the United States not because they were inefficient or unpopular, but because companies like General Motors acquired them in order to put them out of business. We now drive their cars, with umbilical cords that stretch to depleting oil fields in distant places where we are not much appreciated, spend much of our lives caught in traffic jams, burn up our emotional energy in road rages, drive through award-winning ugliness, breathe air contaminated with byproducts of combustion, attend the funerals of the thousands annually killed in highway crashes, continue to pay exorbitant taxes to protect our access to other peoples' oil, and patch over the problems caused by monumental design and planning mistakes attributable to flaws in our political economy by which private mobility and its corporate vendors was deemed better than public mobility. No reasons were given; no vote was ever taken. The market, it was said, had spoken, but in truth the public good was hijacked by corporate pirates in three-piece suits. Advertisers, long-before mobilized to sell cars and automotive accessories, joined in the hijacking and geared up for the post–World War II boom that drove our economy for the next half century by selling chrome-trimmed fantasy, social status, roadside wonders, fast foods, and the promise of excitement just over the next horizon.

In this case the political economy of design was neither political in the sense of being the result of public decisions reached through democratic deliberation, nor economic in any honest way. A great deal of the debt for that half-century binge of individualized, oil-dependent, land-eating, polluting, and democracy-corrupting system of transportation will be passed on to our descendants. Any true accounting of the full costs of our automobile culture also would have to include the role of ExxonMobil and other oil companies in delaying action on climate change that they knew to be a reality as far back as 1977. How many people have died because they lavishly funded four decades of climate denial? How many more will perish in the climate mayhem ahead? How many trillions of dollars of damage might have been avoided had they chosen to lead the transition away from the fossil-fuel-powered system they created? Of necessity there will be an accounting of sorts, but not likely a reckoning with truth and reconciliation because we have neither laws nor institutions to adjudicate lethal malfeasance at this scale.

My point is that all design exists in a larger framework of political economy by which costs and benefits are distributed within society and across generations. Whether we acknowledge them or not, the failure to design with physical and ecological realities incurs irrevocable costs as well. Commercial and industrial designers, however, mostly regard their work as politically and ethically neutral or merely a matter of esthetics and novelty. Steve Jobs, for one, learned how to make computers that were considerably more than tools of computation and communication but rather something designed to light up the pleasure centers of the brain. Jobs, in Sue Halpern's words, used "enchanting theatrics, exquisite marketing, and seductive packaging to convince millions . . . that the provenance of Apple devices was magical, too."[1] Lost in the hype and cultish aspects were the lives of underpaid, exploited workers and the mountains of electronic trash thrown out to buy next year's I-whatever, which Halpern muses "may be the longest-lasting legacy of Steve Jobs' art." As Jobs knew, design has powerful effects.

It is a fact well understood by all designers. "Once people come in," as a software engineer at Instagram reports, "the network effect kicks in . . . then it takes on a life of its own."[2] The goal is to make it "enthralling" and "difficult to put down," in a word, addictive. Every person so addicted faces "1,000 people on the other side of the screen whose job is to break down the self-regulation that you have."[3]

Frank Lloyd Wright once bragged that he could design a house for a newly married couple madly in love that would cause them to divorce in a matter of weeks. But Wright, the architect, would have been able to manipulate only materials, geometry, space, and landscapes. Contemporary designers work with much more powerful tools and sometimes with very bad effects.

In *Addiction by Design*, Natasha Schüll describes the use of design to turn gamblers into gambling addicts. One gaming machine designer, for example, "really knows how to get into the head of a fifty-year-old woman and figure out what she wants." The casino owners who buy his machines only want her money, but he knows that her purse is connected to specific parts of her brain that can be manipulated. "Gambling machines," like those he designs, "are complex calculative devices that operate to redistribute gamblers' stakes in a very precise, calibrated, and 'scientific' way . . . [they] operate as vehicles of enchantment, galvanizing what political theorist Zygmunt Bauman has described as 'human spontaneity, drives, impulses, and inclinations resistant to prediction and rational justification,' or in Weber's words, 'irrational and emotional elements that escape calculation.'"[4] Such machines work in the "fashion of psychostimulants, like cocaine or amphetamines. They energize and de-energize the brain in more rapid cycles." In the words of one gambler, "you're in a trance, you're on autopilot . . . the zone is like a magnet, it just pulls you in and holds you there." As long as you have money that is. "It's our duty," as the CEO of Las Vegas Stratosphere puts it, "to extract as much money as we can from customers." The entire design of the modern casino aims to create a womb to keep gamblers oblivious to everything else, until the wallet is drained. "It is not uncommon," Schüll writes, "to hear of machine gamblers so absorbed in play that they were oblivious to rising flood waters at their feet or smoke and fire alarms that blared at deafening levels . . . or even a dying man at their feet."[5] Severely addicted gamblers will stay at it for twelve hours or longer ignoring all bodily needs to satisfy the craving.

The gambling industry described by Schüll resembles in many ways the larger world of modern advertising that drives consumption. At least since Edward Bernays created the prototype for the modern advertising firm, capitalists have intended to make us dependable and dependent consumers, that is to say consumption addicts by design. The sellers often know more about us than we know of ourselves. They track our behavior: bodily responses to various stimuli, eye motions, and our every flinch and fantasy trolling for any information that might be useful in order to sell us more of what we don't need or don't want but can be made to crave. They have designed a system that orchestrates our fears, phobias, and desires and shapes us into more dependable consumers.

Worse, designers can do work that is purely evil. The designers of Auschwitz and its machinery of extermination, for example, participated in "the greatest crime committed by architects."[6] One can make an even more compelling case against weapons designers who created a world still suspended over the nuclear precipice.[7]

The point is that the art and science of design, in other words, should not be exempted from the standards of morality and decency. Designers now are equipped with powerful tools drawn from the disciplines of psychology, neuroscience, sociology, anthropology, computer science, architecture, and interior design. These can be used to manipulate, deceive, and render dependent, or they could be used to help us undo our addictions and mindless consumption and build a convivial, democratic, fair, decent, healthy, pollution-free, and nonviolent world powered by renewable energy and populated with competent people. There is an important distinction between conventional design, which is simply the making of things to appeal to status needs and transient fashion, and ecological design, which is the skill to make things of value that last and fit harmoniously in their ecological, cultural, moral, and historical context.

The art and science of ecological design has come a long way in the decades since Victor Papenek, Sim van der Ryn, John Todd, John Lyle, Bill McDonough, and others launched the green building revolution. Rapid technological development has made solar and wind technologies competitive with baseload coal almost everywhere and without the many costs of mining, refining, transporting, and burning fossil fuels. The same is true of energy efficiency that could, with more accurate accounting and better policy incentives, eliminate perhaps half or more of our present energy use while providing superior quality in a growing economy. Investment in renewable energy worldwide is growing rapidly, and consistently providing higher and safer rates of return than those in coal, oil, and gas. As a result, it is possible to create buildings and cities powered entirely by improved efficiency and renewable energy.

Ecological design aims to calibrate human actions with the way natural systems work as particular places, larger landscapes, and ecologies. It aims to work with, not against, the flows of energy and natural cycles. It aims to conserve, preserve, and regenerate the basis for life and human flourishing. Architect Stuart Walker writes, "if design is to more effectively address sustainability it has to transcend utility and conventional function-led, and especially technology-led approaches."[8] He calls on designers to rise above "the calculated creation of dissatisfaction" and to "think more comprehensively about the products we already produce and their implications." Design, in other words, must be an act of integration, not just specialization, with the goal of creating wholeness and spiritual well-being.[9] In Robert Grudin's words, design, "unlike any other concept . . . calls for us to create a unity of part with whole, a concord of form and function, a finished product that is harmonious with society and with nature."[10]

By that standard, there are some things that should not be designed. But the distinction between what designers can do and what they should do requires a design ethic to inform professional conduct, rather like the Hippocratic Oath in medicine.[11] Engineer, M. W. Thring, for example, proposes a standard that includes all of the consequences of engineering and design including those affecting "the subjective qualities of human life such as self-fulfillment, happiness, inner freedom and love."[12] Specifically, designers should see all of their work, as engineer Seaton Baxter puts it, as a manifestation of "co-evolution with the natural systems of the world" increasing the quality of life while reducing the consumption of resources.[13]

In summary, the basic rules for ecological design are these:

- maximum use of solar energy
- protect diversity of all kinds
- eliminate waste
- use nature as the model
- make it affordable
- design for repair and disassembly
- build in redundancy and resilience
- maximum public participation, and
- beauty[14]

Design, in other words, is a healing art in the broadest sense of the word. It is no accident that the word *health* is related to the words *holy, whole, holism,* and *healing.* Neither, I think, is it an accident that the root words for religion and ecology imply wholeness and connection. Design should embrace the health of people, ecologies, and social institutions as interacting parts of a larger whole.

Further, good design should increase the reservoir of practical ecological competence at the local level allowing us to do more for ourselves and for each other – the things that we once did better for ourselves as competent people, good neighbors, and active citizens. Excessive dependency has made us less intelligent in many respects. Our smartness has migrated upward into our technologies and systems of technology that are the product of collective intelligence leaving us as individuals clueless. Few, if any, know how these remarkable technologies are made or how they work, let alone how to live without them. Leonard Read's 1958 essay "I, Pencil" illustrates the point by showing that not a single person on Earth knew how to make such a simple thing as a lead pencil, or almost anything else.[15] It is possible, in other words, that our individual competence and perhaps intelligence, too, is inversely proportional to the brainpower that goes into our technologies and systems of all kinds designed by teams of designers, each knowing a small part of the final ensemble and perhaps nothing of the larger system of which it is a part or the effects it may have on the wider culture. As oceanographer Carl Safina puts it, "as a species, we are pretty impressive. But as individuals, most of us, given bolts of cloth wrapped in a bow, couldn't sew a decent shirt."[16]

Good design should help ground us in place. It should inform us of where we are and of the terms of ecology and energy flows by which we are sustained in a particular place. In a world where any one place looks much like any other, we are losing sight of the fine print of our lives and how we are provisioned with food, energy, and materials. We are mostly ignorant of the costs and consequences of the systems that provision us and oblivious to their fragility. Good design should help us know where we are and how to be ecologically competent in that place. Those places should be ecologically designed landscapes with multiple functions to retain water for drought periods, manage floodwater, grow food and fiber, sustain wildlife, and absorb carbon. They should be working landscapes that blend agroforestry, mixed-use permacultures, intensive agricultural and gardening zones, viticulture, aquaculture, water purification, and recreation. And they should be managed by local citizens and used to train young people for lives of growing essentials in managed, integrated ecologies.[17]

Third, ecological design should enhance the opportunities for conviviality, celebration, and direct democracy.[18] Communities with front porches, public squares, community gardens and solar systems, neighborhood stores, corner pubs, and open places of worship are more likely to thrive in a long emergency because they create the conditions favorable to neighborliness, community cohesion, and buffer zones from hardships. And good design will engage people in the making of their homes, neighborhoods, towns, and regions. It should increase our civic intelligence and our joy in life. Designers in this way are facilitators in a larger public conversation and architects of better possibilities, not just makers of buildings, landscapes, and gadgets.

The years of climate chaos ahead will magnify the challenges designers must reckon with. The new normal is now a world of progressively higher temperatures, stronger winds, more frequent and larger storms, rising ocean levels, longer droughts, much larger rainfall events, and new diseases.[19] These, in turn, will cause interruptions in supplies of food, energy, and water and trigger social and political turmoil. We must design in the awareness of the fragility of the present world, as Jared Diamond and others warn. Designers must aim for resilience that both safeguards vital systems under emergency conditions and aids in eventual recovery.

The prospect of future warming to which we are now committed will put a great deal of conventional design into question. Taller buildings are vulnerable to higher wind shear, electricity outages, and terrorists. Sealed buildings work only as long as HVAC systems and complicated electronic controls work, which further depends on uninterrupted electricity, availability of expert managers, and long supply chains. Instead of more of engineering virtuosity, designers should "start re-engineering our aspirations, infrastructures and lifestyles for a softer landing in a post-fossil [fuel] world."[20]

Beginning in neighborhoods, towns, and cities the great work of our generation is to make possible that softer landing in a post-fossil fuel and post-consumer economy in ways that are prosperous, fair, durable, resilient, convivial, and democratic. It must be powered by renewable energy. It must be a circular economy that recycles and reuses its wastes. Of necessity it will be more focused on essentials of food, energy, shelter, clean water, education, and the arts, and be rooted in its place and bioregion. It will be built by local people who cherish and understand their places and the place of nature in a sustainable economy. But it must be a political economy, a product of revitalized grass roots as well. If it is to flourish, it must grow out of the union of ecological competence and the practice of authentic democracy.

For those engaged in the design professions, several conclusions follow. First, architects, engineers, landscape architects, product designers, industrial designers, and ecological designers have been engaged in designing the small components of larger national and global systems. But those larger systems, nonetheless, are trending toward catastrophic failure. However ecologically improved any one building, neighborhood, city, or enterprise may be, the entire system is still trending toward disaster. The problem is not in the particular techniques of design, which have become very sophisticated, but in the haphazard structures – economic, political, social – in which design occurs, which slows the effort to take ecological design to the necessary scale. The rules of the larger system permit changes only at the margins, which is to say only slight adjustments in the coefficients of change but none at the level of social structure and system design. Ecological design then still exists as a patchwork in a larger society, not as a coherent solution to the systemic problems of a capitalist society. In Karl-Henrik Robèrt's words,

> The problem of unsustainability [is rooted in] underlying systemic errors of societal design that will make things *worse and worse* until, in the end, it will be impossible for society to sustain itself. . . . Until the systemic errors are addressed, the very conditions for survival and prosperity will continue to systematically decline.[21]

This leads to a second conclusion: the practice of ecological design must be applied to the larger systems of politics, law, and economics. This might occur by processes of extrapolation and emulation that migrate upward where design infiltrates the normal daily experience. Perhaps we can be instructed by architecture that is a kind of crystallized pedagogy that instructs in many ways. Perhaps we will learn through the cumulative effects of green buildings, solar collectors, electric cars, and the technological paraphernalia of sustainability on our psychology and values. But perhaps not. The relationship between technology, architecture, design, and human behavior is indirect and indeterminate. If it were otherwise, brilliant and lovely architecture long ago would have mellowed our more reptilian behaviors.

To really improve the human prospect the precepts of ecological design must inform our politics, governance, law, and economics, not just buildings, technologies, manufacturing, and landscapes. In that more ecologically shaped world economists, for example, would be regarded as designers of the flows of energy, materials, and wastes constituting the economy. Similarly, legislators, lawyers, government officials, and political theorists would also be thought of as designers of the structures of power, law, and regulation that constitute the scaffolding of society. As designers their mission would be to design social systems that work with, not against, natural processes. Imagine a civilization so artfully and carefully designed that it would protect posterity, ecological processes, and the larger fabric of life on Earth, for as long as one can imagine.

Notes

1 Sue Halpern, "Who Was Steve Jobs?," *New York Review of Books*, January 12, 2012.
2 Natasha Singer, "Can't Put Down Your Device? That's by Design," *New York Times*, December 5, 2015.
3 *Ibid*.
4 Natasha Dow Schüll, *Addiction by Design*. Princeton: Princeton University Press, 2012, p. 77; also John Rosengren, "Betting It All," *The Atlantic Magazine*, December, 2016, pp. 67–78.
5 Dow Schüll, *op. cit.*, p. 35.
6 Robert Jan van Pelt, *The Case for Auschwitz*. Bloomington: University of Indiana Press, 2002; and Jennifer Schuessler, "The Evidence Room: Architects Examine the Horrors of Auschwitz," *New York Times*, June 14, 2016.

7 William Perry, *My Journey at the Nuclear Brink*. Stanford: Stanford Security Studies, 2015. Perry writes that "the gravest security threat of our time is the danger of a nuclear weapon being detonated in one of our cities. That is my nuclear nightmare . . .", p. xiii.

8 Stuart Walker, *Designing Sustainability*. London: Routledge, 2014, p. 35; also Victor Papenek, *Design for the Real World*. 2nd edition. Chicago: Academy Chicago Publishers, 1984/1992, p. 252.

9 Papenek, *op. cit.*, pp. 293–299.

10 Robert Grudin, *Design and Truth*. New Haven: Yale University Press, 2010, p. 131.

11 Steven H. Miles, *The Hippocratic Oath and the Ethics of Medicine*. New York: Oxford, 2004. As Miles explains, the Oath was more than a set of principles. In the world of c. 400 B.C., it was regarded as more binding than a mere verbal promise and something like a social institution, in Miles' telling. If violated, it involved perjury before the Gods, which one may presume is not a good thing to commit, pp. 161–168.

12 M. W. Thring, *The Engineer's Conscience*. London: Ipswich Book Co., 1992, p. 232.

13 Seaton Baxter, "Deep Design and the Engineers Conscience," unpublished, 2005.

14 Sim van der Ryn and Stuart Cowan, *Ecological Design*. Washington, D.C.: Island Press; John and Nancy Todd, *Bioshelters, Ocean Arks, City Farming*. San Francisco: Sierra Club Books, 1996; William McDonough and Michael Braungart, *The Upcycle*. New York: North Point Press, 2013, p. 10; Jay Harman, *The Shark's Paintbrush*. Ashland, OR: White Cloud Press, 2013; Grudin, *op. cit.*, pp. 28–29.

15 Leonard Read, *I, Pencil*. Irvington-on-Hudson: The Foundation for Economic Education, 1958.

16 Carl Safina, *Beyond Words*. New York: Henry Holt, 2015, p. 199.

17 John and Nancy Todd, *From Eco-Cities to Living Machines*. Berkeley, CA: North Atlantic Books, 1993.

18 Randolph T. Hester, *Design for Ecological Democracy*. Cambridge: MIT Press, 2006 is a thorough guide to "ecological democracy" and to the use of design to rebuild the sinews of a coherent, participatory, and therefore resilient society.

19 Sue Roaf, David Chrichton, and Fergus Nicol, *Adapting Buildings and Cities for Climate Change*. 2nd edition, London: Elsevier, 2009; Alisdair McGregor, et al., *Two Degrees: The Built Environment and Our Changing Climate*. London: Routledge, 2013.

20 Roaf, *op. cit.*, p. 344.

21 Karl-Henrik Robèrt, George Basile, Göran Broman, Sophi Byggeth, David Cook, Hördur Haraldsson, Lena Johansson, et al., *Strategic Leadership Towards Sustainability*. 2nd edition, Karlsdrona, Sweden: Psilanders grafiska, 2005, p. 7.

PART 1

Systems and design

Approaching sustainability and design from a holistic perspective, beyond any medium specificity, allows us to see design as a creative problem-solving tool.

Considering the components, interactions, and inflows and outflows of systems of design provides a complete picture of the interconnected relationships that make up a whole. This shift in perception leads us away from individual contributions and presents design within a broader context where it concerns strategy and impact. As a starting point for a holistic systems-oriented design perspective, Part 1 of the *Handbook of Sustainable Design* introduces a range of ideas for reflection.

Diana Wright and Marta Ceroni begin the section with *Systems thinking for design*, a summary of more Donella Meadows's contributions within the context of sustainable design. Meadows' work in systems thinking is among the most influential in environmental sustainability. Wright and Ceroni present a systems-based view of unsustainability and lay out the fundamentals of working with systems. By understanding the larger systems that engage with sustainability and identifying points to intervene, design becomes a catalyst for impact and positive change. Additionally, the chapter poses questions for designers to facilitate a deeper understanding of systems in their work.

Expanding on ideas presented by Wright and Ceroni, John Bruce examines scale, leverage points, and methods in *Design strategies for impact*. Through his work as an artist, designer and educator he asks "How might we consider personal motivations and embodied moments of learning and knowing in relation to collective actions and their accumulation toward the scale of movements for positive systemic change?"

In *Applied sustainability*, Wendy Jedlička and her collaborators, Jeremy Faludi, Pete Markiewicz, Tim Frick and Mark McCahill, present practical applications of systems thinking methodologies in a sustainable design practice. Jedlička et al. introduce practical tools such as Life-cycle Assessment, Impact, and Costing; frameworks and methodologies such as The Natural Step™, ABCD Backcasting, The Living Principals and others. Finally, Jedlička et al. walk the reader through applying various methods to the design process with examples from product design, print and packaging, and digital design.

A key concept to understand when considering systems thinking and sustainable design is scale. Scale is not limited to growth but also includes physical, temporal, geographical, knowledge and paradigm scales. Andrea Steves and Rebecca Silver explore these ideas in *Sustainable design for scale*. Understanding the limits and challenges of working with scale helps designers understand the impact of decisions on a larger perspective. Steves and Silver provide processes and tactics for understanding systems thinking for scale and optimizing design for impact.

As we look at systems, designers can also engage with design services instead of single products. *Systems and service design for the circular economy* by Rhoda Trimingham, Ksenija Kuzmina, and Yaone Rapitsenyane presents this collaborative approach to sustainable design and economy. The Ellen MacArthur Foundation defines the circular economy as "one that is restorative and regenerative by design, and which aims to keep products, components, and materials at their highest utility and value at all times, distinguishing between technical and biological cycles." The authors of this chapter highlight two approaches to working in this sector – designing product service systems instead of just products and reconceptualizing process as a service. Several case studies explore the range of sustainability and business advantages to engaging with service and system design.

Thinking about systems allows us to see all the areas that intertwine with our design. Most notably, in sustainable design, we cross into ecology. As designers working with sustainability, it is also important to understand the context of ecological theory. Joanna Boehnert concludes Part 1 with *Ecological theory in design: participant designers in an age of entanglement*. Unpacking ecological theory and ecological literacy around the participant designer, Boehnert argues that the "participant designer must understand why the political economy matters for regenerative design to enable change on a scale necessary to address society's most severe problems."

Together the concepts presented in Part 1 represent the breadth of ideas in the design practice. For every action, there is a reaction and for every reaction, another place for designers to intervene in the system. Understanding how our designs and actions function in the world is crucial to their success and sustainability.

2
SYSTEMS THINKING FOR DESIGN

Diana Wright and Marta Ceroni

We can't impose our will on a system. We can listen to what the system tells us, and discover how its properties and our values can work together to bring forth something much better than could ever be produced by our will alone.

Donella Meadows (2008)[1]

Sustainability as a systems question

Every day we hear news of record high temperatures, imperiled species and ecosystems, rampant inequality and poverty, and other signs of dysfunctional systems. We also hear news of communities launching renewable energy projects and governments enacting livable city policies or committing to carbon neutrality. Both of these threads – the increasingly obvious impact of industrial humans on the planet and the creative responses of individuals and communities to new challenges – are woven into the life and work of those who design. And design – the act of planning and making – is central to addressing our legacy of environmental impact and moving toward more sustainable ways of living.

Herman Daly,[2] founder of ecological economics, described a sustainable society as one that fills three conditions (Daly, 1990):

- Uses *renewable resources* such as fish and trees at or below the rate at which they regenerate
- Uses *nonrenewable resources* such as minerals, fossil fuels, and fossil water at or below the rate at which renewable substitutes can be put into place
- Emits *pollution and wastes* at or below the rate at which ecosystems can absorb them, recycle them, or render them harmless

The idea of fair access to resources is also key to the social dimension of sustainability. The United Nations Brundtland Commission extended fair access to future generations in defining sustainable development as development that:

- Meets the needs of the present without compromising the ability of future generations to meet their own needs

(United Nations, 1987)

Although we recognize that the word "sustainability" has often been misappropriated and associated with greenwashing, we invite you to recognize the transformational power of these four conditions of sustainability. What if we designed our products and processes so that they satisfied all four of these requirements? Achieving these conditions is truly revolutionary work, and designers play a key role.

Living and operating beyond the capacities of ecosystems and societies to thrive is, essentially, a systems problem. In the words of the late Donella Meadows,

> Unsustainability does not arise out of ignorance, irrationality or greed. It is largely the collective consequence of rational, well-intended decisions made by people caught up in systems – ranging from families and communities to corporations, governments and economies – that make it difficult or impossible to act in ways that are fully responsible to all those affected in the present and to future generations.
>
> *(Meadows, 1998)*

A systems view of unsustainability

Too many of our human-built systems behave unsustainably over time. This was made clear in a pivotal project that traced the root causes and behaviors of unsustainability at the global scale.

In the late 1960s, Italian industrialist Aurelio Peccei and Scottish scientist Alexander King convened a small international group, the Club of Rome, to discuss the dilemma of short-term thinking that leads to what they called the long-term global "problematique" – that cluster of intertwined problems of human poverty and environmental degradation that characterize "the predicament of mankind." They invited Jay Forrester, founder of the new field of system dynamics, to form a team of researchers and computer modelers to dig into the question of why, despite good intentions, diplomacy, and many international development projects, poverty was on the rise, hunger was increasing globally, and ecosystems were being degraded at alarming rates.

System dynamics uses formal mathematical modeling to explore the behavior over time of complex systems. The main lessons from the computer model produced for the Club of Rome are summarized for nonmodelers in the book *Limits to Growth* (Meadows et al., 1972), which was translated into more than 30 languages and sold over 16 million copies (Club of Rome, 2016). The book is one of the best known and accessible systems analyses ever published, and focuses on humanity's choices and the outcomes of those choices on population, economy, and resources on our finite planet.[3] The study was accused of catastrophism because it discussed the possibility of economic and social collapse sometime after 2020–2030 if humanity did not slow down the pace of economic growth and human population. However, the book also explored the policy choices that could lead to a stable world. System dynamics modeling allows exploration of multiple scenarios.

The formal modeling techniques of system dynamics illustrate the long-term unsustainable behavior of key global systems. Systems thinking – the skills to explore, understand, and talk with others about complex systems – is a crucial tool in altering the pieces and the interconnections of those complex systems so we can change their behavior away from unsustainability. This poses unprecedented design and redesign opportunities.

Design and systems

What can design do to help shift us away from unsustainability? A design task often starts with a problem to solve or a need (or desire) to fulfill. We might be asked to design an object or a process, a part of a system or a whole system. How we define the problem and what questions we ask can make the difference between a short-term answer and a long-term sustainable solution.

How we think about problems has a lot to do with the quality of solutions. All too often, we rush through problem solving, overlook the relationships between contributing factors, and fail to elicit and test assumptions before implementing a fix. Systems thinking can help develop questions and illuminate connections that make a difference to both the immediate work and the long-term mission. It provides a holistic design framework for the idea that what to make (or *not* make) and how to make are at the core of creating change toward more sustainable and more equitable ways of living on this planet.

Donella Meadows, lead author of *Limits to Growth*, later wrote "The systems-thinking lens allows us to reclaim our intuition about whole systems and

- hone our abilities to understand parts
- see interconnections
- ask 'what-if' questions about possible future behaviors, and
- be creative and courageous about system redesign."

(Meadows, 2008)

System basics

Stock-and-flow structures, goals, and boundaries

Systems are made up of stocks and flows. The parts of a system that accumulate over time (objects, people, or resources) are referred to in the abstract as stocks. Stocks can be as varied as the number of papers in a folder to the amount of experience in a company's staff to a couple's love for one another. Stocks replenish and deplete through flows of material stuff, energy, or information (Figure 2.1).

A very simple system can illustrate several important points about stocks and flows. Imagine designing a bus stop with a shelter (Figure 2.2). We want the structure to protect people from rain as they wait for the next bus; it is the container for a stock of people (those waiting). The flows of people coming to the bus stop and those leaving on busses determine the size of the stock waiting at any one moment; a stock changes through its inflows and outflows. A small shelter may be fine if busses arrive frequently and predictably (outflow is high) or if very few people come to the bus stop (inflow is low), but it provides very little buffer if busses break down

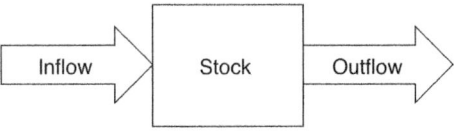

Figure 2.1 Stocks are filled by flows, and drained by flows.

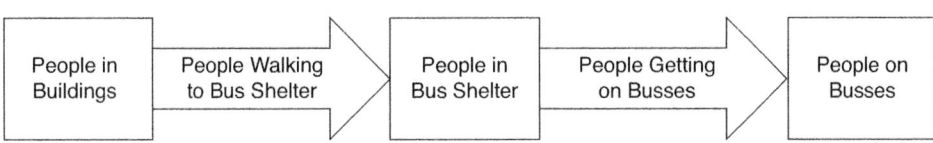

Figure 2.2 People going to the bus shelter, and leaving the bus shelter.

15

or are infrequent. A large bus shelter is a better buffer in a system where the flows of people are large or unpredictable.

Some parts of systems are not tangible material items, yet they are crucial to how the system behaves. Think about the stock of trust a community has in its leaders. This is a reservoir that can be filled and drained just like a water reservoir. Acknowledging such nonmaterial parts of a system and recognizing the interconnections between them and other system elements leads to a fuller picture and a better understanding of possible system behaviors.

In addition to the stocks and flows, the second feature of a system is its purpose, goal, or function. The purpose of a toaster is to produce warm, crisp toast on demand. The goal of a community center is to provide a gathering place with facilities for people to exercise, enjoy performances, or do other kinds of activities. When we look more closely, most things we design sit within a larger system that may pursue a different goal. The higher-level purpose of the toaster may be to make a profit for the manufacturer, or to establish a new fashion in home appliances, or to change the way we think about energy consumption. The greater goal of a community center may be to improve community health, or boost area businesses, or glorify a local politician. The purpose can evolve. As the community center is being built, its purpose is to provide short-term construction jobs or job training for the community; once complete, its purpose shifts to encompass its programs on community health and well-being.

You can see that there is a third aspect of how we talk about systems: boundaries. Very few systems have clear boundaries. The community center donors may require a state-of-the-art, energy-efficient design that reduces energy use and greenhouse gas emissions, but if the building is constructed on the community's only agricultural land, how have you, the designer, contributed to the long-term health and well-being of the community? Have you attained one goal at the expense of another? Is the trade off necessary? Land use planning and policy design are filled with examples of "unintended consequences," unforeseen results that too often are undesirable. The boundaries of the designed system are drawn too narrowly, focusing exclusively on one aspect and excluding other important dimensions. Here's how ecologist Garrett Hardin describes the challenge:

> When we think in terms of systems, we see that a fundamental misconception is embedded in the popular term "side-effects." . . . This phrase means roughly "effects which I hadn't foreseen or don't want to think about." . . . Side-effects no more deserve the adjective "side" than does the "principal" effect. It is hard to think in terms of systems, and we eagerly warp our language to protect ourselves from the necessity of doing so.
>
> *(Hardin, 1963)*

Skill

Identify the stock-and-flow structures, goals, and boundaries of the system in which your design project is situated.

Systems questions

What are the stock-and-flow structures (including nonmaterial stocks) and purpose(s) of the project?
Is it likely that the purpose, goal, or function of the project will change over time?
Does the project sit within a larger system or multiple systems?
What are the system boundaries of the project?
What are potential unintended consequences (both positive and negative) of the project?

Structure creates behavior possibilities

A toaster can heat or cool back to room temperature. It can even catch on fire (an unintended behavior), but it cannot drive down the road. The structure of the toaster system determines the range of possible behaviors, although which behavior manifests at any one time may depend on outside events or forces, such as a person turning on the toaster. The fact that structure drives behavior is a key insight of system analysis.

System structures can produce stable and consistent behaviors, for example when stocks are big relative to the size of their flows. Stocks that don't deplete quickly over time, such as a well-managed bank account or a shop's inventory, act as buffers. In times of uncertainty, we may appreciate such stability. But stability can be undesirable; we may see it as inertia and delay, as when a company has a large number of employees with outdated skills who cannot retrain quickly. Designers may have the opportunity to intervene in their systems, adjusting the size of stocks to find the sweet spot between desirable stability and undesirable inertia.

As we have seen, linking several stocks through flows creates structure. The stock of people waiting at the bus stop is linked to the stock of people on the busses through the flow of people getting on the busses. That bus stop stock is also related to the stock of people in the nearby buildings and streets through the flow of people leaving work or school to catch the bus. We can imagine a fairly simple diagram that shows people leaving one stock (an office building, for example) and entering the bus stop stock by way of the flow of people walking to the bus stop. Most systems have some of these simple interconnections that create linear causality: office building empties and causes bus stop to fill (or A causes B). In some cases, the relationships may not be easy to see, but once identified, the resulting behavior is generally easy to predict.

Also common are the interconnections of circular causality, where A changes B which then feeds back to affect A, a pattern called a feedback loop (Figure 2.3). In everyday language "feedback" is something you request from a friend or trusted colleague, a reaction to your work. You'll use that reaction to improve or change your work. In systems terms, you are creating a feedback loop, in this case a learning cycle.

Two basic behaviors are related to these patterns of circular interconnection.

Reinforcing loops – When a change in one part leads to a change in another part that then increases the change in the first, we see the circular and amplifying nature of the reinforcing feedback loop. A reinforcing loop is also known as a positive feedback loop, not because it is necessarily good, but because the changes, once started, move each other in the same mathematical direction (Figure 2.4).

Think of what happens when all the trees on a piece of land are cut. The tree leaves no longer shelter the soil from the force of the rain and the roots no longer hold the soil. For a short time, dead leaves and twigs on the ground may protect the soil, but if some plants don't sprout quickly that protective covering washes away. Once the soil is bare and exposed to the force of the rain,

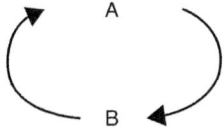

Figure 2.3   Feedback loop where A affects B, which then affects A.

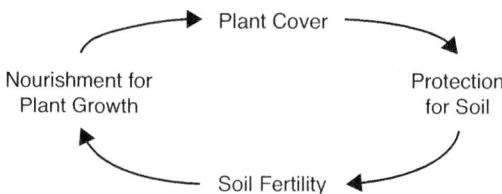

Figure 2.4 Reinforcing loop of reduced plant cover and soil erosion.

seeds that are sprouting and nourishment present in the soil are washed away, reducing the chance to regenerate tree cover. Erosion begets more erosion, and it's all downhill (literally) from there.

This example of a reinforcing loop degrading the stocks of soil fertility and plant cover can, with some effort, run the other way. If you stabilize the soil and plant trees, you'll end up building more soil.

The same pattern of "some begets more" runaway behavior is easy to see in the height of city buildings racing their neighbors for the sunlight and views, or the garishness of advertisements competing for audience attention. Sleep deprivation and coffee consumption is a familiar example, especially on college campuses. As a student spends hours studying until late at night, fatigue sets in and the student drinks coffee to keep going. The coffee reduces the ability to sleep, which makes the student increasingly tired the next day and in need of even more coffee. Eventually, the system with the reinforcing loop bumps up against some limit – the soil erodes down to bedrock, the cost of building ever higher becomes unaffordable, we get so sick of the advertisements that we turn to other media, or the student "crashes." We can choose to limit reinforcing loops, or they can run into limits not of our choosing.

Reinforcing loops are not necessarily bad. Though we see "vicious cycles" we can also find plenty of examples of "virtuous cycles." Practice makes (more) perfect is one – whether it is a young child learning to read or a musician playing the violin, more practice increases the skill and pleasure, which then entices the person to practice more. Soon the person may not even think of it as practice, just pleasure. The adoption of renewable energy technologies has shown the same reinforcing loop behavior. A renewable energy economy may involve three sets of actors: individuals who buy the technology (solar panels, for example), the companies that manufacture the technology, and the government that creates incentives to encourage both the buyers and the sellers. The beauty of this system is that the reinforcing loop can start anywhere. Maybe the citizens lobby the government to create incentives for home owners to install solar panels, or the government issues research and development grants to companies for new solar panel technology, or the companies reduce their prices to encourage buyers. With companies producing and people buying solar panels and government creating appropriate incentives and regulations, distributed electricity production is more easily adopted by more people, which then encourages more companies to get into the market and builds government support for the activity.

Balancing loops – When a change in one part of a system leads to a change in another part that then decreases or damps down the change in the first part, we recognize the balancing feedback loop. A balancing loop is also known as a negative feedback loop, not because it is necessarily bad, but because the changes move each other in opposite mathematical directions. More of one creates less of the other (Figure 2.5).

Whereas reinforcing loops generate runaway behaviors, balancing loops produce stabilizing behavior that keeps things in check by reducing the gap between a current and a desired condition. These are also called goal-seeking loops. One example is a thermostat that senses a difference between the actual room temperature and the target temperature. A difference in temperatures

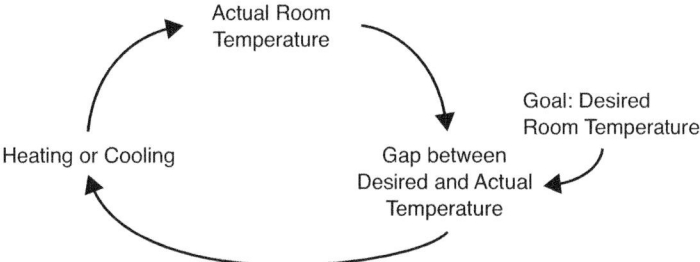

Figure 2.5 Balancing loop of heating or cooling a room.

triggers a heating or cooling device to turn on to reach the desired temperature. Once the difference in temperatures is reduced, the thermostat turns off the heating or cooling device.

As with reinforcing loops, balancing loops may produce desirable behaviors or they may not. The expression "status quo" if often associated with frustrated efforts to move the state of a system away from the current one. Hard-to-shift status quos are often the result of multiple balancing loops aligned to create the same result: discouraging stability.

Many feedback behaviors are fueled by flows of information. The process of design itself takes place in a feedback fashion, through prototyping, gathering information, and redesigning toward a set of goals. When information is withheld, the feedback is delayed and the system cannot adjust. One of the more powerful things that designers can do is shine a light on information flows. Think about who does and does not have access to information. Information can take many forms including producer stories, emissions data, and price. Markets are not very good at pricing goods to include effects on the environment and on social fairness. Sustainable design can engage in production processes that are fair and that price goods like water and carbon, raw materials, and ecosystem services so that they are treated with parsimony.

Skill

Identify linear connections and nonlinear feedback loops of circular causality.

Systems questions

What reinforcing feedback loops are at play in the design?

What balancing feedback loops are at play in the design?

What information flows are crucial to the system's function and who does or does not have access to the information?

Problematic system behaviors

Once we recognize that behavior is determined by system structure, we can examine structure whenever we see unwelcome behaviors appearing again and again. If the pattern is common and persists despite our best efforts, there is probably a structural reason for it. As we learn to identify the systems around us we also recognize the common patterns of behavior – both good and bad. Some of these are so common that analysts refer to them as archetypes or system traps, and have given them names such as "success to the successful" and "drift to low performance." We'll look at three common system structures that produce very familiar dynamics, or behaviors, over time.

Escalation – When the size of one stock is determined by the goal of surpassing the size of another stock and vice versa, then reinforcing feedback loops carry the system into perpetual growth. This escalation can be in the speed of computers or the power of competing military forces. The goal of each participant is to outdo the other. The arms race may be for good or for ill, but the escalation can lead to extremes surprisingly quickly.

If the structure of the system is not changed, the behavior will continue until it is stopped by crashing up against a limit; physical growth cannot go on forever. Foresight and the ability to change a system's structure are key to reigning in the damage an escalating system can do. We can reset a goal, or break the reinforcing growth loop by stepping out of the competition, or we can build in a balancing loop to control the escalation. Designers can examine the goals of a project and highlight the possible limits or opportunities for new balancing loops.

Fixes that fail – This archetype is 'also known as "policy resistance" because' we see it so often in rules that fail to achieve the stated purpose. When stakeholders have separate and competing goals for one part of a system, these goals can create a tug-of-war that may not settle on any acceptable outcome. Think about cars. Drivers want speed and good looks, government wants safety, and society wants lower pollution. Over the years, car design shifts from an emphasis on speed, to safety, to efficiency, and back to safety. As government invests in better roads to reduce accidents, drivers buy faster cars and have more accidents. Car designers create heavier cars to increase safety, but fuel consumption goes up, leading to more pollution (also a safety and health issue). Any new policy or initiative just pulls the car-health-pollution complex farther from the goals of the other stakeholders, often with a result that no one likes.

One way out of this multiway tug-of-war is to look at the boundaries of each party's vision of the system and then redefine broader goals that everyone can endorse – mobility, health, and autonomy, for example. Designers can ask questions about the boundaries of the system that shine a light on a mindset that may be holding us back, for example that we humans should be behind the wheel of the car, then innovate new solutions, such as a self-driving car.

The tragedy of the commons – This trap develops when people have access to a common resource and each person's decision to use the resource creates a cost that is borne by the whole group while the benefit goes entirely to the individual. In this case, each will want to increase his own use because the individual's gain is greater than his portion of the shared cost. The resource might be the grass on the town's common pasture (as in the classic example described by ecologist Garrett Hardin [1968] or the capacity of a river's plants and other organisms to biodegrade wastewater. In each case, the addition of more users reduces the resource, but the cost of that use (slightly less grass for each cow, slightly lower biological activity in the river) is spread across all users, whereas the gain goes entirely to the new user.

In systems language, the feedback from the condition of the resource is weaker than the feedback from the benefit to the individual. We see the same pattern play out in Internet use. We are each enticed by activities and applications (streaming movies or playing the latest Internet game) that require more and more bits per second of data transmission. As one person on a Wi-Fi network increases demand for bandwidth by downloading a large file, the other users get a slightly smaller share of the remaining bandwidth and experience a slightly slower connection.

This trap is even more tragic when the condition of the resource erodes or degrades from the increasing use (or abuse). The soil on the town common erodes as more cows are added, thus decreasing the total capacity of pasture to grow grass. The ability of the river to biodegrade wastes decreases as the high levels of pollution kill key species. In these cases, the consequence of overuse by all is that the resource eventually becomes available to none.

The way out of this trap is to establish a feedback loop between the condition of the resource and each user's decision. Such feedback loops can be physical (putting a factory's water supply intake downstream from its wastewater discharge) or economic (dynamic pricing that increases the price of our Internet connection the more we use it) or social (rewarding resource conservation and discouraging resource overuse). Imagine building a feedback mechanism into everything we design; as the resource declines, each person's decision to use it becomes costlier.

Skill

Identify common patterns of system behavior.

Systems questions

What traps are present in the system you are concerned with?
What strategies are available to change the structure behind these problematic system behaviors?

Key characteristics of systems

Beyond driving the immediate behavior, the structure of a system determines the strength of three system characteristics of interest to designers – hierarchy, self-organization, and resilience.

Hierarchy (nesting)

Think about designing fabric for clothing. A system that makes fabric is one part of a system that makes clothes. At the same time many systems, such as fiber and dye manufacturing, are components of the fabric-making system. Systems are made up of subsystems and are, themselves, part of even larger systems. This nesting of systems is important to issues of sustainability and has two implications for the work of designers: understanding connections and building a team approach.

We see the connections between related systems that create a new fabric when we ask where the fibers come from and under what social and ecological conditions those fibers are grown or manufactured. Clothes designed to protect people do not increase overall well-being if the fabric they are made from exposes people to dangerous chemicals or destructive working conditions during the manufacturing process. Although it is true that everything is related to everything else, subsystems are more tightly related within their own structure than to other subsystems or to the greater system. Recognizing this can give relief when we are feeling overwhelmed by the connectedness of everything. We can work on redesigning one subsection without having to tackle everything else at the same time.

A second implication of nesting systems is that we can build alliances with those who are improving the other subsystems (or the greater system). We can honor them, rejoice in their accomplishments, and collaborate so that our work supports their work (and vice versa). Part of a pre-project system analysis is to describe the hierarchy of systems, who is working on which subsystems (potential allies), and how tightly or loosely related are the subsystems. We may find that the scope or scale or boundaries of the project need to be redrawn to accomplish our goals.

Self-organization

Systems change over time, often without intentional human intervention. Sometimes it is the relatively subtle shift in dominance from a reinforcing loop to a balancing loop. Sometimes it is the ability of a system to rearrange itself in response to changes, giving rise to new structures (e.g., institutions) or repurposing old ones. Systems can learn, diversify, and evolve; in other words, they can self-organize.

Architects recognize this, for example, when a commercial building includes features for use as housing at a later date. As a community shifts from needing commercial space to needing residential space, the building owners can easily repurpose space at little cost because the designer anticipated the possibility of future change and created a structure that can evolve to be useful as demand shifts. The local community, as a whole, is able to successfully self-organize because of the flexibility designed into the built capital.

Designing for change is crucial to long-lasting success. Change will happen and our designs will either adapt or become useless, and if we anticipate change, we may be able to help create the change we want to see rather than the change we dread.

Resilience

The ability of a system to recover from a short-lived shock or disruption is an indicator of resilience. A resilient system can restore itself, repair minor damage, and bounce back to functionality, surviving in a variable environment. The opposite of a resilient system is a brittle system, perhaps finely tuned and highly precise, but fragile.

Resilience usually arises from multiple balancing loops of varying strength and working on varying timescales, all sharing the same system goal. A diversified farm with an imaginative farmer can be a resilient system. Weather that causes one crop to fail may produce an exceptional harvest of another. The farmer may find new markets for the surplus and achieve his or her goals of making a living, feeding the community, or being a good steward of the working landscape. The diversified farm can add to the resilience of the larger community system, improving its ability to withstand economic ups and down. Designing for resilience may require letting go of a certain amount of control over exact forms or functions.

Skills

Identify hierarchy, self-organization, and resilience in your current reality and your design or redesign.
Learn how to design adaptively in systems that change and reorganize themselves.
Design in ways that increase a system's capacity for self-organization and resilience.

Systems questions

What subsystems are a part of or are affected by the design project?
How is the project nested within other systems?
Who are potential allies working to design or redesign other parts of the larger system?
Will the design adapt or become obsolete as the world around it changes?
What parts, connections, or goals will make the design more resilient?
Will the design contribute to more resilient people, communities, or physical systems?

Engaging with systems through design

The design of anything – from a sandwich to an ocean liner – has multiple temporal and spatial dimensions. In production, a design uses materials and energy and it involves people and other creatures; think about the design's cradle-to-cradle material flow, its embodied energy, and its role in creating greater sustainability (or greater destruction). Over its life, a design requires energy and materials, and has an impact on what users do and think while using it. After its first life, its materials go somewhere (reused, recycled, or dumped somewhere that is already occupied by other beings and other systems). When we look at the things we make and ask how we can use design to move toward a more sustainable way of being on this planet, we recognize both the microscale questions about the production, use, and afterlife of the design itself, and the macroscale questions about how having and using the design enables people to create a more sustainable society.

High-leverage design

As a designer, you may find yourself wanting to know how your solutions will affect the larger system and how best to use your understanding of systems. In one of her most popular essays, "Leverage Points: Places to Intervene in a System," Donella Meadows highlighted places in a system where interventions can bring long-lasting and deep impact (Meadows, 1997):

Places to Intervene in a System (*in increasing order of effectiveness*)

12 *Constants, parameters, numbers (such as subsidies, taxes, standards).*
11 *The sizes of buffers and other stabilizing stocks, relative to their flows.*
10 *The structure of material stocks and flows (such as transport networks, population age structures).*
 9 *The lengths of delays, relative to the rate of system change.*
 8 *The strength of negative feedback loops, relative to the impacts they are trying to correct against.*
 7 *The gain around driving positive feedback loops.*
 6 *The structure of information flows (who does and does not have access to information).*
 5 *The rules of the system (such as incentives, punishments, constraints).*
 4 *The power to add, change, evolve, or self-organize system structure.*
 3 *The goals of the system.*
 2 *The mindset or paradigm out of which the system – its goals, structure, rules, delays, parameters – arises.*
 1 *The power to transcend paradigms.*

The list is a reminder to go beyond structural interventions, such as tweaking interest rates or quotas set for pollutants, and focus on interventions at the level of system behavior, such as the capacity of a system to self-organize, or even at the level of goals and mindsets (or paradigms) at work in the system.

The leverage points framework has been proposed in sustainability science as a way to reprioritize research toward deep transformation of unsustainable systems and transcending traditional disciplinary boundaries (Abson et al., 2017). Next we describe the top leverage points in Donella Meadows' framework and invite readers to refer to her original work for more details.

Rules and incentives – Laws are the hardwiring of social systems. They incentivize certain behaviors, discourage others, and too often bring with them a number of unintended consequences when they address one piece of the system at a time. There's power both in recognizing rules and incentives in a system and in transforming existing reward structures. Too often we focus on designing solutions for a problem without recognizing the incentives that created the problem in the first place. For example, agriculture specialists in the lake region of Macedonia designed smartphone apps for alerting apple farmers about pest outbreaks. The goal was to help farmers reduce pesticide use through targeted applications, and so reduce the dangerously high contamination levels in fish and local waters. Whereas farmers responded positively to the app, the national government continued to offer financial incentives to convert new land to apple orchards. This increased the total area in orchards and added more pesticides to the very same ecosystems and communities already under threat (Ceroni, 2012).

Goals – Changing the ultimate goal of a system is one of the most powerful ways to shift a system away from unsustainable behavior. Not to be confused with a system's stated goal, this is what the system produces in the end, as a result of its own workings. Because we are born into systems and we inherit them from the previous generation, we rarely examine the purpose of a family, a school, a company, a monetary system, or an economy. What makes you decide whether to design or not design? What is the ultimate purpose of your design? John Sylvan, the inventor of Keurig's coffee pods had a goal of creating a single-serving, fresh-brewed coffee system. He did not expect that the product would be so successful and would result in nine billion single-serving plastic containers going into the waste stream in 2014. As the system he developed achieved his original goal with tremendous success, he may have realized that he had another (perhaps higher) goal for the system, which was to produce single-serving, fresh-brewed coffee with low environmental impact. By his personal admission, he wished he had never conceived the coffee pod (Hamblin, 2015).

Mindsets – At the top of the list of interventions are designs and actions that shift commonly held beliefs about how the world works and what is possible. A shared view of nature as a set of exploitable resources can only lead to a system that turns natural resources into marketable goods and discards byproducts as waste. But what if partnership with nature became the most commonly held idea of how to run our productive processes? A goal of zero waste would not only feel right and desirable but would become a consequence of the business structure. The notion of design itself reflects a mindset of intentionality, a premeditated answer to a problem based on a set of assumptions about the usefulness, the adoptability, and the continued life of an innovation.

Is unsustainability, at its core, a problem of bad design?

Design and technology are tightly interconnected and it is common to encounter a sense of bold optimism in technological solutions as the silver bullet that will move us closer to sustainability. The authors of the Hannover Principles seemed keenly aware of this mindset:

> Building on the principle of humility, the design philosophy here should realize its inherent limitations in trying to plan and direct both human and natural processes. Design may encourage a sense of permanence and community, but it cannot legislate it. Similarly, no assumed laws of nature can be the only criteria for evaluating a design. The solution must present an aesthetic statement which sets up human society as a conduit toward the further understanding of nature, not as an affront or an enemy to it.
>
> *(McDonough and Braungart, 1992)*

Design – whether in interiors, fashion, or mobility – more than any other human endeavor exposes the shared values of a culture over time.

Throughout this chapter we have maintained an analytical approach to systems thinking. But whereas you can design a part of a system and the structure of a system, the system itself may become uncontrollable as a result of multiple agents acting within multiple nested systems, each optimizing toward its own goals with the result being behavior that is not predictable from an analysis of the subsystems. Working with systems might feel more like dancing than planning or designing (Meadows, 2001).

Analysis alone won't get us far; letting go, listening, and learning are also part of understanding the needs of your client, your community, and your world. These are also key skills in systems thinking.

Designers as systems thinkers and leaders

Cultivating a systems mindset is a continuous practice in recognizing behaviors in seemingly unrelated systems and uncovering hidden goals and mindsets. It might be through a series of aha! moments and getting stuck and unstuck while problem solving that one builds a systems view. How will we recognize that we are thinking systemically? When we are comfortable redefining the problem or the goals of what we do, when we observe new solutions emerge, when new partnerships or new stakeholders come to the table, and when we increasingly work with others for higher impact and more inclusive and far-reaching goals.

The action side of thinking systemically is acting collectively. Collective action is more than a desirable goal; it is an emerging field focused on organizing parts of systems (typically institutions and organizations) around a shared goal (Kania and Kramer, 2011). Intentional networks of organizations, business, legislators, funders, and community members are the fastest growing approach to accelerating change to sustainability in food, energy, arts, restorative justice, and more. As a designer of sustainable solutions, you may find yourself at the center of a collaborative effort or a node in a network of people and organizations that is collectively transforming a system. The question of how to work effectively in teams may shift to how to "lead effectively in systems." On the practical side, how do you talk about "systems stuff" when you might be the only person in a group who holds a system perspective? David Peter Stroh points to the power of telling "system stories" that can help shift a group's perception in three main directions (Stroh, 2015):

- From seeing just their part of the system to seeing more of the whole system
- From hoping that others will change to seeing how they can first change themselves
- From focusing on individual events (crises, fires) to understanding and redesigning the deeper system structures that gives rise to these events

Stroh also suggests that one of the most powerful ways to practice systems thinking and help others in the practice is to ask systems questions, such as:

- What is the case for the status quo?
- What might we have to give up for the whole to succeed?
- What might be the unintended consequences of our proposed solutions?

Being fully conscious of systems and their workings can help us recognize our own taken-for-granted assumptions and illuminate deeper inquiry. Leading in systems has a lot to do with the inner journey of sustainability as reflected in a comment by Bill O'Brien, CEO of Hanover Insurance: "the success of an intervention depends on the interior condition of the intervenor" (Scharmer and Kaufer, 2013).

Notes

1 More than 1,000 freely accessible writings by Donella Meadows are available online at donellameadows. org.
2 For more resources on sustainable development and Herman Daly's work, refer to the Center for the Advancement of the Steady State Economy, steadystate.org.
3 A digital version of *The Limits to Growth* is available on several websites: www.donellameadows.org/ wp-content/userfiles/Limits-to-Growth-digital-scan-version.pdf and http://collections.dartmouth.edu/ published-derivatives/meadows/pdf/meadows_ltg-001.pdf

References

Abson, D.J., J. Fischer, J. Leventon, J. Newig, T. Schomerus, U. Vilsmaier, H. von Wehrden, et al. (2017) "Leverage points for sustainability transformation" *Ambio: A Journal of the Human Environment*, *46*(1): 30–39. doi:10.1007/s13280-016-0800-y

Ceroni, M. (2012) "The Economic Case for Long-term Protection of the Ezerani Nature Park, Republic of Macedonia" *United Nations Development Programme Report to the Ministry of Environment*, Republic of Macedonia.

Club of Rome. "About Us: History" (www.clubofrome.org/about-us/history/) Accessed May 31, 2016.

Daly, H. (1990) "Toward some operational principles of sustainable development" *Ecological Economics*, *2*(1): 1–6.

Hamblin, J. (2015) "A brewing problem" *The Atlantic*, March 2, 2015 (www.theatlantic.com/technology/ archive/2015/03/the-abominable-k-cup-coffee-pod-environment-problem/386501/) Accessed May 31, 2016.

Hardin, G. (1963) "The cybernetics of competition: A biologist's view of society" *Perspectives in Biology and Medicine*, 7(1): 58–84.

Hardin, G. (1968) "The tragedy of the commons" *Science*, *162*(3859): 1243–1248.

Kania, J. and Kramer, M. (2011) "Collective impact" *Stanford Social Innovation Review*, Winter (http://ssir. org/articles/entry/collective_impact) Accessed May 31, 2016.

McDonough, W. and Braungart, M. (1992) "The Hannover Principles: Design for Sustainability" Prepared for EXPO 2000 – The World's Fair, Hannover, Germany. William McDonough Architects (www. mcdonough.com/wp-content/uploads/2013/03/Hannover-Principles-1992.pdf) Accessed May 31, 2016.

Meadows, D.H. (1997) "Places to Intervene in a System" *Whole Earth Review* (Winter), revised and republished as "Leverage Points: Places to Intervene in a System", Sustainability Institute (1999) (http:// donellameadows.org/archives/leverage-points-places-to-intervene-in-a-system/). Accessed May 31, 2016.

Meadows, D.H. (1998) "Internal Guidelines Document of the Sustainability Institute" (now doing business as the Donella Meadows Institute), reprinted in "Letting Go, Opening Up, Letting Come: A Strategic Plan for the Sustainability Institute, August 2010" (www.donellameadows.org/wp-content/userfiles/ Strategic-Plan-August-2010.pdf) Accessed May 31, 2016.

Meadows, D.H. (2001) "Dancing with systems" *Whole Earth Review*, Winter (http://donellameadows.org/ archives/dancing-with-systems/) Accessed May 31, 2016.

Meadows, D.H. (2008) *Thinking in Systems.* Chelsea Green, White River Junction.

Meadows, D.H., Meadows, D.L., Randers, J. and Behrens, W.W. (1972) *The Limits to Growth.* Universe Books, New York.

Scharmer, O. and Kaufer, K. (2013) *Leading From the Emerging Future.* Berrett-Koehler, San Francisco.

Stroh, D.P. (2015) *Systems Thinking for Social Change.* Chelsea Green, White River Junction.

United Nations. (1987) *Report of the World Commission on Environment and Development: Our Common Future* A/42/427. United Nations, Geneva.

3

DESIGN STRATEGIES FOR IMPACT

John Bruce

The questions which one asks oneself begin, at last, to illuminate the world, and become one's key to the experience of others. One can only face in others what one can face in oneself. On this confrontation depends the measure of our wisdom and compassion. This energy is all that one finds in the rubble of vanished civilizations, and the only hope for ours.

James Baldwin, Nobody Knows My Name

In this chapter, I examine approaches of design strategy that initiate and support embodied learning and knowing within nuanced moments of individual experience, and consider how impact might be defined in light of these approaches. My discussion also examines design strategies in relation to learning and knowing, as these events perform as transitions through the various scales of a system.

What we discover and come to know through embodied learning shifts our perspectives and motivates our actions. Let's consider a simple game I have been playing for many years: Ask a question that almost everyone in the room can answer. Who taught you how to ride a bicycle? When was your first kiss? What was the first record album you bought with your own money? For me, it was Pink Floyd's *Dark Side of the Moon*. I walked about a mile and a half to Kmart on a sunny afternoon in 1976. My anecdote goes on with delicious details regarding how I had acquired the money in my pocket, my walk to make the purchase, the unwrapping at home, and, of course, the moment of dropping the needle on the record. Alone in my bedroom, I possessed an embodied ownership of this event. Feelings surrounding a particular kind of agency are inextricably bound to this collection of signifiers. This experience is how I learned something particular about music and myself. My experience was an active event, not simply a passive part of growing up. This energy – a visceral dialogue between head and heart, is both harmonious and confrontational. To experience is to experiment with the unfamiliar – to risk, and confront the perils of the new (Yi-Fu Tuan). This casual parlor game of inquiry is not simply a means of extracting information, but rather an invitation for individuals to visit sites of *knowing* within themselves, revealing a rich constellation of experiential detail contributing to the impact of learning. Design for impact is an invitation.

Recently, I have been asking a question that usually not everyone in the room can answer: Who has been present with someone as they took their last breath and died? At casual, social gatherings of around a dozen people, usually two or three (depending on the context) offer accounts of such an experience. These are always rich in detail and cast a particular gravity in the space. Just before it becomes too heavy, I ask: How many have experienced mediated and constructed images of dying? Movies, TV, stories in books and articles? Certainly everyone. How many images: dozens, hundreds, thousands, tens of thousands? These are rarely nonfiction, moving images at the moment of active dying. Returning to the two or three people who shared their account of being with dying, I ask: How might you compare such mediated images to those of your firsthand experience? Apples and oranges, I am told, over and over again. Mediated experiences and visceral firsthand experiences produce different kinds of learning. What can we know about *being with* dying from each experience? What can we know about dying from each experience? These are thorny and complicated questions. What can we learn from them about generating meaningful experiences through design interventions in order to shift perspectives? What do they tell us about the impact of *knowing* in other spheres of culture and society?

"We perceive our lives, up here, in our head, in our ego," tapping his head, Ram Dass, the spiritual teacher and author of the seminal book *Be Here Now*, tells me during a long exchange a few years ago while I was conducting research for a film project about experiences at the end of life (Figure 3.1). Ram Dass continued, moving his hand from his head and tapping the center of his chest, "it is in our hearts where we hold what we learn from our experiences, where the resonant effects of learning create meaning." As humans, our mortality is a clear fact held in our consciousness, yet our conscious mind also works to keep us from knowing about dying. Distance, or systems delay, allows for a confusion of cause and effect. Distance (sometimes in the form of time), conveniently complicates relationships among the elements within a system. Humans, especially in the West, decouple information regarding our mortality from how we might *know* about dying in ways that impact how we live together. Separateness – of the mind from the body, of individuals from themselves and each other and the planet, of gender and race and nation states, and so on – signals the distances we create that maintain gaps in our capacity to

Figure 3.1   Ram Dass, from the film *End of Life*, by John Bruce and Paweł Wojtasik.

learn and to know. No matter what sphere of impact – issues related to sustainability and beyond, the affect of design relies on strategies that bridge separations. Conjunction is the desired goal for design strategies for impact as a means for the exchange of meaning. Connection, as differing from conjunction, requires the capacity of entities to fit together within known signifiers of understanding. Conjunction requires participatory engagement – sharing, co-creating, reflecting, and allowing for emergence. Franco "Bifo" Berardi states in *And: Phenomenology of The End*, "conjunction, therefore, can be viewed as a way of becoming other. Singularities change when they conjoin, they become something other than what they were before, in the same way as love changes the lover," (Berardi 2015, p. 18). The process of conjoining is an experiment and experience of risk within the unknown – an opportunity to learn (unlearn and relearn), and to know.

What is impact and how is it measured?

Impact is a word like force. It implies strong movement and change. Impact can have a covert relationship to the site of creative intervention responsible for instigating resultant change. Leverage points – places to intervene in a system – might be located at various scales within a system in which we seek to shift the perspectives of individuals and motivate behavior. When we consider leverage points at a human scale within a system we must also consider other hierarchies of elements – geographic, physical, social, psychological – that inhabit the levels of scale smaller than and greater than the human scale. It is critical to question the particular and potential sites where design initiatives might take place in relationship to the various scales within a system and where impact might be desired. A design approach for impact at a particular scale can be trickier than simply adding up humans and considering the larger scale of the group, community, or society. Or, inversely, considering the images, words, ideas, personal moments, organs, cells or atoms of the mind and body. Contemplating movement between scales might offer the most critical insight to how and where design strategies might have impact. A holon, a word not commonly used outside of the academy, refers to something that is simultaneously a whole and a part (Koestler 1967). As a design strategist, it is more insightful for me to consider the complexity of dynamic relationships through the idea of holons. Rather than looking at situations as being composed of known things and processes, holon theory allows for the analysis of and imagination for a wide variety of perspectives and data points – cultural and scientific, about psychological and social realities.

Sustainability is a word I often avoid using. I prefer other language in order to get at the countless ways in which design can impact fields from environmental sustainability to economic and social benefit when it is rooted in *knowing*. I began teaching at Parsons School of Design in 2012, leading a course titled Ethics and Economics of Sustainable Design. It was a respectable course name, exuding a particular gravity, especially given that it was a required course for undergraduates of the Strategic Design and Management program. Most students arrived thinking the class would be about recycling and being nice to workers. My predecessors had been teaching it with the usual doom and gloom brought about by the industrial revolution, followed by how to "green things up." This wasn't a terrible approach, and one that was familiar to me having earned my MBA a few years earlier at Pinchot – an experimental graduate program focused on sustainable systems founded by Gifford Pinchot III and Libba Pinchot. During my time as a member of the sixth cohort of Pinchot, in the early 2000s, I was still abuzz with the notions proposed in *Natural Capitalism*. For me, these were radically new ways of seeing the world in terms of defining resources and value (Hawkin, Lovins, and Lovins). Encountering the work of Donella Meadows, I was introduced to a formal understanding of thinking in systems and contemplating the full range of human emotions impacting our decisions and actions. Alongside Maslow's hierarchy of needs, Gifford Pinchot III shared what he called the *HappoDammo Ratio*

$$\textit{HappoDammo Ratio} = \frac{\textit{happiness created by an activity}}{\textit{damage created by that activity}}$$

Figure 3.2 HappoDammo Ratio by Gifford Pinchot III.

(Figure 3.2). Pinchot's approach for charting a path forward began with considerations of the pursuit of happiness – *Happo* – and its relationship to how much and what kind of damage this pursuit might bring about – *Dammo*. Pinchot's *HappoDammo Ratio* was a light-hearted optimistic equation during a time when the endeavor of sustainable practices circulated with vernacular that was predominantly dire, earnest, and humorless. Pinchot (2010) stated,

> Given that most of happiness comes from relationships and most of consumption uses stuff symbolically rather than for its intrinsic value, it won't be hard to make 1000-fold improvements in the ratio of happiness to stuff. These innovations will often be very popular, cost-effective, and profitable. In this direction lies hope and true prosperity.

My interpretation of Pinchot's idea is that motivations for behavior would not come from didactic narratives of "doing good," and rather would emerge in the nuanced, personal spaces of understanding that resulted from the movement between head and heart during moments of visceral experience. User-centered design, having gained traction in the 1980s, is an approach relying upon the careful consideration of individual needs and desires. Bottom-up perspectives – in popular discourse as human centered design driven by empathetic ethnography – coalesce with top-down systems of infrastructure, intricately arranged and interdependent. A productive tension exists among the often difficult to map constellation of relationships held within bottom-up and top-down perspectives. Herein lies the work of the design strategist.

How might we consider personal motivations and embodied moments of learning and knowing in relation to collective actions and their accumulation toward the scale of movements for positive systemic change?

Scale, movements through systems, and impact

Strategic insight – seeing in systems, understanding how the experience of one person can be reproduced to affect many – requires an ability to comprehend potential movements through various system scales. It is no wonder that the iconic film *Powers of Ten* by Charles and Ray Eames is so often used as a teaching tool for understanding scale and systems. It begins with an overhead, medium shot of a man and woman lying on a blanket in the grass, enjoying a picnic. As the camera zooms up and out we see the park, the neighborhood, the city, the state, the region of the United States, the North American continent, and the Earth. This journey continues outward through the solar system, and beyond. Reversing direction, the film zooms back to Earth and the park, and then plunges our view into one of the people on the picnic blanket – zooming into the skin, the cells, the atoms, and the subatomic matter. Scale is a much trickier idea than the connotations resulting from a capitalist perspective. Notions of size can fool us into believing that scale refers only to categories of hierarchy in units, especially in regard to populations, markets, and policy, as defined by boundaries and borders. It is important to reckon with the existence of scale as the consequence of connections (Latour 2016).

It is perhaps helpful to consider impact as reverberation. Acoustically, reverb is reflection (movement) of sound and the multiplying affect of these reflections absorbed by objects, most noticeable as the reflections continue after the source has stopped. Reverb relies on the generative capacities within an ecosystem to produce sustained presence of a sonic intervention. Similarly, embodied and experiential learning capable of transformation – knowing, relies on connections and conjunctions – energy moving in and through holons, to produce potentialities often not visible or recognizable in a current state view.

How might our personal decisions and actions connect us to issues regarding sustainability – climate change, economic and social equity, food and water security, urban living, political forces, access to education, and the like?

Individuals untouched directly (seemingly) by issues regarding sustainability are removed from experiential opportunities for learning. Distance and delay in system dynamics are gaps, barriers, filters, or baffles to learning and *knowing* that could otherwise shift perspectives and behaviors. Examples, albeit oversimplified, include: to throw away trash means it's out of sight, out of mind, and out of the range of responsibility; a *good deal* reflected by the price of a product that is produced far away obfuscates any notion of true cost and the people attached to the labor embodied in the product; to smoke cigarettes despite explicit warnings of illness or death is reasonable because death is at a distance that is impossible to grasp. Distances and delays also complicate the ways we might measure impact. Defining metrics without embracing the detailed complexity and nuanced moments of individual experience can dangerously result in binary equations of cause and effect, and thus metrics become goals that are unattainable, despite being desirable. And in turn, initial efforts can be blamed for failure to meet such unattainable goals, and abandoned for short-term tactics in attempts to yield measurable results more quickly. In this case, the tail wags the dog. Measuring the more complex sequences of learning and knowing – metrics focused on movements in and through systems – can produce better insights for informing generative iterations of design interventions.

Design strategy employs a number of approaches in order to gain insight to conjunctions at human scale. The persona – a typical tool in design strategy – is a composite character serving as a model of the stakeholders who will most benefit from the value of a design intervention. As a tool it is useful for considering a detailed potential journey of *one person* as she confronts the perils and thrills of the new, considering each nuanced moment of experience: the place of first encounter; the modes of engagement, exchange, and understanding; and the evolution resulting in an ideal outcome. It's an infuriating exercise at first. No one likes to limit the experience of their value proposition to one person and a singular set of circumstances with so many idiosyncratic details. Along with potential benefits, there are dangers in employing personas. A lack of rigorous research can allow for the creation of personas that are merely wishful thinking, and lead to what I call design magic realism. Personas are useful for insights into current state ecosystems, yet can fail to indicate potential invitations for experiences of embodied learning and knowing. Personas compiled from research focused on *what is*, rather than *what could be*, are another example of how easy it is to get caught up in thinking about complex situations as being composed of known things and processes – reliably performing characters, cultural trends, borders, established business models, and so on. Personas drawn from a distance are predictable as they move through convenient systems scenarios based on historical patterns. If one can understand why something worked so well in the past, one might be able to recreate a similar success. It's comforting to trust patterns and abhor black swans. Perhaps there is merit to the claim that 99% of all design is mimic. Like a safe bet with good odds, following a pattern is an easier strategic argument. Securing buy-in, or any kind of traction, ahead of a proven concept is a challenging endeavor if your narrative does not rely on an historical precedent. Much of design's mimicry is useful. However, the potential for design to affect genuine social value demands strategy beyond mimic.

How might design anthropology not only reflect but also participate in movements through systems scales of interdependent experiences as learning and *knowing*?

Prototypes, probes, and emergence

Design research borrows from traditional anthropology, attempting to gain insight into motivations and behaviors by analyzing and interpreting the present and the past "present" moments. Unlike most practices of social science ethnography, designers are less concerned with perfecting an understanding of historical scenarios, and work to leverage insights, even imperfectly, in order to project future possibilities (Hunt 2010). Design anthropology participates in the transformative process by making virtual experiments within the context of social realities, anticipating the existence of emergent qualities within ecosystems (Smith and Otto 2016). These experiments or interventions are particularly salient in how they might address distances and delay within system dynamics. A typical reductionist mistake when addressing gaps that might exist in systems is to imagine a complete puzzle image (ideal outcome) that is simply missing one of the puzzle pieces (Wheatley 2012). This is old-school design intervention: Identify the problem, and create the solution. Certainly, problems exist that beg for solutions. However, this is not an effective starting point for design research and strategy. Design research participates in generative knowledge through activities beyond capturing and analyzing existing information. The process is not simply observation and extraction of data. The potential of emergent qualities within systems provides opportunity for design research to experiment in the unknown, and participate along a fractal path of discovery to support "emerging, wavering, and ephemeral values" (Kilbourn 2013). In this way, the process can produce *reverb*, generative movements in and through holons. The provocation of emergence can yield critical insights as well as new value. Perhaps a more simple way to describe *emergence*: The essence of the ingredients for chocolate chip cookies – flour, sugar, butter, chocolate, etc. – is easy to understand, while the emergent value of these combined nodes of this system – the resultant cookie – cannot be known through the elements alone (Wheatley 2012). To embrace emergence demands that we avoid the reductionist approach where impact is viewed as a concretized and fully recognizable state of being to be reverse engineered in order to define strategic intervention. The future most likely looks like something we cannot fully imagine, and values supporting such a future are equally as mysterious as considered from our current state.

Prototypes can assume many forms and perform many roles in the design process, and are not limited to penultimate manifestations of the final design articulation. The probe is an effective investigative prototype method that I employed during the four years of my research in experiences at the end of life. Video resulting from my fieldwork was periodically shared with small, curated audiences in order to provoke their responses to imagery of intimate scenes of dying people, as our project wished to explore the power of proximity to dying as having the potential to shift relationships around mortality. Our curiosity centered on possibilities of reverberation for closing distances and speeding up delays in systems of knowing mortality in light of the impossibility of knowing the experience of death. The potential discursive power of art – the film – would eventually exist to play a role in a larger system of design intervention, including modes of engagement and utility through symposia and education. The film functions as an experience located at a certain, early stage along a spectrum of holistic awareness and interaction with mortality. Resonant effects of the project will ideally produce a constellation of benefits related to evolved behaviors of being more present with oneself and with others. Some of the images from our project were rendered and presented in ways that are perhaps not typical or expected within Western, entrenched ideas of dying from movies and television, as our process of gathering and assembling images willfully resisted imposing narrative meaning onto the accounts of dying. All documentary filmmaking begins from a place of failure in that no document is objective or without inflection. In this sense, there is always some degree of mediation. The *End of Life* project is designed to minimize mediation while maximizing invitation for viewers to experience embodied learning toward knowing, in this case in a realm very much within the unknown. Our activities as filmmakers were motivated by cocreated experiences in context – in relationships – with the subjects of the project. We were not there to simply observe or extract information. I am present, along with my collaborator Paweł Wojtasik, in the film. We participated in what each person was able to do or not do, what they were able to say or not say. Our presence contributed to the environment and conditions of the subjects, serving as elements within a new realm of existence. We exchanged information, and also acted within events both mundane and extraordinary. Stylistically, as a film, the inclusion of our presence within the sound and image plane is slightly odd, as we are not interviewers, nor is our presence negotiated by any preexisting relationship – we are not old friends or blood relations. Our process attempted a form of mediation for collapsing distances and allowing intimate proximities, thus the images captured and presented produce affect to not only reflect a kind of learning and knowing, evolving for us the filmmakers, but also serving as an invitation for the viewer as their own visceral experience. Images from this fieldwork at times provoked a desire in viewers to turn away, or feel that their act of watching was a violation of privacy. Images of dying, and the associated issues of our own mortality, are uncomfortable. The act of the viewer to stay with the film, to remain within its durational episodes of sometimes awkward witnessing, corroborates the process of the filmmakers – transference of learning and knowing.

Probes for my research and film work concerning the end of life became increasingly complex. I would assemble sequences of various clips that juxtaposed different kinds of imagery, sometimes using video clips from sources other than my own fieldwork in order to create experimental contexts for probing sessions. One particular clip of Ram Dass featured a medium close-up frame showing him staring into the camera. During the actual recording of the video, Ram Dass was staring into my eyes as I kneeled alongside the camera positioned on a tripod at his exact eye level as he was seated in a wheelchair. There are no cuts or camera movements in this segment. Occasionally, Ram Dass tilts forward to reveal sunspots and skin growths on the top of his head. A small, round adhesive bandage is fixed to his nose. He strokes his beard once or twice, and sips a glass of water. There are several moments when he seems to be about to speak, and then does not. His expression changes slightly as the sound of an airplane passes overhead. Another moment the sound of chimes, with a slight shift in his eyes. As time passes, nearly seven minutes in total, the absence of typical actions in the video clip give way to a new set of actions – smaller moments that become much larger. After seven minutes of not speaking, Ram Dass finally says, "In our culture, almost everybody is afraid of death." Some viewers of the segment were agitated. They expressed frustration around feelings of being manipulated. They demanded to know the exact prompt Ram Dass was given by me in order to produce such a performance. Other viewers reported becoming more aware of their own breathing, their own micro movements, and of small sounds in the viewing room that might have otherwise gone unnoticed. And even others shared accounts of initial anxiety giving way to a meditative release and eventual peacefulness. On one occasion, I showed the clip of Ram Dass after showing a five-minute video segment that was not from our fieldwork. The segment was professionally produced and featured a young woman, Brittany Maynard, who had elected to exercise her right to die with dignity as granted by the state of Oregon. This piece was a tear-inducing testimonial by the woman and her family. The video employed music and cross-fades to synthesize various locations and moods. The piece has an agenda. It wishes to make a point, convey didactic information, and motivate specific behavior.

The person and events are real, and policy issues surrounding death with dignity are in play. It functions as communication design to inform, while also provoking an emotional response. A narrative has been assembled so that the subject matter is relatable, albeit from a safe distance. The emotions produced might be intense, while there are no stakes for most viewers. This is not their situation, their mortality. Both videos address mortality through radically different forms of communication design: The piece about Britney Maynard details the context and events that will lead to the moment of her death; and the video of Ram Dass employs a single, durational moving image portrait presented with no introduction or information so that he could be any old man strangely hesitating to speak. The affect of the Ram Dass video resides within its ability to invite the viewer to experience a deeper awareness of their senses, test their ability to be present, and challenge the awareness of their own mortality. Both videos address mortality while employing radically different strategies for very discrete intended outcomes. For the purposes of my probe, it was useful to learn where the site of impact was located for viewers within their personal psychosocial ecosystems, and to hear their reactions to the probing experience. This example of probing as a form of prototype enabled my research work to inform the subsequent design of more refined media artifacts that would perform within scaled strategies for impact. These initiatives – an installation and a feature-length film, to date, are invitations for visceral engagement with consciousness of our own mortality and the ways we as a society serve the various stages of the end of life. Studio courses within the Transdisciplinary Design program at Parsons School of Design leverage our research in collaboration with external partners in health care, exploring ways to shift behavior and systems toward greater compassionate care for the ill and dying.

Products and services in the marketplace can serve as probes for experiences of generative learning and knowing, functioning in ways far beyond their market value and utility. The Light Phone, released in the United States in 2017, is a credit card-sized phone that only makes and receives phone calls (Figure 3.3). I serve as one of the key strategists for the company. Talking on the phone is not the value of the product. The Light Phone is a probe into our 24/7, *always on* selves. Hyper virtual-connectivity has become a normalized way of life for many, and has accelerated the replacement of the "sequence of places and events associated with family, work, and relationships," with "electronic commodities and media services through which all experience

Figure 3.3   The initial Light Phone by Joe Hollier.

has been filtered, recorded, or constructed" (Crary 2013). Joe Hollier and Kaiwei Tang, the Light Phone creators, were driven by the idea of limited features in an era of ramped innovation relying on ever-increasing turbo-charged functionality. The Light Phone is, as an early tagline states, *designed to be used as little as possible* (Hollier 2016). During prelaunch, the discourse at cocktail parties revealed polarized reactions: "I want one, now" and "the last thing I want to do with a phone is talk." The Light Phone is almost a joke: Why would anyone reinvent the telephone, and do so in ways dramatically reductive? And of course, many early opinions simply rejected the idea of any existence away from smartphone connectivity, ever. Certainly, the notion of a phone so limited in functionality – not even capable of text messaging – seems preposterous at a time when smartphone usage and participation in any kind of exchange, beyond face to face, are one and the same. The initial Light Phone product is intended as a second phone, not a replacement for the smartphone. The form factor is completely matt white or matt black with no other surface texture, color or detail except for when it is powered on and the keypad illuminates. It's something that one might expect to see slowly floating in the space station scene from the film *2001: A Space Odyssey*. It's monolithic, and wafer-thin. It's the past and the future. The Light Phone is technology that addresses our relationship with technology (a term other than *techne* must surely be imminent to accurately reflect our contemporary condition). These relationships can include the overuse of technology, and can result in potentially harmful addictions. The Light Phone user, leaving their smartphone at home, determines through an app which calls are forwarded to their Light Phone. The value proposition is simple: Break the addiction to constant virtual connection and "checking," and break free of distractions so that you can enjoy the present. The "do not disturb" feature of smartphones and simple will power are arguments against the Light Phone. However, the power of the object – the Light Phone itself – is palpable as a prompt (or talisman) for conscientious shifts in behavior. Untethering from the Internet leash in our pocket can be a fear-inducing act at first. It feels risky to step away from the pulse of instant information and to venture into the unknown expanse of limited connectivity. The Light Phone is an invitation to experiences that belong to the user, uniquely, and are free of any dictated experiences related to the product's functional utility. Leaving one's smartphone behind for an afternoon in the park, a romantic meal, or perhaps running an errand from the West Village to the East Village in lower Manhattan – a 20-minute stroll without scanning your inbox at every corner – these "Light" moments open spaces of opportunity to learn.

The impact of the Light Phone emerges as a result of space and time safe from smartphone distractions – a place of discoveries within the mystery of the present moment without the fear of missing out or the paralysis of infinite options. The value proposition is located within an unexpected reclaiming of conversation at human scale, newly adventurous and risky despite being mundane on the surface. Sherry Turkle (2015) speaks to these ideas in her book *Reclaiming Conversation: The Power of Talk in a Digital Age*:

> In order to feel more, and to feel more like ourselves, we connect. But in our rush to connect, we flee solitude. In time, our ability to be separate and gather ourselves is diminished. If we don't know who we are when we are alone, we turn to other people to support our sense of self. This makes it impossible to fully experience others as who they are.

Design not only adds new *things* of value, but also, and perhaps more profoundly, serves to take things away, affecting change for positive impact. Design interventions that support activities for learning can involve removing barriers, baffles, or filters that block or warp the agency required to move closer to moments of *knowing*.

Sustainability is a curious notion in regard to the Light Phone. The component parts of the initial Light Phone product include plastic and the usual electronics found in such devices, hence the material aspects of the product are not innovative in regard to environmental stewardship. At the same time, this tiny start-up, working with the manufacturing giant Foxconn, is stirring up lots of conversations around what it means to be human during our current state of vociferous engagement with technology. The reverb, even at very early stages of the Light Phone's market presence, signals alignment and resonance with a wide variety of stakeholders dedicated to mindfulness and activism for evolving environmental and social consciousness toward a more enlightened future.

The trouble with identity, the productivity of being uncomfortable

All acts of organization, at any scale – an atom, an organ, a person, a business, a political party, or a nation – begin with identity formation. What might be determined to be inside the container of identity? What might be determined to be outside the container? Learning and knowing motivate these decisions. Based on defining characteristics, the organization assumes a position in relation to other things identified to be *outside*, whether near or far (Wheatley 2012). As design strategists, we attempt to understand context by defining ecosystems in order to frame our inquiry. We map the constellation of elements germane to the landscape of a project, and consider what might be shared among the elements within this bound environment. In what ways might the membrane of each organized node – the boundary of its identity – be permeable? Holons – things that are simultaneously a whole and a part – are bound nodes within a larger ecosystem. Anticipating the ways in which membranes might be permeable, and imagining not only the results of the shifts in criteria of identity but also the qualities of the rupturing process – the uncomfortable moments of displacement, disorientation, or even great groundlessness are critical for identifying potential leverage points in the system. Stated more simply, invitations to transition beyond boundaries – movements into the unknown or space of the other – are opportunities to affect change. Design for impact relies on provocations toward new experiences. Risk! And despite how much it is touted by political candidates as a shimmering goal, *change* is almost always an uncomfortable experience, as risk can be mysterious, unknown, and dangerous. We expect that our efforts for positive change will immediately result in feeling good. A prevalent cultural idea, especially in the West, is that happiness requires absolute comfort. If we are to face basic truths around situations less than ideal – the negative externalities of industrialization or hyper virtual-connectedness, social and economic inequity, our mortality, etc. – we must also accept accountability. Any such act of acknowledgement would require asking questions that provoke feelings of being uncomfortable. This kind of unpleasantness has come to be socially unacceptable, viewed as a threat to the unfettered happiness of those with enough power to deny accountability (Schulman 2012). Design for impact requires a keen understanding of the possible moments of being uncomfortable during movement through holons, and anticipating this journey with all its potential for delay in causal relationships and warps in perception.

Embodied learning might be spurred in a number of ways along the journey through a system of holons. The origins of the Japanese tea ceremony serve as an interesting case study for this kind of experience design. Historically, tea ceremonies have provided the context for a variety of social functions, including the meeting between the leaders of opposing forces at war. The entrance to the ceremonial chamber was constructed at a height of around three feet, and thus required guests to enter the space in a position of bowing. The affect was intended to generate both an embodied humbleness and a gesture of equality, at least in the moment (Sadler 2008). Design that employs elements of *slight strangeness* creates ways to be open to new experiences that might shift psychological and social dispositions. These spaces not only provide opportunity and support for new products or services, but also more importantly serve as pathways into unmapped territories where new value systems might emerge (Dunne and Raby 2001). Rather than a singular tectonic disturbance, a series of encounters with *slight strangeness* allows for several incremental shifts or small ruptures in the membrane of identity and belief. A more holistic, and perhaps insidious, transgression is an important goal of design strategy for impact.

Calculating the degree of how far an experience might stretch the trust and willingness of participants requires creative research and testing. For an installation version of the *End of Life* project (Figure 3.4), a meticulous script was written and rehearsed resulting in various iterations, as we designed elements of *slight strangeness* for the overall affect of experience. Rather than a white box gallery, the exhibition was installed in a suite on the 27th floor of the Equitable Life building – a modernist office high-rise in the Koreatown neighborhood of Los Angeles. No other tall buildings are in this part of the city, thus the views from the upper floors are dramatic, and somewhat unusual for most Angelenos. Rather than a looping media presentation for random visitation during typical gallery hours, the experience required a reservation with specified available times, only once per day at sunset. Upon making a reservation, guests were given instructions on where to park their car and where to meet an usher waiting for them in the lobby. Upon arrival, the usher, of gender nonspecific appearance and dressed in all gray attire in a slightly odd combination of styles, would check-in guests from a gold sheet of paper. His disposition was flat, almost stoic. Guests were asked to wait until all attendees for the evening – a maximum of 10, had arrived. The building's midcentury elevators operate with a velocity that gives passengers a slight rush of vertigo. During the ride up, the usher would nonchalantly hum, at a nearly imperceptible volume, Beethoven's *Ode to Joy* at a slowed-down pace. After following the usher down a series of hallways, guests paused until the door to the suite was unlocked in a somewhat ominous manner. The walls of the small room were painted dark blue. Guests were invited to take in the view, as the sun was now setting, and also invited to use the restrooms if needed, before settling

Figure 3.4 Usher greeting guests for the *End of Life* installation, curated by Equitable Vitrines, Los Angeles 2016.

into chairs. Finally, the usher would announce that the initial audio and visual elements might seem unusual, and to rest assured that these are not technical difficulties. This instruction was added to the script after lots of testing that revealed audiences of the video panicked due to the first six minutes of the piece having a black screen – no images – with audio only. Such panic was too disruptive to the experience, as viewers would assume the media or equipment was broken, and stop watching. Six minutes of a black screen proved to be too strange, unless released from assumptions surrounding such discomfort. Guests knew that they were attending an installation titled *End of Life*. They knew that it was a film based on people experiencing the end of life. As artists employing experience design, our curiosity involved an invitation for viewers to explore their own bodies and senses in regard to their relationship with their own mortality, and to move beyond the entrenched and unconscious distancing we so often assume. The design challenge demanded modes of unlearning and incremental acts of risk in order to arrive at a genuine place of personal exploration. Where might we go from here?

Conclusion

Sometimes I read backwards. Not each word or sentence. After reading the title, I'll skip to the last paragraph of a chapter or article, looking for big ideas and keywords to hold as questions while I take in the rest. I'll continue backwards from the end, a paragraph or section at a time, working my way toward the beginning. Sometimes I'll halt my backwards march, move to the beginning, and proceed in a normal forward fashion. I don't employ this method for pleasure reading, and especially not for fiction. I appreciate the labor involved in the writing of intellectually rigorous works. I mean no disrespect for the typical scholarly approach of presenting a hypothesis followed by a well laid out argument. At the same time, I cannot always adhere to the writer's assumption that my engagement will be spurred within a certain order of elements, my understanding optimized by a linear sequence of revelations. There is a great deal of design in writing and reading. As a young painter, I'd turn my paintings upside down in order to experience their composition free of expected spatial narratives. When the canvas was too large, I'd turn myself upside down. How might we see ways to explore and take chances in order to discover, even when this results in the path being uncomfortable?

Design strategy for impact begins with iterative acts of inquiry. Designing great questions (and ways to "ask" them) is as important as the design of any product, service, or experience of creative intervention. Embodied learning that moves us toward new places of knowing relies on our curiosity being supported by carefully crafted invitations to experiment and take risks. Decisions motivating our actions appear to be activities of our conscious mind, yet involve the more holistic capacities of meaning-making potential that include our unconscious. Dynamic connections, as well as distances and delays, motivate movements through complex constellations of influences and opportunities. Scale, as a consequence of connections, supports the reproduction of impact as reverberations in and through psychological and social realities. Creative interventions are effective where design anthropology participates in genuinely collaborative investigations within ecosystems to provoke emergence and generatively shift perspectives, behaviors, and systems for positive change. Conditions for interventions rely on the permeability of boundaries that can allow for the disruption of defined identities. Design can disarm conservative acts of defending identity, and thus allow for supported moments of being uncomfortable – spurring an openness for new experiences. Sustainable design requires strategies that enable us to step into futures – to experiment and play in the unknown; and potentially to learn, unlearn, and relearn.

References

Baldwin, J. (1961). *Nobody knows my name: More notes of a native son.* New York: Dial Press.

Berardi, F. (2015). *And: phenomenology of the end.* Los Angeles: Semiotext(e).

Bruce, J. A., and Wojtasik, P. (Directors). (2016). *End of life* [Motion picture]. USA: Haos Film.

Crary, J. (2013). *24/7: Late capitalism and the ends of sleep.* London: Verso.

Dunne, A., and Raby, F. (2001). *Design noir: The secret life of electronic objects.* London: August.

Eames, C. (1977). *Powers of ten and the relative size of things in the universe.* Eames Office. Retrieved August 09, 2016, from www.eamesoffice.com/the-work/powers-of-ten/

Hawkin, P., Lovins, A. B., and Lovins, L. H. (1999). *Natural capitalism: Creating the next industrial revolution.* Boston: Little, Brown and Co.

Hollier, J. (2016). *The light phone.* Retrieved August 01, 2016, from www.thelightphone.com/#light

Hunt, J. (2010). "Prototyping the social: Temporality and speculative futures at the intersection of design and culture," in Alison Clark, ed. *Design anthropology: Object culture in the 21st century.* New York: Springer, p. 35.

Kilbourn, K. (2013). "Tools and movements of engagement: Design anthropology's style of knowing," in W. Gunn, T. Otto and R. C. Smith, eds. *Design anthropology: Theory and practice.* New York: Bloomsbury.

Koestler, A. (1967). *The ghost in the machine.* London: Hutchinson.

Latour, B. (2016, October 7). *On a possible triangulation of some present political positions.* Seminar presented at the Graduate Institute for Design, Ethnography and Social Thought, at The New School, New York, NY.

Maynard, B. (2014). *My right to death with dignity at 29.* Retrieved August 12, 2016, from http://edition.cnn.com/2014/10/07/opinion/maynard-assisted-suicide-cancer-dignity/

Pinchot, G., III. (2010, February 16). *The HappoDammo Ratio.* Retrieved August 9, 2016, from www.pinchot.com/2010/02/the-happodammo-ratio.html

Sadler, A. L. (2008). *The Japanese tea ceremony: Cha-no-yu.* Tokyo: Tuttle.

Schulman, S. (2012). *The gentrification of the mind: Witness to a lost imagination.* Berkeley: University of California Press.

Smith, R.C. Vangkilde, K.T., Kjaersgaard, M.G., Otto, T., Halse, J., Binder, T. (2016). "Cultures of the future: Emergence and intervention in design anthropology," in R.C. Smith, K.T. Vangkilde, M.G. Kjaersgaard, T. Otto, J. Halse, and T. Binder, eds. *Design anthropological futures.* New York, NY: Bloomsbury.

Tuan, Y. (1977). *Space and place: The perspective of experience.* Minneapolis: University of Minnesota Press.

Turkle, S. (2015). *Reclaiming conversation: The power of talk in a digital age.* New York: Penguin Press.

Wheatley, M. J. (2012). *So far from home: Lost and found in our brave new world.* San Francisco, CA: Berrett-Koehler.

4
APPLIED SUSTAINABILITY

Wendy Jedlička, Jeremy Faludi, Pete Markiewicz, Tim Frick
and Mark McCahill

Understanding the whole picture

Sustainability, it must be acknowledged, is not a destination, but a journey. At what point do we want to 'sustain' – at a point of depletion or abundance?

In order to move toward a more sustainable, or better yet restorative, operating model decision makers use a variety of systems thinking methodologies to help them manage both big picture goals and the seemingly endless pile of small details that make up the mechanism for attaining those goals.

Working holistically with systems has many steps, parts, and processes. It's possible that not all steps a designer discovers in a systems methodology can be undertaken at the time of their given project. But, all steps *can* and *must* be accounted for. Sustainability leaders didn't earn their status because they're doing everything perfectly. They're recognized as leaders because they acted on things they could change, made plans for things that couldn't be changed right away but could be in the near future, and made the commitment to keep an eye out for things that will need changing once the technology (or opportunity) is right. As the trail has been well blazed, to do anything less is to fall short, and while knowingly or not, is to participate in greenwashing.

A brochure printed on recycled stock with soy ink is not intrinsically sustainable, and as such can't be called a sustainable solution if these two attributes were all that were considered. Is the stock Process Chlorine Free (PCF)? Instead of using recycled stock of unknown origin, could a certified alternative be used that promotes forest restoration (FSC certified)? How much soy oil is in the 'soy' ink? It's permitted to have as little as 7% soy content and still be called 'soy' ink. What are the environmental impacts of the soy used to make the inks: GMO seeds; petroleum-based insecticides, herbicides, and fertilizers; downstream eutrophication from runoff? Is the printer ISO 14000 certified, part of the Sustainable Green Printing Partnership (sgppartnership.org), or PIM Great Printer Environmental Initiative certified (pimw.org)? What source of energy was used to print the brochure, mill the paper, or manufacture the ink? How was the brochure laid out on the press sheet? Was the imposition set up for maximum stock utilization with minimum trim? Moreover, is a brochure even the right medium for reaching out to the target audience – creating a mound of waste if that audience routinely trashes unsolicited print materials unread on the way back from the mailbox? All of these, and more, are points to consider that a systems thinking methodology, when used correctly, would help a designer organize and work though the details needed to create a solution that really is more sustainable.

Life cycle: assessment, impact, costing

Life-cycle Assessment (LCA) is a term used to describe methods of assessing (but not limited to) environmental impacts connected to a product's life from raw material extraction, processing, manufacture, distribution, use, and disposal (cradle-to-grave). Increasingly LCAs are attempting to include repair, maintenance, recycling, and rebirth scenarios as well (cradle-to-cradle). Sometimes designers use LCAs either too early in the design process or interpret the data without looking at the full picture – thinking the LCA number delivered is the whole answer. In this section we'll look at what an LCA is about, as well as examine when it's advantageous to undertake this effort.

Today there are a growing number of methods used to characterize and categorize an object's life-cycle impact on the environment (resource flows, pollution, etc.), which makes comparing different LCA studies a challenge. Understanding the basics of how an LCA works, and then understanding what a particular LCA tool was designed to measure are important parts of the process.

There are a variety of LCA types as well as tools. Each type defines the beginning and end of the study. Variants on LCAs that can be used for product, print, and packaging projects include cradle-to-grave (resources and efforts through manufacture, use, and disposal), cradle-to-gate (resources and efforts only through manufacture), cradle-to-cradle or closed loop production (resources and efforts through manufacture, use, disposal, and rebirth), and ecologically based LCAs (similar to the previous LCAs but measures a broader range of ecological impacts to uncover direct and indirect human impacts on ecological resources and ecosystems).

Life-cycle Assessment (LCA) tools in the broadest definition, calculate the environmental impact of an object over its lifetime. Data used for these tools varies depending on what the software has been designed to draw from. An LCA in general though is a multistep procedure divided into four main steps:

1 *Goal and scope definition* (define functional unit and system boundary). What exactly will the LCA measure? There are quite a few efforts out there trying to give a single 'yes' answer. But what is the real question? Water isn't generally an issue people worry about – it's not toxic. But not enough of it, or too much of it, can be a real problem. An LCA may measure water used in the processes undertaken to make a product (growing and washing potatoes to make chips), but maybe not in the delivery of a product (suggesting materials required in the packaging to form a water vapor barrier to keep chips crunchy).

2 *Life Cycle Inventory (LCI)* is part of the LCA process involved with data collection. This data focuses on all flows in and out of the object's system, including: raw resources or materials; energy by type; and emissions to air, water, and land per specific substance. LCA tools usually take on the task of handling the LCI data and putting it into usable forms to prepare for interpretation.

3 *Life Cycle Impact Assessment (LCIA)* is the step in the LCA process charged with interpreting results, asking 'what does this mean?' Although LCA software will generate values for various resource flows and impacts, depending on the software used, what those numbers mean is not given a 'good' or 'bad' value judgment – the numbers simply 'are.' For example, a product may require a specific volume of natural gas as part of the manufacturing process (this data is part of the inventory [LCI]); in the LCIA phase, greenhouse gas (GHG) emissions from the combustion of natural gas would be calculated. Using natural gas, with a lower GHG index, could be a great alternative to coal. But if that natural gas is obtained through hydraulic fracturing (fracking), it begins to look less like a final solution and more like an interim step. The Athena Sustainable Materials Institute notes that "variables in LCIA include the

system boundary (how far upstream, downstream and side-stream does the analysis go), the functional unit (what is the volume/mass/purpose of the object being assessed), and specific LCIA methods such as allocation (how are impacts assigned to the product and by-products, on what basis)" (Athena Sustainable Materials Institute, 2016).When comparing two LCA studies, these factors are a critical part of understanding what needs to be accounted for to maintain an apples-to-apples comparison.

4   *Interpretation* (Compare alternatives, optimize, and critique.) An LCA only provides us a look into how our question fits with the data available. How we interpret that data is where we make forward progress.

The key to using any alternative is that it must be appropriate for the application, and the whole life cycle, of any option must be considered. This means an option, for example, can't just be recycle 'able' it has to actually be able to be recycled, otherwise it's still just future garbage. Whether a material is taken for recycling, however, may not be a factor that appears in a particular LCA tool, as recycling schemes vary from community to community.

In 2006, Biota introduced their premium water in a bottle made from compostable plastic, polylactic acid (PLA), a decision they felt would help deal with ever-increasing numbers of plastic beverage bottles in the waste stream and environment. However, whereas the numbers looked good on paper, the reality was that recyclers in the areas where Biota was sold at the time weren't ready to accept PLA (as of 2017 there are still no individual resin identification code numbers for bioplastics), and there were few industrial composting facilities able to accept PLA if it was collected for composting.

Additionally, as the bottles looked the same as competing water bottles made from Polyethylene Terephthalate (commonly referred to as PET), the PET recovered in Biota's distribution areas often became contaminated with PLA and so the resulting material recovered was either less valuable, at best, or completely unusable. The situation became so bad that recyclers in the affected areas called for a moratorium on all PLA bottles until such time as proper facilities could be established (Verespej, 2006).

In this example, PLA would have been a choice better applied to a structure that didn't have a healthy recovery program. And, in fact, the recyclers that had called for the moratorium on PLA bottles were encouraging manufacturers to use it for clamshell packaging, which at the time was not being recycled, to help build markets for PLA more quickly.

In this example, the interpretation of any LCA needed to include scope outside of the numbers delivered in order to make a good decision about whether to use PLA for bottled water or not.

Life cycle costing

Life Cycle Costing (LCC) should not be confused with LCA and LCI. Rather than consider environmental (and social) impacts, LCC looks at the sum of all recurring and one-time (non-recurring) costs over the full life span or a specified period of a good, service, structure, or system. This assessment includes purchase price, installation cost, operating costs, maintenance and upgrade costs, and remaining (residual or salvage) value at the end of ownership or its useful life (Athena Sustainable Materials Institute, 2016). LCC though can be a handy tool to use when considering using a sustainability-focused option over a more mainstream one. It's fairly common for nonmainstream alternatives to be more expensive upfront, but then taking into account long-term operating costs the alternative is usually much more attractive – if the alternative chosen is appropriate for the application. For example, Toyota's Prius, a gas/electric hybrid passenger car, can be a bit more expensive to purchase up front, but over the car's life, the cost to operate the vehicle is a fraction of its petroleum-only competitor (U.S. Department of Energy).

The right tool at the right time

One of the big mistakes designers make is to dive into an LCA before they really understand what it is they're trying to ultimately accomplish. LCAs should absolutely be part of the early design process, but it shouldn't always be the first tool a designer reaches for, as these assessments need to be run on each component that makes up the object. Understanding who the end product will serve, and what it really needs to do first, will help the designer choose the right design tool at the right time. LCAs done at the wrong time, or with the wrong intent (intentions like 'we want to make this out of bioplastic no matter what because compostability is attractive to our target market'), can potentially cut designers off from serendipitous (and more innovative) solutions.

Consider this example: If a designer decides to make a steel toaster oven, then running LCAs early (especially to establish some baselines on existing products and components) can be both enlightening and cost-effective – the components involved in producing this type of product are well established. But if the problem is simply to – roast food – then the time and cost put into problem solving for steel toaster oven ideas would have blocked avenues that could have led to a solar oven (a fantastic solution where electricity infrastructure is unreliable or nonexistent). The critical first step for any design problem is to really understand whom the end product will serve, what the end result needs to accomplish, and what the setting for distributing (or situating) the end solution will be (selling environment [market in general, store types, competitors] and community makeup [use culture, end-of-life options]).

Ongoing challenges

Although the number and variety of certifying bodies and assessment tools is expanding at a staggering rate, like any product or service, not all are of equal value. A designer may work to get certification for their product, but what is the quality of that certification? Who is the certifier? For LCA tools, many draw from similar data sources, some of which have not been updated for some time. Additionally, some LCA tools simply don't have the capacity to measure all aspects of an object. In the case of packaging for example, inks, varnishes, glues, and other decorations or adhesives may not be part of a packaging LCA tool's calculation mix. Yet how a carton is decorated, coated, or held together can have an impact on its recyclability.

Using systems thinking methods

Though the process of completing an LCA (or several) is super important for making efforts more sustainable, they are only tools used in service of doing things in a more sustainable way, they aren't the whole picture. Holistic systems thinking approaches using established sustainability principles are the foundations for numerous applications and tools to plan and design (or redesign) organizational strategy, processes, product and services, as well as business and community models.

What is considered a 'systems thinking' methodology is not universally agreed upon. The basic concept is that a systems thinking methodology is something that gets users to think in ways they wouldn't have considered on their own – and more holistically.

Figure 4.1 illustrates the wide variety of methodologies used to break complex problems down and what their strengths are. If a designer is working on a community development project,

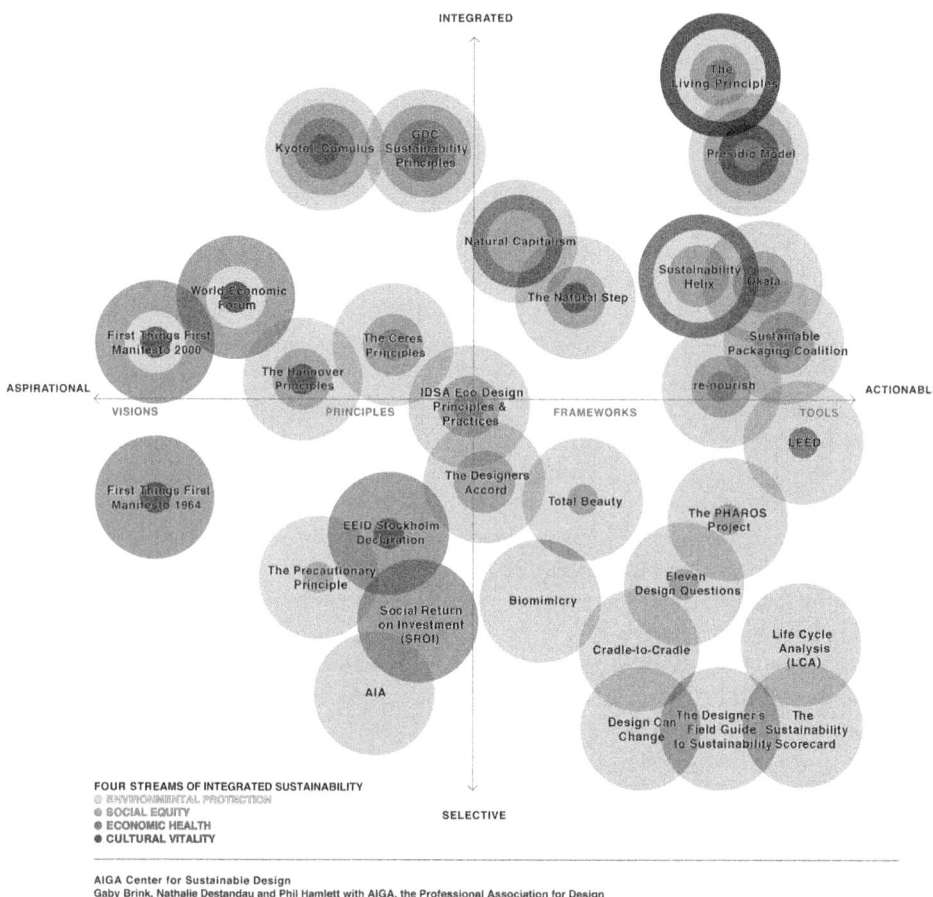

Figure 4.1 The landscape of sustainability systems: visions, principles, frameworks, tools (Brink, Destandau, and Hamlett, 2009).

a more aspirational methodology might be more useful. Creating a product? Culture as well as materials and processes (environmental concerns) might be issues the designer would want a tool for to help create a solution that was more than simply less bad, but one that would be really effective in its targeted market.

Today there are dozens of systems thinking approaches designed to take basic ideas further depending on their intended outcomes. When embarking on a project, the designer might take advantage of an iterative approach to problem solving using a pair of methodologies to be sure both social and ecological concern areas are fully addressed. Or they might pick a methodology where social, environmental, economic, and cultural issues are more fully integrated into one system.

The Natural Step™

One of the early systems thinking methodologies put into practice, and still in use today, is The Natural Step™ (TNS). TNS is a systems thinking framework created in 1989 by

Swedish oncology scientist Karl-Henrik Robèrt. Robèrt's framework identifies four system conditions for conducting human activities more sustainably. These system conditions were derived from a scientific approach looking at socioecological systems, including the laws of thermodynamics and social studies. The four systems conditions of TNS – Take, Make, Break, Needs – state:

In a sustainable society, nature is not subject to systematically increasing . . .

1   concentrations of substances from the earth's crust (such as fossil fuels and heavy metals – what we TAKE [dig-up/drill/extract] from the lithosphere),
2   concentrations of substances produced by society (such as antibiotics, endocrine disruptors, CO_2, and waste/pollution – what we MAKE and leave behind in the biosphere),
3   degradation by physical means (such as deforestation, permanent depletion of aquifers, and ecosystem destruction – what we BREAK of ecosystems), . . . and in that society . . .
4   there are no structural obstacles to people's health, influence, competence, impartiality and meaning. (All human NEEDS are met worldwide. There can be no eco-justice without social-justice.)

(The Natural Step, 2016a)

For a quick assessment of any idea, these four simple systems conditions can be useful. As an example, this could be used to assess new technology for recycling single-use plastic bags. Everyone likes recycling, right? But a quick check against the four TNS system conditions and one would realize that plastic bags in their current use/form need a serious rethink and should be phased out all together. In fact they are being banned outright in countries around the world (reusethisbag.com, 2016). Plastic bags are currently made from fossil products, increasing concentrations of substances in the biosphere from the lithosphere (take and make). They add to degradation of ecosystems when not properly disposed of (break). And they produce negative health impacts affecting those who are the least able to deal with them (needs). For example, in Bangkok plastic bags are a measurable addition to sewer system obstructions regularly turning major thoroughfares into muddy rivers during seasonal downpours. At only about 50 centimeters above sea level and criss-crossed with canals, Thailand's densely populated capital has been in a battle against flooding and the encroaching sea for some time. However, with Bangkok's chronically poor record of recycling, making plastic bags easier to recycle is nice, but finding an alternative that either decomposes quickly with no special composting facility required, or banning the single-use bags outright in favor of more workable solutions, is a more strategic move (Thibaut, 2016).

ABCD planning method (backcasting)

Like any system though, the devil is in the details. Where does your responsibility start and stop? What do you measure? How do you apply your findings? One of the methods for managing these questions is to use backcasting to help better define the issues. Backcasting (working backward up the effort chain) from the desired result, one might use a more general methodology to weigh the viability of early ideas in the brainstorming process. Then, once some likely ideas are identified, a more detailed methodology or a scorecard-based methodology would be employed to refine ideas, with an LCA applied to these refined ideas to verify the solutions are on the right track.

The ABCD planning method for backcasting, often used with the system conditions of The Natural Step™, works well with any systems thinking methodology. The ABCD method guides users through four basic steps:

A = Awareness and visioning

Provides the common language and 'whole-systems' context creating a vision of what the end effort would look like in a more sustainable future.

B = Baseline mapping

Uses sustainability principles from a systems thinking methodology to conduct a sustainability 'gap analysis' of the major flows and impacts from the effort under review.

C = Creative solutions

Brainstorm potential solutions to issues drawn out in the baseline analysis.

D = Decide on priorities

Once opportunities and potential solutions are identified in step C, prioritize options that move the effort toward a more sustainable solution, while making sure to optimize flexibility as well as economic, social, and ecological benefits.

(The Natural Step, 2016b)

Whatever tools are chosen to work with a backcasting method, like a game of Chutes and Ladders, it's very possible at any point for some or all of the process to loop back to earlier stages for further refinement. Unlike the board game though where the goal is to simply finish as quickly as possible, taking steps backward to reassess options guided by new information offers a variety of benefits. Looping back could filter through all of the systems methodologies/frameworks used in the process, or, loop back within a single step until a solution is derived that often outperforms the original end goal envisioned, creating a restorative solution rather than one that's just 'less bad.'

Living principles for design framework

Let's take the idea of pairing backcasting and a systems thinking methodology further using the Living Principles for Design framework (LP framework) (Figure 4.2). Created and published initially through the AIGA (American Institute of Graphic Arts) the Living Principles uses the basic ideas found in the Triple Bottom Line approach (people, planet, profit) and adds culture to the mix, with the idea that if you can't get people to do whatever your idea is (like recycle plastic bags), the rest (like new technology for recycling plastic bags) may at best be only a short-term solution.

Using backcasting in tandem with the Living Principles lets designers plug in their initial problem, look at it through various lenses, then reassess what the problem really is.

Using the example of plastic bags in Bangkok, Thailand in general has a thriving street food culture with millions buying their meals through these vendors each day. In the past, street food vendors would have used banana leaves to serve their food, but plastic bags and other plastic containers have replaced these biodegradable food service options.

The shift from biodegradable options to plastics is the same across the region, resulting in huge impacts on the world's oceans. China, Indonesia, Philippines, Vietnam, and Thailand have been identified as responsible for as much as 60 percent of plastic waste finding its way into the Ocean (Thibaut, 2016).

The question then really isn't just how to make a better plastic bag, or even a better bag recovery system, but to look at why vendors no longer use biodegradable options that served this same function for generations. What advantages do plastic bags offer? Are those advantages being artificially

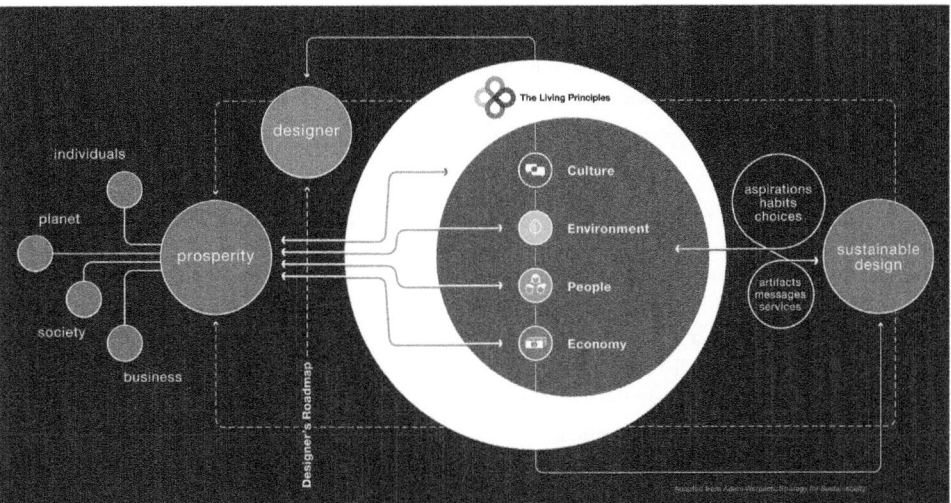

Figure 4.2 The Living Principles for Design framework is a catalyst for driving positive cultural change. It distills the four streams of sustainability – people, planet, profit and culture – into a roadmap that is understandable, integrated, and most importantly, actionable (Brink, Destandau, and Hamlett, 2009).

supported due to lack of producer responsibility or end-user accountability? Can other systems that were less problematic be made more competitive, making plastic bags less attractive?

In the example of overuse of single-use plastic bags, a community could ban the bags outright, but if no solutions are made available that are appropriate for that community's culture, the work around people create for themselves could be even worse. San Francisco, for example, has banned single-use plastic bags, and in their place heavier weight plastic bags are popping up with a disclaimer printed on them stating that the bag is a "reusable bag" with no further information about recovery of the bag for recycling, or a system of return to the business issuing the bag. These 'reusable' plastic bags have simply become heavier, more resource intensive garbage (Alexander, 2016).

These are the ideas that come up when culture is made part of a systems thinking effort, and where backcasting is used to help redefine the questions.

In Figure 4.2 we take the idea of 'prosperity' being one of the goals for embarking on a design effort (make money, satisfy need). Who are the stakeholders? (Individuals, the Planet, Society, Business). Who is the agent of transformation? (Designers). What are the streams the designer would follow? (People, Planet, Profit, Culture). And what is the desired end result? (Sustainable Design). Conversely, working backward from a desired result (Sustainable Design) what might the path be to achieve the goal of Prosperity and who might be impacted by the decisions made? (Individuals, the Planet, Society, Business). What might change to make that happen? (Artifacts, Choices). Example: A designer might embark on a solar energy project as a way to achieve energy independence for a community (move away from dependence on fossil fuels) with reduced environmental impact (Sustainable Design). But once solar becomes commonly used, the community that once relied on coal, now enjoys lower energy costs as well as reduced health issues (and cost) and so greater quality of life and prosperity for all stakeholders. (Spear, 2013) Using the LP-Framework in reverse (backcasting) allows designers to approach a problem from a variety of desired outcomes and perspectives.

Applied methods in industry

Different types of projects require different types of tools and methods. In this section we explore three different approaches of how different systems thinking frameworks can be applied to projects in product design, packaging and print design, and digital media.

Whole systems mapping for product design

A challenge to designing sustainable products is that every product category has different priorities for sustainability, so there is no one-size-fits-all answer. Portable electronics are different from major appliances, which are different from clothing and shoes, which are different from furniture, etc. As with all eco-friendly design, you need to know your priorities for sustainability, both to avoid greenwashing and to get the best return on the time and money you spend. For example, giving a smartphone a recycled plastic case can be a waste of time unless you have already sourced electronics with lower resource use and toxicity or increased the phone's life span, because the plastic case likely causes less than 1 percent of the phone's lifetime impacts. Also because of the plastic's miniscule impacts, trying to market a phone with a recycled plastic case and status quo electronics would be greenwashing.

Even when two different product categories do have the same priorities for sustainability, the solutions are usually very different. For example, smartphones and furniture both have materials as their biggest environmental impact, but furniture can solve this through sourcing sustainably harvested wood or 100 percent recycled metal, whereas smartphones rely on electronics that no one today produces renewably. Even the strategies to extend a product's life depend on what that product is: Durability can give furniture decades of life, because furniture does not go obsolete in the same way; but durability cannot save a smart phone from obsolescence – it will not be used for decades, even if it works perfectly well. Upgradeability is durability for electronics.

To prioritize for your product, use the key tools of systems thinking and quantitative analysis that have already been described. Quantitative analysis methods are methods that provide multi-level scores, not just yes/no certifications. Multiple levels of scores allow you to compare different design ideas against each other to find good, better, and best. Life-cycle Assessment (LCA) is the most rigorous analysis method, but it traditionally only measures environmental impacts. Some certification systems, such as cradle-to-cradle for simple products or EPEAT for computers and some other electronics, and Living Principles for print design, are less rigorous and fine-grained than LCA, but also measure social factors.

One design method, the Autodesk Sustainability Workshop's Whole Systems and Lifecycle Thinking method (or just Whole System Mapping method) weaves together both systems thinking and LCA into a four-step process:

1 *Visually draw out your product's whole system.* Include all major subassemblies, product packaging, life-cycle stages (raw materials, manufacturing, use, and end of life, including transport and other details), how the user interacts with the product, and anything the product needs for use (like electricity or ink). If you're inventing a new product from scratch, estimate the system based on similar products.
2 *Quantitatively analyze the system, using LCA or a point-based certification system to find the worst sustainability problems.* Fixing the worst impact in the system becomes your goal for redesign. Also write down your top business goals (e.g., cost and function) alongside your sustainability goal, so you don't compromise them.

3   *Brainstorm on your goal, using the visual system map.* Use the map to avoid getting fixated on one part of the product and be sure you have alternatives to every component or step in the system map. Use the map to generate more radical ideas by brainstorming how you can skip steps or eliminate components in the system. The more you skip, the more radical your ideas will be. You can also use other systems thinking design methods here.

4   *Use the same quantitative sustainability analysis (LCA or certification scores) to judge the brainstorm results.* These will be very imperfect estimates, but they are still better than guesswork. Pick your winning design idea(s) based on how well they satisfy both your sustainability and business goals.

You can see a video of this method at www.sustainabilityworkshop.autodesk.com/products/whole-systems-and-lifecycle-thinking.

Frameworks for packaging and print design

Though most consumers look at many packaging and print pieces as nothing more than future garbage, without packaging in particular to make moving our goods possible, there would be no modern economy. With the huge diversity of industries that packaging and print professionals serve, packaging and print will play a critical role in moving all of our efforts to a more sustainable operating model.

In the 2016 Smithers Pira report "Ten-year Forecast of Disruptive Technologies in Sustainable Packaging to 2026," author Terence A. Cooper notes "sustainability is no longer just nice to have, but is now seen as a necessity for attracting consumers and protecting market share – i.e., it is now an expectation, not a differentiator" (Butschli, 2016).

Primary questions for product, print, and packaging design are

- To whom will the result be marketed/targeted?
- What does the package or print piece have to do? (Just transport? Store and dispense? Be tamper evident? Communicate? Sell?)
- What is the selling or viewing environment like (physical environment plus competitive environment)?
- What laws and initiatives will the package or print piece have to satisfy (including product and package labeling requirements, producer responsibility, and environmental marketing claims)?
- What materials are appropriate? (Assess via LCA and supply chain analysis.)
- What are the supply chain options being considered? (What sorts of certifications are available to vendors on the chain?)
- What are the transport/delivery options being considered?
- What are the material recovery schemes available in the target markets?
- What opportunities for rebirth are possible for the target markets?

In addition to satisfying effective design basics, a well-designed package or print piece would also satisfy the Sustainable Packaging Coalition's vision and framework that defines what a sustainable result should be. (Note: This framework also applies to product design as well.)

A sustainable result:

1   Is beneficial, safe, and healthy for individuals and communities throughout its life cycle
2   Meets market criteria for performance and cost

3   Is sourced, manufactured, transported, and recycled using renewable energy
4   Maximizes the use of renewable or recycled source materials
5   Is manufactured using clean production technologies and best practices
6   Is made from materials healthy in all probable end-of-life scenarios
7   Is physically designed to optimize materials and energy
8   Is effectively recovered and utilized in biological and/or industrial cradle-to-cradle cycles
(Sustainable Packaging Coalition, 2005)

In the case of packaging in particular: For the most effective and sustainability-focused solution, the best methods include input from packaging professionals at the start of the product design process. When packaging and product are created together as a 'team' the product can be designed in such a way as to require minimal or no packaging. Too often designers and engineers shave product materials down to the fractional penny in order to save on production costs or to meet the product's own sustainability goals, only to have those savings consumed many times over to create more robust (and expensive) packaging to get the now more fragile product to market. The smart producer knows that materials are best optimized to create quality products, not extensive (and expensive) packaging.

Charged with the traditional tasks of protecting, informing, and selling, a package can either make or break the best product, as 70 percent of all purchase decisions are made in the store (WPP). But even the most savvy packaging designer can only get the consumer to buy the product once – the product needs to do its part to complete the equation, resulting in buyer satisfaction and repeat sales.

Digital media and the triple bottom line

Although digital media professionals may not create tangible objects, their products have significant environmental impacts in energy consumption and e-waste. Whereas websites on the surface seem 'weightless' compared to physical media, they consume significant amounts of energy in creation and distribution. Websites are served from data centers that draw a huge amount of electricity. Due to inefficiencies in the system, the average data center in the United States uses between 13 and 16 times the energy actually required to access their stored content (Glanz, 2012). Additional energy is used to transmit the files through the Internet. Finally, desktop computers use significant amounts of power to display websites compared to other home electronics, not least because they are frequently on all the time. Ignoring the carbon footprint of the web, or assuming it is automatically 'greener' than physical media is a good example of *not* applying systems thinking.

It is important to understand that site engineers can't magically fix a bloatware design and make it more efficient. Design decisions directly impact the carbon footprint of the Internet. The problem begins, and must be solved, at the design level. One of the biggest areas of waste is in web design. In his 2012 *Observer* article "Graphic Designers Are Ruining the Web," author John Naughton argues that designers are contributing to excessive energy waste through lush visuals, poor file optimization, and lack of support for mobile. Based on current estimates, the average website is tenfold larger than it was a decade ago (Naughton, 2012), mostly due to visual design elements.

An important point to realize is that the web is not 'electric paper.' Visual design patterns and techniques which work well for print can quickly turn a website into an energy hog, reduce the quality of user experience, and exclude people with less than cutting-edge technology. Most efficiency gains come from reworking the user interface of a site, according to web performance guru Steve Souders (Souders, 2012). On the other hand, it is unnecessary to recycle web assets – sites can be instantly updated to new versions on demand. In short, the rules for sustainable web design are different from print and industrial design, but many of the underlying principles are the same.

Designers who don't think about the sustainability of their web projects also make less inclusive sites, violating equity and social justice parameters found in strategies like Triple Bottom Line (TBL). A fancy brochure produced by an NGO reads the same regardless of where you read it. But a graphic-heavy website, built to mimic print designs (impressive as it may be to the client), often won't work in the target country where Internet infrastructure is not at the same technological level. This inattention to the differences between web and print design is insensitive to the digital divide between different countries. Agencies developing websites need to follow a policy of progressive enhancement, ensuring that content is available regardless of bandwidth, location, or software.

A simple systems thinking methodology typically used for business efforts, like TBL, can help a designer think about digital design in a more holistic way. TBL asks three basic questions:

- How will decisions impact people? (accessibility, inclusion, social justice)
- How will decisions impact the planet? (environment, resource use)
- Is the effort economically as well as socially and environmentally sustainable? (profit)

Following are some areas digital media professionals can use to help their websites apply the principles of TBL (Markiewicz, Save the Planet through Sustainable Web Design, 2012).

1   Carbon footprint sites can help designers understand the impact and costs of their work. Examples include EcoGrader (ecograder.com) as well as Web Bloat Score (webbloatscore. com). To compare their site to the mainstream, designers can use Steve Souders' HTTP Archive (httparchive.org). (planet, profit)
2   User experience (UX) strategies help site visitors complete tasks faster and more efficiently, which in turn reduces Internet resource consumption. Designers should consider replacing an 'artist to developer' model with a UX work flow, which automatically adds audience-centric thinking to design. (people, planet)
3   Iterative design strategies replace a waterfall work flow with a series of prototype sites, each developed and tested. This allows discovered problems with efficiency to feed back onto the design process. (people, planet, profit)
4   Progressive enhancement, in its original form proposed by Steven Champeon, achieves several goals of sustainability. By starting with a basic accessible content, and enhancing visual look and feel based on the user's computer, it maximizes the audience diversity. By starting from the basics, it naturally focuses on efficient design principles. (people, planet, profit)
5   Mobile first has even greater potential to improve Internet sustainability. As developed by Luke Wroblewski, it resets the design focus from power-hungry desktops to smaller, more efficient mobile devices. As Internet use increasingly shifts from desktop to mobile, a mobile-first strategy ensures that digital media solutions work to be more careful with energy demands. This demands in turn that designers rethink the role of graphics as communication tools for the small screen. Designers can test mobile friendliness with tools like the Google Search Console (search.google.com/search-console/mobile-friendly). (people, planet)
6   Responsive Web Design is a set of strategies developed by Ethan Marcotte that allow the same website to dynamically adjust itself to desktop or mobile via CSS media queries. This strategy, combined with Progressive Enhancement, ensures that the same content gets

delivered to its audience in the way most effective on the user's hardware (alistapart.com/article/responsive-web-design). (people, planet)

7   Web standards like HTML5 and CSS3 allow developers to 'send the recipe' for a sophisticated, yet efficient, design, rather than downloading and rich media plugins common in the Flash era. (planet, profit)

8   Search engine optimization (SEO) makes a website easily indexable by search engines. This quite literally cuts down on the power needed by Google to index sites. Making sites more search friendly – for example, by incorporating semantic HTML tags and relevant keywords –reduces the number of bits users burn to find what they want. SEO firms that tie link quality and user support to durable site traffic are helping shape a more sustainability-focused Internet (Audette, 2011). (planet, profit)

9   The Web Index, from World Wide Web creator Tim Berners-Lee looks beyond the efficiency of websites to their relative impact on key areas of sustainability in different countries – inclusiveness, transparency, and value to their users. NGOs creating websites for multiple countries should consult the Web Index to ensure their sites provide maximum benefit to their intended target audiences (thewebindex.org). (people, planet, profit)

Digital media professionals also need to investigate their hosting strategy. Many web hosts claim they are green. As one would do with any potential vendor, be sure to investigate what they mean by green, whether they have any certifications backing up their claims, and if there are any complaints about a potential host engaging in greenwashing. Responsible green hosts (e.g., AISO.net) lay out their sustainability practices in a mission statement, allowing their green claims to be validated.

Like any design project, the critical first steps to create sustainable digital media are clear goals, as well as a clear understanding of what the end user really needs and how they'll access or use the product. In applying then even one of the most basic systems thinking methodologies like the Triple Bottom Line one can begin to develop a more sustainable digital product.

Conclusion

Throughout this chapter we've provided a variety of examples and helpful ideas from product, print, packaging, and digital design using systems thinking methodologies and tools. Though there are new methodologies and tools coming out all the time, best practices dictate that designers use one (or two in sequence) to guide their project – with the goal of trying to meet all of the criteria outlined in the methodology. One of the biggest mistakes designers make when working toward doing things in a more sustainable way is to cherry-pick the parts they find the easiest, and ignore the harder parts.

As mentioned at the beginning of the chapter, it's possible that not all steps a systems methodology uses to manage a project can be undertaken at the time of the project. But, all steps *can* and *must* be accounted for. To move toward a more sustainable operating model is a process. Act on things you can change, make plans for things that couldn't be changed right away but could be in the near future, and, make the commitment to keep an eye out for things that will need changing once the technology (or opportunity) is right.

We find ourselves in this place of depletion through billions of small, shortsighted decisions. By using holistic tools such as LCAs and systems thinking methodologies, we can move to a place of sustainable abundance by making a billion better-informed and forward-looking decisions.

Works cited

AIGA. (2010, October). The Living Principles Framework. *The Living Principles Roadmap.* New York, NY. Retrieved May 30, 2016, from The Living Principles for Design: www.aiga.org/roadmap/

Alexander, K. (2016, September 09). *Plastics Industry Pushing to Halt Bag-Ban Momentum.* Retrieved January 08, 2017, from San Francisco Chronicle: www.sfchronicle.com/bayarea/article/Plastics-industry-pushing-to-halt-bag-ban-momentum-9213882.php

Athena Sustainable Materials Institute. (2016). *LCA, LCI, LCIA, LCC: What's the Difference?* Retrieved May 23, 2016, from Athena Sustainable Materials Institute: www.athenasmi.org/resources/about-lca/whats-the-difference/

Audette, A. (28 March 2011). *Why Quality Is the Only Sustainable SEO Strategy.* Inc. Third Door Media. Retrieved June 16, 2016, from http://searchengineland.com/why-quality-is-the-only-sustainable-seo-strategy-69244

Brink, G., Destandau, N., and Hamlett, P. (2009, October). *Genealogy of the Living Principles.* New York, NY: AIGA, Center for Sustainable Design.

Buckminster Fuller Institiute. (n.d.). *About Fuller.* Retrieved May 30, 2016, from Buckminster Fuller Institiute: https://bfi.org/about-fuller

Butschli, J. (2016, June 07). *Package Sustainability Now an Expectation.* (PMMI Media Group). Retrieved June 18, 2016, from Greener Package: www.greenerpackage.com/supply_chain/package_sustainability_now_expectation

Cradle to Cradle Products Innovation Institute. (2014). *Cradle to Cradle Products Program.* Retrieved May 30, 2016, from Cradle to Cradle Products Program: www.c2ccertified.org/

Denver AP. (2011, June 18). *Corn Bottle Pioneer BIOTA Locked in Legal Battle.* Retrieved May 25, 2016, from denver.cbslocal.com: http://denver.cbslocal.com/2011/06/18/corn-bottle-pioneer-biota-locked-in-legal-battle/

Glanz, J. (2012, September 22). *Power, Pollution and the Internet.* Retrieved June 08, 2016, from *The New York Times*: www.nytimes.com/2012/09/23/technology/data-centers-waste-vast-amounts-of-energy-belying-industry-image.html?_r=0

Jedlička, W. (2008). *Packaging Sustainability: Tools, Systems and Strategies for Innovative Package Design.* Hoboken, NJ: John Wiley & Sons, Inc.

Jedlička, W. (2009). *Sustainable Graphic Design: Tools, Systems and Strategies for Innovative Print Design.* Hoboken, NJ: John Wiley & Sons, Inc.

McDonough, W., and Braungart, M. (2002). *Cradle to Cradle: Remaking the Way We Make Things.* New York, NY: North Point Press.

Markiewicz, P. (2012, March). *Green Design vs. Sustainable Web Design – Some Data.* Retrieved June 18, 2016, from Sustainable Virtual Design: https://sustainablevirtualdesign.wordpress.com/2013/05/28/green-design-vs-sustainable-web-design-some-data-2/

Markiewicz, P. (2012, August 17). *Save the Planet Through Sustainable Web Design.* Retrieved June 10, 2016, from Creativebloq: www.creativebloq.com/inspiration/save-planet-through-sustainable-web-design-8126147

The Natural Step. (n.d.). *Applying the ABCD Planning Method.* (T. N. Step, Producer). Retrieved June 17, 2016, from The Natural Step: www.thenaturalstep.org/sustainability/applying-the-abcd-planning-method/

The Natural Step. (2016a). *Applying the ABCD Planning Method.* Retrieved February 01, 2017, from The Natural Step: www.thenaturalstep.org/sustainability/applying-the-abcd-planning-method/

The Natural Step. (2016b). *Four Basic Rules Define Success.* Retrieved February 02, 2017, from thenaturalstep.org: www.thenaturalstep.org/our-approach/

Naughton, J. (2012, February 18). *Graphic Designers Are Ruining the Web.* Retrieved June 08, 2016, from The Guardian: www.theguardian.com/technology/2012/feb/19/john-naughton-webpage-obesity

Souders, S. (2012, February 10). *The Performance Golden Rule.* Retrieved June 10, 2016, from stevesouders.com: www.stevesouders.com/blog/2012/02/10/the-performance-golden-rule/

Spear, S. (2013, September 06). *5 Reasons Solar Is Beating Fossil Fuels.* Retrieved February 01, 2017, from EcoWatch.com: www.ecowatch.com/5-reasons-solar-is-beating-fossil-fuels-1881792573.html

Sustainable Packaging Coalition. (2005). *Definition of Sustainable Packaging.* Retrieved June 17, 2016, from Sustainable Packaging Coalition: www.sustainablepackaging.org/content/?type=5&id=definition-of-sustainable-packaging

Sustainable Packaging Coalition. (2016). *How2Recycle/Labels.* Retrieved June 17, 2016, from How2Recycle: http://how2recycle.info/labels

Swedish Institute. (2013). *The Swedish Recycling Revolution*. Retrieved June 16, 2016, from Sverige (Sweden): https://sweden.se/nature/the-swedish-recycling-revolution/

Thibaut, M. (2016, September 06). *Flooding Threat as Plastic Bags Clog Bangkok's Bowels*. Retrieved January 05, 2017, from phys.org: http://phys.org/news/2016-09-threat-plastic-bags-clog-bangkok.html

U.S. Department of Energy. (n.d.). *Can a Hybrid Save Me Money?* Retrieved May 24, 2016, from fueleconomy.gov: www.fueleconomy.gov/feg/hybridCompare.jsp

Verespej, M. (2006, October 23). *Group Fights PLA Bottles*. Retrieved May 25, 2016, from plasticsnews.com: www.plasticsnews.com/article/20061023/NEWS/310239995/group-fights-pla-bottles

5

SUSTAINABLE DESIGN FOR SCALE

Andrea Steves and Rebecca Silver

Scale and limits on a finite planet

Designers have profound power to change the world with their actions. This power manifests especially when the results of their design actions scale. Whether designing a new smartphone, e-commerce site, customer service system, or skyscraper, each design action triggers a chain of reactions, governed by design specifications. These reactions in turn cascade into multitude ecological impacts: finished materials will be produced from depleting natural resources, data will be stored in energy-intensive data centers, and building foundations will be dug that disrupt terrestrial ecosystems. The power of design, when multiplied this way, brings with it great responsibility.

In our collective 25 years of designing products, processes, and systems for some of the largest companies in the world, one of the biggest challenges we have faced is designing sustainably at scale. Drawing on our own experiences working across multitude sectors, including technology, retail, electronics, apparel, health care, and consumer packaged goods, throughout the chapter we explore the implications of designing at scale to maximize natural and human ecosystem vitality, as well as economic utility. Designers must take a unique multidisciplinary approach when confronting scale challenges, as they collaborate with business managers and technical experts to meet the demands of launching ideas into the global economy. This collaborative approach influences both our own design practices and the structure of this chapter, which we've tried to summarize in examples and best practices.

We live, and design, on a finite planet, with ecosystems, resource stores, and communities that have limits. According to a report from the United Nations Environment Programme, during the twentieth century "the extraction of construction materials grew by a factor of 34, ores and minerals by a factor of 27, fossil fuels by a factor of 12, and biomass by a factor of 3.6" (United Nations Environment Programme 2011). This repeated pattern of extraction leads to mass resource exhaustion if the rate of consumption is faster than the rate of rebound and replenishment. The Millennium Ecosystem Assessment, initiated by the United Nations in 2001, stated that humans, in our aim to meet demands for natural resources such as fuel, timber, and fresh water, have altered ecosystems more extensively in the last 50 years than in any other comparable period. The Overview of the report states that

> The changes that have been made to ecosystems have contributed to substantial net gains in human well-being and economic development, but these gains have been

55

achieved at growing costs in the form of the degradation of many ecosystem services, increased risks of nonlinear changes, and the exacerbation of poverty for some groups of people. These problems, unless addressed, will substantially diminish the benefits that future generations obtain from ecosystems.

(The International Resource Panel)

In our consumerist and capitalist society, natural resources are often viewed through a lens of production and economic utility, where ecosystems and resource stores become a "standing reserve" to be used to produce economic value in the present (Heidegger 1977). Yet, this "standing reserve" is being depleted, and many, including the United Nations Environment Program, highlight the need to decouple resource use and economic growth. The idea that constant growth is necessary continues to persist even as we uncover increasing evidence of limits, such as resource exhaustion or pollutant saturation. We believe designers have the opportunity to challenge these conventions and assumptions. As we design products that improve lives and increase living standards, how can we avoid the negative socio-environmental impacts of depleting resources, polluting ecosystems, and disrupting the health and economic welfare of communities that rely on these ecosystems for meeting their daily needs?

As we think about designing on a finite planet, we need to expand our definition of design beyond just "making things." Design at scale includes a range of design actions, and doesn't always mean making something new or physical. It could also include the creation of a service, optimization of a process or system, the development of an idea or concept, or even the "unmaking" of something. Designing for sustainability at scale should be taken to mean that we might enact any of these mentioned design actions with the added application of sustainability principles and practices.

What is scale?

When we think about scaling in design, we typically think about scaling up and creating *multiples of things* through mass production – more units, more versions or variations, more customers, more target global markets. This way of thinking dates back to the Industrial Revolution, and the concept of "economies of scale," where an increase in production can lead to proportionate savings. But when approaching a design challenge from the lens of sustainability, we need to think beyond scaling up, and consider how design utility might be scaled without disrupting fragile and limited resources. We approach scaling from five different modes:

Physical scale

The increase or decrease in the scale of physical goods, including the number of units of finished products produced, materials which went into making the product, the waste left over after manufacturing, and physical waste remaining once the product no longer has utility for the consumer.

Temporal scale

The life span of the designed product (physical, digital, and service), including the resources needed to use and maintain the product over time, and what second lives, or expanded utility, the product might serve (if it is reused or recycled). A product's usefulness – or how it might become less useful, or obsolete, over time – is another aspect of temporal scale. For example, a physical product might become less useful as our culture shifts away from ownership of physical products, replacing paper with screen-based media.

Geographic scale

The geographic footprint of the designed product (physical, digital, and service), in terms of where its raw materials come from, where it may be manufactured, where it may be sold and used, and where it may be processed once discarded by the user (as waste or as a recyclable product).

Knowledge scale

The scaled dissemination of information, often brought about through the design of new communications technologies and services, such as through mass production of books via the printing press (historic example), and increased global access to information via online and social media platforms (modern example).

Shifting scale paradigms

Shifting the scope of production at scale, through products and services that offer mass customization and mass personalization, from single products/services that serve many customers toward producing individual/customized products for individual customers on a massive scale.

Why does scale matter?

To understand designing at scale is to first understand the limits we confront when scaling the production, use, and disposal of products and services. Limits challenge notions of continuous growth. Reaching limits results in the failure of systems to function and flourish in perpetuity, often resulting in devastating consequences. Consider how limits have been historically reached as the result of design actions through a brief taxonomy of limit archetypes with particular relevance to design: exhaustion, saturation, material properties, technology, process flows, time and understandability, and predictability.

Limits of exhaustion

Limits of exhaustion result from the depletion of renewable and nonrenewable resources to levels beyond where the resource can be replenished. Historically, there are numerous examples where resources were exhausted (or are near exhaustion) due to activities driven by design actions.

The Aral Sea in Uzbekistan was once the fourth largest inland water body on Earth. From the 1960s through the 2000s, the Aral Sea was depleted, as the rivers that feed it were diverted to grow cotton and other crops – losing around 60 percent of its area and 80 percent of its volume (Chapagain, Hoekstra, and Savenije 2005). Uzbekistan was a major cotton producer and water consumer, the second largest cotton exporter in the world with 41 percent of its cultivated land used for growing cotton. This ecological disaster was believed to have displaced over 100,000 people, impacting the health of five million throughout the entire region (Conant 2006). There are a number of other examples: near extinction of land mammals like African elephants poached for ivory,[1] near extinction of aquatic species like North Atlantic Right Whales hunted for oil,[2] depletion of elements like helium, phosphorus and indium used for industrial and agricultural processes, and limits of critical metals used in production of electronics such as cell phones (Graedel et al. 2015).

Limits of saturation

Whereas limits of exhaustion are a complete depletion of a resource, limits by saturation are effectively the opposite. These limits are reached when a system is overburdened with a pollutant, often as a byproduct of industrial activities. Greenhouse gas emissions are a prime example. These emissions, largely resulting from fossil fuel combustion (for industrial agriculture, transportation, heating buildings, etc.), have created a cumulative buildup of heat-trapping gases in the Earth's atmosphere, leading to global climate change. Other examples include nutrient pollution, where nutrient-saturated "dead zones" in aquatic bodies are caused by agricultural runoff and saturation of particulate matter from the combustion of fossil and natural fuels (used for transportation and cooking fuel).

Limits of materials and material properties

Every material has physical limits, both in terms of supply and capabilities. Each material has unique properties, which govern material use and processing capabilities, durability, and recyclability (and thus temporal utility). Particularly relevant to designing sustainability at scale are material limitations to recycling and degradability. Many materials cannot easily be recycled, do not easily decompose, and present limits to waste treatment in landfills and composting facilities. Furthermore, even when materials are recycled, they cannot be recycled infinitely. Mixing materials (where they're unable to be separated for reuse) and toxic materials present additional constraints to recycling and waste handling, especially if toxic materials are improperly disposed of.

Paper is an easily understood example: it can only go through a recycling process between five and seven times because the quality of fibers degrades over time, presenting limits to reuse. Furthermore, just because paper is a theoretically recyclable material doesn't mean it can always be recycled. There are a number of factors that limit the extended use of recycled paper, including the availability of paper to be recovered and the price of that paper, the quality of the recovered paper (whether it has impurities such as adhesives, foils, or dirt and other waste), the facilities available, and more (Blanco, Miranda, and Monte 2013). These constraints can limit the effectiveness of closed-loop systems and circular economies (where material flows are designed to be reused in a subsequent process). Similar challenges exist with other recyclable materials, including electronic waste. E-waste contains toxic materials, which can be hazardous to human health if disposed of improperly. Bonding two materials together also presents issues for recycling: for example, blended textiles (like cotton-polyester blends) can't be recycled.

Limits of technology

Like limits for materials, there are limits to capabilities of production, information, and technologies to solve specific challenges and perform certain types of work. These limits are primarily gaps between design ideas and technical feasibility.

Although renewable energy is becoming more cost effective, presently (in 2017, the date this text was published), it's challenging to power large population centers (cities) with 100 percent renewable electricity due to two factors: dominant renewable energy sources are intermittent (wind speed and solar radiation fluctuate) and renewable energy can't be stored in batteries at utility scale. Reliable, available, and cost-effective large-scale batteries and storage technologies are necessary to enable a 100 percent renewable-energy-powered economy at current consumption levels.[3] Another technological limit is encountered when resource-intensive processes limit the overall sustainability of reclaiming a material, for example, if a process requires more life-cycle energy and material inputs to recycle than what might be saved through recycling. Until processes that are less energy and/or material intensive are invented, this problem will persist.

Limits of process flows

Material or information flows are limited by a lack of infrastructure, process, or movement in a system (a bottleneck), constraining the amount of material (physical or informational) that can flow through the system. Process flows can also limit the theoretical potential versus actual potential for recyclables and compostables, where reverse logistics are complex, or where there are not enough facilities (or enough demand for the recycled material) to process the waste at the rate it is being generated. For example, a designer might think they are making an ecologically sound decision by using a bio-based material, like biopolymers, but these materials may not be able to be recycled due to lack of recycling infrastructure for these materials. Finally, process flow limits also constrain the ability to scale down as well as to scale up. For example, manufacturers may require minimum production order quantities from customers, which may prohibit small customers from specifying certain efficient or eco-friendly materials and technologies that are only available at a larger scale.

Electronics such as cell phones, tablets, and laptops further illustrate this principle. Many electronics use metals in very small quantities, making recyclability impractical due to the complexity of collecting, separating, sorting, and aggregating these components at common recycling points. Looking at a different industry, textile waste is difficult to recycle because of the variety of textile fiber types and qualities, the difficulty in identifying fibers after consumption, and the challenges in aggregating single-type fibers for recycling. Designers encounter process constraints when sourcing specialty materials, such as those with organic or recycled content, when order quantities aren't large enough to meet supplier minimums.

Limits of time

Another boundary that scaled systems can run up against is limits of time. There is often a bias toward the present and near term, as distant futures and the future value of resources are difficult to conceptualize. For example, the mining of heavy metals creates short-term financial value when these metals are sold, but it may be difficult to account for the costs associated with the long-term, often intergenerational, burden of cleaning up waste from former mine sites. (www.aadnc-aandc.gc.ca/eng/1100100027364/1100100027365).

Additionally, time delays may cause gaps between supply and demand for resources and processes, where supply can't scale up and down at pace with demand, or vice versa. This delay is particularly relevant when sourcing and consuming resources, which take time to recover and rebound, like when a forest needs time to regenerate after logging. Another case of the lag time between supply and demand manifests when customers specify sustainably certified products. When these products are unavailable, producers may seek to obtain certification in order to increase available supply, but may be constrained by the time it takes to bring these products to market. For example, it takes years to obtain organic certification; thus organic crop farmers must incur the costs of growing organic for years before they can reap any benefits from achieving certified organic status.[4]

Limits of understandability and predictability

As designers, there are limits to our own understanding and to our ability to predict outcomes. These cognitive limits can result in unintended consequences or externalities (costs sheltered by the public rather than embodied in the cost of a product) stemming from the designs we create or actions we take. These unintended consequences can manifest at any stage of a product or service's life cycle: materials may have defects, products may be manufactured under dangerous working conditions, technologies may fail, users may handle products in hazardous ways, and waste may be handled improperly, leading to devastating outcomes.

When consumers throw out their computers, smartphones and other electronic waste (e-waste), the hazardous heavy metals and toxic substances contained in the waste, such as lead, mercury, and cadmium,[5] can lead to negative unintended consequences. E-waste is commonly shipped around the world for disposal, often to regions with weak or nonexistent laws governing how this waste is handled. Without strict laws and enforcement, investigations have demonstrated this e-waste may be manually disassembled, sometimes by women and children,[6] burned, releasing hazardous chemicals into the atmosphere, or dumped into local water sources. At the time of publication of this chapter, the United States has no federal laws that ban the export of e-waste.[7]

The challenges of designing at scale

This consideration of limits leads us to imagine why scale might matter in the context of design. The short answer is societies have reached limits before, as a result of activities driven by design actions. Unpacking this statement further we postulate that most practicing designers will create products and services that reach broad physical, temporal, and geographic scales, whether working for a large company, a design consultancy, or independently. This demands an agile practice that considers the broader life-cycle consequences of design output at scale. Simply put, there's a big difference in the challenges inherent to producing one isolated prototype versus a million finished goods that will be distributed all over the world.

Product multiplication or diversification

A company might release multiple versions of the same product or service family, either in parallel or in sequence, increasing complexity of finished product models. At scale, designs may be manufactured or manifested as thousands, hundreds of thousands, or millions of units, when producing both physical goods, such as apparel or packaging, and digital goods, such as mobile applications or computer software. Furthermore this multiplier effect may be exponential, if similar designs are produced by other creators and companies. This challenge is further exacerbated by trends, such as fast fashion, that accelerate disposability and redundancy of multiples. In this context designers must attempt to think beyond a single artifact, by carefully considering how a solution produced at scale may push limits of exhaustion and saturation.

Furthermore, product variations can introduce physical scale challenges, pushing the limit of materials and material properties. It is common practice that a company or designer may create a product family that includes different model variations, with a multitude of sizes, flavors or scents, colorways, quality levels (good, better, best), feature sets (e.g., a base-level car and one with premium add-ons), or brand extensions (e.g., Coke, Diet Coke, Coke Zero, and Vanilla Coke). Furthermore, a company or designer may launch new releases of the same base product on a seasonal or yearly basis, potentially integrating new technologies. For example, think of an iPhone, which includes new features, fixes and improvements, style variations, and is designed to fit changing consumer trends, including colors, physical design, and materials. Each of these variations expands the number of cases in which sustainable design must be integrated, scaling the number of scenarios the designer must consider.

Variance in production

Multiple technologies or suppliers may be used to produce the same finished good or service, increasing complexity of product parts and logistics/distribution. The challenge here for the sustainable designer is to understand all of the production pathways, or supply chain complexity. For a single finished product model, multiple suppliers may produce duplicates of the same material, part, or finished product types, and these products may be sourced from around the world, with (ideally) no perceivable differences in aesthetic or functional quality in the eyes of the brand or the consumer. However, the designer might need to understand the differences between suppliers – for example, are their labor practices equivalent?

Geographic differences

Geographies (whether by continent, country, state, or local municipality) have socioecological variances by region (as just mentioned), as well as idiosyncratic cultural norms, regulatory and infrastructural challenges, increasing complexity of compliance, and environmental/social impact. Further, the global footprint of products presents a large barrier to understanding the impacts of design, as it's hard to manage what you can't see.

There are many impacts for sustainability introduced by geographic differences, and we'll touch on just a few. Varying material content and environmental regulations among different markets can add complexity, as a designer might be asked to create one product that will satisfy regulations for many countries at once. In the case of electronics, some regional regulations might require specific labeling of toxic substances, while other regulations might require removable batteries. Geographic differences in both breadth and enforcement effectiveness of environmental and social regulations must merit different design considerations and standards; for example, lax labor standards in a region may require designers and brands to demand a strong, independently verifiable code of conduct from its manufacturers, and to manage compliance with this code of conduct directly rather than relying on governmental agencies to do so. Unique connectivity systems by geography, such as transportation and distribution infrastructure (some of which might be more sustainable) or divergent recycling infrastructure might also require design adaptation.

Most importantly, as natural resources and human populations are not equally distributed around the world, socio-environmental stresses (and risks) also differ regionally creating challenges for moderating and mitigating negative impacts associated with scaled design solutions. Divergent stressors include lack of availability of fresh water, human population proximity to polluting sources (through air, water, and land), fragile habitat proximity to disruptive forces (via pollution or land use change), and electricity grid makeup (whether electricity is produced from green sources like wind and solar or from fossil fuel sources like coal and natural gas). Environmental stressors are directly tied to the availability and enforcement of regulations, which help to ensure resources are managed appropriately and effectively.

To manage this a designer may need to understand the differences between production regions, which can be difficult to accomplish: is one supplier located in a water-stressed area (where a lot of water may be used to produce a product)?

The tragedy of the commons

The tragedy of the commons is an economic theory that arises within systems of shared resources, such as our finite planet. Individuals act independently in their own self-interest and may exhaust shared resources, known as "the commons" (Hardin 2009). Under this concept, the positive or negative utility (meaning benefits or usefulness) of a service or object is not felt equally by individuals. Consider a smartphone, designed by a U.S. corporation, whose metals are mined in Mongolia, that is manufactured in China, packaged in paper sourced from Brazil, and shipped to a user in the United States – this is a very typical although simplified scenario. The end user benefits from the use of the phone. The corporation profits from the sale of the device. The mining corporation in Mongolia, the miners who work to extract metals, and in China, the factory and factory workers, all receive economic compensation for labor and materials. However, the user might be unaware of the conditions at the mine site, pollution caused by waste products, or air pollution issues caused around the factory – the negative and positive utility is unevenly distributed among the actors in this situation. Furthermore, there may be information gaps that prevent the end user from even thinking about the fact that their smartphone might be causing harm on the other side of the world. This physical and temporal separation can lead to gaps of knowledge or understanding.

Invisibility

As we just described, the effects of the tragedy of the commons can stem from information gaps. Inherent to the challenge of designing on a global scale is a disconnect between designers, their customers, the places where their products are made, and other links in the product's value chain. As in our last example, a user's smartphone may contain minerals that were mined in Mongolia, far out of sight. The phone is made, packaged, and shipped within a web of global infrastructure and manufacturing. During its use, the phone will rely on telecommunications infrastructure, power, and servers, which a user never sees, and at end-of-life, the phone (or the materials, minerals, and components it contains) could end up on the other side of the Earth. This temporal and physical separation creates information gaps that might not otherwise arise if designer, consumer, and manufacturer were all members of the same close-knit community.

Similarly, a product or service user only sees the finished product in front of them and rarely do they see or experience the product at scale. We don't see a product's embodied energy, water, and materials, nor do we experience the labor that went into making or handling the product. Compounded over all users, say, in a city or town, there is a scalar mismatch between individual experience of waste and collective waste production. People go through their day-to-day actions, disposing of waste in their individual trashcans, but often don't think about the places their waste goes or the people who handle their waste. In fact, in many cases, the infrastructure that takes our waste away is so reliable, we don't have to think about, smell, or see it (Ehrenfeld 2013).

This invisibility makes the job of the designer even more challenging. Rarely are designers given enough data to know exactly what challenges, socioecological or otherwise, will result from their design actions. It can be challenging to obtain all the information to fully understand the supply/value system, especially when these systems are highly dynamic, or when one lacks the leverage to obtain this information. Further complicating this problem, many of the socio-environmental impacts stemming from designed products and processes are not tracked. Aside from regulations in some regions, which may mandate accounting for energy consumption, water use, emissions, and waste, corporations and consumers may not be incentivized to measure their consumption and waste generation, which in turn contributes to collective negative human health, environmental, and social impacts. Designers, then, must continuously strive for informational transparency, asking questions and working to fully understand the impacts of their design actions.

Systems thinking for scale

Given the complexities introduced by scale and limits, there's a mandate for designers to begin each challenge by reflecting deeply on the context and consequences of their actions, and to use their influence to exert positive influence over the entire system. By exploring context and systems further, we begin to break down how to solve scale design challenges through the lens of sustainability.

Designers can uncover the context of a design challenge by questioning underlying assumptions and goals. *Who is it for, who does it benefit, and who does it affect? What need does the design solution solve and why is it unique? How will it be made/manifested and where will it be used and distributed?* And finally, *how does your solution address challenges of sustainability?* Though some of this information may be given up-front in an initial design brief or problem statement, it's the designer's role to dig deeper into these questions in order to create successful sustainable solutions.

When designing at scale, designers might find themselves making decisions that don't seem like design decisions. Designers might find themselves solving problems that looks more like problems of politics, business, urban planning, user behavior, or infrastructure, and may need to collaborate with experts in these areas to collectively solve challenges.

Every design depends on larger economic, social, and ecologic systems. Thus, it's critical to approach design actions from a complex systems standpoint – where the connections between the parts of the complex system become more important than the components, or sum of components, of the system itself. For example, an automobile isn't just steel, wheels, and windows – but together these parts form a system that transports people from place to place. Similarly, this automobile is part of a larger system that includes roads, gas stations, and destinations. Collectively this transportation system enables shifts in human behavior, and creates positive impacts such as increased access to remote natural areas and negative impacts such as air pollution.

These all-encompassing systems shift the boundaries of design challenges, requiring us to account for the interaction between a design object and larger ecologic, human, and technologic systems, and to understand this interaction as a set of interdependent relationships, rather than as isolated pieces. This relational approach is key to holistic design thinking. Through this lens, the designer moves beyond simple concerns of object performance (does it work? will it break?) to understand how the object affects and is affected by the broader system, and the stakeholders who take part in the system.

A common pitfall all designers working toward sustainability face is the avoidance of burden shifting – the transfer of pollution, toxicity, or other unsustainable outcome from one issue or region to another. For example, if a designer switches from one raw material to another for a design, like switching from a traditional plastic to a bioplastic, the product's environmental footprint will shift from emitting greenhouse gases, and thus contributing to climate change, when producing petrochemicals (inputs to traditional plastics) to land degradation when producing agricultural products (inputs to bioplastics). An example of burden shifting is what the Center for Environmental Health (CEH) has called the toxic shell game. Bisphenol-A (BPA), an industrial chemical used to make plastics since the 1960s, was found to be a hormone-altering chemical and thus called into question in the late 1990s, and became a public concern in the late 2000s (Erickson 2008). BPA is estrogenic, mimicking estrogen in the body, which could have a number of harmful impacts such as playing a role in the growth of breast cancer. BPA has been restricted by a number of different legislative efforts; for example, the U.S. FDA banned its use in bottles. Yet some environmental groups, such as CEH, are concerned that alternatives proposed to BPA are just as risky, and furthermore, may be untested. This toxic shell game creates a major challenge for designers trying to move to more sustainable alternatives, and illustrates several scale challenges – including distraction from identifying a root systems issue that causes a problem in the first place. In the case of BPA, designers began to reach for nonplastic alternatives altogether, particularly in the design of water bottles.

Tools for considering context and mapping systems

By mapping systems and understanding system dynamics, designers can begin to understand how and when burden shifting may occur. The tools described in the following sections can help designers to both identify the root causes of scale challenges and also to manage and solve for these challenges.

Stakeholder mapping

A useful tool to understand the people embedded in each design challenge is to draw a map or visual of the stakeholders affected by design actions at scale. First consider the solution's customers or users: who they are, and what are their primary needs in terms of the product. Then add to the stakeholder map by including yourself and the company you may be designing for: what's your job and why are you bringing this solution to market? Further build out the map by including the network of suppliers (workers, factory owners, farmers) who contribute to bringing a solution to market, and providers who may help to service or dispose of a product when it's broken, needs to be cleaned, or no longer works. Finally consider who else has a stake in the solution you're creating – what NGOs might represent the environment as a stakeholder? What governments might regulate the solution? Are any populations affected by pollution from your solution? Once this map is complete, carefully consider how your design actions can negatively and positively influence these actors, and how your solution creates benefits or liabilities for each of these stakeholders.

Systems mapping

By developing systems maps and models, designers (often working closely with Life-cycle Assessment and supply-chain professionals), may be able to draw linkages between disconnected parts of a value chain. This begins with gathering as much information as possible about system stocks and flows. When designing physical products this might mean understanding how a material is made or sourced, where the material comes from (is cotton sourced from an area with plentiful water versus drought), and any trade-offs in properties (durability, for example), as well as end-of-life options (many biomaterials are not recyclable, for instance).

Leverage points

Leverage points, designed by Donella Meadows, are defined as "places within a complex system (a corporation, an economy, a living body, a city, an ecosystem) where a small shift in one thing can produce big changes in everything."[8] Consider the widely cited statistic that 70 percent (or debatably 80 percent) of a product's impacts are determined by design decisions. In other words, designers have a large amount of power, opportunity, and responsibility. This statistic supports the idea that intervening in a system, at a point of leverage, can have cascading effects and change the scaled impact of a product. Designers can use the idea of leverage points early on in their process, when digging into a design brief or setting initial parameters, and when deciding where to focus, which can unlock disruptive change rather than incremental steps.

Life-cycle Assessment

Life-cycle Assessment (LCA) is a systems mapping and assessment framework that identifies and evaluates the entire life cycle of a specific product or service, including the environmental aspects.[9] As a scientific methodology, LCA should follow rigid standards defined by the International Organization for Standardization (ISO) to ensure validity.[10] Through the LCA process, once the life cycles processes, including flows of materials, waste, water, and energy consumption for a product or service system are mapped, LCA practitioners and designers, can use scientifically vetted tools to assess the environmental impacts that stem from each part of the product life cycle, in order to identify places in the system with particularly acute impacts (hot spots). LCAs are primarily used to map existing products, and the results from these existing products can then be interpreted to inform the design of new, similar products. Performing an LCA is typically a time-consuming and laborsome process, and due to this resource intensity its application should be judicious. LCAs can be very useful to evaluate products produced in large multiples and particularly those products produced in versions, as opposed to one-off products produced in smaller or limited runs.

Most existing LCA tools are not optimized for designers, as the LCA process necessitates the inclusion of information that designers may have trouble getting access to (such as how much water is used by a manufacturer to manufacture a textile for a t-shirt) or have difficulty understanding (such as the name, or CAS number, for specific chemicals used in textile dyes). You don't always have time to stop everything and assess, but that doesn't mean you can avoid it. Here designers may turn to existing LCAs, looking for examples of previously completed studies that have a similar context (product/service, geographic profile, use case, etc.) to the solution the designer seeks to create.

LCA alternatives

If an appropriate LCA can't be found, designers can turn to less granular impact assessment tools, which highlight key sustainability impacts for specific product categories. For example, the Sustainability Insights tool developed by the Sustainability Consortium, a nonprofit organization led both for-profit brands and higher education, identifies key areas of impact for over 100 product categories, and provides guidance for how to address these impacts.[11] Though these approaches are less accurate than completing an LCA unique to your solution, designers can focus their efforts on improvement rather than spending the time and resources to complete a new study from scratch.

Product footprinting and virtual products

Designers can also begin to account for some of these elusive, invisible impacts through accounting of virtual product inputs. These virtual inputs might include materials you can't see when looking at a saleable artifact (such as waste generated in a manufacturing process), the embedded and embodied product components that were consumed in the process, or the products that are off-site from the user (as in digital infrastructure for digital devices). Whereas many defined methodologies for virtual elements are nascent, several types of footprint analysis, such as those for carbon and water are available. Product footprint methods allow practitioners to calculate the life-cycle impact of a product for a specific impact category, such as carbon or water. Like LCA, footprint methods should also follow ISO standards for carbon[12] and water,[13] to be valid.

Processes and tactics for addressing scale

There is no one-size-fits-all method for designing sustainably at scale, as the context for each design action introduces unique process variability and complexity to each challenge. Whereas a streamlined process would be antithetical to the challenges imposed by designing sustainably at scale, consider the following best practices, which incorporate team dynamics, design process considerations, and tactics.

Scale design challenges even present unique opportunities for cross-sector collaboration, where different companies up and down a value chain come together with other key stakeholders (like NGOs with specific goals and expertise) to collectively solve common pervasive problems in a cooperative, rather than competitive, manner. An example of this is the Sustainable Apparel Coalition,[14] a cross-sector working group of apparel and footwear brands, their suppliers, and environmental NGOs, who are collaborating to collectively address environmental challenges in the apparel industry, by working together to increase transparency. They've collaborated to develop the HIGG Index, an assessment tool for brands and their suppliers to measure environmental, social, and labor impacts.

Scaled design challenges are rarely presented with all the information necessary to solve problems effectively, let alone integrating sustainability into these solutions. Designers must integrate the practice of continuous investigative inquiry into their process, in order to reveal the broader system that drives design challenges and successful solutions. When possible begin each scale design problem with an exploratory research phase that seeks transparency, and ask the question: *Do I have all the information I need?*

As designers dig into a problem and scaled design challenges unfold, surface-level assumptions are often challenged and larger problems revealed. Designers must be adaptive in their practice, creating flexible space to address deeper problems and respond to unforeseen challenges.

Each scale design challenge introduces unique complexities, dependent on the type of scale and limits that are embedded into the system of the design action. Using the scale framework introduced at the beginning of the chapter, next we explore several tactics that can be employed to address solutions that confront each type of scale (this is by no means an exhaustive list).

Tactics for physical scale solutions

Large product volumes can offer the scale to support more sustainable choices for individual physical products and design solutions:

Utilize volume

Designing at scale creates the opportunity to utilize volume to make sustainable choices across a portfolio of solutions. For example, sustainable materials, like organic cotton or recycled nylon, may be less widely available in the variety of colors and textures that designers desire due to the high cost of producing low volumes. At larger scales, it may be possible to have more sustainable materials – even custom materials – created for a product, without confronting challenges of order minimums.

Reduce complexity

As we've discussed, physical and geographic complexity often persist for products, buildings, and services with many parts, variations, or suppliers. Adding to this complexity is the multitude of environmental impacts associated with each part or variation, making it difficult to design for sustainability the more complexity expands. To counter this, and make it easier to address sustainability challenges in the process, designers can seek to reduce complexity by systematically mapping these variables, and looking for opportunities to reduce the number of variables whenever possible.

Dematerialize

Dematerialization is a design tactic that means doing more with less. Dematerialization tactics range from simply reducing waste (increasing material efficiency) to replacing a physical product (and its the associated impacts) with a digital service, thus "dematerializing" the product. This practice has become more common with the advent of digital services, enabled by mobile and Internet technologies.[15] As a rule of thumb, this replacement form of dematerialization works well for scale solutions, as digital services are able to reach global customer bases more rapidly and easily than physical ones. However designers should be careful to avoid burden shifting when employing this tactic. Digital services relying on cloud Internet services and electronics demand huge amounts of energy throughout their life cycles.

Tactics for temporal scale solutions

Designers should consider the full life span of a design, including how it may be used, disposed of, and the secondary value of the product through reuse.

Design for real recyclability

Many products confront a technological and process flow limit when attempting to be recycled. Though many materials are theoretically recyclable, this by no means signifies whether the infrastructure or technology exists to recycle these products and materials. Designers should never assume that materials are able to be recycled, and must consider the context of where the objects will be used and discarded, and what commonly available recycling infrastructure may be available there. Ideally designers will opt to only select materials that are commonly able to be recycled. This is particularly relevant to goods distributed across a vast geographic scale, such as mass-produced consumer packaged goods (like cleaning products, personal care products, and packaged food), which can pose packaging waste challenges due to the complexity and diversity of recycling systems. One illustration of this concept in the United States is that plastic parts of consumer products must be labeled by polymer resin type, indicated through a number, 1–7,[16] but the ability to recycle these products varies, not only by type, but also by how the products are constructed. In the United States recycling facilities commonly recycle plastics 1 (PET) and 2 (HDPE), whereas other plastic types are either less commonly recycled (4, LDPE), or not recycled at all (3, PVC, and 7, Other).[17] Additionally, if plastics are mixed, or plastic parts are bonded to other parts and can't be separated for recycling they may also be difficult to recycle. When designing for recyclability, designers should be cognizant of these limitations, and consider only specifying commonly recycled types of plastics, which can be removed for recycling once a product is disposed of.

Design for product take back and refurbishment

For some physical products, buildings, and other solutions, there may be significant secondary economic, ecologic, and social value embedded in the solution's materials and modular components, even once the solution reaches the end of its first useful life (consider the resale value of car parts once the car no longer runs). Relatedly, parts in a larger product or solution may have different life spans and may either be more or less durable than other product parts (for example laptop batteries may not last as long as the laptop as a whole). In these cases there may be an opportunity to either extend the life of or to resell a solution by refurbishing or replacing the worn parts or components. When the company who originally sells the product collects products for refurbishment at the end of their life, this is called product *take back* (note that companies may also choose to take back products due to regulations or for other reasons). The process of taking back and refurbishing products is complex, as the infrastructure to manage these programs may be inconsistent – or nonexistent – and this complexity may be compounded by product versions. Designing product take-back programs requires team coordination up and down the value chain, and also mandates that refurbishable parts must be easily disassembled, identified, and fixed or replaced. Due to these complexities, and the associated expense this incurs, this type of program typically only works where there is economic value to be gained through replacement/ refurbishment, and where solutions are either produced in large runs of multiples, or where high value materials in parts can easily be separated from the whole.

Tactics for geographic scale solutions

Keep the passport tight

Many products have a diverse supply footprint, where materials and components for the same physical product or solution are sourced from a complex web of global suppliers. This is especially relevant to products with high comparative labor costs and lower mechanistic or technical requirements, like apparel and accessories. As a general rule of thumb, the more suppliers and locations a solution pulls from, the more complex it becomes to manage environmental and social impacts embedded in this supply web. To counteract this, designers should work with their teams and value chain to "keep the passport as tight as possible,"[18] opting for fewer exchanges of hands, a more tightly curated supplier base, for more supply chain visibility and stronger relationship building with suppliers. As an example, the apparel brand Loomstate pioneered the Chetna Coalition, an international supply chain organization of 16 ethical textile brands, fashion brands, and production facilities that works directly with cotton-growing communities in India to strengthen sustainability practices in grower regions.[19] This improved relationship in turn drives higher quality for finished materials.

Produce products in regions with strong environmental regulations

For products for which materials cultivation and production processes create high environmental, health, or social impacts in some regions (like in the EU and United States) strong regulations may be enacted to prevent these negative outcomes. However these regulations may demand high costs to manage, incentivizing producers and brands to outsource production to regions with fewer regulations. This is particularly relevant to products that require toxic chemicals for production, like leather goods and textiles. Designers can avoid this trap by carefully evaluating the supply location of the materials and suppliers they select, opting to source from regions where strong regulations are in place, and should ask their suppliers for the locations of their production facilities, and for the countries of origin for materials. Some designers and brands may also choose to work together to strengthen regulations in specific geographies. Designers and brands can review guidance on which countries and regions have fewer regulations in place through the Environmental Performance Index (EPI) developed by Yale and Columbia Universities, and higher impact risk from watchdog organizations such as the Fair Labor Organization,[20] and which provides a global view of environmental performance by country.[21] This knowledge can then be used to make informed sourcing decisions.

Tactics for knowledge scale solutions

Select sustainable attributes

Products, parts, services, and other design outputs may meet or include *sustainable attributes*, or technical indicators that guarantee specific sustainably preferable criteria have been met. This includes attributes that are certifications (both regulated and independently verifiable), like certified organic, as well as those that aren't represented by a certification but do convey specific criteria that have legal definitions, such as those defined in the Green Guides by the FTC in the United States (and similar organizations in other countries).[22] These attributes hint at embedded environmental and social impacts of product and service systems, which designers may otherwise have an inability to assess effectively. Attributes differ by service and product category, and can be used to communicate sustainable benefits to consumers. For example, the Global Organic Textile Standard, or GOTS, is an independent global certification with a system-wide scope. The certification ensures that textiles have met a set of environmental and social criteria extending through the entire chain of custody for the product (each point the product changes hands), all the way from the farm where raw materials are cultivated through to manufacturing and incorporation into garments.[23] Designers should however be cautious of those attributes that contain no legal definition, such as "natural," or even "sustainable," and can be misleading to consumers and designers alike.

Learn from extreme examples

A major process challenge of designing sustainably at scale is determining how best to test a solution's efficacy before scaling up. Just as designers use prototypes or sample runs to test material fit and usability, prototypes or pilot runs can also be used to inform decisions about sustainability at full scale. One approach toward prototyping with sustainability in mind is piloting to reach extreme goals (design for 100 percent efficiency, zero waste, etc.) to test boundaries or limits, then to analyze what happened and scale best practices. By pushing toward these extremes it allows designers to understand the possible, while uncovering key pitfalls that may be encountered along the way. For example, Adidas and Stella McCartney have released several lines of "zero waste" apparel, which uses high-efficiency design and cutting techniques to ensure that 100 percent of fabric is used in either the products (95 percent goes into the products) or as a repurposed secondary material (5 percent).[24] Lessons learned from this high-efficiency approach were then used to reduce waste across broad categories of products in subsequent seasons.

Visualize the invisible

As a practice, designers should always seek to understand invisible wastes in their process – runoff from fertilizer, embodied energy, labor, materials, etc. The best way to understand these "invisible" infrastructures and wastes is to reestablish personal relationships (and understanding) by going to see these processes for oneself. Go visit a manufacturing facility, garbage dump, recycling facility, or power plant. This is one of the key principles of the Toyota Production System, developed by industrial engineers Taiichi Ohno and Eiji Toyoda between 1948 and 1975. *Genchi Genbutsu* means "go and see," and holds that one must go to the place where the work is done in order to fully understand a situation (Ohno 1988). Furthermore, designers have unique abilities to bring otherwise hidden connections to light, through their powers of visualization.

Conclusions

One of the most important design opportunities when working at scale is the chance to rethink underlying assumptions. Designers commonly go down the path of minimizing impact when targeting sustainability, such as reducing the amount of a material, or swapping out a material. Reduction is often a good starting point, however, the strategy of "doing less bad" can also be a trap. A small change made to a design – such as a small reduction in packaging – might feel like a big impact when scaled up to millions and millions of units. However, designers should be careful to not pass up opportunities to completely shift the premises of a design problem – in this example, perhaps packaging is not needed at all. Furthermore, sustainable design requires we also think about how to scale down, and one way to move beyond "doing less bad" is to actually design less. In some cases, sustainable design requires a recognition of the influence that a product might have. Some products set a precedent or invent a new category, and have the potential to change consumer behaviors or expectations altogether.

Almost all scale sustainable design challenges require teamwork to complete and cannot be solved by design alone. Due to the complex and multidisciplinary nature of each scale sustainable design challenge, designers must incorporate both environmental and systems sciences, understanding of consumer behavior, the business sciences of value-chain and supply-chain management, politics, ethics, and more. In other words, our hope is that designers will continue to integrate STEM (Science, Technology, Engineering, and Math) into the design practice.

Beyond just "doing less bad," scale considerations drive the imperative for positive, scaled change through design. We argue for pivoting from the standard three Rs of sustainable production and consumption – reuse, reduce, recycle – as they often just lead to incremental improvements, and don't effect widespread change. Instead of just reusing materials, or using recycled materials ("less bad"), in lieu of scale complexities designers should aim to avoid creating negative impact in the first place – or perhaps even seek opportunities to do good. We propose a new set of three Rs for designers to strive toward: reflect, replenish, and resilience.

- *Reflect:* Think deeply and carefully about the consequences of your design actions, and imbue them with positive, scaled impact.
- *Replenish:* Breathe new vitality into and restore a previously existing and/or exhausted valuable cultural or ecological resource through your design actions.
- *Resilience:* Instill the capacity for design outputs to grow and repeatedly bounce back in the face of unforeseen challenges.

Scale clearly introduces complexity and uncertainty into design challenges. Thus, in addition to these three Rs, designers might consider challenging basic assumptions from the very beginning to design more sustainably from the very start.

Questions for consideration

Using something you are working on or a product you use every day as a starting point for thinking about scale: how might the project or product scale – across geographies, and over time? What challenges might scale bring about? What kind of limits might you confront? What will happen in 20, 50, 100, or 1,000 years? If the environment was your client, how would the design change? And how could you integrate the three Rs – reflect, replenish, resilience – into your design practice, now, and in the future?

Notes

1 http://wwf.panda.org/what_we_do/endangered_species/elephants/
2 From World Wildlife Federation, sourced on July 28, 2016: http://wwf.panda.org/what_we_do/endangered_species/cetaceans/about/right_whales/north_atlantic_right_whale/www.rsc.org/images/Endangered%20Elements%20-%20Critical%20Thinking_tcm18-196054.pdf
3 From Scientific American, sourced on August 4, 2016: www.scientificamerican.com/article/battery-storage-needed-to-expand-renewable-energy/
4 From USDA, sourced on August 4, 2016: www.ams.usda.gov/services/organic-certification/faq-becoming-certified
5 www.ncbi.nlm.nih.gov/pmc/articles/PMC2796756/
6 *E-waste hazard: The impending challenge*, Indian Journal of Occupational and Environmental Medicine National Institutes of Health: www.ncbi.nlm.nih.gov/pmc/articles/PMC2796756/
7 From PBS, sourced on August 12, 2016: www.pbs.org/newshour/updates/america-e-waste-gps-tracker-tells-all-earthfix/
8 http://donellameadows.org/archives/leverage-points-places-to-intervene-in-a-system/
9 From United Nations Environment Programme, sourced on August 12, 2016: www.unep.org/resourceefficiency/Consumption/StandardsandLabels/MeasuringSustainability/life-cycleAssessment/tabid/101348/Default.aspx
10 www.iso.org/iso/catalogue_detail?csnumber=37456
11 The Sustainability Consortium, accessed on August 12, 2016: www.sustainabilityconsortium.org/product-categories/
12 www.iso.org/obp/ui/#iso:std:iso:ts:14067:ed-1:v1:en
13 www.iso.org/iso/catalogue_detail?csnumber=43263
14 http://apparelcoalition.org/
15 www.salon.com/2013/08/27/the_dematerialization_of_society_in_the_digital_age_newscred/
16 www.epa.gov/recycle/how-do-i-recycle-common-recyclables#pla
17 https://www3.epa.gov/epawaste/conserve/tools/warm/pdfs/Plastics.pdf
18 This comment was inspired by an interview with fashion designer Maria Cornejo, by chapter author Rebecca Silver, conducted in 2014.
19 www.loomstate.org/chetco
20 www.fairlabor.org/
21 http://epi.yale.edu/
22 www.ftc.gov/news-events/media-resources/truth-advertising/green-guides
23 www.global-standard.org/certification.html
24 www.ecouterre.com/adidas-by-stella-mccartney-spotlights-sustainability-at-london-fashion-week/

Bibliography

Ackoff, R. L., and E. Vergara. 1981. "Creativity in Problem Solving and Planning: A Review." *European Journal of Operational Research*. Elsevier. www.sciencedirect.com/science/article/pii/0377221781900448.

Blanco, A., R. Miranda, and M. C. Monte. 2013. "Extending the Limits of Paper Recycling – Improvements Along the Paper Value Chain." *Forest Systems* 22 (3): 471.

Chapagain, A. K., A. Y. Hoekstra, and H. H. G. Savenije. 2005. "The Water Footprint of Cotton Consumption. Value of Water Research Report Series No. 18." UNESCO-IHE, The Netherlands, *http://waterfootprint.org/media/downloads/Report18.pdf*

Conant, E. 2006. "Return of the Aral Sea." *Discover-New York.* Buena Vista Magazines.

Ehrenfeld, J. R. 2013. "The Roots of Unsustainability." *The Handbook of Design for Sustainability.* books. google.com. https://books.google.com/books?hl=en&lr=&id=6m5jAgAAQBAJ&oi=fnd&pg=PA15 &dq=The%2BRoots%2Bof%2BUnsustainability&ots=3jo_Bl2bIo&sig=PKua8Fdq6Zp4oNzI3Dxby 4QoQmc.

Erickson, B. E. 2008. "Bisphenol a under Scrutiny." *Chemical and Engineering News.* cen.acs.org. http://cen. acs.org/articles/86/i22/Bisphenol-Under-Scrutiny.html?type=paidArticleContent.

Graedel, T. E., E. M. Harper, N. T. Nassar, P. Nuss, and B. K. Reck. 2015. "Criticality of Metals and Metalloids." *Proceedings of the National Academy of Sciences of the United States of America* 112 (14): 4257–62.

Hardin, G. 2009. "The Tragedy of the Commons★." *Journal of Natural Resources Policy Research.* Taylor & Francis. www.tandfonline.com/doi/full/10.1080/19390450903037302.

Harrison, N. and H. Mayer. 2004. "The Harrison Studio: Helen Mayer Harrison, Newton Harrison & Associates." Position Papers.

Heidegger, M. 1977. *The Question Concerning Technology, and Other Essays.* Harper & Row.

The International Resource Panel. n.d. "UNEP (2012) Responsible Resource Management for a Sustainable World: Findings from the International Resource Panel."

Ohno, T. 1988. *Toyota Production System: Beyond Large-Scale Production.* Taylor & Francis.

United Nations Environment Programme. 2011. "UNEP 2010 Annual Report." UNEP/Earthprint.

6

SYSTEMS AND SERVICE DESIGN AND THE CIRCULAR ECONOMY

Rhoda Trimingham, Ksenija Kuzmina and Yaone Rapitsenyane

Introduction

People in the western world are now living in a service economy due to a general economic shift from making products to providing services (Bhamra and Lofthouse, 2007). In addition, services are being increasingly embodied in the products we buy (Bhamra and Lofthouse, 2007). Thus far this has been driven by business motives (Goedkoop et al., 1999; Mont 2002) rather than environmental concerns, as by adding services to their products companies can obtain higher producer-customer interaction and increase competitive advantage (Bhamra and Lofthouse, 2007). But, there are a growing number of practitioners who are looking to systems and service approaches as a means of achieving consumer value alongside greater sustainability improvements. In these approaches consumer need and value is addressed in place of product functions. Impacts that affect the sustainability of a product occur across its life cycle, including material selection, use and end-of-life. Systems and services provide an opportunity to reduce life-cycle impacts (Trimingham, 2015). There is a continuum of products and services which includes the following:

- Pure tangible products such as a bottle, dress or artwork
- Tangible product with accompanying services such as a car with a guarantee
- Hybrid of products and services such as a restaurant
- Major service with minor products and services such as an airline
- Pure service such as babysitting

(Bhamra and Lofthouse, 2007)

In recent years design for sustainability has looked towards systems innovation and a service view to achieve greater sustainability improvements (Trimingham, 2015). The services that are of interest to sustainable design are known as eco-services, or sustainable Product Service Systems (PSS). Moving from manufacturing products to providing services is also known as the functional economy, and has been linked to the creation of a more environmentally sustainable economy (Bhamra and Lofthouse, 2007), dematerialisation and the creation of value whilst consuming less resources.

In 2003, McDonagh and Braungart argued that sustainable design needed to take a 'whole system' view, where increased consumption does not lead to increased negative environmental impact. They modelled human-made systems on natural processes where resources are cyclical and fed back into the system rather than becoming waste. They coined this as the cradle-to-cradle approach. The Brezet model of innovation (1997) highlights the benefits of taking a systems thinking approach and is expanded on by Cheschin and Gaziulusoy in Chapter 30. Recently, cradle-to-cradle thinking has evolved into circular economy thinking but is still grounded by the ethos that human-made systems should reflect cyclical natural systems as much as possible. The circular economy refers to an industrial economy that is "restorative by intention; aims to rely on renewable energy; minimises, tracks and hopefully eliminates the use of toxic chemicals; and eradicates waste through careful design" (Ellen MacArthur Foundation, 2010). The concept of the circular economy is grounded in the study of non-linear, particularly living systems and is based on the following principles:

- Design out waste
- Build resilience through diversity
- Work towards using energy from renewable sources
- Think in systems
- Think in cascades

(Ellen MacArthur Foundation, 2010)

Sustainable product service systems

The overarching aim of sustainable PSS is that they focus on consumer need through addressing functions that lead to consumer satisfaction with reduced environmental impacts (Clark et al., 2009). There is less need for a physical product and a reduced focus on product ownership. This way of defining sustainable PSS based on their focus of satisfying consumer needs through the utility they provide has been adopted by numerous authors (Clark et al., 2009; Fiksel, 2006; Kang and Wimmer, 2009; Morelli, 2003; Ness, 2007; Rapitsenyane, 2014; UNEP, 2002). PSS is also referred to as servitization (Baines et al., 2007; Hernandez-Pardo et al., 2013; Kang and Wimmer, 2009; Martinez et al., 2010, Mont, 2002; Tukker, 2004). The function-oriented innovation nature of PSS as opposed to a product-oriented innovation presents opportunities for a shift from ownership to fee-based access to shared resources (Tukker and Tischner, 2006). Although there is a distinction between Product Service Systems and servitization (Rapitsenyane, 2014), these terms are not isolated from one another (Baha et al., 2014; Morelli, 2003; Smith et al., 2014). In the context of conventional manufacturers, PSS can be viewed as a strategy through which manufacturers can servitize their businesses (Baines et al., 2007; Rapitsenyane, 2014). PSS can be viewed as an integration of new product development and new service development (De Lille et al., 2012). The aim of simultaneously addressing product and service components of value creation is to shift the business focus "from designing (and selling) physical products only, to designing (and selling) a system of products and services which are jointly capable of fulfilling specific client demands, while re-orienting current unsustainable trends in production and consumption practices" (Manzini and Vezzoli, 2003). The reorientation of unsustainable trends in production and consumption provides the rationale for this kind of strategy to be called sustainable Product Service Systems. A utility focus allows a company to concentrate on adding value rather than tangible features. These values can represent convenience, comfort, information or emotional and cultural values (Rapitsenyane, 2014). PSS must therefore be socially constructed alongside stakeholder participation (Morelli, 2006; Tukker and Tischner, 2006). PSSs deliver value through three orientations (or focus of value): product orientated, use orientated and result orientated (Tukker, 2004). These are also referred to as services providing added value to product life cycles; services providing enabling platforms for customers; and services providing final results to customers (UNEP, 2002). An overview of these orientations can be found in Table 6.1.

Table 6.1 Types of eco-services (adapted from Bhamra and Lofthouse, 2007)

	Product Orientated services	*Use Orientated services*	*Results Orientated services*
Features	• Customer ownership of the physical good • Services enhance utility	• Ownership of the product resides with the service provider • Consumer gains the functions of the product without ownership	• Product owned and run by supplier • A result is offered rather than a specified product or service • How customer need is satisfied is irrelevant, as long as it is satisfied
Environmental benefits	• Increase product lifespans and therefore save energy and materials over time	• Reduction of products needed • High use intensity • End of life disposal becomes the responsibility of the service provider • Resource reduction	• Incentives to optimise service life and efficiency • Significant reductions in material and energy consumption • Profits are tied to efficiency
Business benefits	• Income from the service • Customer tie-in • Reduced costs	• Economic gains from less resources • Shared costs throughout the lifecycle	• Reduced costs • Improved customer-supplier relationship
Examples	• Warranties • Maintenance agreements	• Photocopiers • Leasing arrangements • Car share	• Pest management service • Gardening service

The advantage with PSS is that value can be created with consumption of less resources (Kang and Wimmer, 2009). Values inherent in PSS are either tangible, where customers see a financial benefit of choosing PSS over product ownership, or intangible, where value comes from the experience of using PSS (Tukker, 2004). Table 6.2 highlights PSS categories and win–win potential, demonstrating positive sustainability and business impacts.

Service design

The promotion of services as a means to add value to product offerings has also seen the development of service design as a discipline in its own right. Service design has essentially removed the product offering altogether, however it is still viewed as a process of value creation (Vargo and Lusch, 2004). The proposition, rather than being product focussed, is in the form of resources that may include services, information, knowledge or skills of staff (Vargo and Lusch, 2004). Service design is human centred and uses design tools and techniques to work with others, to explore and redefine models of public services from the user perspective and to emphasise human involvement through the process of co-creation (Parker and Heapy, 2006). The role of the user is to co-create value by directly interacting with these resources and contributing their own skills and resources if necessary (Kuzmina et al., 2012).

Service design may be defined as an approach that is used to innovate or improve services making them more effective (Moritz, 2005; Stickdorn and Schneider, 2010). It can facilitate

Table 6.2 Sustainability and business added value from PSS (Rapitsenyane, 2014)

PSS categories and win–win potential			
Services providing added value to product life cycle	*Services providing enabling platforms for customers*	*Services providing final results to customers*	*UNEP (2002)*
Product oriented	*Use oriented*	*Result oriented*	*Tukker (2004)*
Minimising costs for a long-lasting serviceable product (economic)	Maximum use of a given product	Optimisation of use reduces energy and material consumption (environmental)	
Design for end-of-life (environmental)	Fewer products needed for a community of people in a given period of time	Product life extension services (economic and social)	
	Low service provider costs	Application of end-of-life strategies to components and materials to save on material and component costs (environmental and economic)	
	Product life extension services		

change in services including within the public sector where design processes and skills form an approach to tackle pressing economic, social and environmental issues (Cottam and Leadbeater, 2004; Mulgan and Albury, 2003; Thomas 2008). For example during the Dott07 project (a year of community design projects in the north-east of England), a service design approach was used to address the sustainability agenda within educational institutions. It brought together stakeholders in a process of problem solving to co-develop and codesign resources that solved specific environmental problems (Thackara, 2007).

The impact of service design thus far has been broad, found within government, communities, health care and education (Sangiorgi, 2011; Thackara, 2007). It has been used to change behaviours and build capacities of users and service providers to engage with the service process of co-creation, reconfiguring relationships and resources of the service (Pacenti, 2011; Szebeko, 2011). Some examples of service design have seen alternative service scenarios that bring communities together and encourage new sustainable behaviours such as sharing spaces or health support to address social and environmental issues (Cipolla and Moura, 2011; Cottam and Leadbeater, 2004).

Case studies

Three very different case studies are presented highlighting the breadth of possibilities for sustainable innovation through taking a systems and services approach. The common denominator is that they are designer-led and the strategies embedded within each project stem from design thinking. The first case study focusses on building capabilities within small to medium enterprises (SMEs) to encourage them to explore the use of sustainable product service systems approaches to increase competitiveness. The second case study presents more user-focussed outcomes of an action research project that had a specific focus on refillable packaging within the personal care market. The final case study looks at how design approaches can be used to explore change in education toward sustainable development by reframing it as a service.

Supporting the adoption of sustainable product service systems in Botswana (Rapitsenyane, 2014)

This case study presents the results of a workshop-based study with designers and SMEs in the leather manufacturing industry in Botswana carried out to support a doctoral thesis supervised at a British university. Its purpose was to explore the use of design knowledge to build service-orientated capabilities in traditionally product-orientated companies to enable these companies to operate, grow and be competitive in a predominantly knowledge and service economy.

Methodology

A multiple case study approach was adopted with a purposefully selected sample of three SMEs in the leather industry in Botswana. All SMEs were micro (employing one to six people), operated in different market segments, and mostly served business-to-business customers. Two sustainable designers were also involved in the study. Data were collected through site visits, workshops and interviews. Data were also collected from the designers through interviews following the workshops. The purpose of the workshops was to expose SMEs' design capabilities in a conscious process of developing PSS offerings alongside the brought-in designers. Data gathered for each case study were transcribed and analysed in N-vivo. The purpose of the analysis was to explore interactions between designers and SMEs. Activities were targeted at overcoming barriers to PSS differentiation. Thematic analysis was adopted (Braun and Clarke, 2006) to identify themes and patterns.

Findings

Six themes were identified during the study which build a framework for exploring PSS offerings within SMEs (see Figure 6.1):

Identify value to initiate engagement – different situations prompted SMEs to engage with new knowledge related to PSS. Both internal and external factors stimulated this engagement. These included the need to launch new product offerings and the desire to explore new market opportunities. Financial benefit was a key driver to engaging SMEs.

Building understanding – of how design can be used to drive companies towards adopting PSS. Central to engaging companies with this were codesign approaches to infuse growth possibilities, and offer a balance to the dominant business perspective.

Reflections and familiar experiences – designers built enhanced capabilities through improving the confidence of SMEs to engage with PSS. This was a result of an educative mentorship approach and through visualization of possibilities.

Empower and coordinate – the definition of a development process for the company to empower them to generate solutions includes identification and deployment of relevant tools to guide logical and systematic solution development.

Organisational outlook – This included designers linking the need to be creative to company visions, shifting SMEs' focus from defining value strictly in tangible terms. An exploration of aspects bearing on a company's activities, such as stakeholders, user needs, value of brand, and relationships aided these conversations.

Proposition for adding value – including strategies adopted by each company to differentiate themselves. A key feature was that designers were regarded as key stakeholders in facilitating the process of developing propositions. Strategy explorations included customer-retention strategies, external partners, opening new markets, services providing added value to product life cycle and services providing enabling platforms to customers.

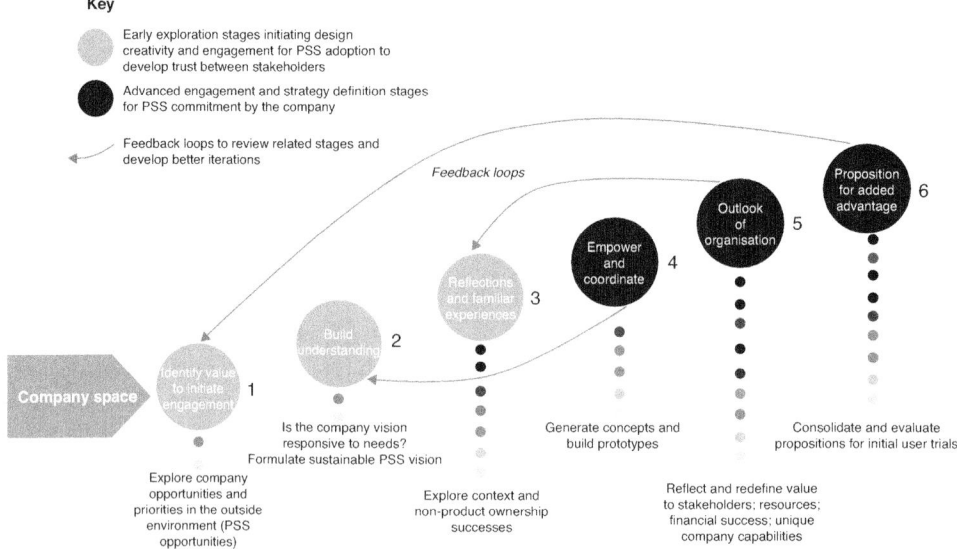

Key

Early exploration stages initiating design creativity and engagement for PSS adoption to develop trust between stakeholders

Advanced engagement and strategy definition stages for PSS commitment by the company

Feedback loops to review related stages and develop better iterations

Figure 6.1 A design capabilities shifts process towards service-oriented differentiation (Rapitsenyane, 2014).

Within the leather manufacturing companies that took part in the case studies benefits of a sustainable PSS approach were seen. These included highlighting new business models (for example rental of leather goods), opening up new markets, enhanced understanding of consumers and increasing business opportunities. Across all six themes the role of design in influencing a shift towards service orientation was identified (Figure 6.1). SMEs still lack the innovation language often found in design. A codesign approach is required in order to unify the business needs of profits with the human-centred approaches required to support servitization through the interpretation of needs in a product or service (Baha et al., 2014).

Refillable packaging (Lofthouse et al., 2009)

In recent years the environmental impact of packaging has become a prominent issue in the United Kingdom, as it is a very visible product in the waste stream, making up between 15% and 25% by weight of household dustbin waste (INCPEN, 2003). The use of refillable packaging has long been cited as a possible solution to this problem, and their potential is clearly recognised by bodies such as the Waste and Resources Programme (WRAP) and the Department of Environment Food and Rural Affairs (DEFRA). This case study presents the results of a study to investigate their feasibility (using a PSS approach) within the personal care market.

From a sustainability perspective the main drivers for using refillable packaging systems stem from the potential to minimise packaging for refills, which reduces material use and ultimately slows resource depletion. The lighter weight of refills also reduces the environmental impact of distribution, as less energy is required to transport the product, which in turn leads to cost savings. In addition less material will end up in landfill when the refill is disposed of.

Methodology

The overall aim of the project was to develop a refillable packaging system for 'body wash' products (i.e. shower gels and or bubble baths) and to investigate its feasibility with respect to consumer acceptance (female customers, aged 21–40) and sustainability improvements. In order to achieve the project aim, a broad range of qualitative methods were used to collate background understanding, develop design concepts and test the viability of the design solutions.

Following the completion of the background research, which aimed to better understand refills and how they are perceived by consumers and industry, a series of educational activities, creativity techniques and design activities were combined together to form the 'creative workshop' programme. The creative workshop aimed to encourage invited participants to think about the different types of refills available, outline the attributes of body wash products, feed in other sources of inspiration, and provide the group with the time to generate ideas which met the refillable packaging systems brief (Lofthouse, 2007). As a result of these workshops, a wide range of ideas for delivering body wash products through a refillable packaging system were generated. These were worked up into concepts for evaluation. Prototypes were trialled with consumers via a two-hour focus group programme, which combined together a series of different activities. The activities aimed to understand how the users felt about the prototypes – whether they liked them, engaged with them and/or accepted them, and more specifically, what elements they instinctively understood and needed to be explicitly explained. Data was collected by video and audio recorders, and after being transcribed qualitative analysis was carried out by hand using a 'coding and clustering' method (Robson, 1993; Strauss and Corbin, 1990).

Findings

With respect to consumer perceptions of refills, a number of attributes which led to the consumer having either a positive or negative experience of refills were identified (see Table 6.3).

Table 6.3 Attributes leading to a positive or negative experience of refillable packaging (Lofthouse et al., 2009)

Attributes leading to a positive experience	Attributes leading to a negative experience
Good product quality	Expensive refills in giveaway parent pack
Convenient delivery	Inconvenience/requiring additional planning
Good value	Take up more space
Less packaging and or product waste	Hassle of maintenance
Easy to use	Increased waste
Clean and hygienic	Poor product quality
Takes us less space	Bad delivery
Light to transport	Bad quality packaging
No mess	'Fiddly' to refill
Cheap	Concerns over how long refill will be available
Quick to use/refill	Incompatibility between systems
Incentives/rewards for use	
Suitability for purpose	

From an economic perspective refillable packaging can lead to an overall reduction of packaging costs, and often leads to higher profit margins either because they are designed to use minimal materials or to be reused by the same or another customer. Many types of refills can also encourage increased levels of customer loyalty, which can lead to increased revenue. Refills also offer the opportunity to present consumers with greater choice, flexibility and customisation. Companies can also highlight reuse and resource efficiency through the use of refills, as a way of demonstrating responsible behaviour.

However, a number of organisational barriers stand in the way of refillable packaging; these include: the commitment required by the retailer to provide space for both the parent pack and refill used in many types of refill system (leading to an increase in stock keeping units); possible requirement of extra space for storage, cleaning; additional logistics requirements. Issues which lead on to potential additional costs which might arise from additional staffing, include cleaning/refurbishment, return logistics and the need for additional manufacturing lines. From a marketing perspective another barrier associated with refills is the potential difficulty in establishing and retaining brand loyalty and customer buy-in. It may be difficult to convince customers to make the initial investment required to take part in some refillable systems. However initial findings from this study do suggest that if the consumer is already engaged with a brand, they will be a lot more likely to adopt and 'refill' alternatives offered to them, especially if they lead to additional cost savings.

The findings from this study have dramatically increased levels of understanding about the potential implications of PSS, in the form of refillable packaging, and how it might be successfully utilised by business. It has been seen that to be truly successful refills must perform for the consumer, the environment and business. This means they must offer good quality, be very easy to use and appropriately delivered, be clearly communicated, be offered through a brand consumers like, and represent good value whilst radically reducing the amount of 'stuff' produced and moved around. To do this the design brief must incorporate both consumer and environmental needs as well as business requirements. Failure to consider both these elements is likely to lead to failure.

Service design and its role in changing education (Kuzmina et al., 2012)

The current sustainability crisis provides an urgent need for an intentional change that entails a transformative process of deep alteration to the nature of education, individuals and institutions within the educational system (Nelson et al., 2007; UNESCO, 2009). Traditionally, education is viewed as the preparation of individuals for economic life (Sterling, 2003), however there is an emerging view of the need for education to reflect alternative views of society and incorporate social and environmental responsibility, cooperation and contextual knowing (Capra, 1994; Sterling, 2003). This doctoral research investigated if a service design approach could be used to analyse and transform education towards education for sustainable development.

Methodology

A study of six British state schools of primary education was carried out. The schools were selected with differing levels of engagement with the sustainability agenda, varying size and from differing economic areas. The focus was on understanding educational change towards sustainable development from the service provider's perspective. Ethnographic methods were used to gather data, including interviews and observations. Additional questionnaires were carried out with school staff. The data were analysed using grounded theory methods (Strauss and Corbin, 1990). Meaning-making occurred when the data was brought together and analysed through the concept of the service.

Findings

The use of service design as a concept to explore change in education towards sustainable development reframed the problem as a change needed in the provision of the service by the provider to its user (as opposed to its general perception as a learning process). In this case the provider is the school, and the user is the student and the wider community. Analysis highlights that schools approach change in an integrative way through developing resources around environmental and social issues alongside users whilst engaging them in meaningful learning process. This frames the change towards sustainable development in schools to be partly dependant on the development of capabilities within the service provider and providing them with opportunities to engage with change in a holistic and enduring manner.

From the research a number of service design strategies were developed. These were informed by the data from the schools that already followed an integrative approach to sustainable development and by the service design thinking that places user's needs at the centre of the change process.

Making complex issues accessible: an emerging role of service design to promote sustainable education within schools is to make such issues accessible to the main user of the service – students. Schools should approach this through real life learning, placing needs and capabilities of students at the centre of its service and relating it to relevant social and environmental issues.

Acquiring resources: a 'sustainable resource' is one that is acquired during the process of solving a problem related to a social or environmental issue. This supports real-life learning for users and becomes a tangible representation of the school's values. It can be based on real ownership (playground made of recycled materials) or be symbolic (projects based within the community).

Support from stakeholders: support from all stakeholders in the provision of sustainable education increases participation and provides motivation. Support is created by opening up opportunities for participation and leading activities.

Building desired identity: a school's perception of self as a contributor to sustainable development allows it to build ethos and identity. Leadership plays a crucial role and this leads to the prioritisation of sustainable development projects.

Self assessment: schools that undergo continuous assessment with regards to attaining sustainable development goals helps to support building identity, leadership and the need to acquire further resources.

The research outlined the relationship between learning processes as a service offering, institutions as service providers and students as users of the service. The research used the integrated framework as an analytical lens to present it from a service perspective. This highlighted that change was needed in both the service offering (expanding it to include sustainable development) and in the service provision process through involvement with users as co-creators of the service. It identified that the capacity and capabilities of the service provider were also an important factor in the success of the service.

Implications for design

PSSs are a business strategy that take into account product and service life cycles (Tan et al., 2006). In this way, the concept is representative of a holistic approach to sustainability innovation (Rapitsenyane, 2014). A view of the whole landscape of the problem, environment and relationships between factors is necessary in this holistic view especially if looked at from the design perspective (Rapitsenyane, 2014). A whole system design approach is necessary to aid such decisions (Fiksel, 2006) and move away from its traditional focus on material products (Morelli, 2003). Characteristics of a system include the problem being investigated, the context in which the system is to be operated, relationships between factors and stakeholders and their interactions (Charnley et al., 2011).

The characteristics of PSS imply the need for cross-disciplinary knowledge co-creation and problem investigation across the entire components of a system (Rapitsenyane, 2014). It assumes a life-cycle focus that concentrates on functionality and value to consumers and reducing environmental impacts (Goedkoop et al., 1999; Tukker and Tischner, 2006). The focus on consumer values and satisfaction inherent in PSS and service design presents a need to reorientate consumer behaviour towards them and demands customer involvement as co-producers (Kang and Wimmer, 2009; Morelli, 2003; Manzini and Vezzoli, 2003).

The importance of design in the performance of companies has been reported by various authors with varying levels of application. Kotler and Rath (1984) argue the use of design by companies' marketing departments as strategic in matching customers' requirements to product-related attributes. This provides a link between user needs and the solution to be proposed. A leadership position for design in new product development, as argued by Perks et al. (2005), expands beyond traditional design tasks to include direct interface with customers. This role addresses the gap often found between design teams and the marketing departments (von Stamm, 2004). The versatility of designers being able to cover such stretching roles stems from superior design capabilities like interpreting, coordinating and facilitating (Turner, 2000), and can be related to Mozota's (2006) four powers of design: design as differentiator, design as integrator, design as transformer and design as good business. The use of design in this way can allow use of user-oriented innovation models to create new business opportunities, ultimately increasing market share. The resistance from manufacturers to create new business opportunities by adopting PSS, often needing mindset change (Rapitsenyane and Bhamra, 2013) can be managed through a capabilities view to service oriented differentiation.

Conclusions

There are a wide range of business and sustainability advantages to engaging with services and systems, if consumer needs can be met and the systems can be designed to work effectively.

The two approaches highlighted in this chapter are a move from product only offerings to sustainable Product Service Systems, and reconceptualising processes as services in order to reframe the issue of change towards sustainable development and clarify connections between stakeholder and social and environmental issues.

Within both approaches designers can work alongside stakeholders to transform their approaches towards sustainable development and introduce the notion of value co-creation and develop user-centred capacities within project teams. This opens opportunities for new design activities requiring that design capabilities be cultivated to be deployed differently; to enable service oriented differentiation in traditionally product oriented companies or to highlight service characteristics within previously process orientated situations. This type of innovation can be driven by users, suppliers and other actors in the value chain.

References

Baha, E., Groenewoud, A., and van Mensvoort, K. (2014). Servitization of products as an approach for design-driven innovation. Paper presented at the *Proceedings of ServDes Conference*, Lancaster University.
Baines, T., Lightfoot, H., Evans, S., Neely, A., Greenough, R., Peppard, J., Roy, R., Shehab, E., Braganza, A., Tiwari, A., Alcock, J., Angus, J., Bastl, M., Cousens, A., Irving, P., Johnson, M., Kingston, J., Lockett, H., Martinez, V. and Michele, P. (2007). State-of-the-art in product service systems. *Proceedings of the*

Institution of Mechanical Engineers – Part B – Engineering Manufacture (Professional Engineering Publishing), 221(10), pp. 1543–1552.

Bhamra, T. and Lofthouse, V. (2007). *Design for Sustainability: A Practical Approach*. Gower, UK: Routledge.

Braun, V. and Clarke, V. (2006). Using thematic analysis in psychology. *Qualitative Research in Psychology*, 3(2). pp. 77–101.

Brezet, H. and van Hemel, C. (1997). *Ecodesign: A Promising Approach to Sustainable Production and Consumption*. The Hague: TU Delft, Netherlands.

Capra, F. (1994). *Ecology and Community*. Lecture presented to administrators and faculty of Mill Valley School District. Berkeley: Centre for Ecoliteracy.

Charnley, F., Lemon, M., and Evans, S. (2011). Exploring the process of whole system design. *Design Studies*, 32, pp. 156–179.

Cipolla, C. and Moura, H. (2011). Social innovation in Brazil through design strategy. *Design Management Journal*, 6, pp. 40–51.

Clark, G., Kosoris, J., Hong, L.N., and Crul, M. (2009). Design for sustainability: Current trends in sustainable product design and development. *Sustainability*, 1(3), pp. 409–424.

Cottam, H. and Leadbeater, C. (2004). HEALTH: Co-creating Services, *RED paper 01*. London: Design Council.

De Lille, C., Abbingab, E.R., and Kleinsmann, M. (2012). A designerly approach to enable organizations to deliver product-service systems. Paper presented at the *Proceedings of International Design management Research Conference*, Boston.

Ellen MacArthur Foundation. (2010). *Circular Economy Thinking*. Available from: www.ellenmacarthurfoundation.org [Accessed on 14 October 2014].

Fiksel, J. (2006). Sustainability and resilience: Toward a systems approach. *Sustainability: Science Practice and Policy*, 2(2), pp. 14–21.

Goedkoop, M., van Haler, C. te Riele, H., and Rommers, P. (1999). *Product Service-Systems, Ecological and Economic Basics*. Report for the Dutch Ministries of Environment (VROM) and Economic Affairs (EZ).

Hernández-Pardo, R., Bhamra, T.A., and Bhamra, R. (2013). Designing sustainable product service systems in SMEs. *The International Journal of Design Management and Professional Practice*, 6(4), pp. 57–71.

Hernández-Pardo, R.J., Bhamra, T., and Bhamra, R. (2012). Sustainable product service systems in small and medium enterprises (SMEs): Opportunities in the leather manufacturing industry. *Sustainability*, 4, pp. 175–192.

INCPEN. (2003). *Reusable Packaging*. Available from: www.ifl sites.co.uk/resource/pv5.exe [Accessed on 15 July 2003].

Kang, M. and Wimmer, R. (2009). *Product Service Systems Beyond Sustainable Products*. Seoul: International Association of Societies of Design Research.

Kotler, P. and Rath, G.A. (1984). Design: A powerful but neglected strategic tool. *Journal of Business Strategy*, 5, pp. 16–21.

Kuzmina, K., Bhamra T., and Trimingham, R. (2012). "Service design and its role in changing education", in Miettinen, S. and Valtonen, A. (Eds), *Service Design With Theory*. Lapland University Press: Finland.

Lofthouse, V.A. (2007). Creative idea generation for refillable body wash products. *Proceedings of ICED 2007, the 16th International Conference on Engineering Design*, DS 42.

Lofthouse, V.A., Bhamra, T.A., and Trimingham, R.L. (2009). Investigating customer perceptions of refillable packaging and assessing business drivers and barriers to their use. *Journal of Packaging Technology and Science*, 22(6), pp. 335–348, Full text: http://www3.interscience.wiley.com/cgi-bin/fulltext/122388099/PDFSTART .

McDonagh, W. and Braungart, M. (2003). *Cradle to Cradle: Remaking the Way We Make Things*. New York: North Point Press.

Manzini, E. and Vezzoli, C. (2003). A strategic design approach to develop sustainable product service systems: Examples taken from the 'environmentally friendly innovation' Italian prize. *Journal of Cleaner Production*, 11, pp. 851–857.

Martinez, V., Bastl, M., Kingston, J., and Evans, S. (2010). Challenges in transforming manufacturing organisations into product-service providers. *Journal of Manufacturing Technology Management*, 21, pp. 449–469.

Mont, O. (2002). Clarifying the concept of product-service system. *Journal of Cleaner Production*, 10(3), pp. 237–245.

Morelli, N. (2003). Product-service systems, a perspective shift for designers: A case study: The design of a telecentre. *Design Studies*, 24, pp. 73–99.

Morelli, N. (2006). Developing new product service systems (PSS): Methodologies and operational tools. *Journal of Cleaner Production*, 14, pp. 1495–1501.

Moritz, S. (2005). *Service design: Practical access to an evolving field.* MSc thesis, Koln International School of Design, Koln, Germany.

Mozota, B.B. (2006). The four powers of design: A value model in design management. *Design Management Review,* 17, pp. 44–53.

Mulgan, G. and Albury, D. (2003). *Innovation in the Public Sector.* Strategy Unit, Cabinet Office: United Kingdom.

Nelson, D., Adger, N.W., and Brown, K. (2007). Adaptation to environmental change contributions of a resilience framework. *The Annual Review of Environment and Resources,* 32, pp. 395–419.

Ness, D. (2007). "Sustainable product service systems: Potential to deliver business and social benefits with less resource use", *Greening the Business and Making Environment a Business Opportunity,* Bangkok: June, pp. 5–7.

Pacenti, E. (2011). "How service design can support innovation in the public sector", in Meroni, A. and Sangiorgi, D. (Ed.), *Design for Services.* Farnham: Gower, pp. 97–105.

Parker, S. and Heapy, J. (2006). *The Journey to the Interface: How Public Service Design Can Connect Users to Reform.* London: Demos.

Perks, H., Cooper, R., and Jones, C. (2005). Characterizing the role of design in new product development: An empirically derived taxonomy★. *Journal of Product Innovation Management,* 22, pp. 111–127.

Rapitsenyane, R. (2014). *Supporting SMEs Adoption of Sustainable Product Service Systems: A Holistic Design-led Framework for Creating Competitive Advantage.* PhD, Loughborough University.

Rapitsenyane, Y. and Bhamra, T. (2013). The place of sustainability through Product Service Systems in manufacturing SMEs in Botswana: A Delphi study, In *Proceedings of the 16th Conference of the European Roundtable on Sustainable Consumption and Production (ERSCP) & 7th Conference of the Environmental Management for Sustainable Universities (EMSU),* June 4–7, Istanbul.

Robson, C. (1993). *Real World Research – A Resource for Social Scientists and Practitioner – Researchers.* Oxford: Blackwell Publishers Ltd.

Robson, C. (2011). *Case Study Research Design and Methods* (third edition). Chichester: Wiley & Sons.

Sangiorgi, D. (2011). Transformative services and transformation design. *International Journal of Design,* 5(2), pp. 29–40.

Sangiorgi, D., Gillen, J., Junginger, S., and Whitham, R. (2011). "A service design inquiry into learning and personalisation," in Meroni, A. and Sangiorgi, D. (Eds), *Design for Services.* Farnham: Gower, pp. 139–146.

Smith, L. A., Maull, R. S., Ng, I.C.L. (2014). Servitization and operations management: a service dominant-logic approach. *International Journal of Operations & Production Management,* 34(2), pp. 242–269, doi: 10.1108/IJOPM-02-2011-0053

Stamm, von B. (2004). Collaboration with other firms and customers: Innovation's secret weapon. *Strategy & Leadership,* 32, pp. 16–20.

Sterling, S. (2003). *Whole Systems Thinking as a Basis for Paradigm Change in Education: Explorations in the Context of Sustainability. Centre for Research in Education and the Environment.* University of Bath PhD thesis, Bath.

Stickdorn, M. and Schneider, J. (2010). *This Is Service Design Thinking.* Amsterdam: BIS Publishers.

Strauss, A., and Corbin, J. (1990). *Basics of Qualitative Research: Grounded Theory, Procedures and Techniques.* London: Sage Publications, Inc.

Szebeko, D. (2011). "Co-designing services in a public sector," in Meroni, A. and Sangiorgi, D. (Eds), *Design for Services.* Farnham: Gower, pp. 42–54.

Tan, A., McAloone, T.C., and Andreasen, M.M. (2006). What happens to integrated product development models with product/service-system approaches. Paper presented at the *Proceedings of the 6th Integrated Product Development Workshop,* IPD2006.

Thackara, J. (2007). *Wouldn't Be Great If . . .* London: Design Council.

Thomas, E. (Ed.). (2008). *Innovation by Design in Public Services.* London: Solace Foundation Imprint.

Trimingham, R. (2015). "Sustainable design," in Edwards, C. (Ed.), *The Bloomsbury Encyclopedia of Design.* London: Bloomsbury Publishing, ISBN 9781472521576.

Tukker, A. (2004). Eight types of product-service system: Eight ways to sustainability? experiences from SusProNet. *Business Strategy and the Environment,* 13, pp. 246–260.

Tukker, A. and Tischner, U. (2006). Product-services as a research field: Past, present and future. Reflections from a decade of research. *Journal of Cleaner Production,* 14(17), pp. 1552–1556.

Turner, R. (2000). Design and business who calls the shots? *Design Management Journal* (Former Series), 11, pp. 42–47.

UNEP. (2002). *The Role of Product Service Systems in a Sustainable Society.* Available from: www.unep.org/resourceefficiency/Business/SustainableProducts/ProductServiceSystemsSustainability/tabid/78847/Default.aspx

UNESCO. (2009). Bonn declaration. *UNESCO World Conference on Education for Sustainable Development.* [Online] Available from: www.esd-world271-conference-2009.org/fileadmin/download/ESD2009_BonnDeclaration080409.pdf [Accessed on 25 January 2012].

Vargo, S.L. and Lusch, R.F. (2004). Evolving to a new dominant logic for marketing. *Journal of Marketing,* 68, pp. 1–17.

7

ECOLOGICAL THEORY IN DESIGN

Participant designers in an age of entanglement

Joanna Boehnert

In a 1964 paper titled 'Ecology – A Subversive Science' Paul Sears proposed that if ecology was taken seriously it would "endanger the assumptions and practices accepted by modern societies" (11–12). Five decades later aspects of this disruptive vision have infiltrated mainstream design. Prominent design theorists talk about participant designers, the circular economy, biomimicry, bioregional design, transition design and many other concepts that support sustainable design. Responsible organizations claim to address sustainability agendas as an integral part of every design brief. In progressive places, the various design disciplines are developing new norms informed by the environmental sciences and ecological theory. And yet despite the hard work by many designers concerned with sustainability, this transition is not happening fast enough to stop the trajectory of increasingly serious environmental harms. Ecological theory is still relatively new to design theory and so all ideas need to be disentangled from the ecologically illiterate assumptions of modernity.

Humankind has initiated a new geological epoch known as the Anthropocene. The *anthropos* (Greek for 'humans') are dramatically affecting Earth system processes and are now responsible for cascading crisis conditions (including but not limited to climate change). Whereas there is much debate on the nature of the challenges associated with sustainability, one thing is certain: designers and other disciplines must develop less ecologically destructive ways of living on this planet. This goal requires a thorough understanding of the nature of environmental problems and the various ways in which these problems can be addressed.

The Earth sciences (geosciences) describe a wide assortment of environmental problems with great precision. These sciences include ecology, biology, geology, geography, atmospheric sciences, hydrology, soil sciences, etc. Earth system scientists warn that three planetary boundary conditions have been breeched (Steffen et al. 2015). The evidence on climate change is unequivocal. The science is contested by the contingent of climate deniers and hard-core anti-environmentalists that dismiss environmental harms entirely. What is almost as controversial are interpretations of the causes of environmental problems and the many different proposed solutions.

Ecological theory is a foundation for informed decision making and problem solving on environmental issues. It is a body of knowledge that proposes more functional ways of conceptualising human-nature relations as a basis for the design and development of more sustainable ways of living on this planet. It supports a transition from a dualistic, reductionist and exploitative perspective to a worldview that is participative, relational and complex. Observations in the

Earth sciences are a catalyst but the vital work that ecologically literate sustainability advocates must now do involves philosophical, cultural, social, technological and political transformations. Design has an important role to play in these transitions.

Considering the severity of many unintended consequences of design and development, questions to be investigated by ecological theorists include: 'what gives some people the right to commit ecologically damaging activities that destroy the lives of others, now and in the future?' A responsible enquiry based on this question shatters many basic assumptions about what constitutes good design. As Sears predicated, ecological thought is disruptive. For this reason it is not always welcome in places where it is urgently needed.

Ecological theory

Ecological thought challenges the intellectual tradition wherein the environment is available to be endlessly exploited and where humanity must conquer the non-human natural world to survive. The design of sustainable ways of living requires a different perspective. Ecological thought emphasizes the intricate interconnectivity and interdependency between humans and the non-human natural world. The term 'non-human nature' accentuates the fact that humans are also part of nature. Non-human nature actively influences the course of history (i.e. consider how new germs have transformed societies). A complex web of life-sustaining ecosystems enables humankind to flourish – or not. For several decades now scientists have warned that many of the ecosystems services that we depend on have been seriously damaged and destabilized by human activities. Effective responses to these problems depend on thorough analysis of their origins. A review of the historical circumstances and the ideas that have enabled environmentally harmful development and design is a starting point.

Historical attitudes towards nature

Attitudes towards nature have a variety of philosophical origins. Some of the most powerful and enduring ideas were those that emerged during the scientific revolution (circa sixteenth to eighteenth centuries) and the Enlightenment (eighteenth century). During this period Francis Bacon's (1561–1626) empiricism, Rene Descartes' (1596–1650) rationalism and Isaac Newton's (1643–1727) mechanism emerged as the dominant constructs that influence the ways that nature is understood. Sustainability educational theorist Stephen Sterling claims that this worldview had "an ontology that emphasized a mechanistic cosmology, which was primarily determinist, and materialist; and an epistemology that was objectivist, positivist, reductive and dualist" (2003, 143). Enlightenment science holds that valid knowledge is derived from empirical evidence (based on observations, experiments and measurement tools). This approach to science has made dramatic technological progress possible – but it has also had other consequences.

Ecofeminist and historian of science Carolyn Merchant alleges that Francis Bacon (known as father of the scientific method) created a powerful cultural metaphor of nature as female and as a force to be mastered, controlled and made to submit. This way of describing nature is dramatically different from earlier ideas:

> The removal of the animistic, organic assumptions about the cosmos constituted the death of nature – the most far-reaching effect of the scientific revolution. Because nature was now viewed as a system of dead, inert, particles moved by external, rather than inherent forces, the mechanical framework itself could legitimize the manipulation of nature.
>
> *(Merchant 2001, 281)*

The scientific revolution created a new conception of the world as passive, available for utilization and in need of being controlled. Bacon wrote that nature was to "take orders from Man and work under his authority" (quoted in Harding 2006, 26). Many ecological theorists allege that this conceptualisation created the framework for exploitative human–nature relations.

Origins of ecological thought

The word 'ecology' was coined in 1866 by Ernst Haeckel (1834–1919) as "the science of relations between an organism and the surrounding outer world". Haeckel was a biologist, a philosopher and also a talented artist who created detailed drawings of microscopic life forms, plants and animals. Thus the study of ecology was linked to image-making from its conception. Unfortunately, ecology has also been linked to racist and oppressive philosophical interpretations. This includes some of Haeckel's own theory. Later, Jan Smuts (1870–1950) coined the concept of 'holism' and used references to nature to advance racist political policies, including racial segregation in South Africa. Nature was mobilised by Hitler and the Nazi regime in the 1930s and 40s as a means of presenting the Aryan or Germanic master race as genetically superior *Übermensch*. The ways in which erroneous interpretations of nature have been used to justify the exploitation of certain groups of people is an ongoing problem.

In the early twentieth century physicists Einstein, Heisenberg and others conducted experiments that proved that an observer is a participant that influences experimental results. This breakthrough challenged the subject/object dualism in the scientific tradition. Quantum physics revolutionized the understanding of observation, perception, participation, relationship and influences. These insights took many decades to influence ecological thought and will take even longer to become embedded in design. Over a century later design theorists describe how 'participant designers' (Slavin 2016, Ito 2016) are part of the world that they aim to influence in an 'age of entanglement' (Oxman 2016, Hillis 2016). I will describe what it means to be a participant designer later in the chapter.

Meanwhile, over the course of the twentieth century ecology developed into a science concerned with feedback mechanisms with the intention of understanding and ultimately controlling natural processes. These reductionist, positivist and instrumentalised approaches to ecology are still prominent. This paradigm has been challenged with increasing clarity over the past sixty years as more integrated, systemic and holistic ways of understanding human–nature relations have been articulated and put into practice.

Characteristics of ecological thought

A critique of reductionist science with its atomism, dualism and anthropocentrism is a basis for ecological theory. Ecological theorists claim that reductionist science erases complexity: "knowledge gains in rigour what it loses in richness" (Santos 2007, 27). Furthermore, it reduces the complexity to alienated elements such that "knowledge gained from observation of the parts is necessarily distorted" (Santos 2007, 28). Vandana Shiva developed this argument in 'Reductionist Science as Epistemological Violence' where she claims: "reductionist science is also at the root of the growing ecological crisis, because it entails a transformation of nature such that the processes, regularities and regenerative capacity of nature are destroyed" (1988, unpaginated). Theorists such as Eugene Odum, Barry Commoner, E. F. Schumacher, Herman Daly, Murray Bookchin, Val Plumwood, Vandana Shiva, Fritjof Capra, and others have developed ecological theory in this tradition. A commons based ecological theory approaches ecology as a commons, to be understood as a community or a network forming an integrated whole.

The ecological paradigm offers a more comprehensive foundation for building sustainable ways of living on this planet. Thomas Kuhn famously described paradigms as the "entire constellation of achievements – concepts, values, techniques, and so on shared by the members of a given community" (1962, 175). The concept emphasizes how worldviews, frameworks and constructs are changeable. When a paradigm is no longer fit for purpose, more appropriate interpretative models replace it. Ecological thought offers a type of rationality, ethic, ontology and epistemology that acknowledges ecological context and prioritizes mutually beneficial human-nature relations. The ecological paradigm proposes deep-reaching shifts in ways of understanding human relations within our ecological context.

Ecological rationality

Ecological thought describes a historic and systemic undervaluing or dismissal of non-human nature in modernist thought. This has lead to a consistent underestimation of complexity. Philosopher and ecofeminst Val Plumwood describes "a cult of reason that elevates to extreme superiority a particular narrow form of reason and correspondingly devalues the contrasted and reduced sphere of nature and embodiment" (2002, 4). Plumwood describes a contemporary 'crisis of reason' propelled by attitudes and assumptions that dismiss the context that makes reason possible in the first place. Some enabling factors include the backgrounding of the activity and agency of nature and the remoteness and the distant consequences of actions in industrial society. Ecological rationality proposes more inclusive and holistic forms of reason that do not ignore the context on which it (we) depend.

Ecological ethics

Early ecological theorist Aldo Leopold advocated an extension of ethics to include the natural world. All ethics, according to Leopold, are based on "a single premise: that we are members of a community of interdependent parts" (2001 [1949]: 98). He proposed a simple ethic: "A thing is right when it tends to preserve the integrity, stability, and beauty of the biotic community. It is wrong when it tends otherwise" (2001, 110). The simplicity of this proposal is appealing but as the impacts of technological innovation, development and design have wide-reaching consequences – ecological ethics are far from simple. Ethical decision making is dependent on institutional, technical and communicative processes that make it possible to anticipate unintended consequences. With extended boundaries of concern, putting ecological ethics into practice is complex and political.

Ecological ethics are complicated by the remoteness of industrial processes, poor communicative links and unintended consequences. As unintended consequences are often distant (in time and space) or entirely unknown, ethical design practice requires concerted efforts to understand causality and risk in order to take greater precaution. All too often it is more financially rewarding for industry to deny the existence of unintended consequences than to anticipate and confront problems before they happen. As new technology and innovation emerge faster than the social mechanisms and institutions to ensure unintended consequences are investigated and avoided, ethics are compromised. The result is more (and often amplified) unsustainable development.

Ecological ontology

Ontology is the study of the nature of being. Ecological ontology is our constitutive embeddedness within and as part of larger ecological systems on which we depend. Each of us is nested

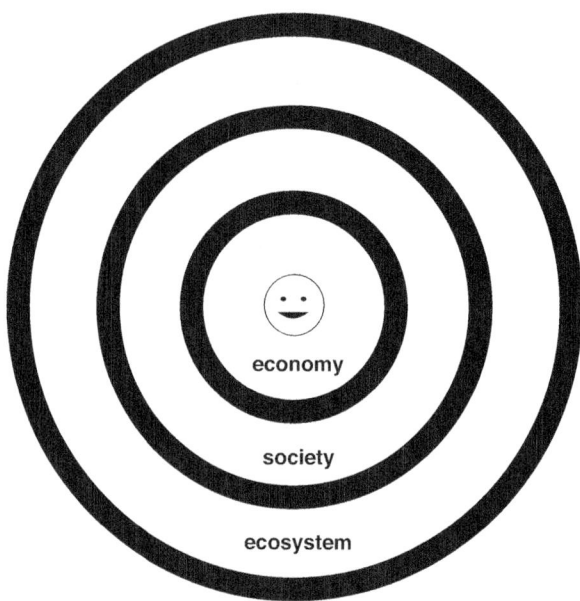

Figure 7.1 The ecosystem, society and economy as nested systems (EcoLabs 2014).

within the ecological context. Ecosystems come in many sizes, each nesting within larger systems (from microscopic to planetary). The ecological, social and economic systems can also be understood as nested systems (see Figure 7.1). The economic order is nested within social order. The social order, in turn, is nested in the ecological order. The Earth will continue to evolve regardless of what happens to the social and the economic orders. Clearly ecological systems on various scales can be degraded and destabilized (i.e. significantly less biodiversity, dead seas, desertification, toxicity, etc.). Ecological economists argue that the economic system has not been constructed to respond to feedback from the systems in which it is embedded (the social and ecological systems) and on which it depends. By formulating ecological ontology as a hierarchy of nested systems ecological theorists describe how dysfunction arises when the systems humans design do not reflect ontological interdependence and interconnectivity.

Ecological epistemology

Epistemology is the study of the nature of knowledge and ways of knowing. In the book *Steps to an Ecology of Mind* (1972) anthropologist and cyberneticist Gregory Bateson described an 'epistemological error' in the current dominant worldview. Bateson wrote: "most of us are governed by epistemologies we know to be wrong" (493) and initiated the revision of epistemological premises in ecological thought. Within the context of a society with powerful industrial capacities, risks associated with this 'epistemological error' are severe:

> I suggest that the last 100 years or so have demonstrated empirically that if an organism or aggregate of organisms sets to work with a focus on its own survival and thinks that is the way to select its adaptive moves, its 'progress' end up with a destroyed environment. If an organism ends up destroying its environment, it has in fact destroyed itself.
>
> *(1972, 457)*

Humans are part of the natural world and are dependent on it for survival, but the dominant epistemological tradition denies this relationship. The narrowing down of ways of knowing to focus only on our own interests is one aspect of epistemological error.

> When you separate mind from the structure in which it is immanent, such as human relationship, the human society, or the ecosystem, you thereby embark, I believe, on fundamental error, which in the end will surely hurt you.
>
> *(1972, 493)*

Epistemological error is characterized by a number of fallacies that include: (1) the assumption that humans are separate from the non-human natural world, (2) the assumption that this separation creates a 'natural' competition, and (3) the assumption that competition and domination are the primary means to success. These premises have wide-ranging implications.

The concept of epistemological error describes a crisis of perception. An ecological paradigm implies a shift in perception. Since design is a practice that is often concerned with perception, learning and encouraging people to do things in new ways, there are many ways design can help facilitate this shift. Communication design is especially well suited to nurture ecological perception by drawing attention to patterns, context, comparisons, causality, connections and complexity. In illustrating these types of relationships, "graphic design has unique potential to nurture the ability to 'see systems' – supporting both ecological perception and ecological literacy" (Boehnert 2014, 1). Whereas graphic design deals most directly with perception, all types of design both reflect and also influence how people understand and relate to the material world.

Language, communication, objects and cities are all constructed in ways that reflect the ideas and assumptions of the people involved with their creation (along with economic priorities that influence what type of work is done). Bateson explains that the world "partly becomes – comes to be – how it is imagined" (1980, 223). Designed artifacts, spaces, systems and communications are extensions of our ways of knowing. Epistemological error is thereby encoded into communication, artefacts and systems structures – reproducing cultural assumptions and making it difficult to identify alternatives.

This perspective limits human capacities to perceive, engage with and respond to complex problems. Sterling explains that "the dominant western epistemology, or knowledge system, is no longer adequate to cope with the world that it itself has partly created" (2003, 3). Ecological theory reveals epistemological blind spots and proposes alternatives. This "shift from mechanism, which has dominated western thinking for over three hundred years to a new organism; from the machine metaphor to the systemic metaphor of ecology" (2003, 8) is increasingly evident. Designers are in a good position to embed this vision into new communication, products and environments.

Alternative epistemologies

Feminist, class, race and indigenous scholars and activists have described how conceptual frameworks justify exploitation. Feminist theory critiques androcentrism and the supposed value neutrality of hegemonic ideologies and perspectives. Donna Haraway argues that all knowledge is situated: meaning that knowledge emerges out of a particular social, cultural and material context (1988). Feminist theory describes how conceptual frameworks and institutional practices reproduce oppressions: "Injustice does not take place in a conceptual vacuum, but is closely linked to desensitizing and Othering frameworks" (Plumwood 1999, 197). 'Othering' is the process through which the interests and needs of certain groups of people are denied the same considerations and rights as those with greater privilege.

Obviously women are not the only social group encountering oppression and many people face multiple and intersecting injustices. Ecofeminists extend feminist theory work to include non-human nature. They maintain that social injustices and environmental injustices are both enabled by othering frameworks. Since intersectional feminist strategies and other anti-oppressive work have in places worked to help make women's and other groups' needs and interests visible and actionable (these are ongoing struggles) – these strategies can also inform the work that needs to be done to confront the forces that deny the interests of non-human nature.

At least 7,000 indigenous societies around the world maintain a variety ecological episte-mological traditions based on a "substantive reliance of interrelatedness of nature" (Lauderdale 2007, 741). TEK (traditional ecological knowledge) offers unique ways of conceptualizing human-nature relations often embedded in oral traditions. Indigenous people typically cele-brate nature's regenerative capacities with an ethic of care that is based on relationships and kinship. For this reason, many ecological theorists agree that traditional indigenous knowledge has "inclusive approaches to current environment problems and critical ideas on how to . . . create more equitable, less oppressive structures from which to approach the numerous crises" (Lauderdale 2008, 1836). Though it is true that not all indigenous peoples have always been sound ecological stewards, they have often cultivated place-based knowledge that has sup-ported relatively ecologically sustainable ways of living. In many places indigenous peoples now struggle against those who threaten their existence with land grabs, pollution and resource extraction on their territories. Biopiracy (meaning the theft of property, traditional knowledge and biological/genetic resources) is one of the many examples of the continuation of half a millennium of colonialism.

Epistemic selectivities

The ecological paradigm is still marginal. As a disruptive vision that exposes many common practices in society as deeply unsustainable, it is unwelcome by those with a vested interest in the status quo. Scholars studying the continued marginalization of environmental concerns refer to 'epistemic selectivities' as the dynamics that legitimize certain epistemological perspectives at the expense of others. Epistemic selectivities are "mechanisms inscribed in political institutions which privilege particular forms of knowledge, problem perceptions, and narratives over others" (Brand and Vadrot 2013, 218). It is often psychologically easier for the materially privileged and powerful to ignore facts and even entire ways of thinking that threaten their sense of entitlement. In this way, people with relative amounts of power avoid feeling complicit with the injustices that are a consequence of unsustainable development.

The emergence of ecological literacy

The design and development of sustainable futures demands specialized knowledge and skills informed by ecological knowledge within the various disciplinary traditions. David Orr coined the concept of 'ecological literacy' in 1992 as a type of education that imparts an understanding of our ecology context and of environmental problems along with new capacities to respond effectively. Orr argues that environmental problems are linked to how we think:

> The disordering of ecological systems and of the great biogeochemical cycles of the earth reflects a prior disorder in the thought, perception, imagination, intellectual pri-orities, and loyalties inherent in the industrial mind. Ultimately, then, the ecological

crisis concerns how we think and the institutions that purport to shape and refine the capacity to think.

(Orr 2004, 2)

Orr explains that environmental problems "are mostly the result of a miscalculation between human intention and ecological results, which is to say that they are a kind of design failure" (2002, 14). These design failures signal "inherent problems in our perceptual and mental abilities" but also suggest that improvements can be made through design (2002, 14). Design can be a powerful transformative practice when it is informed by an in-depth understanding of ecological theory. Thus, ecological literacy must become a pedagogic priority in design education. According to Orr, ecologically literacy involves: an understanding of why it is necessary to work with (rather than against) natural forces; a basic familiarity with ecological processes; a historical understanding of how humankind has become so destructive; and capacities to work towards solutions (1992, 93–94). Ten years later Orr proposed more specific features of ecological design. He described it as a community process that aims to increase local resilience, as accepting limits, as eliminating the concept of waste, and as having to do with systems structure (2002, 180–183). These goals typically demand interdisciplinary collaborations beyond the scope of traditional design education. Ecologically literate design is systems aware, enabling, collaborative and participatory. With ecological literacy, the scope of change required to address environmental problems becomes evident. But the awareness of the ecological impact of our actions is only the beginning of the journey. Ecological literacy demands critical skills in diagnosing the forces that reproduce what is unsustainable. Ecological literacy is a basis for ethical and informed decision making in a technologically advanced civilization.

Participant designers

The notion of the participant designer implies a profound transformation. With this perspective, designers are "participants within the systems they exist in. This is a fundamental shift – one that requires a new set of values" (Ito 2016, para 17). MIT Media Lab Director Joichi Ito describes an internal shift that influences the ways designers work:

> As participant designers, we focus on changing ourselves and the way we do things in order to change the world. With this new perspective, we will be able to tackle extremely important problems that don't fit neatly into current academic systems: instead of designing other people's systems, we will redesign our way of thinking and working and impact the world by impacting ourselves.
>
> *(2016, para 28)*

The participant perspective acknowledges that designers are part of the world that we want to influence. This view sits in sharp contrast to the narrower perspective where designers focus on 'the user'. Kevin Slavin claims: "This is the inversion of User Centric Design. Rather than placing the human at the center of the work, the systems that surround us – systems we depend on – take the appropriate center stage in their complexity, mystery, in their unpredictability" (2016, para. 36). Participant designers are learning to work in transformative ways by

> engaging with the complex adaptive systems that surround us, by revealing instead of obscuring, by building friction instead of hiding it, and by making clear that every one of us (designers included) are nothing more than participants in systems that have

no center to begin with. These are designers of systems that participate – with us and with one another – systems that invite participation instead of demanding interaction.

We can build software to eat the world, or software to feed it. And if we are going to feed it, it will require a different approach to design, one which optimizes for a different type of growth, and one that draws upon – and rewards – the humility of the designers who participate within it.

(Slavin 2016, para. 40 and 41)

The type growth that Slavin refers to here should be qualitative, regenerative growth (in shared prosperity) – with simultaneous *de-growth* in much of what is currently counted as economic growth – but has devastating ecologically and social consequences (known abstractly and over-simplistically as 'economic externalities'). Challenging the nature of growth is an essential part of developing sustainable future ways of living.

Nature's patterns and processes

Nature's patterns and processes provide time-tested models for the design of sustainable ways of living. Ecological theorist Fritjof Capra describes six "principles of organization, common to all living systems, that ecosystems have evolved to sustain the web of life" (2003, 201). The Center of Ecological Literacy lists six processes and patterns in ecological systems:

> *Networks* – All living things in an ecosystem are interconnected through networks of rela-
> tionship.
> *Nested systems* – Nature is made up of systems that are nested within systems. Each individ-
> ual system is an integrated whole and – at the same time – part of larger systems.
> *Cycles* – Members of an ecological community depend on the exchange of resources in
> continual cycles.
> *Flows* – Each organism needs a continual flow of energy to stay alive. The constant flow of
> energy from the sun to Earth sustains life and drives most ecological cycles.
> *Development* – All life – from individual organisms to species to ecosystems – changes over
> time. Individuals develop and learn, species adapt and evolve, and organisms in ecosys-
> tems coevolve.
> *Dynamic balance* – Ecological communities act as feedback loops, so that the community
> maintains a relatively steady state that also has continual fluctuations. This dynamic bal-
> ance provides resiliency in the face of ecosystem change.

(2016)

Patterns in nature are also the building block of biomimicry (see Chapter 33). Design that works with nature's patterns and processes is regenerative for humans and non-human nature alike. Nature's patterns and processes framework can be applied at all levels of systems that humans design – including political and economic systems.

Ecological literacy and the political economy of design

In the context of a deeply unsustainable culture, ecological literacy offers a more comprehensive critique than the abused concepts of 'sustainability' and 'sustainable development'. Sustainability has been associated with development since the 1987 United Nations Brundtland Commission report *Our Common Future*. Meaning 'ecological care' and 'development' simultaneously the term has been described as conflicted. Critics claim that the concept ensures the "conservation of development, not for the conservation of nature" (Sachs 1999, 34). This contradiction has noted from the beginning:

> With sustainable development there are no limits to growth. Greens and environmentalists who today still use this concept display ecological illiteracy. There is a basic contradiction between the finiteness of the Earth, with natural self-regulating systems operating within limits, and the expansionary nature of industrial capitalist society. The language of sustainable development helps mask this fundamental contradiction, so that industrial expansion on a global scale can temporarily continue.
>
> *(Orton 1989, unpaginated)*

Increasing levels of consumption with evermore people wanting more resource intensive stuff cannot happen indefinitely. Ecological literacy acknowledges thresholds and builds capacity to address problems where shallow approaches to sustainability fail. Though the Earth's generative capacities can sometimes be remediated, there are also finite resources and planetary boundaries that must be taken into account.

Ecological literacy informs the debate on sustainability by emphasizing the contextual and collective nature of sustaining civilization over time. Sustainability is not the feature of one product, but is the condition of an entire culture relative to its gross impact on ecological systems. The per capita ecological footprint of consumption is 4.9 global hectare (gha) in the United Kingdom and 8.2 gha in the United States (Global Footprint Network, 2016). These nations collectively use respectively over three and five times the sustainable levels of resources. Cumulatively these two nations have ways of living that are deeply unsustainable. Pollution and climate change already have very real consequences (especially for the poor who bear the brunt of environmental harms). There will be even more dramatic consequences for future generations. Whereas some individuals personally use fewer resources and create less pollution, it is the gross impact of the system that matters. For this reason sustainability is a political problem. It is about structural choices (that determine how much greenhouse gases are released and the types of development that are enabled) – and not simply a matter of individual consumer choices. The designer concerned with creating sustainable ways of living needs to think not only about the ecological circumstances relevant to a particular design problem she is addressing – but how she participates in a political context that is changing to meet environmental challenges. Environmental problems are also political problems so the political economy of design matters. Economic priorities have a determining role in the degree to which design can address ecological problems. Designers concerned with sustainability need to consider why it is that ecological sustainability is so difficult in the current political context.

Some clarification on ecological entanglement

Although design increasingly engages with ecological entanglements, certain ways of thinking continue to enable continued harmful, unsustainable design and development. MIT Press *Journal of Design and Science* (January 2016), published an article with a section titled 'The End of the Artificial' where Joichi Ito claims that "unlike the past where there was a clearer separation between those things that represented the artificial and those that represented the organic, the cultural and the natural, it appears that nature and the artificial are merging" (2016, para. 20). In the same journal, Danny Hillis states:

> We humans are changing. We have become so intertwined with what we have created that we are no longer separate from it. We have outgrown the distinction between the

natural and the artificial. We are what we make. . . . We are at the dawn of the Age of Entanglement.

(2016, para. 1)

It is true that plastic debris is clogging up the guts of marine animals, greenhouse gases in the upper atmosphere are destabilising the climate system and there are endless examples of similar entanglements. The artificial and the organic are definitely interacting in countless ways on all scales across the Earth – but the 'end of the artificial' concept has more to do the legacy of epistemological error and the particular type of political economy that emerged from this error than the so-called merging of the ecological and the artificial. Contrary to the ideas presented in this journal, the entanglement must not be theorised as the coalescing of the natural and the artificial.

The ways that we talk about nature influence how we understand and value it. If the artificial things that humans have designed and constructed over the past century are conceptualized of the same order as natural patterns and processes that have made it possible for humans to flourish over millenniums – this influences the ways we understand and value natural processes (in ways that are unhelpful). The ecological sphere has evolved over millions of years to enable life-sustaining conditions on this planet. In stark contrast to the ecological, the artificial has not endured the test of time. It has not evolved to work in harmony with the ecological. In many places it disables or disrupts the dynamic balance ecosystems need to sustain or regenerate their processes. The climate system is the most dramatic example of this severe disruption. The artificial includes toxic elements and destructive technologies that threaten not only the most complex and exquisite ecosystems and animals on the planet but civilization itself.

Nature is of a different order than the artificial because it is the *context* of the artificial. Just because it is now possible to 'edit' nature (genetic engineering, synthetic biology, geo-engineering) does not mean the organic and the artificial are the same, or that they have equivalent value. We might redesign nature into what appears to the most cavalier amongst us as a 'better' place, to suit human needs and desires – but we cannot predict with certainty the consequences of the most dramatic interventions. (This is what is described as the 'instrumentalisation' of human-nature relations: where natural processes are controlled, exploited.) On the other hand, nature has experimented for millions of years to refine the evolutionary moment that we find ourselves in now, one that we are quickly degrading. Since humans have already caused irreparable damage to the climate system, to biodiversity and to a vast array of ecosystems and species, now is not the time to build new theory that will further dismiss ecological concerns.

In a context that already denies the primacy of the ecological, the claim that the ecological and the artificial are merging is a convenient and 'useful' assumption. It is a claim that facilitates the interests that profit from new technologies and associated market growth. Meanwhile, the denigration and dismissal of the ecological context is not an easy assumption to break considering the powerful interests that are served by certain types of industrial development and the historical circumstances that have led to epistemological error and ecologically destructive types of development. The flattening of the natural and the artificial is an error of order and value. The ignoring of the severity of the consequences of many types of industrial development emerges from this mindset. This is part of the epistemological error that must be challenged. The error is simultaneously in ways of thinking, in design and in the political economy.

Design is a social practice that reflects the assumptions of designers as well as priorities embedded into the political economy. There are toxins and greenhouse gases that are entangled with 'the natural' in deeply damaging way. Ecological theory provides a basis for making distinctions between good and bad entanglements. Knowing the difference between life-sustaining and life-destroying entanglements is essential for designers to move beyond the ecologically disastrous errors of modernity.

Conclusion

Ecological rationality, ethics, ontologies and epistemologies challenge conceptions of nature as ripe for abuse. Ecological thought rejects modernist rationality that "depends on what it destroys for its survival" (Plumwood 2002, 236). It should be evident that "no rational society rewards members to undermine its existence" (Orr 1992, 6), but clearly those who exploit natural and human 'resources' are rewarded financially in the current economic context. Ecological thought offers a more coherent paradigm as a basis for sustainable transformations. The participant designer understands herself as embedded within and interdependent with her ecological context. Yet effective design solutions do not simply emerge from this understanding. They become possible through her capacities to analyze and identify the interests that are systemically de-prioritized in this particular context along the concepts that legitimize environmental and social harms and injustices. The participant designer must understand why the political economy matters for regenerative design to enable change on a scale necessary to address society's most severe problems.

References

Bateson, G. (1972) *Steps to an Ecology of Mind.* Chicago, University of Chicago Press.

Bateson, G. (1980) *Mind and Nature.* London, Bantam Books.

Boehnert, J. (2014) Ecological Perception: Seeing Systems. *DRS 2014: Design's Big Debates*, Umea. June 16–19.

Brand, U., and Vadrot, A. B. M. (2013) "Epistemic selectivities and the valorisation of nature," *Law, Environment and Development Journal*, 9, 202–222.

Capra, F. (2003) *The Hidden Connections.* London, Flamingo.

Center for Ecoliteracy (CEL). (2016) Applying Ecological Principles. (www.ecoliteracy.org/article/applying-ecological-principles) Accessed 30 May 2016.

Global Footprint Network. (2016) Global Footprint Network: Footprint Basics – Overview. (www.footprintnetwork.org/en/index.php/gfn/page/footprint_basics_overview) Accessed 30 May 2016.

Haraway, D. (1988) "Situated knowledges: The science question in feminism and the privilege of partial perspective," *Feminist Studies*, 14(3), 575–599.

Harding, S. (2006) *Animate Earth.* Dartington, UK, Green Books.

Hillis, D. "The enlightenment is dead, long live the entanglement," *Journal of Design and Science*, MIT Media Lab, MIT Press (http://jods.mitpress.mit.edu/pub/enlightenment-to-entanglement) Accessed 30 May 2016.

Ito, J. (2016) "Design and science," *Journal of Design and Science*, MIT Media Lab, MIT Press (http://jods.mitpress.mit.edu/pub/designandscience) Accessed 30 May 2016.

Ito, J., Slavin, K., Neri, O., and Hillis, D. (2016) *Journal of Design and Science*, MIT Media Lab, MIT Press. (http://jods.mitpress.mit.edu/) Accessed 30 May 2016.

Kuhn, T. (1962) *The Structure of Scientific Revolutions.* Chicago, University of Chicago Press.

Lauderdale, P. (2007) "Indigenous peoples and environmentalism," in Anderson, G. and Herr, K., eds., *The Encyclopedia of Activism and Social Justice.* London, Sage Publications.

Lauderdale, P. (August 2008) "Indigenous peoples in the face of globalization," *American Behavioral Scientist*, 51(12), 1836–1843.

Leopold, A. (2001) "The land ethic," in Zimmerman, M., Callicott, J.B., Sessions, G., Warren, K., and Clark, J., eds., *Environmental Philosophy*, 3rd edition. Upper Saddle River, NJ, Prentice Hall.

Merchant, C. (2001) "The death of nature," in Zimmerman, M., Callicott, J.B., Sessions, G., Warren, K., and Clark, J., eds., *Environmental Philosophy*, 3rd edition. Upper Saddle River, NJ, Prentice Hall.

Orr, D. (1992) *Ecological Literacy.* Albany, State of New York Press.

Orr, D. (2002) *The Nature of Design.* Oxford, Oxford University Press.

Orr, D. (2004) *Earth in Mind*. London, Island Press.

Orton, D. (1989) Sustainable development or perpetual motion? *The New Catalyst*, 23, Spring.

Oxman, N. (2016) "Age of entanglement," *Journal of Design and Science*, MIT Media Lab, MIT Press (http://jods.mitpress.mit.edu/pub/AgeOfEntanglement) Accessed 9 October 2016.

Plumwood, V. (1999) "Ecological ethics from rights to recognition: Multiple spheres of justice for humans, animals and nature," in Low, N. ed., *Global Ethics and Environment*. London, Routledge.

Plumwood, V. (2002) *Environmental Culture*. Oxon, Routledge.

Sachs, W. (1999) *Planet Dialectics*. London, Zed Books.

Santos, B. de S. (2007) *Cognitive Justice in a Global World*. Plymouth, Lexington Books.

Sears, P. (1964) Ecology – A subversive science. *Bioscience*, 14(7) 11–13.

Shiva, V. (1988) "Reductionist science as epistemological violence," in Nandy, A. ed., *Science, Hegemony and Violence*. Oxford, Oxford University Press.

Slavin, K. (2016) "Design as participation," *Journal of Design and Science*, MIT Press (http://jods.mitpress.mit.edu/pub/design-as-participation) Accessed 30 May 2016.

Steffen, W., Richardson, K., Rockstrom, J., Cornell, S.E., Fetzer, I., Bennett, E.M., Biggs, R., *et al.* (2015) "Planetary boundaries: Guiding human development on a changing planet," *Science*, 347(6223), 736–747.

Sterling, S. (2003) *Whole Systems Thinking as a Basis for Paradigm Change in Education*. PhD, University of Bath.

PART 2

Global impact

As illustrated in Part 1, it is impossible to consider any action as singular to maintain a holistic view sustainable design. Raw materials originate from all corners of the Earth and are manufactured worldwide into products that crisscross oceans for consumption and disposal. Even individuals who try to live within local economies are influenced by and exert influence on the global marketplace. A holistic definition of design is not limited to the field of study but includes its interactions with the international community. Part 2 of the *Handbook of Sustainable Design* focuses on shared impacts of designing, consuming and living in a global society.

Douglas Bourn begins the section with an overview of *Global perspectives for sustainable design*. Presenting globalization as a complex phenomenon, Bourn argues "any discussion of its impact on a particular economic sector and lifestyle needs to take into consideration an understanding of power and inequality, recognizing diversity and the plurality of voices that may exist around an activity and the value of these different world outlooks." The chapter outlines Bourn's work on global perspective frameworks in four themes – Global Outlook, Globalization, and the Imagination; Understanding Power and Inequalities in the World; Belief in Social Justice; and Critical Dialogue, Reflection, and Transformation.

Sustainable design faces challenges across the globe in growth-oriented economies, and a fundamental question emerges "how to reduce energy and material consumption in socio-economic systems that are dependent on economic growth for their sustenance." Harold Wilhite explores this question in the chapter *Politics and sustainability*. Wilhite argues that a narrow focus on efficiency in the global context leads to "weak sustainability," and that 'smart' designs must strive for a reduction in resources and consumption overall.

Helena Norberg-Hodge shares how her personal experience of working in Ladakh has shaped her perspectives on globalization in her chapter *Design for localization*. Encouraging designers to use natural, place-based, human-scale and diverse elements, she demonstrates the need to build decentralized local economies. Norberg-Hodge provides contextualized examples from her work with the Ladakh Ecological Development Group (LEDeG) for the global reader.

Thinking about global impact requires a cosmopolitan understanding of culture, cooperation, and partnership. Denielle Emans and Kelly Murdoch-Kitt share their pedagogical experiences partnering design students from different sides of the world in their chapter *Intercultural collaborations in sustainable design education*. Their framework presents sustainability in the classroom while trying to work on unified goals with international partners that cultivate global perspectives and empathy. The chapter includes four activities that design educators and other stakeholders can use to prepare their students for global stewardship.

Erinn G. Ryen, Callie W. Babbitt, and Alex Lobos explore the environmental, social, and economic trade-offs of consumer electronics design in the chapter *Lifecycle thinking and sustainable design for electronics*. The chapter combines systems thinking ideas presented in Part 1 with concrete global supply chain examples and outlines the complex global lifecycle of consumer electronics from resource extraction to e-waste. Ryen et al. present several design strategies to combat challenges in an area of sustainable design that relies very heavily on precious resources and production from across the globe. The authors acknowledge that current design approaches may not suffice in the ever-changing consumer trends sector and explore how to "leverage user-oriented sustainable design to create greater benefits while reducing environmental risks."

Some environmentally concerned citizens believe that going "paperless" or "digital" is the best solution for reducing waste. However, virtual data still produces a tremendous amount of waste – just a different kind. Arman Shehabi explores the environmental impact of data servers, cloud storage, online and electronic information, and electricity in his chapter *Data clouds and the environment*. While not filling our landfills with solid waste, the pollution from these factors has consequences and requires consideration at the individual and global scale.

Using GIS (Geographic Information Systems) and remote sensing tools, urban planners identify properties and possible uses for geographic spaces to increase regional sustainability. Luiz Felipe Guanaes Rego, Maria Fernanda Campos Lemos, and Luís Carlos Soares Madeira Domingues reflect on their experience using GIS in Resende, Rio de Janeiro, Brazil in the chapter *Increased urban sustainability using GIS*. Advanced technology paired with satellite capability allow designers to understand geographic conditions and the impact of their decisions on a local and global level.

International forces affect our daily lives whether we live in rural Australia, remote Africa or downtown New York. Circumstances beyond our nation's borders influence our choice of apparel, food supply, musical taste, and job market as well as the causes supported by local government. Part 2 builds a case for exploring the field of design through its relationship with politics, culture, resources, and humanity worldwide.

8

GLOBAL PERSPECTIVES FOR SUSTAINABLE DESIGN

Douglas Bourn

Introduction

The United Nations Sustainable Development Goals launched in 2015 make implicit reference to themes around globalization such as consumption, industrialization and economic growth, but they do not directly address the impact of global forces on people's lives and communities. This reflects the ongoing tension that has existed since the Rio Summit of 1992 on sustainable development in the relationship between global economic and cultural forces and the goal of living more sustainably. Yet a constant theme of promoters of a more sustainable lifestyle is the need for societies and economies to recognise the influence of global forces that are encouraging a faster pace of life and greater consumerism. Therefore, as this chapter will suggest, discussing sustainability themes within design has to include engagement with an understanding of the impact of globalization.

Where globalization has been discussed within the design fields, for example in architecture and marketization of products, it is often equated with homogenisation. Buildings and places are becoming more and more alike, populated with the same global consumer brands. Wherever you go in the world, the same global products and brand names can be seen.

The design industry could also be said to be one sector of the global economy that has directly benefited from globalization through global forms of technology and as a communicator of global brands.

This chapter aims to address the tensions and issues by reviewing the literature on globalization, looking particularly at the debates around homogeneity and identity. It will suggest that globalization should be seen as a complex phenomenon and any discussion of its impact on a particular economic sector and lifestyle needs to take into consideration an understanding of power and inequality, recognising diversity and the plurality of voices that may exist around an activity and the value of these different world outlooks. The chapter will further suggest that globalization is a reality of peoples' lives and presents opportunities for broadening horizons and outlooks. This 'global perspectives' approach could be valuable for sustainable design because it provides a pedagogical approach with which to make sense of, and engage with, the world in which we are now living.

The global perspectives framework outlined in this chapter is based on four themes, outlined elsewhere by this author (Bourn, 2015): global outlook, globalization and the imagination;

understanding power and inequalities in the world; belief in social justice; and critical dialogue, reflection and transformation. The themes addressed in this chapter have been influenced by the discourses in and around development and global education, global citizenship education and education for sustainable development.

Debates on globalization

Globalization is an ever-present feature of people's everyday lives, particularly in large cities, whether they live in Cape Town, Beijing, New York or New Delhi. A major feature of discussions within design and architecture about globalization is the debate between the particular or the indigenous and the general, homogenous and global (Tyrrell, 2008). Globalization, as will be suggested, needs to be seen in much more complex terms. The contradictions and challenges that globalization poses can be seen as 'opening spaces for new identities and contestation of established values and norms' but 'may be detrimental to the achievement of true social justice' (Stromquist and Monkmann, 2000: 21).

Towards the end of the twentieth century, there was a major reconfiguration of the economic, political and social landscape of the world. This included the fall of the Berlin Wall, the rise of market globalization and neo-liberal philosophies, and the growth of instant access to communications and information with people throughout the world. Castells (1996) refers to this as the 'rise of the network society'. There are many interpretations as to what is meant by globalization but some of the most influential theorists have been Harvey, Held and McGrew, and Giddens. Harvey (1989) refers to globalization as resulting in cultural de-territorialisation and time space compression. Held and McGrew (2000) refer to globalization as being about a complex process of transformation of economic, political and cultural social relations. Giddens (1991) described globalization as the 'intensification of worldwide social relations which link distinct localities in such a way that local happenings are shaped by events occurring far away and vice versa' (p. 64).

What these definitions have as their common focus is a sense that the world has become smaller, more accessible and as a consequence has greater impact on local activities and economies. Baylis and Smith (1999: 7) summarise this well by seeing globalization as 'the process of increasing interconnectedness between societies such that events in one part of the world more and more have effects on people and societies far away'.

There have been many interpretations of what the impact of globalization on societies and economies means. As Wiseman (1998) suggests, an adequate understanding of globalization requires an integrated approach which illuminates global economic relations in terms of changing social, political and cultural landscapes. Lewin (2009) suggests three themes to the discourse on globalization:

- *Economic* – in terms of the borderless nature of the production and marketing of goods
- *Political* – including the declining role of the nation state
- *Global communications* – instant access to knowledge, information and dialogue

Impact on production of goods

Of particular importance in the world of design is the impact of global forces on how products are made. Today the manufacturing industry is fragmented around the world. Globalization has resulted in raw materials mined from several parts of the world being shipped to another for manufacturing and then perhaps on to somewhere else for further refinement and then to somewhere else for distribution. At the end of the useful life of a product, it is then often shipped around the world again to be dumped in areas that are often the furthest away from Western consumerist eyes. For example, watches may be designed in Switzerland but their components are often produced and assembled in other countries. Another example is the famous Barbie doll which is owned and manufactured by the American company Mattel, uses plastic derived from Saudi Arabian oil which is then turned into pellets made in Taiwan. The nylon hair is made in Japan and attached to the doll in China, with final packaging made in the United States. All of this is overseen and managed from Hong Kong (Morgan, 2001). This global distribution of manufacturing is influenced by a number of factors including cheap labour, easy transport connections, specialist skills and level of government regulation.

For example, China, the engine room of most manufacturing in the world today, produces the vast amount of its goods for the West. This means that the ways in which products are made has also radically changed as a result of globalization. Many countries in Western Europe and North America are no longer the leading places for the manufacture of products particularly in areas related to consumer goods.

The complex way in which products are now made means that there is a need for an understanding by those responsible for managing the production of materials of what globalization means in terms of supply chains. This theme has been noted by employers as can be seen from this quotation from a representative from a leading UK retail employer:

> In the past it was simple. You selected your suppliers from your area, and they used the materials that were to hand. This delivered your project in such a way that the project's impact on the environment was automatically as low as it could realistically be. This is no longer the case. Nowadays, the complexity of materials and components from an ever increasing global supply chain means that your management must have a thorough knowledge of the entire supply chain and exactly how it fits together, in order to make the right decision.
>
> *(Brown, quoted in Bourn, 2008: 22)*

Globalization and complex identities

This sense of fluidity and flexibility and the taking on of new and adaptable skills is one direct consequence of globalization. This has of course had a major impact on many aspects of the design industry where computer technology skills in many areas are more important than traditional craft based skills.

Globalization therefore should also be seen in terms of constant change, of opening up societies, economies, cultures and political systems to new, different and often very powerful external forces that can have a profound impact at both a local and national level.

In areas such as design, it is also important to understand globalization in terms of its impact on, and relationship to, cultures around the world.

Globalization has had a profound effect on people's individual lives, through cultural influences on their lifestyle, and how they perceive their relationship to communities and societies. As Nayak (2003) has suggested, global forces can be seen to have major impacts upon a person's sense of identity. Ray (2007) refers to a myriad of cultural influences that challenge one's own sense of identity and belonging within a community. France (2007) refers to globalization leading to increased individualisation of societies, dis-embedding of traditions and emergence of uncertainty and fluidity. Dolby and Rizvi (2008: ix) refer to globalization leading in some people's minds to a 'dislocation from traditional moorings'.

The influence of global forces can be seen in how individuals define themselves in terms of their sense of being and place. What we wear, the food we eat, the music we listen to and the jobs we have are all influenced by factors beyond national boundaries. It could be argued, many of the things that are part of our daily lives today, such as the use of the Internet, email, and mobile phones, would not have been possible without globalization.

Homogeneity and global brands

In a number of the discussions related to design and globalization (Adam, 2013), there is a common comment that global influences have led to homogeneity and 'bland product conformity' (McDermott, 2007: 120). Many cities now look the same, the food people eat and the clothes they buy and wear are often the same whether in Shanghai, New York, Rio or Dubai. Adam has commented on the consequences of this global brand culture:

> The global culture of design is supported by architects who study what other architects are creating, no matter where. With fabulous photographs in slick magazines and professional journals, trend-conscious designers can scan and span the globe, sharing high-style concepts rendered in stylish materials.
>
> *(Adam, 2013: 139)*

This sense of homogeneity is also seen as linked to the theme, in globalization discourse, of de-territorialisation (Kearney, 1995: 553). Hernandez (2006) goes further and suggests that de-territorialisation makes it difficult to sustain a distinctive local cultural identity due to our daily lives being evermore linked to influences elsewhere in the world.

Companies and retail outlets for example recognise the diverse markets they are appealing to by making reference to specific cultural preferences, whilst at the same time promoting a sense of the value of global uniformity (Adam, 2013: 150).

This is where the power and influence of the media and the advertising world plays a central role, with global brands being promoted as showing how we want to be and live. This pressure is based on an assumption that the Western image is the most popular, the one that everyone aspires to, resulting in marginalisation of indigenous images and localised cultural perspectives.

Identity, plurality and criticality

There is a danger of oversimplifying the impact of globalization on design and cultures. People and communities are not just empty vessels ready to absorb the latest fashion message. They have their own sense of identity, and what tends to happen in many cultures is a complex relationship between the local and global. In many communities around the world, communities have resisted the global juggernaut and there has been a new flowering of the promotion of specific local identities. In some cases, this can result in negative reactions, through forms of xenophobia and the rise of populist and nationalist movements. Secondly, however, globalization has enabled voices, often from disenfranchised and oppressed communities, to put their viewpoints and outline their grievances on a global stage. The influence of social networking and instant access to communications have played a major role in this (Castells, 2009). Examples can be particularly seen in Latin America with the emergence and coming to power of voices that have challenged dominant Western assumptions on economic growth.

Another response to the challenge of globalization has been a form of hybridisation where identities and outlooks have incorporated a range of influences which are often ever-changing and fluid (Scholte, 2005). Baumann (2005) refers to cloakroom communities that come into being for a period of time for a specific purpose, then are gone again. What tends to happen is that when communities and cultures feel threatened by global forces, there is a desire to see as Baumann (2005) refers to metaphorically for people to be like hapless sailors, searching for small havens to anchor and find safety.

A more direct result of this hybrid approach within architecture has been the emergence of the movement around 'critical regionalism'. This approach can be seen in a range of environmental projects where, whilst recognising the global influences to design, buildings are adapted to take account of specific local and cultural factors. Examples include the Menara Meisiniaga Tower in Kuala Lumpur and the St. Mary Axe building in London, better known as the Gherkin (Adam, 2013: 223, 231).

These different responses to globalization need also to be seen in the context of the dominance of economic pressures as a result of marketization, which can all too easily lead to one size fitting all. This has been noted by Clifford (2009: 147) in relation to engineering where he notes that all too often engineers have ignored sustainability and designed equipment, processes and technologies without taking into account local factors such as culture, environment, gender and local production methods. An example is cooking stoves which are very important for many rural populations around the world. In response to the challenges of climate change, Western designers have come up with alternatives but have not taken into account specific local climatic conditions or costs. Where local communities are directly involved in both the design and development of alternative approaches, then there is more likelihood of success (Clifford, 2009: 147).

Different worldviews and postcolonialism

Within many areas of design, when reference is made to wider world influences, they are often promoted in terms of 'the other', outside of the dominant Western discourse. This often leads to the promotion of such designs in terms of 'the exotic'. An often-used example is that 'fashion' is seen as the result of global influences and 'costume' relates to the indigenous and usually non-Western style.

Katherine Ladd (2015) in her study on African artisans and design shows this most clearly by questioning the ways in which Western companies and aid agencies emphasise authenticity to the detriment of the economic needs of local communities or creative development. Traditional African craft products, she notes, have always been influenced by different cultures. The example she refers to in Burkino Faso in West Africa, funded by aid agencies, resulted in a marginalisation of the craft skills of the artisans. Moreover, she stated that the approach taken by Western agencies was to perceive craft skills as existing in 'timeless societies that needed to be revived and preserved' (Ladd 2015: 131).

This example highlights the importance of bringing into the debates on globalization and design, the influences of colonialism, empire and consequent power. Key figures promoting this critique have been Edward Said (1978) and his work on Orientalism, Homi Bhabha (1994) who brings in the recognition of hybridity, and Gayatri Spivak (2003) and her use of the term 'subaltern'. This theme, usually termed postcolonialism, is concerned with dealing with the effects of colonisations on cultures and societies. Central to the thinking of many proponents of postcolonialism is the recognition of different histories, moving beyond dominant Western notions of modernity. This approach to the notion of culture can help to move us beyond reducing culture to forms of exoticism, as a static form.

The debates from postcolonialism are important in considering globalization because of recognition of the influence of powerful forces in the world, the existence of divisions, and resultant notions of supremacy. Secondly, postcolonialism provides a way to make a distinction between difference and diversity, to move from a multicultural approach to one that recognises the fluid and ever changing natures of people's own identities and cultures.

Globalization, neo-liberalism and globalism

What cannot be denied is that globalization is here to stay. Whilst globalization is an important concept through which to analyse the dominant social and economic trends in the world today, there is a danger of equating it with one ideological perspective. Beck is very helpful in this regard because he makes a distinction between 'globalization' as an analytical tool and the ideological manifestation of 'globalism' which he sees as the ideology of the 'world market place' (Beck, 2000: 26). This is the ideology of neo-liberalism where every aspect of global change is reduced to an economic force. Harvey (2005) defines neo-liberalism as a theory of

> political economic practices that proposes that human well-being can best be advanced by liberating individual entrepreneurial freedoms and skills within an institutional framework characterised by strong private property rights, free market and free trade.
>
> *(Harvey, 2005: 3)*

There is a danger of reducing all of the debates around globalization to the neo-liberal economic discourse, important as this, and not recognising the complex ways in which societies and communities around the world have been influenced by these major changes in the world over the past three decades. What above all needs to be recognised is the complex, fluid and ever-changing nature of economies and communities. As Baumann states, we are living in 'fluid' times with 'porous borders' (Baumann, 2005).

Globalization may have accelerated flows of cultures across borders. It has also transformed knowledge into a commodity to which the most powerful in society usually lay unjustifiable claim (Dei, Hall and Rosenberg, 2000: 4). Whilst globalization may appear to be destroying many indigenous cultures, there is evidence from many countries in the Global South of a growing resistance to the dominance of Western thinking.

Framework for global perspectives

Central to this chapter so far has been the recognition of the complex nature of globalization; and that its influences need to be seen in more than just economic or cultural terms. Globalization, whilst providing many challenges to many communities around the world, can lead to an opening up of minds and opportunities. There have been a number of approaches around the world that aimed to develop a framework or pedagogical approach to how people and communities make sense of and engage with the challenges of globalization. One example in the UK, taken from higher education, refers to global perspectives as an approach that

- values methodologies, techniques and academic analyses from other cultures;
- challenges and discards prejudice;
- considers with sensitivity the effect of our actions on others locally and globally, both now and in the future;
- questions eurocentric, rich world, restricted perspectives and takes into account viewpoints and circumstances from all regions of the world;
- presents learners with the capacity to calculate the risks of decision making;

- acknowledges the global forces that affect us all, and promotes justice and equality;
- empowers learners to bring about change; and
- provides an international curriculum and seeks opportunities to develop students' international awareness and competence.

(Bourn and Shiel, 2009: 669)

Other examples use the term global citizenship as a way of encouraging critical thinking alongside the promotion of a sense of common humanity and universal outlook. Andreotti (2006) makes a distinction between a 'soft' approach, being about a cosmopolitan approach and a 'critical' approach, being a more advocacy and questioning approach. Research at Alberta University in Canada found that using terms like global citizenship were helpful in engaging academics and students in debates on global understanding, social justice and personal social responsibility (Shultz, 2010).

To make sense of the impact of globalization on design and to consider how best to respond to the challenges, a framework is suggested here building on earlier work by this author (Bourn, 2015). This framework should be seen as an approach that people engaged in sustainable design could consider within their practice and work.

The framework is based on four themes:

- Developing a global outlook: globalization and the imagination
- Understanding of power and inequality
- Cosmopolitanism and global social justice
- Commitment to dialogue, reflection and transformation

These themes bring together influences from discourses within global and development education in Europe and North America (see Kirkwood-Tucker, 2009; Peterson and Warwick, 2015; Maguth and Hilburn, 2015). These discourses have as their common theme the value and importance of learning about the wider world through a lens that recognises and understands the causes of inequality in the world and what, as individuals and communities, one can do to make a more just and sustainable world.

This approach has also begun to be considered within a number of professions, most notably health and engineering, with the growing realisation that these are global professions and that people working in these areas need not only a knowledge of global influences, but the skills to engage in a critical way and have a values base that recognises the importance of fairness, justice and equity (Neal and Bourn, 2008; Willott et al., 2012; Murdan et al., 2014).

Developing a global outlook: globalization and the imagination

The world of the twenty-first century is a global one. To engage in this global world, people need to have an understanding of how it works and what their potential contribution can be. Terms such as being 'world or globally-minded' can be a useful way of describing this outlook, which could include a sense of personal responsibility, an awareness of cultural pluralism, a sense of efficacy and a sense of interconnectedness (Merryfield, 2009). Marquardt suggests that if people have a global mindset they will

seek to continually expand their knowledge, have a highly developed conceptual capacity to deal with the complexity of global organisations, are extremely flexible, strive to be sensitive to cultural diversity, are able to undertake decisions with adequate information and have a strong capacity for reflection. A person with a global mindset thinks and sees the world globally, is open to exchanging ideas and concepts across borders.

(Marquardt quoted in Jameson, 2006: 6)

This global outlook or mindset has been posed by Appadurai (2005) as a potentially positive force that can encourage an emancipatory form of engaging in the world, a new imagination. He sees the imagination as acting as a social force in globalised interactions, allowing people to draw on different media and other cultural resources to construct new identities and to challenge boundaries.

This form of imagination or 'social imaginery' is carried in images, characteristics, metaphors, stories and in the context of globalised societies of the twenty-first century, the mass media. But imaginations are however are not constant, they are ever changing. Globalization could therefore be argued to have resulted in a new form of social imagination or global outlook related to life-style, taste and personal identity. This has had consequences in how individuals and communities respond to challenges to their own sense of freedom and personal space. The globalised world of the twenty-first century is one of change – ideas and economies are in a state of flux and constant motion. This means that there is not one 'global outlook or global imagination' but competing ones, interpreting and responding to daily challenges.

For example, there may be a dominant neo-liberal imaginery of globalization or 'globalism' as Beck (2000) refers to it. But there are also counter narratives and imagineries that challenge this, whether they be anti-capitalist movements, indigenous communities or extreme fundamentalist notions related often to a distorted perspective of a specific religion.

It can also perhaps be argued that within the neo-liberal imaginery of globalization, there are potentially spaces, opportunities and openings to begin to articulate different imagineries that pose the social and cultural value of interconnectivity, of collective action and common goals of humanity and social justice; and through education, a more informed and potentially more democratically based society.

The implications of this global outlook or global imaginery approach for design could be seen in the following areas:

- Access to information, resources and images from across the world, through the Internet, can play a role in encouraging counter stories, production of artefacts and materials that challenge dominant perceptions.
- 'Oppositional imaginations' can be based on real-life daily experiences and understanding of inequality.
- This global outlook and imaginery has also meant that for many economies around the world, the consumer has become more powerful in terms of determining which products are purchased. The emergence of the fair trade movement is one of the most obvious examples of this.

Understanding of power and inequality

The second theme of this global perspectives framework is understanding the influence of global forces, power and inequalities in the world and their relationship to design. Globalization, as suggested, has a differential impact upon societies and cultures around the world. What is evident is that the disparities between the rich and the poor have grown on a global scale. The inequalities that exist in the world may well be a direct result of global forces, but the ways in which they are maintained are ever changing and much more complex than say fifty years ago.

The contradictions in how globalization can be seen could be summarised in the following from Stiglitz:

> Globalization can be a force for good: the Globalization of ideas about democracy and of civil society have changed the way people think, while global political movements have led to debt relief and the treaty on land mines. Globalization has helped hundreds of millions of people attain higher standards of living. . . . But for millions of people Globalization has not worked. Many have actually been made worse off, as they have seen their jobs destroyed and their lives become more insecure.
>
> *(Stiglitz 2002: 248)*

Whilst globalization may have benefitted the industrialised West and been the driver for economic growth in East Asia, for many countries in sub-Saharan Africa for example, the impact has often been to the detriment of local and indigenous cultures, forms of trade and production of goods. This can be seen, for example in the decline of locally designed and produced clothes. For example, on the streets of Cape Town or Lagos you are more likely to see young boys wearing soccer-themed shirts produced in China, than locally sourced or locally designed clothes.

The consequence of globalization for areas such as design, as in many other aspects of life, is the domination of powerful forces that promote particular styles and approaches. Power, as Foucault suggests, is dispersed. It is not a thing but a relationship. It is therefore more than just, say, the state and is exercised throughout society (see McNay, 1994). This means recognising and understanding the ways in which this power is dispersed and used, and the role that ideas and the media play in ensuring the domination of particular ideologies and viewpoints. Discussions on power also lead to themes such as inequalities in the world, and the causes of these divisions. This involves recognition of how historical, social, cultural and economic forces have shaped and informed these power relations. This is where the discourses around postcolonialism are particularly relevant.

These themes can be taken forward within design in terms of:

- promoting the implications of power relations through appropriate visual images;
- recognising and valuing a range of cultural styles and approaches, particularly indigenous community approaches;
- consideration of the impact of financial factors and costs and who has funding and who has not.

Cosmopolitanism and global social justice

Debates on globalization inevitably lead to discussions of whether the world appears to be getting smaller, and what is common to all human beings around the world. Some voices in this debate lead to discussion of global citizenship, whilst others refer more to talking about a common humanity or a common belief in social justice.

The term 'cosmopolitanism' has often been used to summarise these debates. Whilst there are many interpretations of the term, there is a common assumption of a link to a sense of a common humanity, and a recognition that all human beings should be treated equally, which goes beyond the national state (Wallace Brown and Held, 2010: 1). From this, cosmopolitan thinking is often associated with the protection of human rights and a sense of global justice.

Martha Nussbaum (2002), a leading figure within the discourses on human development, sees cosmopolitanism as including an ethics of compassion, of shared values and respect for reason and moral choice.

However, there are dangers in one single view of values, respect and compassion being portrayed, as Harvey (2009) suggests, hiding class and cultural divisions. Sharon Todd (2009) suggests that a way through this is to recognise plurality of thought and critical thinking in helping to make sense of a global outlook.

Perhaps a more useful term than cosmopolitanism is 'global social justice', as it poses a sense of change, movement and aspiration rather than a static view of the world. Brock (2009: 119) suggests that global justice should be perceived as relating to every person having the right to be adequately positioned to enjoy the prospects for a decent life, including enjoying basic freedoms and opportunities for social and political action. But as Odora Hoppers (2008: 608) suggests, who determines what is fair and what are our basic needs? She suggests that concepts of justice need to incorporate a cultural dimension, not only listening to and recognising the views of others, but directly engaging in forms of interaction that invoke the cultural worlds of the players.

This means recognising that any design, particularly of say a building, in itself will pose wider questions related to the extent to which the concerns of the people are reflected, understood and incorporated. All too often, global forces can result in the loss or diminution in influence of local and indigenous voices and cultures. Within the context of understanding global forces and the challenges for sustainable design, an important consideration therefore is the recognition of the importance of indigenous knowledge, and that knowledge and ideas are constructed according to specific social and cultural traditions.

These themes therefore mean that in consideration of the construction of buildings, the promotion of artefacts and design approaches in general need to

- Recognise that a range of voices and perspectives need to be understood and where appropriate, ensure local and indigenous cultures are incorporated.
- Consider the potential value that a belief and commitment to social justice can play as an important motivational role in helping to clarify and identify the purpose of what is being designed.

Commitment to dialogue, reflection and transformation

The themes suggested in this global perspective framework pose major questions about how people learn, understand and engage with the influence of global forces on their lives. What this framework is suggesting is that this can pose challenging questions to the individual, to their own worldview, how they construct their own ideas and make sense of the world around them.

It is suggested here that individuals in engaging with global themes need to recognise and understand different types and forms of information, to weigh up the evidence, and thus to be critically reflective before engaging in any form of action (Brookfield, 2012: 13). Implicit in this approach is the recognition that engaging in dialogue and understanding global forces and processes means taking an approach that moves from a fixed view of the knowledge and skills needed to one that recognises complexity, difference and uncertainty. It also means moving from absorption of information and acceptance of existing models of learning to challenging, questioning and moving positions and views. Finally, it means moving from structured and universal views of the world to complex, multifaceted and different means of interpretation (Neal and Bourn, 2008).

Andreotti suggests that a role for educationalists is to 'reclaim their role as cultural brokers' by increasing 'their awareness and capacity to analyse and see the world from different perspectives, learning to listen and to negotiate in diverse and complex environments.' Andreotti suggests that the role of the educator should be to keep 'possibilities open and equip learners to engage critically with each possibility, to listen and to negotiate ethically with others, and to analyse and take responsibility for the implications of their choices' (Andreotti, 2010: 9–10).

Global forces tend to encourage a culture of instant decision making and constant change. A consequence of this culture is that critical thinking and time to reflect, question and consider options and different viewpoints gets lost. Therefore, time and space for dialogue and reflection needs to be an essential component of global perspectives within sustainable design.

A very effective way of encouraging critical reflection and dialogue is through the use of visual images as a way of encouraging questioning of perceptions of poverty and inequality in the world. This is where sustainable design can make an important contribution, by posing images and ideas that reflect a range of world viewpoints.

Many education systems around the world, for example, may use artefacts as a way of demonstrating forms of design. But all too often the social context of how these artefacts were used is not addressed. Also there are dangers of 'essentialism', of seeing materials and designs in some form of 'traditional' state and not addressing the fact that designs all over the world are ever subject to external influences and forces.

Taking forward these themes, there needs to be

- recognition of the plurality of ideas and to understand the basis of these differing viewpoints;
- engagement in a process of personal reflection and dialogue with others to clarify one's own views and understand the views of others;
- understanding of the potential power and influence of visual imaginery in how ideas are constructed and designs are developed;
- ensuring that artefacts and other design products are all influenced by differing social, cultural and economic factors that need to be understood.

Globalization and sustainable development

Globalization enables many of the world's environmental problems and issues to be seen as ever present in people's everyday lives. But where there has been debate about the relationship between globalization and sustainable development, this has tended to be seen in economic terms, in terms of how economic growth can help and support sustainable development (Waller-Hunter and Jones, 2002), or in negative terms with an ever-widening divide between the two concepts (Sachs, 1999). There has also been a tendency for the concept of sustainable development to be seen as primarily about the environment, with the focus in its implementation on policies and practices around the world in terms of the natural environment, and less concerned with human development. Even when Stibbe (2009), for example, refers to the concept of sustainability as including social justice, well-being and social transformation, it is framed within an environmental outlook. One person in the UK who has thought in a broader context is Stephen Sterling, who relates sustainable development to systems thinking. He states that we need to move from 'things to processes, from static states to dynamic, and from parts to wholes' (Sterling, 2004). He sees sustainable development as being potentially transformative, constructive and participatory.

Ito and Nakayama (2014), in reviewing sustainable development practice in schools in Japan, note that any form of engagement and learning in this area must aim to have an element of transformation, of encouraging understanding about different ideas and thinking which will stimulate reflection and a rethinking of the individual's own values base and behaviour. Sustainable development approaches in many areas, including design, have tended to focus more on 'reducing negative impacts on the environment' rather than looking at sustainability in a more holistic sense.

Where sustainable development is seen in an interdisciplinary way, as an approach to learning and change in society, then there is potential linkage with the global perspectives approach outlined here. As Scott and Gough have suggested, sustainable development should be seen not as some form of end state but as a way of describing an 'adaptive approach to managing human-environment co-evolution' (2004: 253).

In terms of the themes posed in this chapter, it could be argued that there is potential synergy between some of the conceptual bases for sustainable development and global perspectives, if the approaches say of Sterling and Scott and Gough, mentioned earlier, are taken into consideration.

Chris Shiel in her work on global perspectives at Bournemouth University in the UK has referred to global perspectives as incorporating within higher education four themes: global issues, global process, internationalisation and sustainable development (Shiel and Mann, 2006). Shiel also takes these themes forward by posing an approach for global perspectives that includes a recognition of the interconnected lives people lead, the importance of critical reflection and challenging assumptions, with the skills and understanding to wish to make a difference in the world (Shiel, Williams and Mann, 2005).

Taking the agenda forward

The launch of the United Nations Sustainable Development Goals in 2015 has undoubtedly given a new impetus to the themes addressed in this chapter. For example, it provides openings and opportunities to bring to the fore themes addressed in this chapter concerning the relationship between lifestyle and culture, global citizenship and human rights:

> By 2030, ensure that all learners acquire the knowledge and skills needed to promote sustainable development, including, among others, through education for sustainable development and sustainable lifestyles, human rights, gender equality, promotion of a culture of peace and non-violence, global citizenship and appreciation of cultural diversity and of culture's contribution to sustainable development.
>
> *(UN, 2015)*

These themes build on past initiatives that aimed to bring global and sustainability themes closer together, such as the Earth Charter, an international initiative that has had support from many civil society organisations and some governments around the world (Newman, 2009).

This chapter has outlined the importance of global forces, globalization and the development of a global outlook in considering future training and education in sustainable design. What is needed is for a greater recognition that addresses global and sustainability themes together within an area such as design, poses wider questions that go beyond technological development or being conscious of one's ecological footprint. As the chapter has aimed to demonstrate, having a global perspectives approach raises issues about power and inequality, about what a global outlook means, having a strong values base built on social justice and a sense of common humanity but at the same being open to new ideas, to be critically reflective and be prepared to engaged in dialogues that may question your own assumptions and worldviews.

Globalization has opened up many societies and communities to a wealth of influences, including economic, social, cultural and political forces. Sustainable development is recognised by policymakers around the world as a necessary focus for human development. But all too often the two areas are not looked at together. As a result, globalization discussion tends to go down a route of economic growth and technological development, whilst sustainability programmes tend to emphasise the environmental protection side. Only by bringing the two themes more closely together and framing them within a pedagogical approach such as that of 'global perspectives', can an area such as sustainable design effectively engage with the impact of global forces.

References

Adam, R. (2013) *The Globalisation of Modern Architecture*, Newcastle-upon-Tyne, Cambridge Scholars.

Andreotti, V. (2006) Soft versus critical global citizenship education, *Policy and Practice*, 3.1: 40–51.

Andreotti, V. (2010) Global education in the 21st century: Two different perspectives on the post of post-modernism, *International Journal of Development Education and Global Learning*, 2.2: 5–22.

Andreotti, V. (2012) *Actionable Postcolonial Theory in Education*, New York, Palgrave.

Appadurai, A. (ed.) (2005) *Globalization*, Durham, NC, Duke University Press.

Bandyopadhyay, S. and Montiel, G.G. (eds.) (2013) *The Territories of Identity – Architecture in the Age of Evolving Globalisation*, Abingdon, Routledge.

Baumann, Z. (2005) *Liquid Life*, Cambridge, Polity Press.

Baylis, J. and Smith, S. (eds.) (1999) *The Globalization of World Politics – An Introduction to International Relations*, Oxford, OUP.

Beck, U. (2000) *What Is Globalisation?* Cambridge, Polity Press.

Bhabha, H. (1994) *The Location of Culture*, London, Routledge.

Bourn, D. (2008) *Global Skills*, Coventry, Learning and Skills Improvement Service.

Bourn, D. (2015) *The Theory and Practice of Development Education*, Abingdon, Routledge.

Bourn, D. and Shiel, C. (2009) Global perspectives – Aligning agendas, *Environmental Education Research*, 15.6: 661–667.

Brock, G. (2009) *Global Justice*, Oxford, Oxford University Press.

Brookfield, S. (2012) *Teaching for Critical Thinking*, San Francisco, Josey-Bass.

Castells, M. (2009) *Communication Power*, Oxford, Oxford University Press.

Castells, M. (1996) *The Rise of the Network Society*, Blackwell, Oxford.

Clifford, M. (2009) Appropriate Technology and Appropriate Design, in Stibbe, A. (ed.) *The Handbook of Sustainable Literacy*, Totnes, Green Books, 144–149.

Dei, G.J., Hall, B.L. and Rosenberg, D.G. (ed.) (2000) *Indigenous Knowledges in Global Contexts*, Toronto, University of Toronto Press.

Dolby, N. and Rizvi, F. (Eds.) (2008) *Youth Moves – Identities and Education in Global Perspectives*, New York, Routledge.

France, A. (2007). *Understanding Youth in Late Modernity*, Berkshire, Open University Press.

Giddens, A. (1991) *Modernity and Self-Identity: Self and Society in the Late Modern Age*, Cambridge, Polity Press.

Harvey, D. (1989) *The Condition of Postmodernity*, Oxford, Blackwell.

Harvey, D. (2005) *A Brief History of Neoliberalism*, Oxford, Oxford University Press.

Harvey, D. (2009) *Cosmopolitanism and the Geographies of Freedom*, New York, Columbia University Press.

Held, D. and McGrew, A. (eds.) (2000) *The Global Transformation Reader*, Cambridge, Polity Press.

Hernandez i Marti, G. (2006) The Deterriorialisation of Cultural Heritage in a Globalised Modernity, *Journal of Contemporary Culture*, vol. 11, Insttitut Ramon Lull, Barcelona, 92–107.

Ito, Y. and Nakayama, S. (2014) Education for sustainable development to nurture sensibility and creativity, *International Journal of Development Education and Global Learning*, 6.2: 5–21.

Jameson, J. (ed.) (2006) *Leadership Practices in Lifelong Learning in a Global Society*, London, DEA/Centre for Leadership.

Kearney, M. (1995) The local and the global, the anthropology of globalization and transnationalism, *Annual Review of Anthropology*, 24: 553.

Kenway, J. and Fahey, J. (eds.) (2008) *Globalizing the Research Imagination*, London, Routledge.

Kirkwood-Tucker, T. (ed.) (2009) *Visions in Global Education*, New York, Peter Lang.

Ladd, K. (2015) *Hand Made With Love*, London, Artifact.

Lewin, R. (ed.) (2009) *The Handbook of Practice and Research in Study Abroad: Higher Education and the Quest for Global Citizenship*, New York, Routledge.

Maguth, B. and Hilburn, J. (ed.) (2015) *The State of Global Education-Learning With the World and Its People*, New York, Routledge.

McDermott, C. (2007) *Design: The Key Concepts*, Abingdon, Routledge.

McNay, L. (1994) *Foucault: A Critical Introduction*, Cambridge, Polity Press.

Merryfield, M. (2009) Moving the Centre of Global Education: From Imperial Worldviews that Divide the World to Double-Consciousness, Contrapuntal Pedagogy, Hybridity and Cross-Cultural Competence, in Kirkwood-Tucker, T. (ed.) *Visions in Global Education*, New York, Peter Lang, 215–239.

Morgan, J. (2001) *Development, Globalisation and Sustainability*, Bath, Nelson Thornes Ltd.

Murdan, S., Blum, N., Francis, S.A., Slater, E., Alem, N., Munday, M., Taylor, J. and Smith, F. (2014) *The Global Pharmacist*, London, UCL School of Pharmacy and Institute of Education.

Nayak, A. (2003) *Race, Place and Globalisation*, Oxford, Berg.

Neal, I. and Bourn, D. (2008) *The Global Engineer*, London, Engineers Against Poverty.

Newman, J. (2009) Values, Reflection and the Earth Charter, in Stibbe, A. (ed.) *The Handbook of Sustainable Literacy*, Totnes, Green Books, 99–104.

Nussbaum, M. (2002) Capabilities and social justice, *International Studies Review*, 4–2: 123–135.

Odora Hoppers, C. (2008) *South African Research Chair in Development Education – Framework and Strategy*, Pretoria, University of South Africa.

Peterson, A. and Warwick, P. (2015) *Global Learning and Education*, Abingdon, Routledge.

Ray, L. (2007) *Globalisation and Everyday Life*, Abingdon, Routledge.

Sachs, W. (1999) *Planet Dialectics: Explorations in Environment and Development*, London, Zed Books.

Said, E. (1978) *Orientalism*, London, Routledge.

Scholte, J. (2005) *Globalization: A Critical Introduction*, Basingstoke, Palgrave.

Scott, W. and Gough, S. (eds.) (2004) *Key Issues in Sustainable Development and Learning*, London, Routledge/Falmer.

Shiel, C. (2007) Developing and Embedding Global Perspectives Across the University, in Marshal, S. (ed.) *Strategic Leadership of Change in Higher Education*, London and New York, Routledge, 158–173.

Shiel, C. and Mann, S. (2006) 'Becoming a Global Citizen,' in *Bournemouth University Global Local Education (BUGLE)*, internal news publication.

Shiel, C., Williams, A. and Mann, S. (2005) 'Global Perspectives and Sustainable Development in the Curriculum: Enhanced Employability, More Thoughtful Society?' in *Enhancing Graduate Employability: The Roles of Learning, Teaching, Research and Knowledge Transfer, Proceedings of the Bournemouth University Learning and Teaching Conference*.

Shultz, L. (2010) What do we ask of global citizenship education? A study of global citizenship education in a Canadian University, *International Journal of Development Education and Global Learning*, 3.1: 5–22.

Spivak, G. (2003) *Death of a Discipline*, New York, Columbia University Press.

Sterling, S. (2004) Higher Education, Sustainability and the Role of Systematic learning, in Corcoran, P.B. and Wals, A.E.J. (eds.) *Higher Education and the Challenge of Sustainability*, Netherlands, Springer, 49–70.

Stibbe, A. (ed.) (2009) *The Handbook of Sustainable Literacy*, Totnes, Green Books.

Stiglitz, J. (2002) *Globalizations and Its Discontents*, London, Penguin,

Stromquist, N.P. and Monkman, K. (eds.) (2000) *Globalization and Education*, Oxford, Rowman and Littlefield.

Todd, S. (2009) *Towards an Imperfect Education: Facing Humanity, Rethinking Cosmopolitanism*, London, Paradigm.

Tyrrell, R. (2008) Sustainable Design: A Counterpoint to Globalization, in Al-Qawasmi, J., Mahmoud, A. and Djerbi, A (eds.) *Regional Identity in the Age of Globalization*, vol. 1, Dharan, CSAAR Press.

United Nations. (2015) *UN Sustainable Development Goals: Goal 4*, available at: https://sustainabledevelopment.un.org/sdg4 (last accessed 21 April, 2016).

Wallace Brown, G. and Held, D. (ed.) (2010) *The Cosmopolitan Reader*, Cambridge, Polity Press.

Waller-Hunter, J. and Jones, T. (2002) Globalisation and sustainable development, *International Review for Environmental Strategies*, 3.1: 53–62.

Willott, C., Blum, N., Burch, W., Page, B. and Rowson, M. (2012) *The Global Doctor*, London UCL and Institute of Education.

Wiseman, J. (1998) *The Global Nation: Australia's Response to Globalisation*, Melbourne, Cambridge University Press.

9

POLITICS AND SUSTAINABILITY

Harold Wilhite

Introduction

The sustainable design of cities, buildings and products engages designers with a number of environmental challenges. The monster of all challenges is climate change, the main source of which is carbon emissions emitted from fossil fuel-based energy production and consumption. Design has an obvious and important role to play in creating designs intended for low energy, both in the production of materials needed to realize the products designed, and in the case of buildings, in the achievement of building-related energy services such as thermal comfort, light and hot water. In this chapter I will argue that a transition to sustainable design is hindered by many of the same obstacles faced by energy planners, manufacturers, householders and other actors in today's growth-oriented political economies: how to reduce energy and material consumption in socioeconomic systems that are dependent on economic growth for their sustenance. Given this context, in the rich and emerging economies around the world, reduction in energy extraction, production and consumption is to be accomplished by greater energy and environmental efficiency; however, as I will argue, efficiency is not sufficient to achieve deep reductions in growth economies where the energy saved in one activity is used to foster growth in another (the so-called rebound effect; see Winther and Wilhite 2015). The narrow focus on efficiency leads to weak political incentives for carbon dioxide (CO_2) reduction and other forms for 'weak sustainability', paraded out under headings such as ecological modernization, green economy and green energy (McNeill and Wilhite 2015). I will discuss and critique mainstream 'green' policy approaches to reducing the energy impacts of everyday life and the related emphasis on 'smart' designs for cities, buildings and technologies as the panacea for meeting the low energy and low carbon challenge. I will argue that in order to be truly sustainable, 'smart' designs should aim for a reduction – not just greater efficiency – in the energy needed to provide energy services (such as light, heat and hot water) for the households living in them.

The chapter is organized as follows. In the next section I briefly summarize the now incontrovertible evidence for the need for rapid reductions in energy use and carbon emissions. In the subsequent section I discuss and critique 'green' policy approaches to reducing the energy impacts of everyday life, with their emphasis on 'smart' designs. Finally, I examine how 'smart' can be reinvented in ways that are compatible with user know-how and the need for reduced energy use.

The urgency of a transformation to low carbon societies

In a recently published book on the political economy of low carbon transformation (Wilhite 2016), I review the evidence for the relationship between human activity and climate change, arguing that from mid-twentieth-century global energy use and climate emissions have grown in step with growing national economies in the rich countries of the world. Though methane, hydrofluorocarbons and other pollutants contribute to climate perturbation, the major contribution to climate change is related to the emissions of CO_2 from the conversion of fossil fuels to useful energy. The most recent projections from a number of different sources are converging on a likely global temperature rise of at least 3 degrees Celsius (37 degrees Fahrenheit) or more within the next 50 years and proposing that this will have major impacts on microclimates; on Arctic and Antarctic ice with consequent effects on sea levels and ocean chemistry; severe disturbance of forest ecosystems and species death, with half of global species dying out by 2050 (Lynas 2007); as well as potential devastating effects on food production and food harvesting, both on land and in oceans. In a 2015 article published in *Nature*, Trusel et al. (2015) found that should the global temperature increase to around 3 degrees Celsius above the preindustrial era, the ice shelves that hold back the continental ice sheets would dissolve over the next few centuries. This would trigger an ecological collapse that would go on for thousands of years, raising sea levels by as much as 3 meters by the year 2300. The authors' predict that our descendants living in the year 5000 will continue to suffer the consequences of today's fossil fuel burning, as sea levels continue to rise up to 9 meters above current levels. These findings graphically illustrate the accuracy of the conclusions of the 2014 Intergovernmental Panel on Climate Change (IPCC) report: 'failure to rapidly reduce climate-gas emissions will result in severe, pervasive and irreversible impacts for people and ecosystems'.

The recognition of anthropogenically driven climate change and the necessity to do something about it is nothing new. The report of the World Commission on the Environment (WCED 1987) put climate change on the international political agenda four decades ago. The report indicated that in order to prevent severe climate change global carbon emissions would need to be reduced by 80 percent within a half century (the report assigned 60 percent reductions to the rich countries of the world and 20 percent to developing countries). Against this background, it is noteworthy that in the period from 1990 to 2010, global carbon emissions grew by 70 percent. In the United States there has been a slight decline in total emissions from an extremely high starting point compared to the rest of the world (three times the per capita French emission level, and ten times that of India); however, this decline does not account for the outsourcing of emissions to other parts of the world through global imports. Sixty percent of all goods consumed in the United States are now produced elsewhere (CSE 2015). Europe has also exported emission generation to other parts of the world. Seventy percent of European consumer goods are now produced outside Europe, mainly in Asia.

There are many reasons for the displacement of manufacturing and other goods production to Asia, including generally weaker regulations on both working conditions (cheap labor) and restricting environmental impacts. Another important factor is that global carbon emission schemes such as the Clean Development Mechanism (CDM) assign CO_2 emissions to the countries in which the emissions related to the production of goods are emitted rather than to the countries in which the goods are consumed. This is unfortunate from a global CO_2 emissions perspective because it reduces the motive, and obligation, of high-consuming countries to reduce their consumption. Every proposal to associate emissions with points of consumption rather than production has been squashed by the high-consuming countries because it would add to their CO_2 emission accounts and obligations to reduce emissions. There is also a practical problem in such an accounting system, because it would involve tracing products back to their countries of origin and to the fuels that contributed to production, difficult in the many cases in which a final product such as a car or washing machine is composed of parts manufactured in different countries using differing fuel sources in production.

Another issue is that middle classes are growing in Asia and Latin America and demanding many of the same kinds of energy-using buildings, appliances and products used in the rich countries of the world, adding to global energy use and carbon emissions. The European Environmental Agency (EEA 2015) predicts that global energy use and carbon emissions will only decline slightly in the next 25 years. Measured against what was known to be needed in 1992, the transition to a low carbon economy can thus far be declared a failure.

The heart of the dilemma is that economic growth demands energy and that capitalism thrives on cheaply available fossil fuels. Economic growth in North America and Europe has been sustained through three types of geographical expansionism: colonialism, international trade and transnational investment. Under colonialism, countries in Asia, Africa and Latin America were a source of virtually unlimited cheap (or even free) labor and raw materials for colonial enterprises. In the post–World War II era, transnational corporations based in the OECD countries have been given liberal operating conditions in most developing countries in return for a promise of jobs and technology transfer. More recently, credit-based production and consumption in the rich and 'emerging' economies (such as China, India and Brazil) has allowed economies to grow through mortgaging the future. According to Cross (2000), debt-based consumption did not come into being until the end of the nineteenth century, but it increased rapidly in the early twentieth century. By 1924, in the United States 70 percent of new cars were bought on credit, as was 70 percent of furniture, 75 percent of radios, 80 percent of phonographs and 80 percent of household appliances. From the 1950s, in the United States, household debt steadily increased, quadrupling between 1980 and 2010 (Klein 2014: 75). Total debt grew from about 1,5 times U.S. national output in the early 1980s to nearly 3,5 in 2007. The financial sector's share of U.S. profits increased from about 15 percent in the early 1950s to almost 50 percent in 2001 (Faulkner 2013: 291). From 1970 in the United States, average incomes have declined, but purchasing power has increased due to credit and debt-financed consumption. Huber (2013) argues that debt-consumption and other characteristics of the ways national economy is conducted have been absorbed into the ways that middle-class households conduct their household economics. The combination of postwar neoliberalism and the rapid growth in single-family housing have contributed to the transformation of home life into what Huber refers to as minicapitalist, private sphere in which accumulation of money and goods is made possible through debt financing.

Over the 40 years from the birth of the concept and politics of energy conservation, economic and technical efficiency in the rich countries of the world has increased, but the energy saved has been used to fuel economic growth. The result is a relatively flat energy use over the past four decades, when from a climate perspective, deep reductions are needed. This is not simply an economic issue, because the ideology and practices of growth have fostered high energy habits in every sector of society, associating better lives with more and bigger homes, cars and other commodities. If the global economy recovers from its current recession and returns to growth rates of 4–5 percent per year, it will be 80 times bigger in 2100 than it was in 1950 (Jackson 2009). It is impossible to imagine that the global ecosystem can continue to thrive, or even to survive the massive demands on resources or the wastes generated by an economy of that size. In the 2013 'State of the World' report by the World Watch Institute, entitled 'Is Sustainability Still Possible?' (WWI 2013), an impressive set of authors state decisively that a significant reduction in the environmental impacts of economic activity will not be possible within the economic growth paradigm. In order to achieve the societal transformation necessary to reduce the size of economies and the amounts of energy and materials used to support everyday practices, design will need to play an important role. I will return to this design challenge later in the chapter, but first flesh out the mainstream 'green' frameworks that take growth for granted.

Green economy and ecological modernization

Energy use is the product of intensity (the inverse of efficiency) and volume (or amount). The proposition that efficiency alone can reduce energy in a growth economy is, in the words of Wilhite and Norgard (2004) a 'delusion' in energy policy, or as formulated by Bluhdorn (2007: 80), an exercise in 'energy metaphysics'. Still, this delusion persists in mainstream efforts to achieve sustainable energy use. Many of these can be fit under the headings 'green economy' or 'ecological modernization' (Spaargaren and Mol 1992; Huber 2007). Ecological modernization is a 'readaptation of industrial society within the global geo- and biosphere by *modern means* such as a scientific knowledge base and advanced technology in order to upgrade the earth's carrying capacity and make development more sustainable' (Huber 2007: 360). Ecological modernization has formed the basis for both international and national policies for reducing carbon and energy and has been integrated into national 'green energy' programs and many 'green city' programs. These efforts have emphasized sustainable resource management, clean and energy efficient technologies, product design that includes environmental concerns, extended producer responsibility (or its cognate corporate social responsibility), recycling, low-emission production processes, and add-on purification technologies in emission control and waste processing. In ecological modernization, the environment is conceptualized as a source of 'services', such as fishing, mineral extraction, clean water, sewage treatment, forestation, protection of genetic materials of animals, insects and plants, that support human societies and which need to be better managed (Daly 1992; Salleh 2010).

The problem from a climate change perspective is that carbon and other climate-gas emissions emanate from energy use associated with virtually every form of economic and social activity. Growth in the economy fosters a demand for growth in energy and environmental services. With a few exceptions, ecological modernization theorists do not pose economic growth as a problem, but rather as a part of the solution to reducing environmental consequences of human activity (see Gibbs 2006 and Baker 2007). A few of its proponents advocate that growth is not merely compatible with the environment but actually capable of enhancing it, the argument being that growth will provide the capital to address environmental problems (Hajer 1995). Robertson (2004) and others have shown how ecological modernisation has been seamlessly incorporated into global development institutions, national governments and corporate rhetoric on sustainability without significantly changing their practices. Barry (2007: 450) writes this about Great Britain's interpretation of green economy:

> The notion that orthodox economic growth, employment and investment patterns and the cross-sectoral goals of sustainable development might be in serious tension is excluded from the government's rhetoric on the environment and the 'greening of the economy'; it is certainly not presented as a possibly problematic issue for industrial production processes or for global capitalism or the new orthodoxy of export-led growth. Instead, environmental protection and economic growth are portrayed as a positive-sum game, a 'business opportunity'. . . . The (UK) strategy document studiously avoids what many would see as the real issue with consumption – *i.e.*, how to reduce it rather than simply focus on making it 'greener' or lessen its environmental impact.

Bluhdorn and Welsh characterize the efforts in Europe to incorporate ecological modernization into national political economies as toothless, writing that they have 'rehabilitated the ecologist enemies and made technological innovation, economic growth, capital accumulation and consumerism in principle acceptable – if only they were of the correct, i.e. of the "green" variety' (2007: 194). Essentially, the advocates of green economy would have it both ways: promote increased energy efficiency as a source of income for increased production, innovation and competitiveness on the one hand, and as a means to reduce energy use and carbon emissions on the other. This is a formula that is doomed to fail from a low carbon perspective. Energy efficiency is a means, not an end. It is important that it continues to be a goal for low energy and low carbon policy, but will only contribute to deep reductions if it is framed in a broader set of policy goals that aim at reducing both the size of the economy and the amounts of energy used to fuel everyday practices.

Low carbon design within the logics of capitalism

One of the main thrusts within sustainable design has been framed by European eco-design initiatives. The European Union's Eco-design Directive of 2009 established a framework for mandatory ecological requirements for energy-using and energy-related products, including many of the technologies commonly used in homes, such as cold appliances, windows and insulation materials. This has led to a number of new design initiatives that take a product life-cycle perspective. The aim is to create designs that will reduce the environmental impacts of buildings and technologies in each phase of their product lifetime from resource extraction, through the supply chain and after products are taken into use. EU regulations encourage the selection of materials that have low environmental impacts, reduce the weight or volume of materials used in the product, use cleaner manufacturing processes, reduce packaging, reduce the environmental impacts from consuming and maintaining the product, increase the product life and encourage reuse, remanufacture, recycling and environmentally friendly disposal (Roy 2000: 290).

In a 2015 article, Pettersen argues that these initiatives are important, but that their environmental potential is limited by the logics of capitalism. According to Pettersen, at the level of the firm, eco-design remains a profit-driven strategy in which efforts are typically geared at catering to consumer 'need' and aiming to deliver designs that satisfy needs by lowering impacts in the supply chain and throughout the product life cycle. The needs themselves are not challenged by design firms for fear of losing customers and losing business (Kimball 2011). Luttropp and Lagerstedt (2006: 1396) write that 'increasing welfare and ambitions for growth have changed the scope of product design. . . . In a long-term business perspective the creation of market demands is more profound than the design and production of the product.' Neither the eco-design framework nor other political incentives for eco-design firms encourage business strategies built on designing, producing or marketing low-tech or low-energy designs that are durable and attractive (referred to as 'sufficiency' designs in the industrial ecology literature; see Tukker et al. 2010 and Hargreaves et al. 2013), for example, buildings heated entirely by solar energy or cooled without the need for air conditioning. Roy encapsulates the conservative nature of the eco-design framework: 'Eco-design is essentially an attempt to enable existing patterns of production and consumption to continue into the future, at least in the industrialized North, without destroying the environment. However, eco-design alone is unlikely to be enough to deal with the pressures on the environment posed by global economic development and population growth, especially in the developing South' (2000: 292).

Another important point made by Pettersen (2015) is that designers who have a mainly technical education and training 'are not equipped to understand human activity'. Designers need to be made cognizant of household habits and practices if they are to produce designs for buildings and the systems within them that are in line with householder's know how and which they are capable of mastering. Designer–user interaction could facilitate designs that make sense for the people who will use them. An example of this is an ongoing project in Brussels, where a block of houses is being renovated for low-energy use with the contribution of project managers, design specialists, and the inhabitants (Wallenborn and Wilhite 2014). In this project, inhabitants work together with architects and entrepreneurs in designing for low energy while at the same time the occupants develop know-how on the workings of building systems and their energy technologies. Perhaps most importantly, participants feel a sense of pride and ownership in the completed project. Other examples of participatory experiments involve cohousing and collaborative consumption, such as car sharing and home sharing (Wilhite 2016).

Seyfang and Haxeltine (2012) refer to this participatory approach as a form for 'niche management' that fosters bottom-up governance (Shove and Walker 2010), avoiding the knowledge gaps and alienation many people experience when faced with living with 'smart' technologies. Geels (2011) argues that radical design innovations can only emerge in these grassroot niches, where many experiments are taking place with new patterns of ownership such as leasing and sharing in which producers retain ownership for products throughout their life cycle, which could provide incentives for producers to demand designs for long-lasting products in order to postpone maintenance and disposal costs for the manufacturing of new products, thus decoupling economic value from material and energy consumption. This is consistent with the message of transition theorists such as Ceschin (2013) who argue that innovations at a process or product level are not sufficient to achieve a radical shift in sustainable design for services such as mobility, thermal comfort, and cleanliness that minimize materiality and waste. Radical design innovations must aim at multilevel changes in the 'sociotechnical regime' (meso level), the niche (micro level) and the landscape, meaning the social, political and economic contexts in which actors interact and regimes evolve.

Smart city and building design

One of the main points in my recent book is that the logics of capitalism shape not only national economic policies of all sorts, including green policies, but also extend their reach into the politics and practices of cities, neighborhoods and households. One of the new thrusts in green energy policy is 'smart' design of both cities and buildings. 'Smart' is shorthand for technological systems and controls that optimize energy use and generally minimize the householder's interface with their houses in the production of comfort, light and other energy services. The control of energy systems is delegated to thermostatic controls and sensor-driven components. Design of buildings and their components are standardized and modulated in accordance with an economic system that is interested in making business and profit out of high-tech development. As Koolhaas (2015) writes, 'Architecture has entered into a new engagement with digital culture and capital – which amounts to the most radical change within the discipline since the confluence of modernism and industrial production in the early twentieth century'. This new engagement 'threatens to flatten the architect's range'. It also flattens the involvement of the building occupant in the creation of home energy services such as comfortable indoor temperatures and light. There is now a substantial body of evidence that 'smart' systems do not conform to the ways people prefer to regulate comfort because they are overly complex and lead to 'suboptimal' (from a technology perspective) behaviors by the occupants, such as opening and closing windows to regulate indoor temperatures or overriding automatic thermostat systems (Pickerill and Maxey 2009). Wade (2015) reviews studies around Europe that reveal that in a number of different national settings, smart technologies are not being used as intended and in some cases residents are not even aware that their buildings have smart controls (for example Rathouse and Young 2004; Woods 2006; Revell and Stanton 2014). A nationwide study from Finland revealed that over 60 percent of respondents reported that they either did not use their thermostat at all or changed its setting less frequently than once a month (Karjalainen 2010). In a study of houses with and without thermostat controls in the United Kingdom, Shipworth et al. (2010) found no statistical difference in average living room temperatures in households with and without smart meters.

In an ongoing study in Oslo, Norway, of how people live in 'smart' buildings, researchers found that very few of the families interviewed understand the workings of the smart interface with the mechanical ventilation system or use it as designed (Standal et al. in press). This is consistent with the findings from Wade's (2015) study, referred to previously. The heat engineers she studied who install home heating systems in the United Kingdom reported that many households of all ages and socioeconomic groups had difficulties understanding smart meter interfaces and that they never recommend smart thermostatic controls for older people. For those households who elect to install them, the installers recommend a simple method for regulating thermostats that ignores or overrides the programming required by the smart device.

In her book entitled *Smart Utopia*, Australian Yolande Strengers (2013) cites evidence of widespread skepticism to the idea of living in a smart house and ceding control of comfort to smart technologies (Vyas and Gohn 2012). She also supports the evidence from European studies that people living in smart houses often do not use them in ways intended by designers (Valocchi and Juliano 2012). According to Strengers, one of the reasons for these problems is that smart technology designers imagine a household energy consumer as 'resource man': a male who makes decisions for the entire household, is well educated, is interested in energy data, is techno-savvy, and responds rationally to price signals. 'Resource man' is the prototype *homo economicus* of late capitalism. Unfortunately, this imagined householder does not correspond to most men and women of any age, place or social class. In the emerging 'smart utopia' designers and manufacturers script designs in accordance with green capitalism, delegating agency to technology, making experimentation and control by residents more difficult and raising concerns about public access to information about how people live in the privacy of their homes. In the words of Koolhaas (2015), smart buildings are

> listening, thinking, and talking back, collecting information and performing accordingly. The door has become automated, transformed into an extension of the smart phone, with each opening and closure logged; elevators predict your intended destination by listening to your conversations and tracking your routines; toilets diagnose potential illness, building a catalogue of the user's most intimate medical data; windows tell you when they should be opened and closed for maximum environmental efficiency. You house may soon insist on an early bedtime to stop irresponsible consumption of energy.

There is an urgent need to rethink 'smart'. The emphasis should be on design principles that correspond to and engage with people's know-how about heating, cooling and ventilating. This will involve a challenge to 'the fundamental opposition we now face . . . between architecture's long-established power to articulate the collective and the digital's apparent ability to merge with the self' (Koolhaas 2015). Stewart Brand (1994) anticipated the problems with smart in his concept of 'the scenario buffered building' and his statement that 'All buildings are predictions. All predictions are wrong.' From the perspective of both user interface and sustainability demands, buildings should be built in ways that make them malleable and adaptable. This was the case in pre-smart design, where flexibility for ventilating, insulating and shading are important. Smart design disables flexibility and householder agency in interacting with the building in ways that suit their needs for light, air, sociability and so on. Smart is dumb if it means locking buildings and people into predetermined patterns and disabling creative low-energy and user-adapted comfort solutions. Technology has a very important role to play in sustainable design, but designers must be careful to insure that occupants can exercise their know-how and interests in the production of home services.

The new directions in sustainable design calling themselves smart give the impression of being apolitical, but this is deceptive. As I have argued, the pursuit of efficiency, optimization, standardization and automatization are decidedly political and largely undemocratic from the perspective of limiting user agency. Sustainable design must be cognizant that the politics of sustainable production, provision and consumption are saturated with incentives, infrastructures and technologies that are designed to satisfy the demands of economic growth, individualization and rapid product turnover. Each of these domains (production, provision and consumption) will need to be reregulated and political incentives for low energy choices provided that go against the grain of capitalist development. Still, design can play an important role in moving and influencing technologies, products and practices from within and from below; for example, by redesigning cities to enable the use of nonmotorized transport such as walking and bicycling; redesigning living spaces such that they are more compact and are amenable to sharing, and in warmer climates, can be cooled without central air conditioning; and redesigning products for durability and longevity. In this sense design can provide niches for innovative experimentation that have the potential to demystify sustainable living; enable contraction, sharing and collaboration; as well as influencing political debates on new pathways toward sustainable futures.

References

Baker, S. 2007. Sustainable development as symbolic commitment: declaratory politics and the seductive appeal of ecological modernisation in the European Union. *Environmental Politics* 16: 297–317.

Barry, John. 2007. Towards a model of green political economy: from ecological modernisation to economic security. *International Journal of Green Economics* 1(3/4): 446–464.

Bluhdorn, I. 2007. Democracy, efficiency, futurity: contested objectives of societal reform. In I. Bluhdorn and U. Jun (Eds), *Economic Efficiency – Democratic Empowerment*. Lanham, MD: Rowman & Littlefield/ Lexington, pp 69–98.

Bluhdorn, Ingolfur and Ian Welsh. 2007. Eco-politics beyond the paradigm of sustainability: a conceptual framework and research agenda. *Environmental Politics* 16(2): 185–205.

Brand, Stewart. 1994. *How Buildings Learn*. New York: Viking Press.

Ceschin, Fabrizio. 2013. Critical factors for implementing and diffusing sustainable product-service systems: insights from innovation studies and companies' experiences. *Journal of Cleaner Production* 45: 74–88.

Cross, Gary. 2000. *An All-Consuming Century: Why Commercialism Won in Modern America*. New York: Colombia University Press.

CSE. 2015. Assessing US climate action plan. Report by the Centre for Science and Environment, Delhi. Available at www.cse.org. Accessed 17 October 2015.

Daly, Herman. 1992. Allocation, distribution and scale: towards an economics that is efficient, just and sustainable. *Journal of Ecological Economics* 6: 185–193.

DEFRA. 2005. *Securing the Future: Delivering UK Sustainable Development Strategy*. London: Department of Environment and Rural Affairs.

Dryzek, J. 1997. *The Politics of the Earth*. Oxford: Oxford University Press.

EEA. 2015. Trends and projections in Europe 2015: tracking progress towards Europe's climate and energy targets. European Environmental Agency Report 4/2015. Available at www.eea.europa.eu/publications/trends-and-projections-in-europe-2015. Accessed 24 October 2015.

Faulkner, Neil. 2013. *A Marxist History of the World: From Neanderthals to Neoliberals*. New York: Palgrave.

Geels, Frank W. 2004. From sectoral systems of innovation to socio-technical systems: insights about dynamics and change from sociology and institutional theory. *Research Policy* 33: 897–920.

Geels, Frank W. 2011. The multi-level perspective on sustainability transitions: responses to seven criticisms. *Environmental Innovation and Societal Transformation* 1(1): 24–40.

Geels, Frank W. 2014. Regime resistance against low-carbon transitons: introducing politics and power into the multi-level perspective. *Theory, Culture and Society* 31(5): 21–40.

Gibbs, D. 2006. Prospects for an environmental economic geography: linking ecological modernisation and regulationist approaches. *Journal of Economic Geography*, 82: 193–215.

Goedkoop, M., van Halen, C. teRiele, H., and P. Rommes. 1999. Product services systems, ecological and economic basics. Report 1999/36. VROM, The Hague.

Hajer, M. A. 1995. *The Politics of Environmental Discourse: Ecological Modernization and the Policy Process.* Oxford: Clarendon Press.

Halme, M., Jasch, C., and M. Scharp. 2004. Sustainable home services? Toward household services that enhance ecological, social and economic sustainability. *Ecological Economics* 51(1–2): 125–138.

Hamilton, Clive. 2010. Consumerism, self-creation and prospects for a new ecological consciousness. *Journal of Cleaner Production* 18: 571–575.

Hargreaves, T., Longhurst, N., and G. Seyfang. 2013. Up, down and round: connecting regimes and practices in innovation for sustainability. *Environmental Planning A* 45(2): 402–420.

Huber, Joseph. 2007. Pioneer countries and the global diffusion of environmental innovations: theses from the viewpoint of ecological modernization theory. *Global Envionrmental Change* 18: 360–367.

Huber, Mathew T. 2013. *Lifeblood: Oil, Freedom and the Forces of Capital.* Minneapolis: University of Minnesota Press.

IPCC. 2014. Climate change 2014: impacts, adaptation, and vulnerability. Available at www.ipcc.ch/report/ar5/wg2/. Accessed 20 September 2015.

Jackson, T. 2009. *Prosperity Without Growth: Economics for a Finite Planet.* London and Washington, DC: Earthscan.

Karjalainen, S. 2007. Why is it difficult to use a simple device: an analysis of a room thermostat. In A. Sears and J. Jacko (Eds), *Human-Computer Interaction Handbook: Fundamentals, Evolving Technologies and Emerging Applications, Part I, HCII.* New York: Laurence Erlbaum Associates, pp 544–548.

Kimball, Lucy. 2011. Rethinking design thinking: Part 1. *Design and Culture* 3(3): 285–306.

Klein, Naomi. 2014. *This Changes Everything: Capitalism vs. the Climate.* New York: Simon & Shuster.

Koolhaas, Rem. 2015. The smart landscape: intelligent architecture. *Artforum*, April. Available at: https://artforum.com/inprint/issue=201504. Accessed 1 June 2016.

Luttropp, Conrad and Jessica Lagerstedt. 2006. EcoDesign and the ten golden rules: generic advice for merging environmental aspects into product development. *Journal of Cleaner Production* 14: 1396–1408.

Lynas, Mark. 2007. *Six Degrees: Our Future on a Hotter Planet.* London: Harper Collins.

McNeill, D. and H. Wilhite. 2015. Making sense of sustainable development in a changing world. In A. Hansen and U. Wethal (Eds), *Emerging Economies and Challenges to Sustainability.* London: Routledge.

Pettersen, I. N. 2015. Fostering absolute reductions in resource use: the potential role and feasibility of practice-oriented design. *Journal of Cleaner Production.* Available at http://dx.doi.org/10.1016/j.jclepro.2015.02.005. Accessed 17 October 2015.

Pickerill, Jenny and Marsh Maxey. 2009. Low impact development: the future in our hands. Published Under the Creative Commons Attribution-Non-Commercial-Share Alike 3.0 licence. Available at http://creativecommons.org/licenses/by-nc-sa/3.0/

Rathouse, K. and B. Young. 2004. Domestic heating: use of controls. Defra Market Transformation Program, United Kingdom.

Revell, K. M. A. and N. A. Stanton. 2014. Case studies of mental models in home heat control: searching for feedback, valve, timer and switch theories. *Applied Ergonomics* 45: 363–378.

Robertson, M. 2004. The neoliberalisation of ecosystem services: wetland mitigation banking and problems in environmental governance. *Geoforum* 35: 361–373.

Roy, Robin. 2000. Sustainable product-service systems. *Futures* 32: 289–299.

Salleh, Ariel. 2010. Climate strategy: making the choice between ecological modernisation or living well. *Journal of Australian Political Economy* 66: 118–143.

Seyfang, Gill and Alex Haxeltine. 2012. Growing grassroots innovations: exploring the role of community-based initiatives in governing sutainable energy transitions. *Environmental Politics* 16(4): 584–603.

Shipworth, M., Firth, S. K., Gentry, M. I., Wright, A. Shipworth, D. T. and K. J. Lomas. 2010. Central heating thermostat settings and timing: building demographics. *Building Research and Information* 40(4): 481–492.

Shove, Elizabeth and Gorden Walker. 2010. Governing transitions in the sutainability of everyday life. *Research Policy* 39(4): 471–476.

Spaargaren, G. and A. Mol. 1992. Sociology, environment and modernity: ecological modernisation as a theory of social change. *Society and Natural Resources* 5(4): 323–344.

Standal, Karina, Wilhite, Harold, and Solvår Vagø. In press, 2017. Household energy practices in low-energy buildings: a qualitative study of an Oslo housing cooperative. *Energy Research and Social Science.*

Strengers, Yolande. 2013. *Smart Energy Technologies in Everyday Life: Smart Utopia?* Basingstroke and New York: Palgrave Macmillan.

Trusel, L. K., Frey, K. E., Das, S. B. Karnauskas, K. B., Munneke, P. K., van Meijgaarda, E., and M. R. van den Broeke. 2015. Divergent trajectories of Antarctic surface melt under two twenty-first-century climate scenarios. *Nature Geoscience.* Available at: www.nature.com/ngeo/journal/vaop/ncurrent/full/ngeo2563.html. Accessed 13 October 2015.

Tukker, A., Cohen, M., Hubacek, K., and O. Mont. 2010. The impacts of household consumption and options for change. *Journal of Industrial Ecology* 14(1): 13–30.

Valocchi, Michael and John Juliano. 2012. Knowledge is power: driving smarter energy usage through consumer education. IBM Business Report. Available at http://smartgridaustralia.com.au/SGA/Documents/Consumer_Behaviour_Report. Accessed 30 June 2015.

Vyas, Charul and Bob Gohn. 2012. *Smart Grid Consumer Survey.* Boulder, CO: Pike Research.

Wade, Faye. 2015. An ethnography of installation: exploring the role of heating engineers in shaping the energy consumed through domestic central heating systems. Thesis submitted for the Degree of Doctor of Philosophy in Energy and Human Dimensions, UCL Energy Insitute, Bartlett School of Environment, Energy and Resources, University College London.

Wallenborn, G. and H. Wilhite. 2014. Rethinking embodied knowledge and household consumption. *Energy Research and Social Science* 1: 56–64.

WCED. 1987. *Our Common Future.* Oxford and New York: Oxford University Press.

Wilhite, Harold. 2012. The energy dilemma. In K. Bjørkdahl and K. B. Nielsen (Eds), *Development and the Environment: Practices, Theories, Policies.* Oslo: Universitetsforlaget, pp 81–99.

Wilhite, Harold. 2016. *The Political Economy of Low Carbon Transformation: Breaking the Habits of Capitalism.* New York and London: Routledge.

Wilhite, Harold. and J. Norgard. 2004. Equating efficiency with reduction: a self-deception in energy policy. *Energy and Environment* 15(3): 991–1011.

Winther, T. and H. Wilhite. 2015. An analysis of the household energy rebound effect from a practice perspective: spatial and temporal dimensions. *Energy Efficiency Journal* 8(3): 595–607.

Woods, J. 2006. Fiddling with theormostats: energy implications of heating and cooling set point behavior. *Proceedings of the 2006 ACEEE Summer Study.* Washington, DC: American Council for an Energy Efficient Economy.

WWI. 2013. *Is Sustainability Still Possible? State of the World 2013.* World Watch Institute. New York: Island Press.

10

DESIGN FOR LOCALIZATION

Helena Norberg-Hodge

Design may not be the first thing that comes to mind when you hear the word economy. However, just as everything else about our lives is inextricably linked to economic activity, so is design, in all its senses. Awareness is increasing that the current global economic system no longer serves the needs of the majority of people and that it is fundamentally unsustainable. A growing number of voices are speaking out against this system and advocating a different way forward – a new economy.

For me, the key element of this new economy is scale. To create genuinely sustainable societies, we need to encourage a fundamental shift toward economic localization – or what I call "the economics of happiness." A new global system, based on interlinked self-reliant economies, would embody distinctly different values than the ones that underpin the status quo. Localized economies put people and planet at the center, adapting financial structures and commercial activity to place and culture. They honor and enhance diversity in all ways – cultural, biological and agricultural. Localization fosters a multitude of meaningful jobs and forms the foundation for strong, resilient communities. This in turn provides for a true sense of belonging, purpose and connection, ultimately increasing psychological well-being. Today, designers have a choice: they can either contribute to the global system that values exploitation, consumption and waste or join in a shift toward the local, where it is life itself that is of the highest value.

The current global economy

What we have today is a model of development that is dangerously distanced from the needs of cultures and places, and rigidly imposed from the top down. At the moment, the global economy and the growing domination of technology are not only severing our connection to nature and to one another but also breaking down biological and cultural diversity. In so doing, we are threatening our very existence.

Over the last 30 years, the power of corporations has increased dramatically and there has been a shift in the social and environmental movements away from focusing on political change towards market solutions. The environmental movements of the 1970s were very clear about the need for regulations, for instance to ban certain pesticides and other sources of pollution. There was also a demand for a shift away from subsidizing nuclear power and fossil fuels and toward decentralized, renewable energy. In terms of development, there was recognition of the importance of supporting self-reliance, rather than creating dependence on aid. Gradually, however, the thinking shifted so that by the late 1980s there was an increasing emphasis on green consumerism. The message was "if you care for the environment, you need to pay more for organic food." If you want to reduce pollution "pay more for a green car". In terms of aid and development the thinking had shifted to argue that aid (even for self-reliance) was patronizing. The new slogan was trade, not aid.

Through the deregulation of trade treaties, global corporations get ultimate freedom. Most production has shifted away from Western industrialized countries and is now concentrated in the global South. The transport alone represents a significant increase in energy consumption. In addition, because the production is often in developing countries with lax environmental standards, it ultimately leads to practices that are wasteful and toxic. These countries are relatively new to the onslaught of corporate-driven, global-scale production and thus do not have the capacity to protect themselves from the damage that ensues.

There is no doubt that much of the thinking behind globalization came from corporate-funded think tanks. However, because much of it sounded perfectly sensible on the surface, many well-meaning individuals, organizations and governments supported it. The situation we now find ourselves in is that almost every choice that is ecological and socially just costs more money, even though local, natural products should logically be cheaper.

We have not chosen this path consciously. We have all been victims of a system that values profit over life and has gained power over us by twisting our perceptions, undermining human connections and our sense of self-worth. On a global level, the process began with force – slavery, colonialism, genocide. Now in most of the North, and increasingly in the South, control of our minds and hearts is gained through manipulation. In the modern era, the primary tool is seduction – using our innate need for recognition, approval, connection and love to fuel consumerism. Children are especially vulnerable as advertisers work to channel their desire for love into a desire for the objects that keep the consumer economy running.

From a very young age, we are exposed to a series of myths and basic assumptions that form the backbone of the growth economy. Through various channels, including education and mass media, even the most well-intentioned individuals fall victim to the deceit. Even those working from within the system cannot see clearly the forest for the trees. In both the global North and South, the message is that a rising GDP (Gross Domestic Product) is necessary to create jobs; that economic growth, development and technological progress are continually improving our lives. It begins to look as if we value things over people and money more than the living planet around us.

Given this, it is not a surprise that this system is dramatically increasing resource and energy use at a completely unsustainable pace. We know that if the entire human population were to consume at the rate of those living the industrialized West, which is what the proponents of globalization try to convince us is possible, we would need multiple planets to support the consumption and waste.

We are told, because of overpopulation, we need to shift to high-rise living, in isolated family units. But, in many unseen ways, today's centralized systems take up much more space. The relationship between the vast urban centers of today and their physical requirements is analogous to the way we use more land the higher up on the food chain we eat. A beef cow does not take up nearly as much room in itself as a vegetable garden, but when you take into account the fields of grain to feed the cow, the water to irrigate the fields, and the land that dried up because of the diversion of that water, it is clear that a cow actually takes up more land. A large city takes up less physical space than the same population dispersed into small communities, but it lives higher on the energy chain. Per capita consumption in the cities is also higher. The freeways, the transport, the used-car lots, the oil fields, the food-processing plants, the pollution of air, water, and land mean that contemporary urban centers use more resources and ultimately more space than decentralized communities closer to nature.

Our current economic path systematically destroys not only the environment, but jobs and livelihoods as well. Unfortunately, we rarely hear about the ways that so-called progress contributes to social and psychological breakdown. The news doesn't report that globalization is bankrupting governments at every level – that the perverse logic of corporate capitalism forces them to subsidize global corporations while cutting back on the social programs their citizens need.

There is a massive global push by corporations and governments to come up with the latest and greatest solutions to the environmental and social crises we face, while largely ignoring that they arise from the same source. Even many of the most ecological architects and designers, economists, green activists, and concerned academics are convinced that market-based solutions, often a result of the latest developments in design and technology, are the answer to saving our planet and offer a sustainable future for our species. Unfortunately, most of these solutions are a version of the same corporate thinking that serves to fuel the very problem they are trying to abate. Depending on market-based solutions means relying on a marketplace that is heavily tilted in favor of the biggest players.

For instance, corporations have been very successful at convincing the public that free-market transactions, rather than global regulation, are the best means of reducing carbon emissions. This approach not only preserves the power of corporations, it augments it. Carbon trading, for example, essentially gives industries the right to pollute, for a price – making the atmosphere on which all life depends a commodity that can be sold to the highest bidder. This, at a time when the biggest transnational corporations are wealthier than entire countries.

Similar market-based approaches have been suggested for "protecting" the planet's remaining rainforests. But as Brazilian activist Camila Moreno points out, proposals like these promote the privatization and commodification of what has always been common land. She asks, "Is that what we want as an international public policy, that the last public forests and public lands on earth – where there is biodiversity, where there are indigenous people – be from now on connected to financial markets?"[1]

Fair trade standards are another example of a market-based solution that enables global players to buy where it is cheap and sell where there is greatest profit. These standards make people feel they are exercising their purchasing power for good, but the reality is that we are still trapped within the exploitative system. Of course, we want all trade to be fair, but is this actually achievable when engulfed in an unfair game? When dependent on foreign markets, this is a precarious existence for the producer, and consumers sometimes fare no better. Countries in both the North and South would be far better off if they were to use their resources for themselves and prioritize supporting local businesses that provide for local needs.

Market-based strategies have also taken off in the realm of renewable energy. Though there is no question that renewables must replace fossil fuels as the primary source of energy, our current needs must be greatly reduced in order for that to be feasible. It is simply not realistic to assume we can carry on needlessly transporting trinkets and cheap clothing around the world or, worse, trading identical goods. Many countries routinely export and import similar quantities of the exact same foods – bread, milk, meat, potatoes – in what has been called "the great food swap." Nonetheless, renewables are often portrayed as a means to maintain the current structures of the global economy – changing little but the fuel that runs it. Thus, a headline on the website Eco-Watch proclaims, "Renewable energy and economic growth go hand in hand."[2]

Thanks to billions of dollars in government subsidies, the renewable energy field has already attracted the interest of large corporations. For example, the Spanish energy multinational Iberdrola – the fourth largest electric power provider in the United Kingdom and a major player in U.S., South American, and European energy markets – is also one of the world's biggest wind energy companies; Canadian natural gas corporation Gaz Metro (co-owned by tar sands giant Enbridge) also has major investments in industrial wind projects. The renewable energy projects that these and other global corporations invest in are large-scale and centralized, thus keeping the energy supply tightly in corporate hands.

The destruction we're seeing today – environmentally and socially – is a result of the *scale* of the economy and the corporate values that drive it. It does not have to be this way. For more than four decades, I and my organization Local Futures have been raising awareness about the multiple benefits of a systemic shift in direction away from globalization towards localization. My initial insight into the importance of strong local economies for sustainability and well-being came from my time in Ladakh.

Learning from Ladakh

I was a young student of linguistics when I first went to Ladakh in the 1970s. I had gotten a job as a translator for a film crew and my task was to learn the Ladakhi language as quickly as possible. I immediately fell in love with the people and the landscape. As a foreigner, but speaking the language fluently, I quickly gained a unique vantage point as both insider and outsider.

The Indian government had just built a new road to the capital city, Leh, and opened the region to development and tourism. During my first year there, many of the tourists I met were fatalistic. They were sure that crime, pollution, and unemployment would be inevitable consequences of the area's exposure to the outside world. In their eyes, progress was a natural and inexorable process that could take only one form. But I could not agree. I felt sure the destruction I saw starting to occur was neither necessary nor inevitable. Rather, it was a result of specific policies and perceptions that could be changed. I was convinced another way must be possible.

Just at that time, I came across a copy of *Small Is Beautiful*, by the economist E. F. Schumacher, which strengthened my conviction that development does not have to mean destruction. I had seen how people in the modern sector were starting to buy imported coal and wood to heat their homes in winter. To them, of course, this seemed an absolute improvement over burning sparse supplies of animal dung to combat the severe winter temperatures. However, as was already becoming apparent, the problems with transporting these fuels across the Himalayas were immense and prices were rising every year. There was no way a family in the traditional subsistence economy could afford regular supplies throughout the winter; the only means of buying these fuels was to plug into the money economy of Leh. This was contributing significantly to the drift away from the land into the capital, creating a dependence on an inflationary economy based on nonrenewable resources.

I began writing letters to both the state and central Indian governments, pleading for policies that would build on the strengths of the traditional culture and promote the use of renewable energy. In 1978, after several meetings with the Indian Planning Commission, I requested and received permission to organize a small pilot project to demonstrate some simple solar technologies. Solar energy was an obvious choice since the region receives more than three hundred days of sunlight a year.

The focus of the project was to find an effective way of heating the houses, but we also built a demonstration solar oven and a greenhouse. Fortunately, an elegantly simple solar technology for heating houses was available, named the Trombe wall after its French designer. We found that this system could be easily adapted to the traditional architecture and available materials. A double layer of glass is attached to the outside of a south-facing wall, which is painted black to absorb the sun's rays. The ceilings and other walls are insulated with straw.

The Trombe wall proved to be ideally suited to Ladakh. Mud brick is an excellent medium for absorbing and storing solar energy; and the rays of the low winter sun effectively heat the room, while those of the high summer sun barely touch the wall, keeping the room cool and comfortable. The whole system cost about three hundred dollars to install or the price of one *dzo* (a yak-cow hybrid, highly valued as a working animal). As the average heating bill could otherwise be as much as two hundred dollars a year when using fossil fuels such as coal, the cost of the wall could be recovered in less than two heating seasons.

Before we built our first Trombe wall, many people were somewhat skeptical and laughed at the idea. "Don't be silly," they said. "The heat will leak out as soon as you open the door." And when we were building the walls, the straw insulation was a source of great amusement to the masons, who called it "a home for mice." However, over the years interest in Trombe walls and other solar technologies has increased.

Early on, in response to the demonstration Trombe walls, the radio programs and dramas, a group of concerned Ladakhis became interested in exploring a more sustainable development path. They represented Ladakh's leading thinkers, people of great integrity and dedication. Many of them had traveled outside Ladakh, received a modern education, and yet retained respect for the values of their traditional culture. In 1983, we officially registered as the Ladakh Ecological Development Group (LEDeG). With a current staff of forty, LEDeG has become the most influential nongovernmental organization in the region. LEDeG continues to develop and demonstrate a whole range of appropriate technologies.

In addition to the Trombe walls, we began to build greenhouses and these caught on like wildfire over the years. There is virtually no village in the whole region now where you will not find these mud-brick greenhouses. These simple and adaptable structures have contributed enormously to agricultural productivity because they not only allow people to grow vegetables throughout most of the winter, but to start seedlings, which enable farmers to produce tomatoes, peppers and beans, despite the cold climate and short growing season.

Other solar technologies included ovens for cooking and baking, water heaters – both simple batch and thermosyphoning systems. We also developed hydraulic ram pumps, made by our own technical staff entirely from standard plumbing parts. These raise water using the power of gravity instead of imported petroleum. One of the first pumps we installed lifted water 150 feet to the top of a monastery to the amazement and appreciation of the monks, who previously had to carry water on their backs. Other projects included improved traditional water mills – that could not only grind grain faster, but also provided mechanical power for driving tools. We also built micro-hydro installations for domestic lighting in the villages.

All these technological alternatives made sense economically, environmentally and culturally. By encouraging a more human-scale and decentralized development pattern, they actively supported Ladakh's culture rather than destroying it. And they are not "technologies for the poor," only suited to the underprivileged. As we did our best to make clear, nonpolluting appropriate technologies based on renewable energy are *not* something second-rate, but highly effective and efficient solutions to the long-term needs of both developed and developing countries.

All our projects involved the participation of the beneficiaries. Before we installed a turbine, for instance, the villagers themselves would have helped to choose a site, improved an existing water channel and made a holding tank. One or two villagers then came to our workshop in Leh for six months to learn how to run and maintain the installation. After the turbine was in place, the village was responsible for building a small powerhouse.

LEDeG's headquarters – the Center for Ecological Development in the heart of Leh – was inaugurated by Indira Gandhi in 1984 and consecrated by His Holiness the Dalai Lama. The building itself is an example of how traditional Ladakhi architecture can be "updated" to meet changing expectations and needs. Part of it is solar heated, and solar water-heating panels on the roof provide hot water.

The center helped bring our work and the thinking behind it to the attention of Ladakh's decision-makers and visitors from abroad. It generated considerable interest not only within Ladakh itself, but throughout the rest of India. Visitors ranged from government officials, journalists, teachers, and tourists, to Ladakhis from all walks of life. Here Ladakhis could meet foreign tourists face to face and on equal terms. This facilitated real communication between the two cultures, demystifying the West and showing the Ladakhis how much value the foreigners attached not only to traditional Ladakhi culture, but also to the work we were doing.

Although I felt that solar heating could provide a clear improvement in living standards, I would not have considered it appropriate for an outsider like myself to introduce this technology had not other less-sustainable heating methods – like coal and oil – already begun to pollute the environment. Since they had, I felt that people should have the information to make a choice; the Ladakhis had received no information whatsoever about solar energy or other forms of renewable energy. We demonstrated that higher standards of living did not have to mean abandoning economic independence or traditional values. With experience, however, we realized that demonstration was not enough. There was a need to actively support and propagate such alternatives, and to lobby the government to divert subsidies away from capital- and energy-intensive installations toward decentralized technologies based on renewable energy.

In the last decade, as India has opened its door to foreign investment, large amounts of money have poured into Ladakh, so that now there are two distinct opposing trends in the region. As in so many parts of the world, there is now an ecological movement that promotes renewable energy and genuinely sustainable development, but at the same time much bigger sums of money are promoting conventional development.

We have played a part in raising awareness of the need for a long-term ecological perspective on development, for progress based on self-reliance and self-respect. The terms "ecology" and "solar energy" are now widely used and understood throughout Ladakh, and there is a growing number of people who make the environment and Ladakh's future well-being a conscious priority. But there is still a lot to be done if this work is to fully succeed in preventing Ladakh from ending up a polluted, depleted and divided region as so many places in the South have become under conventional development.

From global to local

Today, humanity faces a stark choice. We can continue on the path of globalization and deregulation, handing over ever more power to a volatile global market dominated by unaccountable banks and corporations. Or, we can start moving in the opposite direction, toward localization, reclaiming our power as citizens and reconnecting to each other and the Earth.

Localization does *not* mean isolation or nationalism. In fact, international collaboration will be imperative if we are to successfully relocalize. Scaling down economic activity to a more local level will be less capital-intensive and will work with, rather than against, the real needs of both people and planet. Encouragingly, there are countless localization initiatives around the world that are *already* demonstrating its multiple benefits.

It is important to understand that this is not a battle of good versus evil, but rather it is about awareness of systemic issues and understanding the bigger picture. We need grassroots and political engagement in the form of resistance and renewal – resistance to further globalization, along with the renewal of localized systems in food, energy, finance and other sectors of the economy. I'm convinced that this is the most strategic path toward genuine sustainability.

What we have today is almost as far from a free market as you could get, with regulations and subsidies continually furthering the expansion of multinational corporations to the detriment of local businesses and the communities they support. Imagine if governments did not subsidize fossil fuels, which they do to the tune of more than $500 billion a year globally. Suddenly it would become a lot less profitable to transport goods around the world to take advantage of lower labor costs. Redundant trade, where a country imports and exports identical products, would also cease to be a reasonable business transaction. Likewise, large corporations – from mega-farms to oil companies to clothing brands – are eligible for a range of capital allowances and other tax breaks that are out of reach for small businesses. It is verging on the absurd that we continue to believe we have a free market capitalist system after the recent bank bailouts.

Scaling back the economy would reign in the power of these corporations and free up government spending for social programs and supporting local enterprise. It would also foster businesses that, by their very nature, have a smaller ecological footprint than those which rely upon redundant trade and which offer more meaningful employment. Because localization is all about adapting the economy to place – local culture, local environment, local needs – there is not one global blueprint.

Localization involves active steps toward decentralization. Since extreme dependence has already been created on both national and international levels, it would be irresponsible to "delink" economies and cut off assistance from one day to the next. We cannot, for example, suddenly halt our purchase of coffee or cotton from those countries in the Third World whose economies totally depend on such trade. But we *can* immediately begin supporting aid programs that will enable farmers to return to growing food for local consumption, rather than cash crops for export to the West.

Parallel to economic decentralization we need to decentralize the production of energy. Again, this ought to happen both in the West and in the Third World, but because the energy infrastructure of most developing countries is still relatively limited, the widespread application of solar, wind, biomass, and hydropower technologies in these regions would be comparatively easy. Until now, however, it simply has not happened. Instead, the West has pushed its own industrial model, based on large-scale, centralized power production. One of the most effective ways of turning destructive development into genuine aid would be to lobby for widespread support and subsidies for decentralized applications of renewable energy.

Changes at the policy level are needed to ensure that society determines the rules for business, rather than the other way around. A first priority is to insist that our governments get back to the same tables where they signed our rights away to global corporations. New treaties are needed that will take back that power – in part by requiring businesses to be place-based or localized, thereby making them more accountable to those they affect. Rather than continuing to promote the large and global, government policies would strive to support local and regional business instead. The following are some of the policies that would need to be enacted.

Financial policies

The banking and financial system needs to be re-regulated to limit the creation of phantom wealth and to curtail the unregulated flow of capital. At the same time, the local investment sector needs to be freed of outdated laws that make it almost impossible for people to invest in their communities through retirement funds and securities exchanges.

Taxation

In almost every country, tax regulations systematically discriminate against small- and medium-scale businesses. Smaller-scale, sustainable production is usually more labor intensive and heavy taxes are levied on labor through income taxes, social welfare taxes, payroll taxes, etc. Meanwhile, tax breaks (accelerated depreciation, investment allowances and tax credits, etc.) are afforded the capital- and energy-intensive technologies used by large corporate producers. Reversing this bias in the tax system would not only help local economies, but would create more jobs by favoring people instead of machines.

Decentralized, renewable energy

Currently, renewable energy technologies receive less than a fifth of the amount of subsidies given fossil fuels. Reversing this imbalance would result in less pollution, more jobs, and long-term cost savings.

In addition to these changes in top-down policies, a global-to-local shift requires diverse, local, bottom-up initiatives of the kind that are already emerging. Unlike actions to halt the global economic juggernaut, these small-scale steps require a slow pace and an intimate understanding of local contexts, and are best designed and implemented by local people themselves. If supported by policy changes, such initiatives will, over time, inevitably foster a return to cultural and biological diversity and long-term sustainability.

Designing for localization

It is clear that we are at a crossroads. For decades, we have been on a path emphasizing economic growth, but another way is becoming more visible. It is unfortunate that so much of the sustainability movement has been swept along on the first path, believing that there is no alternative to the global growth paradigm. Many leading figures have advocated for urbanization under the banner of greening cities. Some have even come out in favor of synthetic foods and nuclear power to sustain an ever-growing urban population. Yet, as I explained earlier, continued centralization and urbanization is fundamentally unsustainable and a sure way to expand each individual's ecological footprint.

For genuine sustainability, we need to head in the opposite direction. We need to decentralize in every way, including our patterns of habitation, our energy sources and food production. We need to reestablish close links between people and their natural environment and make sure that the design elements of these communities are as natural as possible.

The fundamental elements of design for local economies are natural, place-based, human-scale and diversified. The definition of "natural" should be fairly straightforward, but it has also become twisted by greenwashing. Even in some eco-villages, communities are building with high-tech, synthetic materials that have high embodied energy. Petrochemical foams, concrete and plastic are heavily employed in an effort to make low-energy dwellings. These homes tend to be so well sealed to modulate temperature that sophisticated ventilation is then needed. Combining natural materials – clay, hemp, stone, etc. – with sophisticated know-how could give us both healthy buildings and energy savings all along the chain from the production of materials through transport to end use.

Real sustainable design also needs to be place-based – adapted to and reflective of the local environment and the local culture. This can be as simple as building houses to take advantage of passive solar or as complex as planning developments around ecological features, so that wild habitats are preserved. It also includes thinking through what truly reflects the values and needs of the local community. For example, what public art is on the streets? Does it allow for participation of the community? Does it encourage solidarity and inclusion? In recent years, there has been a growing movement for "place making" that asks these questions and more. Advocates in this movement are transforming spaces in cities and towns to encourage community interaction instead of ever more traffic and pollution.

Another key feature of sustainable design is that it is human-scale. This is especially relevant in the realms of energy and food production. In both sectors, the green movement has largely fallen for the "bigger is better" myth. Renewable energy is most often found in vast wind farms or "solar ranches," which centralize energy production in what was once wild habitat. Organic farms have grown to hundreds of acres, producing monocrops destined to be transported thousands of miles. In both cases, scaling-down and decentralizing has a range of social and ecological benefits. First of all, more jobs would be created in these sectors. There would be less wastage of energy and food, and more space left for wild nature. Designers can participate in the decentralization of these sectors by advocating for human-scale production.

Encouraging diversity is also essential in designing for localization. At a biological level, diversity is the basis for life on this planet. At an economic level, it provides richness and resilience for communities. At a cultural level, it encourages solidarity and tolerance. And at a psychological level, it fosters happiness. Unlike the consumer monoculture of the global system, local economies both require and support diversity. The emerging concept of the modern artisan economy is a good example of this. Arising both through planning and through innate human ingenuity, these human-scale, diversified economies can be found in many parts of the world.

In a recent survey by the Artisan Economy Initiative in Portland, Oregon, researchers found successful businesses of all sorts, including clothing and jewelry manufacturing, graphic design, furniture-making and food production, among others.[3] The 126 businesses surveyed employed more than 1,000 people collectively and contributed over $250 million to the Portland economy. Because these business are local, this money circulates within the community generating more benefits instead of being immediately siphoned off to distant corporate headquarters and shareholders. The positive changes in Portland and elsewhere came about because increasing numbers of people from various walks of life woke up to their deep need for connection to others and to nature. They rediscovered which values truly mattered to them. As various initiatives started demonstrating the benefits, more people were drawn in, and a virtuous cycle of reinforcement developed.

What we need now is to globalize localization – creating small-scale on a large scale. To do so, Portland and other communities like it would benefit from more education about the dominant system and the need for policy change. Localists need to develop a policy plan and not just within individual cities, regions or countries; we also need to think through our foreign policies and international trade links.

There are many ways for designers to get on board with the global-to-local shift. For those interested in pursuing and working toward this broad shift and genuine sustainability, the first step is to connect with and seek out like-minded people. We need to remember that individuals do not drive this system and that solutions will not come from individual behavior change, but from a collaborative systemic movement. There is no value or reason in playing the blame game, both toward others or ourselves. Guilt only serves to paralyze those who have the best intentions, which ultimately worsens the trends that globalization promotes.

Wherever you are, whatever job you do, you can support decentralization. You can raise awareness among your friends and colleagues about the need for policy change and the need to support local initiatives. If your job and lifestyle allow you to choose, then go for natural over high-tech materials, be attentive to how your designs fit in the local context, take a step back and look at the bigger picture.

Although trying to make a positive difference in the face of global corporate power can feel overwhelming at times, change can happen quickly when we share information and insight. Once a broader understanding catches on, it can spread like wildfire. Design for sustainability is not just a passing trend, it can and should be a way towards ensuring that life on this planet can continue to thrive. It can and should be a part of creating an economics of happiness.

Notes

1 Moreno, Camila, interviewed on Democracy Now, December 18, 2009, "Environmental and Indigenous Activists Criticize Proposed Deal to Save Rainforests", www.democracynow.org/2009/12/18/environmental_and_indigenous_activists_criticize_proposed. Accessed November 4, 2015.
2 Batistelli, Paul, "Renewable Energy and Economic Growth Go Hand in Hand in Massachusetts", EcoWatch, Sept. 20, 2013, http://ecowatch.com/2013/09/20/renewable-energy-economic-growth-massachusetts/. Accessed November 10, 2015.
3 https://artisaneconomyinitiative.files.wordpress.com/2014/10/portland-made-collective-survey-report.pdf

11

INTERCULTURAL COLLABORATIONS IN SUSTAINABLE DESIGN EDUCATION

Denielle Emans and Kelly M. Murdoch-Kitt

Introduction

This chapter explores the productive potentials of intercultural design collaboration for sustainability in terms of teamwork, communication, and creative innovation. The research has evolved from an ongoing pedagogic study by two graphic design faculty: Denielle Emans and Kelly M. Murdoch-Kitt (respectively teaching at VCUQatar in Doha, Qatar and Rochester Institute of Technology, in Rochester, New York, when this chapter was written. Kelly now teaches in the penny W. Stamps School of Art & Design at the University of Michigan). Building off their prior research in Intercultural Design Collaborations (IDC), these two educators examine university-level design partnerships involving team-based projects and virtual communication in order to advance sustainable design.

The authors make a case for teaching design students to collaborate on sustainability topics across cultures. Introducing intercultural collaborations into sustainability projects prepares students for twentieth-first-century design practice as well as global citizenship. The firsthand knowledge that participants gain from their interactions changes their interest in – and perceptions of – worldwide sustainability issues. By learning how different communities respond to environmental, social, and economic challenges, students develop enhanced interpersonal communication skills and strive for the highest order of thinking: contextually sensitive design innovation.

Design and sustainability

Sustainability is an emotionally loaded concept that provokes both positive and negative reactions from students and nonstudents alike. Passionate cries for environmental change are often met with sighs of passivity due to a perceived 'drone' of environmental consciousness. But with global employers and world leaders identifying sustainable development as among the most important issues of the future, socio-environmental topics will continue to impact designers' personal and professional lives.

Though definitions vary, the term *sustainability* is used within this chapter to describe the well-being of humanity and the planet: environmental, social, and economic. For pragmatic purposes, this overarching concept helps describe the complex challenges facing the Earth and her fragile population. The 'social' aspect embedded within the description recognizes the impacts of contemporary power structures on sustainability while also highlighting justice and equity as a core feature of an inclusive agenda for change. At the same time, it embraces the notion that no single designer, group, program, or organization can solve the world's increasingly complex environmental or social problems alone.

Whereas a multitude of research exists regarding sustainability on a global scale, there are only a small number of individual case studies that focus on how design can promote lifestyle changes or shift power dynamics, particularly in non-Western contexts. The existing research rarely acknowledges the importance of emotional states as part of the individual adoption of new habits, or the impact of communication models that urge transformation through dialogic methods. As such, individuals' behaviors – along with their ramifications – continue to go unchecked and unchanged in cities around the world. Prevailing attitudes include feelings of hopelessness ("I can't make a difference on my own"), resistance ("I don't want to be bothered to change"), disinterest ("I don't really care one way or the other"), or frustration ("I resent that I keep hearing about this all the time").

In 2016, the United Nations began a coordinated effort to address climate change and environmental protection through economic strategies targeting poverty and inequality with education, health, and job opportunities. As students and educators, what are ways to support these efforts in the design classroom? What are ways to unpack the complexities of sustainability at the local level (neighborhoods, individual towns, and cities) and extend the efforts to large-scale initiatives (metropolitan, multinational, and global)? What techniques can galvanize students to become the change makers the world so desperately needs?

With professional practices of design increasingly recognized for innovative strategies, services, and systems, designers have a significant role to play in the United Nations' 2030 sustainable development goals. Not only can design help dematerialize services and products, but it can also influence individual attitudes and behaviors by generating positive feelings, engaging interactions, and meaningful services. By shaping trends and decision making, human centered design research and creative inquiry can support an inclusive agenda for sustainable development.

Intercultural competence for sustainability

Without becoming myopic, revelatory problem solving for global change requires unified goals and diverse perspectives characteristic of teamwork and collaboration. With the United Nations' seventeen strategic sustainable development goals propelling the discussion forward, countries across the world have committed to transforming areas of critical importance for humanity and the planet. But while creating for – and alongside – different cultures is increasingly commonplace, the success of global initiatives relies on intercultural competencies. In other words, the ability to communicate and collaborate alongside international partners will play a pivotal role in the effectiveness of global sustainability efforts in the future.

Intercultural competence is a learned skill defined by actively seeking to understand the norms and expectations of other cultures for productive teamwork. Supported by open-mindedness and alternative thinking, communication and interaction between team members broadens global perspectives and drives creativity, rather than hindering it. This methodology is particularly impactful when people from different cultures come together to address pressing issues such as water scarcity, overconsumption, or environmental degradation.

Complex sustainability problems involving multiple actors require skills of cross-cultural competence to succeed. Research suggests that learning about cultural differences – along with personal attitudes, behaviors, and biases – is vital to intercultural collaboration. Developing sensitivity to the traditions, views, and needs of others through intimate teamwork increases skills in empathy, adaptability, and understanding. Students who learn cross-cultural competence develop the ability to question how their environmental, social, and economic choices impact communities beyond their local context. Instead of being content with understanding a sustainability topic through a personal viewpoint, learning from partners with different social and cultural backgrounds, challenges the status quo and broadens critical awareness.

However, students often lack experience in the interpersonal skills required to succeed as members of interconnected, interdisciplinary, and multicultural teams. Of course, these competencies can be learned through trial and error, but this often involves miscommunication or cultural insensitivities that hinder the collaborative process. The opportunity to strengthen cross-cultural collaborative capabilities at the university level may increase productivity in situations where time and resources are limited. For this reason, higher education has a responsibility to prepare design students with the tools and thinking needed to respond to twenty-first-century environmental and social challenges.

Intercultural design collaborations: structural overview

Intercultural Design Collaboration (IDC) at the university level provides students with the opportunity to produce collaborative projects with cross-cultural partners, using virtual communication tools. The inclusion of sustainability within an IDC experience increases the development of students' cross-cultural competencies and supports global citizenship as a core feature of twenty-first-century design practice. The multifaceted process of an intercultural design collaboration involves discussions, activities, and projects introducing students to systems design and sustainable-thinking through the lens of diverse cultural perspectives.

Taking the time to acquaint each student to one another, by face and name, using synchronous virtual communication tools, lays the foundation for fruitful relationships. During introductions, students should be ready with a question for their cross-cultural partner, keeping in mind that awkward pauses may naturally occur due to slow Internet connections. As discussions continue over time, it is also important to move beyond surface-level, 'get to know you' questions that the groups start with during the first meeting. These types of questions tend to keep partners at a distance or show a lack of genuine interest. Faculty can help facilitate the process, by prompting students to find interesting correlations between students or the two cultures. Of course, this process requires initial planning from the faculty leading the collaboration, but the benefits are noticeable.

One method is to ask partners to prepare an interesting story (funny or scary) about a cultural holiday to share with one another. Laughter, awe, and even shock have the remarkable capacity to reduce tensions and build empathy. For instance, sharing scary memories about Halloween (in the United States) and silly stories about Garangaou (in Qatar) serves the function of initiating respect for cultural similarities and differences when students realize both holidays involve children knocking on their neighbors' doors to receive sweet treats.

Preparing students ahead of time for the intense juggling act of intercultural collaboration involves multiple reminders about differences in time and language, along with positive reinforcement from faculty on both sides. In an effort to ease potential tensions, in-class discussions should encourage students to confront their opinions, assumptions, and (so-called) facts about their soon-to-be partner city. Structured in-class activities should tackle perceptions about the other culture in an open and supportive environment before virtual introductions to the other class. Working through biases and stereotypes in the internal setting alleviates potentially insensitive conversations with partners and identifies areas for later discussion; it also offers opportunities for significant growth in critical thinking and global sensitivity.

Let's begin by looking at an initial introduction between two different groups of students, in two very different parts of the world: Doha, Qatar, and Rochester, New York.

25 January: We faculty each watch the clock as we fumble – on opposite sides of the earth – with our video chat software, gathering our troops so that all students can be seen by the computer's built-in camera. We send some harried messages as we scramble to get the video image to work, while our students anxiously chatter in the background. We connect our computers to projectors in our respective classrooms so students can get a good look at each other, and suddenly, with a flash of blue light, we are connected.

Most of the students seem a bit shy to see and talk with each other for the first time, but there is often one outgoing personality who will break the ice and get everyone laughing. Each class has prepared one question for the other class, so the students take turns sitting right in front of the camera so they can be clearly seen and heard, and answer the other class' question – usually along the lines of "What's your favorite food?"

The students in Doha wonder why the American students look so tired. "It's 8 AM here," one of them explains. "And we had a LOT of work to do last night." The Doha students nod, relating to the universal travails of the university-level design student, and acknowledging the time difference. The students in Rochester can't believe their Doha counterparts are sitting around the conference table eating french fries! "We love all kinds of foods!" one of them explains. "We get these from the cafeteria on campus," another student tells the astonished Americans.

Introductions out of the way, the nervousness begins to subside and the students start chatting more casually about the sustainability topics they might explore together this semester. It's hard to hear over the din; with two excited classrooms talking simultaneously, and often with a little delay in the audio, but the enthusiasm is obvious. They've survived the test of first impressions, and everyone is relieved. Now, the real work can begin.

Collaborative projects involving intercultural team members require patience, openness, trust, and willingness to listen. When students initially begin a project together, they often experience a range of emotions from paralyzing intimidation to wild excitement. Because English is often the unifying language between the two classes, insecurity may increase anxiety or hesitation for some students, while others may jump at the opportunity to practice their conversation skills. More often than not, introductions bubble over with unfettered enthusiasm as students revel in the idea of connecting with designers in another part of the world and learning about their daily lives.

Beginning discussions that touch on personal interests help alleviate preliminary fears of collaborating with a stranger, but more importantly, a shared objective – such as a joint project – can serve as a bonding agent for team development. The unifying function of pairing teams through mutual goals is further amplified when team members share a similar design vocabulary, processes, and methodologies. Faculty who calibrate the overall tone of the exchange to include 'difference' (as a positive force for creativity) help set the stage for generative partnerships. Successful collaborations rely on equally committed partners who work to foster an atmosphere of trust and acceptance through teamwork. Confidence among teammates deepens further when students begin to see their partners as valuable contributors to their project development or success.

Communication: dialogue, critique and virtual tools

Whereas international partnerships increase respect for cultural diversity as a problem-solving tool, learning to cope with ambiguity and uncertainty is also part of the process. Miscommunications are a natural expectation due to differences in language, vocabulary, and nonverbal behaviors. Continuous communication is a vital ingredient to productive collaborations, but students can still become disenchanted by the process if not adequately supported through positive reinforcement. Although it is important to encourage students to communicate outside of class time, scheduling time for discussion within the course framework ensures dialogue will continue to evolve between partners. As intercultural design projects progress, it is the ongoing responsibility of the instructors to temper the ebb and flow of classroom dynamics through internal dialogue, particularly when students' attitudes and behaviors shift due to project complexity.

Although managing time differences is a continuous challenge in a cross-cultural learning environment, students who extend communication boundaries beyond asynchronous written communication are often more successful. Live virtual critiques can add positive pressure to the mix, and hold students accountable to their project progress. Depending on the time difference between countries and the maturity level of the students, a critique may feel one-sided if one partner initiates and the other does not reciprocate. In other cases, feedback is brief or superficial ("we like your idea, good job!"). Sometimes, this lack of in-depth feedback is due to students' fear of insulting their partners; faculty should reinforce the expectation of critical, yet *constructive* feedback as important. Students in both classes can also benefit from receiving feedback from another design instructor, but this may require faculty to share responsibilities across both classes to manage the workload.

A shared space for students to communicate and collaborate virtually, such as a Google+ community or a Slack private group, is a productive method for students to give and receive feedback on sustainability projects. Shared virtual spaces allow students to comment directly on visuals, but require project alignment to minimize the feeling of 'extra work.' 'Private' to the general public, yet freely accessible between the two collaborating classes, these virtual communities increase dialogue and critique between students. Email-based dialogue, on the other hand, should be used sparingly because it does not enable faculty oversight or hold students accountable for critical analysis.

Developing global perspectives: design projects and sustainability

University design curricula that incorporate intercultural design collaboration for sustainability into generalized and specialized courses set the stage for multifaceted design opportunities from many angles. Systems thinking, coping with ambiguity, critical analysis, and viewing problems from different perspectives are skills essential to all design students – and are the hallmarks of successful, team-oriented, twenty-first-century design practitioners. These competencies – particularly learning to see from a vastly different cultural perspective and learning to work productively with someone from another culture on sustainability challenges – will prove indispensable to participants in their professional design careers.

By working together to understand a sustainability problem from multiple viewpoints, students develop systems-based thinking and diverse problem-solving approaches. Shared socio-environmental topics deepen cultural exchange when students begin to understand how 'context' plays a vital role in human centered design research methodologies. In other words, while sustainability challenges are often context-specific, the 'international' perspective of one partner can directly contribute to the growth of the other. A motivational factor to help cross-cultural partners see a direct correlation between teamwork and project development is to encourage the whole group of students to start by exploring one particular topic, such as water sustainability. Based on the interests that emerge through this activity, pairs and teams will form to work together on design projects throughout the semester.

One initial activity is to ask students in both classes to examine their daily behaviors with a resource, such as water. From early morning rituals to late-night study sessions, students should document and analyze their various relationships with water using photography, video, illustration, and copious note taking. Not only is this activity useful for students to begin to understand themselves and their behaviors, but sharing their findings and insights with a partner from the other class prompts conversations about similarities and differences in each culture. Imagine, for example, the differences in how water is used and perceived in Rochester, New York, versus Doha, Qatar. In sharing their insights, students often stumble upon other relevant topics related to sustainability. After all, sustainability issues are interconnected.

Let's take a peek into the lives of two students – one located in Doha and the other in Rochester – and what they can learn from each other through a sustainability issue, such as water use:

> *Doha, 5 February: Ahmed turns off the alarm on his phone and reaches for the bottled water on his bedside table. After quickly showering and pulling on some clean clothes, he stops at the local mosque on his way to school for Salaat Al Fajr, making his obligatory ablutions before prayer. Climbing back into the car, he thinks it could use a wash to clean away the fine layer of sand built up over the past few days. His mind wanders as he drives to university while the sun rises higher in the sky. By the time he arrives at school, he has forgotten all about having the car washed and is now totally focused on what he'll grab for breakfast. On his way to his first class, he stops off at the campus Starbucks to get a mocha and a gooey pastry. He has to duck into the men's room to wash his hands. As he sips his coffee, he pulls out his laptop and uses his extra 10 minutes before class to make some final edits to the project he will be presenting that day.*
>
> *Eight hours later, in Rochester, NY: Eliza wakes to the smell of coffee that her roommate is brewing in their small campus apartment. She rolls out of bed, realizes she's almost late for class, runs her fingers through her hair, and grabs a clean sweatshirt out of the laundry basket – at least she hopes it's clean. Eliza never has time to put her clothes away after washing them in the dorm laundry facility, and sometimes gets her clean and dirty piles confused. Her roommate hands her a travel mug full of coffee as she makes her way through their tiny kitchen and assures her that she has already added milk and sugar. Eliza thanks her as she fills up her reusable water bottle from the kitchen sink and steps out the door. As she heads outside, she realizes it has snowed – quite a bit – and she ducks back in to grab some boots. As she shuffles across campus, she thinks at least the university ski club will be fun this weekend. It's always so much more fun to ski on real snow than the man-made stuff.*

Both of these students have many direct – and indirect – interactions with water in their day-to-day lives. From personal hygiene (or lack thereof, because they are college students) to transportation, water visibly impacts their lives in a variety of ways. Though students might discuss the cultural implications of Starbucks on a global scale, there is a larger conversation to be had around the virtual water content invested in the coffees both sleep-deprived students use to fuel their day. Ahmed would never dream of filling a reusable water bottle from the tap which spouts desalinated water, and Eliza would think twice before purchasing what, to her, is a pricey bottle of Evian. Whereas Ahmed's bottled water is an everyday necessity in Doha due to health concerns with desalinated water, Eliza probably does not think twice about where her tap water comes from or if she should be concerned about its quality.

In a discussion on the class's shared online community, both Eliza and Ahmed find they are interested in some of their parallel consumption behaviors – coffee, for example – which leads them to start considering food production as a potential topic for further research and design exploration. Consequently, these two will become a cross-cultural partnership. Two other students, Mariam in the Doha class and Peter in the Rochester class, are interested in local food consumption. The four decide that it might be a good idea for them to work as a larger team. Partnerships within the same geographic classroom are encouraged because daily interactions with a colocated peer support continued critical thinking, discovery and analysis. Although it is not a prerequisite for every design team, sophisticated problem solving and design development often occurs when cross-cultural teams also share partners within the same class.

Support from a student within the same class helps bridge the sometimes inconsistent communication that can occur with a cross-cultural partner due to logistical or interpersonal reasons. For instance, concern about language barriers coupled with a student's natural level of introversion may make an international partnership feel overwhelming to some participants. In these cases, teammates within the same class – with complimentary personality types – facilitate the cross-cultural aspect of the collaboration when students feel shy or fearful to engage. Partnerships with a colocated peer also help students understand and more gracefully manage the differences they may encounter when working with the other class. They serve as a sounding board for issues, but also prompt faster development of the essential interpersonal skills needed to succeed in the global discussion.

Let's examine a sample activity between two sets of international partners:

Doha, 10 April: Ahmed teams up with Mariam (from his Doha class), along with Eliza and Pete (two students in the Rochester classroom) to do the 'Sustainability Safari' activity. Armed with cameras, phones, notepads and a lot of curiosity, the pairs will hunt for a restaurant or vendor who serves local foods in their respective cities. Ahmed and Mariam aren't really sure where to begin; most of the restaurants they like serve food from different parts of the world, and they know that the climate and geology of Qatar make farming pretty difficult. After some discussion, Mariam asks her driver to take them to Souq Waqif, a market selling traditional goods and items from across the region. They are excited to find local dates, as well as camel milk chocolate! They record their interviews with the vendors using video and take lots of photos so they will have good documentation to share with Eliza and Pete in Rochester.

Rochester, 10 April: Meanwhile, Eliza and Pete set out to find local foods in Rochester. Pete initially suggests that they go to the place that created the first garbage plate, a well-known dish in Rochester. Eliza tries to explain to Pete that just because that particular dish is known locally, it is not necessarily made from food that is grown locally. They contemplate going to the Public Market downtown, but after some research they discover that much of the produce sold there is grown elsewhere and shipped to Rochester for resale. Neither of them has a car, so they get another friend from the class to drive them to one of the local farmers markets. They are both amazed at the amount of fruits and vegetables grown in the area, and so the students spend some time talking to farmers at a few of the booths. Eliza buys a smoothie from one of the vendors, and learns that most of the ingredients in it are local, and that the vendor also composts all of her leftover produce scraps! Eliza thinks this will be an interesting detail to share with Ahmed and Mariam.

As illustrated in this example, sustainability topics offer students the opportunity to expand their critical thinking and global awareness. By collectively examining two distinct cities, each facing different sustainability challenges, students begin to consider issues such as pollution, equity, and distribution from a wider perspective. Through project activities, students go on to learn a great deal more about each other as well as the sustainable features of their cities. All of this rich information will inform the projects they create together during the rest of the design collaboration.

Approaching sustainability in the classroom with international partners may seem like a daunting task, but the long-term benefits of preparing students for global stewardship far outweigh the challenges. In addition to expanding multicultural sensitivities, the openness of team members to the creative ideas of international partners often results in design outcomes surpassing original project objectives. For most students, regularly communicating with another designer is both motivational and stimulating. Shared interests or goals increase commitment to course content and inspire students to view issues from multiple perspectives.

By introducing another designer into the creative process, students begin to develop trust, resiliency, and adaptability as part of their design process. Intercultural design collaborations in sustainability support the idea that students have a stake in each other's success, and that successive rounds of design often result in stronger final outcomes. In addition to facilitating another's design journey, participants support their peers' growth in developing an enhanced set of interpersonal skills. Cultivating empathy and respect for different customs, habits and ideologies lead to more informed and fruitful design concepts. All of the experiences – benefits as well as challenges – better prepare students for a twenty-first-century working environment; wherein teamwork, adaptability, and communication are essential qualities to solving global sustainability challenges.

Activities

The following activities are intended to provide practical, easy-to-use approaches to intercultural collaboration in a broad range of design classrooms. These activities are among many examples that have served not only to bring students closer together, but also provoke discussion, stimulate thinking, and lead to new ideas in addressing global sustainability topics. Each activity brings new challenges and skills to light – for example, creating audience personas from first-person interviews is potentially a huge moment of cross-cultural sharing, understanding, and dialogue. For all activities, student-to-student communication is critical as they learn to engage in action research and share outcomes remotely with another design student.

The faculty's primary task is to integrate sustainability concepts into the core of each project, balancing intercultural learning experiences with quality design outcomes. Because faculty teach a range of courses that reflect varying levels of design development, activities incorporate ideas that respond to a variety of class needs, from foundation courses to graduate level. Similarly, because some courses enable more flexibility than others in learning outcomes or structure, projects can be tailored to different levels of involvement. All of these activities are starting points to which educators and students might add and invent new approaches, with the mutual goal of understanding – and perhaps improving – some of the world's most difficult sustainability challenges.

Activity 1: photography exchange

Project overview

Through a photographic journey, this assignment asks international partners to examine the environmental similarities and differences between their two cities. Guided by two oppositional concepts (such as 'natural' and 'man-made'), partners swap image collections to engender discussion, comparison, and analysis. The word pairing intends to highlight the contrasting features found within each city and provides partners with a relatable starting point. Students should gain an appreciation for the unique features of their surrounding environment, and experience a different landscape, through visual methodologies and dialogue with partners.

Guiding steps for students

> *Step 1, Photograph* – Using an assigned word-pair, photographically illustrate two contrasting concepts in your city. You and your partner will use the same word-pair to explore multiple facets of your cities, from beautiful green spaces to dilapidated signage.

Step 2, Take notes – Critically examine the influences of economy, commercialization, history, and culture on your city during the photographic process. Take notes to share with the class and your partner.

Step 3, Discuss – Share your collection of images and notes, along with 'new' thinking about your city with your partner. Compare and contrast the two cities verbally and visually, working to understand the critical influences that appear in the photography.

Note: The exchange of imagery and written elements can serve as a starting point for an extended design project, such as a poster project.

Project variation

A variation on the photography exchange project is to conduct an ethnographic photo-swap of a day-in-the-life; focusing on a specific sustainability topic, such as water. In this case, students should photograph all of their daily interactions with water, noting their water usage over a 24-hour period (including eating/drinking, kitchens, bathrooms, etc.). The resulting images and discussion should help students examine their personal water usage, compare findings with their partner, and provide a snapshot into one another's personal lives.

Although this variation of the project helps partners unpack their daily interactions with water, the images produced are generally not as aesthetically pleasing as in Variation 1. These images are often more of a documentary style and are imbued with more personal day-to-day elements, exposing unlikely photographic subjects (such as peoples' bathrooms and kitchens). To conduct the Variation 2 photography exchange, replace step 1 with 'daily water usage' and follow steps 2 through 4 for the intercultural exchange making sure to focus on the idea of 'water' as opposed to 'city' as the point of comparison between partners.

Activity 2: poster pairs

Project overview

This project examines the sustainability successes of two partnering cities and uses positive reinforcement (elicited through the notion of 'success') to encourage sustainable behavior. Students will use posters to promote a sustainability-related event (real or fictional) in their home city, as well as create a version for the partnering city. By incorporating the creation of personas into the project, students develop cultural insights into another country. This project helps students learn what has been successful in other cities regarding sustainability initiatives and asks them to consider how they might apply the idea to their own city. Students also learn how different audiences and cultures require different communication tactics by creating a poster for the partnering city. The benefits of this project may be more evident in the long-term, as students begin to adapt their critical thinking lenses to evaluate their surroundings based on discussions and exchanges with cross-cultural partners.

Guiding steps for students

Step 1, Research – Conduct research about a sustainability initiative happening in your city. Photograph the location, interview people involved, and write a brief description about the initiative (at least two paragraphs). Connect your research with a real or fictional event in your city to promote in a poster format.

Step 2, Share – Share the visual and anecdotal research with your cross-cultural partner and take notes about his/her initiative and event.

Step 3, Persona – Create two audience personas (based on your interviews during the research phase) to share with your cross-cultural partner. Personas are characterizing descriptions of 'users' from your own culture who will eventually view and interpret your posters. In your description of the character, focus on the individual's behaviors, motivations, interests, and needs, as well as his/her attitude toward sustainability. Make sure to provide your partner with additional cultural insight and nuance BEYOND initial features described in your personas. You and your partner will use the collection of personas to design two posters, one for each city.

Step 4, Design – Showcase a sustainability-related event by developing two posters; one poster for each city. The first poster will focus on an event in your city and should appeal to an audience that is disengaged from the sustainability movement (perhaps feeling hopeless or that 'change' is not possible). The second poster should shift to account for your cross-cultural partner's personas in order to meet the needs of their unique context.

Phase 2

If there is time, a 'design-remix' embedded within the poster pairs project can deepen intercultural competencies. The process involves students working independently on a poster; passing initial efforts off to the cross-cultural partner; working with the poster they received, and then passing the poster back to the original maker.

Step 6, Remix-Round 1 – Hand over your initial poster files to your cross-cultural partner and, at the same time, collect your files from your partner. Develop the posters further taking into account the personas developed by your partner. Keep in mind that trusting someone to work with, and even drastically change your ideas and design files, is an important lesson to learn as a designer. This happens all the time in professional practice; it is good to get used to the process now.

Step 7, Re-Remix-Round 2 – Send the updated files back to your cross-cultural partner, and collect your own updated files. Conduct another round of updates, refining the ideas with one last round of careful design decisions. Time permitting, files can be exchanged for subsequent rounds of design/edits.

Step 8, Exhibit – Share final outcomes with partners and display all posters in an exhibition context to promote the sustainability initiatives of both cities.

Activity 3: sustainability safari

Project overview

This project explores how to shift negative feelings associated with socio-environmental concerns into proposals that urge appropriation of sustainable practices. The aim of the project is threefold: first, for students to come away with a better understanding of their emotional responses to social or environmental concerns they encounter within their city. Second, to examine the interrelationship of design with sustainability through hands-on exploration, synthesis, and brainstorming. Finally, to generate a collection of relevant input to share with community leaders who are instrumental in improving each city's sustainable development agenda.

Guiding steps for students

Step 1, Research – Within each class, create mind-maps about the topic of sustainability. Discuss and share ideas, paying attention to the emotions evoked by social, environmental, and economic concerns. How do certain themes make you feel? What ideas make you feel disenchanted by the notion of sustainable practices? Or empowered to make change? Based on the emerging discussions, create small working groups around a particular sustainable challenge.

Step 2, Safari – Based on mutual interests of the working groups formed in step 1, investigate a sustainability challenge outside of the classroom in the form of an urban 'safari.'

For example:

- find an item for sale that was produced locally
- find a locally owned and operated business
- find a restaurant or vendor who serves local foods
- find an example of creative reuse or upcycling
- find a green space in the city (e.g., park, landscaping, footpath, etc.)
- use public transportation, walking, or cycling as a method to get from point a to b

Step 3, Ethnography – Engage in mobile ethnography, recording all your experiences through notes, photos, videos, sketches, etc. Carefully monitor and record your emotional states during different phases of the project (e.g., fear when getting on a public bus and realizing that there's no route map; excitement when ordering a local dish from a street vendor).

Step 4, Synthesize – Returning to the classroom, visualize and synthesize notes from the experience following a service design methodology, including techniques such as journey mapping and mental modeling. Share your findings with your partner. Conduct a comparative analysis of sustainable behaviors and systems between your city and your partner's city. Together with your partner, indicate opportunities for design intervention(s). Consider the individual emotional responses to the activity, along with the locations best suited for the potential intervention(s).

Step 4, Develop – Present findings within the two classes and collect critical feedback from global partners outside of the individual partnership. Through cocreative brainstorming, groups should respond to the feedback and develop their design recommendations and finalize the proposal.

Step 5, Present – Share final proposals in the form of visual presentations to invited university and community leaders. Each group should describe the sustainability challenge, research process, emotional states, and proposals for design intervention(s). Highlight the differences between the two cities, indicate how proposals meet the needs of each unique context, and discuss how partners influenced concept development.

Activity 4: sustainable city visual narrative

Project overview

The purpose of this project is to facilitate discussion, exploration, and creativity within cross-cultural teams who share a mutual interest in a sustainability topic. The project works best when students are communicating not only with their cross-cultural partner(s) but also when they have peer support within their home class. Based on the shared sustainability interest, students identify a location in their city to document with video, audio, photography, and notes while discussing their findings with cross-cultural partners. After comparing and contrasting each city, cross-cultural partners brainstorm together to develop visual narratives that function as stand-alone pieces, but also link together thematically as a series when shown together. In other words, the project requires cohesion across the group of narratives, yet also enables students to generate individual portfolio pieces. By encouraging collaborative practice, this experience helps cross-cultural teams take initiative, cultivate leadership skills, and learn together. Students of all levels benefit from connecting with design students from another culture, as well as building transdisciplinary connections that could continue to serve them at the university level.

Guiding steps for students

Step 1, Determine – Begin by determining a personal sustainability interest that you are passionate about and want to explore in your city. Choose cross-cultural partners based on the mutual interest and discuss how sustainability practices occur (or are needed) in each country.

Step 2, Locate – Identify a location in your city that pertains to your team's sustainability interests and also lends itself to good cinematography. Document your chosen location with video, audio, photography, and notes. Present your findings to your cross-cultural partner(s), making sure to explain culturally specific details (such as your transportation method or historic details about the particular area of the city).

Step 3, Brainstorm – Your task is to create a cohesive series of time-based visual narratives about your group's sustainability interest. Although each member will develop their own stand-alone visual narrative, the series produced by the group must demonstrate cohesiveness. This may occur stylistically, typographically, or in some other manner. Work together as an intercultural team to brainstorm ideas about ways to create cohesion for the series and finalize your approach before beginning to storyboard your individual narrative.

Step 4, Storyboard – Your goal is to convey a message and/or communicate a story about your sustainability interest to a diverse audience in both countries (your country and your partner's country). Create a storyboard to outline the sequences of shots and return to your original location to pinpoint ideal lighting for film and photography.

Step 5, Develop – Create a visual narrative through a time-based design medium by integrating video, images, and text into sequential motion. The final outcome should be self-communicative, meaning that it should speak for itself and clearly communicate ideas about your topic. The piece should make the audience want to learn more, question their behaviors, or peak their curiosity about sustainability in both cities.

Step 6, Critique – Present in-progress work within the two classes and collect critical feedback from global partners outside of the individual partnership. Groups should respond to the feedback and finalize individual narratives, while considering the cohesiveness of the series.

Step 7, Present! – Together with your cross-cultural team members, present your series to both classes and invited guests using virtual tools. Bring popcorn and discuss the benefits and challenges of working together on a mutual interest in a sustainability topic.

References

Blair-Early, A. (2010) "Beyond Borders: Participatory Design Research and the Changing Role of Design" *Visible Language, 44*, 207–218.

Canniffe, B. J. (2011) "Designing in and for Communities: Breaking Institutional Barriers and Engaging Design Students in Meaningful and Relevant Projects" *Iridescent: Icograda Journal of Design Research*, 1, 202–215.

Chick, Anne and Micklethwaite, Paul (2011) *Design for Sustainable Change*. Switzerland: AVA Publishing.

Friedman, K. (2012) "Models of Design: Envisioning a Future Design Education" *Visible Language*, 46, 132–153.

Heller, S. and Talarico, L. (2011) "An Education Manifesto for Icograda" *Icograda Design Education Manifesto*, 82–85.

Hofstede, Geert (2003) *Culture's Consequences: Comparing Values, Behaviors, Institutions and Organizations Across Nations*. Thousand Oaks, CA: SAGE Publications.

Hunt, J. (2011) "Icograda Design Education Manifesto" *Icograda Design Education Manifesto*, 86–89.

Katzenbach, Jon R. and Smith, Douglas K. (2015) *The Wisdom of Teams: Creating the High-Performance Organization*. Boston, MA: Harvard Business Press.

Klebnikov, S. (6 July 2015) "What Employers Are Looking for When Hiring Recent College Grads" *Forbes* (www.forbes.com/sites/sergeiklebnikov/2015/07/06/what-employers-are-looking-for-when-hiring-recent-college-grads/#2fbc7add21e5).

Murdoch-Kitt, K. and Emans, D. (2015) "Experiential Elements of High-to-Low-Context Cultures" *LearnxDesign: 3rd International Conference for Design Education Researchers*, 3, 1301–1318.

Norman, D. (15 March 2010) "Why Design Education Must Change" (www.core77.com/posts/17993/why-design-education-must-change-17993).

Papanek, Victor (2005) *Design for the Real World: Human Ecology and Social Change*. Chicago: Chicago Review Press.

Parker, Glen M. (1990) *Team Players and Teamwork: The New Competitive Business Strategy*. San Francisco, CA: Jossey-Bass.

Patton, B. R. and Downs, T. M. (2003) *Decision-Making Group Interaction: Achieving Quality* (4th ed.). Boston: Pearson Education.

Rosen, E. (2009) *The Culture of Collaboration: Maximizing Time, Talent and Tools to Create Value in the Global Economy*. San Francisco: Red Ape Publishing.

Sawyer, K. (2007) *Group Genius: The Creative Power of Collaboration*. New York: Basic Books.

Tharp, T. (2009) *The Collaborative Habit*. New York: Simon & Schuster.

Whyte, J. and Bessant, J. (2007) "Making the Most of UK Design Excellence: Equipping UK Designers to Succeed in the Global Economy" Innovation Studies Centre, Tanaka Business School, Imperial College, London.

United Nations. "The Sustainable Development Agenda" (www.un.org/sustainabledevelopment/development-agenda/).

12

LIFE-CYCLE THINKING AND SUSTAINABLE DESIGN FOR EMERGING CONSUMER ELECTRONIC PRODUCT SYSTEMS

Erinn G. Ryen, Callie W. Babbitt and Alex Lobos

Introduction

Rapid globalization and technological innovation has created a consumption conundrum: increasing production and consumption of goods and services has the potential to improve worldwide economic development and quality of life, but often at the cost of overextending natural resources and damaging global ecosystems. Rapid proliferation of consumer electronic products is a prime example of this challenge. In 2015, global spending on electronics was estimated to exceed $1 trillion by the Consumer Technology Association. This investment in digital infrastructure has created significant expansion in social and economic systems. For example, "smart" appliances and electric grids hold promise for resource conservation and climate change mitigation (Graedel and Allenby 2010). In developed economies, electronic products are the backbone of innovation and foster the transition to knowledge economies (Dutta and Mia 2009). Deploying electronics globally has also been transformative in developing and middle-income economies, as a factor in achieving Sustainable Development Goals: ending poverty, enabling quality education, and fostering economic growth (Batchelor et al. 2003).

Though advancement and abundance of electronic products worldwide has revolutionized business and society, it has also created unprecedented sustainability challenges. During their production, use, and disposal, these devices – computers, smartphones, televisions, etc. – have environmental, social, and human health impacts that must be balanced against their potential sustainability benefits. Similarly, as design efforts are enacted to minimize the environmental footprint of electronic products, new trade-offs may emerge. Therefore, it is necessary to consider how consumer electronics contribute to environmental impacts from a "life-cycle" perspective. This chapter provides an overview of the environmental, social, and economic trade-offs that span the life cycle of consumer electronics and describes how design strategies seek to address these challenges. However, it also must be recognized that existing design approaches may not suffice as electronics increase their evolutionary trajectory toward embedded, convergent, multi-functional devices and as these products continue to transform how we live, work, and play. Thus, the chapter also highlights nascent opportunities to leverage user-oriented sustainable design to create greater benefits while reducing environmental risks.

Figure 12.1 Representative life cycle of a consumer electronic.

The life cycle of consumer electronics: environmental, social, and economic challenges and opportunities

A product life cycle is traditionally thought of as a linear system: extracting and refining raw materials, manufacturing parts and components, packaging and transporting the final product, using the product over its life span, and then ultimately managing it at end-of-life, whether by disposal or by closing the resource loop with reuse or recycling (Figure 12.1). Life cycle thinking provides a systematic approach to quantifying resource limitations and environmental impacts of the processes that occur along this entire chain. Further, taking a life cycle perspective can offer unexpected insights into the environmental "hot spots" or problem areas for a product that can then be targeted for design improvements. In the sections that follow, key environmental issues spanning the consumer electronic product life cycle are detailed.

Resource extraction and refinement

The first step in producing consumer electronics is *resource extraction*, wherein raw materials and minerals are extracted from nature, and then processed, refined, transformed, or combined with other materials to create the building blocks of our products (i.e., parts and components) (OTA 1992; Matthews et al. 2015). For example, resources like crude oil and metal ores are removed from the Earth and then processed further to produce the plastics, metals, ceramics, semiconductors, and composites used in electronics. In most cases, these raw materials are taken from "primary" sources: virgin raw materials extracted directly from nature, rather than from "secondary" sources, or recycled material streams.

Electronic devices are composed of a diverse set of materials, including up to 60 elements (UNEP 2009). Electronics are largely comprised of bulk materials like plastics, aluminum, steel, copper, and glass (Widmer et al. 2005; Oguchi et al. 2011), but they also contain low concentrations of toxic substances (lead, arsenic, mercury) (Widmer et al. 2005), high value materials like precious metals (gold, silver, platinum) (Widmer et al. 2005; Chancerel et al. 2009; UNEP 2009; Oguchi et al. 2011), critical and scarce materials (e.g., indium, cobalt, gallium), and rare earth elements (neodymium, praseodymium, cerium) (Chancerel et al. 2013; Sprecher et al. 2014). The diversity of materials needed has implications at this stage, but as well as for how the product is potentially recycled (see the section on End of Life).

The geographic location and manner in which we extract and refine raw materials for use in electronic components are associated with numerous social and environmental impacts. A key example is gold, which is commonly used in electroplating and wire bonding of electrical components, particularly on the printed circuit boards (PCBs) that are ubiquitous to electronics (Goodman 2002; Wang and Gaustad 2012). Following increased demand, gold prices rose three-fold from 1995 to 2015, going from $386 to $1,170 per troy ounce (USGS 2000; 2016). In 2015, 37% of domestic gold consumption was used for electrical and electronic devices (USGS 2016), as compared to 4% in 1999 (USGS 2000).

The demand for gold and other metals, though providing significant economic benefits for mature and developing countries, has increased pressures on developing countries to develop mineral deposits, which are often adjacent to ecologically sensitive areas or poverty stricken regions (Reed and Miranda 2007). For example, small-scale or artisanal mining of gold in developing nations like Ghana is an important sector in local economy (Obiri et al. 2016), as it has been a central industrial activity for over 200 years (Aryee et al. 2003; Obiri et al. 2016). The socioeconomic benefits of gold mining are not without trade-offs: for example, residents who cede farm lands to the mining companies reduce their ability to improve their livelihood with farming (Obiri et al. 2016). In one instance, residents of the Tarkwa mining area in Ghana, laid off from the gold mines, participated in illegal mining activities to maintain their livelihoods (Obiri et al. 2016).

Further, without adequate policy oversight, negative social impacts from mining activities includes displacement of people, prostitution, alcoholism, and social and political unrest (Reed and Miranda 2007). The term "conflict minerals" has been used to identify mineral resources being extracted from regions like the Democratic Republic of Congo (DRC), where ongoing civil conflict is closely tied to mining activities and the resulting corruption, poverty, and land use disputes in the region (Figure 12.2). In addition to gold, tin, tungsten, and tantalum are typically classified as conflict minerals, all of which are used in the production of consumer electronics (Fitzpatrick et al. 2015).

In addition to socioeconomic impacts, mining metals like gold has resulted in adverse impacts to the environment and health of communities in developing countries. Mining can result in toxic substances being leached into the ground and surface water and accidental releases to the surface water from tailings dam breaches (UNEP 2013). Gold mining activities have been associated with surface water impacts such as uncontrolled releases of cyanide and acid mine drainage into water bodies, as well as levels of arsenic, manganese, lead, cadmium, and mercury exceeding permissible global guidelines (Obiri et al. 2016). Land impacts from mining activities include piles of waste, excavation pits becoming a breeding ground for mosquitos, and the destruction of agriculture land (Aryee et al. 2003). In addition to the local environmental, social, and health impacts, the processes involved with the mining and refinement of metals is a very

Figure 12.2 Often, gold mines in the Congo are filled with child miners such as Patrice, 15, who started working at this mine when he was eight years old.

By Image Journeys, Sasha Lezhnev. CC BY-ND 2.0.

energy intensive process, and as a whole, these activities consume 8% of the global energy supply (UNEP 2013).

Beyond precious metals like gold, a growing concern is the use of critical metals and rare earth elements in electronics (Chancerel et al. 2013) both because of their potential scarcity and the economic impacts that may result if supply limitations occur (Alonso et al. 2012; Bustamante et al. 2014). Currently, China controls nearly all the production of the rare earth elements (Jacoby, and Jiang 2010). Due to the geographic limit to supplies of rare earth metals, electronics supply chains are vulnerable to disruptions, which if one occurred, could have a rippling impact on global prices and demand, similar to how civil and political unrest in Zaire in the late 1970s disrupted the global cobalt supply (Alonso et al. 2007; Bustamante et al. 2014). Thus, having a secure and stable supply of these materials is important to the downstream product manufacturing stage.

Component and product manufacturing

In the manufacturing stage, raw materials are combined with energy, water, and other materials to form components and to assemble final products. The microchips or integrated circuits (ICs) contained in all electronics are one of the most important components to consider because of their environmental significance. ICs are fabricated on small semiconductor dies, for which the manufacturing process consumes high volumes of water (approximately 17 liters per square centimeter of semiconductor), etchants, dopants, photolithographic chemicals, acids/bases, semiconductor-grade silicon, elemental gases, and energy from electricity and direct fossil fuel use (Williams et al. 2002; Williams 2004). In large part, the energy intensive nature of this process derives from the high purity and high volume of chemicals required in semiconductor grade materials (about 280 kilograms of chemicals per kilogram of input silicon, Williams et al. 2002). Additional energy is used during the purification of chemicals and gases during semiconductor manufacturing (Williams 2011). Energy consumption from fossil fuel use in turn leads to broader environmental impacts, such as greenhouse gas emissions (GHG), natural resource depletion, acid rain, and ecotoxicity (Huijbregts et al. 2006; Kok et al. 2006). Health concerns during manufacturing include worker exposure to chemicals during the semiconductor fabrication process (Williams 2004; Williams 2011). Though the evidence is mixed, a literature review suggests that semiconductor fabrication processes may enhance worker risk for cancers such as hematologic malignancy, brain tumors, and breast cancer, in addition to reproduction abnormalities and dermatologic and respiratory problems (Kim et al. 2014).

Beyond semiconductor fabrication, the production of other components and the final assembly of electronic products are also energy intensive. For example, manufacturing a single laptop computer requires between 3,000 and 4,000 megajoules of primary energy and emits about 250 kg CO_2, which is roughly equivalent to the greenhouse gas emissions from driving 600 miles in an average passenger vehicle (Deng et al. 2011; U.S. EPA 2016). It is positive to note that over time, production efficiencies can result in lower product environmental footprints, particularly for mature technologies, like computers or printers, resulting in reduced energy and carbon emission impacts (Ryen et al. 2015). Similarly, technological innovations and decreasing costs have driven up computing efficiency (in computations per kilowatt-hour) for all electronic devices; roughly doubling every 1.5 years from 1946 to 2009 (Koomey et al. 2011). However, a *rebound effect* is often observed, whereby these efficiency gains translate to reduced costs leading manufacturers to add functionality and consumers to increase consumption, rather than to a net decrease in environmental impact (Deng and Williams 2011; Kasulaitis et al. 2015).

Product use

Whereas significant impacts occur upstream, the phase when products are actively used by consumers is often the one that receives the greatest attention. During the use phase, when consumers watch TV, send texts, or surf the Internet, energy consumption creates a significant environmental impact. As technology advances, use of electronic devices becomes an integral part of modern society and everyday living, influencing how we communicate, pay bills, read books, shop, work, watch television programming, exercise, play, and very soon even drive our cars. This social transformation coincides with demand for increased product functionality, and often results in increased energy use that leads to negative environmental outcomes. Globally, energy production is largely dominated by combustion of fossil fuels, including coal, natural gas, and petroleum. Not only are fossil-based technologies highly inefficient at converting primary energy resources into electrical energy, they are also extremely harmful to the environment, resulting in GHG, acid rain, smog forming, and toxic emissions.

At an individual product level, electronic devices themselves are becoming more efficient, particularly by the implementation of Energy Star efficiency standards for low power standby modes (Brown et al. 2002; Roth and McKenney 2007). Typically, trends indicate that after new products are introduced, their energy intensity declines over time as the technology matures. For example, the energy impact from the use of well-established mature technologies (e.g., desktop computers, basic mobile phones, cathode ray tube TV) has decreased about 31% per product since the early 1990s (Ryen et al. 2015). However, whereas the devices themselves are becoming more efficient, the net energy impact has actually grown, which is attributable to two key factors. First, consumers do not purchase and own a single product, but rather they accumulate multiple devices. In 2010, residential consumers in the United States had over three and a half televisions, four and a half phones (basic and smart), and two cameras per household, not to mention the many other devices used for communication and entertainment purposes (Ryen et al., 2014). Second, not only has the number of products in an average household more than doubled between 1990 and 2010 (CEA 2008; 2010), the number of available functions overall has similarly increased, whereby added functionality often translates to greater power consumption and time in use. From the early 1990s to the late 2000s, the average active power mode per device increased 38% (Ryen et al. 2015).

Actual consumer use of devices has also confounded energy efficiency attempts. For example, about 50% of the U.S. population only watches television one hour per day, but a small fraction of heavy watchers (the 14% who view almost eight hours of TV per day), actually consume 34% of all the energy associated with TV use (Sekar et al. 2016). Energy use in electronic products is driven by two issues: the power demanded for operation in a given mode (off, on, standby) and the time spent using the device in that mode. Unfortunately, not all of the energy consumed in watching TV or using computers is associated with the most energy efficient devices. Older, outdated models that have been repurposed in children's rooms, basements, and attics can also drive up energy consumption over time (Ryen et al. 2015). Added functionality also drives energy use up, requiring greater innovation aimed at changing consumer behavior to minimize time in use. In addition, consumption continues to increase for mobile devices powered by rechargeable lithium-ion batteries. In these devices, overcharging and undercharging a battery can reduce the life of the battery (Hill 2015; Keating 2015), leading to unnecessary energy consumption.

End of life: reuse, recycling, and disposal

Due to the rapidly shortening product innovation cycles, devices are being replaced at an increasing pace (Williams and Hatanaka, 2005; Babbitt et al. 2009). Unfortunately, increasing product ownership, decreasing product life span, and shortened innovations cycles have led to an increasing number and type of products entering the waste stream each year. Obsolete devices like computers, TVs, mobile phones, and appliances are referred to as e-waste (Robinson 2009). Predicting the volume of e-waste generation is complicated and depends on product life spans and technological innovations, but it is expected to continue to rise as economies mature and technologies expand (Robinson 2009). Yang and Williams (2009) forecasted that 92 to 107 million computers would reach obsolescence in the United States by 2020. E-waste is also believed to the fastest growing waste stream in Europe (Khetriwal et al. 2009), although these estimates will be outpaced quickly in developing economies as product adoption expands worldwide.

The social, economic, and environmental impacts in this end-of-life (or EOL) phase center on the management of resources and waste. As noted earlier, a linear product life cycle ends with disposal and management of the resulting waste (OTA 1992). Only recently have more circular strategies been employed to recoup embedded materials and embodied energy in products through recycling, reuse, or repurposing (Ellen MacArthur Foundation 2013). However, closing the loop on EOL electronic products faces a number of economic, social, and environmental barriers, both for formal and informal management systems.

Formal e-waste management systems

Formal e-waste management encompasses recycling, reuse, and disposal activities that take place within the bounds of applicable laws and use appropriate and safe material handling and treatment systems to minimize emissions of harmful chemicals and protect human health. For example, literature review (Williams et al. 2008) suggests the risk of heavy metal (lead and mercury) emissions from sanitary landfills in formal waste management systems results in minimal risk, due to the existing leachate capture and control systems. However, landfill is a less preferable option for e-waste management, as it results in a loss of all material, energy, and value originally put into the product in the material extraction and manufacturing stages. Reuse, on the other hand, retains the energy and material values embodied in the product (Manomaivibool 2009) and may create socioeconomic opportunities. For example, official trading of obsolete computers in some countries like Peru appears to be driven by reuse markets rather than recycling activities (Kahhat and Williams 2009). Device reuse extends a product's life span, which has been noted as a strategy to lower the net life cycle energy impact (Deng et al. 2011). Formal reuse activities also provide a source of jobs and enable economic and social development by enhancing education, fostering businesses, and diminishing the digital divide (Williams et al. 2008).

Although formal recycling systems only can recoup about 10% of the initial energy invested in manufacturing consumer electronics (Deng et al. 2011), this is a necessary avenue for products that become outdated and functionally obsolete. Even reused products will ultimately require downstream recycling when no useful life remains. Formal recycling systems create social benefits directly through jobs and local income from material recovery (UNEP 2009), and indirectly by displacing virgin raw material extraction in socially vulnerable regions. Environmental benefits of recycling are associated with recovering valuable and useful materials (Robinson 2009), potentially up to 95% of materials from a computer and 45% from a cathode ray tube monitor (Ladou and Lovegrove, 2008) with relatively low environmental impacts compared to primary material production (Aizawa et al. 2008; UNEP 2009). By keeping the materials in productive use, countries are able to reach new goals of achieving a circular economy (Ellen MacArthur Foundation 2013). Finally, formal recycling systems are critical to enhancing domestic supply chains of scarce and critical metals, thus reducing supply chain risks and vulnerability to sources in other countries (Chancerel et al. 2013).

Informal e-waste management systems

In contrast, informal reuse, recycling, and recovery operations may also create benefits and impacts, but they are far more challenging to manage, as they are typically associated with illegal imports and exports of nonreusable electronics that are recycled using inefficient technologies with no environmental or worker health and safety controls. Although there is concern that only a small portion of obsolete electronics is actually reused, some countries like India have a viable repair and reuse market for products and components due to the low labor wages (Manomaivibool 2009). Electronics are critical educational and economic tools, so reuse activities (by extending the product life span) in developing countries enable the access to technology (Williams et al. 2008). Informal reuse and recycling activities benefit poorer countries by creating "backyard" industries that recover precious metals and provide sources of income (Williams 2008; 2011).

These benefits are not without significant costs. Whereas toxic materials found in electronic products (lead, arsenic, mercury) are not of concern during the use phase, their uncontrolled releases into the land, air, and water during informal processing result in negative human health and environmental impacts (Figure 12.3). Informal recycling practices rely on primitive methods like open burning of plastic cables to recover copper wiring or high concentration acid leaching to recover precious metals in a printed circuit board (Manomaivibool 2009). The resulting emissions of heavy metals, acid residue, dioxins, furans, and particulate matter lead to adverse health impacts in workers and even children living or working in the area (Ladou and Lovegrove, 2008; Williams et al. 2008). Numerous field studies in regions with informal recycling processes have been conducted

Figure 12.3   Dismantling electronic waste in New Delhi, India.
By Matthias Feilhauer, Thousandways. CC BY 2.0.

in Guiyu, China, which have found soil contamination like polybrominated diphenyl ethers (Wang et al. 2005) and polycyclic aromatic hydrocarbons (Yu et al. 2006). In addition to land impacts, high concentrations of heavy metals (cadmium, copper, lead, and zinc) have been found in the surface water (Wong et al. 2007) and fine particles in the air (Deng et al. 2006). Health impacts have been noted with elevated level of brominated flame retardants in workers (Bi et al. 2007) and elevated lead levels in the blood of children in the Guiyu area (Huo et al. 2007). Though originally a concern in a few isolated regions in China, the potential impact of informal e-waste disposal is now a global concern, with informal export and management taking place around the world.

Current design solutions for improving the sustainability of consumer electronics

Given the complex environmental challenges that span the entire life cycle of consumer electronics, it is clear that sustainable solutions must also apply this holistic perspective and map onto the product life cycle at the point where the greatest benefit can be achieved. It is also critical to be able to identify, measure, and reduce the environmental repercussions of electronics at early stages of the product life cycle, which places a particular responsibility on product designers to be proactive in seeking sustainable alternatives to environmentally harmful incumbent materials and technologies.

Environmentally and socially responsible material selection

Reducing the environmental and social impacts of material extraction and enhancing the ultimate recyclability of an electronic product both hinge on selecting appropriate materials to comprise the diverse parts and components within consumer electronics. Design efforts to select environmentally benign materials have largely been driven by regulatory initiatives to eliminate hazardous compounds from electronic products and thereby reduce the potential for these materials to be released if the product if disposed or recycled without appropriate environmental and safety controls. The European Union's Restriction of Hazardous Substances (RoHS) Directive plays a major role in this domain, as it limits use of specific hazardous substances in electronics (e.g., lead, mercury, cadmium, hexavalent chromium, and several flame retardants). Similarly, growing attention to conflict minerals and sustainable material supply chains has led to regulations and industry initiatives to account for how and where metals used in electronics are sourced. For example, the Dodd-Frank Act of 2010 (United States) requires that companies publicly report their use of conflict minerals obtained in or near the Democratic Republic of Congo.

Companies like the social entrepreneurship firm Fairphone have created initiatives aimed at sourcing responsibly mined materials for their eponymous smartphone (Figure 12.4A) and improving social conditions in mining regions. Material selection has also been emphasized as an opportunity to minimize impacts from manufacturing electronics by extending life span and encouraging users' emotional attachment to their products. For example, the iameco personal computer (Figure 12.4B) demonstrates the use of durable steel supports coupled with Forest Stewardship Council Certified hardwood to create a chassis that is long-lasting, easy to repair

Figure 12.4A Fairphone.
Photo by Till Westermayer, Creative Commons.

Figure 12.4B iameco computer designed for small-medium enterprises.
Photo by Artyom Schetnikov, Public Domain.

or return to a like-new finish, and visually attractive and engaging to users, intended to create product loyalty and extend replacement cycles (Fitzpatrick et al. 2014; Hickey et al. 2014).

Implementing sustainable material selection strategies is often confounded in the design stage due to the lack of information provided to designers to enable comparisons that adequately balance life cycle considerations. As a result, design tools have been developed in an attempt to streamline this process (see comprehensive review by Leal-Yepes, 2013). For example, the Electronic Product Environmental Assessment Tool (EPEAT) created by the Green Electronics Council provides a scoring rubric where specific electronic product categories (computers, displays, televisions, and printers) are numerically rated based on a suite of criteria, including compliance with the RoHS directive, elimination of known hazardous materials, and inclusion of renewable, bio-based, and recycled content materials. More in-depth design tools built on analytical or software platforms (e.g., AutoCAD, Solidworks) also provide capability to assess material selection using formal Life-cycle Assessment (LCA) methodology. These software tools often link to life cycle databases that provide comprehensive information about embodied energy, toxicity, greenhouse gases, and recyclability of materials selected for electronic product manufacturing. When coupled with 3-D models, these tools can be leveraged to quantify life cycle trade-offs of multiple material alternatives in the design phase.

Life span extension and energy efficient product use

The life cycle environmental footprint of consumer electronics clearly shows that the greatest impacts occur either during product manufacturing or use (Deng et al., 2011; Ryen et al. 2015), underscoring the need to radically improve these life cycle stages. However, the product designer often has limited ability to influence upstream manufacturing processes (e.g., silicon wafer fabrication) or downstream consumer behavior. Moreover, manufacturing design strategies to reduce energy consumption can be negated by consumer behavior. Thus, design interventions have to balance both life cycle priorities and the designer's scope of influence. Key opportunities exist, however, to indirectly enhance environmental performance by creating products that are used longer or directly improve device performance with reduced energy consumption.

Extending product life span has three key facets: (1) designing a product that is physically durable and likely to withstand use over long periods; (2) ensuring that a product is repairable and upgradable to keep technology current to meet evolving demands; and (3) ensuring that a user will continue to want the product, even if new models are available. Ideal strategies are those that address each of these goals at the same time. For example, using timeless, durable materials like aluminum or steel for product housing eliminates the likelihood that a user may change preference in color or pattern (i.e., compared to painted plastics) and increases the ability to maintain and refurbish the device's appearance and functionality. A product that is upgradable is one that has clear, easy access to the most vulnerable components and for which information is provided for users to perform needed maintenance and repair. If a user gains the experience of repairing their own device and invests time and money into its upkeep, they are also more likely to continue using it as long as it technically meets their needs, as opposed to purchasing a replacement. Standardization is a critical strategy in design for life span extension, including use of standard connectors and fasteners to access internal component) and consistency and uniformity in connectors and power supplies (particularly between multiple generation of the same product) (Rifer and Brody-Heine 2009).

Modularity has also emerged as a strategy for life span extension. Project Ara is a mobile phone concept by Google and Motorola in which phones are viewed as a system of interchangeable components (rather than as a single product) that can be chosen and assembled based on the interest and preferences of the user (Pierce 2016). The phone has a skeleton that hosts basic functionality (Figure 12.5). From there, individual users select the modules that they need in order to obtain a phone that fulfills their needs. With this model, there is no unused technology and each component is easy to replace or upgrade without having to dispose of the entire device. Modular concepts may ultimately promote a closed loop and lead to circular economies wherein components can be easily replaced and be sent back to their manufacturers. For the end user there is significant satisfaction and potential emotional attachment in putting together a mobile device that is truly customized.

While life span extension can reduce the initial environmental investment during manufacturing, continuing to use less efficient devices can create unintended consequences, particularly if newer models have enough of an efficiency gain to offset the added energy required for their production (Gutowski et al. 2011). While this scenario is rare for consumer electronics, it is a motivator to couple life span extension strategies with energy efficiency solutions. Technological approaches to energy efficiency focus on reducing the power demand when the product is in active or standby modes and enably automatic power savings modes and features. Product labeling, as commonly seen for the Energy Star program, communicates the energy and cost savings to consumers to influence decisions at the point of sale. As consumers increasingly purchase battery-powered mobile devices, use phase energy efficiency largely depends on specifying robust battery systems that have higher capacity and longer life spans.

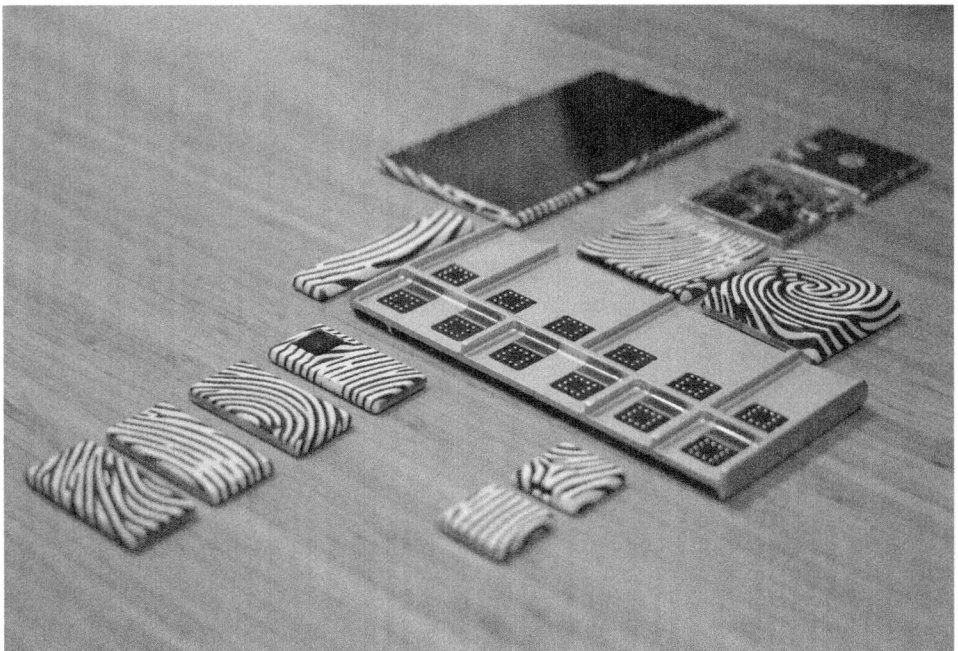

Figure 12.5   Project Ara spiral 2 prototype.
By Maurizio Pesce. CC BY-SA 2.0.

Design for end-of-life

The social and economic implications of informal e-waste management have driven significant policy efforts that have translated to widespread design for recycling (DfR) approaches. While e-waste policy varies widely around the globe, the European Waste Electrical and Electronic Equipment (WEEE) Directive has been a key regulatory mechanism for ensuring collection, recycling and recovery for all electronics (including both consumer electronics and appliances). In the U.S., e-waste policy is far more disparate and at an earlier stage, with no federal regulation and only partial coverage by a limited set of states. The similarity of both policy landscapes, however, is the emphasis on extended producer responsibility (EPR), whereby manufacturers take on the responsibility, albeit indirectly, for the products they put on the market, by bearing costs of recycling proportional to the volume of products they sold. Although not a direct driver for DfR innovation, these systems create greater public awareness and demand for greener electronics while also offering the potential to reduce compliance costs through design changes that can minimize the expenses of e-waste handling and processing.

DfR strategies have emerged in parallel to the development of recycling infrastructure and business practices, and thereby reflect the needs of these businesses. Typically, e-waste recycling takes place in a series of interconnected steps: (1) initial disassembly and de-pollution, wherein potentially harmful components (e.g., lithium-ion batteries) are removed; (2) disassembly and manual sorting to segregate high value components (printed circuit boards, hard drives, metal casings); (3) automated sorting and size reduction (e.g., shredding) of specific products or components, particularly for which disassembly is not technically or economically feasible; (4) consolidation of large volumes of products, components, or materials through brokerages and shipments;

and (5) chemical separation and extraction of materials of interest for sale on the commodity market (primarily precious metals, including gold, silver, platinum; as well as bulk metals, including aluminum, steel, copper).

Given the importance of manual disassembly, separation, and material identification, the responding design strategies have focused on improving ease and efficiency with which products can be quickly taken apart to yield the valuable materials inside, many of which are the last to be removed when the product is disassembled, as is the case for printed circuit boards. Therefore, recycling can be enhanced through design changes aimed at identifying or labeling materials, particularly using recycling symbols for varied plastic types; applying consistent design elements among manufacturers and across multiple product generations; standardizing parts and fasteners for ease of access with standard (rather than specialty) tools; eliminating glued or embossed parts that are unseparable; and embedding access information into the product itself, for example, by numbering the access points in the order in which they should be removed to reach a specific component for recycling (Masanet and Horvath, 2007; Huang and Truong, 2008; Rifer et al. 2009; Rifer and Brody-Heine 2009).

Reconciling design solutions with consumer trends

In the examples provided here, traditional sustainable design strategies can be classified into two broad categories: (1) production or supply-side or (2) user-centered or demand-side strategies. *Production or supply-side* strategies center on greening the production process, which is important for consumer electronics because many of the impacts occur during this phase. On the other hand, *user or demand-side* strategies relate to the consumer and his/her interaction with the product. Clearly both approaches are vital: production strategies are needed because many upstream impacts are not under the control of the user (the consumer). However, even if a product is designed to be energy efficient or upgradable, the consumer's behavior patterns, choices, or general unawareness of environmental impacts can negate well-intentioned designs. For example, a television may be considered 'green' if it is made with recycled materials and has a low standby power mode. But improvements are counteracted if a consumer decides to purchase multiple products per household or fails to drop off their product at a recycling facility. Thus, there is clearly a disconnect between green design and manufacturing choices versus sustainable purchasing and use behavior (Komeijani et al. 2016).

This disconnect is reflected more broadly in evolution of product design at an industry level. Traditional product design focused on individual aspects of artifacts and their functionality in regards to solving specific user needs. This approach provided effective solutions for common problems in daily life, but also promoted consumerism and growth of the consumer's material landscape and environmental footprint (Chapman 2009). As manufacturers became more efficient at product development, they were able to move beyond basic user needs to start looking at organic connections between consumers' activities and the different dimensions of their environment, from social to family to work to leisure, to name a few. This transition reflects a shift from "product" design to "experience" design. For example, while designing a stand mixer focuses on specific tasks such as mixing dry and wet food ingredients, today small appliances' manufacturers go beyond improving tasks, addressing emotional interests such as health and well-being when preparing a special family meal. Advances in technology and connectivity are key in enabling these types of holistic experiences where physical and emotional needs are addressed between multiple products and services.

For electronics, this transition is currently in progress, particularly in the evolution from individual products to complex product ecosystems that involve smart products, grid-based platforms, and social media, all of which can enhance user experience and interaction. This interconnection of smart devices is being defined as Internet of Things (IoT), and it allows for products to move from segregated artifacts to interconnected components with ubiquitous intelligence and interaction that serve multiple users across multiple aspects of life (Xia et al. 2012). These advanced technologies allow for products to "talk" to each other and ultimately learn user behavior in order to provide more consistent and efficient operation within and among devices in a given system. It is also important to note that whereas the use of advanced technology was primarily focused on individual electronic products in the past, there has been a fundamental shift to integrate "smart" features into any kind of consumer device. Simple, everyday products such as lightbulbs or hand tools now have smart features and digital interfaces, and automobiles, which used to work primarily on mechanical components, now have their electrical system count for at least 50 percent of the total number of parts. The very definition of consumer electronic or e-waste has fundamentally changed.

Though the emphasis of this systemic approach currently focuses more on software and user interaction, the potential for more sharing of physical product attributes can ultimately lead to reducing redundancy in components manufacturing and use and net decreases to resource consumption. For example, radio frequency identification (RFID) technology can track and alert users on energy usage or performance issues. Other concepts include assembling appliances into higher-level systems to achieve efficiency gains, for example, where the heat generated by a refrigerator's compressor or a cloths dryer could be used for warming up an oven. Though this concept is novel and makes sense in principle, manufacturers need to design products to share these resources while maintaining consumer acceptance. For example, consumers wouldn't appreciate wide insulation tubes running through the kitchen or consuming valuable space if hidden inside cabinets.

Sustainable behavior design

As electronic product systems provide engaging ways for consumers to enjoy life, there is the potential for increasing sustainable benefits via user behavior. Products that promote sustainable behaviors are far more effective in reducing environmental impact versus products that only rely on their innate performance and don't account for user involvement (Figge and Hahn 2004). For example, incorporating features in a smartphone that enhance emotional attachment; using slip proof, durable materials to prevent/minimize damage from dropping the device; and using materials/framework and cues to regulate heating and cooling and optimize battery life (Figure 12.6) results in 30% savings in the net annualized energy demand from producing and using a cell phone (Komeijani et al. 2016).

As tempting as some smart technologies can be, it is also important that users maintain an active and conscious role in product use, so that they develop greater awareness of how their behaviors and decisions impact sustainability issues. Products that are "too smart" and make all decisions for the user, can create a negative impact if users take for granted that their products are always sustainable. The rebound effect may occur if users make environmentally friendly decisions for their product, but also increase their frequency of use or the amount of products that they own.

Convergent device design

Another approach to designing, producing and using devices with lower energy impacts centers on enhancing concepts of functional convergence and multifunctionality. In ecological systems, invasive species have multiple functions and are thus able to adapt and survive with limited

Figure 12.6 Design changes to physical form and electrical systems can create a charging port that is difficult to detach while the phone is charging, but easily removed when the battery is fully charged. Advances in smart grid technology may allow for systems that delay the start or reduce the speed of charging based on when the power grid is supplying electricity from the cleanest mix of energy sources. Further, enhanced interface and application design can help consumers understand how charging decisions relate to battery life and economic costs.

Image by Mona Komeijani.

resources or under extreme conditions, often outcompeting native species for an ecological niche. Whereas invasives are viewed as a negative in ecological systems, "invasive" multifunctional products may offer a disruption to the current redundancy in product ownership. Consider the smart phone, which originated from multiple single function devices (computer and phone) and then converged physically into smaller devices that provide multiple and parallel functions. Now, a household can listen to music; communicate by emailing, faxing, texting or voice; play games; or watch video programming on one device (a smartphone, or a tablet, or the "Phablet" (DesMarais 2011)). A digital, streamlined household that replaces existing single-function devices and shares fewer highly convergent devices, can lead to as much as 40% savings in annual net energy impact (Ryen et al. 2015). To realize this potential, new design challenges emerge, such as ensuring that small, mobile convergent devices can offer high enough quality and user experience to truly displace larger, more energy intensive technologies.

Design for systems-level sustainability

Clearly, there are numerous opportunities for innovating design to achieve smart, sustainable products that have a smaller environmental footprint. However, the greatest potential for sustainable electronics may not be through products themselves, but rather through rethinking how these products can be designed and used to achieve broader sustainability goals. The indirect benefits from consumer electronics use include energy efficiency through home automation and smart appliances, reduced transportation impacts from telecommuting, enhanced logistics and distribution networks, and dematerialization through electronic media (Hilty et al. 2006). Beyond these well-known benefits, new areas are emerging where sustainable systems design can be leveraged through consumer electronics. Two examples are described next.

Figure 12.7   Raptor reloaded prosthetic hand.
By Kevin Jarrett. CC BY 2.0.

Digital fabrication

Three-dimensional (3D) printing offers the potential for consumer electronics to facilitate design and collaboration that does not depend on large-scale manufacturing. For example, E-Nable, a worldwide community that develops customized hand prosthetics (Figure 12.7), was started by a South African man who reached out to the maker community to create a comfortable prosthetic hand for his son. Other users saw potential in developing an organized collaborative community that could connect people with CAD knowledge and printing resources with children in need of prosthetic solutions. This kind of cooperation can only be possible with Internet connectivity and democratization of additive manufacturing, as well as the human passion that moves it forward. On the other hand, it is important to keep in mind potential issues of creating parts and products outside regulated guidelines for safe and environmentally friendly manufacturing, as well as EOL management impacts from generating unwanted 3D prints as part of the trial and error development process.

Combining sustainability and personal health

In terms of promoting user behavior, an industry making significant impact is health-tracking devices. It is increasingly common to see consumers wearing devices that measure their daily activity, water and food intake, heart rate, and in some cases, even provide feedback on their mood (see Figure 12.8). By combining this information with social media and gamification, these

Figure 12.8 Fitbit Surge activity tracker.
By Sam Sailor. CC BY-SA 4.0.

devices are effective in increasing health and physical activity. Activity tracking has become effective through the combination of short-term goals, like achieving a certain amount of daily steps, with long-term goals such as losing weight, being able to run a 5-kilometer race, or reducing cholesterol. Connection to social media adds accountability and provides an outlet for reaching out to other users to share successes, setbacks, or suggestions. In terms of sustainability, new trade-offs emerge. Whereas proliferation of digital devices leads to greater manufacturing and waste impacts, these factors may be offset by the broader benefits associated with personal health. For example, people who feel motivated to be healthier are most likely to use human-powered transportation such as biking or walking, or prefer to look for organic, local, foods, potentially resulting in far greater systems-level benefits.

Design enablers for sustainable electronic product design

The strategies needed to ensure that future sustainable electronic product design can be realized cannot happen in isolation. Concurrent changes in enabling systems, like policy, process improvement, and design education are also required. For example, policy mechanisms that encourage green design through requirements that companies procure sustainable electronics (e.g., EPEAT purchasing standards) must also be coupled with institutional best practices in disposing of these devices at end of life so that they enter proper reuse or recycling streams (Babbitt et al. 2011). Similarly, the current extended producer responsibility policy landscape in the United States can at best be described as a "patchwork," where only a fraction of states have implemented an e-waste law with recycling targets (Ogunseitan et al. 2009). More clear and consistent voluntary and mandatory policy instruments are required to span the life cycle challenges of consumer electronics.

Sustainable electronic product design also relies on new approaches to education and multidisciplinary collaboration. Design education is undergoing a dramatic transformation moving from traditional models with a narrow focus on skills, form, and function development (Spangenberg et al. 2010) to new models enabling dynamic methods and an integrated approach to empower multiple disciplines to collaborate together. Multidisciplinarity is critical for consumer electronics because sustainability problems are too complex to be successfully addressed by a single discipline. New curricular approaches can overcome the challenge associated with integrating sustainability principles into the design phase, by engaging teams from broader disciplines (engineering, design, sustainability, business, etc.) to work together in project-based assignments. Therefore, different perspectives can be applied to a single problem, ensuring that solutions can understand complex systems, create life cycle solutions, and work effectively with diverse stakeholders (Lobos and Babbitt 2013). Students who are exposed to this collaborative model also are likely to be more successful in the workforce, as they learn to speak a common language, which is key for working in any manufacturing environment.

Conclusion

Sustainable design requires a life-cycle approach to address environmental, social, and economic challenges, particularly for products like consumer electronics, which are experiencing shortened innovation cycles and rapid adoption. Design is the bridge to ensuring sustainable production and consumption practices at each stage of product manufacturing, use, and end-of-life. Life-cycle thinking enables designers, manufacturers, and consumers to think beyond the environmental footprint of a single product and to instead improve the performance of consumer electronics as a whole or to design electronics that can be leveraged to achieve broader systems-level sustainability benefits. Eco-design strategies must evaluate and balance impacts that can occur in all life-cycle stages, and also consider how those strategies may be enacted or prevented by planned or unanticipated user behavior. For example, extending product life span can create significant environmental savings, but certainly faces an uphill battle against the rising tide of technology innovations and consumers' desire for the next and newest product. On the other hand, designing durable and repairable products can create emotional attachment with users and even facilitate a second life through reuse and repurposing. Optimizing sustainability, design, and user experience requires new kinds of collaborations in education, design, policy, manufacturing, and consumer engagement. The benefits can be significant, leading to net reductions in electronic products' environmental footprints, new social and economic opportunities, and innovative avenues to retain and circulate resources throughout the economy.

References

Aizawa, H., Yoshida, H., and Sakai, S.I. (2008) "Current results and future perspectives for Japanese recycling of home electrical appliances" *Resource Conservation Recycling*, *52* 1399–410

Alonso, E., Gregory, J., Field, F., and Kirchain, R. (2007) "Material availability and the supply chain: Risks, effects, and responses" *Environmental Science & Technology*, *41*(19), 6649–6656.

Alonso, E., Sherman, A.M., Wallington, T.J., Everson, M.P., Field, F.R., Roth, R., and Kirchain, R.E. (2012) "Evaluating rare earth element availability: A case with revolutionary demand from clean technologies" *Environmental Science & Technology*, *46*(6), 3406–3414.

Aryee, B.N., Ntibery, B.K., and Atorkui, E. (2003) "Trends in the small-scale mining of precious minerals in Ghana: A perspective on its environmental impact" *Journal of Cleaner Production*, *11*(2), 131–140.

Babbitt, C.W., Kahhat, R., and Williams, E. (2011) "Institutional disposition and management of end-of-life electronics" *Environmental Science & Technology*, *45*(12), 5366–5472.

Babbitt, C.W., Kahhat, R., Williams, E., and Babbitt, G.A. (2009) "Evolution of product lifespan and implications for environmental assessment and management: A case study of personal computers in higher education" *Environmental Science & Technology*, *43*(13), 5106–5112.

Batchelor, S., Evangelista, S., Hearn, S., Peirce, M., Sugden, S., and Webb, M. (2003) *ICT for Development, Contributing to the Millennium Development Goals: Lessons Learned From Seventeen infoDev Projects.* Washington, DC: The World Bank.

Bi, X., Thomas, G.O., Jones, K.C., Qu, W., Sheng, G., Martin, F.L., and Fu, J. (2007) "Exposure of electronics dismantling workers to polybrominated diphenyl ethers, polychlorinated biphenyls, and organochlorine pesticides in South China" *Environmental Science & Technology*, *41*, 5647–5653.

Brown, R., Webber, C., and Koomey, J. (2002) "Status and future directions of the energy star program" *Energy*, *27*, 505–520.

Bustamante, M.L., Gaustad, G., and Goe, M. (2014) "Criticality research in the materials community" *JOM*, *66*, 2340–2342.

CEA (Consumer Electronics Association). (2008) "Coming to a neighborhood near you" *Vision*, September/October (www.ce.org) Accessed 15 August 2011.

CEA (Consumer Electronics Association). (2010) "Just the stats: Latest industry numbers" *Vision*, July/August (www.ce.org) Accessed 15 August 2011.

Chancerel, P., Meskers, C.E., Hagelüken, C., and Rotter, V.S. (2009) "Assessment of precious metal flows during preprocessing of waste electrical and electronic equipment" *Journal of Industrial Ecology*, *13*(5), 791–810.

Chancerel, P., Rotter, V.S., Ueberschaar, M., Marwede, M., Nissen, N.F., and Lang, K.D. (2013) "Data availability and the need for research to localize, quantify and recycle critical metals in information technology, telecommunication and consumer equipment" *Waste Management & Research*, *31*(10 suppl.), 3–16.

Chapman, J. (2009) "Design for (emotional) durability" *Design Issues*, *25*(4), 29–35.

Deng, L., Babbitt, C.W., and Williams, E. (2011) "Economic-balance hybrid LCA extended with uncertainty analysis: Case study of a laptop computer" *Journal of Cleaner Production*, *19*(11), 1198–1206.

Deng, L., and Williams, E. (2011) "Functionality versus 'typical product' measures of technological progress: A case study of semiconductor manufacturing" *Journal of Industrial Ecology*, *15*(10), 108–120.

Deng, W.J., Louie, P.K.K., Liu, W.K., Bi, X.H., Fu, J.M., and Wong, M.H. (2006) "Atmospheric levels and cytotoxicity of PAHs and heavy metals in TSP and $PM_{2.5}$ at an electronic waste recycling site in southeast China" *Atmospheric Environment*, *40* 6945–6955.

DesMarais, C. (2013) "Phablets craze goes bigger and adds dual SIM support" *PC World.com*, 26 January 2013. (http://www.pcworld.com/article/2026484/phablets-craze-goes-bigger-and-adds-dual-sim-support.html#tk.nl_today). Accessed 15 July 2016.

Dutta, S., and Mia, I. (2009) *The Global Information Technology Report 2008–2009: Mobility in a Networked World.* Switzerland: World Economic Forum and INSEAD.

Ellen MacArthur Foundation. (2013) *Towards a Circular Economy: Economic and Business Rationale for an Accelerated Transition.* (www.ellenmacarthurfoundation.org/assets/downloads/publications/Ellen-MacArthur-Foundation-Towards-the-Circular-Economy-vol.1.pdf) Accessed 5 July 2016.

Figge, F., and Hahn, T. (2004) "Sustainable value added: Measuring corporate contributions to sustainability beyond eco-efficiency" *Ecological Economics*, *48*, 173–187.

Fitzpatrick, C., Hickey, S., Schischke, K., and Paher, P. (2014) Sustainable life cycle engineering of an integrated desktop PC; A small to medium enterprise perspective. *Journal of Cleaner Production*, *74*(1), 155–160.

Fitzpatrick, C., Olivetti, E., Miller, T.R., Roth, R., and Kirchain, R. (2015) "Conflict minerals in the compute sector: Estimating extent of tin, tantalum, tungsten, and gold use in ICT products" *Environmental Science & Technology*, *49*(2), 974–981.

Goodman, P. (2002) "Current and future uses of gold in electronics" *Gold Bulletin*, *35*(1), 21–26.

Graedel, T.E., and Allenby, B.R. (2010) *Industrial Ecology and Sustainable Engineering.* Upper Saddle River: Prentice Hall.

Gutowski, T.G., Sahni, S. Boustani, A., and Graves, S.C. (2011) "Remanufacturing and energy savings" *Environmental Science and Technology*, *45*(10), 4540–4547.

Hertwich, E. (2005) "Consumption and the rebound effect: An industrial ecology perspective" *Industrial Ecology*, *9*(1–2), 85–98.

Hickey, S., Fitzpatrick, C., Maher, P., Ospina, J., Schischke, K., Beigl, P., Vidorreta, I., Yang, M., and Williams, I.D. (2014) "A case study of the D4R laptop" *Proceedings of the ICE – Waste and Resource Management, 167*(WR3), 101–108.

Hill, S. (2015) "Should you leave your smartphone plugged into the charger overnight? We asked an expert" *Digital Trends*, 31 January 2015. (www.digitaltrends.com/mobile/expert-advice-on-how-to-avoid-destroying-your-phones-battery/#ixzz3vqqy4Pha).

Hilty, L. M., Arnfalk, P., Erdmann, L., Goodman, J., Lehmann, M., and Wager, P. A. (2006) "The relevance of information and communication technologies for environmental sustainability – A prospective simulation study" *Environmental Modelling & Software, 21*(11), 1618–1629.

Huang, E. M., and Truong, K. N. (2008) "Breaking the disposable technology paradigm: Opportunities for sustainable interaction design for mobile phones" in *Proceedings of the SIGCHI Conference on Human Factors in Computing Systems*, Florence, Italy, 5–10 April 2008, 323–332.

Huijbregts, M., Rombouts, L., Hellweg, S., Frischknecht, R., Hendriks, A. J., van de Meent, D., and Ragas, M.J. (2006) "Is cumulative fossil energy demand a useful indicator for the environmental performance of products?" *Environmental Science & Technology, 40*(3), 641–648.

Huo, X., Peng, L, Xu, X., Zheng, L., Qiu, B., Qi, Z., Zhang, B., Han, D., and Piao, Z. (2007) "Elevated blood levels of children in Guiyu, an electronic waste recycling town in China" *Environmental Health Perspectives, 115*, 1113–1117.

International Telecommunication Union (ITU) website (www.itu/int/themes/climate) Accessed 19 October 2010.

Jacoby, M., and Jiang, J. (2010) "Securing the supply of rare earths" *Chemical Engineering News, 88*(35), 9–12.

Kahhat, R., and Williams, E. (2009) "Product or waste? Importation and end-of-life processing of computers in Peru" *Environmental Science & Technology, 43*(15), 6010–6016.

Kasulaitis, B.V., Babbitt, C.W., Kahhat, R., Williams, E.W., and Ryen, E.G. (2015) "Evolving materials, attributes, and functionality in consumer electronics: Case study of laptop computers" *Resources, Conservation and Recycling, 100*, 1–10.

Keating, L. (2015) "Can charging cases shorten a smartphone battery's lifespan?" *High Tech Times*, 11 December 2015 (www.techtimes.com/articles/115529/20151211/charging-phones-battery-shorten-life.htm).

Khetriwal, D. S., Kraeuchi, P., and Widmer, R. (2009) "Producer responsibility for e-waste management: Key issues for consideration – learning from the Swiss experience" *Journal of Environmental Management, 90*, 153–165.

Kim, M. H., Kim, H., and Paek, D. (2014) "The health impacts of semiconductor production: An epidemiologic review" *International Journal of Occupational Environmental Health, 20*(2), 95–114.

Kok, R., R. Benders, R., and Moll, H. C. (2006) "Measuring the environmental load of household consumption using some methods based on input–output energy analysis: A comparison of methods and a discussion of results" *Energy Policy, 34*, 2744–2761.

Komeijani, M., Ryen, E. G., and Babbitt, C. W. (2016) "Bridging the gap between eco-design and the human thinking system" *Challenges, 7*(1), 5.

Koomey, J., Berard, S., Sanchez, M., and Wong, H. (2011) "Implications of historical trends in the electrical efficiency of computing" *IEEE Annals of the History of Computing, 33*(3), 46–54.

Ladou, J., and Lovegrove, S. (2008) "Export of electronics equipment waste" *International Journal of Occupational Environmental, 14*, 1–10.

Leal-Yepes, A. M. (2013) "Evaluating the effectiveness of design for the environment tool to help meet sustainability and design goals." A Thesis of the Rochester Institute of Technology.

Lobos, A. (2014) "Timelessness in sustainable product design" in *The Colors of Care: Proceedings of the 9th International Conference on Design & Emotion*, eds. J. Salamanca, P. Desmet, A. E. Burbano Valdes, G. Ludden, J. Maya, Universidad de Los Andes, Bogotá, 169–176.

Lobos, A., and Babbitt, C.W. (2013) "Integrating emotional attachment in electronic product design" *Challenges, 4*, 19–33.

Malmodin, J., Moberg, Å., Lundén, D., Finnveden, G., and Lövehagen, N. (2010) "Greenhouse gas emissions and operational electricity use in the ICT and entertainment & media sectors" *Journal of Industrial Ecology, 14*(5), 770–790.

Manomaivibool, P. (2009) "Extended producer responsibility in a non-OECD context: The management of waste electrical and electronic equipment in India" *Resources, Conservation and Recycling, 53*(3), 136–144.

Masanet, E., and Horvath, A. (2007) "Assessing the benefits of design for recycling of plastics in electronics: A case study of computer enclosures" *Materials & Design, 28*(6), 1801–1811.

Matthews, H. S., Hendrickson, C., and Matthews, D. (2015) *Life Cycle Assessment: Quantitative Approaches for Decisions that Matter.* (www.lcatextbook.com) Accessed 1 July 2016.

Obiri, S., Mattah, P. A., Mattah, M. M., Armah, F. A., Osae, S., Adu-Kumi, S., and Yeboah, P. O. (2016) "Assessing the environmental and socio-economic impacts of artisanal gold mining on the livelihoods of communities in the Tarkwa Nsuaem municipality in Ghana" *International Journal of Environmental Research and Public Health, 13*(2), 160.

Oguchi, M., Murakami, S., Sakanakura, H., Kida, A., and Kameya, T. (2011) "A preliminary categorization of end-of-life electrical and electronic equipment as secondary metal resources" *Waste Management, 31*(9), 2150–2160.

Ogunseitan, O.A., Schoenung, J.M., Saphores, J.-D.M., and Shapiro, A.A. (2009) "The electronics revolution: From e-wonderland to e-wasteland" *Science, 326*, 670–671.

Pierce, D. (2016) "Project Ara lives: Google's modular phone is ready for you now" *Wired Magazine*, 20 May 2016 (www.wired.com/2016/05/project-ara-lives-googles-modular-phone-is-ready).

Reed, E., and Miranda, M. (2007) *Assessment of the Mining Sector and Infrastructure Development in the Congo Basin Region.* Washington, DC: WWF Macroeconomics for Sustainable Development Program Office.

Rifer, W., and Brody-Heine, P. (2009) "A new look at design for EOL: Game changing outcomes of the Close the Loop study" in *Proceedings of the 2009 IEEE International Symposium on Sustainable Systems & Technology*, Tempe, AZ.

Rifer, W., Brody-Heine, P., Peters, A., and Linnell, J. (2009) *Closing the LOOP: Electronics Design to Enhance Reuse/Recycling Value, Final Report.* Green Electronics Council.

Robinson, B. H. (2009) "E-waste: An assessment of global production and environmental impacts" *Science of the Total Environment, 408*(2), 183–191.

Roth, K., and K. McKenney (2007) *Energy Consumption by Consumer Electronics in U.S. Residences.* Final report prepared for the Consumer Electronics Association (CEA) Cambridge, TIAX LLC.

Ryen, E. G., Babbitt, C. W., Tyler, A. C., and Babbitt, G. A. (2014) "Community ecology perspectives on the structural and functional evolution of consumer electronics" *Journal of Industrial Ecology, 18*(5), 708–721.

Ryen, E. G., Babbitt, C. W., and Williams, E. (2015) "Consumption-weighted life cycle assessment of a consumer electronic product community" *Environmental Science & Technology, 49*(4), 2549–2559.

Sekar, A., Williams, E., and Chen, R. (2016) "Heterogeneity in time and energy use of watching television" *Energy Policy, 93*, 50–58.

Spangenberg, J. H., Fuad-Luke, A., and Blincoe, K. (2010) "Design for sustainability (DfS): The interface of sustainable production and consumption" *Cleaner Production, 18*, 1485–1493.

Sprecher, B., Kleijn, R., and Kramer, G. J. (2014) "Recycling potential of neodymium: The case of computer hard disk drives" *Environmental Science & Technology, 48*(16), 9506–9513.

U.S. EPA Greenhouse Gas Equivalencies Calculator, https://www.epa.gov/energy/greenhouse-gas-equivalencies-calculator. Accessed July 2016.

U.S. Geological Survey (USGS). (2000) *Mineral Commodity Summaries 2000.* Reston, USGS (http://minerals.usgs.gov/minerals/pubs/mcs/2000/mcs2000.pdf) Accessed 24 July 2016.

U.S. Office of Technology Assessment (OTA). (1992) *Green Products by Design – Choices for a Cleaner Environment.* Washington, DC, US OTA (www.princeton.edu/~ota/disk1/1992/9221/9221.PDF) Accessed 10 July 2010.

UNEP. (2013) *Environmental Risks and Challenges of Anthropogenic Metals Flows and Cycles.* SBN: 978-92-807-3266-5, Job Number: DTI/1534/PA, UNEP (www.unep.org) Accessed 5 July 2016.

United Nations Environmental Programme (UNEP). (2009) *Recycling – From E-Waste to Resources.* Berlin, UNEP and United Nations University (www.unep.org) Accessed 5 July 2016.

USGS. (2016) *Mineral Commodity Summaries 2016.* Reston, USGS (http://minerals.usgs.gov/minerals/pubs/commodity/gold/mcs-2016-gold.pdf) Accessed 24 July 2016.

Wang, D., Cai, Z., Jiang, G., Leuang, A., Wong, M. H., and Wong, W. K. (2005) "Determination of poly-brominated diphenyl ethers in soil and sediment from an electronic waste recycling facility" *Chemosphere, 60*, 810–816.

Wang, X., and Gaustad, G. (2012) "Prioritizing material recovery for end-of-life printed circuit boards" *Waste Management, 32*(10), 1903–1913.

Widmer, R., Oswald-Krapf, H., Sinha-Khetriwal, D., Schnellmann, M., and Böni, H. (2005) "Global perspectives on e-waste" *Environmental Impact Assessment Review, 25*(5), 436–458.

Williams, E. (2004) "Energy intensity of computer manufacturing: Hybrid assessment combining process and economic input-output methods" *Environmental Science & Technology, 38*(22), 6166–6174.

Williams, E. (2011) "Environmental effects of information and communications technologies" *Nature, 479*(7373), 354–358.

Williams, E., and Hatanaka, T. (2005) "Residential computer usage patterns in Japan and associated life cycle energy use" in *Proceedings of the 2005 IEEE International Symposium on Electronics and the Environment,* 177–182.

Williams, E., Kahhat, R., Allenby, B., Kavazanjian, E., Kim, J., and Xu, M. (2008) "Environmental, social, and economic implications of global reuse and recycling of personal computers" *Environmental Science & Technology, 42*(17), 6446–6454.

Williams, E. D., Ayres, R. U., and Heller, M. (2002) "The 1.7 kilogram microchip: Energy and material use in the production of semiconductor devices" *Environmental Science & Technology, 36*(24), 5504–5510.

Wong, C. S., Wu, S. C., Duzgoren-Aydin, N. S., Aydin, A., and Wong, M. H. (2007). "Trace metal contamination of sediments in an e-waste processing village in China" *Environmental Pollution, 145*(2), 434–442.

Xia, F., Yang, L. T., Wang, L., and Vinel, A. (2012) "Internet of things" *Communications System, 25* 1101–1102.

Yang, Y., and Williams, E. (2009) "Logistic model-based forecast of sales and generation of obsolete computers in the US" *Technological Forecasting and Social Change, 76*(8), 1105–1114.

Yu, X. Z., Gao, Y., Wu, S. C., Zhang, H. B., Cheung, K. C., and Wong, M. H. (2006) "Distribution of polycyclic aromatic hydrocarbons in soils at Guiyu area of China, affected by recycling of electronic waste using primitive technologies" *Chemosphere, 65*(9), 1500–1509.

13

DATA CLOUDS AND THE ENVIRONMENT

Arman Shehabi

Systems thinking in the cloud

Imagine you are sitting with your laptop reviewing some design mock-ups from a client while streaming music and occasionally chatting online with a friend. Stretched out on your couch, that laptop resting appropriately on your lap, with your hands firmly holding a warm cup of coffee. How would you apply systems thinking to understand the environmental implications of this scenario? How did that coffee finally make it into your hands? The coffee beans had to be grown and harvested, then shipped possibly across the globe. The beans were then roasted and packaged before being transported to your local market where you purchased them and then brewed on the new coffeemaker that Grandma gave you for your birthday. At each stage in the coffee production process, energy and materials are consumed, and that consumption has an impact on the environment. A similar evaluation could be performed on your laptop computer – as was discussed in the previous chapter – including the mining and production of different materials contained in the laptop, the manufacturing of the laptop, the transport of that laptop onto your lap, and the final end-of-life for the laptop once it's discarded and dissembled, with some parts being recycled and some parts ending up in a landfill.

Environmental sustainability strives to eliminate impacts on the environmental that will have an undue burden on current and future generations. Designers must have the perspective of environmental impacts across the entire life cycle of a product or service. Beyond just looking at when the product is used, consider the impacts from each phase in the product's life, from the extraction of materials, to the manufacturing process, including the product end-of-life, and all the transportation that occurs between each step. From a design prospective, many of the impacts can be distilled down to how we use materials and energy to provide products and services in our society. Some materials are finite resources, such as many of the rare earth metals required in our electronics, and the extraction practices to collect resource materials, be it mining, drilling, or cutting, can be ecologically damaging. Other materials can be toxic when they find their way into the air, water, or soil. Similar impacts are seen with energy. Energy often starts from a finite resource, such as coal or oil, causes environmental damage during extraction, and releases pollutants when used. Often the use of energy and materials are intertwined. Throughout this chapter the environmental impacts from the Information and Communication Technology (ICT) that allow us to have digital data in "the cloud" are viewed through the lens of the material and energy requirements for these services.

Direct environmental impacts of ICT

Back to that image of you sitting on the couch. Applying systems thinking to understand the behind-the-scenes impacts in this scenario is a challenging endeavor, but the warmth of that coffee in your hands and the weight of your laptop resting on your lap help remind us that these are products to evaluate. But what about the other "products" with you on the couch? Those design mock-ups sitting in your computer's inbox, along with the music and your friend's emojis, are all the result of intangible products that we can't see and hold in the same way, but nevertheless still have an impact on the environment. Consider what happens once you plug your laptop into the electrical wall socket and it begins drawing electricity. Similar to the life cycle impacts from your cup of coffee, the impacts from electricity are unapparent while you're using it. Rather, the impacts occur behind the scenes and require a systems approach to properly capture. The electricity coming out of the wall socket traveled along transmission lines from a power plant miles away where the electricity was generated from a primary fuel. If that primary fuel was a finite resource like coal or natural gas, as is most of the electricity generated around the world, the burning of that coal emits a host of toxic air pollutants that stay airborne for days and travel many miles, polluting the air and creating a health hazard for the surrounding regions. Additionally, the burning of those fossil fuels exacerbates the effects of global climate change by releasing carbon dioxide into the atmosphere. Even if the electricity is generated from cleaner sources, such as wind or solar, the systems approach reminds us that the nonnegligible energy and material resources required for the building and operation of these facilities must also be included.

The electrical plug is not the only connection on your laptop that is creating behind-the-scenes impacts. Your laptop needs electricity to perform the functions that occur within your computer, but more and more of these functions are being outsourced to "the cloud." The cloud is colloquially used to describe any computer activity that occurs away from the user, and is how we apply the term in this chapter. Music and movies are now streamed from a provider rather than stored on personal computers. Computer programs and software that used to reside and operate on individual machines are instead reached through an Internet connection where they reside and operate on a remote server. Chances are that the laptop resting on your lap in much smaller and lighter than the previous one you owned. The outsourcing of local computer functions to the cloud reduces the need for a beefy computer processor or an even larger storage drive. Though your computer now doesn't need electricity to perform these outsourced functions, they are still happening, and all those computations, storage, and streaming activities that are happening elsewhere demand electricity.

Where does that Internet connection go – and how does it demand electricity – when you tap into the cloud for your email, pictures, videos, or online software? The wireless receiver in your laptop first communicates with the local router in your room. The glowing green light on that router is a reminder that it is another step in the ICT pathway that requires electricity to operate. The signal is then sent along transmission lines to a series of increasingly consolidated network access points; from the beige sidewalk utility box on the corner that handles internet traffic for your block to an indiscrete telecom building in your neighborhood, then on to increasingly larger buildings that serve your city and broader region. Each access point is equipped with an amount of network equipment proportional to the amount of data that passes through that location. All that network equipment requires electricity to operate.

Ultimately the signal will end up at a data center: the core – and the brains – of the cloud. Data centers come in all shapes and sizes, but odds are that the data you've stored in the cloud, such as your email or pictures, is located in a large warehouse-size cloud data center that serves millions of users. These data center buildings are unlike most other buildings. They are often the size of multiple football fields and completely enclosed with no windows. From the outside these buildings might simply look like a very large storage facility. Once inside though, these buildings reveal a sea of blinking lights, created by row after row of Information Technology (IT) equipment. This IT equipment includes thousands of computer servers and data storage equipment, as well as network equipment that allows for communication within the data center itself and to the outside world (and ultimately back to your laptop, phone, tablet, watch, and other connected devices). All of this IT equipment requires electricity to operate. Lots of electricity.

The IT equipment is not the only source of electricity demand in data centers. Just as your laptop warms your lap, all that IT equipment also gives off heat while operating. And with such a high concentration of IT equipment in a single place, the heat generated is enormous. Data centers must blast air conditioning continuously throughout the space to make sure the IT equipment functions properly and doesn't overheat. The buildings also require additional electrical equipment to deal with power conversions and to ensure consistent high-quality power. When combined with more conventional building power demand such as lighting, the non-IT auxiliary equipment in a data center can consume as much power at the IT equipment itself, essentially doubling the energy associated with data centers.

Data centers in the United States require about 70 billion kWh of electricity every year,[1] equivalent to the electricity consumed in about 7.5 million U.S. homes and more electricity than is consumed in many individual states. Just to keep the buildings running, data centers account for about 1.5% of all global electricity use.[2] A remarkably high number for a single industry with relatively few buildings that doesn't even begin to include energy and materials required in the greater electronics systems. Accordingly, data centers have received significant attention for their energy use. In properly comparing energy and environmental impacts associated with different services, however, proper systems thinking requires first estimating the impacts from any alternative services and then "normalizing" values to ensure that the sustainability comparison is apples to apples. This practice can lead to surprisingly counterintuitive results.

Here's an example: the small continuous power draw from the local router in your living room contributes more of an energy impact to your laptop's use of the cloud than any other part of the infrastructure, including the energy hogging data centers themselves. Though large data centers consume an extraordinary amount of energy, they also serve a high number of users. The only user of your local router is you, and maybe your housemates. When the energy use of each component in the cloud infrastructure is normalized on a per-user basis, the ICT equipment within the "last mile" rise to have the greatest impacts. This equipment often includes personal devices, like the router in your living room, or even your laptop itself.

This "last mile" insight is important when considering alternatives to using the cloud for data services. For example, rather than using Gmail or some other cloud service for email, assume your boutique design firm decided to host their own servers to provide email and project files – still a common practice among many small businesses. A handful of servers would be set up in a small room or closet, along with some additional storage and network IT equipment. Your company might also need to purchase a small window air-conditioner, to make sure the room doesn't get too hot for the IT equipment, and an uninterruptable power supply (UPS) to make sure power glitches don't corrupt your data. Unfortunately, this small, localized data center would be grossly inefficient relative to its cloud counterpart. The UPS and air-conditioner would most likely be relatively inefficient at such a small size. Trying to match the UPS and air-conditioner efficiency of the cloud would cost thousands of extra dollars in equipment but, because of the small setup, only provide pennies in electricity savings. Aside from the auxiliary equipment, the IT equipment in your local data center would be necessarily oversized since it would have to be large enough to handle requests from all your employees, but with only a handful of employees, most of the time that equipment would be sitting idle ready to work. The equipment would be doing nothing but consuming electricity and forcing the UPS and air-conditioning to operate.

Utilizing the cloud is not an impact free activity, and sustainable design dictates these services should not be used without restraint. However, cloud utilization is often the most efficient ICT pathway to provide a digital computation, storage, or network service, when considering the other inefficiencies that would be introduced from instead of using a personal server or bulked up computer. Cloud computing in many ways benefits from the centralization of a utility: the large scale provides both technological opportunities and economic incentives to maximize efficiency. When cloud data centers spend millions of dollars each year on their electricity bills, even small efficiency measures that would look negligible to an individual consumer, such as upgrading equipment for a 1% efficiency gain, can look appealing to their bottom line. As a consumer of cloud services, individual sustainability efforts should focus on choosing cloud service providers that commit to powering their data centers with cleaner, renewable electricity, to help ensure that the electricity that is consumed in cloud data centers results in the least amount of environmental damage. Additionally, individual sustainability effort should focus on maximizing the efficiency of personal electronic devices by eliminating unnecessary device idling and striving to have them only consume power when needed.

The recent rapid growth of information and communication technology with data digitization has generated a lot of attention toward the significant amount of electricity consumed by this ICT infrastructure; from the data centers to the end users' devices that access them. Although this direct electricity consumption is significant, the ways in which these data services are used and interact with other parts of society can result in much larger indirect impacts. Using the cloud for data services is a way to minimize your ICT impacts. But there is still an impact. Through innovative design, new data center services could be developed that improve global sustainability. Alternatively, if the potential ramifications across the economy are not properly considered, new ICT services could also emerge in ways that have significant deleterious environmental impacts – impacts that are only indirectly associated with data centers, but much larger than the direct impacts themselves. These indirect impacts are much more broad and difficult to quantify. It can even be difficult to know if the impact will have a positive or negative environmental effect. The following discussion of potential life-cycle and indirect impacts are derived from the outline and taxonomy developed by Horner et al. (2016)[3] to characterize these indirect effects. Both the magnitude and uncertainty of impacts increase moving down this list, in that the impacts become less understood, but the influence across society becomes potentially greater.

Life-cycle impacts of ICT equipment

Similar to the electricity demand required to operate ICT infrastructure, the equipment associated with that infrastructure carries a necessary environmental burden proportional to the growth in cloud technologies and services. The infrastructure of ICT is made up of millions and millions of servers and other IT equipment that are housed in data center buildings around the world. Material and energy were required to build those data centers. Material and energy were required to build all those servers. And material and energy are required to build the replacements for those servers, which are replaced every few years. Since servers pretty much run nonstop and demand a lot of electricity while being used, the "embodied energy" of these devices – that is, the energy used in obtaining and transporting all the materials needed to manufacture a server, the energy used actually building the server at the server factory, as well as the energy used to ultimately recycle or landfill the server – is much lower than the electricity used to actually operate the server during its lifetime. Embodied energy, however, is not the only sustainability concern in the life cycle of servers. The material demands include certain rare earth materials with limited environmental availability that are sometimes located in conflict zones where purchasing these materials can indirectly support political regimes with human-rights violations. Additionally, many of the materials within the electronic circuitry of the servers contain heavy metals and toxic substances. The improper extraction of these materials and disposal of electronics can lead to health hazards from pollutants leaching into soil and groundwater. These toxic components can also become airborne if certain components are incinerated without the correct protections in place; which can be a challenging issue when electronic waste is often sent across the globe for disposal in countries with less restrictive health and environmental disposal regulations.

These life-cycle impacts become much more magnified when considering the end-use devices of ICT, like your computer, laptop, tablet, or cell phone. These issues with rare earth and toxic materials are similar, but the number of end-use devices is in the many billions and rapidly increasing[4] so that the total amount of materials and energy needed to manufacture these devices – as well and the impacts of disposal once discarded – is significantly greater. Nobody likes to have the cell phone or laptop battery die, so end-use devices are typically designed to use a minimal amount of electricity, and these devices are becoming more efficient as they become increasingly more mobile. The low amount of electricity required to operate these devices during their lifetime belies this embodied energy, which contributes much more to the total life-cycle energy use. For example, the energy to manufacture the laptop sitting on your lap was probably about four times greater than all the electricity you will ever use to operate it.[5]

Strategies to limit the environmental impacts embodied with ICT equipment across the life cycle includes designing the equipment to minimize the need for rare earth and critical materials and finding strategies to improve the efficiency of the manufacturing process. The fairly short lifetimes of ICT equipment magnifies the life-cycle impacts, since every replacement comes with a whole new set of life-cycle impacts. The short lifetime is in many ways unique to ICT equipment. There are few items that people buy for hundreds of dollars – sometimes thousands – with a full expectation that the item will be obsolete in just a few years. Designing ways to extend the lifetime of ICT equipment through reusing certain components can help address life-cycle impacts by reducing the frequency of manufacturing replacements. Finally, for components that cannot be reused or recycled, better disposal protocols can minimize unintended exposure to any potentially toxic substances.

Design intervention for indirect impacts

So far in this chapter we've only discussed the environmental impacts associated with ICT itself. Though much of this ICT infrastructure is behind the scenes and not apparent to most users of cloud services and other digital services we all enjoy, this infrastructure represents a vast amount of equipment easily observable to many. The enormity of the material resources and electricity demanded from this equipment makes it the most conspicuous impact of ICT and as a result these impacts have received the most attention when discussing ICT infrastructure. That infrastructure, however, is the foundation for a system that allows us to collect, transfer, and react to information at speeds that would be inconceivable a generation ago. This system of interconnectivity creates new opportunities for improving efficiency and optimization strategies that can reduce the waste of resources throughout the life cycles of all of our goods and services, building operations, and transportation methods. The acceleration of information flow also creates the possibility to increase the environmental damages throughout many aspects of society that together may dwarf the damages directly associated with the ICT infrastructure itself. The different ways that ICT may indirectly impact environmental sustainability has been characterized by Horner et al. with a taxonomy of efficiency, substitution, rebound, economy-wide, and systematic transformational impacts. Each type of impact, discussed in more detail in the next section, is an opportunity for the next generation of designers and innovators to steer the growth of ICT along a more environmentally sustainable pathway.

Efficiency impacts

Efficiency is a metric to describe an amount of resource required to provide a service. The miles-per-gallon rating in a car, for example, indicates how much gasoline (a resource) is required to move the car (a service). Being efficient at doing your homework indicates that you can complete your assignments (a service) without wasting too much time (a resource). There is actually an amazing amount of energy and material inefficiencies around us all the time. Just think of all the items in your apartment right now not providing a service, but instead just waiting to be used. When you review some design mock-ups on your laptop, you really only need an illuminated screen to see the images, but many of the internal components are still operating in the back-ground; the processor is running and the wireless antenna is communicating with your router. Your router is drawing power, along with your television and many other electronic devices, even though you don't need them right at this moment. These devices still must draw power when you don't need them because you may need them at any moment and your devices don't know when that moment may come. But what if they did know? The interconnectivity created by ICT creates the opportunity to make devices and services "smart."

Examples of this type of ICT efficiency are already being seen across the economic sectors of building operation, transportation, and manufacturing. Smart homes can tailor to your heating, cooling, and lighting needs by sensing your location and even anticipating your future locations based on your past actions. It's possible to imagine a fully networked building where the lighting and air-conditioning or heating are just right in the room where you are, but off where you aren't, and adjust as you move through the building without you ever noticing any change. Building operations consume more than a third of all energy in the United States, and account for more than two-thirds of all electricity consumption.[6] Leveraging communications through the cloud to gain small efficiency improvements across a large portion of the building stock can result in significant energy saving on a national or global scale. In the transportation sector, the Global Positioning System (GPS) that helps prevent us from getting lost (an efficiency improvement itself) is being paired with cloud-based software by the delivery companies, such as UPS and FedEx, to find the most efficient routes for drivers, which has famously led to those delivery trucks being known to rarely make left-hand turns in busy cities.[7] Smart manufacturing is the application of ICT to minimize resources by tailoring activity to real-time demand, so that machines only operate when needed and just the right amount of products are produced. Efficiency through ICT is – by definition – always an improvement in reducing resource use, but the amount of efficiency that will actually be enabled by ICT is unknown and will depend on how ICT is ultimately applied.

Substitution impacts

Substitution is the idea that ICT can create new services and products that replace existing services and products. Electronics books (e-books) are a good example of ICT-generated substitution. When you read a book on your laptop or tablet it is consuming electricity, and you probably purchased and downloaded that book from a website that contributed to electricity demand of the ICT network. But consider the alternative service. Consider how that book would have been "delivered" to you absent of the cloud. A printed version of the book would have to be made, requiring material resources like paper and ink as well as manufacturing energy. The book would then have to be loaded on a truck and transported to a bookstore, consuming gasoline and creating vehicle emissions in the process. You would then need to go to that bookstore – possibly driving to get there – to purchase the book. The "dematerialization" of goods through digital substitution is one of the more promising sustainability opportunities that can emerge from ICT services, since manufacturing and transporting physical products always consumes more energy than transporting the intellectual content of those goods through the Internet.

Telework is another example of ICT providing a more sustainable substitution. Fast Internet connections, access to data in the cloud, and video conference technologies have all reduced the need to be physically present at events and in offices, thereby substituting ICT energy in place of the much larger energy associated with driving and flying for travel. Utilizing ICT services as a substitution for an existing service, however, is not always a move toward improved sustainability, and often it can be difficult to properly weigh the different impacts of comparable services. The shift toward electronic billboards that act as large video screens consume more electricity to operate than the old poster billboards they have replaced, though a systems analysis comparing the impacts across the lifetimes of the billboards, including the production and replacement of new posters, would be needed to make and accurate comparison and will be probably vary by the specifics of each billboard scenario.

Rebound impacts

Rebound is a concept in economics used to describe how consumers can react to changes in the cost of goods and services that reduce the benefits gained from ICT efficiency and substitution technologies. Direct rebound refers to the consumption of a specific product based on how the price of a product affects its demand. Simply put, people will consume more of something as the cost of consumption drops. Any efficiency and substitution benefits achieved through ICT will experience some level of direct rebound. If GPS navigation and self-driving technology make driving more efficient through some combination of taking up less time, costing less, or generally being a more pleasant experience, people will be have an incentive to drive more. If purchasing a book as an e-book is only a few simple clicks away, there's a good chance you'll end up buying more books than if you had to schlep across town to a bookstore. The growth of video streaming of movies and television from the cloud has received much attention as an energy efficiency form of video viewing, when comparing the energy and material resources associated with ICT infrastructure relative to going to a theater or renting a DVD, but the ease of viewing with streaming may result in more movies being watched, which ultimately reduces the net efficiency benefits. The impact of direct rebound is limited by saturation. At some point, regardless of cost or ease of purchase, you're not going to watch any more movies, read any more books, or have anywhere else you could drive. Indirect rebound impacts consider the impacts of what else might be done with the extra time or money gained through ICT efficiency or substitution. Spending less time and money by streaming a movie at home rather than going to the movie theater means that people will have more time and disposable income to purchase other goods and engage in other activities that may have a larger – or smaller – environmental impact than the original trip to the movie theater that was avoided.

Economy-wide impacts

Economy-wide impacts consider how other economic sectors adjust to new products and services that emerge from ICT. The ability to purchase items through the Internet can cause a contraction in storefront stores – like bookstores – while promoting growth in services associated with shipping and delivery, such as packaging, delivery trucks, and warehouse hubs. The growth in easily accessible GPS has allowed for services like Uber and Lyft to emerge, which changes how we move around cities and affects other methods of transportation. Video streaming services may create a decrease in movie theaters while expanding the demands for bigger and more powerful home entertainment systems. Understanding net impact on environmental sustainability from these macroeconomic shifts is challenging to estimate, but the far reach of these effects indicates a potentially significant impact on society's use of resources.

Systematic transformational impacts

Systematic transformational impacts consider how the combination of all the impacts described throughout this chapter ultimately may change how our society develops around future technologies. The growth of automobile ownership in the mid-twentieth century, for example, transformed how we built our cities and where we lived with suburban development. Technologies emerging from ICT, such as fully autonomous vehicles, 3D printing, and virtual reality may all create the next generation of systematic transformation impacts. These impacts could completely change how we approach sustainability, but the actual impact will depend on the specifics of the technology and how it is integrated into society. GPS systems may allow for the growth of autonomous vehicles, which could lead to a sustainable transportation future. The desire for private vehicle ownership would be replaced with on-demand vehicles that are tailored for specific tasks and for the number of riders to be efficient as possible. The layout of transportation infrastructure would evolve to meet the needs of this new fleet: imagine a city with no parking spaces and roads that allow for cars to drive very close to each other at high speeds. Conversely, GPS systems could also allow for the growth of autonomous vehicles to evolve toward a sustainability dystopia. Without the need for actual drivers, cars could become increasingly larger to provide more comforts to passengers. Larger and more comfortable cars could lead to greater acceptance of longer drive times and greater distances between homes and businesses. In this scenario, everyone would be riding around in their personal mobile homes all day and night. The ICT infrastructure and electricity required to meet the computational demand of an all autonomous vehicle society would be enormous, but – in terms of scale – would be relatively insignificant to the environmental impacts that would result from these larger societal shifts that could emerge from the technologies.

ICT design for sustainability

The evolution of ICT through the Internet and the cloud is rapidly transforming society in many ways, from how we communicate, to commerce, to entertainment. These far reaching impacts are enabled by the ability to use cloud technologies for a variety of services. The cloud is essentially a tool, and how we use that tool can have broad environmental implications – both good and bad. The most direct impacts are the use of resources required to build, maintain, and operate the ICT infrastructure; from the large cloud data centers all the way to your computer (as well as every other computer, tablet, and phone connected to the Internet). These direct impacts – the electricity consumed to operate each point in the ICT system – are relativity well understood and have received substantial attention. Whereas the electricity to operate ICT infrastructure is by no means insignificant – estimated to represent about 5% of all global electricity use[8] – the enormity of the equipment involved, and how it touches nearly every part of the global economy, indicate that other more indirect impacts from utilizing cloud technologies could be much greater.

The application of this ICT infrastructure is still at the nascent stages of development, creating lots of opportunities to influence how it will ultimately become integrated throughout different sectors in the global economy. Innovative thinking and good design can help harness ICT to steer global energy and resource consumption toward more sustainable pathways. Many of the impacts associated with ICT are challenging to quantify and can change with such rapidly evolving technology. Promoting sustainability through ICT will require considering all of the different ways ICT can influence our use of resources and our interaction with the environment. ICT should be leveraged to improve sustainability within the areas of transportation, building energy use, and manufacturing, along with addressing the rapidly growing ICT sector itself, while also being mindful of the potential unintended consequences that can arise from such a far reaching and influential technology.

Notes

1 Shehabi, A., Smith, S. J., Horner, N., Azevedo, I., Brown, R., Koomey, J., Masanet, E., Sartor, D., Herrlin, M., and Lintner, W. 2016. *United States Data Center Energy Usage Report*. Lawrence Berkeley National Laboratory, Berkeley, CA. LBNL-1005775.
2 Koomey, J. 2008. Worldwide electricity used in data centers. *Environ. Res. Lett.* 3: 034008.
3 Horner, N., Shehabi, A., and Azevedo, I. 2016. Known unknowns: Indirect energy effects of information and communication technology. *Environ. Res. Lett.* 11: 103001.
4 Evans, D. 2011. *The internet of things how the next evolution of the internet is changing everything*. Technical report, CISCO Internet Business Solutions Group, www.cisco.com/c/dam/en_us/about/ac79/docs/innov/IoT_IBSG_0411FINAL.pdf
5 Apple, Inc. 2016. *Environmental Responsibility Report, 2016 Progress Report, Covering FY2015*.
6 USDOE. 2016. *Buildings Energy Data Book*. U.S. Department of Energy. Building Technologies Program, US Department of Energy, Washington, DC. http://buildingsdatabook.eren.doe.gov/
7 Lee, K.H. and Vachon, S. 2016. The carbon economy: A brave new world? In K.H. Lee and S. Vachon, eds., *Business Value and Sustainability* (pp. 97–133). Palgrave Macmillan, London.
8 Van Heddeghem, W., Lambert, S., Lannoo, B., Colle, D., Pickavet, M., and Demeester, P. 2014. Trends in worldwide ICT electricity consumption from 2007 to 2012. *Comput. Commun.*, 50: 64–76.

14

INCREASING URBAN SUSTAINABILITY USING GIS

Luiz Felipe Guanaes Rego, Maria Fernanda Campos Lemos and
Luís Carlos Soares Madeira Domingues

Introduction

The continuous interaction between natural (relief, soil, climate and hydrology), structural (streets, buildings and infrastructure) and social environments (political, economic, cultural systems) define the city as a complex, multidisciplinary being. Cultivating interdisciplinary dialogue is necessary for an efficient and sustainable city project.

Cities are made by people, over time, reflecting their history, conflicts and culture. No transformation towards sustainability is legitimate without collective agreement, achieved through democratic and inclusive decision-making processes. Consequently, overcoming the challenge of an urban project requires collaborative project strategies, designed in a nonhierarchical authorship model.

The relationship between developed (full) and undeveloped (empty) spaces, permeated by the flow of people, goods, and information further defines the concept of the city. This relationship occurs at different scales – regional, urban and block. At the regional level, urban and rural areas interact with each other. At the urban scale, industrial, commercial and residential areas function alongside areas of leisure and preservation. At the block scale, buildings function together with the undeveloped spaces surrounding them, including plots of land, streets, plazas and squares. City planners must maintain a pluralistic view.

The relationship between developed and undeveloped spaces is correlated with population density and land development. These relationships influence the activities in the urban space, flow pattern, landscape appropriation and the local microclimate. Thus, the planning and management of cities require a systemic approach.

Defining the layout of the city – the planner's end goal – is but one part of the urban planning process, which is inextricably linked to social, economic, political and cultural mechanisms. The urban form cannot be separated from the urban planning process if the intention is to promote an effective and lasting transformation. Planning for land usage, population density, commerce, people, natural resources and legislation are essential for a robust urban design solution. When considering the interdependence among project, planning and management, an integral understanding of the urban landscape is fundamental.

Finding an urban design solution depends upon a precise understanding of the urban reality and an inclusive, interdisciplinary approach. However, a planner cannot comprehend the city better than its residents, given their diverse experiences living within the space. The inclusion of residents in the project from the diagnostic phase can ensure the accuracy and legitimacy of solutions.

The city can only be understood with a good diagnostic system that incorporates flexibility, monitoring, and provision for a constantly changing system, particularly considering climate change. The city design incorporates flexibility in their solutions, monitoring the dynamics of the urban system and the results applying new strategies throughout the territory.

Including a Geographic Information System (GIS) in the urban planning process is a viable solution to overcome the previously mentioned challenges and to build sustainable cities. Reflecting on the authors' experience in the city of Resende, in the state of Rio de Janeiro, Brazil, this chapter examines the relationship between planning and management processes in an urban/GIS project.

GIS potential for sustainability in city planning and design

Geographic Information System (GIS) use cartographic and geographical representations of environments on digital platforms to answer spatial questions. The system does not analyze the spatial data, but rather provides the necessary information for an expert to study the space, identify its natural and anthropogenic components, and explore solutions that promote sustainable development.

The types of questions asked determine how a GIS is used. Before beginning the planning and implementation stages of an urban project, it's necessary to raise questions that determine methods. The scale of the geographical data follows a hierarchical model and determines which spatial questions can be answered.

For example, before designing an urban sector, you first need to define solutions to specific questions. In the early stages of the project, one can use an average cartographic scale (1:10.000 to 20.000). In the transitional phases of the project, questions about components of the city, such as river basins, protected areas, and occupancy patterns could be defined on a more precise cartographic scale (1:2.000 to 5.000).

GIS employs a variety of tools (arithmetic, spatial relations, editing) to construct map layers reflecting the different types of information that provide visual solutions to spatial questions. Spatial representations range from simple maps that can answer a single question to a complex set of map layers constructed to answer a set of questions.

The construction of a geographic database from reputable sources is fundamental to successful GIS analysis and requires information from reputable sources with clearly defined metadata. The geographic data scale must be compatible with the level of detail reflected in the spatial analysis questions. It is essential to clarify that the problems arising from multiple cartographic representations at different scales are not solved in a GIS environment. Rather, the individual analyzing the problem must address the concern of scale. However, analyzing spatial questions by creating map layers at different scales can make it easier for the expert to integrate and analyze "interscaled" data.

The GIS allows the inclusion, manipulation, and development of metadata from dynamic maps, for example, climate or communication maps. The inclusion of this data is necessary to show the continuous transformation of a complex territory, such as a city or metropolitan region and supports a flexible approach to territorial management. GIS is particularly important at the regional and metropolitan scale, where it is necessary to integrate multiple municipal plans (e.g., environment, mobility and sanitation) and develop a common socioeconomic strategy.

Thus, GIS maps can be very complex. For example, one project can include numerous municipal, ecological and water storage plans. The benefit of GIS is the ability to visualize the different administrative and political goals to encourage communication among the various sectors of public administration. Each project represents a multidisciplinary perspective to solve inconsistencies in plans from municipalities within the same region.

Depending on the GIS version and package, the GIS offers a three-dimensional perspective on a landscape, population density, and bioclimatic data. By maximizing all capabilities of GIS, the residents can view a 3D representation of the urban plan and participate in the urban planning process. For example, in addition to complex metadata, a polygonal layer representing the city's master plan could be made available to residents. This layer could offer a spatial representation of proposed legislation. This 3D system also allows for monitoring current construction and adjusting territorial planning, as necessary.

A GIS can also be introduced to the public to enter real-time data. For example, residents can record crimes in the GIS-enabled map to ensure a faster police response. Participation by private citizens may increase the efficacy of the system overall. Residents could also record instances of illegal logging, illegal dumping, blackouts, and other areas of public concern to promote efficiency in urban management and improve their quality of life.

The ability to use GIS to store information and updates allows a realistic depiction of the city. It also offers the opportunity to create new strategies for a territory based on real-time information, allowing for ongoing analysis. Overcoming the challenge of integrating disciplines in the planning and management of cities has a lasting impact on construction and governance.

Including GIS in the urban planning and administration process is a primary condition for community participation and engagement in regional and municipal decision making. Allowing the public to participate in the creation of GIS data gives legitimacy to democratic governance. Social control, transparent government and facilitating smooth changes in state mandates are additional benefits of this approach. The system of public participation facilitates plans with greater autonomy.

Bases and procedures for applying GIS in city planning and design

GIS offers two models, the vector and GRID model. These models provide maps with various degrees of detail on different cartographic scales. Deciding which model to use depends on the stage of the project as well as the scale – regional, urban and block. The two systems are complementary. Understanding the two systems makes it possible to use technology to support urban sustainability.

Vector model

In the vector model, geometrical representations are not limited to the spatial relationships between objects. Both numerical attributes and spatial relationships provide critical insight into spatial questions. For example, one can illustrate a flat projection of a building with a measurable area, showing the distance from and overlap with other objects.

There are three ways to express spatial attributes – topological, describing objects at the neighborhood level; metric, representing objects in terms of distance; and prepositional, describing objects relative to others, such as "in front of" or "above."

In the vector model, geometrical representations are not limited to the spatial relationships between objects. Both numerical attributes and spatial relationships provide crucial insight into spatial questions. For example, one can use GIS to identify areas considered at risk of landslide in Rio de Janeiro due to heavy rains, soil conditions and urban decay. Creating a GIS representation of this scenario would require gathering information on highly developed areas, land, population density and household income within a single GIS map.

Both skill in understanding how to use the system and how to interpret data, as well as characteristics of the patterns, are paramount to analyzing and understanding (making sense of) these relationships. Vector models are best suited to a point in time. Flows are represented by lines and can be customized to show different relationships.

GRID (RASTER) model

The GRID model has no objects, but rather a continuum of geo-referenced units called pixels, which occupy the entire analysis section. The pixel is represented by a spatial resolution corresponding to its real world physical area. The smaller the pixel, the greater the level of detail and the larger the resulting scale. There are three types of analysis – satellite imagery, thematic data and geographical synthesis based on arithmetic operations.

Satellite imagery generates colors for the attributes based on reflectance value of landscape elements. Quick Bird,[1] Landsat[2] and MODIS[3] are three types of sensors that generator satellite images. You can extract data from the GIS system and convert it to a vector. For example, the image can assess the soil detected to determine its appropriateness for different construction projects. The map can be cross-referenced with environmental fragility maps to evaluate the possibility of an accident.

The second type of GRID method uses geo-referenced points to generate nets on geographic data. Most maps generated in GIS use point data. Rainfall, temperature and altimetry data determine the surface and color of these maps. One highly relevant use of this feature when conducting chemical, toxicological analysis involves using interpolation methods linked with socioeconomic and infrastructure data to identify areas with high pollution.

Finally, GRID maps can be synthesized to generate qualitative data. For example, several layers of data can be analyzed to calculate the incidence rate of a phenomenon. Analysis of natural disasters, such as flooding, landslides and fires and economic factors such as expansion and economic activity require a multidisciplinary approach. For example, a flood risk model on a graded map showing the areas of flood risk and the locations of past floods will provide an empirical basis for solutions proposed by urban planners.

In summary, one can infer that both vector and GRID models accurately represent the pluralistic spatial relationships that occur in the urban environment.

The experience with the municipality of Resende, Rio de Janeiro, Brazil

From January 2008 to April 2009 the authors of this chapter worked with the Center of Technical Assistance to Municipalities of the Pontifical Catholic University of Rio de Janeiro (NAT/PUC-Rio) on the GIS for the Physical-Territorial Management of the Municipality of Resende, Rio de Janeiro (RJ), Brazil project. This project explored the possibilities of incorporating a GIS with urban planning, in a real-world setting.

The location of the study, Resende, is a city in northwest Brazil. Specifically, it's located in the central region of the Paraíba do Sul River. A determining factor in selecting Resende was its location, equidistant from the country's two largest cities, Rio de Janeiro and São Paulo. At the beginning of the twentieth century, the region contributed more than 50% of the municipal GDP, followed closely by the services sector. It occupies 1,098 km², which corresponds to 2.5% of RJ's territory. Resende has a tropical climate and presents a great variation of altitude, from 394.6 meters in the city center to 2,791.6 meters in the Itatiaia Park region, a conservation unit of the Atlantic Forest.[4] Per the Brazilian Institute of Statistical Geography (IBGE), the city had an estimated 119,769 inhabitants in 2010 and 119 persons per square kilometer.

The primary objective of the project was translating urban data for compatibility with the GIS system. The primary source of the data was the Municipal Participative Master Plan (PDP).[5] Secondary goals included selecting and importing data into the GIS for analysis. The end goal of the project was to improve the efficiency, precision and local implementation of urban planning strategy by analyzing current information, considering alternatives to the current approach and developing effective legislation (e.g. land use law, construction plan, building plans) for the city. The project considered legislation implemented between 2009 and 2011. The authors were a part of this team with NAT/PUC-Rio.

The limitations and challenges of this project and, specifically, importing data in GIS, include lack of sources, unclear data, the simultaneous finalization of the PDP during this project, competing priorities and "scope creep" or adapting the project scope to accommodate new demands.

The implementation of GIS in Resende and the Brazilian urban context

To better understand urban planning in contemporary Brazil, it is important to consider Brazil's rapid urbanization and social issues in the twentieth century. The urban population increased from 44.7% in 1960 to 81.2% in 2001. The impact of the transformation is better understood with whole numbers. Over a period of 36 years between 1960 and 1996, the urban population increased from 31 million to 137 million, for a total of 106 million new residents.

Heavy urbanization with accelerated growth of the Brazilian economy increased social injustice and inequality in cities. These injustices are well-known and present in the region in many forms. Distribution of wealth between central and peripheral areas in cities is a primary concern. Urban control and expansion continue without reference to local conditions. Urban development is disconnected from actual urban conditions and ignores the fact that most of the population has very low income and investment in spaces.

The City Statute,[6] Brazilian federal law 10257, gives the municipality the exclusive power to legislate on matters of local interest, to augment federal and state legislation as appropriate and to control land usage distribution. Each local municipality is responsible for the development of the city's social functions, the well-being of inhabitants and ensuring that public property meets societal needs. These activities are conducted in agreement with the criteria established in the municipal's PDP, which the Brazilian constitution names the primary instrument guiding urban policy.

Resende's city statutes served as a primary reference for the NAT team, paying special attention to opportunities to incorporate sustainable development principles in the development standards. The PDP provided an excellent informative basis from to structure the territorial management system in GIS for Resende.

GIS – urban design coordination strategies in the city of Resende

To ensure consistency between planning and implementation, this was an interdepartmental effort with the Urban Planning team, the Ecological-Economic Zoning team, Environmental Vulnerability Mapping team, Environmental and Urban Legislation team, and the Geographical Basis team, thus implementing an interdisciplinary approach to work.

The team started the analysis with current city materials, by identifying information gaps and directing the process for using GIS to select additional information. After the analysis of the material, the GIS feeding stage began, which consisted of transferring diagnostic information, documents that were reformatted to suit GIS, and finally, the translation of proposed PDP strategies.

The Information Matrix Plan (IMP)

The Information Matrix Plan (IMP) served as the foundation of project methodology. The team developed the IMP for analysis, classification and delivery of information within the GIS. The IMP served as a visual of the most significant information prepared by the urban planning team and the other project teams. Regular seminars and workshops among the teams of NAT/PUC-Rio complemented this process.

The team developed the IMP based on the selection of information per the following criteria: (1) relevance to the GIS system in Resende, (2) relevance to territorial management, applicability and efficiency as determined by the municipality's technical staff, (3) existence of data, and (4) feasibility of installing the information in GIS and reliability of data.

The team added additional criteria to the IMP throughout the course of the project. One such addition was a description of the information in each row and column of the matrix, to facilitate translation into the GIS system. These additions made it easier to map data in the territorial management process.

Table 14.1 reports and describes this process: (1) the urban planning topic to be addressed in the GIS, (2) how the layer is represented and manipulated in the GIS, (3) attributes related to that information, (4) the scale of information and licensing considerations, (5) the frequency of information updates, and (6) the source of the data and possible association with other layers and sources of information. These items were deployed in the vector environment of geographic data storage.

The IMP became an instrument to support the larger PDP, creating a plan to visualize each topic, either with simple maps or detailed maps with multiple layers as its basic characteristics (e.g. geometry, attributes, scale and periodicity). This system allowed urban planning information to be parsed by the GIS software.

An equally important function of the matrix is its visual representation of simple maps (single layers) and complex maps (multiple, integrated layers) within the system.

After translating the final bit of information in the GIS, the team developed a system to classify the layers and attributes of the geo-referenced data for urban planning using the translated content from the PDP that was developed for the GIS.

For this purpose, the team developed charts (titled *Indications of subsidy for urban planning through the GIS base in Resende*) for each of the main GIS information sets related to urban planning – territorial organization, urban legislation, roads, land use, housing, public facilities and urban voids). Each chart contained the following information: (1) the purpose of the information in territorial planning, (2) the possibility of being used with other information in the system, and (3) the challenges associated with updating the information in the system and its future development. The chart for "urban voids" is presented in Table 14.2 as an example of this stage of the process.

Deployment by the GIS expert

The IMP is a methodological tool that allows the urban planner to determine the scope of analysis, define spatial questions, and consider the various dimensions (e.g., political, environmental, social) in a territory. From these elements, a group of GIS experts selects the geographic databases that generate information layers, simple maps and, eventually, complex maps that illustrate spatial proposals.

Creating a geographic database usually represents more than 70% of the total cost of deploying a GIS. This process may involve reconciling information in different scales, generating specific attributes to verify calculations, updating existing cartographic bases and generating digital versions of paper maps.

Table 14.1 Structure of the Information Planning Matrix

IPM structural columns	Item	Description (layers)	Attribute (database)	Geometry (GIS features)	Scale	Periodicity
Objective of the columns	Description of the theme usually applied to territorial planning (layer association)	Subdivision of the theme in the smallest coherent portions of information	Additional information, texts, tables, images, etc., associated with the geo-referenced layer	Graphic components of the representation of the layer in the GIS	Suggested scale for representation of the information compatible with the system	Time interval at which it is advised to verify and update the information in the database
Example of matrix of information supply related to territorial planning	Cultural heritage and historical-symbolic references	Assets protected or preserved by legislation Reference spaces for local culture not yet preserved by legislation	Date of the act of protection or preservation (including the protection entity) and its restrictions; Specific characteristics (reasons to consider it an asset and the uses it currently holds); Association with images and other texts	Polygon points (depending on the scale of representation or level of accuracy of the original information)	1:2000–1:5000 (prioritizes the features of the property) 1:25000–1:50000 (prioritizes the location of the property in context of the neighborhood or municipality)	1–5 years

Table 14.2 Indications of subsidy for urban planning through the GIS base in Resende: Urban Voids (example)

Urban Voids	Remark	The layer "urban voids" is included in the GIS system in Resende, including the description and location of each void, as identified in the Strategic Plan for Occupancy of Urban Voids and Containment of Spreading (SPOUVCS).
	General function	It facilitates the control and proper management of vacant urban areas that hold value for the future of the city. The manager establishes guidelines to determine the possible role of these areas, monitor threats and consider opportunities. Therefore, the *PEOVUCE* and a monitoring system for these areas are necessary conditions to achieve this objective.
	Potential of articulation	Monitoring the void spaces in conjunction with the road system allows a more effective field inspection. The associated analysis allows greater insight into the value of each space.
	Challenges of maintenance and future development	Attention to detail regarding the limits of the data is important. Effective monitoring will require constant updates to the system, including maintaining records of developed land and the prompt registration of formerly vacant spaces.

For this project, the team adapted data set to 1:25.000 (the Brazilian mapping standard developed by IBGE) to scales greater than 1:2000. The transformation process included conducting fieldwork with GPS support and acquiring and interpreting high-resolution aerial photos. The photos, in grid format with a spatial resolution of 50 cm, were orthorectified to ensure the reliability of data and to interpret the rugged terrain.

The team also used aerial photos to render an up-to-date cartographic representation of the region. Though the scale was compatible with the analysis, 1:2000, it was outdated, because it did not include the recent municipal expansion. It is also worth mentioning that this representation was generated in CAD. Converting the representation from CAD to GIS format was a lengthy process. The process involved inserting attributes that verify geometric measurements, a necessary step to perform GIS analysis.

The NAT team started working on GIS in the second phase of the project when the PDP was nearly complete. Consolidating the geo-referenced database involved creating cross-links between layers, and multiple spatial products to create the final product, the PDP. Consolidating the geo-referenced database ultimately resulted in a revision of the nearly-completed PDP.

To demonstrate how layers, intersect, one could examine the process of mapping urban voids in the diagnostic phase. The urban voids are regulated by the Strategic Plan of Urban Void Occupancy and Sprawl Containment (PEOVUCE), which established adequate standards of control and management of the areas still empty within the city. Intersecting the urban voids map with the transportation system map added to the analysis of land occupation trends and supported the city's expansion planning.

The overlay of thematic maps is an old practice and has always been used by the urban planner. GIS strengthens this technique by offering a more structured set of information, allowing systematic control of results, and allowing cross-linked information, such as coverage and usage patterns.

Analyzing complex maps does not ensure the desired result, and it is important that the urban planner seeks the advice of multidisciplinary experts and includes the views of residents to validate conclusions. In the case of the Resende municipal project, the final product represented different hypotheses and proposals of thematic synthesis, including how environmental zones are influenced by the transportation system. Other examples include a map showing occupancy trends and road conditions to demonstrate the influence of a high-speed train and a depiction of the macro-zoning of the urban area. These concepts were presented to the public for feedback, and that feedback was used to develop the final model.

In Brazil, a master plan (PDP) becomes law after several steps, beginning with a review by local representatives. Following this review, city council members hold a public hearing, in which the PDP is officially ratified. Thus, the establishment of the PDP is a political decision. The municipality of Resende hired the PUC-Rio research team to develop a draft law for the PDP, which was finalized and prepared for the ballot. The team expects to reevaluate the initiative in Resende in the future, to ensure future expansion plans are compatible with the initial proposal and to assess if the project has contributed to more balanced and sustainable management practices.

A municipal GIS system, able to manage the information generated in the process of creating the master plan, greatly simplifies the task of monitoring results in the municipality and adjusting to ensure the initiative's success. This is just one of the benefits of the GIS system in the municipality. Essentially, the GIS creates the basis for smart city management and boosts urban sustainability.

The GIS legacy in the municipality

The implementation of the GIS management system represents a smart city and urban management in the municipality. When the team wrapped up its participation in Resende, local technicians were trained to manage the GIS system. Their duties will include updating the GIS system with new information and resolutions from the with different public management departments.

Because the urban plans were updated immediately, the master plan, and land use guidelines could be used for comparative analysis and licensing new construction.

The system has increased the efficiency of the data management and decision-making process and the population's access to urban planning information. Residents can view their homes and neighborhoods online in the city plan along with metadata for their properties and other properties in the neighborhood, with these initiatives, citizen engagement and participation in the decision-making process has greatly increased.

For the system to reach its full potential, it depends on its continued use by the public. More than technology, becoming a smart city depends on fostering a culture of acceptance and continued use of GIS technologies and a culture of collaboration. The GIS facilitates the implementation of these processes, but without it, the connection between the municipality and public is weakened.

Conclusion

The current crisis between society and the natural environment created the concept of the Anthropocene – a picture of the human impact on the planet's biosphere. In this context, cities have multiplied (as shown by UN forecasts) and by 2025 half of the planet's population will live in cities that occupy just over one percent of the developing land.

Cities, therefore, play a fundamental role in understanding anthropic impact on the environment. Municipalities can seek spatial and urban solutions that promote good quality of life, equity, and low environmental impact.

Geo-technology contributes to a more efficient management of urban space, in conjunction with city planning and management. It provides an appropriate analytical environment for the development of diagnostics and scenarios of the future and the monitoring of the urban dynamics and the effects of current interventions in the city. The GIS applied to the urban project can also facilitate an inclusive, interdisciplinary, and collaborative approach that is essential to the design of more sustainable cities. It also provides the basis for the adoption of other technologies, particularly information and communication technologies (ICT), which guide the city toward smart development and management.

Maintaining updated physical-territorial visualization of urban plans and projects allows ongoing monitoring and improvement on analytic and practical strategies. Thus, the GIS system democratizes the municipal management system through the dissemination of information about the territory and the collaborative processes. This process establishes the basis for engaging residents in the decision-making process and giving them control over the territory.

The application of GIS and its effectiveness in urban design, planning, and management require an understanding of the tool, the environment to be mapped and the technical and institutional capacity of the municipality. Therefore, the structure of the municipal administration, the regulatory framework, and the local urban context determine the conditions.

The case of the municipality of Resende, as presented in this chapter, highlights some applications of geographical syntheses that can be translated to spatial analysis. The case study confirmed the multidisciplinary nature of implementing GIS to support the development of a municipal master plan. It reconciles the conceptual basis in modeling of geographic databases that support complex spatial analysis.

The work of the NAT/PUC-Rio team in the second phase of the project, demonstrated the potential to transform the system in Resende. This transformation was due to the transparency of technicians and public managers, the consistency among plans and the general demands territory management. Therefore, the appropriation of the GIS in Resende had an immediate transforming effect on public management.

The success of a GIS in supporting the planning and sustainable management of urban space is not dependent on the technology, but on the competence of the technicians involved in the process. Multidisciplinary expertise, an institutional culture that values planning and management processes, including monitoring and evaluation, and active residents who participate in the management process all facilitate the success of GIS. Transparent governance that is committed to the success of the GIS system and to using it in the interest of the public while being guided by socio-environmental principles is vital to a successful GIS/urban planning project.

Notes

1 QuickBird was the first in a series of satellites developed by DigitalGlobe with high spatial resolution and accuracy. Its multispectral and panchromatic sensors capture images with 23 m horizontal (CE 90%) spatial accuracy and 60 cm spatial resolution in natural and artificial colors. It has great data storage capacity and temporal resolution.
2 Landsat has the largest collection of satellite data. Developed by NASA and the U.S. Geological Survey, it is used on government, military and commercial projects worldwide.
3 MODIS (or Moderate Resolution Imaging Spectroradiometer) was developed by NASA and is used on the Terra (previously known as EOS AM-1) and Aqua (previously known as EOS PM-1) satellites.
4 The Atlantic Forest is an area of significant importance for the municipality and the region.
5 By law, all sectorial plans (e.g., mobility, sanitation, housing) are submitted to generate this master territorial plan, which is municipal urban management's primary instrument. The master plan is mandatory for all municipalities in Brazil with more than 20,000 inhabitants. Specifically, it is required in urban areas, tourist sites and locations deemed to have significant environmental impact.

6 Federal law (10257), which deals with the urban development of cities, was approved in 2001. It addresses the challenges of proposing urban reconstruction, under new principles, with new methods and concepts, and new tools. The Statute's innovations are divided into three areas – new urban-planning instruments aimed at inducing the different forms of land use, the possibilities of regulating urban property with ambiguous borders, and the idea of including citizens in the discussion of the city's future.

References

Brasil. Estatuto das metrópoles (http://legislacao.planalto.gov.br/legisla/legislacao.nsf/Viw_Identificacao/lei%2013.089-2015?OpenDocument) Accessed 16 August 2016.

Brasil. Ministério das Cidades. *Estatuto da Cidade: guia para implementação pelos municípios e cidadãos*. Ministério das Cidades/FASE, São Paulo, novembro de 2004.

Burrough, Peter, and McDonnell, Rachel. (1998) *Principles of Geographical Information Systems*. Oxford: Oxford University Press.

Harvey, David. (2014) *Cidades Rebeldes: Do Direito à Cidade à Revolução Urbana*. São Paulo: Martins Fontes. 1ª edição.

Jenks, Mike, and Dempsey, Nicola. (2005) *Future Forms and Design for Sustainable Cities*. New York: Architectural Press.

Kinder, David, Higgs, Gary, and White, Sean. (2003) *Socio-Economic Applications of Geographic Information Science*. London: Taylor and Francis.

Longley, Paul, Goodchild, Michael F., Maguire, David, and Rhind, David. (2005) *Geographic Information Systems and Science*. New Jersey: Wiley.

Moura, Ana Clara Mourão (2003) *Geoprocessamento na Gestão e Planejamento Urbano*. Belo Horizonte, Brazil: Interciência.

PNUMA (Programa das Nações Unidas para o Meio Ambiente). (2003) *Manual geociudades. Metodología para La Elaboración de los Informes GEO Ciudades*.

Rolnik, Raquel. (1997) *A cidade e a lei: legislação, política urbana e territórios na cidade de São Paulo*. São Paulo: Studio Nobel.

Silva, Heliana Vilela de Oliveira. (2008) *O Uso de Indicadores Ambientais para Aumentar a Efetividade da Gestão Ambiental Municipal*. Rio de Janeiro: COPPE, D.Sc., Planejamento Energético.

Thomas, Randall. (2003) *Sustainable Urban Design*. London: Spon Press.

PART 3

Values, ethics, and identity

Both designers and consumers have an existence demarcated from what are believed to be their actual values. An individual may oppose child labor practices, deforestation, and pollution, but purchase $5 shirts, disposable electronics, and "value" meals. In many cases, consumers are ignorant as to the origin of their products. In other situations, the pull of seductive advertising and the glamorization of consumerism are too strong to resist. Part 3 of the *Handbook of Sustainable Design* examines using design to realign our values, ethics, and identities in accessible ways.

The chapters in this section span the globe and draw from vastly different cultural experiences. Much like the previous section, they each address issues of global impact. But this group of chapters investigates how we construct individual and cultural identities and design for our individual and collective values. One could argue that "doomsday" examples and lists of scientific facts on climate change have had little effect on overall behaviors toward sustainability. The contributions in Part 3 focus on connecting empathy with a deeper awareness of our actions and their impact to facilitate change.

In contrast to more traditional commercial-based design approaches, practitioners in Human Centered Design (HCD) seek to understand the empathetic needs and emotions of the user. Bruce Hanington contextualizes HCD in light of sustainability in his chapter *Empathy, values, and situated action: sustaining people and planet through human centered design*. In doing so, the "user" becomes not only an individual but also part of the community and society as a whole. Hanington includes methods for HCD research and a framework of four levels of human centered design aimed at sustainable change.

Theresa J. Edmonds continues the theme of compassion in her chapter *Practicing empathy to connect people and the environment*. Edmonds' work contemplates how designers can cultivate empathy that fosters an interconnected view of individuals and the environment. Practicing design "in these ways illuminates the world as a complex, interrelated system and emphasizes the importance of responding to needs, collaborating across differences, and seeking guidance from ethical and moral teachings."

Edmonds' work invites personal reflection, which is also explored by Yoko Akama in her chapter *Surrendering to the ocean: practices of mindfulness and presence in designing*. Akama considers "ways to practice mindfulness that foregrounds being and becoming with, instead of accounting and obligating, where sustainability means a surrendering to impermanence and interrelatedness." The chapter is not an instructional guide to mindfulness and design practices, but rather a philosophical memoir to Akama's personal practice.

The efforts of humanitarian design are often considered helpful and potentially life saving for individuals in need, but equally detrimental when it means disregarding cultural and regional considerations. Brita Fladvad Nielsen draws on her work with refugee camps in Ethiopia to explore these challenges in her chapter *Confronting the five paradoxes of humanitarian design*. The ethics of who is helping whom, how, and in what ways present challenges when evaluating the impact of design. The chapter illustrates how we need to rethink relief on multiple levels to confront paradoxes in the environment, short-term thinking, self-reliance, multiple agendas, and scalability.

Maria Rogal and Raúl Sánchez work with design students through Design for Development (D4D), an international initiative started by Rogal. D4D brings design students from the United States to work with "indigenous entrepreneurs, farmers, artisans, and other groups from southern Mexico seeking to tell their collective stories through their products and services." In their chapter, *Codesigning for development*, Rogal and Sánchez discuss working with design movements pushing to "design for the other 90%" while also being critical of colonialist issues. The term codesign suggests an equally collaborative partnership where, much like explored in the previous chapter, designers must work carefully to preserve cultural values and intentions.

Traveling across the globe again, Benny Ding Leong and Brian Lee write about their research in the chapter *The Internet of life: changing lifestyles and sustainable values in fast-developing China and India*. Leong and Lee's work strives to identify "the values and meanings for which people yearn, while simultaneously considering the contextual constraints that have shaped and will shape their preferences." Their perspectives shed insight into the world of millennials driving the Asian economy that will have a profound impact locally and globally. Although their research is on the effects of Internet technologies and the Internet of Things (IoT) in China and India, the overall themes in their findings extend to cultures in both the developed and developing worlds. Understanding lifestyle values in this context enables designers to redirect consumers toward a "socially and culturally acceptable path toward sustainability."

Fashion helps construct individual and collective identities. The fashion industry carries deep ties to ethical and values-based decisions in designing, manufacturing, selling, and wearing. In *Fashion, the city, and the spectacle* Dilys Williams considers how identity is formed both individually and culturally through dress and place. Williams describes how "the social fit of our clothes involves intuitive, personal stories and knowledge, which are less easily transferable and yet, it is these elements of fashion that stitch a city's social forms and visual narratives together, connecting matter with meaning."

Finally, the closing chapter of Part 3 considers the individual designer's career. The person or entity behind the employer is among the many issues facing today's innovators. *Designing individual careers and work environments for sustainable value* by Cynthia Scott offers tools to help designers identify their own values and explains how to align those values by creating meaningful employment. Here, sustainability applies not only to the betterment of the planet but also to sustaining oneself. Creating meaningful work is important, as are the values encompassing the work environment. Sustainable design is not only about the outward contributions but also about examining one's own personal values.

Throughout this section, different approaches are taken to deepen our understanding of personal and cultural identities and how they translate into our ethics and values toward one another and the planet. These chapters invite us to slow down and reflect on our practices, understanding of the world, as well as fellow designers and consumers. In a world where we make countless split-second decisions with consequences that extend decades into the future, this reflection is becoming increasingly necessary. The multicultural approaches in this section are complementary to a design practice that cultivates a holistic and inclusive approach to design for sustainability.

15

EMPATHY, VALUES, AND SITUATED ACTION

Sustaining people and planet through human centered design

Bruce Hanington

Introduction

Human centered design (HCD), or user centered design (UCD), is an integrated research and design approach led by the motivation to responsibly and responsively address the genuine needs and desires of people affected by design intervention. The approach stands in contrast to technology-led or purely commercial, marketing-driven approaches, and extends throughout the design process through a set of creative research methods and processes aimed at enhancing design outcomes and therefore human lives affected by design. Clearly implied here is an adherence to Herbert Simon's definition of design being "to devise courses of action aimed at changing existing situations into preferred ones" (Simon, 1996). Contextualizing human centered design in terms of sustainability would assume changing situations into those preferred not only by individual users, but also by communities of people and society at large, and with respect for the natural environment.

Whereas sustainability is defined throughout other sections of this book, it should be noted that in this chapter the term is used broadly, encompassing environmental, social, economic, cultural and humanitarian responsibility (see Pilloton, 2009). People should be empowered with agency to live their lives with fulfillment and self-worth, and with the economic means to maintain sustainable levels of health, education and general well-being, with respect for personhood and culture. Elements of design oriented in this direction are encompassed under "social design," which is focused on real change for the betterment of human life and the planet. When human centered design is used as a mechanism toward positive social and environmental change, the approach has much to offer in these broader terms of sustainability.

Human centered design can itself be sustainable, at least when practiced well, and with balanced respect for people, planet and profit. First, it is inherently participatory. Human centered design reaches people and communities where they are, validating their genuine needs and desires through responsible design. Second, participation by stakeholders can ensure greater chances of successful design delivery, and therefore less waste of time, money and resources in processes and outcomes. It engages people, to guide both design of the right thing, and to design the thing right. Third, human centered design can result in products, tools and services specifically focused on facilitating or encouraging sustainable behaviors, or behavior change. And finally, engaged participation in the process of human centered design can motivate people to committed action.

This chapter provides a context for human centered design through a brief history and overview of currently defined practice, coupled with a more specific understanding of the approach motivated toward sustainability. Methods for conducting human centered research and design will be discussed, highlighting those with greatest potential in the context of sustainability. A framework of four levels of human centered design aimed at sustainable change will be presented. In conclusion, benefits and outcomes of human centered design will be discussed, including critique and future of the approach.

History and focus of human centered design

Aside from specific terminology, human centered design is not entirely new. The evolution of tools, shelter (architecture), clothing and other products aimed at meeting human needs and conditions obviously have a lengthy history. For as long as we have been making things to accomplish human goals we have been "human centered." However, the notion of formally assessing and designing for the capabilities and limitations of people as an explicit approach has a shorter history, and one that differs in emphasis between industrial design and human computer interaction, the two disciplines in which human centered design primarily evolved.

Much of human centered design history can be tied to milestones in technological innovation. Motivated by assembly line production being perfected in the early 1900s, design interventions claiming to improve work for people took a mechanistic view aimed at increased efficiency. The use of scientific management principles known as Taylorism borrowed directly from manufacturing and factory processes, extending into the domestic realm to rationalize work flow in the kitchen and other areas of home management. Analyses using time and motion studies, for example, would inspire solutions for the "efficient kitchen" (see Frederick, 1920; Lupton and Miller, 1992). However, this approach had little to do with the nuance of how work was actually conducted or individually preferred, failing to account for the personal meaning of activities centered around care of home and family, the chore of cleaning, or the satisfaction of preparing meals according to embedded traditions or desired routines.

The formal discipline of Human Factors emerged during World War II with the study of "manned systems." At that time, "attention was focused on operations analysis, operator selection, training, and the environment associated with signal detection and recognition, communication, and vehicle control. Concurrently, human factors work in industry was focused on efficiency, task analysis, and time-and-motion studies" (Human Factors and Ergonomics Society, n.d.). However, in the peace following World War II, human factors concerns broadened to include systems design in industrial and consumer arenas, eventually with impact in transportation, manufacturing, farming, health care, technology, organizational design and other critical aspects of life. The Human Factors and Ergonomics Society (HFES) was formally established in 1957.

As early as 1955, the industrial design pioneer Henry Dreyfuss advocated for what would eventually become known as human centered design in his landmark book, *Designing for People*. Dreyfuss was recognized for ergonomically driven design, taking into account both physical fit and cognitive ease of use in such ubiquitous consumer products as the classic round Honeywell thermostat and the standard desk set telephone. Dreyfuss was largely responsible for a significant shift in thinking from the fitting of "man to machine," which dominated pre–World War II engineered products, to fitting machines to man, or, products to people (Dreyfuss, 1955; Lupton, 2014). This shift in thinking saw the need for products and systems to map or adapt to human capabilities and limitations, rather than forcing people to work within the constraints of technology.

However progressive, designing for people in the early years was still dominantly focused on the meeting of ergonomic and usability criteria, essentially a reductionist view of people as one element in a mechanistic system of inputs and outputs. The efficient completion of tasks was still addressed primarily on the basis of ergonomic principles of fit, safety and comfort. It was not until the 1980s that signals began to emerge that incorporated a broader view of the human in industrial design. For example, *semantics* as a design approach channeled away from the simple mantra of form follows function, with a focus on making products meaningful, easy to use and enjoyable to experience (Krippendorff and Butter, 1984; Krippendorff, 2005).

Likewise, the primary focus of early Human-Computer Interaction (HCI) was on workplace efficiency and measurable usability. The rise of complex consumer electronics in the home saw the emergence of interaction design as distinct from industrial design, and subsequent attention being paid to the emotional impact of technology products, and therefore a more holistic view of people. Rosalind Picard's landmark book on *Affective Computing* was first published in 1997, extending her prior MIT technical report published in 1995. Picard's work recognized the critical role that emotions play in decision making, perception and learning, advocating for why we must give computers the ability to recognize and understand human emotion, and even to have and express their own emotions (Picard, 1995, 1997).

Similarly, in 2000, Patrick Jordan advocated for a revised view of human factors in his book *Designing Pleasurable Products: An Introduction to the New Human Factors* (Jordan, 2000). Jordan promoted a broad look at design, crafting a framework of experiential pleasures of human-product interaction based on the work of anthropologist Lionel Tiger (1992). The text was among the early works to recognize that usability had moved from being what marketing professionals call a "satisfier" to being a "dissatisfier." In other words, people were no longer pleasantly surprised when a product was usable, but were unpleasantly surprised by difficulty in use. Recognizing that the human response to products and systems is comprised of more than physical fit and information processing, the "new" human factors explicitly promoted a more holistic view of people.

This more holistic view of people was gradually encompassed under "user experience," a term first coined by Donald Norman at a Computer-Human Interaction (CHI) conference in 1995. This led to similarly accepted terms such as experience design, design for experience, and ultimately the established shorthand of "UX" for user experience design, which is still in use today. A broader understanding of people and how to design for them advocated under user experience saw affective human factors as coexisting with cognitive and behavioral concerns more traditionally associated with product and system usability.

In 2004 John McCarthy and Peter Wright published *Technology as Experience*, building heavily on the premise of John Dewey's notion of lived experience, suggesting that we not only *use* technology, we *live* with it. It stands to reason that if we are to design according to the popularized term "user experience," we must take into account the "emotional, intellectual, and sensual aspects" of the interactions we are creating. This aspect of felt human experience, viewing technology as creative, open and relational, again presented a challenge to traditional notions of human computer interaction as merely fulfilling functional usability needs (McCarthy and Wright, 2004).

The current International Organization for Standardization (ISO) definition of human centered design is covered under ISO 9241-210:2010, "Ergonomics of human-system interaction – Part 210: Human-centred design for interactive systems" and reads in part as follows:

> Human-centred design is an approach to interactive systems development that aims to make systems usable and useful by focusing on the users, their needs and requirements, and by applying human factors/ergonomics, and usability knowledge and techniques. This approach enhances effectiveness and efficiency, improves human well-being, user

satisfaction, accessibility and sustainability; and counteracts possible adverse effects of use on human health, safety and performance.

(International Organization for Standardization, 2010)

Within the ISO standard, user experience is noted as

[a] person's perceptions and responses resulting from the use and/or anticipated use of a product, system or service. User experience includes all the users' emotions, beliefs, preferences, perceptions, physical and psychological responses, behaviors and accomplishments that occur before, during and after use.

(International Organization for Standardization, 2010)

The ISO lists three factors that influence user experience: system, user and the context of use.

This has led to a shift away from usability engineering to a much richer scope of user experience, where users' feelings, motivations, and values are given as much, if not more, attention than efficiency, effectiveness and basic subjective satisfaction (i.e. the three traditional usability metrics).

(User Experience, n.d.)

Just as the evolution of *concerns* has moved from a limited view of people as operational elements in a feedback loop to more holistic perspectives, so too have the *methods* of human centered design. Earliest methods were focused primarily on testing of human factors criteria, often after the fact when products were already designed, prototyped, engineered or even manufactured. This involved mostly testing methods focused on engineering performance measures such as task completion times and error rates; in essence, early forms of usability testing. Other design criteria, including physical and cognitive performance data based on statistical averages, were often supplied by human factors practitioners, shipped to designers in formats challenging to incorporate into the creative design process.

Participatory design methods growing out of Scandinavia played a significant role in changing the mindset of how human centered design would be practiced, and introduced an inherently social process. As outlined in a short history by Kuhn and Winograd (1996), beginning in Norway in the 1970s, participatory projects engaged union workers directly in the introduction of computing into workplace design. These early approaches established a philosophy and methods instrumental in advancing the causes of participatory design; most notably, that design be conducted as a collective effort by "skilled, experienced users and design professionals" (Ehn, 1992). Users possess intimate practical knowledge and engage in processes that designers must strive to understand; yet designers have unique insight into technical possibilities that users may not see. Likewise, success was contingent upon methods beyond technical specifications and interviews, expanding to site visits, joint discussions and shared learning, design-by-doing, mock-ups and organizational games (Ehn, 1992).

The precedent of participatory design in Scandinavia slowly gave rise to similar movements in North America. Greenbaum and Kyng (cited in Kuhn and Winograd, 1996), identify four core design issues that can essentially be credited for laying the foundation for many human centered research methods in established practice today. These foundational elements can be assumed to extend beyond the context of work, to leisure, home and social life:

1   The need for designers to take work practice seriously – to see the current ways that work is done as an evolved solution to a complex work situation that the designer only partially understands.

2   The fact that we are dealing with human actors, rather than cut-and-dried human factors – systems need to deal with users' concerns, treating them as people, rather than as performers of functions in a defined work role.

3   The idea that work tasks must be seen within their context and are therefore situated actions, whose meaning and effectiveness cannot be evaluated in isolation from the context.

4   The recognition that work is fundamentally social, involving extensive cooperation and communication.

The rise of participatory design and the search for ongoing ways of creatively engaging "users" (people) in design inspired further changes to the practice of design research, most notably the introduction of methods earlier and earlier in the process, often referred to as the "fuzzy front end." Eventually turning to the established methods of anthropology and psychology, designers gravitated toward ethnographic methods, based largely on the appealing features of rigor within a recognized qualitative approach, the very contextual nature of anthropological inquiry, and a compatible set of interests residing in social concerns. To illustrate, the following definition of ethnography easily serves the interests of design: "The study of people in their natural settings; a descriptive account of social life and culture in a defined social system, based on qualitative methods (e.g., detailed observations, unstructured interviews, analysis of documents)" (Bowling, 1997).

However, ethnography as practiced in its pure form is an anthropological method often involving extensive hours, months or even years of immersive experience within a culture under study. It is therefore necessary to distinguish *design ethnography*, which attempts to approximate the immersion techniques of ethnographers, but without the same investment of time. Nonetheless, a significant premise of design ethnography is that it is highly contextual. The argument for understanding context to engage with and design for people is underscored by situated action, arguing that peoples' actions are a continuous dialectic dependent on material and social circumstance, and moment-to-moment interactions between people and with their environment (Suchman, 1987). Situated action again understands people in a codeterminant relationship with the world, far more complex and humane than a linear input–output exchange.

The evolution of concerns and methods detailed here is one that witnessed the move of human centered design from a traditional view based on measurement and evaluation of individual interactions with products, to creative means designed to engage people in unique, participatory ways, to adapted methods that assess human experiences in context as guiding inspiration within the design process. All of these methods can be placed on a trajectory that moved from testing users as an element in a mechanistic system to one of participatory inclusion of people in a process; a move that also saw changes from a quantitative scientific approach to more qualitative social methods; to contextual methods more holistically focused on empathically responding to the composite needs and desires of human beings.

Human centered methods for sustainable design

Methods of human centered research and design that are appropriately focused on sustainable behaviors and concerns are inherently participatory, contextual and creative. Current forms of design ethnography, practices of participatory design, and creative design workshops provide a baseline of approaches from which to work, with a broad range of methods encompassed within each, and wide latitude for the adaptation and creation of new methods uniquely catering to varied situations.

Methods employed under the broad umbrella of design ethnography include various forms of observation, experience sampling and diary studies, simulation exercises, conversational interviews and directed storytelling (Hanington and Martin, 2012). Many ethnographic methods in design are converged under the general rubric of *contextual inquiry*. This means gaining an empathic view into peoples' lives through direct exposure, visiting them in their homes and places of work. These methods are used primarily in the exploratory phase of research, whereby designers need to gain knowledge of products and people, coupled with genuine empathy for those affected by proposed design interventions.

At the most contextual level, participant observation immerses the researcher as a member of the cohort under study. This investment is rare in design, with more typical forms of observation ranging from distant "fly on the wall" to more intimate shadowing. Experience sampling consists of collecting self-reported information through smartphone or paper diary studies, often by signaling participants at random intervals to gather a longitudinal cross-section of information. Simulation exercises place people in approximated versions of human or environmental conditions to garner empathy through firsthand experience; for example, restrictive attire that simulates age-related physical deficits of the elderly, or navigating space using a wheelchair. Contextual inquiry typically combines observation with conversational interviews, and may include a touchstone tour whereby participants verbally guide the design researcher through their environment, possessions or a system they use. Directed storytelling prompts participants to offer a rich narrative, based on their personal experience of a product, service or system.

Participatory methods as they are practiced today rely heavily on creative tool kits. Elizabeth B.-N. Sanders has coined the term "make tools" to describe an array of materials aimed at fostering creative engagement with research participants, while also the name of her company (make-tools.com). Whereas self-report instruments are adept at capturing the past, and observation captures the present, make tools are valuable in facilitating the communication of desired futures (Sleeswijk-Visser et al., 2005). For example, collage kits allow people to project their thoughts, needs and desires onto a visual artifact for discussion; flexible modeling kits composed of modular forms, feature sets or component parts allow participants to configure fantasy or desirable objects to express their preferred actions and experiences. The use of these tool kits facilitates conversations, through projective and constructive techniques that overcome the limitations of verbal or written expression. (Hanington and Martin, 2012).

In facilitating the projection of desirable futures by people, Sanders has since extended the participatory codesign process to combine making with telling (stories) and enacting (role playing). Collectively this process constitutes a participatory prototyping cycle (PPC), enabling people to make ideas tangible, talk about them in personal detail, and provide context to an imagined future through the acting out of scenarios with the artifacts they have made, their own bodies and simple props at hand (Sanders, 2013).

Design workshops provide an efficient and dynamic venue for creatively exploring topics with people to guide design inspiration. In contrast to focus groups based primarily on discussion led by a single moderator and often in response to existing products or conditions, design workshops center on imaginative activities facilitated by a team. Encompassing make tools or other means of flexible communication, participants are encouraged to craft visual or physical representations of past, current and desired future experiences. A cornerstone of workshops is shared output, with rich descriptions of generated work provided by participants through presentation and discussion. Conversation in a group context is eased by the investment made in personal artifacts, although nonetheless is reliant on a positive environment led by competent facilitators.

Human centered sustainable design

The potential of human centered *sustainable* design lays in the creation of products and services that motivate or empower people to action, in harmony with the planet and other living things. Design can intervene from simple to complex ways, ranging from the creation of rewarding interactions for sorting waste, or designing apps for vetting responsible corporate sources for products, to providing the scaffold for motivated action such as the sourcing of locally produced goods, through to design roles in larger community efforts such as volunteerism or cleaning up blighted neighborhoods, and even the design-led creation of global scale shared-service networks.

A model of human centered sustainable design first and foremost must take an expansive view of people and their context, well beyond the limited notion of "users" who merely interact with products, communications and services in an input-feedback-action loop. Furthermore, whereas human centered design has always emphasized an awareness of people, a sustainable model positions the natural world as the context in which all design occurs. In other words, as articulated by Irwin:

> The "designed" or "built" world is always embedded within the social world and both of these are always embedded within the "natural" world or environment. The built, social, and natural worlds are nested, interconnected, and interdependent spheres in which countless continual interactions take place. Placing the design of products, communications, and environments (both physical and digital) within the greater contexts of society and the natural world compels students [and designers] to frame design problems within ethical and environmental contexts.
>
> *(Irwin, 2015, see Figure 15.1)*

Beyond the physical design of artifacts are the emergent areas of design for services and social innovation. Design for service focuses on the totality of experience between providers and users of a service, encompassing products, communications and environments within a larger ecology of interactions. Design for social innovation expands the exploration of problems and needs beyond the traditional commercial context, to address social, cultural and economic concerns.

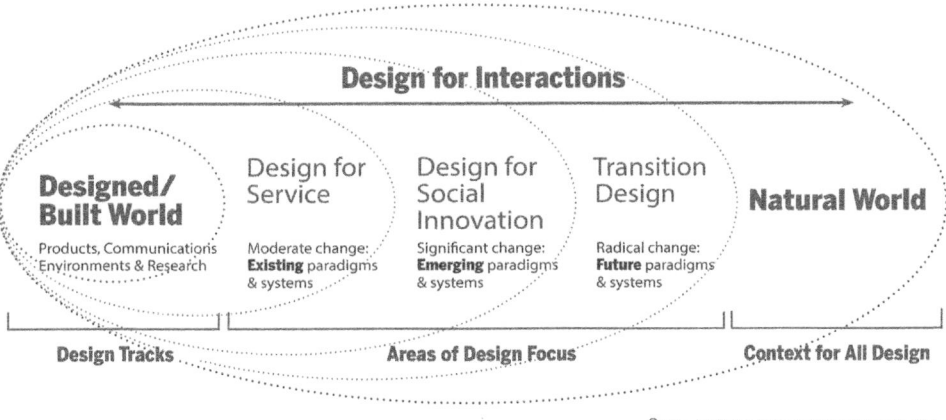

Figure 15.1 Situating design in a social and environmental context: program framework, Carnegie Mellon University School of Design ("Program Framework," n.d.).

Table 15.1 Human Centered Design at Four Levels of Change

	Individual	Social	Practice	Systems
Unit	Person	Community	Society	Planet
Scale/impact	Actions	Activities	Socially embedded routines	Established norms
Establishment	Established/ traditional	Emergent	Emerging	Future/aspirational
Target/focus	Product	Service	Social innovation	Transition
Theory/practice	Human factors	Participatory design, design ethnography	Practice theory	Transition design/ multilevel perspective
Methods examples	User/product studies, testing	Maketools, ethnographies, personas	Participatory action research (PAR)	Design-led workshops, organizational change

Human centered design can be used to create sustainable products, communications and environments. It can be used to support people already motivated toward sustainable behaviors, by providing them with the tools they need in a form agreeable to them to fulfill sustainable actions, goals and desires. A human centered design approach can also be used to motivate people who are unaware or unmotivated to engage in sustainable behaviors, through forms of behavior change resulting from design intervention, whether or not they are aware of their changed behavior being more desirable. And finally, human centered design can be used to increase conscious *awareness* of actions, ideally inspiring the transfer of desirable behaviors to other contexts.

Human centered design can be advocated as an approach to achieve change at four levels, all geared toward sustainability at various scales. These extend from the *individual*, to *social*, *practice*, and *systems* levels, with increasing leverage points for enacting change. All four may be targeted at sustainable change, but at different levels of scale, from individual actions through societal or even global norms. Each level is also increasingly capable of making substantial change; social more so than individual, practice more so than social, and ultimately the systems level being capable of having the most impact. This implies an increasing level of complexity too, from most simple to most complex. And finally there is a chronological element, the individual level being the most traditional with an established past, through to the systems level being the most aspirational for a future not yet entirely seen (see Table 15.1).

Individual

The individual view of human centered design is oriented around the mantra of "useful, usable, and desirable" (Sanders, 1992), and is perhaps the most traditional and well-established approach. This posits that all products need to have a fundamental purpose in achieving goals (useful), are usable in that people can make sense of them based on intuitive or instructed interactions to achieve their goals (usable), and that they are desirable, insofar as people must be attracted to or otherwise motivated to use something. This approach has a longer history, dating back to Vitruvius' framing of architecture as embodying qualities of *Firmitas*, *Utilitas*, and *Venutas* (Strength, Utility, and Beauty), with *Venutas* elevated to a status of desirability that transcended aesthetic appeal into the experiential realm (Vitruvius, transl. 1960).

The individual level is based primarily on satisfying immediate goals through human-product interactions. Depending on the product, this would entail ensuring ergonomic criteria were met for fit, safety and comfort; usability principles were adhered to in terms of recognized human input, feedback and other heuristics, and that there were basic desirable components to the product attracting the user and motivating them to interact.

With the relative simplicity of meeting human centered design criteria at the individual level, the potential for sustainable impact is also reduced. For example, the human centered design process at this level might address the human factors integrity of an app or website that allows users to accurately locate local venues for disposing of recyclable waste, through appeal and usability of the interface. Though not without the potential of connecting people socially, when design emphasis is on users as individuals creating individual actions, the scale of impact is less significant than change occurring at the social, practice or systems level.

Social

At social levels, the audience or target of change is focused on the community. This moves beyond simple and individual product interactions, to goal-fulfilling *activities*. As an emergent approach with a relatively recent history, human centered research and design here demands an empathic understanding of the people for whom a design intervention is intended, often articulated in sets of composite personas, developed from design ethnographies and participatory design research. Although individual actions may be relevant, it is the move to communal activity that most matters and has the potential for greater impact than individual-level human centered design.

Design processes and outcomes at the social level correspond to the emergent discipline of design for services. For example, a design team following a human centered process to explore how to optimize volunteer experiences to strengthen communities developed a service platform, Seedlinks, to encourage volunteerism.

> Seedlinks helps people who care contribute to their communities. The platform leverages data and the digital world to encourage action in one's local community and measure impact. It serves as a space for neighbors to identify local community challenges, create and contribute to local projects, share knowledge, and nurture relationships.
>
> *(Hanington, 2013; see also Sykes, n.d.)*

Practice

Practice, borrowing from practice theory, leverages the power of semiconscious routines embedded in everyday life. Given that diverse people maintain a high degree of consistency in their habitual practices, such as eating, sleeping, cleaning and commuting, the challenge for human centered design is to change behaviors that are already deeply ingrained. A naïve view of people would assume that simply conducting empathic research and responding with appropriate prototypes and products could produce significant, situational change. However, in well-practiced human centered design the complexities of behavior are recognized, as are the connections between artifacts, meaning and human endeavor. Whereas a simple design prototype alone may not bring about desired change, contextualized interventions built upon situated awareness of current attitudes and actions may catalyze individuals and communities toward socially and environmentally sustainable behaviors embedded in routine practice.

The method of Participatory Action Research (PAR) is instructive here. PAR is a cyclical, collaborative research process that seeks to intentionally change the community, party or policies that are involved in a research investigation. The method stands in contrast to many "objective" social science methods, which maintain a distant and noninfluential relationship between researchers and the people under study (Hanington and Martin, 2012).

For example, a project involving the design of a health literacy game engaged community members so that designers could understand current behaviors and motivations toward healthy living. Inspired by their own change in behaviors, the research participants appropriated their own version of the game and took it to other communities, work and summer camps, spreading the message of healthy living. The design research team was in turn inspired to expand the game into an educational program to run in local charter schools, with a goal of motivating healthy eating and lifestyles among children and teens (McGaffey et al., 2010; Hanington and Martin, 2012). With an overtone of empowerment, emancipation and activism, PAR has the potential to extend behaviors into socially embedded routines; for example in the preceding case, weight loss and healthy lifestyles among an expansive number of people and communities.

To affect significant change at the practice level, Max Neef's fundamental human needs and human-scale development model serve as an appropriate reference (see Neef, 1991). Neef outlines fundamental needs as subsistence, protection, affection, understanding, participation, leisure, creation, identity and freedom. As applied in strategic sustainable development, human scale development is described as "focused and based on the satisfaction of fundamental human needs, on the generation of growing levels of self-reliance, and on the construction of organic articulations of people with nature and technology, of global processes with local activity, of the personal with the social, of planning with autonomy, and of civil society with the state." Human centered design aimed at the satisfaction of fundamental needs in harmony with sustainable development is ambitious, yet significant if achieved through behaviors embedded in practice (Fundamental Human Needs, n.d.).

Systems

The systems level of human centered design is oriented toward transition design, or design-led societal change toward more sustainable futures. "Transition design is a nascent area for design research, practice, and study where speculative, long-term visions of sustainable lifestyles fundamentally challenge existing social, economic and political paradigms" (Irwin, 2015). The worldview here is one of interconnectedness, and suggests the need for a multilevel perspective (MLP).

A multilevel perspective posits that socio-technical transitions result from a dynamic relationship across three levels of analysis: landscapes, regimes and niches. Landscapes are the socio-technical context in which things occur, and which may pressure regimes through global trends. Regimes are social norms, rules and systems that comprise mainstream society. Niches are innovations and ideas that may challenge regimes. Transition occurs as a matter of coevolution and mutual adaptation of developments across these three levels (Southerton and Watson, 2015).

Systems-level change is the most aspirational level of human centered design. Thus far there is also the least evidence of human centered design operating at this level. However, the potential for design to intervene here would be through design-led workshops and other forms of generative and participatory design aimed at significant organizational change, and the globally networked spread of such change. To this end, systems change may be reliant on the cumulative effects of successes at the social and practice levels. Participatory design also has the potential for socio-technical coevolution. Just as designers shape behavior through the prompt of designed artifacts, people reconfigure new uses through the unanticipated and creative potential of objects and services, with novel applications unforeseen by design.

An example of systems level change would be the Transition Town movement, essentially a set of networked grassroots community projects that aim to increase the self-sufficiency of communities, towns and cities, to reduce the negative effects of peak oil, climate change and economic crises. As a movement with potential for human centered design, the transition movement attempts to mitigate "the converging global crises by engaging communities in home-grown, citizen-led education, action, and multi-stakeholder planning to increase local self reliance and resilience" (The Transition Town Movement, 2013). However aspirational, sustainable systems have the potential to become established as eventual norms, ultimately demonstrating "the normative power of the actual." In other words, once people live certain ways for enough time, the individual and social practices embedded in systems become taken for granted as normal.

Conclusion

Human centered design has the potential to catalyze significant change. Conducting research with people using effective methods can forge an understanding of what to design and why (or why not). It empowers designers not only with a knowledge set about people, products and services, but also with an empathic understanding of the very human situations into which they are designing. Human centered design can help bring about products and services that can be used effectively and efficiently to achieve goals and make lives better.

At a fundamental level, there is also fair evidence that human centered design is beneficial in terms of time, money and resources. The expense of getting the product wrong, of having it rejected by users, fail in the marketplace, or adversely affecting the brand reputation of an entire company is clearly detrimental and costly. This also has clear repercussions in sustainable terms: A failed product may literally end up in the landfill; manufacturing processes and materials may have been wasted; people may be offended by culturally insensitive products; or there may be economic fallout from lost jobs. In short, getting it wrong is unsustainable. Human centered design, in ideal form, can prevent costly mistakes up front by ensuring that the right product or service is being designed, and that it is being designed "right," through careful and thorough research with stakeholders, constituents, *people*, and increasing the likelihood of a sustainably designed outcome.

Human centered design has its proponents, as well as detractors. There is certainly evidence that human centered design as an approach has improved the quality of products and services, not only in their ability to fulfill human goals, but to do so with a responsible level of fit, comfort, and safety, with intuitive design that guides people through use effectively and efficiently. The approach can also be credited for the emergence of new, creative innovations in products and services that might not have existed without the advocacy that comes from human centered design, understanding people to create the things they need, things that are sustainable, and sometimes to *not* create things that are unwanted, unneeded or unsustainable.

However, on the other hand, an extreme, mono-view of designing exclusively for peoples' needs and desires without forethought can be legitimately criticized for coming at the expense of the planet and other living things. An overfocus on the (instant) gratification of human wants and needs, without consideration for costs such as negative social impact or environmental degradation, presents a contaminated version of human centered design with inherent risks for the future of people and planet.

Alternate views of human centered design have been presented with arguments as to its limitations. For example, Donald Norman in 2005 wrote an article titled, "human centered design considered harmful" which was widely misconstrued as a renouncement of the approach he has long advocated (Norman, 2005). Norman later clarified his position through better defining his advocacy for Activity-Centered Design (ACD) (Norman, n.d.), with roots in Activity Theory.

ACD is focused on activities comprised of composite tasks and people in the fulfillment of goals, rather than a narrow evaluation of individual tasks or users in isolation. In other words, it offers a framework for designers to focus on systems that should support the activities that people do, or want to do (Rowland, 2013).

Human centered design in the context of sustainability, then, needs to be carefully balanced, or redefined in new terms that continue the evolution of concerns beyond individual need (want) fulfillment, to the betterment of lives at the social, practice and systems level, in balance and harmony with other living things and the natural world as a context in which all things occur. To this end, some have advocated for more descriptive terms, such as values-based design, or life-centered design (see From Human-Centered to Life-Centered Design, 2014; Design for All Life, 2015). Under any term, there are promising signs that human centered sustainable design will continue to evolve, with promise for an approach that has the potential to motivate positive change for people and planet.

References

Bowling, A (1997). *Research methods in health: investigating health and health services.* Buckingham: Open University Press.

Design for all life: is it time to re-examine human-centered design? (2015). [www.core77.com/posts/31264/Design-for-All-Life] Accessed December 21, 2016.

Dreyfuss, H. (1955). *Designing for people.* New York: Simon and Schuster.

Ehn, P. (1992). "Scandinavian design: on participation and skill." In: P. Adler and T. Winograd, eds., *Usability: turning technologies into tools.* Oxford: Oxford University Press.

Frederick, C. (1920). *Household engineering: scientific management in the home.* London: G. Routledge & Sons, Ltd.

From human-centered to life-centered design. (2014). [http://schedule.sxsw.com/2014/events/event_IAP21775] Accessed December 21, 2016.

Fundamental human needs. (n.d.). [https://en.wikipedia.org/wiki/Fundamental_human_needs] Accessed December 21, 2016.

Hanington, B. (2013). MDes students win best social impact at Microsoft Design Expo. [http://design.cmu.edu/content/mdes-students-win-best-social-impact-microsoft-design-expo] Accessed December 21, 2016.

Hanington, B. and Martin, B. (2012). *Universal methods of design: 100 ways to research complex problems, develop innovative ideas, and design effective solutions.* Beverly, MA: Rockport Publishers.

Human Factors and Ergonomics Society (n.d.). [www.hfes.org] Accessed December 21, 2016.

International Organization for Standardization. (2010). *Ergonomics of human-system interaction: Part 9241–210.*

Irwin, T. (2015). "Redesigning a design program: How Carnegie Mellon University is developing a design curricula for the 21st century." *The Solutions Journal,* 6(1) January, 91–100.

Jordan, P. W. (2000). *Designing pleasurable products: an introduction to the new human factors.* London: Taylor and Francis.

Krippendorff, K. (2005). *The semantic turn: a new foundation for design.* Boca Raton: Taylor and Francis.

Krippendorff, K., and Butter, R. (1984). "Product semantics: Exploring the symbolic qualities of form." *Innovation,* 3(2), 4–9. [http://repository.upenn.edu/asc_papers/40] Accessed December 21, 2016.

Kuhn, S. and Winograd, T. (1996). "Participatory design." In: T. Winograd, ed., *Bringing design to software.* Reading, MA: Addison-Wesley. [http://hci.stanford.edu/publications/bds/14-p-partic.html] Accessed December 21, 2016.

Lupton, E. (2014). *Beautiful users: designing for people.* New York: Princeton Architectural Press.

Lupton, E. and Miller, J. A. (1992). *The bathroom, the kitchen, and the aesthetics of waste: a process of elimination.* Princeton Architectural Press.

McCarthy, J. and Wright, P. (2004). *Technology as experience.* Cambridge, MA: MIT Press.

McGaffey, A., Hughes, K., Fidler, S., D'Amico, F., and Stalter, M. (2010). "Can Elvis Pretzley and the Fitwits improve knowledge of obesity, nutrition, exercise, and portions in fifth graders?" *International Journal of Obesity* (London), 34(7), 1134–1142.

Neef, M. (1991). *Human scale development: conception, application and further reflections.* New York: Apex Press.

Norman, D. (n.d.). HCD harmful? A clarification. [www.jnd.org/dn.mss/hcd_harmful_a_clari.html] Accessed December 21, 2016.

Norman, D. (2005). Human-centered design considered harmful. [www.jnd.org/dn.mss/human-centered.html] Accessed December 21, 2016.

Picard, R. (1995). Affective computing. *M.I.T Media Laboratory Perceptual Computing Section Technical Report*. No. 321.

Picard, R. (1997). *Affective computing*. Cambridge, MA: MIT Press.

Pilloton, E. (2009). *Design revolution: 100 products that empower people*. New York: Metropolis Books.

Program framework. (n.d.). [www.design.cmu.edu/content/program-framework] Accessed December 21, 2016.

Rowland, F. (2013). Activity-centered design – some thoughts. [https://ebiinterfaces.wordpress.com/2013/03/13/activity-centered-design-some-thoughts] Accessed December 21, 2016.

Sanders, E.B.-N. (1992). "Converging perspectives: Product development research for the 1990s." *Design Management Journal*, 3(4) Fall, 49–54.

Sanders, E.B.-N. (2013). "Prototyping for the design spaces of the future." In: L. Valentine, ed., *Prototype: design and craft in the 21st century*. London: Bloomsbury.

Simon, H. (1996). *The sciences of the artificial*. Cambridge, MA: MIT Press.

Sleeswijk-Visser, F., Stappers, P. J., van der Lugt, R. and Sanders, E.B.-N. (2005). "Contextmapping: Experiences from practice." *CoDesign* 1(2), 119–149.

Southerton, D. and Watson, M. (2015). Multi-level perspective and theories of practice: a mistaken controversy? [http://en.forumviesmobiles.org/arguing/2015/11/25/multi-level-perspective-and-theories-practice-mistaken-controversy-2972] Accessed December 21, 2016.

Suchman, L. (1987) *Plans and situated actions: the problem of human-machine communication*. New York: Cambridge University Press.

Sykes, S. (n.d.). Seedlinks. [http://sarahsykes.us/portfolio/seedlinks/] Accessed December 21, 2016.

Tiger, L. (1992). *The pursuit of pleasure*. New Brunswick: Transaction Publishers.

The Transition Town Movement. (2013). [http://transitionus.org/transition-town-movement] Accessed December 21, 2016.

User experience. (n.d.). [https://en.wikipedia.org/wiki/User_experience] Accessed December 21, 2016.

Vitruvius, P. (transl. by Morris Hicky Morgan, 1960). *De architectura: the ten books on architecture*. New York: Courier Dover Publications.

16

PRACTICING EMPATHY TO CONNECT PEOPLE AND THE ENVIRONMENT

Theresa J. Edmonds

In a verdant valley of China's Sichuan Province, the Min River winds between mountains and plains. More than two millennia ago, faced with seasonal floods and droughts that threatened the viability of farmlands and survival of human populations in the area, the government commissioned a project to alleviate those extremes. The resulting Dujiangyan irrigation system, awarded UNESCO World Heritage site status in 2000, has been in continuous operation since 256 BCE with little maintenance (UNESCO 2000). In addition to its longevity, the Dujiangyan irrigation system is remarkable for its regulation of water flow with minimal interventions in the river's topography.

The project's architects worked ingeniously with the river's natural bend to filter sediment and rocks away from irrigation channels, while the addition of a V-shaped dike harnesses the flow of water into inner and outer branches. In the rainy season, it directs 60% of the water towards the Yangtze River, and in the dry season it directs 60% of the water towards irrigation for farmland (China Heritage Project 2005). This design reflects a process that involved careful observation over an extended period of time, a respect for the river and local ecosystem's integrity, and a willingness to work with rather than against the natural patterns of seasons and topography.

The designers integrated human needs into the larger system to which they belong. Furthermore, they met the needs of diverse people in the area: irrigation for the farmers and protection from flooding for those living along the river.

Further down the Yangtze River, the Three Gorges Dam provides a contrasting approach and set of results. The Three Gorges Dam is at once an engineering marvel and an "environmental catastrophe" (Hvistendahl 2008). Premier Li Peng, one of the dam's proponents, said of the project, "The damming of the Yangtze is of great political and economic significance. . . . It proves to the whole world the Chinese people's capability of building the world's first-rate hydroelectric project" (Cleveland 2010). In relation to these priorities, and as a source of renewable energy, the project is a success. However, Wang Xiaofeng, who oversaw the project for China's State Council, countered this perspective, saying, "We simply cannot sacrifice the environment in exchange for temporary economic gain" (Hvistendahl 2008). Although it produces about 18,000 megawatts of non-fossil fuel power, the dam has also displaced 1.3 million people, changed the local climate, and threatened the area's biodiversity (Hvistendahl 2008).

Whereas the Dujiangyan irrigation system reveals the possibility of integrating human needs with those of the greater ecosystem, the Three Gorges Dam reflects the common view that human well-being is in conflict, or at least in competition, with the well-being of the environment. Under this view, humans simply need to apply a solution, which often takes the form of increased control, uniformity, and predictability. Underlying this mentality is the perception that, as the writer, environmental activist, and farmer Wendell Berry, puts it, "'the environment,' a word . . . which means 'surroundings,' [is] a place that one is in but not of" (Berry 2000). The implications of this distinction are far-reaching.

Both of these projects involve human interventions to address flooding, but in the case of the Dujiangyan irrigation system, those modifications led to greater flourishing and a design that has continued serving its purpose for 2,200 years. In the case of the Three Gorges Dam, the desire to demonstrate technological, political, and economic power led to destruction of human life and the environment, even though it was framed as a project for human and environmental prosperity. The outcomes reflect the approaches, which in turn reflect the perceptions and values behind those approaches.

These relationships are reflected in the three modes of change necessary to move towards a "life-sustaining society" as articulated by Joanna Macy, the eco-philosopher and scholar of Buddhism and general systems theory. The modes of change are (1) engaging in holding actions – "political, legislative and . . . direct actions" that attempt to slow down the destruction taking place, (2) redesigning structures and systems – in favor of practices that support life and well-being, and (3) shifting perception and values – "shifts . . . in our hearts, our minds, and our views of reality" (Johnstone and Macy 2012, 31).

This chapter explores the relationship between the mode of change most familiar in sustainable design – redesigning structures and systems – and the mode of change that involves shifts in our perception and values. First, we consider why sustainable design must integrate a shift from viewing people and the environment as separate to seeing them as inextricably connected. Second, we explore how our natural capacity to empathize with others reveals our mutual dependence and further motivates us to expand the reach of our empathy in sustainable design. Third, we discover the importance of engaging with people and places with a respect for their integrity, an attitude of openness and curiosity, and a sense of wonder. Finally, we look at how practicing design in these ways illuminates the world as a complex, interrelated system and emphasizes the importance of responding to needs, collaborating across differences, and seeking guidance from ethical and moral teachings.

Redefining the relationship between people and the environment

Human centered design provides an example for how values and perception inform processes and outcomes. It also demonstrates an understanding of people that, if extended to entire ecosystems, serves as a compelling guide for sustainable design practice. Human centered design recognizes that people are complex, emotional and intellectual beings. The integration of empathic research practices reflects an appreciation of learning about people and places through not only facts and figures, but also all of the senses (Kelley and Kelley 2013, 20). For example, designers seeking to redesign some part of a hospital might spend time experiencing being in a hospital with props and activities that simulate the experience of a patient, a doctor, or an administrator. Rather than simply asking what these stakeholders want changed, they ask questions that seek to understand their underlying needs and values (Battarbee, Suri and Howard 2012). However, empathic research methods do not prescribe how resulting insights are used. It depends on the underlying motivations, which are often multiple. In the case of the Three Gorges Dam, environmental health and human prosperity were included in their motivations, but the demonstration of economic and political power was prioritized as a motivation and design criterion. Our decisions will reflect our motivations and their order of importance in our minds. Therefore, a conversation about sustainable design necessitates examining motivations and the views and values that shape them.

The framing of the Three Gorges Dam project reflects the widespread view that environmental and human well-being are separate and in competition with one another. Under this view, it makes sense to prioritize human prosperity in design and manage any resulting environmental degradation as an unfortunate side effect. However, as Wendell Berry points out, if we begin to look at the relationships between the two, it becomes clear that this view of the world presents troubling contradictions. He says, "If we are willing to pollute the air . . . by that token we are willing to harm all creatures that breathe, ourselves and our children among them. . . . You cannot affirm the power plant and condemn the smokestack, or affirm the smoke and condemn the cough" (Stephensen 2015, 69). This larger view requires that we extend the system boundaries of our design decisions in space and time. The impact of our designs, both positive and negative, radiates out from the people and places we are designing for to other people near and far, as well as future generations, other species, ecosystems, and the whole biosphere. With this perspective, Wendell Berry proposes that the ultimate standard of all professions be the well-being of our communities:

> Suppose that the ultimate standard of our work were to be, not professionalism and profitability, but the health and durability of human and natural communities. Suppose we learned to ask of any proposed innovation. . . . What will this do to our community? Suppose we attempted the authentic multiculturalism of adapting our ways of life to the nature of the places where we live. Suppose, in short, that we should take seriously the proposition that our arts and sciences have the power to help us adapt and survive. What then?
>
> *(Berry 2000)*

This description reveals an apt definition of sustainable design, taking design in its broadest sense. If design is understood as "transforming current situations into preferred ones" (Battarbee, Suri and Howard 2012), sustainable design necessitates defining "preferred" in terms of the "health and durability of human and natural communities." In other words, all other motivations must be subordinate to that ultimate standard. Intrinsic to this definition is the understanding that human lives are inextricable from the larger complex systems of which we are a part.

Therefore, practicing sustainable design includes an underlying shift in how we relate to the world. If we value other things above life and see the world as a collection of static, independent entities, our design decisions are unlikely to support a "life-sustaining society." If instead we value all of life and see the world as a complex system of dynamic, interrelated entities, our design decisions are more likely to support its continuation. Shifting towards the latter relationship cannot occur through the intellect alone without the risk of becoming abstract and irrelevant to our lives and work. It is the difference between reading the obituary of a stranger and a close friend. For the stranger, what we read is all that we know; that person is, in our minds, just the short description. For the close friend, what we read calls to mind the memories of moments shared, the changes in their life over time, and their relationships with other friends and family. Though we intellectually know that both are human beings with rich relationships and personalities that could never be fully described in a short paragraph, we have only experienced a close relationship with one, so our response to reading the two obituaries is entirely different. In a similar way, we have the ability to know places, landscapes, and ecosystems like a close friend – precious in their entirety.

Just as in our interactions with people, our interactions with everything are informed by the kind of relationship we have to them. As Wendell Berry says, "We know enough of our own history by now to be aware that people exploit what they have merely concluded to be of value, but they defend what they love" (Berry, *Life Is a Miracle* 369). This statement holds equally true if "what" is replaced with "whom," which illuminates that the various kinds of exploitation and oppression visible in the world derive from a common source: a division between this and that, me and not me, people and environment, my people and not my people, etc.

Both ancient traditions and modern sciences address the mind's tendency to create divisions and the implications of perceiving the world as divided. They also point to the ways in which we inherently know and feel that we are part of this world and belong here, and that we must respond to the needs of the Earth if we wish to continue living here. Feeling pain at the sight of another person's pain or in the presence of a polluted landscape signals a recognition that our well-being is tied up with the well-being of others.

Expanding our notion of empathy

Our capacity to empathize reminds us viscerally that we depend on one another. However, we do not empathize equally with all people and beings. As the anthropologist Mary Catherine Bateson succinctly puts it, "Sentience proposes similarity, similarity proposes empathy, empathy proposes compassion" (Bateson 2010, 214). This is why she states it is easier for us to empathize with people we love than strangers, and easier for us to care about whales than phytoplankton. The danger in this limited view of "similarity" is that it neglects the web of relationships that support our lives – that the whales cannot exist without the phytoplankton and that we depend on countless strangers for our daily survival and well-being.

Fortunately, the relationship between perceived similarity and empathy is bidirectional. The more we practice empathy in our engagements with others, the more we experience a sense of connection and familiarity. The more connection and familiarity felt in relationship to another, the easier it is to empathize with them. This is why practicing empathy has been shown to reduce prejudice and racism, improve medical patient care and recovery, and yield designs that improve people's lives (The Greater Good Science Center 2016).

Neurobiologist Daniel Siegel's work suggests that we are kinder to people we consider to be "like us," whereas we treat those we consider to be "not like us" with "disdain and disregard" (Siegel 2010, 258). These judgments occur unconsciously and subliminally, so we are often blind to how our perceptions shape our actions.

For instance, George Wiley, an American chemist and civil rights leader, tells the story of a well-meaning community in Colorado that sought out a ban on burning trash. As it was a group of well-off citizens that made the decision, they failed to consider the barrier of cost to families paying for garbage removal, and many families in the neighborhood could not afford it. Trash accumulated in the poorer areas, and the neighborhood became more, not less, polluted (Wiley 1970, 235). Because our perception of difference based on appearance, background, values, etc., often intersects with systemic forms of discrimination, such as racism, sexism, and ableism, actions based on considering others to be "not like us" usually results in the perpetuation of inequality and injustice. These dynamics extend to relationships between not only diverse human beings, but also human beings and the rest of the world. Consider the "disdain and disregard" with which we treat others and how it increases as the perception of similarity decreases: from pets to wild mammals to bugs to plants to microorganisms. And yet, if we stop to look more closely, we were born and continue to live thanks to countless beings of all varieties. Failing to recognize this, we disregard them and see them as less valuable than ourselves.

This perception of difference reinforces the second way in which empathy can be dulled. Because the independent individual is such a primary idea in Western culture, feelings of distress regarding the state of the world can sometimes be pathologized as an individual shortcoming. At the same time, there is a prevalent belief amongst many environmentalists and activists that the public simply does not care about sustainability. Therefore, they attempt to address this perceived apathy by increasing the volume and alarmist tenor of information:

> Reformers and revolutionaries decry public apathy. To rouse people, they deliver yet more terrifying information, as if people didn't already know that our world is in trouble. They preach about moral imperatives, as if people didn't already care. Their alarms and sermons tend to make people pull the shades down tighter, resisting what appears too overwhelming, too complicated, too out of their control.
>
> *(Brown and Macy 2014, 20)*

This approach and its underlying assumptions tend to increase feelings of shame, guilt, and fear, further repressing the care that actually exists. Furthermore, the implicit assumption in these modes of working towards sustainability is that few people care about the environment. As Dan Becker, the Sierra Club's Global Warming Director from 1989–2007, expressed, "there's no one else to protect the environment if we don't do it" (Nordhaus and Shellenberger 2004). This belief reinforces the notion that the environment is a separate thing, valuable only in that it delivers resources and receives our waste products. Even valuing the beauty of nature and wanting to preserve it for that reason reflects a valuation system based on human desires, rather than inherent value.

Increasingly, the assumption of public apathy is being challenged by expressions of pain in response to environmental degradation around the world. Glenn Albrecht, professor of sustainability at Murdoch University in Perth, Australia, even coined a term – "solastalgia" – to describe "the pain experienced when there is recognition that the place where one resides and that one loves is under immediate assault" (Smith 2010). It has been used to describe the range of emotions – "anxiety, despair, numbness, 'a sense of being overwhelmed or powerless,' grief" – felt by peoples facing acute alterations to their homes, such as Ghanaian farmers encountering changing rainfall patterns and New Orleans residents returning home after Hurricane Katrina (Smith 2010). Albrecht believes solastalgia is a "global condition, felt to a greater or lesser degree by different people in different locations but felt increasingly, given the ongoing degradation of the environment" and the increasing awareness of its extent due to the international flow of information (Smith 2010).

Joanna Macy, who has developed a set of practices over more than forty years to closely examine this pain arising from ecological degradation, has found that what many perceive as apathy is not an inherent lack of care, but "the inability or refusal to experience pain" (Brown and Macy 2014, 20). Apathy, which comes from the Greek word *apatheia*, meaning "not suffering," is often a state of repressed pain. Usually, fear is the culprit – fear of feeling pain, fear of feeling hopeless, or fear that, as one person told her, "If I open the door to those feelings, I'll be plunged to a place so low I don't think I'll ever get back" (Johnston and Macy 2012, 69). Unfortunately, this fear and resistance impact all aspects of our being, including dampening our creativity and empathy, which are both essential in the design process:

> Without empathy, our natural capacity to sense and identify with the joy and suffering of others is cripple. Instead, we tend to project our repressed fears and anger onto other people. . . . Free play of the imagination requires trust in life and courage to walk where there is no path. It takes us beyond our perceptions of what is to what might be, opening

us to new ways of seeing and new ways of being. . . . This crucial source of all creativity
is blocked when we resist images, ideas or feelings that might trigger moral pain.

(Brown and Macy 2014, 33)

Without empathy, not only are we diminishing our capacity to respond to the state of the world,
through our creativity and imagination, but we are also preventing ourselves from seeing where
that pain comes from. As Macy succinctly puts it, "the anguish we feel for what is happening
to our world is inevitable and normal and even healthy" (Pachamama Alliance 2015, 23). She
continues, "Pain is very useful. Just don't be afraid of it. Because if we are afraid to feel that, we
won't feel where it comes from, and where it comes from is love, our love for this world. That's
what is going to pull us through" (Pachamama Alliance 2015).

This kind of love – a love for the world that propels people into action – has a close relationship to compassion. The etymology of the English word "compassion" translates directly
to "suffering with," which implies that compassion cannot arise if one is not open to feeling
suffering. Therefore, while intellectual recognition of the loss of life which sustainable design
hopes to alleviate is important, it alone is not sufficient. Emotional recognition must also be felt.
As psychology professor J. William Worden explains, there are two phases to processing grief:
the first is accepting a loss, and the second is feeling the pain of that loss. He says, "When we
feel this emotion, we know not only that the loss is real but also that it matters to us. That's the
digestion phase – where the awareness sinks to a deeper place within us so that we take in what
it means" (Johnstone and Macy 2012, 71).

Through practices that engage individual and group work, Joanna Macy has found that
"When people are able to tell the truth about what they know, see, and feel is happening to their
world, a transformation occurs. There is an increased determination to act and a renewed appetite
for life" and furthermore, people "feel tremendous relief at realizing [their] solidarity with others"
(Johnston and Macy 2012, 70). The recognition of suffering inherent in compassion can then
become a powerful source of motivation to seek ways to alleviate that suffering.

In his book, *What We're Fighting for Now Is Each Other*, the writer Wen Stephensen interviews
people and groups working on climate justice. Amongst these passionate individuals is Grace
Ann Cagle, who speaks about the source of her motivation and perseverance in her work on
climate justice:

If it weren't for the connection I feel to the earth, I would quit. Because it's really difficult. I'm not directly fighting for my house or my family, but the earth is in imminent
danger, and so are my friends, and it takes this sense of being united, together, and this
feeling of caring not just for each other but for the earth. And where does that come
from? It comes from somewhere deeper. The whole reason I'm doing this . . . is the
continuation of life.

(Stephensen 2015, 168)

Fully encountering the dangers facing life on Earth and feeling connected, "united, together,"
are the two sides of the coin that Joanna Macy describes: the pain and the love, the suffering and
the compassion.

Buddhism, like other ancient wisdom traditions, has a deep-seated respect for and understanding of compassion. The Buddha was motivated to teach "for the good of the many, for the
happiness of the many, out of compassion for the world" (Rahula 1974, 46). The Pali word for
compassion is *karuna*, which Buddhaghosa, a fifth century Theravadan Buddhist commentator

and scholar, explains includes feeling the suffering of others and actively responding without discrimination:

> When others suffer it makes the heart of good people tremble (*kampa*), thus it is *karuna*;
> it demolishes others' suffering, attacks and banishes it, thus it is *karuna*; or it is dispersed
> over the suffering, is spread out through pervasion, thus it is *karuna*.
>
> *(Jenkins 2000)*

To say that the heart trembles when we see others suffer is a striking depiction of the "feeling with" and "suffering with" aspects of empathy and compassion. Compassion, in contrast to empathy, additionally includes being "active and materially effective" in alleviating the suffering of others (Jenkins 2000). Furthermore, it is not limited or bounded, but rather "dispersed" and "spread out" for all beings. In other words, in its most matured form, *karuna* does not discriminate; it is equally felt for and extended to all.

The People's Climate March, which took place on September 22, 2014, in New York City, exemplified in its media design an understanding of many of these principles. The tagline for the event was "To change everything, we need everyone" (Peoples Climate March 2014). This event sent both a literal and embodied message of unity in diversity. It celebrated the unique relationship different coalitions and groups have to climate change, as well as the universally shared experience of being a human on this planet. Rather than preaching alarm and fear, it spoke of urgency and solidarity. The designers of the messaging, media, and event had a clear intention of bringing diverse people together to express their compassion for the world, and the result was powerful.

Being motivated by a felt sense of caring empowers a different way forward. It does not guarantee the right outcome, but it does direct our attention towards learning all that we can about the people and places in which we are designing. When this happens, we are designing for the sake of sustaining life about which we personally care. If we want our designs to reflect a respect for the integrity of a place, our ways of engaging with the communities in which we are designing must do so too.

Experiencing the integrity of people and places

Rachel Carson, the scientist and author of *Silent Spring*, is celebrated for her groundbreaking research and writing on the impacts of synthetic pesticides. She was also a devoted aunt to her nephew Roger, with whom she shared a different but equally important kind of research and writing. Though her early death prevented the completion of what she referred to as "the wonder book," her essays about experiencing nature with Roger and deepening the sense of wonder reveal an essential complement to her scientific work.

In one of these essays, she writes about the many moments spent with Roger exploring the coast of Maine. One rainy night, when Roger was twenty months old, she carried him down to the beach. As they encountered the place together, she recounts, "Together we laughed for pure joy – he a baby meeting for the first time the wild tumult of Oceanus, I with the salt of half a lifetime of sea love in me. But I think we felt the same spine-tingling response to the vast, roaring ocean and the wild night around us" (Carson 1998, 15).

Through these experiences, she came to believe that "for the child, and for the parent seeking to guide him, it is not half so important to *know* as to *feel*" because "Once the emotions have been aroused – a sense of the beautiful, the excitement of the new and the unknown, a feeling of sympathy, pity, admiration or love – then we wish for knowledge about the object of our emotional response. Once found, it has lasting meaning" (Carson 1998, 56). In other words, a felt connection to the world cultivates curiosity and contextualizes knowledge. Furthermore, being open to experience what is unknown increases the possibility that we will learn something genuinely new, rather than simply confirming prior beliefs.

Many individuals and peoples who have made common cause with protecting their homes reflect a similar appreciation for the importance of feeling connected and part of the place they live, whether defined locally or globally. One way that this is reflected is in the gratitude practices of many cultures. Robin W. Kimmerer, a botanist of Potawotomi descent, describes "the givea-way" or *minidewak*, a ceremony passed down by her ancestors that begins many gatherings and celebrations in which the host or the one being honored gives gifts to everyone (Kimmerer 2010, 142). This ceremony reflects and cultivates a culture of gratitude, in which wealth is measured not by how much one can get but by how much one can give away.

Even the word *minidewak* encodes this meaning. It translates to "they give from the heart," and *min* comes from the root word for "gift" as well as "berry." Kimmerer reflects that perhaps the common root reminds them through language to take inspiration from berries. She says, "They remind us that all flourishing is mutual. We need the berries and the berries need us. Their gifts multiply by our care for them, and dwindle from our neglect. We are bound in a covenant of reciprocity, a pact of mutual responsibility to sustain those that sustain us" (Kimmerer 2010, 144). Whereas biology tells us about the importance of symbiotic relationships in nature, if that knowledge remains strictly intellectual, it will not necessarily translate to living in accord with that understanding. Having a practice that reflects and cultivates the feeling of gratitude has a much farther-reaching effect. For example, the Potawatomi speak of the land as *emingoyak*, "that which has been given to us," "a gift that must be reciprocated with our own" (Kimmerer 2010). In contrast, in English, we tend to use words like "natural resources" or "ecosystem services," which suggest that the land is "our property, our entitlement, which becomes valuable only when consumed" (Kimmerer 2010, 144). However, our experiences of being in places we love challenge this narrow view of land's value, as evidenced in Carson's description of her adventures with Roger. Putting aside our tendencies to evaluate and analyze, we experience the world and people as valuable in their own right.

In Brian Doyle's piece called "A Newt Note," he describes such an experience during a day exploring the Oregon coastal forest with his children. His "proem," somewhere between prose and poem, captures an exuberance and insatiable curiosity that takes the reader on a joyous romp. They find "banana slugs waaay longer than bananas," dance on "the biggest stump in the history of the world," and find "a newt! O my god! dad! check it *out!*" He writes, "the point of this story" is "that one day when my kids and I were shuffling through the vast wet moist forest we saw so many wonders and miracles that not one of us ever forgot any of the wonders and miracles we saw" and asks, given this, how can we not "spend every iota of our cash and creativity to pro-tect and preserve a world in which kids wander around gaping in wonder" (Doyle 2010, 168)? Though in different language, Doyle's message mirrors that of the Potawotomi's *minidewak* – that life is a gift, and that we are bound to one another in reciprocity.

The rhetoric and practices of wonder and gratitude suggest that our capacity to discover and appreciate the people and places around us is inexhaustible. It bears a striking resemblance to the Buddhist articulation of wisdom, or *prajna*, which translates literally to "before knowing" (Thanissara 2015, 39). *Prajna* conveys an "understanding of things as they are," their "true nature, without name and label," "known and loved as most intimate, most precious" (Rahula 1974, 49; Thanissara 2015, 39).

This orientation to the world protects us from falling into the rigid categories that, once identified, stop us from looking or listening further. John Daido Loori describes the tension between biology's classification of living things and his relationship with the specific living beings he knows. He considers the tree outside his door not only as the plant called a white pine, but also as a familiar friend:

> But what do these categories really say about the white pine I see each day as I come out of the front door of my cabin? It's been a friend for more than two decades. It has witnessed my comings and goings. I've watched it dance in the mountain's fierce winds. I've seen it shelter birds in a snowstorm, provide a branch for a red squirrel, feed a ravenous woodpecker. This tree, just like me, is an ever-changing individual. It is easily recognizable from another *Pinus strobus* growing right next to it. How many individuals do we miss in our daily experience because we've stopped seeing and started knowing?
>
> *(Loori 2004, 71)*

To stop seeing and start knowing is the root of discrimination and exploitation, of people and the planet. Analyzing and categorizing is useful, but it can mistake a whole, unique, evolving being for a subset of their characteristics. Building the capacity to continue "seeing," and not converge to "knowing" too soon yields a greater sense of connection and appreciation for complexity. The world shifts from being a collection of two-dimensional entities (objects) to being a complex web of alive and coevolving beings (subjects).

Consider the implications of these modalities of getting to know a place for sustainable design practice. They suggest that engaging with all of our senses, without expectations for what we might find, has the potential to reveal a place more completely, whether it be a landscape or city. Directing our attention in this way uncovers the relationships between people and place, making it clear that lives and their impacts unfold in particular places. Therefore, sustainable design must be situated in specific local, regional, and global contexts. For example, Jacqui Patterson, director of the Environmental and Climate Justice Program at the NAACP looks at the impact of closing coal plants from the perspective of not only the regional and global communities, impacted by the combustion of green house gasses, but also the individuals whose livelihoods depend on them. She says, "We don't talk about closing any coal plant without making sure that every worker has a different way to make their living" (Stephensen 2015, 98). Such a commitment to addressing what might appear as peripheral impacts to shutting down a coal plant reveals the perspective that it is not an inconvenient side-project but integrated as an essential part. In this way, sustainable design needs to address, in research and response, a respect for the integrity of people and places.

Responding to needs in an interrelated world

Recognizing our ability to empathize as a sign of our relatedness suggests an underlying shift towards a different way of seeing the world: from a collection of separate objects with fixed characteristics to a living system with emergent properties and relationships.

By nature, consciousness and language divide and objectify. In the Buddhist conceptualization of the mind, the group of "ever-changing physical and mental forces or energies" that comprise "consciousness" is called *vijnana*, which means "to divide" (Rahula 1974, 20). Consciousness itself is "knowledge that results from separation, separation of subject from object and one object from another" (Pine 2004, 64). This division is necessary for thinking and communicating, but becomes restrictive if those boundaries and categorizations are all that we see. For example, the word "chair" is useful for identifying and communicating that it is an object to sit on. However, "chair" does not describe all of its relationships and changes through time. A particular chair could be made of wood, so it used to be part of a tree. Perhaps a father and daughter made it, so anytime the daughter sits in it she thinks of her father. Someday, that chair will become something else – the foundation of her child's fort, perhaps. Even so-called objects have interrelated and dynamic lives.

The importance of classification through differentiation laid the foundation for the view of the world encouraged by nineteenth century thought leaders in Western culture. They saw the world as a collection of fixed objects with fixed relationships. They shared the belief that, "As Francis Bacon and others proclaimed, we modern humans with our vast intelligence [have] only to determine the laws governing matter for us to gain control over the entire affair" (Swimme and Tucker 2011, 105). As it became clear that not only did this view fail to yield them control, but it also failed to describe the impermanent and cocreative nature of living systems, a new paradigm came forward.

In the twentieth century, biologists sought to more fully describe the "self-renewing processes of life" and so, Austrian biologist Ludwig von Bertalanffy gave birth to what is known as General Systems Theory. It describes reality as "dynamically organized and intricately balanced systems," "wholes instead of parts, processes instead of substances" (Brown and Macy 2014, 39). Systems cybernetician Norbert Wiener offered a compelling metaphor to understand the shift from viewing reality as a collection of independent objects to a deeply related web of subjects. He said, "We are not stuff that abides . . . we are patterns that perpetuate themselves; we are whirlpools in a river of ever-flowing water" (Brown and Macy 2014, 41).

Though this conception of the universe is new to the modern Western mind, other cultures and traditions have similar portrayals that are thousands of years old. In Buddhism, there is a popular image used to describe the simultaneous unity and differentiation of all things. In *The Flower Garland Sutra*, the "diamond net of Indra" depicts the nature of reality as "a vast net of gems that extends throughout the universe" in three-dimensional space and the fourth dimension of time. At each point of the net, there is "a multi-faceted diamond which reflects every other diamond, and as such, essentially 'contains' every other diamond in the net (Loori 1999, 34). The universe is understood as utterly interrelating and interpenetrating, at once differentiated and unified. Stunningly, modern studies of systems – from the mind to societies – discover that health and resilience looks a lot like this representation of the nature of reality.

For instance, neurobiologist Daniel Siegel has found that the mathematics of complex systems aptly describes the psychology of the mind. Just as systems become more stable and adaptive as their complexity increases, so does the mind. Harmony emerges with the linkage of differentiated parts, very much like the "vast net of gems." If these two essential properties – differentiation and linkage – are out of balance, the system tends towards chaos or rigidity, which show up as mental unease or illness. These dynamics also describe healthy relationships. As Siegel says, "resonance requires that we remain differentiated – that we know who we are – while also becoming linked. . . . As a therapist, if I do not track the distinction between me and other, I can become flooded with my patients' feelings, lose my ability to help, and also burn out quickly" (Siegel 2010, 63).

Notably, in relation to practicing sustainable design, understanding the world as nested complex systems means that moving one part of the system impacts the whole. In John Daido Loori's words, "we are all totally, completely, and intricately interconnected throughout time and space" (Loori 2004, 236). This conveys the extent of our responsibility and therefore the necessity to understand to the best of our ability how our design decisions will impact communities today and in the future. As Wendell Berry describes, this involves a humility and willingness to not know the answers:

> We've acknowledged now that the problems are big, now where's the big solution? When you ask the question "What is the big answer?" then you're implying that we can impose the answer. But that's the problem we're in to start with. We've tried to impose

the answers – the answers will come not from walking up to your farm and saying "This is what I expect from you." You walk up and you say, "What do you need?" And you commit yourself to say alright I'm not going to do any extensive damage here until I know what it is you're asking of me. And this can't be hurried. This is the dreadful situation that young people are in and I think of them and I say, well, the situation you're in now is a situation that's going to call for a lot of patience, and to be patient in an emergency is a terrible trial.

(Berry 2013)

This humble and responsive orientation to the world counters our culture of certainty and decisiveness. Instead, it draws upon the openness and receptivity discussed earlier so that our designs respond to genuine needs rather than imposing a solution. It necessitates expanding our capacity to be attentive to all that is in front of us. It also suggests that we need each other – diverse others – to understand all dimensions of the situation. We need to work collaboratively from many disciplines: field biologists, community leaders, designers, poets, entrepreneurs, artists, and human beings from all backgrounds and views.

In this light, engaging with moral and ethical teachings can also offer guidance, especially when understood as emerging from an examination of how to live harmoniously within the human and larger communities of which we are a part. John Daido Loori explains how the Buddhist precepts relate to underlying wisdom and compassion:

The precepts are about creating activity in the world in a way that is in harmony with it. It is what we call compassion. The first realization of unity is wisdom, the realization of oneness. The manifestation of that wisdom in the world of separation is compassion, which is the functioning of the precepts.

(Loori 1999, 102)

The precepts are the moral and ethical teachings in Buddhism, equivalent to the Ten Commandments in Judaism and Christianity. They are not just guidelines for a peaceful society, they are understood to be the manifestations of "compassion for the world" (Rahula 1974, 46). Fully developed compassion, in the Buddhist sense, is pure action in harmony with wisdom, the insight into radical interrelatedness. It is not calculated or sentimental, but rather "functions freely, with no hesitation, no limitation. It happens with no effort, the way you grow your hair, the way your heart beats, the way you breathe. . . . It does not take any conscious effort. Someone falls, you pick them up" (Loori 1999, 72). In this way, compassion is the natural response to witnessing suffering in this world.

Carl Pope, executive director of the Sierra Club, suggests that "our existing ethical principles are perfectly adequate" to inform actions on issues like climate change, but that "we hesitate because the scale of the human endeavor – in time and space – has now far outpaced the local context in which ethical principles arose and have been traditionally applied" (Pope 2010, 294). Pope's quote implies that we must work to extend the scale on which we practice our existing ethical principles. The principle of not killing others must extend beyond the small group of people we know to encompass billions we will never meet, as well as microorganisms invisible to the naked eye. The principle of being generous and not stealing must extend beyond the here and now of our neighborhood to include not stealing – not taking more than we give back – from other species and future generations we will not personally live to see (Loori 1999, 102).

Our decisions also need to take into account the diversity of people, reaching across the boundaries that our mind so readily makes between "us" and "them." We can counter these tendencies by "looking at relationships as moving in two directions for mutual benefit" and to develop, as writer and social activist bell hooks calls it "a politics of accountability" in which "we are all compelled to move beyond blame to see where our responsibility lies" (Bateson 2010, 215; Thanissara 2015, 139). Engaging in this way can lead to unlikely and powerful partnerships, such as the Indian-Cowboy Alliance that formed to oppose the Keystone XL pipeline (Thanissara 2015, 158).

As designers, we can engage with empathy not only as a tool to meet the needs of people, but also as a capacity that reveals our interdependence with the whole world. Therefore it does not make sense to pit human needs against environmental needs, or the needs of one community against another. As Bikku Bodhi says, "What is equally essential is to facilitate the transition . . . to a new paradigm that gives priority to preserving the integrity of human beings and the natural world" (Thanissara 2015, 105). This paradigm reveals the world as alive, complex, and constantly evolving. It makes clear that sustainable design is not about one-size-fits-all solutions, but a responsive, situated, and integrated approach to transformation. Recognizing that people and the environment are not two separate things, it becomes natural to extend our existing ethical principles to include all of life, present and future. Though it can feel daunting to take such a large view in our personal lives and work, it also means that even small actions can have an important impact.

I was riding the bus recently, immersed in my thoughts, when I heard one passenger say to another, "That was a really great thing to do." I realized the woman had just bought someone who did not have money two bus tickets – one for now and one for later. "You would have done the same," she replied. "Maybe, but I don't think I would have thought of it," said the fellow passenger. "Well, now you've got an idea," she said, smiling. I noticed myself and many other passengers smiling too.

We cannot predict the full impacts of our actions or how they will influence others. What feels most important is to continue remembering that we care, and to try our best to find ways to support the life of this incredible planet.

References

Bateson, M. C. (2010) "Why Should I Inconvenience Myself?" in Moore, K. D. and Nelson, M. P. eds, *Moral Ground: Ethical Action for a Planet in Peril*. San Antonio, TX, Trinity University Press, 211–216.

Battarbee, K., Suri, J. F. and Howard, S. G. (2012) "Empathy on the Edge: Scaling and Sustaining a Human-centered Approach in the Evolving Practice of Design" (www.ideo.com/images/uploads/news/pdfs/Empathy_on_the_Edge.pdf) Accessed 18 June 2016.

Berry, W. (2000) *Life Is a Miracle: An Essay Against Modern Superstition*. Washington, Counterpoint.

Berry, W. (2013) "Wendell Berry, Poet & Prophet" on Moyers B. *Moyers & Company* (billmoyers.com) Accessed 4 October 2013.

Brown, M. and Macy, J. (2014) *Coming Back to Life*. Gabriola Island, B.C., Canada, New Society Publishers

Carson, R. (1998) *The Sense of Wonder*. New York, Harper Collins.

China Heritage Project, The Australian National University. (2005) "Taming the Floodwaters: The High Heritage Price of Massive Hydraulic Projects" *China Heritage Newsletter* (chinaheritagenewsletter.anu.edu.au) Accessed 3 November 2014.

Cleveland, C. (2010) "Three Gorges Dam, China" *The Encyclopedia of Earth* (http://editors.eol.org/eoearth/wiki/Three_Gorges_Dam) Accessed 10 December 2016.

Doyle, B. (2010) "A Newt Note" in Moore, K. D. and Nelson, M. P. eds, *Moral Ground: Ethical Action for a Planet in Peril*. San Antonio, TX, Trinity University Press, 167–168.

Epstein, M. (2005) *Open to Desire: The Truth About What the Buddha Taught*. New York, Penguin Group.

Greater Good Science Center (2016) "What Is Empathy?" *University of California Berkeley* (http://greatergood.berkeley.edu/topic/empathy/definition) Accessed 10 December 2016.

Hvistendahi, M. (2008) "China's Three Gorges Dam: An Environmental Catastrophe?" *Scientific American* (www.scientificamerican.com/article.cfm?id=chinas-three-gorges-dam-disaster&page=3) Accessed 10 December 2016.

Jenkins, S. (2000) "Do Bodhisattvas Relieve Poverty? The Distinction between Economic and Spiritual Development and Their Interrelation in Indian Buddhist Texts" *Journal of Buddhist Ethics*, 7, reprinted in Queen, C. ed., *Action Dharma: New Studies in Engaged Buddhism*, New York: Routledge Curzon (2003), 38–49.

Johnstone, C. and Macy, J. (2012) *Active Hope: How to Face the Mess We're in Without Going Crazy*. Novato, New World Library.

Kelley, T. and Kelley, D. (2013) *Creative Confidence: Unleashing the Creative Potential Within Us All*. New York: Crown Business, USA.

Kimmerer, R. W. (2010) "The Giveaway" in Moore, K. D. and Nelson, M. P. eds, *Moral Ground: Ethical Action for a Planet in Peril*. San Antonio, TX, Trinity University Press, 141–145.

Loori, J. D. (1999) *Teachings of the Insentient: Zen and the Environment*. Mt. Tremper, Dharma Communications Press.

Loori, J. D. (2004) *The Zen of Creativity: Cultivating Your Artistic Life*. New York, Ballantine Books.

Nordhaus, T. and Shellenberger, M. (2004) "The Death of Environmentalism" *The Breakthrough* (thebreakthrough.org) Accessed 20 March 2014.

Pachamama Alliance (2015) *Awakening the Dreamer Manual* (http://hub.pachamama.org/resources/symposium-materials/manual) Accessed 22 June 2016.

Peoples Climate March (2014) "To Change Everything, We Need Everyone" (peoplesclimate.org) Accessed 10 December 2014.

Pine, R. (2004) *The Heart Sutra*. Berkeley, Counterpoint.

Pope, C. (2010) "Ethics as if Tomorrow Mattered" in Moore, K. D. and Nelson, M. P. eds, *Moral Ground: Ethical Action for a Planet in Peril*. San Antonio, TX, Trinity University Press, 294–300.

Rahula, W. (1974) *What the Buddha Taught*. New York, Grove Press.

Scharmer, O. C. and Kaufer, K. (2013) *Leading From the Emerging Future: From Ego-System to Eco-System Economies*. San Francisco, Berrett-Koehler Publishers, Inc.

Siegel, D. (2010) *Mindsight: The New Science of Personal Transformation*. New York, Random House, Inc.

Smith, D. B. (2010) "Is There an Ecological Unconscious?" *The New York Times Magazine* (www.nytimes.com/2010/01/31/magazine/31ecopsych-t.html) Accessed 2 December 2016.

Stephensen, W. (2015) *What We're Fighting for Now Is Each Other: Dispatches From the Front Lines of Climate Justice*. Boston, Beacon Press.

Swimme, B. T. and Tucker, M. E. (2011) *Journey of the Universe*. New Haven, Yale University Press.

Thanissara (2015) *Time to Stand Up: An Engaged Buddhist Manifesto for Our Earth*. North Atlantic Books, Berkeley.

UNESCO (2000) "Mount Qingcheng and the Dujiangyan Irrigation System" *United Nations Educational, Scientific, and Cultural Organization* (whc.unesco.org) Accessed 17 August 2016.

Wiley, G. (1970) "Ecology and the Poor" in Environmental Action Organization, *Earth Day – The Beginning*. New York, Arno Press.

17

SURRENDERING TO THE OCEAN

Practices of mindfulness and presence in designing

Yoko Akama

Sea, salt and sand

Sustainability has been a contemporary vanguard for necessitating ethical questions in design. For some time, I have been questioning what it means to be an ethical designer and becoming increasingly troubled by persistence for a common framework for all designers to pursue the 'right', 'better', 'more effective' or 'sustainable' approach or outcome (see Akama 2012 and Lisa Norton's reply in *Design Philosophy Paper*). Utilitarian ways to measure and standardize accountability, such as the Triple Bottom Line, Life Cycle Analysis, Corporate Social Responsibility, and versions of similar models, also suggest this desire for universality. My concern comes from such pervasiveness for consistency. When this dominates, it becomes an ethical monologue, creating a silent and peripheral 'other'. Speaking from the periphery, I consider ways to practice mindfulness that foregrounds being and becoming with, instead of accounting and obligating, where for me, sustainability means a *surrendering* to impermanence and interrelatedness.

Pursing questions on ethics can lead to two contrasting views. Thomas Kasulis (2002), a seminal scholar in Asian philosophy, proposes *integrity* and *intimacy* as different orientations that exist in most cultures to help us think about different ways of relating, understanding and being-in-the-world. He suggests that either the *integrity* or *intimacy* orientation dominates as 'tradition' or 'mainstream' in society, but qualifies that no one culture can purely be one or the other, allowing both orientations to be part of subcultures even when one of them dominates.

The integrity view sees the ethical relation as existing externally between two independent entities. This relation has to be constructed according to an agreed value or principle, for example, treating another as autonomous agents with the right to self-determination. Kasulis observes that the quest for generalizable paradigms has roots in Plato and Aristotle that sought eternal, transcultural truths as philosophy, in the Renaissance and Enlightenment's universal application of science and mathematics, and the twentieth century's emphasis on formal logic and empiricism. This search for common foundations developed as a way to bridge contexts, culture, time and geography and became the dominant thinking in Europe. This seems to underlie the desire for a consistent ethical framework, discussed in the introductory paragraph. Kasulis explains that formal principles between person 'a' and person 'b' constitute the integrity view. In this framework, it makes little difference who a and b are, which allows the relationship 'R' to be made universal $a(R)b$. 'R' remains constant in relations such as $b(R)c$, $a(R)d$, and R can be expressed as a principle.

When *a* and *b* enter into a relation *R*, it is an external relation where *a* and *b* are essentially unchanged. Kasulis calls this orientation *integrity*-based reasoning because the two parties have their own integrity outside the relationship. He describes integrity as having virtue, honesty and honor and the etymological root suggests being indivisible and inviolable. Someone with integrity does not compromise his or her virtue because of circumstances.

In further explaining the integrity orientation, I find his analogy of sand and seawater very evocative. Sand and seawater have a strong relationship. Sandbars affect the formation of waves, waves sculpt the sand from the ocean floor that is then deposited on the shore. Yet their relationship maintains its respective integrity – seawater remains seawater and sand remains as sand. In other words, its constitution remains the same because their relationship is external in its combination. When this analogy is used to describe people, Kasulis suggests principled people believe in external set of values and standards that are applied to different situations. These principles, not the situation, guide behavior. We see this reflected in the concept of rights, beginning with human relationships, extended into non-human beings as environmental ethics. Taking this into design and sustainability, there are celebrated scholars who propose what could be called an integrity view where principles guide a designers' behavior. For example, Tony Fry's (2009) book *Design Futuring: Sustainability, Ethics and New Practice* argues for a complete reconceptualization of design for new forms of living; and Ezio Manzini's (2006) article *Design, Ethics and Sustainability: Guidelines for a transition phase* speaks about making conscious, ethical choices in the steps towards sustainability. These are highly recommended for readers in need of guidance in design, ethics and sustainability. Toni Robertson and Ina Wagner's (2013) chapter on *Ethics: Engagement, representation and politics-in-action* also offers a range of ethical principles as questions that guides negotiation when undertaking any participatory design work. Such academic writings reflect an integrity-orientation where knowledge is logical, external, and independent from the known, enabling it to become portable and transferrable between contexts.

In contrast to *integrity*, Kasulis proposes the notion of *intimacy* that begins with the assumption of interdependency that inherently already has a connection. Where integrity's ethics attempted to preserve the integrity of those involved, the intimacy orientation seeks to highlight or enhance the intimacy between people. This means to be engaged in the contextual specificities of the overlap. This connection then becomes important, determining and changing the *very nature* of those involved. Using a similar analogy of the sea, Kasulis describes the relationship between water and salt that becomes seawater when merged. Their independent identities as salt and water disappear to become seawater as an intimate relationship where *each surrenders parts of its own nature*, in becoming the relational whole of the ocean. The ethics of intimacy is not about forging new relations between discrete individuals, nor is it logical, external and contractual where one needs to behave ethically in terms of principles and responsibilities. Rather, intimacy's etymology as *innermost*, or Latin's *incorporat*, is 'an incorporating: a drawing into the body. We enter into intimate relations by opening ourselves to let the other inside, by putting ourselves into internal relations with others or recognizing internal relations that already exists' (Kasulis 2002: 43).

The intimacy orientation resonates with my experience of being Japanese, which interestingly, Kasulis notes is more dominant in Japan. We will see how mindfulness informed by Zen Buddhism also reflects this orientation. Furthermore, the intimacy view also exists in 'subcultures' of dominant paradigms, such as feminist discourses that take the position that we are already entangled in a web of systems and influences, and any interventions are from 'within' and cannot be seen as external, isolated or independent. For example, Erin McCarthy (2010) builds on Kasulis' framework and incorporates Japanese and feminist philosophies to argue an ethics of care as embodied intimacy that foregrounds relationality and interdependence. Harraway (2008: 70) describes that things and living beings matter, but that 'mattering' is 'always inside connections', where 'interdependency is not a contract but a condition; a pre-condition' (Puig de la Bellacasa 2012: 198). Care, according to Puig de la Bellacasa, is a precondition of interdependency because care itself is relational. It recognises the inevitable interdependency, not something forced upon by moral order. This is also Nancy's (2000) co-ontology of 'being with', where plurality is irreducible, and the singular 'I' does not precede the relation of 'we'. The intimacy orientation resonates with my view on sustainability where we are already entangled with and part of other constituents of the world.

Taking the intimacy orientation into design, designing is also inherently social, relational and embodied – it is enacted for and with other people. If we foreground designing that cannot be disentangled from this ecological, relational world in which it originates from, performed within and 'intra-venes' in (following Barad 2003), we can reorientate its focus from what designing does in and to the world, to also consider what it means for a designer to be part of this continual becoming of our world. In other words, rather than proposing abstractions of design as common principles, guiding questions, models or methods for how design/designers *should* act (integrity view), I consider ways to pursue how we, as designers, are changing and intra-vening in one's own life through mindfulness practice. One could even suggest that it is not the world that we need to change or design, because to change also necessitates our own reorientation and transformation, simultaneously. I emphasize concurrence here because catalyzing change is neither 'inside' within us or 'outside' in the world in binary ways, but rather, mindfulness meditation removes such mind-created constructs so that we can *become* impermanent, interrelated and intimate, not just being aware of it. What I share in this chapter is an intimacy orientation in practices of mindfulness, informed by my Japanese cultural background, constituted by practices of *unlearning*, *emptiness* and *surrender*, contextually shaped by the kinds of designing I have done, and continue to do.

A circle: dialogue across difference

I am Japanese by birth and was educated in England, Japan and the United States, currently working in Australia. My design research practice, over many years, has been shaped by working with regional communities in Australia; in strengthening their resilience for disaster preparedness and with Indigenous Nations to enact their sovereignty and self-determination. This context is central in defining my design practice, as well as shaping unlearning, surrender and emptiness as a path towards mindfulness, motivated by a concern for our ecological world and what futures we are designing and participating in together. This chapter is written in first-person to reflexively bring the situation of ourselves as 'knowers' into an epistemic frame and critically interrogate the social relations within which we as 'knowers' know how knowledge is produced (Nakata 2007). The structure moves through several layers, starting with mindfulness framed by various scholars in cognitive psychology, Asian philosophy and Zen Buddhism. Then, I share how I am *unlearning* dominant orientations in design that promote methods and technique, entrenched in habits of problem solving and attribute linear and causal impacts of design. Lastly, *emptiness and surrender* speaks of a way to erode, 'molt' or 'throw away' predetermined constructs, attachments and self-consciousness to foreground absence-centred, receptive and intimacy orientation and speaks to spiritual dimensions in my designing. It is a circle. Due to length, only brief fragments from my practice weave through each section to bring specificity and illustration of my practice. Extensive accounts of the project and context can be read in the published works cited.

There are several major challenges to note before we begin that ironically highlight the limitation of this writing. Firstly, discussion on mindfulness can only make sense through experience and practice, echoing Zen Buddhism that shaped its evolution. This means readers who are looking for instructions for mindfulness and its application in design will be sadly disappointed as I do none of these here (I recommend joining meditation groups as a way to start practicing). I say this upfront because design and research expects what methods enable and enact, and accounts of design's materiality and its impact, which all stem from a paradigm of design that privileges an active and conscious mode of change and engagement. Foregrounding a peripheral view of design, as I do here, speaks of receptive, passive, reflexive mode. Design research is an evolving paradigm and creative practice, and we must continue with a path beset with fear, risk and scepticism to disrupt existing power and knowledge structures to allow fragile ideas and understandings to emerge (Rendell 2013).

Secondly, mindfulness constituted by *unlearning, emptiness* and *surrender* stem from non-being or absence as a ground of reality (Nishida in Dilworth et al. 1998). 'Absence' in English connotes negative and undesirable qualities such as non-existence or a lack, like deficiency or exclusion. In other words, absence is defined by being the opposite quality of presence, revealing the dualistic constructs that are common in English language. *Sunyata* (in Sanskrit), *Wu* (in Chinese) and *Mu* (in Japanese) are various ways 'emptiness' are expressed, central to Mahayana Buddhism, Taoism and Zen Buddhism. In these spiritual cultures, emptiness is taken *as is*, not qualified by its opposition to a 'positive' quality, or interpreted nihilistically as 'abyss' or 'meaninglessness'. Mindfulness and Zen Buddhism has been associated with nihilism, but many philosophers whose work I draw upon, like Suzuki and Kasulis, deal with these misunderstandings expertly.

Lastly, the preceding concerns speak of the emphasis given to subject-centred and active-mode of orientation. Henri Bortoft (1996), a philosopher of science, draws on the science of Johann Wolfgang von Goethe, better known for his poetry and plays, to explain how human beings have two major modes of organisation: the action mode and the receptive mode. Using developmental psychology, he explains how infants in the receptive mode gradually develop the action mode through their interaction with the physical environment that becomes dominant. The action mode refers to a consciousness that discriminates, analyses and divides the world up into objects. Recognizing and distinguishing one thing from the other immediately separates oneself from the thing – we stand outside of it. This is institutionalized by the structure of language, such as English, that favors the active, subject-centred mode. In comparison, the receptive orientation emphasizes holistic, non-verbal, nonlinear and intuitive perception. It is being open to events as they happen, and to take in and work with what is. In order to reverse the way in which we engage with the world from an analytical, sequential and logical mode of consciousness, Bortoft explains that we must turn our awareness from the singular object and encounter the whole. 'This turning around, from grasping to being receptive, from awareness of an object to letting an absence be active, is a reversal which is the practical consequence of choosing the path which assents to the whole as no-thing and not mere nothing' (Bortoft 1996: 17). In the context of design, this receptive mode could be considered as a way to embrace unknown and uncertainty, incorporate ambiguity and serendipity, and foreground embodied and sensory perception, to deepen our interrelatedness as a whole being.

I pursue a discussion on mindfulness by building on various scholars across time and geography, so this is not a simplification of 'East' versus 'West', yet as just demonstrated, I acknowledge the dominance of certain ways of thinking in these cultures. However, what might appear as opposite poles is merely a difference in position on a circle. Seeing difference as oppositional results in no cultural dialogue or philosophical empathy. McCarthy explains (2010: 6) the temptation in integrity-dominant culture 'is the tendency to frame differences in terms of "us versus them," or "you versus me." Even in the intimacy orientation, we have "insider versus outsider," wherein the intimacy group seeks to protect the members of its group from outsiders.' Rather, like Kasulis and McCarthy that aims to create a ground for understanding by working across and through difference and respecting distinct characteristics, I see integrity and intimacy orientation, active and receptive mode, subject and absence-centred connected fluidly as a circle. Like day and night, relations are interdependent. Lao Tzu helps us see into the interfusion of being and non-being: 'Being does not remain as such, nor does nonbeing. They are always ready to change from one state to the other. This is the "fluidity" of things. . . . But as soon as his mind "stops" with either of them, it loses its own fluidity' (in Suzuki 1958: 158). The challenge of any orientation is not to stop, to hold on to power or to silence its counterpart, but to be in perpetual, cyclical motion.

Mindfulness

There are various approaches and rich descriptions of mindfulness. A single definition is not possible, just like love, happiness and compassion as states of being-in-the-world are different according to context and person. Accepting this plurality is a significant start because it enables numerous ways mindfulness can be expressed and practiced. Acceptance of plurality also means to abandon any absolutes or assumed a priori. To me, mindfulness is a constant practice of being and becoming.

However, some characteristics have informed my approach to mindfulness. For example, a celebrated Zen scholar and practitioner, Thich Thien-An, elucidates how mindfulness can give insights into harmony of nature: 'Since everything is interrelated, since all things depend one upon another, nothing is absolute, nothing is separate, but all are part of the one indivisible whole' (1975: 32). He suggests mindfulness as a pathway for self-realisation and to discover new ways of relating to others. This speaks of an ecological consciousness and the interdependent system of all things. Another renowned Zen philosopher, Daisetz Teitaro Suzuki (1958: 9), describes a kind of awakening that is 'attuned to the pulsation of Reality.' When the mind is ready, 'you at once return to your original home . . . you discover your new real self. From the very beginning nothing has been kept from you, all that you wished to see has been there all the time before you, it was only yourself that closed the eye to the fact' (Suzuki 1969: 92). Others like Carl Jung have grappled with Zen to consider the meaning of 'becoming whole (*Ganzwerdung*)' in relation to psycho-therapy to highlight that 'the conscious is only part of the spiritual, and is never therefore capable of spiritual completeness . . . the attainment of completeness calls for the use of the whole' (in Suzuki 1969: 27–28). We can see from these scholars an awareness of 'no thinking' (*mushin*) that is at the heart of mindful meditation where the practitioner 'overcomes the perception of things in terms of past/present/future and experiences the phenomenon just as it is' (Kasulis 1981: 80). This involves changes to the practitioner immersed within an unending experience of flux and impermanence, which changes what is being experienced to enable a transformative process (Kasulis 1981; Varela et al. 1993).

Mindfulness also rejects logic and rational analysis. The avoidance of words and texts is strongly seen in Zen Buddhism's orientation to mindfulness. Suzuki (1969: 61) cautions not to get 'entangled in intellectual subtleties, not to be carried away by philosophical reasoning that is so often ingenious and full of sophistry', further reminding us 'to know that words are words and nothing else'. The mind only trained to analyze, 'in spite of its practical usefulness . . . goes against our effort to delve into the depths of being' (Suzuki 1958: 271). Through constant practice, it is possible to achieve a state of emptiness – no-mind – 'stripping off all the artificial wrappings humanity has devised, supposedly for its own solemnization' (Suzuki 1958: 271). Intellectual and cognitive orientation can only get us so far, just as reading and thinking about mindfulness alone also has its limitations. Here, I see a resonance between designing and mindfulness, which can only be undertaken through practice. Practice here meaning direct experience, embodiment and a presence of being and becoming.

However, it is important not to confuse what I discuss with 'mindfulness' framed by psychology and a different world view that often sees its usefulness to change behavior towards a desired outcome. Thich Nhat Hanh (1991: 4) shares two ways to wash the dishes. 'The first is to wash the dishes in order to have clean dishes and the second is to wash the dishes in order to wash the dishes.' This simple story teaches us the difference between one that is outcome and future-focused and one that brings us closer to ordinary experience. The former state is 'not alive during the time we are washing the dishes . . . sucked away into the future – and we are incapable of actually living one minute of life' (Hanh 1991: 5). When this view of mindfulness is taken into design, it is a means of improvement, to solve problems or to achieve goals (see e.g. Akama and Light 2015; Niedderer 2013). Here, 'mindfulness' has been turned into a technique for relaxation, stress relief, attention and judgment, which have little connection to mindfulness that originates from spiritual teachings of Buddhism. Most interesting here is to see 'mindfulness' used to further consolidate the dominance of the action-mode that analyses, divides and separates consciousness. The receptive, intimate, interdependent and spiritual orientations is a mindfulness practice that I discuss via Zen Buddhism, foregrounded in my design practice.

Unlearning

Working with communities was not my design or research training. My degree in visual communication led to my employment as a graphic designer to create various communication artefacts related to human rights, education and environmental issues for international NGOs in the United Kingdom. These are issues that motivated me then, and continue to do so now. However, this design education and industry apprenticeship was highly specific to crafting design solutions in response to defined problems, typified by a practice of producing finished outcomes (e.g. posters for campaigns). These objects became proxies for my involvement in these issues, designed and deployed from a distance, and this disconnect catalyzed my pursuit for designing with communities.

Designers are often poorly prepared to engage in community work because, as the preceding account illustrates, their education or apprenticeship is geared towards industry practice to craft solutions in response to a narrowly defined 'problem'. Design's problem-solution paradigm is entrenched, stemming from theories of design that evolved during the late 20th century in Europe (Bousbaci 2008) where the dominance of rational thinking emerged from philosophical modernism and Enlightenment (Kasulis 2002). Giard and Schneiderman (2013: 132) echo this view and observe how design education is still framed within the precepts of industrialisation, based on 'growth, materiality, and a fixation on the artefact'. Feminist and postcolonial theory can expose the mechanics of established canons and occupied theories because the dominant is often unable to recognize its own power, privilege and penetration (Minh-Ha 1989). Similarly, I cultivated my practice of designing with communities by unlearning entrenched and dominant world views of design.

The first thing I had to unlearn was my training in design to 'solve problems' and attach agency and change to design alone, especially when the issues were complex and compounded. During a pilot study to address lack of disaster preparedness among residents living in regional areas of Australia, our research team developed visual and tactile methods to share local knowledge and facilitate dialogue. This grass-roots approach aimed to build awareness and cultivate neighbourly relations for survival in fire. However, when the methods, trialed and evaluated, were passed on to our partner organization in the hope they would continue its use, we were surprised to hear that no further community workshops were held. Even though they were convinced of its performance and value, there were numerous factors that prevented our partner organization to continue community preparedness workshops, such as changes in staff and cuts in funding. Also, many residents had a sense of dependency on the fire authority for instruction and fragmented social relations among neighbours. These revealed entrenched issues and the need for a long-term approach to truly embed transformation for the community to take ownership of change. Methods, design or designers alone cannot 'solve' this 'problem'. These realisations were significant lessons for my *unlearning* that turned the research around to examine the invisible 'infrastructures' (Star and Ruhleder 1996) such as relational, socio-material practices. Our methods then became incorporated into a nationwide training program in the Emergency Management sector as a way to reveal, reflect and address power dynamics and community fragmentation in order to build capacity towards a systemic, community-centred approach (see Akama 2015b).

Methods, like process, tools and techniques are celebrated in design, especially in codesign, service design and design for social innovation – the very field that seeks to champion social change. Pragmatic interventions of design are highlighted to focus on 'whatever design can do to start, boost, support, make robust and replicate social innovation' (Manzini and Rizzo 2011: 202) rather than acknowledge the 'mess', contingency and turbulence that accompanies most change work. This speaks to the dominant form of design that privileges the active-mode of doing and action, rather than a passive, receptive mode of reflection, which has the unfortunate consequence of framing design as causal in a linear manner, isolated and discretely 'bounded' in projects, artifacts, methods, models or performance. Methods alone do not have agency – they are performed among groups of people, a context rife with contingency where needs emerge, dynamics change and all constituents of change process is continually reconstructed (DiSalvo et al. 2013; Light and Akama 2012). This is the messiness of change that cannot be planned or neatly categorized. Designers' embodied knowing shifts from moment to moment, often in response to the inter-subjective nuances of the group whilst influencing the dynamic. In other words, to notice such nuances means the need for us to develop sensitivity and awareness in these situations. When designing is enacted in the between-ness among heterogeneous influences, incremental details of transformative processes can often remain hidden by their very nature of being silent, internal, ephemeral, dispersed, all of which are difficult to notice as part of change (Akama 2015a). This requires a cultivation of an absence-centred, receptive orientation.

There are things we need to *unlearn* in design. In practicing mindfulness, I necessarily begin with unlearning because it is the first step to short-circuit entrenched habits. Cognitive scientists Varela et al. (1993: 29) suggest that an approach to mindfulness is a 'letting go of habits of mindlessness, as an *un*learning rather than a learning' and 'it is a different sense of effort from the acquiring of something new'. The mind can be cluttered with habitual patterns, which 'constantly tries to grasp some stable point in its unending movement and to cling to thoughts, feelings, and concepts as if they were a solid ground' (Varela et al. 1993: 26). They claim that the first significant discovery of mindfulness meditation is not a piercing insight but an awakening 'of just how disconnected humans normally are from their very experience' (Varela et al. 1993: 25). Even though designers might wish to attribute purposeful change as a result of their specific interventions, our habit of looking for tangible change, our training to solve problems and our expectations for controlling mess can become barriers to notice invisible conditions entangled with people, place, culture, materiality, local knowledge, histories and emotions that are all constituents of transformation. Disruptions, accidents, chance and surprise are also features of change. This highlights the need to let go of a 'spacesuit' made of 'habits and preconceptions, the armor with which one habitually distances oneself from one's experience' (Varela et al. 1993: 25) to realize our own disconnect, and *surrender* to the flux and flow of change as a necessary process of our own transformation.

Emptiness and surrender

When the neo-liberal agenda emphasizes growth, productivity and accumulation, to which design undoubtedly contributes to, it may sound odd to talk about emptiness and surrender, but this is the teaching of Zen. The Japanese word for mindfulness is *mushin*, composed of two words, *mu* ('nothingness' or 'emptiness') and *shin* ('mind-spirit-heart'). In translating *mushin*, various scholars have used terms such as 'no-thought', 'no-mind', or 'no-form', and in a language that privileges an active-mode of consciousness (Bortoft 1996) and one that separates mind from body and spirit, it is impossible to find an equivalent term that comes close. The English etymology of mindful is 'gemyndful', meaning 'of good memory' (www.etymonline.com), again emphasizing mind-training or cognitive improvement. However, when mindfulness is viewed as a skill or training, it is likely to escalate a distanced and analytical view of the world (Varela et al. 1993), moving further away from the original Buddhist teachings of *sunyata* (emptiness).

Mu as nothingness is not a negation but to erode, 'molt' or 'throw away' mind-created constructs, attachments, intellectualization, self-assuredness and past conditionings (Kasulis 1981). These must be surrendered. 'The person of no-mind sees the objects of the world as neither real nor unreal, as neither independent substances nor dreams or illusions. Here, then, lies the connection between no-thought and non-form: without denying the forms encountered in daily life, the Zen Buddhist, nonetheless, does not cling to them or take them to be the one reality' (Kasulis 1981:44). In other words, *Mu* is not nihilistic as a denial of thinking or annihilation of consciousness, but to question the very category of thinking and words, to neither affirm or deny, accept or reject, believe or disbelieve and bring one's full participation in direct experience (Kasulis 1981). Surrender here is supplication, evoking Kasulis' story of the interrelatedness of salt and water that surrenders parts of its nature to become the whole of the ocean, and not interpreted within a combative frame as 'beaten' and 'quitting'.

Mushin in Japanese speaks of the inseparability of the mind, body and spirit. As mentioned earlier in the chapter, spiritual dimensions underpin mindfulness in Zen Buddhism. Spirits, life force, soul, gods and ancestors (referred to as *tama* or *kami*) are frequently used in conversation in Japan and can be found in the most quotidian. It is not strange for someone to pray to a fox, light incense to waft bad spirits away or contemplate life when the cherry blossoms scatter in the spring wind. Shinto is the indigenous spirituality of Japan before Buddhism's arrival from China, and sees interrelatedness of all beings and non-beings. For example, the sacred rope, *shimenawa*, encircles human and non-human forms that inspires awe and wonderment, such as an ancient tree, rock, spring, or hung to indicate a threshold to a cave, mountain or the grounds of a Shinto shrine. Kasulis (2004) explains that this rope is a symbolic connection to remind us of our interrelatedness, functioning like a 'bookmark' for connecting people to the awe-inspiring power of *kami* or *tama* that permeates. *Shimenawa* or *torii* gate are thresholds to prepare the visitor to being enveloped and permeated by awe, mystery and wonderment. It is thought that, as one enters through the *torii* gate, awe also enters (Kasulis 2004). In other words, one must clear a space, through surrender and emptiness – *mushin* – for awe and wonderment to permeate. The *shimenawa* and *torii* gate signals a preparation for this mutual entry. This means if one crosses over the threshold in haste and in stress, lost in the busyness and details of the everyday, one would only encounter the same state at the shrine, disconnected from the capacity for awe and wonderment of life.

Advocates in sustainability argue various interpretations of spirituality as an ethical perspective, a meaning-seeking path and an intimacy with the divineness of the natural world, which has significant implication in reorienting damaging consequences of modernity (Walker 2013). Yet, spirituality has been an absent presence and a tricky topic to discuss in design and research. A sustainability proponent, Stuart Walker (2013), alludes to this reason in his article, *Design and Spirituality*. He describes how spirituality was politically, socially and culturally eroded in northern Europe through religious reform, eradication of traditional ways of life, and the rise of scientific methods such as Empiricism and Utilitarianism. The devastating consequences of this led to the 'modern' worldview, based on the assumption that the physical universe is all that exists, confined to observation and inferences to the physical world. This view 'virtually expunged the relevance of spirituality from public and often private life' where spirituality became 'bereft of their roots' (2013: 91) and non-physical aspects of human dimensions – intuition, sense of transcendence and spirituality – were eclipsed during a time of rapid technological innovation and industrial modernization. Walker's compelling argument for spirituality as personal meaning of ethics, values and attention to inner development, aims to invoke substantive change in design to redress the imbalance of the contemporary world that is preoccupied with consumption.

I do not live in Japan, yet, living in Australia for fifteen years has not diminished the spirituality of my every day. In fact, it has become more pronounced by inhabiting a landscape that inspires awe and wonderment. My work with Aboriginal and Torres Strait Islander peoples further heightens my spirituality, awe and wonderment, even though our journeying together is often confronting to challenge hegemonic colonial legacies. I am part of a team to design various mechanisms for participation to promote necessary discussions on self-governance, Indigenous sovereignty, cultural renewal and political identity, and these have taken shape as events, digital platforms and a variety of creative materials (see Akama et al. 2017). These materials and processes can be considered as mediators, interfaces or in-betweens to support 'sticky' relations such as trust, respect and closeness to flourish (Bush and Tiwana 2005) among and between Indigenous and non-Indigenous people. Though the things I design are aided by the active-mode of doing and action, I am simultaneously foregrounding a receptive, absence-centred orientation in a cyclical way to have a heightened relational sensitivity to invisible dynamics, and intuitively feel resonance with Indigenous culture, instead of being anxious about further colonializing their knowledge through research (Tuhiwai-Smith 1999). With every invitation to meet or visit Wiradjuri people, I am foregrounding my culture, as they do, in building relationships, which, in many cases, are evolving into friendships. This includes my spirituality, humility and reverence for beings and nonbeings I encounter. When an Elder teaches me weaving as a practice of Indigenous sovereignty, my nimble fingers learning this technique evokes my grandmother's hands that stitched kimono for all her children. When I am invited on their Country on field trips, interview or document their events; I am also emplaced. We sit by the foreshore of Murrumbidgee River enveloped in warm sunshine, feel the light river breeze and listen to the call of native birds. In my own way, I locate the feeling of connectedness to this country. This means I am continually practicing mindfulness constituted by emptiness and surrender – to erode, 'molt' or 'throw away' intellectual categories, self-consciousness, desirable expectations and conditioning that seeks to grasp at certainty, to analyze phenomena, and to selectively privilege active, physical presence. Like a bowl, ready to receive by surrendering its existing contents, this allows me to be open. Debora Bird Rose (2004: 22), a celebrated anthropologist who works with Indigenous Australians explains, 'openness is risky because one does not know the outcome. To be open is to hold one's self available to others: one takes risks and becomes vulnerable. But this is also a fertile stance: one's own ground can become destabilised. In open dialogue one holds one's self available to be surprised, to be challenged, and to be changed.' We can see here how surrender, emptiness and openness share similar paths in different names. I am intimately woven into the paths of our journeying together because of mutual recognition of our sovereignties. In seeking potentiality in what we might become together, the spiritual dimensions clear a space for awe and wonder to permeate, and create emptiness for my own potentiality and transformation. In doing so, I can further cultivate interrelatedness to mutually explore connection to culture and the kinds of relationships we want to create in our journey forward.

A wave is the ocean

A Zen Buddhist approach to mindfulness is practiced in the every day. Others can be seen in walking labyrinths – the body moving through space calls on the ability to be in the world through affective senses (Vaughan 2004), or meditating silently in calmness and stillness and use the breath to observe wandering, mindless thoughts (Varela et al. 1993). I have shared experiences with friends who practice mindfulness through photography, walking, smoking and gardening (see Akama & Light 2015). There are many paths in practicing mindfulness.

Similarly, my mindfulness practice does not happen only when I am visiting a community or designing with people, as if flicking on a switch. It is attempted and pursued in the various in-betweens of my daily routine, when I practice calligraphy and tai chi, and also elicited when I hear the rain or watch wafting clouds from my office window. These inhibit automation and distancing, to be aware of not being present to bring me closer and more intimate with the world. Thien-An (1975: 38) explains: 'Every day we face problems, some easy, some difficult. . . . Of course, it is more difficult to apply meditation in action than at rest, but it is also of more value . . . when we meet troubles or obstacles in our life, they should be faced with the mind poised in the calm of meditation'. His notion of *poise* is a helpful way to consider designing when there are emergent actions, dynamics and flow that one needs to be responsive to, without being overtly reactive or rigidly adhere to plans already drawn. It reflects a form of composure and preparation to enter and immerse in contingency, such as those we encounter when designing with communities. It is a readying to being fully present.

Thich Nhat Hanh says 'Enlightenment for a wave in the ocean is the moment the wave realizes it is water' (1995: 138). A wave is merely a construct and temporary form shaped by wind, tide and the ocean floor, but it is a movement of water not separate from the ocean. This resonates with the seawater analogy by Kasulis, returning again to his notion of intimacy that surrenders parts of its own nature in becoming the relational whole. This view sees that we are already part of the ecology of beings and non-beings of this planet and beyond. Mindfulness is a practice that attends to this interrelated awareness and be concerned with the literal and indirect impacts of our thoughts, feelings and conduct. A *Cloud Floating in Each Paper* by Thich Nhat Hanh (2016) is a story that reminds us how we are all connected – the sunshine, the rain, the tree, the logger and the paper upon which this ink is printed – and be weary of mind-constructed categories that measure each as separate, like the Life Cycle Analysis or the Triple Bottom Line because the whole is more than the sum of each part.

Being mindful cannot be immediate, and nor will it end with its mastery or perfection. In my hectic work life, I am prone to being more mindless than mindful, so this is a lifelong pursuit. I am and will always be a beginner – the purpose being not to 'attain' mindfulness but a commitment to practice it every day. Similarly sustainability is not an end goal or a linear trajectory, but taking part in the world's continual becoming. Practicing mindfulness catalyzes change to my own practice, be immersed in the ebb and flow of designing whilst being changed by it. When I am present-in-the-moment, I feel most open, receptive and sensitized to phenomena. Instead of a clenched fist, grasping and holding on to certainty, it relaxes into an open palm of emptiness, ready to receive and be part of the world in its continual becoming.

References

Akama, Y. (2012) "A 'way of being': Zen and the art of being a human-centred practitioner" *Design Philosophy Papers*, 1, 1–10.

Akama, Y. (2015a) "Being awake to *Ma*: Designing in between-ness as a way of becoming with" *Co-Design: International Journal of CoCreation in Design and the Arts*, 11(34), 262–274.

Akama, Y. (2015b) "Continuous re-configuring of invisible social structures" in A. Bruni, L. L. Parolin and C. Schubert, eds., *Designing Technology Work Organization and Vice Versa*. Wilmington: Vernon Press, 163–183.

Akama, Y., Evans, D., Keen, S., McMillan, F., McMillan, M., and West, P. (2017) "Designing Digital and Creative Scaffolds to Strengthen Indigenous Nations: Being Wiradjuri by Practising Sovereignty" *Digital Creativity*. doi: 10.1080/14626268.2017.1291525

Akama, Y., Keen, S., and West, P. (2016) "Speculative design and heterogeneity in indigenous nation building" in *Proc. Designing Interactive Systems* 2016, Queensland University of Technology, Brisbane, Australia, 895–899.

Akama, Y. and Light, A. (2015) "Towards mindfulness: Between a detour and a portal" in *Proc. CHI '15*, Seoul, Korea, 625–637.

Barad, K. (2003) "Posthumanist performativity: Toward an understanding of how matter comes to matter" *Signs: Journal of Women in Culture and Society*, 28(3), 801–831.

Bortoft, H. (1996) *The Wholeness of Nature: Goethe's Way of Science*. New York: Floris Books.

Bousbaci, R. (2008) "'Models of man' in design thinking: The 'bounded rationality' episode" *Design Issues*, 24(4), 38–52.

Bush, A.A. and Tiwana, A. (2005) "Designing sticky knowledge networks" *Communications of the ACM*, 48(5), 67–71.

Dilworth, D. A., Viglielmo, H. V., and Zavala, A. J. (eds.). (1998) *Sourcebook for Modern Japanese Philosophy: Selected Documents*. Westport: Greenwood Press.

DiSalvo, C., Clement, A., and Pipek, V. (2013) "Communities: Participatory design for, with and by communities" in J. Simonsen and T. Robertson, eds., *Routledge International Handbook of Participatory Design*. London and New York: Routledge, 182–209.

Fry, T. (2009) *Design Futuring: Sustainability, Ethics and New Practice*. Oxford, UK: Berg.

Giard, J. and Schneiderman, D. (2013). "Integrating sustainability in design education" in S. Walker and J. Giard, eds., *The Handbook of Design for Sustainability*. London: Bloomsbury, 121–136.

Hanh, T. N. (1991) *The Miracle of Mindfulness*. London, Sydney, Auckland, and Johannesburg: Rider.

Hanh, T. N. (1995) *Living Buddha, Living Christ*. London, Sydney, Auckland, and Johannesburg: Rider.

Hanh, T. N. (2016) *Thich Nhat Hanh Quotes*, viewed 30 Sept. 2016, <www.goodreads.com/author/quotes/9074.Thich_Nhat_Hanh?page=12>.

Harraway D. J. (2008) *When Species Meet*, Minneapolis: University of Minnesota Press.

Kasulis, T. (1981) *Zen Action/Zen Person*. Hawaii: University of Hawaii Press.

Kasulis, T. (2002) *Intimacy or Integrity: Philosophical and Cultural Difference*. Hawaii: University of Hawaii Press.

Kasulis, T. (2004) *Shinto: The Way Home*. Hawaii: University of Hawaii Press.

Light, A. and Akama, Y. (2012) "The human touch: From method to participatory practice in facilitating design with communities" in *Proc. PDC*, Roskilde, Denmark, 61–70.

Manzini, E. (2006) "Design, ethics and sustainability. Guidelines for a transition phase" in *Cumulus Working Papers: Nantes*, Helsinki, Finland, 9–15.

Manzini, E. and Rizzo, F. (2011) "Small projects/large changes: Participatory design as an open participated process" *Co:Design: International Journal of CoCreation in Design and the Arts*, 7(3–4), 199–215.

Mccarthy, E. (2010) *Ethics Embodied: Rethinking Selfhood Through Continental, Japanese and Feminist Philosophies*. Blue Ridge Summit, PA: Rowman & Littlefield Publishing Group.

Minh-Ha, T. T. (1989) *Woman, Native, Other: Writing Postcoloniality and Feminism*. Bloomington and Indianapolis: Indiana University Press.

Nakata, M. (2007) "The cultural interface" *The Australian Journal of Indigenous Education*, 36 (Supplement 2007), 7–14.

Nancy, J.-L. (2000) *Being Singular Plural*. Translated by Richardson, R. D. and O'Byrne, A. E. Stanford, CA: Stanford University Press.

Niedderer, K. (2013) "Mindful design as a driver for social behaviour change" in *Proc. International IASDR Conference*, Tokyo, Japan, 4561–4571.

Norton, L. (2012) "Beyond design's ethical void" *Design Philosophy Papers*, 10(2), 169–171.

Pedersen, A., Beven, J., Walker, I., and Griffiths, B. (2004) "Attitudes toward Indigenous Australians: The role of empathy and guilt" *Journal of Community & Applied Social Psychology*, 14, 233–249.

Puig de la Bellacasa, M. (2012) "'Nothing comes without its world': Thinking with care" *The Sociological Review*, 60(2), 197–216.

Rendell, J. (2013) "A way with words: Feminists writing architectural design research" in M. Fraser, ed., *Architectural Design Research*. London: Ashgate, 117–136.

Robertson, T. and Wagner, I. (2013) "Ethics: Engagement, representation and politics-in-action" in J. Simonsen and T. Robertson, eds., *Routledge International Handbook of Participatory Design*. London and New York: Routledge, 64–85.

Rose, D. B. (2004) *Reports From a Wild Country: Ethics for Decolonisation*. Sydney, Australia: University of New South Wales.

Star, S. L. and Ruhleder, K. (1996) "Steps toward an ecology of infrastructure: Design and access for large information spaces" *Information Systems Research*, 7(1), 111–134.

Suzuki, D. T. (1958) *Zen and Japanese Culture*. New York: Princeton University Press.

Suzuki, D. T. (1969) *An Introduction to Zen Buddhism*. London: Rider and Company.

Thien-An, T. (1975) *Zen Philosophy, Zen Practice*. Berkley, CA: Dharma Publishing.

Tuhiwai Smith, L. (1999) *Decolonising Methodologies*. London: Zed Books, CPI Group.

Varela, F. J., Thompson, E., and Rosch, E. (1993) *The Embodied Mind: Cognitive Science and Human Experience*. Cambridge, MA: MIT Press.

Vaughan, L. (2004) *Anfractuous: An Exploration of Creative Practice*. Unpublished PhD Thesis, School of Applied Communications, RMIT University, Melbourne.

Walker, S. (2013) "Design and spirituality: Material culture for a wisdom economy" *Design Issues*, 29(3), 89–107.

18

CONFRONTING THE FIVE PARADOXES OF HUMANITARIAN DESIGN

Brita Fladvad Nielsen

A refugee on average spends 17 years in a refugee camp (UNHCR 2007), while relief assistance delivered by humanitarian actors are typically designed to last only 12 to 24 months (Van Wassenhove 2006). This is a relationship which illustrates the urgent need to focus on designing for long-term sustainability within the humanitarian market. In my work to frame 'humanitarian design' from 2011 to 2015 (Nielsen 2015) I conducted research on the case of providing energy alternatives for refugee camps in Ethiopia. I chose this location because Ethiopia is the largest traditional host of refugees and because this area represents one of the environmentally vulnerable areas where deforestation caused partly by refugee settlements is of high relevance to the future sustainability of these communities and the surrounding area. During my research I realized that the fundamental challenges of humanitarian design at the time being are linked to more systematic challenges of the humanitarian system, and less, to cultural and socio-technical challenges.

When hundreds of thousands of refugees are placed in settlements of already pressured land in regions that are environmentally vulnerable, the direct effect on this on the surrounding land is typically deforestation due to the need for cooking fuel (Whitaker 2002, Lyytinen 2009), and degradation of arable land. Indirect effects are conflict between host communities and refugees, and added conflict in the already conflict-burdened border areas of development countries. Yet, whereas the focus of the international humanitarian sector from 2007 to 2011 was on the *environmental* sustainability of refugee camps, the refugee crisis in Europe seems to have shifted this environmental focus over to a more fundamental, and renewed debate on the holistic sustainability both globally (Fargues 2014, Cutler 2016) *and* locally (Fransen 2015). Globally, the discussion centers on how the refugee system succeeds in serving the needs of displaced populations and the effect on global security and migration, whereas locally, the sustainability discussions embrace economic, social and environmental concerns related to the core of humanitarian assistance, namely dignity.

The idea of human rights as a foundation for impartial delivery of humanitarian aid has remained the core of humanitarian relief since World War II. The acknowledgement that all people are entitled to be treated equally and to be protected in times of war and disaster is key to understanding the efforts of humanitarian actors. A humanitarian actor typically refers to an organization providing humanitarian relief assistance, such as the United Nations (UN), the International Red Cross (ICRC), Doctors without Borders (MSF) and the Norwegian Refugee Council (NRC).

'The Sphere Handbook: Humanitarian Charter and Minimum Standards in Humanitarian Response' (Griekspoor and Collins 2001) is the common reference point for humanitarian actors and explains their mandate as follows:

The right to life with dignity

This right is reflected in the legal measures concerning the right to life, to an adequate standard of living and to freedom from cruel, inhuman or degrading treatment or punishment. We understand an individual's right to life to entail the right to have steps taken to preserve life where it is threatened, and a corresponding duty on others to take such steps. Implicit in this is the duty not to withhold or frustrate the provision of life-saving assistance. In addition, international humanitarian law makes specific provision for assistance to civilian populations during conflict, obliging states and other parties to agree to the provision of humanitarian and impartial assistance when the civilian population lacks essential supplies.

(Sphere humanitarian charter)

Humanitarian design can be used to describe the process of designing products for refugees or other disaster victims, service design for the provision of aid, or strategies that will improve the delivery of emergency aid. Furthermore, by centering on dignity, humanitarian action has obliged itself to provide disaster-affected communities with essential physical goods in emergency situations. Dignity implies that the goal of humanitarian action is both value based and human centered; as is design science (Dorst 2011). This is where design and design thinking become relevant; design being a value-oriented science (Dorst 2011) where we seek to identify which efforts result in *meaningful experiences* for those involved. We cannot say that something is useful or necessary to create, unless it increases the well-being of people and adds to their ability to make sense of their situation (Krippendorff 1989). Following this line of reasoning, 'humanitarian design' should refer to the application of 'designerly' approaches (Cross 2006) to assist crisis-affected people to reach a situation where they can live with dignity.

Successful humanitarian design lies in the designer's ability to make sense of the complexity of the humanitarian market, while balancing the humanitarianism of their design with influential factors in a wider context. It requires a conscious effort of the designer and the design team together with humanitarian practitioners (Santos, Capet et al. 2013) and multiple stakeholders (Nielsen and Santos 2013a) to decide what an 'adequate standard of living' is and what a dignified life entails in a given setting. And precisely the 'setting' will be unpredictable and conditions will vary immensely, making this a more challenging task in the humanitarian market than in a conventional consumer market.

Consequently, before we can move into the depths of humanitarian design's paradoxes and potential, it is necessary to understand the basics of how humanitarian relief works. Humanitarian aid, as opposed to development aid, is intended to be short-term. There is no clear distinction between short-term and long-term, yet humanitarian actors and enterprises explain that they typically work with 12- to 24-month budgets in humanitarian emergencies, and that they are supposed to pull out their efforts after two years. Humanitarian development aid on the other hand is delivered by other organizations, and focuses on long-term development based on a country's identified and stated needs. Typically, humanitarian aid organizations (humanitarian actors) respond to crises by dividing them into phases: preparedness phase, immediate emergency, recovery phase and durable solutions phase (Perry and Lindell 2003). The main purpose of this division is to understand how urgent assistance is needed and to systematize the response. Once an emergency occurs, international donor countries and humanitarian actors join forces to make decisions based on rapid needs assessments on the ground. Countries contributing official donor aid (ODA) are referred to as donor countries. Ideally, the situation was foreseen and regional offices were previously equipped with preparedness shelters, ready to supply humanitarian actors with the necessary supplies of food, water and non-food items (NFIs).

It is agreed that humanitarian innovation must always be measured through its impact (Fladvad Nielsen 2016). However, even if results-based management has been at the core of humanitarian development for decades (Binnendijk 2000), the nature of the impact and how to meaningfully assess the impact within the humanitarian sector remains debatable (Roche 1999, Proudlock and Ramalingam 2009).

Saying that humanitarian design must be directed towards the crisis-affected people does not exclude the application of 'design thinking' to the design of solutions or improvement of organizational structures or policy development for humanitarian relief. Design that improves the delivery of relief can have great impact on the objectives of humanitarian work. Indeed, the manner in which the delivery of emergency aid is accomplished needs rethinking. This concern has been raised by multiple humanitarian actors and researchers (Macrae et al. 1994, Holtzman 1999, Gunning 2000, Betts, Bloom et al. 2015, Santos et al. 2016). The questions raised typically center on the challenge to bridge short-term, urgent needs and short-term solutions delivered by humanitarian relief actors, with the long-term, sustainability focused efforts for the crisis-affected communities.

This chapter specifically centers on refugees as victims of emergencies and potential end users in relation to design efforts seeking to alleviate poverty and ensure life with dignity. The current situation remains that, by the end of 2015, more than 50 million people were fleeing war or famine (NRC 2015). The continuous increase in humanitarian need presents an increasing expense to the nations funding international humanitarian action.

The new humanitarian agenda for design and innovation

As people flee war and famine in ever-larger numbers, international efforts have focused on determining how the exponential growth in crises can be met by the donors of international aid and relief. Humanitarian innovation is one of the concepts that has emerged as a potential solution. There is no common agreement on what humanitarian innovation means. At the beginning of this decade, a common denominator was that humanitarian actors look to private enterprises rather than political leaders to find better solutions to humanitarian needs. 'Humanitarian innovation' has been particularly used with the purpose of making humanitarian action more effective and efficient. Large and small private enterprises are engaged in the provision of everything from electricity, water and sanitation to schools and communication in relief areas. This has been the result of the fast and global increase in requests to mitigate the effects of disasters.

The strengthened bond between humanitarians and private enterprises, seen in humanitarian innovation, is perhaps a result of a mentality shift amongst humanitarian staff. Traditionally, humanitarian values were seen as a mismatch with the values of the business sector and hence the humanitarian sector was reluctant to involve private enterprises at a strategic level. In practice, humanitarian innovation implies, for example, that humanitarian actors open up to the use of credit cards (Barrow 2016) for refugees instead of controlled food rations or donated items. Digital Food Aid and Digital Aid allows access for cell phone companies and MasterCard (UNHCR

2016) to transfer cash so that the aid recipient can choose their own food. World Food Program hopes that this will lead to

- Empowered refugees, as they can make their own choices
- Reduced corruption as the MasterCard solution is transparent
- Increased stimulation of the local market for products and services
- Easier flow of funds from donation to recipient (refugee)

The emergence of solutions such as digital food aid can hence be regarded representations of how humanitarian actors have begun to realize that before certain system-related issues have to be addressed ((UNDP 2016) UNDP, UNHCR). Humanitarian actors are also opening their doors to enterprises, such as IKEA, who have started building emergency shelters in refugee camps (FOUND). On a smaller and more grassroot scale, humanitarian innovation is used to describe enterprises where local industrial managers hire refugees to work side-by-side with local citizens. New collaborations between private sector, policy makers, humanitarian sector, NGOs and their (Omata 2012, Betts and Bloom 2014, Boyer and DuPont 2016) 'new' way of delivering products and services are frequently referred to as humanitarian innovation.

When discussing system-related issues humanitarian actors and scholars raise the need to discuss how emergency aid is delivered, why, and for the benefit of whom, as well as its long-term consequences. Literature criticizing the humanitarian market as a self-sufficient industry and the idealist as unaware of 'real needs' has contributed to this debate (Linda 2011). The United Nations Development Program (UNDP) recently stated that the following key issues (Kumpf 2016) are relevant to design for 2030:

- Invite external expertise
- Focus on the change, not the solution
- Forget creativity; formulate and test hypothesis
- Fewer pilots, more scale
- Embrace politics
- Make systems-thinking practical

The United Nations High Commissionaire for Refugees (UNHCR) trains their staff in innovation processes and uses bottom-up approaches to 'harvest' ideas from all levels of their organizations; while Doctors without Borders (MSF) applied a humanitarian innovation mindset to rethink service provision in situations such as the Ebola outbreak in West Africa in 2014 (Wright, Dalwai et al. 2015) and also designed an ethical framework for humanitarian innovation (Sheather, Jobanputra et al. 2016).

As the definition of humanitarian innovation broadens, designers play an important role to ensure that innovations are engaging, holistic and human centered; and to assist humanitarian actors in reaching an understand of 'real' problem(s) (Simon 1973) of humanitarian emergencies.

Areas where humanitarian design is needed

Practitioners in humanitarian action say that there has been a too high focus on product innovation. Instead, they emphasize the need for service design, systems design and business models that can increase the sustainability of solutions within the three previously mentioned sectors (Fladvad Nielsen 2016). Furthermore, many individual products fail as there is not enough collaboration between the humanitarian supply system and its structural need for scalable solutions, and the individual product designing enterprise. The most prominent and continuously relevant challenges for humanitarian actors are the ones that require long-term focus across the organization of delivering humanitarian emergency aid:

- Water and sanitation – water access and sound sanitation systems are fundamental to the health of crisis-affected populations

  (Biran, Schmidt et al. 2012, Nicole 2015)

- Energy access – access to electricity and fuel for cooking

  (Aberra, Ndiaye et al. 2014, Bartolomei 2016)

- Big data – accountable and meaningful use of data and information sharing with crisis-affected populations as information is key to their feeling of a predictable and safe future

  (Nielsen 2014a, Meier 2015, Chretien et al. 2016)

All of these are heavily systems- and service-dependent. Products that serve smaller issues are of course interesting, yet addressing these successfully in the longer-term is a game changer. The inability to address water and sanitation issues results in epidemics and death; lack of energy resources results in conflict and environmental degradation; whereas the inability of humanitarian actors to successfully gather and use data is hindering them from learning, improving and keeping people safe.

One way that designers can approach these three areas for innovation is to work closely with stakeholders and to allow for the creation of contextual yet scalable solutions that emphasize capacity building (Brinkerhoff 2007). Capacity building is essential to build trustworthy local partnerships that will be responsible for running the service or system of services. Recent studies have shown that enterprises who do not focus on scalability, but internal learning and the constant improvements of their innovations, are the ones who succeed in the humanitarian market. This is also mentioned as the success behind flagship 'design thinking' innovations such as AirBnB and Uber: innovations that are based on unlocking a need and demand in the same area and simply connecting them through simple business mechanisms. This type of innovation may be exactly what the humanitarian sector needs. Still, in order for this to work, we must find a way to move away from the current structure of the humanitairan market. This is because the scalability of Uber and AirBnB relies on the universal basis of customers who can give feedback and make individual choices. Currently, the refugee does not have this ability. The refugee is the end user of a service or a product, yet they are depending on a large bureaucracy to make choices for them. They also lack a way to communicate their satisfaction with a product or a service. This represents a significant difference between the conventional consumer market and the humanitarian market, making it a quasi-market (Le Grand and Bartlett 1993) in which scalability of a design is dependent on the decisions of multiple organizations and not those of end users.

The broader solution to humanitarian design innovation is hence to find a new paradigm (Mawdsley, Savage et al. 2014, Saunders 2014) that addresses the mentioned paradoxes of humanitarian design on a higher level; so that communities can access sustainable services that assist them in achieving self-reliance. This means that humanitarian designers must seek to solve the challenges that are undermining the effective delivery of humanitarian assistance; as well as the accountability issues of humanitarian innovation (Sandvik, Jumbert et al. 2014). In order to succeed, designers need to be aware of the structural paradoxes that humanitarian innovation has only begun to address. Designing beyond these, will help us move from why to how in humanitarian design and innovation.

Design that confronts five humanitarian paradoxes

The new paradigm that I mention previously commonly refers to the post-2015 humanitarian agenda (Kharas and Zhang 2014) and the need to rethink relief (Mawdsley, Savage et al. 2014, Santos et al. 2016). In this context, five paradoxes have emerged from my work on designing energy alternatives for refugee camps in Ethiopia. These five paradoxes illustrate the complexity of humanitarian relief in relation to design and the necessity to rethink relief on multiple levels. A 'paradox' is 'a situation or statement that seems impossible or is difficult to understand because it contains two opposite facts or characteristics. This is a fitting term, because different stakeholders have objectives that pull in different directions, creating mismatches that undermine their overall sustainability (Mays, Racadio et al. 2012). To illustrate the difference between paradox and challenge: financing is a challenge, and not a paradox. Humanitarian actors and nongovernmental organizations are challenged by the fact that funding does not and will not keep up with the requirements for urgent assistance (Scott 2015). It is primarily this increasing funding gap that has led humanitarian actors to call for a 'paradigm shift' or a 'new humanitarian agenda' (Almedom and Tumwine 2008, Foran, Greenough et al. 2012, Mawdsley, Savage et al. 2014). A new agenda highlights 'humanitarian innovation', referring most often to an increased collaboration between private enterprises, public partners and humanitarian actors.

Yet it is not the funding challenge that designers must overcome. Instead, I will argue that there are *five paradoxes* in the way that humanitarian relief is delivered. These represent essential root problems that designers and innovators must understand and overcome. These prevent innovation from delivering impact. These five paradoxes of humanitarian relief are

- The environmental paradox
- The short-term thinking paradox
- The self-reliance paradox
- The multiple-agenda paradox
- The scalability paradox

As you will see, all of these are tied together and linked to the issue of triple bottom line sustainability, which again is the root problem causing the current search for a new humanitarian agenda.

I have chosen to discuss these paradoxes by presenting them with a discussion about design and innovation approaches both theoretically and practice-based. In order to disrupt these challenging relationships within the humanitarian system, we need to break down the paradoxes to understandable approaches. Design approaches are appropriate here, as designers are trained to look for *empathic* approaches in challenging situations. We are also familiar with bridging technology and human inputs through interface thinking and visual simplification.

The environmental paradox

A central challenge and a source of political conflict from humanitarian relief is the environmental footprint of humanitarian action. Refugee settlements will typically be placed in environmentally vulnerable marginal or border areas, with little infrastructure to supply the settlements with water or energy. This happens because of many factors. For example, refugees fleeing war and famine will set up spontaneous camps across the border from where the ongoing conflict is taking place. If the aid community is slow to respond or the country hosting the refugees is late to request assistance, this will often become the location where the official refugee camp will be set up and administered. Moreover, host countries may wish to keep the refugees in areas where they do not want permanent settlements, or there will be other political reasons for not bringing a high number of refugees to an area with sustainable resources. Because the creation of refugee camps that host a large number of people also brings schools and jobs and infrastructure, and consequently an increase in the non-refugee population further straining areas scarce of natural resources, humanitarian assistance in these areas becomes an environmental paradox in itself. Refugee settlements are therefore a root of unsustainable land use in the development world, something that we are witnessing in the host countries surrounding the Syrian refugee crisis (Al-Bakri, Salahat et al. 2013). The degradation of arable land and deforestation are mentioned as significant problems that have warranted attempts at solving them through cross-sectorial efforts administrated by the United Nations Environment Program (Forbes 2015).

The short-term thinking paradox

A market has emerged in the aftermath of disasters worldwide. This market consists of suppliers and customers of products and services seeking to assist the victims of a crisis. This is a market heavily represented by international and national non-governmental organizations (NGOs). It also includes donors, service providers and enterprises that develop, purchase and distribute goods such as food, shelter, medical equipment and energy-generating devices. This market is referred to as the humanitarian market (Nielsen and Santos 2013a). In order to understand the current and potential impact of design for humanitarian emergencies, it is key to understand how humanitarian action functions as a market as this defines how certain products and services are chosen over others.

Urgent needs, such as food, shelter, water and santiation, are the mandate of the United Nations High Commissionaire for Refugees (UNHCR) and other *humanitarian aid distributors* who seek to follow the minium guidelines of the Humanitarian Charter (Sphere 2011). *Development aid* organizations are to be the responsible for longer-term needs, yet as the humanitarian system fails to resettle displaced populations or find long-term solutions, the balance between immediate and long term needs remains blurred. Also, since it is difficult to argue for short-term water and sanitation solutions and the need for more durable and less cost-intensive designs, the distinction between short-term needs and long-term needs as a basis for good humanitarian design is not as central as many designers may think.

An identified feature of the humanitarian market is that humanitarian customers – the UN, ICRC, or another International NGO – typically depend on a 12- to 24-month budget frame. This short budget frame means that the products and services chosen for an emergency setting are designed for a life span that does not match the needs of the people. Also, host countries are reluctant to support the building of higher quality, lasting shelter structures, fearing that refugees will not wish to return to their former countries (Baker 2013, Onishi 2013). Products and services that are focused on the recovery phase will not be chosen due to the short-term thinking of the humanitarian market. Knowing that a refugee on average spends 17 years in a refugee camp (Ratha, Eigen-Zucchi et al. 2016) and that frequently areas stay in a protracted emergency situation, designers must create long-term solutions.

This means being mindful of how the design can last through many years in often challenged infrastructure. Challenged infrastructure means that maintenance and spare parts will be hard to come across, and that there are often no local services to support the product. The innovator has to either add a service design to the product or, preferably, make beneficial partnerships locally to build capacities in the host community or among the disaster-affected population/refugees. Studies have also shown that the (design) enterprises that add services to their product succeed in the humanitarian market. Enterprises can also advocate for humanitarian customers and donors to expand the short budget frame or to offer leasing agreements that allow for humanitarian customers to invest in longer-term solutions for issues such as energy, water and sanitation.

The self-reliance paradox

The underlying goal of 'self-reliance' for the crisis-affected communities is reflected in the linear understanding of emergency relief. By moving from immediate response into durable solutions, the humanitarian system aims to move into a sustainable scenario. The paradox is within the structure of this assistance, which in many ways undermines the affected individuals and communities' ability to depend on themselves. Self-reliance, a factor that is central in peace building, dependent on access both to 'hard' and 'soft' contributions (Galtung 1996). 'Hard' values include access to water and food, whereas 'soft' values include access to education and employment. Yet, the creation of sustainable providers of clean water and the right to work, in what is seen as a temporary settlement, meets political barriers. In particularly refugee-heavy areas, authorities are reluctant to give large refugee settlements access to 'national' resources and to build long-term solutions. Environmental concerns are also mentioned, as the Kenyan government threatens to close down the world's largest refugee settlement (Graham-Harrison 2016). At the same time, the humanitarian actors depend on the already mentioned 12- to 24-month budgets, which do not invite longer-term solutions.

For refugees, this means that they typically get access to school the first six years of primary schooling, and in some cases more (MacKinnon 2014). In many cases, however, they do not have the right to make use of their educations as they do not gain a complementary right to work. Further, refugees become so dependent on the aid provider after many years without the basic right to earn an income (Oliver-Smith 1996) that they may have difficulties managing their personal economy and moving towards self-reliance for themselves and their families.

Further, the humanitarian market can be described as a quasi-market, in which the aid recipient currently has little or no influence on which product or service they are provided. A study among enterprises developing energy and health care products for the humanitarian market showed that humanitarian actors do not select products and services based on assessed end-user needs. Instead, cost per item, short-term thinking and 'trend reports' affect their choices (Nielsen and Santos 2013b). They also have little or no way to provide feedback to the product supplier, resulting in a lack of data available to decide which products or services have had positive impacts.

This is clearly something that should be in the designers' interest to improve through human-centered design processes and ethically sensitive codesign efforts (Hussain 2011). For the designer, it is important to know that the current shift in mindset that is brought about by the humanitarian innovation paradigm does not have unethical consequences. Humanitarian actors are seeking product and service solutions that can challenge this dependency cycle and provide more choices to the refugees.

This means that designers should propose solutions that foster self-reliance by:

- Providing choices for the end user
- Giving feedback about the design in all user-phases
- Basing solutions on the idea of 'the capable refugee' by including capacity building or skills training as a part of the solution
- Connecting the needs of refugees with the services available in host communities
- Contributing to the creation of a sustainable market in the given context (for example through entrepreneurial components)

Regarding sustainable market creation, Betts and Bloom have contributed to the knowledge gap with their publication 'Refugee Economies' (Betts et al. 2014). In this publication they highlight the need to include refugees in income-gathering strategies of their host communities, and to create innovation based on a thorough understanding of existing self-reliance strategies within the refugee's local context. Although I have highlighted the challenge of bridging local and contextual needs with the scalability focus of the humanitarian market, this publication is still a relevant reference point and humanitarian design researchers should seek to contribute to this area by studying design projects that seek to achieve self-reliance for the end-user communities.

The multiple-agendas paradox

Whereas humanitarian objectives seem to be obvious and the issue of dignity indisputable, studies show that each contributor's inability to grasp how they can impact it often results in an ineffective system. This is due to the presence of multiple stakeholders and their conflicting and/or misaligned agendas (Olsen, Carstensen et al. 2003, Beamon and Balcik 2008, Mays, Racadio et al. 2012, Nielsen and Santos 2013b). The final impact of an innovation for the humanitarian system is dependent on the following decisions within the international logistics system:

- The decision of donors to require monitoring and follow up – currently this is not standard and the lack of applicable and comparable data on implemented innovations – beyond handover of a product or service – makes it difficult to decide what to support and what will be needed in the future.
- The decision of donors to support the said innovation – also through the training and assessments needed to make sure it reaches a durable solutions embedded in local practices and local services.
- The agreement of humanitarian non-governmental organizations who often do not share the agendas of the donors.
- Successful collaboration (Ramalingam et al. 2015) and alignment between the suggested product or service and the national policies of the donor country – government objectives, local stakeholder objectives and local NGO workers who in the end will implement the product or service.

Designers who deliver products through the humanitarian preparedness *system* have often no overview about which stakeholders will be involved when their product or service-design is delivered in the field. Due to the large, and unpredictable, number of stakeholders, agendas and decisions in any given emergency, coordination of these agendas is key to the success of the product or solution. If host governments perceive that humanitarian actors are working with separate objectives other than their own, the collaboration needs particular focus and the design will meet difficulties. This means that mapping stakeholder agendas during the designing of the business or service component can be highly beneficial for designers who seek real impact (Nielsen 2015). A simple way to map the stakeholders is to create codesign or collaborative workshops throughout the design process that include as many stakeholders as possible. The stakeholders must include host government representatives, local NGOs, representatives from the main local industrial sectors relevant for the design and finally the camp management. The camp management or the refugee agency is normally working under the mandate of UNHCR. It will be beneficial for the design that these stakeholders influence the final design so that it does not run into contextual barriers or barriers due to misalignment of interests. A misalignment of interest will lead to the human and financial resource support for the design drying out. One such misalignment was visible when Lebanon objected the inclusion of IKEA shelters (Onishi 2013) since they did not want the refugees to stay too long. Respecting host country objectives and trying to involve them in the design process is key and can prevent political barriers from interrupting the implementation process. It will also save cost to realize fundamental challenges early.

The scalability paradox

The push to scale and find one-size-fits all solutions has been mentioned to be a hindrance of good product and service innovations during the last decade, also beyond humanitarian design and innovation (Chesbrough 2006, Voveryte 2011, Stampfl, Prügl et al. 2013, Ramalingam et al. 2015). Since the humanitarian market depends on a large number of products reaching 'the field' rapidly following the onset of a disaster and to stockpile them in high numbers in regional preparedness shelters (Anh and Phong 2014, Nielsen 2014a), an unfortunate pressure has been put on scalability. At the same time, the opportunity that enterprises have to receive a large order from a humanitarian donor adds to the idea that humanitarian sector is, in fact, looking for product innovations. It is far more difficult to understand how services and training can be financed in a refugee camp or other emergency settings. For products and services that need a high degree of local service and maintenance and that seek to influence the potential for self-reliance, as discussed in the second paradox, this raises a number of challenges. For example, my studies in Ethioipa showed that most battery-dependent products are damaged due to the storage times of preparedness shelters and they are difficult to sustain due to the need for training and follow-up. Further, the stoves delivered to refugees rely on affordable and accessible fuel delivery systems, which have been insufficient or not existing. Further, the typical design process' dependence on creating probes (Mattelmäki and Battarbee 2002, Mattelmäki 2006) and prototypes to test out design hypotheses early and also the need to build contextually fitted services is particularly difficult to achieve in the humanitarian market. The pressure to reach as many refugees as possible with a single donation and as fast as possible leads to designs that are pressured to scale-up prematurely. A concrete example is how the solar cell lamp from Tough Stuff (Wright 2013, Ottinger and Bowie 2015) received significant positive attention from the media and humanitairan sector. Yet, due to the high request for their products, they focused too much attention on bringing the product to the market, and too little on improving the product through iterative design loops.

An example of humanitarian design

In 2013, a team of design students and researchers from the Norwegian University of Science and Technology (NTNU) traveled to the Somali region of Ethiopia (Figure 18.1) with the purpose of designing energy alternatives for refugees (Hasselknippe, Reikvam et al. 2014). More specifically these students traveled to Kebri Beyah refugee camp, a typical example of a protracted emergency setting where the resettling of refugees has proven difficult. War-affected communities were placed in the Somali region in eastern Ethiopia, where they have been living as camp refugees since the Somali Civil War began in 1988. The larger region, the Horn of Africa, has been a source of conflict ever since the colonial times and the reasons for the conflict can be traced back to English and Italian interests in this region combined with ethnic conflict (Cassanelli 1982, Lewis 2002). Kebri Beyah is one of three refugee camps in eastern Ethiopia.

Within this region, there are very few natural resources, and hardly any vegetation or water left to sustain the growing population of the town Jijiga, which is located an hour's drive away from Kebri Beyah. For the refugee women who are dependent on firewood for cooking throughout the day, gathering firewood has become not only a time-consuming but also a dangerous affair

Figure 18.1 The arid Somali region, seen from the air.

(Bizzarri 2010). People who gather firewood outside the refugee camps risk getting assaulted or even arrested, as gathering firewood has been illegal in this part of the world since 2012.

The students were invited by the UNHCR Ethiopia and the Ethiopian Gaia Association for the purpose of proposing ideas for how to redesign an ethanol stove. The Ethiopian Gaia Association was founded as a nonprofit organization in 2005 to carry on work with ethanol cook stoves. Gaia has provided thousands of households with clean stoves and ethanol fuel, taking advantage of domestic ethanol production has tried to mitigate this by introducing an ethanol driven stove (Association 2007). As of 2015, Gaia had begun to expand into the Assosa camps in western Ethiopia and is aiming to reach additional camps in both Ethiopia and eastern Africa more broadly. To date, the humanitarian program has distributed more than 7,000 clean cook stoves and over three million liters of ethanol. This stove is simple, user-friendly and safe, considered that training is provided. It represents a highly relevant alternative to the three-stone fire commonly used for cooking. This stove is provided through a charity-model in which private people pay for a stove to be donated. The simplified design process can be described as follows:

Listening and observing

Through observation, interviews and focus group discussion, the students identified several challenges that were less product-related than they had anticipated. One challenge was that there is currently no requirement for the humanitarian actors to follow-up the success of this product, which then become the sole responsibility of the Gaia Association itself. No independent assessment was done to decide whether this is the most appropriate product and that it fits the circumstances. The students found that the women in this camp already had five donated stoves available. And even if the Gaia Association is one of the few working consistently and

Figure 18.2   Refugee woman with her Gaia stove.
Photo: Kathinka Hasselknippe.

impressively to solve the fundamental energy challenge of refugees, there was no direct way for the refugee to give feedback to the designer or anyone else on whether this stove solved their problems. This means that there is little evidence of impact and little useful insight to apply for the students' design process (Figure 18.2).

Identifying real needs

The students discovered that it was not the design of the stove that hindered the refugees from using it; it was the lack of fuel. They only had access to one-sixth of their demand and the stoves therefore were not utilized for the most energy consuming cooking. Instead, the refugees said that they were looking for opportunities to trade what they were given for food and clean water. The fuel was hence a more important commodity to them than the donated stove. The students continued their research by observing how much time and resources each refugee spent on cooking and what other barriers and enablers were relevant.

Stakeholder analysis

The three students went on to conduct a stakeholder analysis and to identify the available resources in the local host community. They spoke to members of relevant ministries, to local technological faculties and visited the largest engineering university. In Jijiga, the neighboring town, they identified several energy technologies developed locally. A local university had developed stoves that were fueled by animal waste. They also spoke to local human waste collectors to find out how their business models were designed. Based on this, they calculated the energy needed to fuel the three refugee camps surrounding Jijiga with fuel for cooking. Then, based on a literature search of ways for refugees to earn additional income, they identified a number of innovative insights that could improve access to energy. Further, they participated in stakeholder workshops with government officials and the Ethiopian Refugee and Returnee administration to understand the priorities for the Somali region. The latter provided support for their decision to move away from ethanol, as the government of Ethiopia planned to use the ethanol produced domestically for purposes other than household cooking.

Idea generation: the day of post-its

Having gathered data from multiple stakeholders including the end users, the students completed an extensive idea generation phase where they included brainstorming on resource availability and matching of needs and available resources in new and innovative ways through sketching and backcasting techniques. The idea generation made them realize that a significant barrier to self-reliance in the refugee-hosting Somali region is that the region is not capable of delivering the fuel necessary for the current stoves that are delivered by Gaia and other organizations. This idea generation also made them look for alternative energy resources such as cooking oil waste and charcoal.

Yet, mapping sessions which they refer to as 'the day of post-its' (Grande et al. 2013), including affinity mapping (Holtzblatt and Jones 1993), made them realize that their goal should be to figure out how the refugee camp could rely on preexisting fuel resources so that they did not have to depend on the unpredictable humanitarian market: "And after yet another elimination process, we were left with these three starting points:

- Access to energy
- Utilization of resources
- The human being as a resource"

Further, the team noted that

> The information we have gathered is so much more than the exact wording of the answers we got in our interviews. Tacit observations, such as the interactions between individuals, how people reacted to seeing us, and even the physical layout of the camp, are elements that might give us a better understanding of the setting and the users we are designing for.
>
> *(Grande et al. 2013)*

Service design + business component

By some simple equations, the students estimated that the combination of human and animal waste in the region surrounding the refugee camps would be enough to supply the camp with fuel. They also knew that the refugee children used to earn an income by herding cattle and camels. Based on this, the business component of their design became that the refugee children, who were already herding livestock, could earn an additional income if they supplied a digester company with animal waste. The human waste collectors could then add to this fuel source. The refugee children's salaries would be paid directly as school money, and the enterprise would earn money by selling energy back to the refugee camp as biogas.

Final prototype design

The product component of the student design is a tarpaulin and leather bag which can be strapped on a cow or a camel, which waste can be collected in (Figures 18.3 and 18.4). The product could be imported, but the students' idea was that also this part should be locally produced and tarpaulin and leather were of the few available materials.

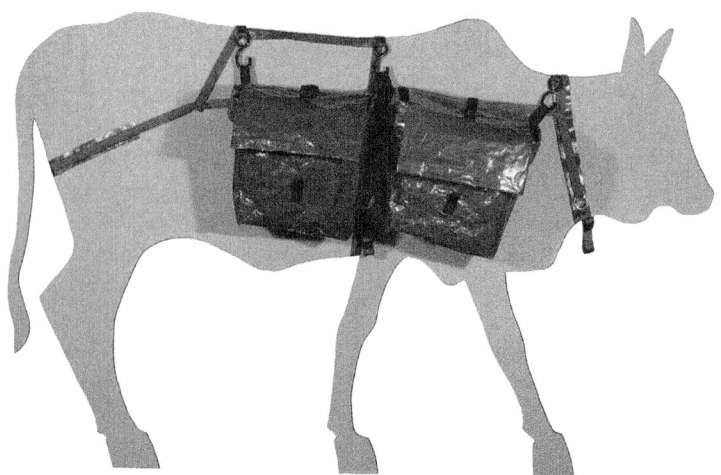

Figure 18.3   Illustrations of the final product prototype.

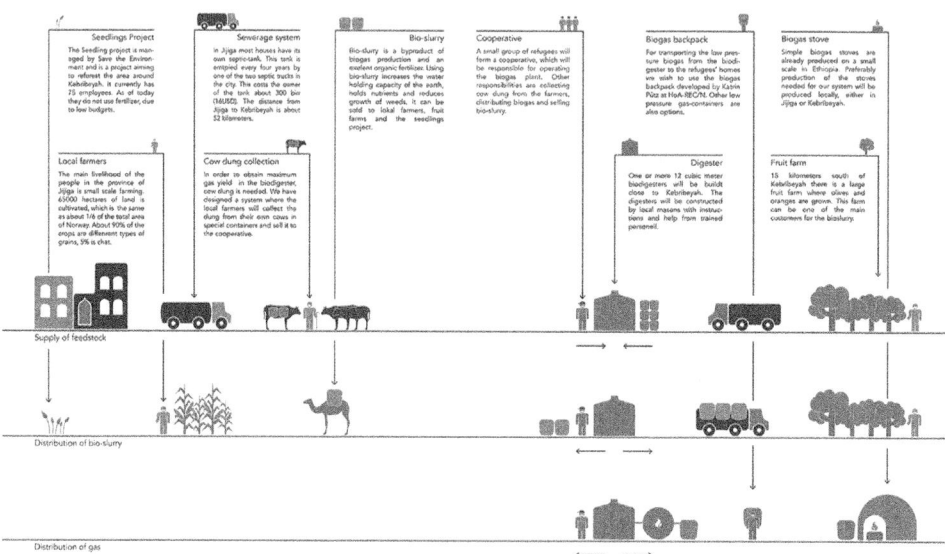

Figure 18.4   Illustration of the system and service.

Lessons learned and implication for humanitarian design

The described student project shows the value of hands-on experience to guide the design process. If the students had not traveled to Kebri Beyah refugee camp, they would have no knowledge of the lack of fuel and of the 'real needs'. The literature that they had reviewed before arriving to the Somali region did not fit with reality. For an enterprise in a Western country designing for humanitarian relief, there will however be several reasons why designers do not prioritize first-hand knowledge at the beginning of the design process. The designer or her employer must balance the costs of bringing a designer to the field. Also, doing design research in a disaster situation like this however raises some ethical and practical challenges. Humanitarian stakeholders and local partners will be reluctant to let designers conduct design research. Refugees and other disaster-affected people are considered vulnerable populations and should only be included when strictly necessary. Further, in a strongly hierarchical setting, which a refugee camp and the humanitarian system itself is, a typical design research process with extensive ethnographic inspiration and participatory approaches will seem invasive and difficult to understand the purpose of for gatekeepers. This makes the end user in a humanitarian setting particularly inaccessible. Further, to gain hands-on knowledge with the safety of her spending time in an often relatively dangerous area. These risks are often mitigated by creating strong partnerships with the UN or the responsible humanitarian actor in the region. This is also a requirement to access any areas managed through the UNHCR.

The need for meaningful approaches

The complexity of humanitarian relief and the inability of the system to fill the needs of suffering populations requires us to pull out of our toolboxes everything we know about designing for challenged infrastructure and development contexts; yet to design for the humanitarian emergency setting requires a mindset and a deep understanding also of the holistic system at play. There is not 'one problem' to solve or any simple means of doing so. Victims of war and other disasters are dependent on an internationally constructed system to help them move from a situation of dependency and into a situation of self-reliance. The humanitarian designer or design team needs the flexibility and experience to balance multiple requirements and considerations.

Within this chapter I have attempted to describe not only a general state of mind, but also the willingness to take in the complexity of humanitarian relief. Despite this complexity, the designers' habit to think open-mindedness, talent for communication and constant agency for the user will be central. Both as a practice in the traditional sense, and on a more analytical level, design has untapped potential when it comes to improving and transforming humanitarian action. Designers working in development contexts have broad experience with resilience-focused projects. By including local partners and spending time understanding local service systems and customs, designers have the possibility to bridge the short-term focused efforts of humanitarian actors with longer-term resilience factors in context. Product design efforts alone will only touch upon the surface when it comes to overcoming the paradoxes. It is the compliance with local services and value chains that will determine the impact of humanitarian design.

References

Aberra, E., Ndiaye, K., and Roess, A. (2014). "The dangers of cooking in Kakuma: How access to cooking fuel compromises the safety, dignity, and well-being of women living in refugee camps, a quantitative analysis." *Annals of Global Health* **80**(3): 208.

Al-Bakri, J. T., J. Salabat, A. Suleiman, and M. Suifan (2013). "Impact of climate and land use changes on water and food security in Jordan: Implications for transcending 'the tragedy of the commons'." *Sustainability* **5**(2): 724–748.

Almedom, A. M. and J. K. Tumwine (2008). "Resilience to disasters: A paradigm shift from vulnerability to strength." *African Health Sciences* **8**(S1): S1–S4.

Anh, T. T. and T. V. G. Phong (2014). "Opportunities to build disaster-resilient shelter and settlements: Lessons learnt from a housing architecture design competition." *Journal of Civil Engineering and Architecture Research* **1**(1): 24–31.

Association, G. (2007). "Indoor Air Pollution Monitoring Summary for the Gaia Association Clean Cook Stove Tests in Addis Ababa, Ethiopia." https://projectgaia.com/.

Baker, A. (2013). "After a long delay, Lebanon finally says yes to IKEA housing for Syrian refugees." *Time.com*.

Barrow, G. (2016). "WFP launches E-cards for Syrian refugees in Lebanon with MasterCard's support." *MasterCard Newsroom*.

Bartolomei, L. (2016). "Refugees and refugee camps." In Nancy Naples, ed., *The Wiley Blackwell Encyclopedia of Gender and Sexuality Studies*. Hoboken, NJ: Wiley-Blackwell.

Beamon, B. M. and B. Balcik (2008). "Performance measurement in humanitarian relief chains." *International Journal of Public Sector Management* **21**(1): 4–25.

Betts, A. and L. Bloom (2014). *Humanitarian Innovation: The State of the Art.* New York, NY: United Nations Office for the Coordination of Humanitarian Affairs (OCHA).

Betts, A., et al. (2014). *Refugee Economies: Rethinking Popular Assumptions.* Oxford: University of Oxford, Refugee Studies Centre.

Betts, A. and E. Bloom (2015). "Refugee Innovation: Humanitarian Innovation that Starts With Communities." [Report], Refugee Studies Centre.

Binnendijk, A. (2000). "Results Based Management in the Development Cooperation Agencies: A Review of Experience." Background Report.

Biran, A., W. P. Schmidt, L. Zeleke, H. Emukule, H. Khay, J Parker, and D. Peprah (2012). "Hygiene and sanitation practices amongst residents of three long-term refugee camps in Thailand, Ethiopia and Kenya." *Tropical Medicine & International Health* **17**(9): 1133–1141.

Bizzarri, M. (2010). "Safe Access to Firewood and Alternative Energy in Ethiopia: An Appraisal Report." Prepared for the World Food Program. www. genderconsult. org/uploads/publications/doc/SAFE_Ethiopia_Appraisa l_Report_Final_Draft_2. pdf Accessed May 12, 2015.

Boyer, G. and Y. DuPont (2016). "The contribution of the private sector to solutions for displacement." *Forced Migration Review* **52**: 36.

Brinkerhoff, D. W. (2007). "Capacity Development in Fragile States." International Public Management With Research Triangle Institute (RTI International), Mimeo.

Cassanelli, L. V. (1982). *The Shaping of Somali Society: Reconstructing the History of a Pastoral People, 1600 to 1900.* Philadelphia: University of Pennsylvania Press.

Chesbrough, H. W. (2006). *Open Innovation: The New Imperative for Creating and Profiting From Technology.* Boston: Harvard Business Press.

Chretien, J.-P., et al. (2016). "Make data sharing routine to prepare for public health emergencies." *PLoS Med* **13**(8): e1002109.

Cross, N. (2006). *Designerly Ways of Knowing.* London: Springer.

Cutler, S. (2016). "Refugee crisis and re-emergence of forgotten infections in Europe." *Clinical Microbiology and Infection* **22**: 8–9.

Dorst, K. (2011). "The core of 'design thinking' and its application." *Design Studies* **32**(6): 521–532.

Fargues, P. (2014). "Europe Must Take on Its Share of the Syrian Refugee Burden, But How?" Migration Policy Centre, http://www.migrationpolicycentre.eu/.

Fladvad Nielsen, B. K. B. S. M. G. J. (2016). "How Can Innovation Deliver Humanitarian Impact." P. Oslo, PRIO.

Foran M., P. G. Greenough, A. Thow, and D. Gilham (2012). "Identification of current priorities for research in humanitarian action: Proceedings of the First Annual UN OCHA Policy and Research Conference." *Prehospital and Disaster Medicine* **27**(3): 260–266.

Forbes, A. (2015). "Mainstreaming Environment and Climate for Poverty Reduction and Sustainable Development," UNDP-UNEP Poverty-Environment Initiative, http://www.unpei.org/sites/default/files/publications/PEI%20handbook-low%20res.pdf.

FOUND, I. "TheGraphic". IET, p14-14, http://ieeexplore.ieee.org/stamp/stamp.jsp?tp=&arnumber=6657845.

Fransen, S. (2015). "The socio-economic sustainability of refugee return: Insights from Burundi." *Population, Space and Place* 23(1). doi: 10.1002/psp.1976.

Galtung, J. (1996). *Peace by Peaceful Means: Peace and Conflict, Development and Civilization.* London: Sage Publications.

Graham-Harrison, E. (2016). "Kenya says it will shut world's biggest refugee camp at Dadaab." *The Guardian.*

Grande, J., et al. (2013). "The Day of Post-Its." http://idethiopia.tumblr.com/page/2. Accessed October 10, 2016.

Griekspoor, A. and S. Collins (2001). "Raising standards in emergency relief: How useful are Sphere minimum standards for humanitarian assistance?" *BMJ: British Medical Journal* 323(7315): 740.

Gunning, J. W. (2000). *Rethinking Aid.* World Bank, Washington, DC: Annual World Bank Conference on Development Economics.

Hasselknippe, K., G. Reikvam, and B. Nielsen (2014). *HCD in a Quasi-Market: Lessons From a Design Project in Kebri Beyah Refugee Camp, Ethiopia.* DS 78: Proceedings of the 16th International conference on Engineering and Product Design Education (E&PDE14), Design Education and Human Technology Relations, University of Twente, The Netherlands, 04–05.09. 2014.

Holtzblatt, K. and S. Jones (1993). "Contextual inquiry: A participatory technique for system design." *Participatory Design: Principles and Practices*, Hillsdale: Lawrence Erblaum, 177–210.

Holtzman, S. B. (1999). "Rethinking 'Relief' and 'Development' in Transitions From Conflict," Brookings Institution Project on Internal Displacement, http://www.brookings.edu/fp/projects/idp/idp.htm

Hussain, S. (2011). "Designing for and With Marginalized People in Developing Countries: Efforts to Undertake a Participatory Design Project With Children Using Prosthetic Legs in Cambodia," Trondheim: NTNU.

Kharas, H. and C. Zhang (2014). "New agenda, new narrative: What happens after 2015?" *SAIS Review of International Affairs* 34(2): 25–35.

Krippendorff, K. (1989). "On the essential contexts of artifacts or on the proposition that 'design is making sense (of things)'." *Design Issues* 5(2): 9–39.

Kumpf, B. (2016). "6 Ways to Innovate for 2030." www.undp.org/content/undp/en/home/blog/2016/6/16/6-ways-to-innovate-for-2030.html. Accessed September 03, 2016.

Le Grand, J. and W. Bartlett (1993). "Quasi-markets and social policy: The way forward?" *Quasi-Markets and Social Policy.* Springer, 202–220. *The Economic Journal* (101)408 (Sept. 1991): 1256–1267, Wiley, http://www.jstor.org/stable/2234441

Lewis, I. M. (2002). *A Modern History of the Somali: Nation and State in the Horn of Africa.* London: James Currey Publishers.

Linda, P. (2011). "The crisis caravan: What's wrong with humanitarian aid." *New York: Picador.*

Lyytinen, E. (2009). "Household Energy in Refugee and IDP Camps: Challenges and Solutions for UNHCR." UNHCR, Policy Development and Evaluation Service.

MacKinnon, H. (2014). "Education in Emergencies: The Case of the Dadaab Refugee Camps." Centre for International Governance Innovation.

Macrae, J., et al. (1994). "War and Hunger. Rethinking International Responses to Complex Emergencies," FAO library & archives, http://www.fao.org/library/library-home/en/

Mattelmäki, T. (2006). *Design Probes.* Aalto, Finland: Aalto University.

Mattelmäki, T. and K. Battarbee (2002). *Empathy Probes.* PDC, Proceedings, http://rossy.ruc.dk/ojs/index.php/pdc/article/view/265

Mawdsley, E., L. Savage, and S.M. Kim (2014). "A 'post-aid world'? Paradigm shift in foreign aid and development cooperation at the 2011 Busan High Level Forum." *The Geographical Journal* 180(1): 27–38.

Mays, R. E., R. Racadio, and M. K. Gugerty (2012). "Competing Constraints: The Operational Mismatch Between Business Logistics and Humanitarian Effectiveness." Global Humanitarian Technology Conference (GHTC), 2012 IEEE.

Meier, P. (2015). *Digital Humanitarians: How Big Data Is Changing the Face of Humanitarian Response.* Boca Raton, FL: CRC Press, Taylor & Francis Group.

Nicole, W. (2015). "The WASH approach: Fighting waterborne diseases in emergency situations." *Environmental health perspectives* 123(1): A6.

Nielsen, B. F. (2014a). "Imperatives and trade-offs for the humanitarian designer: Off-grid energy for humanitarian relief." *Journal of Sustainable Development* 7(2): 15.

Nielsen, B. F. (2014b). "Out of context: Ethnographic interviewing, empathy, and humanitarian design." *Design Philosophy Papers* 12(1): 51–64.

Nielsen, B. F. (2015). "Framing humanitarian action through design thinking." *Technology* 500: 5.

Nielsen, B. F. and A. L. R. Santos (2013a). "Key Challenges of Product Development for Humanitarian Markets." Global Humanitarian Technology Conference (GHTC), 2013 IEEE.

Nielsen, B. F. and A. L. R. Santos (2013b). "Designing for multiple stakeholder interests within the humanitarian market: The case of off – grid energy devices." *International Journal of Learning and Change* **7**(1–2): 49–67.

NRC, I. D. M. C. (2015). "Global Estimates 2015," http://www.internal-displacement.org/publications/2015/global-estimates-2015-people-displaced-by-disasters/

Oliver-Smith, A. (1996). "Anthropological research on hazards and disasters." *Annual Review of Anthropology* 25: 303–328.

Olsen, G. R., N. Carstensen, and K. Høyen (2003). "Humanitarian crises: What determines the level of emergency assistance? Media coverage, donor interests and the aid business." *Disasters* **27**(2): 109–126.

Omata, N. (2012). "Refugee Livelihoods and the Private Sector: Ugandan Case Study." Refugee Studies Centre.

Onishi, N. (2013). "Lebanon worries that housing will make Syrian refugees stay." *New York Times*, 11.

Ottinger, R. L. and J. Bowie (2015). "Innovative financing for renewable energy." *Pace Environmental Law Review* **32**: 701.

Perry, R. W. and M. K. Lindell (2003). "Preparedness for emergency response: Guidelines for the emergency planning process." *Disasters* **27**(4): 336–350.

Proudlock, K. and B. Ramalingam (2009). "Improving Humanitarian Impact Assessment: Bridging Theory and Practice." 8th Review of Humanitarian Action: Performance, Impact and Innovation.

Ramalingam, B., et al. (2015). "Strengthening the Humanitarian Innovation Ecosystem," https://www.brighton.ac.uk/_pdf/research/centrim/humanitarian-innovation-ecosystem-research-project-final-report-with-recommendations.pdf

Ratha, D., Eigen-Zucchi, C., Plaza S. (2016) Migration and remittances Factbook 2016, World Bank Publications, Washington DC

Roche, C. J. (1999). *Impact Assessment for Development Agencies: Learning to Value Change*. Oxford: Oxfam.

Sandvik, K. B., M.G. Jumbert, and J. Karlsrud (2014). "Humanitarian technology: A critical research agenda." *International Review of the Red Cross* **96**(893): 219–242.

Santos, A. L. R. and B. Nielsen (2013). "The Value of Collaborative Design to Address the Challenges of the Humanitarian Sector." Proceedings of the 3rd International Conference on Integration of Design, Engineering and Management for Innovation.

Santos, A. L. R., et al. (2016). "Systemic barriers and enablers in humanitarian technology transfer." *Journal of Humanitarian Logistics and Supply Chain Management* **6**(1): 46–71.

Saunders, N. (2014). "Paradigm shift or business as usual? An historical reappraisal of the 'shift' to securitisation of refugee protection." *Refugee Survey Quarterly* **33**(3): 69–92.

Scott, R. (2015). "Financing in Crisis?" http://www.oecd.org/dac/OECD-WP-Humanitarian-Financing-Crisis%20.pdf

Sheather, J., K. Jobanputr, D. Schopper, J. Pringle, S. Venis, S. Wong, and R. Vincent-Smith (2016). "Case studies: A Médecins Sans Frontières ethics Framework for Humanitarian Innovation," http://hdl.handle.net/10144/615491

Simon, H. A. (1973). "The structure of ill structured problems." *Artificial intelligence* **4**(3–4): 181–201.

Sphere (2011). "The Sphere Handbook: Humanitarian Charter and Minimum Standards in Humanitarian Response." The Sphere Project.

Stampfl, G., R. Prügl, and V. Osterloh (2013). "An explorative model of business model scalability." *International Journal of Product Development* **18**(3–4): 226–248.

UNDP (2016). "Principles of Innovation." www.undp.org/content/undp/en/home/ourwork/development-impact/innovation/principles-of-innovation/. Accessed September 03, 2016.

UNHCR (2007). "Trends in Displacement, Protection and Solutions." UNHCR, Geneva.

UNHCR (2016). "Vodafone Foundation." http://innovation.unhcr.org/vodafone-foundation/. Accessed September 03, 2016.

Van Wassenhove, L. N. (2006). "Humanitarian aid logistics: Supply chain management in high gear." *Journal of the Operational research Society* **57**(5): 475–489.

Voveryte, J. (2011). "Are Bottom of the Pyramid Strategies Scalable." Unpublished Research Project. Social Business Enterprises and Poverty, HEC Paris, France.

Whitaker, B. E. (2002). "Refugees in Western Tanzania: The distribution of burdens and benefits among local hosts." *Journal of Refugee Studies* **15**(4): 339–358.

World Bank (2016). *Migration and Remittances Factbook 2016*, 3rd edition. Washington, DC: World Bank. doi:10.1596/978-1-4648-0319-2. License: Creative Commons Attribution CC BY 3.0 IGO

Wright, N. (2013). "Village Savings and Loan Associations: Market Potential for Clean Energy Products in Kenya, Rwanda and Tanzania," ENERGIA International Network on Gender and Sustainable Energy, October 2013, http://wmi.uonbi.ac.ke/sites/default/files/cavs/wmi/CARE%20wPOWER%20PROFILING%20STUDY%20FINAL%20REPORT%20%282%29_0.pdf

Wright, V., M. Dalwai, R.V. Smith, and J.P. Jemmy (2015). "Médecins Sans Frontières' Clinical Guidance mobile application: analysis of a new electronic health tool." *Public Health Action* 5(4): 205–208.

19

CODESIGNING FOR DEVELOPMENT

Maria Rogal and Raúl Sánchez

Introduction to the chapter

We have two goals for this chapter. The first is to describe and explain some key ideas that designers must add to their conceptual tool kits in order to make the benefits of design available to a much broader range of people, including those who would not normally have access to professional design services. The second is to share examples of these concepts in practice: to describe how a group of designers – Maria and her students – have worked with nontraditional, indigenous groups of people as collaborators and partners rather than clients. They have done this work not only to bring professional design to those who would otherwise not have it, but also to help direct the field of design – its theory and its practice – toward a social and cultural perspective that, for the most part, it currently lacks.

We approach these goals through Design for Development (D4D). D4D is an international initiative Maria began at the University of Florida to bring design students into contact with indigenous entrepreneurs, farmers, artisans, and other groups from Southern Mexico seeking to tell their collective stories through their products and services. D4D's goal is to help these groups succeed – on their own terms – in a crowded, tourist-oriented marketplace that has trouble understanding and valuing the profound knowledge and vibrant identities behind some of the items it offers for sale.

D4D begins with Maria. She is a communication designer with experience in and out of academia and a design educator with an international orientation and reputation. In turn, Raúl's experience and knowledge lie in the humanities, specifically the areas of rhetorical and critical theory with a recent emphasis on decolonial studies. Together, we hope to give readers a comprehensive look at the ideas, practices, and goals of D4D. And we hope to place this information in contexts that can inspire the thinking and practice of contemporary design students and educators. We will begin by discussing some of the theoretical and methodological concepts informing D4D. Then we explain the concepts and practices of D4D in light of decolonial theory and methodology. We continue with a brief description of the region in which D4D operates, the indigenous culture within it, and the issues faced by members of that culture. Finally, we will present two case studies of D4D projects – the Lol-Balché honey cooperative and the Xyaat community ecotourism cooperative – that reflect the concepts and practices described.

New paradigms for design: decoloniality

During the decade that D4D has worked with various groups in the Yucatán peninsula, ideas of social design and design activism have come to the forefront of the field's thinking about its core functions. Such ideas have challenged design's traditionally commercial orientations and applications by arguing that it should imagine greater purposes and goals. In 2007, the Cooper-Hewitt Design Museum in New York staged an exhibition titled *Design for the Other 90%*. Its purpose was to draw attention to the idea of design as a tool for mass empowerment. Likewise, in his 2008 book, *Out of Poverty*, psychiatrist/entrepreneur/author Paul Polak (who had contributed an essay to the Cooper-Hewitt exhibition) lamented the fact that 95% of contemporary design serves only 10% of the population – the wealthiest and most powerful 10% (Polak 2008, 1). In 2009, Alastair Fuad-Luke's *Design Activism* laid out a framework in which design principles could help address "important contemporaneous societal issues" (Fuad-Luke 2009, 1).

Around the same time, designers began launching research and practice networks that integrated design and sustainability. In the United States, an initiative titled The Living Principles of Design created a "roadmap to guide decisions for positive cultural change" (AIGA n.d.). This roadmap offers considerations, concepts, and questions to help designers create sustainable outcomes. AIGA has supported, encouraged, and embraced The Living Principles of Design, throwing behind it the full support of the largest professional communication design organization in the United States.

Internationally, the Milan-based DESIS Network (Design for Social Innovation and Sustainability) emerged from multiple international conversations which asked if and how social innovation could drive sustainability. As DESIS evolved, it identified educational institutions as key to building a new global paradigm for design. Today, DESIS promotes "design for social innovation in higher education institutions" in order to "generate useful design knowledge and to create meaningful social changes in collaboration with other stakeholders" (DESIS n.d.).

Finally, the Cultures-Based Innovation initiative, founded by design anthropologist/scholar/educator Dori Tunstall is a global network of scholars and practitioners using "old ways of knowing to drive transformative innovations that directly benefit communities of high cultural awareness, yet who may experience social or economic distress" (Calliou 2015).

In short, the idea is now becoming mainstream – particularly within the academy – that design can help groups of people who lack money and power address problems that plague them economically, politically, and culturally. These are groups who could not normally afford to commission designers but for whom design processes, strategies, and products might generate sustained and sustainable benefits.

Meanwhile, beyond the field of design, and extending as far back as the late nineteenth century, writers from various countries in Latin America have taken a critical look at the enduring economic, political, and cultural influence of European countries and the United States. Writing in 1925, Peruvian journalist and activist José Carlos Mariátegui expressed contempt for the lingering influence of the decrepit Spanish empire on segments of Latin American culture, particularly the academic classes and other members of what we might call the "cultural elite." He also voiced serious concern over the growing influence of the United States in Latin American economic matters (Ibero-Americanism). Behind Mariátegui's claims stands the influential figure of Cuban writer and revolutionary, José Martí, whose 1891 essay, "Our America," called for a reconceptualization of Latin American culture based on the overthrow of residual European influence, a skepticism toward U.S. economic and political power, and a profound examination of the region's homegrown strengths – including its indigenous cultures and peoples.

The fact that Martí's reconceptualization has not been fully achieved is evident in the contemporary Yucatán peninsula. Despite gestures by Mexican state and federal governments to recognize indigenous groups as integral to the life of the nation, contemporary Maya live and work in a context that the Peruvian sociologist Anibal Quijano refers to as "the coloniality of power." According to Quijano, a state of coloniality exists when "direct, political, social and cultural domination" from the outside is replaced by an internal "association of social interests between the dominant groups . . . of countries with unequally articulated power" (Quijano 2007, 168). This unequal power often breaks down along racial and ethnic lines. And in the case of the Maya in the Yucatán peninsula, it takes place relative to the international tourism industry in and around the region known as the Maya Riviera.

Making contacts

For over a decade, Maria and her students have worked in the Yucatán peninsula. This began with a 2003 Fulbright Hays Seminar, *Environmental Reality and Indigenous Society: Historic and Contemporary Perspectives*, in which she explored how the visual rhetoric of tourism in and around the Maya Riviera shapes dominant notions of the Maya, often obscuring and distorting the lived realities and histories of Maya people and culture. Maria's everyday interactions with Maya entrepreneurs fostered her interest in the socioeconomic impact of these distortions, so she began making ethnographic fieldwork methods, designing-in-context, and codesign essential parts of her practice. No longer satisfied with designing in the cultural vacuum of a studio, Maria created opportunities for her students to learn these methods and practices in context, so that they might inform their own art and design practice. She wanted to teach an approach to graphic design that is socially conscious, responsible, and sustainable.

In 2006, sponsored by two Fulbright awards, she was able to dedicate extended period of time to work in the Yucatán peninsula. She interacted with experts in areas such as migration, forestry, entrepreneurship, and anthropology, all of whom who were interested in collaborating with her to use communication design to make social change. Through this network and its attendant social capital, she was invited by Maya entrepreneurs into their communities, businesses, and homes, where they collaborated in the economic and social development process.

These early visits helped establish the framework for D4D. Key considerations took the form of questions. Was there a need that came from within the community – in other words, not imposed from the outside? Did Maria and her potential collaborators share similar values, support each other's goals, and respect for each other's work, cultures, and ways of being? Was everyone serious about collaboration, and were they committed to codesign? What were the expectations regarding time and effort? What capacities and resources would everyone bring to the collaboration and would they be sufficient? Was everyone willing to commit to complete the project? Was everyone flexible enough to be able to proceed with a rough roadmap and allow for ambiguity? It was important to answer these questions honestly. The decision-making process is further elaborated on in the section entitled "Negotiating."

The Maya people and the Riviera Maya

The Yucatán peninsula's Caribbean coast is an international tourist destination offering beaches, fishing, diving, shopping, nightlife, and other vacation-oriented amusements. It also offers exposure to Maya culture. Or, rather, it offers limited exposure to a tourist-friendly caricature of ancient Maya culture. This exposure is integral to the Maya Riviera experience from Playa del Carmen to Tulum. It informs everything from the souvenirs (some made by local contemporary Maya artisans, others made in China) that one can buy on the main tourist drag in Playa del Carmen, to nearby theme parks (such as Xcaret) built in and around actual archaeological sites.

The Maya presence in the Yucatán peninsula predates the arrival of the Spanish by thousands of years. Large and small archaeological sites dot the landscape, perhaps the most famous being Chichén Itzá, approximately two and a half hours inland from Cancún to the east and one and a half hours from the colonial city of Mérida to the west. The pre-Conquest history of the Maya and other indigenous groups in the region is long, complex, and often difficult to ascertain thanks to the Spanish destruction of most Maya codices. Equally rich is the history of the Maya after the Spanish conquest and after Méxican sovereignty. Unfortunately, due to the ongoing process of coloniality, this history and its influence on contemporary Maya life and culture are often compressed, sanitized, or otherwise distorted to suit the needs of international tourism.

The tourism industry creates problems and stresses for Maya who live and work in the region. They continue to experience long-standing ethnic, class, and political prejudice and discrimination within México. Although many of them live not far inland from or south of the tourist destinations on the coast, most contemporary Maya have not reaped the economic benefits of tourism – certainly not the benefits that major corporations and Méxican and international entrepreneurs have enjoyed. And even those who have experienced some upward economic movement continue to feel social and cultural discrimination. Furthermore, the region's natural resources continue to be exploited for the upkeep and construction of resorts and attractions. Thus, there exists an ongoing and lived tension between, on the one hand, the Mayas' deep and traditional knowledge and concern for the environment and, on the other hand, the region's need for economic development.

D4D's core concepts

Developed and refined over the course of a decade or more, D4D's core concepts – relationality, negotiation, sharing, and representation – have made it possible for specific design issues to emerge in fuller complexity, to the benefit of all involved. This respect for complexity helps designers better understand their roles, both actual and potential, within larger intercultural and transnational social, cultural, and economic systems. By working in the field, as it were, designers explore how to develop innovative and sustainable solutions to mutually identified and understood problems. Although we use regionally and culturally specific examples to illustrate these concepts, the concepts can nonetheless be adapted to other situations. In fact, we believe they must be adapted if the field of design is to expand its theoretical and practical horizons, and if it intends to help define and establish an ethos of cross-cultural egalitarianism across a range of fields and subfields in and out of design proper.

Relationality

Relationality is the idea that beings and objects emerge and are known through interaction. This stands in contrast to Western, modernist epistemologies and ontologies, according to which beings and objects exist in themselves primarily. Rhetorical theorist Andrea Riley Mukavetz argues that "to practice relationality is to understand one's position in the world, one's relationship to land, space, ideas, people, and living beings, and to understand how these relationships have been and will always be at play with each other" (Riley Mukavetz 2014, 112). Similarly, in his widely cited book, *Research is Ceremony: Indigenous Research Methods*, Indigenist philosopher and educator Shawn Wilson explains how in indigenous research paradigms, concepts such as ontology, epistemology, and methodology cannot be considered separate, as they would be in Western and modernist paradigms, because the world is simply not understood as being fundamentally atomistic and agonistic. Consequently, this conceptual interrelatedness carries over into research practice, as ideas of reciprocity and responsibility call upon researchers not to extract information and knowledge from people and places but rather to establish and maintain relationships with and among them. As Riley Mukavetz notes, this approach is not only ethical; it is also "personal and communal" (Riley Mukavetz 2014, 113). It recognizes that the act of doing research – especially research performed *upon* indigenous communities – has been appropriative, violent, and of no use to those it often claimed to want to help.

In recent years, some Western theorists have also begun to question their culture's orientation. More often than not, these questions have arisen from within, as it were, rather than through a thoughtful engagement with the indigenous perspectives we previously summarized. Nonetheless, these theorists have proposed the notion of a radical relationality, not only among people and other beings assumed to have agency, but also among agents and things. For example, in books such as *We Have Never Been Modern* and *Reassembling the Social*, among others, French sociologist of science Bruno Latour has articulated what he and others refer to as Actor-Network Theory, or ANT. ANT is essentially a methodology for conducting empirical research – initially in science studies but applicable across fields that carry out qualitative research – freed from the conceptual restrictions that, according to Latour, commit sociology and anthropology to the reification of established and often inaccurate ideas rather than the discovery of new ones. For Latour and other proponents of ANT, an enduring inability to recognize and describe a functional symmetry among agents and objects – that is, the refusal to see both as actors – limits our ability to understand and describe nothing less than reality itself, since reality is fundamentally relational. Things do not exist in themselves, so it makes no sense to describe them according to epistemological frameworks and research methodologies that operate as though they do.

Negotiating

If relationality offers a conceptual framework, negotiating refers to the discursive process, carried out early on, by which designers and collaborators learn each other's concerns and set the terms for their working relationship. This relationship can be complex and extensive, as some groups are justifiably wary of working with those they consider outsiders. For example, the Lol-Balché Cooperative – a group of beekeepers and honey producers we will discuss in more detail below – had experienced broken promises from outsiders, as well misunderstandings and bad deals. The suspicions they harbored (understandably) as a result meant that finding common ground would be especially important, and the D4D designers would have to work harder to build a relationship that was more active and participatory than that of the typical client and designer.

Negotiating thus helps establish a practice of open and ongoing communication, as designers and collaborators become more comfortable asking questions and bringing concerns or potential problems to the table. In D4D's work with Lol-Balché, ongoing negotiation revealed key instances of miscommunication, but it also allowed participants to correct problems, clarify issues, or make other necessary adjustments before those moments affected the rest of the project.

Negotiating is a crucial and concrete process for establishing a context of mutual respect, fruitful interaction, and open and frank communication between designers and collaborators. It fosters buy-in on all sides, creates a meaningful sense of partnership, and lays a foundation of trust in which continued sharing becomes possible.

Sharing

Sharing is the nonproprietary exchange of information and knowledge. Unlike traditional design practice, designers and collaborators who share information and knowledge contribute these things toward a common goal. Sharing of this kind exposes all participants to deeper understanding of each other's – and sometimes even their own – practices and traditions. For example, D4D designers learned that beekeeping in the Yucatán peninsula is a centuries-old practice handed down from generation to generation, carried out with great care for the natural environment and great affection for the bees.

Sharing also helps expose hidden or underlying barriers to change. For example, when the cooperative's beekeepers saw how artisanal honey is marketed and packaged elsewhere, they were inspired to move forward with the project of bringing their honey to those other markets. As well, sharing allows the group – designers and collaborators – to establish priorities. For example, the features of Lol-Balché's honey, combined with the cooperative's environmental values, emerged as important issues that needed to be addressed in product labeling.

When designers and their collaborators share information without regard to its ownership and without a purely instrumental objective, they arrive at ways to market products and services more creatively and substantively. They transform products and services into something more than mere commodities in the capitalist marketplace. In short, products and services become vehicles of contemporary cultural representation.

Represent

To represent is to communicate messages visually, graphically, and textually. But too often, indigenous groups have little or no control over how they are represented in the larger culture and in the marketplace. For example, marketing materials for tourism companies represent Maya culture as a thing of the past, ignoring the fact that contemporary Maya culture is quite vibrant. When D4D designers collaborate with indigenous communities, they help these communities assert control over how they are represented on the products and services they offer. For example, the marketing materials developed for Xyaat featured real Maya people living their daily lives, not reenacting a caricature of ancient rituals. By asserting control over representation, collaborators tell their own stories, share their own identities, and sell their own products – on their own terms. By designing and printing postcards in three languages (Mayan, Spanish, and English), the Xyaat cooperative consciously asserted itself and its members as simultaneously Mayan, Mexican, and international. For those who consume these products and services, this kind of representation can foster deeper inquiry into the values and identities of other cultures. Rather than absorbing yet another caricature of an indigenous culture, consumers encounter – in the design itself – a culture's own counter-narrative about itself.

Cooperativa Lol-Balché/Kanan Honey

The Maya have practiced beekeeping for generations. One key to this tradition is care for the environment. Many Maya beekeepers believe that in order to produce quality honey, bees must live and work in environment that is natural: free of pesticides and other contaminants. Today, by combining old techniques and values with certain contemporary technologies, Maya beekeepers try to preserve, sustain, and extend this important tradition.

In the southern Mexican states of Campeche, Yucatán, and Quintana Roo, the most sought-after honey is produced from the flowers of the dzidzilché (ts'its'ilche') tree and the tajonal plant.

In 2006, Maria and her students began to work with the Cooperativa Lol-Balché (CLB), a 41-member apiculture cooperative in Santa Elena, Yucatán. Through her previous work with the state of Yucatán's Institute for the Development of Maya Culture (INDEMAYA), and through site visits, Maria had learned firsthand the limited economic opportunities for the rural and mostly Maya communities in the area. This lack of local opportunity forces people to emigrate to the coastal resort areas of Cancún and Playa del Carmen, or to the United States.

During one visit, Maria toured CLB's new honey processing plant, which was in the final phases of construction. Manuel Magaña Ayil, CLB's president, was eager to show how the plant was equipped with state-of-the-art processing technology, which would bring the cooperative one step closer to its goal of exporting products to Europe or the United States. The details of a business model for such an expansion were still in progress, but the basic idea had already been articulated: CLB wanted to have a direct presence in the international market as a known producer of quality honey. This arrangement would be preferable to the existing model in which the beekeepers sell their product only to intermediaries representing large corporations. For these intermediaries and their clients, the honey's quality makes little difference. Thus beekeepers are paid the same price for excellent honey and for acceptable honey. These prices are often so low that the beekeepers cannot make a profit and are sometimes unable to recoup the cost of supplies, labor, and bee maintenance throughout the year.

By establishing a new enterprise through which to sell artisanal Maya honey in new markets, CLB would be able to buy and resell its members' best honey at fair prices. Consequently, the first and most tangible goal of bringing together CLB's beekeepers and Maria's design students was to design and produce an institutional identity and related collateral so that the cooperative could carry out its plan. Although the D4D process includes problem seeking, we only work on projects identified from within the community and which community members are invested in. This is the only way we can ensure we are working on something valuable and meaningful to people, and it increases the likelihood the project will be sustainable for the long-term.

Maria's early experience working at the Inter-American Foundation, a US Government grassroots development agency, taught her that people within a community best know what their needs are, and that design processes work best in helping communities refine these needs. This is all to say that the D4D methodology does not support parachuting, that is, designers "dropping in" on communities for a short time and offering no commitment beyond the creation of an artifact.

Of course, true collaborations require establishing trust. Initially, Maria worked directly with Magaña (CLB's president) and a few of his close advisors, but eventually she was introduced to the rest of the cooperative. Maria approached their first meeting worried that her status as a U.S. citizen might present some obstacles. This concern turned out to be overstated, as several of the members had knowledge of the United States (particularly of U.S. citizens) either through having lived there or through family and friends who had lived there.

Nonetheless, trust was not automatically given. Fortunately, Maria had earned social capital in the area through previous relationships with INDEMAYA field representatives. In short, these representatives vouched for her to CLB, and this helped the collaboration get off the ground. Still, throughout her time on the project, Maria remained conscious of the fact that she was perceived by the members of the cooperative (and others) to wield some measure of power due to her work on a prestigious grant from a Mexican government agency and due to her position as a professor at a major U.S. university. Therefore, through her actions and words, she worked to maintain an ethic of humility, respect, and cooperation.

With an initial trust established, Maria and the beekeepers shared with each other their values, as well as what they thought they brought to the project. In addition, there was an early understanding that the relationship would be long-term – lasting beyond a month, a semester, or year – as it was clear that production, marketing, and getting the product to market would take a long, if undetermined, amount of time. But this time would allow the designers to learn the context and culture of CLB, and to learn it reasonably well. Also, it would mitigate against the prospect of a familiar cliché: the Western academic parachuting into an "exotic" locale with her students and then leaving after a short while, just long enough for everyone to credibly collect a vita line or résumé item.

Instead, the designers and beekeepers would learn more about each other and, with that knowledge, they would carry out a project substantially in-field. Doing so would give the designers a sense of the people and the environment. Relationality plays a significant role in helping to frame the interactions by prompting deeper observation and inquiry and in reflecting to develop findings and further questions. It would give them contact with the individuals with whom and for whom they were working, of course, and thereby expand their sense of what professional design practice should entail when intended for "the other 90%." And it would grant the beekeepers an often-withheld measure of recognition and respect for their work, their values, and their goals.

Working with CLB under these conditions prompted the designers to adopt something of a decolonial attitude, even if it was not identified as such. Perhaps the most important examples of this were the ideas of suspending judgment and surrendering the belief that they knew, in advance, anything meaningful about the people with whom they were working: their culture, practices, desires, motives, etc. This would allow the designers to ask questions that sought genuine information and knowledge, and it would act as a brake against jumping to premature, inaccurate, or plainly false conclusions.

It was important, as well, for everyone to periodically rearticulate the project's purpose and, when necessary, renegotiate terms and conditions. This kept the work's scope and everyone's expectations in plainly view. It also kept the design process as a whole – including crucial feedback loops that enabled additional design iterations – at or near the front of everyone's minds. The feedback loops, planning, revisions, redirections – all of this involves negotiation, an everyday transactional practice that incorporates meeting, discussion, and compromise with people in context.

This need proved particularly important on one evening, early on, when the students gave the beekeepers some initial design concepts for feedback. These concepts were meant as prototypes only, designed prior to any fieldwork or research in context, and intended only as possible points of departure and discussion toward future designs. However, after Maria and the students had presented the concepts and given the beekeepers time to discuss them amongst themselves, the beekeepers settled on one of these as the final design. As Maria later learned, the beekeepers believed the designers had worked hard enough on the prototypes and did not feel comfortable asking them for more. Because the beekeepers were not attuned to design practice – particularly the idea of multiple iterations – it became necessary to renegotiate terms, goals, and expectations so that they could more fully participate in the design process, and so that the designers could receive more substantive feedback.

Moreover, it was important for the designers to adopt a "decolonial" attitude from the very beginning, before their first meeting with LBC, in the two months they spent eagerly conducting research and drafting the prototypes mentioned earlier with another D4D instructor, Doug Barrett. It was an important attitude to maintain upon arriving at the Cancún airport, which is semiotically oriented almost exclusively toward the tourist experience. It was an important attitude to remember as they explored Playa del Carmen in order to see first-hand the misrepresentations and caricatures of Maya culture that they had read and heard about. And it was an important attitude to bring to their data-gathering: the interviews they conducted, the photographs they took, the research notes they wrote, and even the impressions they felt along the way.

In addition to learning the tourist context, the designers needed as well to learn the beekeepers' context. Working next to them would allow designers to understand their collaborators' real needs, and perhaps the real obstacles they faced. For example, ahead of the initial meeting in Santa Elena between the designers and the beekeepers, Maria drove her students in from the *Zona Maya* in the southeastern part of the Yucatán peninsula. The idea was to pass through small towns, making stops along the way, observing small bits of the region's everyday life. The experience would give students an initial (if admittedly cursory) sense of working in context. However, the drive caused them to arrive much later in Santa Elena than expected – well into the evening and after dark, in fact. Despite this delay, the beekeepers expressed desire to meet the designers upon their arrival, in order to welcome them and to launch the project. Consequently, the first meeting between the designers and the beekeepers took place in semi-darkness, in an outdoor courtyard, everyone seated in a circle and taking turns introducing themselves. It became, in short, an even better lesson to the designers about working *in* context and *out* of the studio.

Subsequent meetings were held to let the designers and beekeepers become better acquainted. Designers shared examples of high quality artisan honey (and its marketing) currently sold in the United States and Europe. In doing so, the beekeepers saw real-world examples of honey in different markets, which informed the process and helped them better understand the consumer context. The beekeepers explained the honey business, including its recent ups and downs, as well as their ongoing concerns about its viability. More importantly, they took the designers to their apiaries to show them the process of honey harvesting, which is labor-intensive and involves several beekeepers performing different tasks. After that particular excursion, Magaña told Maria he was impressed and surprised that everyone had been so interested to learn about the process. He thought they would be scared of being stung. Their lack of fear demonstrated to him the seriousness with which each designers took the project. At that moment, the beekeepers revised some of their preconceived notions about the designers, and in doing so it offered the designers a larger lesson about their discipline: that, done correctly, working in context can prompt the mutual empathy that social design (and all communication design) requires.

Eventually, the design prototypes and D4D's growing relationship with CLB lead other cooperatives to want to join the project. Over several years, some members left CLB to form a new cooperative focusing exclusively on larger markets beyond the Maya Riviera. These larger goals would require a larger network of like-minded cooperatives from which to pool larger amounts of high-quality honey. Eventually, this new organization, called Miel Kanan (Kanan Honey) received dedicated support from the U.S.-Mexico Foundation for Science, a binational organization that provides training on small business development and food safety. This new project, funded partially by the Mexican government and various Mexican foundations, made it possible for more beekeepers from more communities to take part. As a result, D4D's role in the project evolved accordingly, continuing to the present day.

Xyaat: Ecoturismo Comunitario Maya

Headquartered in the small inland town of Señor, *Xyaat: Ecoturismo Comunitario Maya* (Xyaat) is a cooperative that brings visitors face to face with contemporary Maya culture, not the caricatures peddled in the tourist zones. It offers real-life encounters and experiences with actual members and features of the Maya community in and around Señor. Its goal is to provide an opportunity for people to experience Maya culture as it is: vibrant and contemporary but also in touch with its ancient and traditional knowledge. At the same time, its members wanted to create homegrown economic opportunities, support community educational programs, and back local environmental initiatives. Señor is home to people with deep and useful knowledge of local medicine, agriculture, the environment, culture, customs, and practices – much of which was, until relatively recently, considered primitive, unsophisticated, and therefore without value. When we began working with Xyaat, their members said they wanted to be represented as modern Maya with a rich history, including that of the Caste War of the Yucatán, and engagement with the land, and a focus on preservation and responsible development and farming. They led the development of a network of community tourism groups in the region, whose purpose was to teach people about traditional medicine, contemporary history, and language, whose purpose was to remain small, manageable, and responsible to the community.

Xyaat had a business model in place and was already connected to a tourism infrastructure, but it lacked a consistent revenue stream. They had a strong sense of who they were, their needs, and had a desire to innovate. D4D's work with Xyaat involved framing its services in such a way as to articulate the cooperative's values, its commitment to aligning tradition and modernity, and its goal to build a sustainable economy and environment.

In order to do this, the designers had to develop an understanding of those values and the practices that embodied them. Activities included meeting with and interviewing the people who are part of Xyaat, participating in the tour of the community and daily practices, and learning more about the many internal and external tensions the cooperative faced in the peninsula. We learned what is important to people, including the Maya language, for most their native language, which is a living language or their history as rebels who fought for autonomy from the Mestizo and Spanish landowners and founded the Zona Maya, a Maya autonomous zone in the southern part of Quintana Roo. The concepts and design decisions emerged directly from the interviews, participatory experiences, working meetings and feedback sessions with Xyaat. They were also informed by experiencing the region as tourists which included interviewing, observing, and gathering materials in Playa del Carmen and Tulum, two main urban centers of tourism. It was important to and often in opposition to the stereotypes being offered by Xyaat's competitors.

Relationality aided in considering multiple points of view and interpretations of sites and people. This was an important reference point when working in the culturally hybrid and cosmopolitan space of the Maya Riviera and served as a way to ground our research and subsequent work. To acknowledge the tensions that existed, including the socioeconomic disparity in the region, the culture of consumption of the environment and Maya/Mexican culture that is part of the tourism industry and modern history of the region, and the irony of the promotion of Maya culture and the general exclusion of Maya people from its benefits.

The resulting communication materials, rather than focusing on anonymous groups of indigenous people, highlighted individuals who were part of the Xyaat experience. One of these was Don Crecencio Pat, who taught rope-making with *henequen*, an agave plant native to the region that is processed into a textile. In general, the designers and cooperative members sought to create materials that would mirror the one-to-one interactions Xyaat would afford its visitors. Each photo selected would highlight a specific expertise, and it would place the guide in a position of power and respect, often through careful selection of camera angle and vantage point. This was a system designed to be scalable, adding more people, and providing the audience with a connection to living people – creating an empathetic relationship – rather than a caricature.

D4D designers also emphasized maps as part of Xyaat's promotional materials and online presence. Free maps are everywhere on the peninsula; they are handed to tourists upon arrival at the Cancún airport. Sponsored by advertisements, and often highlighting the advertisers' particular interests, these tourist maps point out archaeological sites, *cenotes* (sinkholes with clear water), theme parks, attractions, museums, hotels, restaurants, cities, and towns. They track various routes in and around the eastern and central parts of the peninsula: the Route of the Nuns, the Route of the Churches, the Puuc Route, as well as cultural sites of note along the way – usually those deemed noteworthy by the local states (Quintana Roo and Yucatán). In contrast to these, the Xyaat map was designed to signify Señor's proximity as a tourist site, off the beaten path but still accessible. Like others with whom we worked, the members of Xyaat wanted to be recognized not only for their current ventures, but also for their history and in-depth knowledge of place. They were here long before Cancún – just north of the Maya Riviera – was created as an international tourist destination in the 1970s. Their families had been here for centuries. So, this representation and communal ownership of history was critical for representation. The resulting design was a negotiation between participants, as well as a kind of negotiation with the expectations of the tourist zone.

In the context of D4D, relationality is practiced in part through codesign: designers collaborating fully with Maya partners. For example, working with Xyaat designers interviewed the Mayan artisans, historians, environmentalists, and *curanderos* who provide the content of the tours. Through these interviews, which were approached as discussions among equals, the designers began the process of integrating their professional and cultural perspectives with those of Xyaat. In this process, the designers came to understand the Xyaat members' values as well as the messages they wanted to convey about themselves and their culture through their products and services. For example, they learned that historian Don Abundio Yama Chiquil's ancestors fought in the Mayan Caste Wars of the nineteenth century, and that he wanted the history of that conflict to be known and presented to Xyaat's clients in order to give them a deeper sense of modern Mayan history and culture – a sense beyond the pre-Columbian caricatures peddled in the tourist zones.

When designers practice relationality, the work of design is epistemologically reframed. The studio-based tropes and processes of conventional communication design come into question and are even discarded entirely. Former D4D student Morgan Claytor notes that she "learned to be unassuming and humble" in her basic approach to design and beyond. According to Claytor, because D4D designers "spent a lot of time talking about our expectations and assumptions" before going to Mexico, and because they took great pains to learn "the landscape and people," they felt "prepared to achieve a truly collaborative experience" that would honor "the dignity of both parties." This approach subsequently became, for Claytor, "the platform for any successful design relationship."

Conclusions

Like traditional design, D4D is concerned with economics, particularly those of contemporary marketplaces. But it is also concerned with culture, sustainability, and equity. In fact, it is these "larger" issues that prompt D4D's focus on the economic success of its various collaborators. In other words, for D4D, profit is not an end in itself. Moreover, the relatively narrow range of concerns that are normally identified as those of the designer do not nearly test the discipline's capacity to reach into many areas of human activity and effect positive change. In contrast, the mode of design envisaged and enacted by D4D points the discipline toward goals and purposes well beyond the purview of traditional designer/client relations.

Design seen this way is not only about creating an artifact that enhances – or at least does not threaten – the bottom line. It is about the processes of collaboration and creativity among disparate groups of people from different backgrounds with often considerably different knowledges, interests, experiences, and worldviews. It is about understanding others' contexts and collaboratively creating new contexts in order to create new things, new perspectives. It is very much about teaching designers to leave the familiar and often provincial walls of the studio.

The success of D4D is evidenced, in part, by the perspectives of the designers it has trained. For example, Laila Simonovsky notes:

> the research involved in this kind of work is so different from any other – it requires interacting in unfamiliar environments and in a more personal and humanistic way than I am used to. When you're there you learn so much about people and I think for any kind of design you really need to understand who people are and what they want.

Similarly, Doug Barrett, a former student and later a coteacher, explains that "the results of these projects – actually getting to work with people" caused him to ask himself, "how can I make my work more meaningful?" According to Barrett:

> fieldwork gets you to think about designing things in a different way. When we went to Mexico and you're out in this unknown territory, it throws you out of your safety zone. You've got to start thinking and creating outside of that safety zone. It flips the whole design process upside down for you. Working in the field, you realize that there are many ways to do design work.

For Gabriela Hernández, working with D4D turned her research and creative activities toward social design. After graduating with an MFA, she continued to work in Mexico and in her native Costa Rica, seeking ways for graphic designers to collaborate. She has since worked with entrepreneurial women in rural Costa Rica, and in her professional work she collaborates with scientists, NGOs, and others to improve the livelihood of minority groups and disadvantaged communities, and to protect the environment. While Assistant Professor at the University of Houston-Downtown, she worked with students interested in social design and design research, and launched her own social design initiative. Her drive to work with students is vital to help new generations to focus on the value of design to support development, which can bring lasting positive impact into communities.

Every culture designs things. A culture's designs tell stories about it. In emphasizing "design for the other 90%," and in focusing specifically on design's uses for people who have endured (and survived) extended and extensive discrimination, D4D hopes not to give these people a gift but rather to help them direct their particular talents and knowledge – to tell their particular stories – toward venues from which they have, up to now, been turned away or ignored.

Acknowledgements

The authors are grateful to the many participants who contributed to D4D, including the members of Lol-Balché, Xyaat, and Kanan cooperatives, members of the México-Estados Unidos Fundación para la Ciencia, Cristina Acevedo Hernández, Doug Barrett, Alison Brovold, Marcos Canté Canul, Morgan Claytor, Ciara Cordasco, Sarah Corona Berkin, Narayan Ghiotti, Gabriela Hernández Leyton, Marcia Isaacson, Manuel Magaña Ayil, Ana Lilia Mancilla, María Fernánda Matús, Cassie McDaniel, Gabriela Méndez, Ariella Mostkoff, Alex Racelis, Laila Simonovsky, Avery Smith, and Concepción Tec May.

References

AIGA (n.d.) *The Living Principles for Design.* [Online] Available at: www.aiga.org/the-living-principles-for-design. [Accessed 2 October 2016].

Calliou, B. (2015) Email to Maria Rogal, May 7, 2015.

Canada Newswire (2016) *Dr. Elizabeth (Dori) Tunstall Appointed Dean, Faculty of Design.* [Online] Available at: http://news.morningstar.com/all/canada-news-wire/20160926C7566/dr-elizabeth-dori-tunstall-appointed-dean-faculty-of-design.aspx. [Accessed 9 October 2016].

Claytor, M. (2015) Email to Maria Rogal, October 5, 2015.

DESIS Network (n.d.) *DESIS Network: About.* [Online] Available at: http://www.desisnetwork.org/about/. [Accessed 5 October 2016].

Fuad-Luke, A. (2009) *Design activism: Beautiful strangeness for a sustainable world,* London, Earthscan.

Hernández, G. (2016) Email to Maria Rogal and Raúl Sánchez, July 4, 2016.

Jandt, F. E. (2004) *An introduction to intercultural communication: Identities in a global community,* Thousand Oaks, CA, Sage Publications.

Latour, B. (1993) *We have never been modern,* trans. Catherine Porter, Cambridge, Harvard University Press.

Latour, B. (2007) *Reassembling the social: An introduction to actor-network theory,* Oxford, Oxford University Press.

Mariátegui, J. C. (2011) "Ibero-Americanism and Pan-Americanism" in Vanden, H. and Becker, M. eds. and trans., *José Carlos Mariátegui: An anthology,* New York, Monthly Review Press, 281–85.

Martí, J. (1977) "Our America" in Foner, P. S. ed., *Our America: Writings on Latin America and the struggle for independence,* New York, Monthly Review Press, 84–94.

O'Reilly, K. (2009) *Key concepts in ethnography.* Thousand Oaks, CA, Sage Publications.

Polak, P. (2008) *Out of poverty: What works when traditional approaches fail,* San Francisco, Berrett-Koehler.

Quijano, A. (2007) "Coloniality and modernity/rationality" trans. Therborn, S. in *Cultural Studies* 21: 168–178.

Riley Mukavetz, A. (2014) "Towards a cultural rhetorics methodology: making research matter with multi-generational women from the little traverse bay band." *Rhetoric, Professional Communication, and Globalization* 5: 108–125.

Smith, C. E. (2007) *Design for the other 90%,* New York, Cooper-Hewitt, National Design Museum, Smithsonian Organization.

Tuhiwai Smith, L. (2012) *Decolonizing methodologies,* 2nd edition, London, Zed Books.

Wilson, S. (2008) *Research is ceremony: Indigenous research methods,* Winnipeg, Canada, Fernwood Publishing.

20

THE INTERNET OF LIFE

Changing lifestyles and sustainable values in fast-developing China and India

Benny Ding Leong and Brian Lee

Heading toward the digital highway

Tales of the Internet of life

In early February 2016, an orange-red poster appeared in the high-density Dongzhimen subway station in Beijing whose translation read: "Dear Mom and Dad, please don't worry. The world is so big, and there are many forms of life. Life as a *singleton* can be very happy" (Figure 20.1). The poster had been crowd-funded via the Internet by a group of single women in Beijing to protest against family pressure to get married (Yang, 2016).

The poster ignited heated debate over the phenomenon of "singletons," of whom there are nearly 200 million in China (Yang, 2016), many of them living in the nation's roughly 60 million one-person households (OPH). The number of Chinese OPHs has tripled since 1990, and is now greater than those of the United States, Britain, and France combined. Of the major OPH types – *single, married, divorced* and *widowed* – urban singles aged 20 to 34 constitute about 39 percent of the single OPH population (Cheung and Yeung, 2015; Hu and Peng, 2015). Why has there been such marked growth in the number of young, unmarried singles in China when remaining single is still considered taboo?

Recent research has identified two major interconnected causes: first, the rise of the *zhái* (being socially inert and staying home) lifestyle choice (Liu and Jia, 2011) and, second, the encouragement of that lifestyle choice through the social and recreational functions of the Internet (Mao, 2012). This emerging trend is now seen as the cause of an excessively immersive lifestyle among young urban singles in China.

Approximately 4,700 kilometers away from Beijing, the people of Mumbai received a seemingly funny Twitter post in late January 2016: "Roar like a lion. Stop doing 'meow-meow.'" This post is one of the many promotional messages that the Mumbai police have created as part of a social media campaign to fight a rapidly proliferating drug nicknamed meow-meow (Rebello, 2016).

Meow-meow's scientific name is mephedrone. It has cocaine-like psychoactive properties that can induce depression and suicidal behavior. At just one sixth the price of cocaine (about US$2.3 per gram), however, its use by urban youth in India has soared in recent years. There are estimated to be at least 150,000 users, and the drug has spread to all of the country's major cities, including Mumbai, Delhi, Calcutta, Bangalore, Ahmedabad, and Chennai (Sathian, 2015).

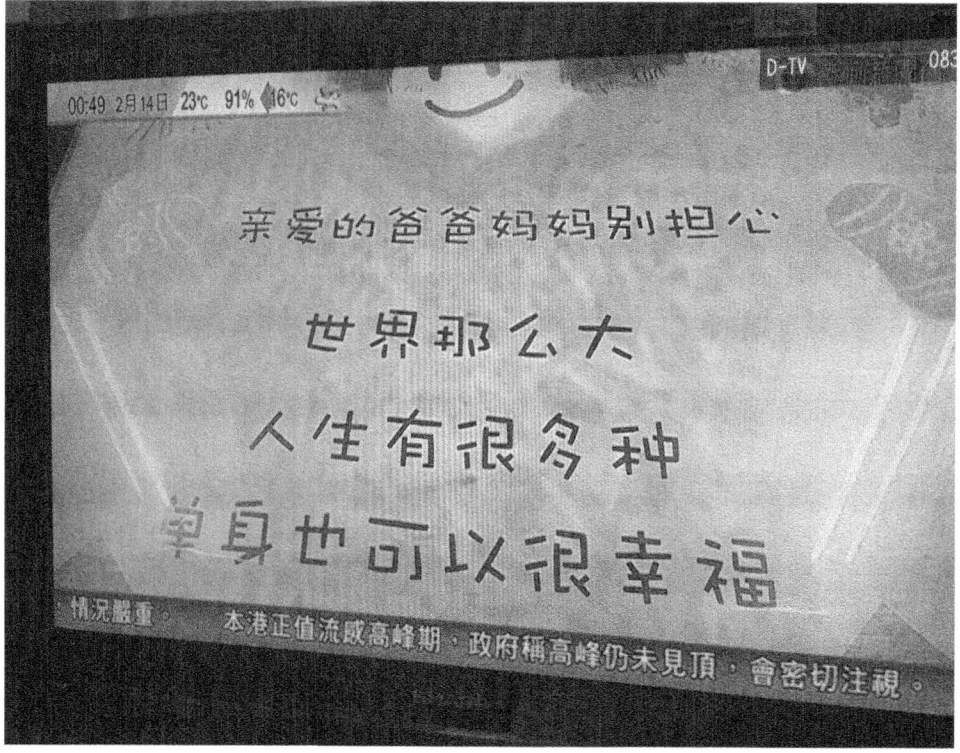

Figure 20.1   A poster promoting singleton life in Beijing.

An interesting question is how the adolescent population of a country such as India, with heavy restrictions on the sale and consumption of drugs, could be so readily threatened by a drug that was virtually unknown before 2010. One answer is that meow-meow has been promoted as a plant fertilizer or bath salts on the Internet (Merchant, 2014), and until early 2015 successfully escaped the list of government-banned drugs. In fact, meow-meow dealers should thank the swiftly developing Internet in India. Without it, no Indian youngster would have even heard of the drug, let alone be able to obtain it easily via an online subscription and home delivery.

The promised land of the Internet

Although Internet proliferation poses obvious threats, as indicated by the meow-meow case cited earlier, both China and India have plans to invest hundreds of billions of dollars (Carsten, 2015; Digital India, n.d.) in further developing their Internet-based economies to enable "win-win" sustainable growth.

In economic terms, the prospects for Internet-based growth are enormous for both countries. For instance, by 2020 an estimated 250 million Internet users in India and 560 million netizens in China will shop online. By the same year, annual retail e-commerce sales in India and China are expected to exceed US\$70 billion and US\$1.55 trillion, respectively (Ojha, 2015; "70% of

China," 2015). More importantly, the development of e-commerce seems to be helping to alleviate employment pressure in the two countries. In 2015, China succeeded in creating 20.5 million direct and indirect employment opportunities (Zuo, 2015), and India managed to generate about 250,000 new jobs in 2016 ("E-commerce Industry," 2016), through the development of e-commerce and related businesses.

In environmental terms, both China and India are looking to alleviate the environmental depredations (such as air and water pollution) that have caused millions of fatalities and economic losses by achieving green and sustainable development goals through advances in information and communications technology (ICT). For example, such initiatives as smart cities and energy-efficient and eco-friendly infrastructure, factories, buildings, transportation, and logistics have been on the rise since 2014 in both China and India (IDC, 2015; Draft Policy, 2015).

Millennials and the Internet life

Learning about change

As the Chinese and Indian governments have fully embraced the cyber-economy, Internet-related products and services have become increasingly prevalent and readily accessible, which is having significant effects on their populations' everyday lives and consumption practices.

Drawing on insights gained predominantly from recent research focusing on the Internet of Things (IoT)-related lifestyle of urban millennials in China and India (Figure 20.3), we elaborate here on our understanding of the *Internet life* phenomena underpinning the Beijing and Mumbai events outlined at the beginning of the chapter.

The future belongs to millennials

As illustrated in Figure 20.2, the aforementioned research incorporated five types of investigation: context scanning (to identify sociocultural happenings and trends via desk research and a literature review), an online survey, observation, in-depth interviews, and guided self-reporting (via a research toolkit comprising a demographic sheet, social media interaction, IoT possession, social networking, and IoT usage pattern tables). Twenty-four participants and 400 survey respondents (millennials aged 20 to 35 years old) were recruited from first-tier cities in India and China.

The reasons for choosing urban millennials as the research informants are straightforward. Millennials are the largest generation since the Baby Boomers (world total around 1.8 billion; China and India about 760 million in total) ("Live World Population," 2016). At the same time, they account for at least 25% of the global workforce (30% in China and 50% in India) (Universum, 2014). Hence, they will play a vital role in shaping business growth. Moreover, urban millennials are entering their prime consumption years, and will be the major consumption force for years to come. Most importantly, they are technologically adept, and thus can be seen as a leading indicator of where life is headed for everyone (Doctoroff and Hong, 2015).

Influences on lifestyles and social practices

Our study results suggest that the IoT is now a part of everyday life for millennials. A review of the Internet usage of millennials in China and India revealed profound effects on their everyday lives and interpersonal relationships.

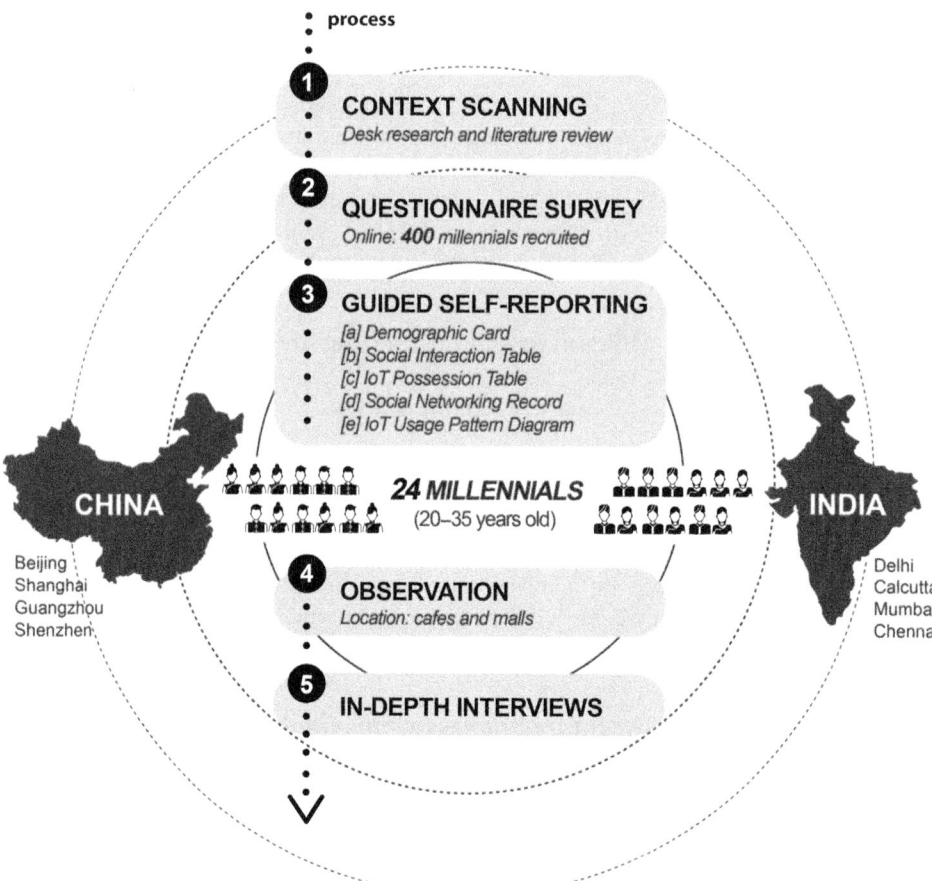

IoT Lifestyle in China and India

Figure 20.2 Framework for investigating IoT-related lifestyle of urban millennials in China and India in 2016.

Daily life nuisances and well-being

The nuisances of the Internet in the daily lives of millennials are easily observed. First, 24/7 Internet access and usage of up to 20 hours a day has blurred the line between work and rest time. Second, concurrent use of the IoT implies that multitasking has become the norm, and decision making in the face of information overload has become a constant challenge. Third, time is becoming fragmented, jeopardizing quality of life. As one participant stated, "Time has become fragmented. The phone disturbs my daily arrangements."

Further, nearly half of the Chinese and one third of the Indian participants reported negative effects on their health and well-being from the prolonged use of IoT devices. The most common problems are eyestrain and neck and back pain. Some Chinese participants reported experiencing headaches, dizziness, tenosynovitis, and insomnia, with some even reporting anxiety and obsessive-compulsive disorder. "I am constantly checking . . . I'm afraid of missing messages," one participant said. Moreover, about two-thirds of the Chinese survey respondents expressed anxiety about "information security" and "information bombardment," whereas over half their Indian counterparts are uneasy about "the need to constantly upgrade systems" and the "risk of system failure."

Effects on social life

In terms of modes of social interaction, most participants in China (10 out of 12) prefer face-to-face interaction, whereas half of those in India prefer virtual. With regard to virtual interactions, online socialization accounts for about 3% of Chinese and Indian millennials' daily IoT usage. Even with such a relatively limited socially active window, however, evidence was found for the following Internet-induced changes in social life.

- Millennials can now connect to distant friends and acquaintances anywhere, anytime.
- Social networks and social life have been expanded exponentially.
- Mixed-mode (online/offline) communication has become the new norm.

Just over half the Chinese (58%) and Indian (54%) millennials surveyed said they are likely to make new friends online. Among the Chinese participants who like making friends online, getting in touch with like-minded circles such as former classmates or schoolmates via social media was the preferred option. The Chinese participants were more cautious about privacy protection than the Indians.

When it comes to physical interactions, although most participants (the Chinese in particular) claimed to value in-depth, face-to-face conversations, the facts on the ground were quite different. During on-site observations, we frequently saw millennials texting and browsing while chatting with friends or acquaintances (Figure 20.3). Instead of focusing on their conversations with the people whom they were with, they engaged with them only occasionally after several-minute intervals, as they were constantly distracted by messages.

The reasons for such social behavior were verified by participants' guided self-reporting of their weekly messaging frequency. Both incoming (about 600) and outgoing (about 140) messages were a reasonable number among the Indians, but their Chinese counterparts dealt with up to 1,100 and 34,000 weekly outgoing and incoming messages, respectively. We also observed three unmarried Chinese participants to remain in their bedrooms for most of the day, accompanied only by their IoT devices, whereas married couples in both countries tended to use their phones and/or tablets in the evening in the living room and bedroom (Figures 20.4 and 20.5), indicating that the quality of couples' physical interactions has likely deteriorated.

Figure 20.3 Observations at cafes in Shenzhen and Delhi showing millennials texting and browsing via their smartphones while chatting.

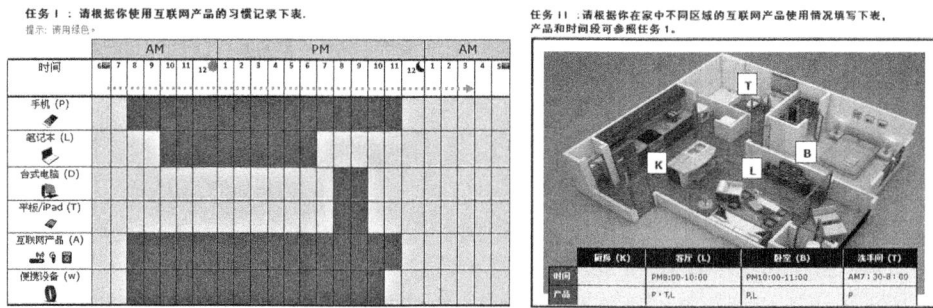

Figure 20.4 Daily IoT usage pattern reported by a Chinese couple.

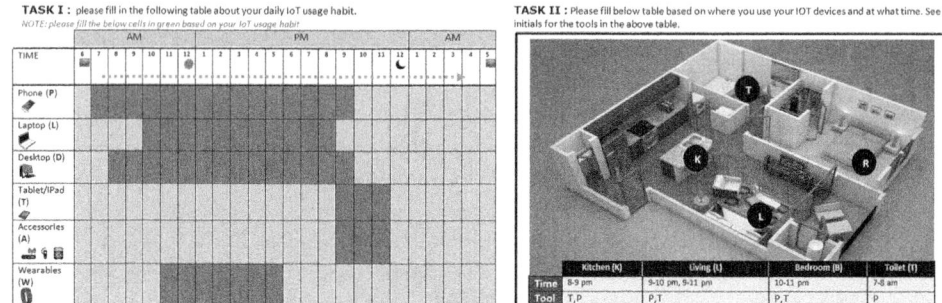

Figure 20.5 Daily IoT usage pattern reported by an Indian couple.

Table 20.1 Number of IoT devices owned by Chinese and Indian urban millennials

	Smartphone	Tablet	Laptop	Desktop	MP3/4	Wearable	Power charger	Other
China	**100%**	79%	**92%**	57%	39%	27%	82%	9%
India	**100%**	36%	**85%**	38%	23%	25.5%	30%	3%

Effects on daily consumption

Online consumption tendency

Most Chinese and Indian urban millennials are now equipped with key IoT devices (see summary in Table 20.1), which makes it easier for them to shop or engage in other types of consumption online.

The results of the guided self-reporting and survey showed two-thirds of the Chinese and one-third of the Indian participants prefer online shopping, with 47.3% and 17%, respectively, shopping online daily or weekly. With regard to information sources for possible consumption, the most popular apps cited by both Chinese and Indian millennials were food and travel apps (average of 4.5 per person), followed by social, shopping, and game apps (average of 3.5 per category per person).

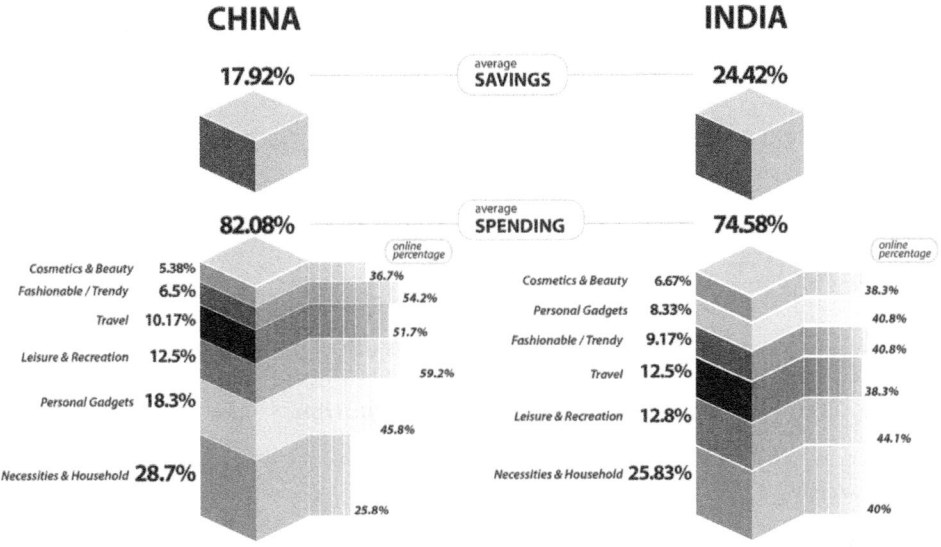

Figure 20.6   Monthly spending patterns of participants in China and India.

Spending patterns and preferences

The diagram in Figure 20.6 provides a breakdown of the monthly spending and saving patterns of the participants in China and India, with the online percentage of that spending indicated.

Two points are worthy of note. First, the average monthly savings rate of the Chinese participants is about 18% of income, with some saving as little as 5–10%, compared with average savings of around 50% in China (Roberts, 2015). Second, the Chinese and Indian participants appear to spend roughly the same amount on leisure and recreation (which includes online games and video-game devices) and travel combined as on basic necessities, whereas the Chinese spend more on personal gadgets than they save. In addition, 40–60% of consumption takes place online for both groups, and most of the participants reported being equipped with at least 12 apps to enhance their online consumption activities.

Reasons for online spending

The quantitative survey results showed 87% of Chinese and 55% of Indian millennials *spend more* when shopping online for several reasons. First, cheaper prices and discounts were the dominating factors for the Indian millennials (56% versus 8% for the Chinese). Similarly, nine of the 12 Indian interviewees said they shop more online when there are specific sales events. Second, because of the extremely flexible, user-friendly mobile payment services (such as face recognition and QR code technologies) offered by WeChat and Alipay in China, a sizable portion (40%) of Chinese participants cited convenience and time saving as the key factors in favoring online-to-offline (O2O) shopping. Third, although "endless choices" was the second most important reason for both the Chinese (22%) and Indian (24%) millennials, pervasive advertising also seems influential, with more than two-thirds of both groups reporting impulsive online shopping behavior. For instance, one Chinese participant said, "There are ubiquitous hints [online] for consuming," and another confessed: "The more I browse, the more I want. Just can't stop!" The only difference between the two groups was that the Indian participants expressed a sense of guilt. Finally, in the in-depth interviews, the Indian participants indicated that the ability to "spend first, pay later" and "peer recommendations" were also factors in spending more online, whereas their Chinese counterparts cited the accessibility of high-quality, authentic products from overseas.

So, will the prevailing "Internet of life" and corresponding changes in consumption and spending affect millennials' values and orientation toward sustainability? In the next section, we discuss the values and value changes of millennials and their influence on sustainable development in China and India.

The moment of truth

Values and value orientation

Values are beliefs that sit deep beneath the habitual and materialistic levels of people's lives. Once learned and established, not only do values act as a "permanent perceptual framework" (value system) guiding individuals' behavior (England, 1978), but they also become an internal reference point for the choices they make every day (Rokeach, 1973). Values are also shared conceptions of what is good and desirable in a given culture (Schwartz, 2006). Hence, values are not universal, but represent a culture's set of core beliefs and characteristics (McCarty and Hattwick, 1992).

To enable comparison of the value orientations of Chinese and Indian millennials, an overarching framework (Figure 20.7) has been synthesized by integrating the value-orientation model proposed by Kluckhohn and Strodbeck (1961) with the Chinese cultural value table in Fan (2000) and cultural and value verbal model in Banerjee (2008). We refer to this framework in discussing the effects of the "Internet life" on the values of Chinese and Indian millennials in the next subsection.

Common challenges for change

Because of rapid industrialization and urbanization, millennials in both China and India have experienced a rapid transition from traditionalism to modernism. Beyond the rapid rise of individualism, utilitarianism, and materialism, there are tensions between the old (the pervasive socialist legacy in China, heterogeneous, deep-rooted traditions in India) and the new (globalized consumerism) (Jacobson, 2004; Zhang, 2015). At the same time, the disappearance of trust and genuine emotions between individuals is eroding interpersonal relationships within the context of China's gender imbalance (Fish, 2015) and India's high degree of social interdependence. Moreover, the rapid growth of the urban population and the expansion of education have led to high unemployment rates among educated youth (over 7 million in China and about 8 million in India) (Doctoroff and Hong, 2015; Waghmare, 2016). In addition, increasing health-care costs and living expenses and growing social inequality are challenging for both Chinese and Indian millennials.

Internet life-related value orientation

Against the foregoing sociocultural backdrop and the rapidly emerging "Internet life" trend observed from our IoT lifestyle research in China and India, we summarize the changing value

Traditional Values (selective)

Figure 20.7 Values orientation framework for comparing Chinese and Indian traditional values.

orientations among Chinese and Indian millennials using the five main categories in Figure 20.7 and in Table 20.2.

On the whole, rapid sociocultural changes and empowerment through Internet and IoT use have led to a clear tendency to pursue quantifiable relationships, efficiency, individuality, freedom, and happiness among Chinese and Indian millennials. Although the latter are more disciplined and better able to harness the Internet to maintain connections with family, obvious *living for today* and *pursuit of novelty* mentalities are displayed by both groups, which implies unpredictable consequences for sustainable development in China and India.

Table.20.2 Changing value orientations

Chinese	Indian
1. Individual and Family	

1. Individual and Family

Chinese:
- Less desire to *self-cultivate* and to seek and accumulate knowledge.
- Certainly *materialistic*; tendency to exhibit unrestrained consumption or guiltless impulse shopping is notable.
- Emphasis on *pragmatic* utilization of Internet-related time and resources.
- Less value placed on *family relationships* while prioritizing daily communication with schoolmates and friends.

Indian:
- *Disciplined* life and *self-cultivation* valued relatively highly.
- *Materialistic* behavior manifested through more spending and impulse buying online or via sales events; display of interest in latest technology and product offers.
- Value a *pragmatic* mix of online/offline social life for mere convenience.
- Value *families and relationships* via frequent online connections.

2. Work Attitude

Chinese:
- Working hard for *personal security* and *independence* (particularly female millennials); comparatively less interest in contributing to society.
- Norms of *thrift* seem to have diminished; greater indulgence via social media, IoT and related gadgets.
- *Relationship* with friends and schoolmates valued for personal or professional purposes.

Indian:
- Working hard for *success* and *wealth*, but desire a balance with *family life*; contribute to society.
- *Saving* is a consumption preference via online sales events.
- Stress on close *relationships* and connections with clients and business friends.

3. Social and Interpersonal Orientation

Chinese:
- *Happiness* and *freedom* are highly valued.
- *Individuality* is emphasized, and uncommitted relationships much more tolerated.
- Obvious tendency to quantify *relationships* in term of cost, ease and purpose.
- Interested in exploring *virtual relationships with strangers*, and tend to trust such relationships.
- Material possessions still key as a representation (*face*) of self-worth.
- Emphasis on sharing personal events and interests with *like-minded social circles*.

Indian:
- *Relationships* and *freedom* are highly valued.
- *Seeking* a *balance* among personal freedom, relationships and a stressful life.
- *Relationship building* is judged primarily in terms of professional, career and community strengthening.
- Preference for *virtual social interaction* is notable because of time and location.
- Technological devices seen as a *symbol* of modernity and social status.
- Value *friends' references* to interesting events and consumption opportunities.

4. Relationship with Nature and Environment

Chinese:
- Less interest in nature-related activities; high priority given to *art-, culture- or professional*-related social activities.
- *Few environment*-related concerns, but conscious of eco-friendly habits.

Indian:
- Display strong preference for *professional-, sports-, and entertainment/game*-related social activities.
- *Environmentally friendly* acts noted.

5. Time/Space Orientation

Chinese:
- *Efficiency* (for leisure or work) is the top criterion for choices made in everyday life.
- *Multitasking* emphasized as a method for increasing time.
- Pursuit of *newness* (technologies, relationships, experiences, etc.) instead of valuing the old and existing.
- Enjoy building or retaining relationships in the *virtual space*.

Indian:
- *Productivity* and *efficiency* greatly valued.
- *Multitasking* at *multi-locations* of IoT usage are the norm.
- *Around-the-clock* (24/7) connections seen as important in strengthening relationships.
- *Living for today* mentality noted in online consumption practices.

Consequences for sustainable development

Unraveling of families

Our research findings show that Internet use plays a significant role in adversely affecting the social involvement of Chinese and Indian millennials. Other research has demonstrated increased Internet use to be associated with significant declines in social contact, the size of social circles, and communication within the family (Kraut et al., 1998). The more that an individual is exposed to the Internet, the greater his or her preference for online rather than face-to-face social interactions, which serves to feed the vicious cycle of compulsive Internet use (Caplan, 2005). Similar to the rise in the number of Chinese singles in recent years, the rapid socioeconomic transformation in India has also boosted the number of singles, single women in particular. Fernandes and Dhar (2015) report that there are about 72 million single Indian women, nearly 70% of them millennials.

Thanks to IoT devices, millennials are finding the singleton lifestyle appealing because it is well-matched with such emerging values as wanting to have control over one's own time and space and to be free and happy. If this trend continues, it is likely to further unravel the family-centric traditions and values of China and India.

Stimulation of consumption

The proliferation of Internet-empowered lifestyles has also resulted in the multifaceted stimulation of consumption in China and India. First, the singleton lifestyle is known to be eco-unfriendly, with research showing OPH to consume 60% more natural gas, 55% more electricity, and 39% more daily necessities annually than a single member of a five-member family (Xu, 2013). Second, driven by the cost advantages of intangible settings, e-commerce is growing rapidly in the two countries, with their combined number of online shoppers targeted to exceed 800 million by 2020. However, online shopping will not displace physical purchasing behavior. Of the US$472.9 billion worth of e-commerce sales in China in 2014, 40% of the increase came from shoppers switching channels from bricks-and-mortar stores to online platforms, with the remaining 60% organic sales growth (Zuo, 2015).

Third, virtual is not equivalent to eco-friendly. For instance, the energy used in e-commerce sales surpasses that of traditional distribution channels by about 10% (largely because of smaller units of delivery, particularly for overseas shipments) (Fichter, 2002). Moreover, extra materials are needed to protect parcels. In 2015 alone, over 20 billion packages were transported via China's express-delivery sector, a 20-fold increase since 2006 ("Over 20 billion", 2016). And that is not to mention the energy-intensive data centers that facilitate highly efficient e-commerce services. They are anticipated to emit as much as 780 million metric tons of carbon dioxide by 2020 (Kaplan et al., 2009). Fourth, the physical shopping experience is regaining popularity with the new development of O2O in Asia, with many consumers now trying out products before purchasing them online (Yiu, 2014). The implications for energy use of the combined increase in goods deliveries and users' personal transportation are likely to be significant. Finally, fashion trends are changing faster than ever owing to increased information sharing via the Internet, thereby indirectly triggering greater consumption (Clark, 2012).

Ripple effects

With information now shared among the 3.39 billion like-minded netizens worldwide, business ideas and practices, whether good or bad, can now be spread and copied around the world within seconds. For instance, Chinese company Alibaba cloned the business models of U.S.-based eBay, Amazon, and PayPal, and then grew rapidly with the help of numerous domestic manufacturers looking for ways to digest their excess inventory ("E-commerce Industry," 2016). Although excess productivity within China initially fed the growth of such cyber-companies as Alibaba and Tencent, they have now begun branching out to rural areas to capture a market worth US$70 billion (Sy, 2015). China's "copy-and-paste" strategy for e-commerce development has to date proved successful. In addition, China has started to exert its influence in India directly by importing various telecom products and equipment, and indirectly by investing US$5–10 billion in digital startups since 2015 (Samidha and Boby, 2016). India also exports its leading IT services and software to China and the world. In the past decade, India's IT services have accounted for 65% of the global offshore IT industry (Bhattacharya, 2011).

Driven partly by substantial investments in ICT, the world's two most populous developing countries now share 24.59% of global GDP (Statista, n.d.). China is also predicted to become the world largest economy, and India the third largest, by 2028 in market exchange rate terms ("The World," 2015). Given their relatively robust performance amid global economic uncertainty, China and India also serve as role models for the rest of the developing world (Santos-Paulino and Wan, 2011), notwithstanding the environmental issues their surging economies have created. Moreover, because of cultural proximity and/or economic and political interdependencies, the developmental trajectories of ten highly populous developing economies, namely, Indonesia, Brazil, Pakistan, Nigeria, Bangladesh, Mexico, the Philippines, Vietnam, Egypt, and Ethiopia, will likely be influenced by the next moves made by China and India ("World Economic," 2014). Hence, we are likely to soon witness the ripple effects of the consumption induced by these two "southern giants." Among those effects may be exponential growth in demand for natural resources and energy and global-scale environmental depletion and degradation. These are the biggest challenge the global community may confront in the near future.

Design for change

The core of the challenge

The challenges facing sustainable development have in fact been a key issue for governments and scientific elites around the world for years. At the core of the sustainability challenge are two influential factors: population growth, which determines the scale of the human impact on the plant, and the aspirations and expectations of growing populations. Corresponding to these factors, three essential ways to minimize the overall environmental impact are to reduce the number of people on the planet, improve the efficiency of technology, and make lifestyle changes (Jackson, 2008).

In the field of design, a number of approaches that aim to reduce the overall effects of consumption and production have also been proposed in the past few decades, for example, eco-design, sustainable product design (SPD) (Charter and Tischner, 2001), eco-effectiveness (McDonough and Braungart, 2002), design for sustainable behavior (Rodríguez and Boks, 2005), system design for sustainability (Vezzoli, 2007), and design for social innovation and sustainability (Manzini, 2010). These various approaches can be clustered into two categories of sustainable design strategy: design for efficiency (DfE), which focuses on the greening of products/services at all lifecycle stages to maximize eco-efficiency or eco-effectiveness, and design for sufficiency (DfS), whose aim is to devise sustainable solutions or system solutions (based on a sustainable product-service system) to meet functional needs and satisfy desires while minimizing the use of physical resources to facilitate sustainable consumption (Tukker et al., 2010).

In the early 1980s, DfE approaches (e.g., eco-design, SPD, eco-effectiveness), which place emphasis on the adoption of technology, were largely preferred. However, not only did increased technology adoption engender rebound effects, but it also induced technology dependence in users. Moreover, the global population is predicted to reach 9.72 billion by 2050, with the 12 most populous developing economies (including China and India) representing nearly 60% of the predicted growth. Any improvements by means of technology adoption are likely to be swamped by the sheer scale of the rising aspirations of upwardly mobile populations in developing economies.

Implications for design

In view of these challenges, particularly those corresponding to the reality of rapidly emerging economies such as China and India, an overarching design strategy called the Middle of the Pyramid (or MoP) strategy has been advocated (Leong, 2010). MoP derives from the earlier Bottom of the Pyramid (BoP) strategy coined by Prahalad (2004).

The MoP strategy is in essence a prioritization strategy for the deployment of DfS and lifestyle design research to mitigate sustainability problems from the consumption end. It helps to shift the focus to three main priorities: (1) the most populous fast-developing countries, where the desires of materialistic consumption are rising; (2) people from the MoP stratum within these economies who are economically, socially, and politically the most resourceful and influential; and (3) those in the MoP stratum who live in the urban areas of rapidly developing economies, who consume three to four times as much as their rural counterparts (Court and Narasimhan, 2010). Once these priorities have been affirmed, DfS efforts can be exerted to enable urban MoP members to set a better example for those in other social strata and for entrepreneurs worldwide who aspire toward more sustainable ways of living, consuming, and producing.

Understanding lifestyles conducive to sustainable change

To envision sustainable consumption as an everyday life practice for the urban MoP in emerging economies, we require a better understanding of the lifestyle aspirations and consumption-related drivers and preferences of these populations.

Lifestyles are important because they are one of the major drivers of consumption (Sonderegger, 1978). Not only do lifestyles serve as "social conversations" to signify social status and psychological aspirations ("Sustainable Lifestyles," n.d.), but they are also cultural signifiers that represent the characteristic consumption patterns of particular groups (Chaney, 1996). It is for this reason that we adopted a lifestyle design research approach for our IoT lifestyle project in China and India. Developed in 2005, the approach, which is also termed "people-centric lifestyle research," is grounded in three basic premises. First, consumption is largely bound up with the habits and routines of everyday life, and thus embedded with pre-invested emotions, attitudes, and values. Second, consumption is not an individual activity, but is framed by particular social and even political contexts within and outside a collective entity (i.e., the household, community). And, finally, but most importantly, incentives for consumption are deeply rooted in culturally conditioned conceptions (Anderson and Golden, 1984; Gronow and Warde, 2001; Miller, 1998).

The research framework depicted in Figure 20.8, which is based on these three premises, has been designed to assist and guide four investigation levels and two perspectives. The four levels are (1) the contextual (structural), (2) the consumption/creation (behavioral), (3) the daily routine (organizational), and (4) the value (ideological) levels. The two perspectives are the spatial and temporal. This framework can be used in conjunction with a variety of research techniques,

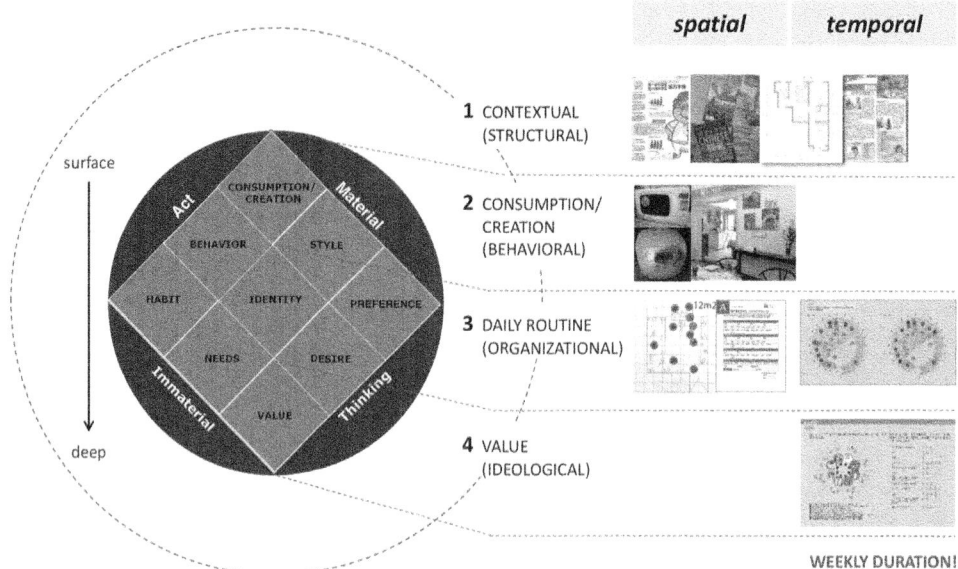

Figure 20.8   A framework for lifestyle design research.

methods, and tools, such as contextual inquiry, guided self-reporting, and in-depth interviews, depending on the nature and duration of the given project.

Design with culture

As the aim of the foregoing approach is to reveal consumption routines, preferences, and aspirations, primarily through the lens of *culture* and *contexts*, it provides another layer of understanding in addition to product-centric or user case studies. The approach is thus particularly relevant to countries such as China and India, where the rapid cultural and structural transition from traditionalism to modernism is particularly challenging (Leong and Manzini, 2006).

In fact, the key design strategies that Chinese e-commerce companies have adopted to win over the domestic market from their competitors are *cultural* and *contextual* in nature. For instance, Alipay has created a service that enables users to forward "red envelopes" (with small monetary gifts, an age-old tradition in China) to friends and family members during Chinese New Year. The service has been very successful and helped to promote the adoption of the company's services more widely. Another example is WeChat (a Chinese competitor of WhatsApp), which has developed a very popular voice-messaging service as an intelligent alternative for the cumbersome entry of Chinese characters (Sander, 2014) to ease the fast-paced, stressful life of the urban Chinese.

Such cultural- or contextual-based thinking can also be adopted for envisioning alternative ways of sustainable living via design. For example, in the case of IoT lifestyle research, culture-related aspirations such as particular preferences for the arts and culture and food-/cooking-related social activities are notable among Chinese and Indian millennials, respectively. One can imagine a system solution that integrates outdoor, food growing/cooking, and cultural activities into a social experience that motivates millennials to move away from their screens and devices to take part in physical and socially oriented activities.

Conclusion

The Internet and IoT devices will continue to permeate and dominate the everyday lives of people in China and India for years to come. They will certainly influence the way we think, live, interact, and consume, and this is particularly true for the millennial generation. Their influence is currently triggering gradual social unraveling and environmental degradation in these two large, rapidly growing economies, which is certain to have consequences for the rest of the world.

Striving for sustainable change through dependence on technology alone does not hold the answer because any improvement effected by technological innovation is likely to be swamped by the sheer scale of the rising aspirations of upwardly mobile millennials and the MoP in fast-developing economies. Better hope lies in effecting lifestyle changes through a better understanding of what is driving such runaway aspirations. To achieve those changes, lifestyle design research that delves deep into people's everyday lives is needed. Identifying the values and meanings for which people yearn, while simultaneously considering the contextual constraints that have shaped and will shape their preferences, is essential for redirecting them and us toward a socially and culturally acceptable path toward sustainability. Doing so is important both for Asia and the rest of the world.

Acknowledgement

In writing this chapter, we received considerable support from the editor and from our research team, Avleen Kaur, Ada Chan Berry Hou, and Peri Kedarnath Kartik.

References

70% of China Internet Users to Shop Online by 2020 (2015, August 26). *China Internet Watch*. (www.chinainternetwatch.com/14344/china-largest-e-commerce-market-the-world-2014/) Accessed 10 August 2016.

Anderson Jr., W.T., and Golden, L.L. (1984). Lifestyle and psychographics: A critical review and recommendation. *Advances in Consumer Research*, 11(1), 405–411.

Banerjee, S. (2008). Dimensions of Indian culture, core cultural values and marketing implications: An analysis. *Cross Cultural Management: An International Journal*, 15(4), 367–378.

Bhattacharya, M. (2011, June 30). *The Information and Communication Technology Sector in India: Performance, Growth and Key Challenges* (DSTI/ICCP/IE-JT03286352) Secretary-General of the OECD.

Caplan, S.E. (2005). A social skill account of problematic Internet use. *Journal of communication*, 55(4), 721–736.

Carsten, P. (2015, May 20). *China to Spend $182 Billion to Boost Internet by End of 2017* (www.reuters.com/article/us-china-internet-idUSKBN0O50JH20150520) Accessed 10 August 2016.

Chaney, D. (1996). *Lifestyles: Key Ideas*. Routledge: London.

Charter, M. and Tischner, U. (2001) *Sustainable Solutions: Developing Products and Services for the Future*. Sheffield, UK: Greenleaf Publishing.

Cheung, K.L. and Yeung, W.J. (2015). Temporal-spatial patterns of one-person households in China, 1982–2005. *Demographic Research*, 32(44): 1209–1238.

Clark, P. (2012). *Youth Culture in China, From Red Guards to Netizens*. New York: Cambridge University Press.

Court, D. and Narasimhan, L. (2010). Capturing the world's emerging middle class. *The Mckinsey Quarterly*.

Digital India: A Programme to Transform India Into a Digitally Empowered Society and Knowledge Economy. (n.d.). *Department of Electronic and Information Technology, Governement of India* (http://deity.gov.in/sites/upload_files/dit/files/Digital%20India.pdf) Accessed 9 August 2016.

Doctoroff, T. and Hong, L.Y. (2015, July). *Chinese Millennials: New Minds in an Old World* (www.forbes.com/sites/forbesasia/2015/07/31/chinese-millennials-new-minds-in-an-old-world/#5e70a26615a8) Accessed 10 August 2016.

Draft Policy on Internet of Things. (2015). *Ministry of India* (https://mygov.in/sites/default/files/master_image/Revised-Draft-IoT-Policy-2.pdf) Accessed 2 August 2016.

E-commerce in Emerging Markets. (2016, March 3). *Economist.* (www.economist.com/news/leaders/21693925-battle-indias-e-commerce-market-about-much-more-retailing-india-online) Assessed 10 August 2016.

E-commerce Industry to Generate 2.5 Lakh Jobs in 2016. (2016, February 5). *The Economic Times* (http://articles.economictimes.indiatimes.com/2016-02-05/news/70373520_1_e-commerce-market-e-commerce-industry-2-5-lakh-jobs) Accessed 10 August 2016.

England, G.W. (1978). Managers and their value systems: A five country comparative study. *Columbia Journal of World Business*, 13(2), 35–44.

Fan, Y. (2000). A classification of Chinese culture. *Cross Cultural Management Journal*, 7(2), 3–10.

Fernandes, J.R. and Dhar, S. (2015, November 22). *All the Single Ladies . . . 73m and Growing* (http://timesofindia.indiatimes.com/home/sunday-times/deep-focus/All-the-single-ladies-73m-growing/articleshow/49875130.cms) Assessed 10 August 2016.

Fichter, K. (2002). Sustainable Business Strategies in the Internet Economy. In J. Park and N. Roome (Eds.), *The Ecology of the New Economy* (pp. 22–34). Sheffield: Greenleaf Publishing.

Fish, E. (2015). *China's Millennials: The Want Generation*. London: Rowman & Littlefield.

Gronow, J. and Warde, A. (eds.). (2001). *Ordinary Consumption*. London: Routledge.

Hu, Z., and Peng, X. (2015). Household changes in contemporary China: An analysis based on the four recent censuses. *The Journal of Chinese Sociology*, 2(1), 1–20.

IDC. (2015, November 13). *China's ICT Market Direction Takes Shape for the 13th Five-Year Plan Period 2016–2020* (www.idc.com/getdoc.jsp?containerId=prCHE40612915) Accessed 2 August 2016.

Jackson, T.D. (2008). The Challenge of Sustainable Lifestyles. In G.T. Gardner, T. Prugh, and L. Starke (Eds.), *State of the World 2008: Innovations for a Sustainable Economy* (pp. 45–60). New York: W.W. Norton & Company.

Jacobson, D. (2004). Indian Society and Ways of Living. *Asia Society* (http://asiasociety.org/education/indian-society-and-ways-living) Accessed 10 August 2016.

Kaplan, J., Forrest, W. and Kindler, N. (2009, July). *Revolutionizing Data Center Energy Efficiency. The Mckinsey Quarterly*.

Kluckhohn, F.R. and Strodbeck, F.L. (1961). *Variations in Value Orientation*. Evanston, IL: Row, Peterson.

Kraut, R., Patterson, M., Lundmark, V., Kiesler, S., Mukophadhyay, T., and Scherlis, W. (1998). Internet paradox: A social technology that reduces social involvement and psychological well-being? *American Psychologist*, 53(9), 10–17.

Leong, B.D. (2010). Context of the Concept of Change: Designing a Greener China via Deeper Understanding of the Material Lifestyle of Urban Chinese. In F. Ceschin, C. Vezzoli, and J. Zhang (Eds.), *Proceedings of Sustainability in Design: Now! Challenges and Opportunities for Design Research, Education and Practice in the XXI Century* (pp. 752–765). Sheffield, UK: Greenleaf Publishing.

Leong, B.D. and Manzini, E. (2006). *Design Vision on the Sustainable Way of Living in China*. Guangzhou, China: Lingnan Art Publishing.

Liu, Y. and Jia, N. (2011, Feb. 18). "剩男剩女", "剩"的是什么......["Left over men, Leftover women", What's "left". . .]. 'Green Ocean' supplement, *Procuratorial Daily*, vol. 398, pp. 5 (http://newspaper.jcrb.com/page/1/2011-02/18/05/2011021805_pdf.pdf) Accessed 10 August 2016.

Live World Population Clock. (2016, June 11). *Population of the World.* (www.livepopulation.com/) Accessed 10 August 2016.

Manzini, E. (2010). Small, local, open and connected: Design for social innovation and sustainability. *The Journal of Design Strategies*, 4(1), 8–11.

Mao Qi. (2012, June). 宅男宅女现象的社会学分析 [Sociological analysis of the phenomenon of 'otaku']. *Journal of Hubei University of Economics* (Humanities and Social Sciences) 9(6): 35–38.

McCarty, J.A. and Hattwick, P.M. (1992). Cultural value orientations: A comparison of magazine advertisements from the United States and Mexico. *Advances in Consumer Research*, 19: 34–38.

McDonough, W. and Braungart, M. (2002). *Cradle to Cradle: Remaking the Way We Make Things*. New York: North Point Press.

Merchant, Y. (2014, December 26). Meow Meow Menace: An Article on Drug Abuse. *Civil Services Strategist* (www.civilservicesstrategist.com/meow-meow-menace-an-article-on-drug-abuse.html) Accessed 10 August 2016.

Miller, D. (1998). *A Theory of Shopping*. Ithaca, NY: Cornell University Press.

Ojha, N. (2015). Adding to Cart: Digital's Impact on Consumer Goods in India. *Bain & Company* (www.bain.com/Images/REPORT_Adding_to_Cart.pdf) Accessed 10 August 2016.

Over 20 Billion Packages Delivered in China in 2015. (2016, January 19). *China Internet Watch* (www.chinainternetwatch.com/16856/china-20-6-billion-couriers-2015/) Assessed 10 August 2016.

Prahalad C. and Fruehauf, H. (2004). *The Fortune at the Bottom of the Pyramid* (First ed.). Wharton School Publishing.

Rebello, L. (2016, January 28). Anti-Drug Twitter Campaign by the Mumbai Police Is So Dope! *International Business Times* (www.ibtimes.co.uk/anti-drug-twitter-campaign-by-mumbai-police-so-dope-1540549) Accessed 10 August 2016.

Roberts, D. (2015, May 1). *The Chinese Can't Kick Their Savings Habit* (www.bloomberg.com/news/articles/2015-05-01/chinese-consumers-cling-to-saving-suppressing-spending) Accessed 10 August 2016.

Rodríguez, E. and Boks, C. (2005). *How Design of Products Affects User Behavior and Vice Versa: The Environmental Implications*. Proceeding of EcoDesign 2005, Tokyo, pp. 54–61.

Rokeach, M. (1973). *The Nature of Human Values*. New York: The Free Press.

Samidha, S. and Boby, K. (2016, January 27). Chinese Investors Bet Big on India, Internet Giants Pour Funds Into Digital Startups. *The Times of India* (http://timesofindia.indiatimes.com/business/india-business/Chinese-investors-bet-big-on-India-internet-giants-pour-funds-into-digital-startups/articleshow/50734979.cms) Assessed 10 August 2016.

Sander, E. (2014, October 9). *How China Leapfrogged the West on Internet Innovation.* (http://europesworld.org/2014/10/09/how-china-leapfrogged-the-west-on-internet-innovation/#.VzGOUoR96Uk) Accessed 10 August 2016.

Santos-Paulino, A.U. and Wan, G.H. (2011, August 30). *Learning From the Southern Giants: China and India* (http://unu.edu/publications/articles/learning-from-china-and-indias-development-strategies.html) Assessed 10 August 2016.

Sathian, S.J. (2015, December 31). Meow Meow and the Walking Dead: India's Newest Drug. *OZY.* (www.ozy.com/fast-forward/meow-meow-and-the-walking-dead-indias-newest-drug/62142) Accessed 11 August 2016.

Schwartz, S.H. (2006). A theory of cultural value orientations: Explication and applications. *Comparative Sociology*, 5(2–3), 137–182.

Sonderegger, R.C. (1978). Movers and stayers: The resident's contribution to variation across houses in energy consumption for space heating. *Energy and Buildings*, 1(3), 313–324.

Statista. (n.d.). *The Statistic Portal* (www.statista.com/) Accessed 10 August 2016.

Sustainable Lifestyles and Education for Sustainable Consumption. (n.d.). The Marrakech Process. *UNEP.*

Sy, N. (2015, May 14). *Chinese E-Commerce Companies Head to the Countryside.* (www.scmp.com/tech/e-commerce/article/1795393/chinese-e-commerce-companies-head-countryside) Accessed 11 August 2016.

Tukker, A., Cohen, M.J., Hubacek, K. and Mont, O. (2010). The impacts of household consumption and options for change. *Journal of Industrial Ecology*, 14(1): 13–30.

Universum. (2014, August). Understand a Misunderstood Generation. *Survey Report.*

Vezzoli, C. (2007). *System Design for Sustainability: Theory, Methods and Tools for a Sustainable 'Satisfaction-System' Design*. Milan, Italy: Maggioli Editore.

Waghmare, A. (2016, May 6). By 2050, Millions of Youth in India Are Going to Be Unemployed: Report Reveals How. *Youthki Awaaz* (www.youthkiawaaz.com/2016/05/lack-of-jobs-and-unemployment-in-india/) Accessed 11 August 2016.

The World in 2050. (2015, February). *PricewaterhouseCoopers* (www.pwc.com/gx/en/issues/the-economy/assets/world-in-2050-february-2015.pdf) Accessed 10 August 2016.

World Economic Situation and Prospects 2014. UN. (2014). *United Nation.* (http://unctad.org/en/PublicationsLibrary/wesp2014_en.pdf) Accessed 11 August 2016.

Xu, A.F. (2013, January 22). 我国2.5亿人卷入单身潮 [250 Million Have Been Drawn Into the Trend of 'Singles'] (http://health.huanqiu.com/health_news/2013-01/3567501.html) Assessed 10 August 2016.

Yang, J. (2016, April 27). "剩女"大战《中国青年报》 [The War of "Shengnu", China Youth Daily] (http://zqb.cyol.com/html/2016-04/27/nw.D110000zgqnb_20160427_1-12.htm) Accessed 11 August 2016.

Yiu, A. (2014, February 2). O2O Has a Bright Future in Asia (www.marketing-interactive.com/o2o-sees-bright-future-asia-market/) Assessed 11 August 2016.

Zhang, X. (2015, September 10). One life for sale: Youth culture, labor politics, and new idealism in China. *Positions: East Asia Cultures Critique*, 23(3): 515–543.

Zuo, M. (2015, December 7). How Online Shopping Is Revolutionizing China's Economy . . . and Even Its Villages (www.scmp.com/news/china/money-wealth/article/1888184/china-e-shopping-nation) Accessed 10 August 2016.

21

FASHION, THE CITY, AND THE SPECTACLE

Dilys Williams

Introduction

Some 900 years ago, an extraordinary occurrence is said to have taken place on market day in the English Midlands town of Coventry; a noble lady rode through the town, on horseback, adorned solely by her hair, which was long enough to ensure her modesty. The apparent outcome of this spectacle was the rescinding of a repressive tax on the city's citizens, whom Lady Godiva sought to support. Whether this is fact or fable, fashion, as city spectacle has long held cultural and political significance; an emotive force, it affects those directly involved and a wider society.

Whilst a long-standing citizen of London, a megacity recognized throughout the world as a site of fashion creation and public performance, my intrigue in fashion as a city spectacle dates from my childhood in a small village. Insights came monthly, delivered by post, in the form of a bunch of pages in landscape format, stapled together to form iD magazine, capturing images of fashion's everyday spectacles on its streets: the shapes, forms and encounters of time, place and culture. This arresting visual commentary shared the concerns, allegiances, excitements and anger felt by the city at that time. Fashion evidenced more than what people were wearing: it also made clear what they were thinking and feeling, representing those who felt unrepresented elsewhere. Since then, through my work as a designer, researcher and educator, I have sought ways in which fashion's ability to give voice to the unrepresented and the unspoken, and its ability to celebrate all that our shared planet and shared humanity offers, can become an intrinsic part of fashion's design.

'Writers, designers and philosophers have long understood the connections to be made between the sense of place, the experience of modernity and the making and wearing of clothing' (Breward and Gilbert 2006). Fashion making and city making are both social processes, they are interlinked and bound together. It is through the dynamic interplay between making of meaning (values and identities) and matter (artifacts of adornment) that fashion becomes personal and vital to each of us.

Cities' and similarly, fashion, provide protection, conviviality and sites of exchange for citizens. Both, in their matter and meaning making draw on nature and humanity's resources, and in so doing mold them. As a social barometer, and major industry employing approximately 60 million of us, and currently the world's second most polluting industry (Fashion United), fashion has the opportunity to make a profoundly vicious or vital contribution to this urban metabolism.

Fashion is about the individual, as maker, wearer, and participant; it is about community, as place and culture; and it is about infrastructures of governance and business. Fashion Design for Sustainability weaves together these elements, moving beyond technical improvements, matter-making, to embrace fashion's long history of social and cultural expression, meaning-making.

Housing almost 55% of the global population (Demographia 2016), urban areas, and more specifically cities, are the home of modern civilization. We are an increasingly urban species and, as such, how we live in cities will determine our ability to live well on this planet (Girardet 1999). 'Cities are our glory and our bane' (Rogers 1998); we adapt them and are adapted by them.

Many of us are familiar with the conventional role of designer within an urban or fashion context. Through Fashion Design for Sustainability there is the potential for a more expansive role, as alchemist and agent for change. This chapter explores the interplay between citizen, designer and city to create spectacles of fashion as crucibles for the fermentation and distillation of values and practices congruent with sustainability in a city.

Fashion and habitus

For the individual citizen, fashion offers the opportunity to be noticed, 'No one's gonna spot you across a crowded room and say "Wow! Nice personality."' Fashion in the shape of possessions acts as part of an 'extended self' (Belk 1988) and it is a vital means for us to facilitate our social animal behavior. Fashion displays of our distinctions and connections, as Rocamora observes, "Strangers who pass each other by in the street create sense and meaning by seeing clothes as a legible surface that can reveal the other's personality" (Rocamora 2009).

Whether a Celine handbag or a pair of running shoes, fashion's shapes and forms, their meanings, makings and materials vary so much that we do well to remember that fashion can be defined much more clearly as our ability to represent ourselves, to gain a sense of belonging and engage in a reciprocal exchange, than if we define it by the specifics of material or stitch process alone. Fashion is a relational and social process; it is location specific: on the body, as well as in place.

Each day, each of us considers, if fleetingly, the world and our place in it as we reach for something to wear, to represent ourselves as we represent our times and locations (Williams 2014). Fashion offers us both highly visible and also unseen views on life as public spectacle and private action. In this way, 'the spectacle is the catalyst for culture making, negotiating the threshold between form and event' (Kessler 2015).

Rocamora (2009) describes fashion discourse 'as made up of a set of values, assumptions and rules that are dominant at a certain time and at a certain place in the field they are produced and reproduced in' indicating the agency of fashion to influence cultures of cherishing or of discarding the 'products' of nature and human endeavour. The creation of meaning is an iterative process involving an individual and an audience able to understand the visual cues, a 'knowing community' in fashion, usually with in an urban context.

Rocamora observes, fashion and city are overlapping fields, coterminous places of experience and practice (2009, 85). As Lynch says, we are ourselves part of the spectacle 'moving elements in a city, and in particular the people and their activities are as important (for the city) as the stationary physical parts.' (Tonkiss 2013). In an open and diversified city, an ethos rises up, is made visible (the spectacle) becomes accepted (normalized) and evolves through its inhabitants in a feedback loop (Corby et al. 2016). Bourdieu describes this as 'Habitus', or socialized norms that guide behaviour and thinking, otherwise described as 'the way society becomes deposited in persons in the form of lasting dispositions, or trained capacities and structured propensities to think, feel and act in determinant ways, which then guide them' (Wacquant 2005, 316, cited in Navarro 2006, 16). For Foucault meaning and matter making overlap, as 'fields' are shaped by wider social forces and relations with other fields (Foucault 2006). The material organization of fashion mediates the production and reproduction of social, cultural and economic arrangements that ultimately make the fashion system and its role within the city system, congruent with sustainability principles or not.

Girardet (1993) characterizes cities as either biogenic or biocidic. Biogenic cities are balanced urban metabolisms that take and give back, through a reciprocal process based on ecosystems thinking. Biocidic cities are urban mechanisms that use ingenuity and technological innovation to expand beyond nature's boundaries. This Descartian approach persists as the dominant model of modern Western thinking with economic growth as its primary goal, whereas Design for Sustainability explores a heterogenous model of future prosperity based on interdependent systems. Foregrounding nature-based systems of prosperity and ideas of humanity based on mutuality (Von Busch and Williams 2011) involves a re-conceptualisation of human progress as a dynamic interplay between economic, social, political and environmental elements. This systems view of life (Capra and Luisi 2014) underpins explorations at Centre for Sustainable Fashion, the research centre that I established, along with others, in 2008, based at London College of Fashion. We explore our coexistence with each other and with nature through fashion's personal, community and societal practices. We recognize that academia as well as industry is predominantly situated in the rational-scientific realm, so seek ways to explore an epistemological dialogue within and beyond between different sources of knowledge to form new understanding, recognizing contributors from inside and outside of traditional research roles.

Our planet, our bodies, and our cities depend on a healthy metabolism and an understanding of what this constitutes is vital to us as designers and as citizens. It is 'crucial to learn the lessons of history and to make sure that our settlements are socially just, participatory and economically viable, whilst being environmentally sustainable' (Girardet 1999). Through the spectacle of fashion, the city displays its ethos in action, all that is, or could be, where such a transformation in values and cultures can take place and be made visible.

Modernity and the loosening of ties

There was for a long time an assumption that 'modernity, urbanization and the growth of fashion went hand in hand.' Simmel and Weber characterize modernity as 'a decisive break with the past – from rural tradition and stasis – to urban change, fragmentation and mobility' (Wilson 1985).

With the shift from metabolic systems to mechanistic systems since the Industrial Revolution notions of time and space have becoming increasingly abstract. This loosening of traditional anchors might be seen as embracing diversity or threatening the basis on which all of our lives depend, nature.

Historically, cities were built on and defined by that which was produced in their location with local resources making the wares produced, bought and sold there distinctive. Today, increasingly cities are the context for the spectacle of fashion retail and consumption of global brands that transcend the locale (Gilbert 2000, Breward and Gilbert 2006).

Sales of fashion contribute to the city's economy directly whilst fashion's indirect effects on tourism, attractiveness as a location to live and do business as well as its contribution to infrastructure make fashion capitals powerful. 'Making a city fashionable (in both narrow and wider senses of the term) is now a common and often explicit aim of urban policy' and part of the global competition between cities (Gilbert 2000).

Broken promise

The spirit of emancipation and liberation that modernity, fashion and urban life offer when viewed through a sustainability lens, lack critical understanding of the vital elements of freedom and well-being. Aristotle spoke of virtue as the key to eudaimonia, loosely translated as 'thriving'. Yet that tradition has faded as happiness is increasingly associated with material conditions, especially income and consumption (Huffington 2015).

The dominant political discourse is about choice and individualism, yet this is an illusion; 'the more our society talks about the individual and individualism, the more alike we all seem to become' (Wilson 1985). The myth of choice instead creates a position where 'individuals in the current era of mass-individualization have not been empowered' (Wilson 1985). Yet the promise of the new continues to generate increasing sales, from increasingly diminishing resources. The crisis of the 'extended self' results in an 'empty self' continuously needing to be filled through consumption (Cushman 1990). As a consequence, the 'I' is never found and is always 'not yet'; the desire of becoming is endless (Spierings and Van Houtum 2008).

We know that cultures of consumption are destructive, Viktor & Rolf refer to the way that capitalist production veils its origins with cultural producers and consumers seduced even as they understand they are being manipulated (Evans 2007).

With the advent of globalized supply chains, there has been a disconnection between the production and consumption of fashion. Cities such as London, Paris, New York and Milan now foreground spectacles of fashion as a commercial, consumerist sport, the sentier[1] and other garment districts a fraction of their former size. London is a case in point, known for the creativity of its independent designers, the majority of these small- and medium-sized fashion enterprises fail within their first five years, crowded out by the high-growth mass production model that includes global marketing and premium retail rents (reference).

However, such is the power of fashion 'as a signifier of urban modernity and of world status' (Yusuf and Wu 2002), that even though production now predominantly takes place elsewhere, processes of fashion branding and city branding continue to be co-dependent (Rocamora 2009). Fashionable is often less about the distinction of product and more about the theatre of retail.

As individuals, we are removed from production, so idly take part in consumption. If the most pleasurable part of fashion is sometimes captured at the point of purchase, then the act of consumption replaces the object itself as the locus of meaning (TRANSFER 2015). So the connection with the object is ever more transient; without meaning it ceases to be valuable and is 'thrown away' or forgotten.

Within this efficient system of production and consumption, enabled by access to cheap resources, our identities become so bound up in the commerce of fashion, that even our values can become reduced to the label of 'ethical consumer' or not. With the same styles available in every city, when we can no longer see our labour through the making of things, our attachment to them lessens. 'Clothing functions as a metaphor for the instability and contingency of modern life' (Anderson 1992).

The media is replete with evidence of the unsustainability of our current ways of living and manufacturing. This 'unsustainability' is not solely a technical problem to be fixed, though technological solutions play their part, it is also a cultural problem, of social dis-ease. We encounter more stimulation of all sorts, but also more anxiety; we have more personal autonomy, but also more personal crises. 'Such is the greatness of fashion, which always refers us as individuals, back to ourselves, such is the misery of fashion, which renders us increasingly problematic to ourselves and others' (Lipovestsky 1994).

Alongside the crises of the individual, some communities face declining levels of trust and social well-being, disconnected from their traditional certainties (Joseph Rowntree Foundation 2016). As Manzini (2015) describes, communities in place are being weakened by hyper-individualised, delocalized society and a notion of looking backwards instead of around. Whilst new connections and communities are forming, not confined to geographical location, the infinite possibilities for citizens to connect via social media platforms and coalesce around shared interests are increasing, though these may lack common values.

As we evolve into 'amplified human beings' (Girardet 1999), sharing our hopes and discontents, large and small, in expanding megacities and through a digital documentary updated many times a day, crossing nature's boundaries and socially acceptable practices, we create a spectacle that resonates far beyond physical city walls. The potential reach for different kinds of spectacle, such as Fashion Design for Sustainability might offer, is all the greater.

Role of the designer

A role for the fashion designer beyond commerce is hard to imagine. The discourse and practice of fashion supports the core values of the market economy: an unsustainable behemoth (Gatzen and Von Busch). To explore the agency of the designer, we must look at the power relationship between the individual, community (whether geographic or otherwise) and wider infrastructures in fashion's supply chain. Though we are confronted by the inequalities in this relationship through NGO and media attention,[2] unjust practices are culturally and symbolically legitimised through the continued endorsement of buying and wearing clothes created in unjust ways. Community plays a critical role in shaping and endorsing this acceptance, our current 'Habitus' (Wacquant 2005).

In fashion, the media is used to condition our perception of what is acceptable, and desirable. As well as driving sales, cultural sway has in the past provided 'the means for a non-economic form of domination and hierarchy, as classes distinguish themselves through taste' (Gaventa 2003). Fashion designers, brands and their media partners play a key role in 'taste-making'. For those exploring fashion in relation to sustainability, cultivating 'taste' is therefore an opportunity to use their agency to evolve the 'Habitus' away from cultures of consumption towards cultures of care.

Fashion design has grown out of a traditional couturier model, a skilled profession and craft from apprentice to master: shaping forms on the body with a selection of materials, colours, textures and construction techniques suitable to the wearer and their lifestyle. This model has been overtaken, though not eliminated, by semi-formalized practices involving fashion design, business and communication graduates and others from a variety of fields. Whilst methods and practices follow broadly similar chronological processes (concept research, materials selection, sketching, pattern making, prototyping, etc.), the focus is on commercial efficiency, delivering and communicating goods to wider markets. The field of Fashion Design and Sustainability needs to develop roles and methods that connect fashion's tradition, its current dominant models and those with an understanding of Design for Sustainability. Together, they offer a means to consider not only *what* the designer makes, but also *how* the designer makes.

Through my practice and research, I have identified three broad 'types' of design role in fashion and sustainability (Williams 2015a) (Figure 21.1). These are not fixed, complete or ranked in terms of efficacy: the suitability of each will depend on context, on the designer's perspective, and the ethos of the business or organization of which they are part. We live and design in a post-sustainability awareness-raising era (Chapman 2012), but will not realize a paradigm shift towards sustainability until we are able to find ways in which every kind of designer can act on that awareness.

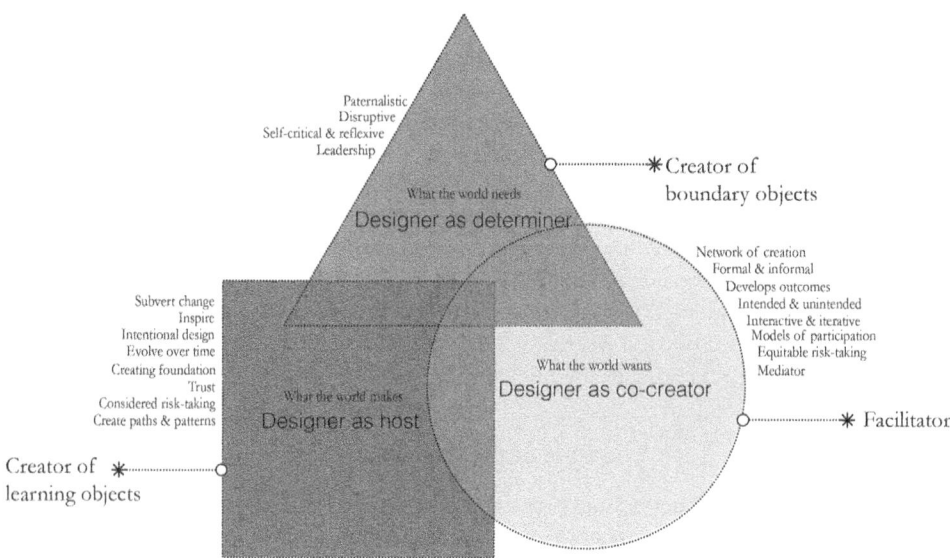

Figure 21.1 Roles of a designer (adapted from Williams 2015a).

Designer as determiner: the creator of boundary objects

This, possibly the most widely recognized and traditional of design roles, is often found where there are already established relationships with production networks, where attire is presented for specified wear and care, and where business is ongoing. It resonates with Schon's notion of designers as creators of boundary objects (1994). Designers create boundary objects when their role remains largely the same whilst the specific form of their work may change, from collection to collection, for example. This role describes how most industrialised practice operates (Williams 2015a) The designer's approach is consistent, whilst specific styles are created in response to a range of factors including what is happening in the world, what others are interested in, and changes in their supply chain. In this context, Fashion Design for Sustainability involves making choices that are informed by sustainability knowledge, often relating to material and manufacturing elements, and passing on such information to the buyer and customer. Whilst 'designer as determiner' might practice within a currently unsustainable business model, this hierarchical position offers the opportunity for highly visible innovative disruption, and changes to what is accepted as fashion design practice. It also includes the potential for design tactics (Rigby 2013) that influence pro-environmental or pro-social behaviour, through 'provotypes' (Fuad-Luke 2009) that provoke new thinking and behaviour.

Designer as co-creator: facilitator

When a designer considers their role as one of co-creator with the wearer, producer or other, this opens up places and spaces for active participation involving a range of agendas, actors, contexts and new applications of fashion. Fashion is intrinsically a co-creation process. It inevitably involves interaction, the nature of which is dependent on the agency of each participant. Codesign has an extended history inside and outside fashion, often taking place informally and without recognition. Through an expanding range and discourse of codesign in Design for

Sustainability, changes in the practices, skills and required capabilities of the designer can emerge, and a revised intention. The visualization of the contribution of each participant in a codesign process varies widely as do the ambitions involved. Codesign might involve protagonists across a production network in more collaborative working practices; it might encompass a feedback loop between maker and wearer; or it might involve a design–with notion involving a partnership between designer and nature.

Designer as host: the creator of learning devices

The role of 'designer as host' involves an inversion of the usual hierarchical designer model, to foreground the agency of others through the creation of conditions for a series of autonomous, authentic progressions of fashion by a variety of actors, often over time (Williams 2014). The design decisions may be intentional or not, and the study of design can be seen here as a means to open up creative opportunity in others. The host or professional designer acts as encouragement to the citizen designer, design being a fundamental part of human capability (Cross 2006). The host is catalyst for a series of actions and encounters to take place, which may involve a specific piece or shape, or may include the transformation of that piece through learning experiences. The host facilitates learning, exploration, adaptation and interaction to 'malleable' situations, shapes and forms. This relates to the notion of 'creator of learning devices' (Schon 1994), which may change the nature and content of a piece beyond the imagination of the host designer, through the enabling function of design, and through the web of relationships that fashion can form. This is a radical departure for fashion design, moving its framework and hierarchical structure into a networked heterarchy (Williams and Fletcher 2010). This mode of design offers the potential for 'mass innovation, not mass production' (Leadbetter and 257 others, 2008), challenging existing ways of 'doing design', and challenging the usually recognized role and status of the designer to become activist or space creator: a designer who hosts and creates a place for the spectacle of, as yet, undetermined outcomes.

For a designer to operate beyond the conventional commercial mode requires a context supportive of values-led design practices, for example Shared Talent (Williams and Fletcher 2010), where designers, makers, buyers and promoters from different cultural and geographic locations were brought together to explore how they might question and realize their ambitions. Education is one of the greatest spaces to challenge our ways of perceiving, doing and making. However, increasingly participants rehearse scenarios that reflect the current business of fashion, leaving little space to try out what might be over what is.

Case studies: fashion-articulating discontents

Mid-to-late twentieth-century fashion designers articulated the pleasures of identity, alongside the anxieties of alienation and loss against the unstable backdrop of rapid social, economic and technological change through their collections. McQueen's Highland Rape, and other collections, engaged incredible skill in the aestheticization of his politically charged concerns. 'In McQueen's work too a warped engagement with politics as trauma sketches a strong sense of disenchantment with the world through the expression of a rough sensuality and refined cruelty' (Evans 2007). Whilst such messages are arresting and understood by those in close dialogue with the designer and others interested in his work, they became, paradoxically, a means towards the designer's recognition in the fashion's establishment: McQueen having undertaken roles at Givenchy, his own label acquired by Gucci group (later Kering), and his work including collaborations with Puma and Target. While protest may be the intent, if the presentation and acquisition of collections is bound by the conventional commercial framework, then fashion is conspiring, as Barthes (2010) suggests, to rid 'human activity of its major scoria alienation, boredom, uncertainty, or more fundamentally: impossibility focusing instead on pleasing and reassuring experiences'.

By the early twenty-first century, the rise of fashion, either casual or professional, gave the impression that it was not questioning the dominance of brands, the commoditizing of identities, or profusion of garments as supposed democracy through fashion (Wilson 1985).

A more profoundly shocking reaction to fashion's modus operandi and long held habits has followed, with some designers refusing to create conventional collections, such as Tigran Avetisyan's 'In loving memory of Spring Summer 2014' sending out pieces from a previous collection daubed in paint saying 'nothing changes' (Fedorova 2016), and others refusing to take part in the seemingly endless carousel of shows and exhibitions and sales. These responses challenge the fashion system to address its complicity in an unjust economic system. Simultaneously, we are also seeing a questioning of existing consumption patterns and the emergence of alternative modes of fashion acquisition and enjoyment, for example through Kate Fletcher's Craft of Use project, a celebration of ordinary and ingenius uses of garments as part of an extended excitement in fashion, beyond the acquisition of the new (2016).

Design for sustainability is a different kind of revolt against the machine, with each of the roles of designer providing a range of entry points into sustainability, whilst not limiting the actions of any designer to one role. In fact, many designers, myself included, cross back and forth between roles over their careers and situations. Such a designer, artist and researcher is Professor Helen Storey, a member of Centre for Sustainable Fashion, who has designed, made and exhibited Dress 4 Our Time (D4OT), a dress that communicates (via digital messaging projected from inside the dress) unseen elements of our changing ecological and social environment that are of collective concern and individual resonance, a dress being a recognizable item to us all. D4OT carries with it a story of our humanity, our shared existence, and visualizes the effect of our current lifestyles. The discourse of sustainability is often hampered by apparent distance, whether geographic, cultural or temporal (Hoffman 2015). In contrast, fashion is 'a relation that affects us all, whether we want it to or not' (Fletcher and Tham 2014). Such a universally recognized item of attire renders a message legible in powerful ways. Taking the role of designer as determiner, it seeks to inform public understanding and instigate action in ways that the raw data of climate change science and the media coverage of social injustice cannot do alone. 'Act, like we have just enough time, live like it runs out today' (Storey 2015). Drawing on expertise from the Met Office collaboration with UNHCR (United Nations Human Rights Council), digital expertise[3] and industry support, the dress became a public art installation at St. Pancras International station, the departure point to the UN COP 21 Climate Conference. The dress has been installed as a public display at the United Nations Palais de Nations in Geneva (TEDx), worn on stage at Glastonbury Festival (LCF 2016), and on public display in The Science Museum in London, engaging audiences in a visceral experience of scientific consensus as a means to galvanize the cultural consensus towards caring for our only home and shared humanity (Science Museum 2016).

This fashion spectacle has broad resonance, it aims to change the actions of many, contributing to the creation of a larger ecological consciousness, an Ecozoic Age (Swimme and Berry 1992).

Through Fashion Revolution, Orsola de Castro, Carry Somers and others, myself included, engage 'the power of fashion to change the story for the people who make the world's clothes and accessories' (Fashion Revolution). Curating physical and digital spectacles in over 90 countries with the social media hashtag #whomademyclothes, Fashion Revolution uses simple design tactics, such as wearing your clothes inside out, to metaphorically and literally show fashion's insides, visibly evidencing the vast range of people who demand more for the people who make our clothes; in 2016's Fashion Revolution week, there were approximately 156 million impressions of

Fashion Revolution hashtags, 1251 brands responded directly to consumers asking #whomade-myclothes, and 3500 producer voices were heard using the #imadeyourclothes hashtag (Fashion Revolution 2016). Fashion Revolution seeks to offer the individual the opportunity to regain a sense of ownership over their fashion messages, whilst pledging allegiance to a community of like-minded fashionistas.

Labour Behind the Label, Greenpeace, and others, have helped and been helped by Fashion Revolution, catalysing citizens to interrogate what fashion offers that they can socially accept and can personally enjoy. With extended supply chains and design detached from production, designers as well as wearers are publically asking questions, with those who have trusted supply chains able to stand by their wares.

This heterachical network of fashion designers, makers, wearers, educators, students and others creates a spectacle of fashion that offers agency to those involved,[4] engaging citizens in a creative process that is challenging the status quo, whilst celebrating the value of people and fashion through a convivial exchange. Fashion Revolution is a global movement of prosumers, with the designer as host activating citizen ethics and action through citizen as designer.

Through a co-creation process, a team from CSF and Sheffield University Psychology department have engaged in research to explore whether 'the motivation behind unsustainable consumerism is the fact that people feel detached from the things that they purchase' (TRANSFER 2015). The TRANSFER[5] research created a participatory exhibition in a Leeds shopping mall, 'to showcase, in full view of the public, the manufacturing process behind a t-shirt, creating a visible and wearable connection between consumers' fashion purchase decisions and the manufacturing processes underlying the products that people desire'. The ability of fashion, as spectacle, to engage in a dialogue about sustainability offers an opportunity to explore sustainability within and beyond the content of the garments themselves. Whilst improvements have been made to the impact of each garment of up to 30%, higher levels of consumption have overshadowed this reduction (Fletcher and Tham 2014, 20), contributing to a negative environmental impact overall, so the project sought to engage potential customers in an active dialogue about how clothes are made, where they are made and by whom, to make the social, environmental and cultural impacts of our day-to-day purchasing decisions more tangible. Through participatory design, a production line was set up inside the shopping centre, where garments were made with customers, whose responses to 'connectedness to clothing questions' were applied to pocket shape, responses to 'impulse buying tendency questions' were applied to text on the back of the garment, and responses to 'environmental concern and environmental behaviour questions' applied to stitching colour. The findings from this research (TRANSFER 2015) offer data about buying decisions; for example 71% of interviewees were identified as being partially disconnected from sustainable clothing purchase and disposal practices. What is more, over the two days 150,000 passers-by witnessed or took part in a collaborative fashion spectacle. These alternative spectacles offer different narratives of fashion in the city, which are visible, identifiable and offer open-ended reflection and debate. As 'year by year, our world becomes more complex, we must remold our old cities and build new communities better suited to our needs' (Mumford 1970). This project seeks small ways to involve community in the shaping of garments, potentially the city, and for these spectacles to contribute to the Habitus' evolution.

As another perspective on the role of designer as co-creator, the acts of reciprocity involved in making together, exemplified by Von Busch's Do-It-Together (2013), seek to make connections within communities through new frameworks for cooperation as sustainability in action. The starting point of Strategic Repair and other mutual benefit projects that I have been leading at The London College of Fashion, was for MA students to act as magpies, seeking out a piece of clothing that holds their attention, but is visibly in need of care (Von Busch and Williams 2011). Taking this piece to a person or place that might actively contribute to its value, the designer (the MA student) then sets about finding ways for these and other participants to physically exchange skills, ideas, or time, so that there is a benefit to all and a visibility to each participant's contribution. This process is far from novel; cities were built as places of exchange and society still manifests many active exchange opportunities, but for fashion design students to engage in creation through such a process is seen by many as radical and unexpected. The culmination of this and other projects that I have run with students is a public display, in places where those involved are invited to participate, and where the social interaction of the pieces' creation is celebrated alongside the social interaction of their display.

If our clothes are to act as signifiers of our selves, then what we stand up *in* should represent what we stand up *for*. To explore this, I have been developing participatory design techniques to encourage a voicing and a wearing of concerns (positive and negative) as part of a wider research project Habit(AT).[6] In asking if what you stand up *in* represents what you stand up *for*, it takes the simple message t-shirt, a concept I know well having worked as women's mainline designer at Katharine Hamnett for many years. Through a number of iterations this research seeks to make fashion spectacles that enable identity, connection and reciprocation to take place. More fully described elsewhere, designers versed in ethnographic methods integrate these approaches within their practice with publics to identify and analyze a design concern at hand and codesign responses (Corby et al. 2016; Williams 2015b). Design methods culminate in a t-shirt designed to conceptually represent the location in question alongside the slogan 'I Stood Up'. Significant interest has been generated, with a range of passers-by self-selecting to take part, putting on the t-shirt, and responding to semi-structured questions about environmental concerns, finally being photographed engaging with this ubiquitous item in a personal way. This creation of a kind of social form, through a fashion object as facilitator, and a pop-up event encourages individual and collective expression. It is the intertwined relationship between form and event, each propelling the other towards the creation of a spectacle in the city, which informs urban life (Kessler 2015). In this case, the t-shirt and discourse through verbal exchange and photography offer a spectacle that demonstrates culture making as a live social exchange in the city. These interactions have produced data about concerns, art works for public exhibition, and positive feedback regarding participatory experience on the part of the citizen designers. This research does not claim to have made any lasting impact on citizen participants, however, it starts to reveal the possibilities afforded by an unconventional role for the designer.

In one iteration, first time voters were invited to an I Stood Up workshop at the House of Lords. A committee room was transformed into a participatory making space for the day with sewing equipment replacing the usual documents for discussion. The event culminated in a debate, chaired by Baroness Lola Young to evidence fashion as a means to connect the political with the public (Till), 'speaking truth to power' (AMFSC 1955). Through such practices, we seek places that open up opportunity and activate performance to create disruptive participation. These interventions do not compel but encourage action, making it safe to speak out, thus redistributing the power in the city's spectacle (Lynch 1984).

As the case studies illustrate, Fashion Design for Sustainability provides a diversity of ways to respond to the complex challenges of our time. They need to be informed by bodies of knowledge, practices and roles that lie inside and outside of traditional fashion design. If, to paraphrase Tonkinwise (2015), design is about providing 'something useful', then the 'usefulness' of the designer is as creator of boundary objects, facilitator of co-creation or as host. Although apparently riskier than current practice, these processes could enable positive and novel outcomes, as the World Bank (2014) notes, 'the risk of inaction may well be the worst option of all.'

Working in conditions of continuous change, partial control, pluralism and participation, maintaining their creative and aesthetic abilities and using them in open and participatory ways can be challenging for designers. In this case, designers are mediators between the agency of the expert and that of the amateur, between the intentional and the improvised, the permanent and the temporary. Success is as much about steering patterns of social behavior as it is about composing physical forms (Lynch 1984).

Conclusion

Action on sustainability in fashion, and otherwise, requires many responses. We know from experience that the science and data of climate change, for example, have done little to change habits and practices. This is not to undermine the absolute necessity of the vital work that continues to take place in these fields, but, as we at CSF have seen, in humanizing data, such as through Nike Making (CSF Nike project), which CSF helped to develop, we can create culture change. Sustainability is a cultural problem; it is about how we live in the world. Fashion 'visualizes the tenor of urban life, like no other visual medium' (Breward and Gilbert 2006).

Fashion alone cannot address the existential crisis (LeGeorge 2016) that many societies currently face, but as it is a vital part of how we explore our sense of selves, it can facilitate reflection and experimentation to re-imagine its practices, industrial and personal, in relation to environmental and social degradation.

Debate inside and outside of the fashion and sustainability discourse reflects a range of ideologies. Change is needed across the political and economic spectrum, and this can happen when people are actively involved in creating a sense of themselves that also creates recognition and belonging to a wider community, city and culture.

Cities have the capability of providing something for everybody, only because, and only when, they are created by everybody (Jacobs 1961). The material object continues to be significant, but it functions as part of a wider set of processes that place people at the centre of the design process, by interweaving place-making and form-making as a medium for communities to contribute to socially and environmentally restorative practices.

As an academic, I consider my duty of care to students, to the community within which I belong and so forth; as a designer setting out, I might have different considerations, and as a designer heading up an international fashion house considerations shift again – and in each case we juggle different kinds of risks, different values, different experiences. But we are part of a shared humanity and through cultures of sustainability visualized in cities, through fashion spectacle, we can create diverse approaches to living well with nature and each other, if we each foreground these, the only elements on which our prosperity can be assured.

Notes

1 Sentier, in the second arrondissement of Paris, is historically known as the garment making district.
2 Examples of media outlets include Friends of the Earth, Greenpeace, Labour Behind the Label, National Geographic and others.
3 Digital expertise provided by Unilever and Holition.
4 Such as Fashion Revolution's 'The 2 Euro T-Shirt' film.
5 TRANSFER full name is Trading Approaches to Nurturing Sustainable Consumption in Fashion and Energy Retail.
6 Habit(AT): fashion in cities as sustainability habits in place.

References

Papers

Belk, R. (1988) "Possessions and the extended self" *Journal of Consumer Research*, *15*, 139–168

Corby, T., Williams, D., Sheth, V., and Dhar, V. (2016) "I stood up: Social design in practice" *Art and Design Review*, *4*, 30–36. Published Online May 2016 in SciRes. (www.scirp.org/journal/adr) (http://file.scirp.org/pdf/ADR_2016051813400901.pdf)

Cushman, P. (1990) "Why the self is empty: Toward a historically situated psychology" *American Psychologist*, *45*(5), 599–611

Gaventa, J. (2003) *Power After Lukes: A Review of the Literature*. Brighton: Institute of Development Studies

Navarro, Z. (2006) "In Search of Cultural Interpretation of Power" *IDS Bulletin*, *37*(6), 11–22

Spierings, B. and Van Houtum, H. (2008) "The brave new world of the post-society: The mass-production of the individual consumer and the emergence of template cities" *European Planning Studies*, *16*, 899–909

Von Busch, O. (2013) "Collaborative craft capabilities: The bodyhood of shared skills" *The Journal of Modern Craft*, *6*(2), 135–146

Williams, D. and Fletcher, K. (2010) "Shared Talent: An Exploration of the Potential of the 'Shared Talent' Collaborative and Hands on Educational Experience for Enhanced Learning around Sustainability in Fashion Practice" in *Sustainability in Design: Now! Challenges and Opportunities for Design Research, Education and Practice in the XXI Century*. London: Greenleaf Publishing Ltd, 1096–1004

Yusuf, S. and Wu, W. (2002) "Pathways to a world city: Shanghai rising in an era of globalization" *Urban Studies*, *39*, 1213–1240

Theses

Rigby, E. (2013) *Design and the Laundry: Changing Behaviour and the Rhythm of Consumption*. PhD project at London College of Fashion. London: British Library

Books

AMFSC, eds. (1955) *Speak Truth to Power, a Quaker Search for an Alternative to Violence*. American Friends Service Committee

Anderson, M. (1992) *Kafka's Clothes: Ornament and Aestheticism in the Habsburg Fin de Siecle*. Oxford: Clarendon Press

Barthes, R. (2010) *The Fashion System*. Vintage Classics

Breward, C. and Gilbert, D. eds. (2006) *Fashion's World Cities*. Berg Publishers

Capra, F. and Luisi, P. (2014) *The Systems View of Life*. Cambridge University Press

Cross, N. (2006) *Designerly ways of knowing*. London: Springer

Evans, C. (2007) *Fashion at the Edge: Spectacle, Modernity and Deathliness*. Yale University Press

Fletcher, K. (2016) *Craft of Use: Post Growth Fashion*. Routledge.

Fletcher, K. and Tham, M., eds. (2014) *Routledge Handbook of Sustainability and Fashion*. Oxon: Routledge

Foucault, M. (2006) *Madness and Civilisation*. Vintage Books; 1st edition

Fuad-Luke, A. (2009) *Design Activism: Beautiful Strangeness for a Sustainable World*. London: Earthscan

Girardet, H. (1993) *The Gaia Atlas of Cities: New Directions for Sustainable Urban Living (Gaia Future)*. London: Gaia Books Ltd.

Girardet, H. (1999) *Creating Sustainable Cities (Schumacher Briefings)*. Green Books

Huffington, A. (2015) *Thrive: The Third Metric to Redefining Success and Creating a Happier Life*. WH Allen

Jacobs, J. (1961) *The Death and Life of Great American Cities*. Originally published: New York: Random House

Leadbetter, C.W. and 257 others. (2008) *We Think: The Power of Mass Creativity*. Profile Books

Lipovestsky, G. (1994) *The Empire of Fashion: Dressing Modern Democracy*. Trans C. Porter. Princeton University Press

Lynch, F. (1984) in Tonkiss, F. (2013) *Cities by Design: The Social Life of Urban Form*. Polity Press

Mumford, L. (1970) *The Culture of Cities*. Thomson Learning

Rocamora, A. (2009) *Fashioning the City: Paris, Fashion and the Media*. B Tauris & Co. Ltd.

Rogers, R. (1998) *Cities for a Small Planet*. Basic Books

Schon, D. (1994) *The Reflective Practitioner: How Professionals Think in Action.* Surrey: Ashgate Publishing Limited

Swimme, B. and Berry, T. (1992) *The Universe Story: From the Primordial Flaring Forth to the Ecozoic Era – A Celebration of the Unfolding of the Cosmos.* Harper San Francisco

Tonkiss, F. (2013) *Cities by Design: The Social Life of Urban Form.* Polity Press

Wacquant, L. (2005) *Habitus. International Encyclopedia of Economic Sociology.* Edited by J. Becket and M. Zafirovski. London: Routledge

Wilson, E. (1985) *Adorned in Dreams: Fashion and Modernity.* London: Virago

Chapter of book

Gilbert, D. (2000) "Urban Outfitting: The City and Spaces of Fashion Culture" in Bruzzi, S. and Church Gibson, P. eds., *Fashion Cultures: Theories, Explorations and Analysis.* London: Routledge

Williams, D. (2014) "Fashion Design" in Fletcher, K. and Tham, M. eds., *Routledge Handbook of Sustainability and Fashion.* Oxon: Routledge

Williams, D. (2015a) "Fashion Design and Sustainability" in Blackburn, R. ed., *Sustainable Apparel: Production, Processing and Recycling.* Cambridge: Woodhead Publishing

Williams, D. (2015b) "Fashion Habit(at)s for Resilience: How Fashion's Habits and Locations Shape Our Cultures and Contribute to Authorship of Our Lives" in *Cultures of Resilience Book 1.* London: Hato Press, 92–95 (http://culturesofresilience.org/wp-content/uploads/resources/CoR-Booklet-forHome Printing.pdf)

World wide web pages

CSF Nike Project (http://sustainable-fashion.com/projects/nike/) Accessed 1 June 2016

Fashion Revolution (2015) The 2 Euro T-Shirt Film (www.unit9.com/project/fashion-revolution/) Accessed 18 July 2016

Fashion United Global Fashion Industry Statistics (https://fashionunited.com/global-fashion-industry-statistics) Accessed 1 June 2016

Fedorova, A. (2016) How Designers Are Responding To Fashion's Overproduction Problem. (https://i-d.vice.com/en_us/article/how-designers-are-responding-to-fashions-overproduction-problem) Accessed 3 August 2016

Gatzen, P. and Von Busch, O. eds., "Letter From the Editors" *Journal of Design Strategies Volume 7* (http://sds.parsons.edu/designdialogues/?post_type=article&p=629) Accessed 17 July 2016

Hoffman, A. (2015) How Culture Shapes the Climate Change Debate. Stanford University Press (www.sup.org/books/cite/?id=25621) Accessed 3 May 2016.

LCF (2016) Dress for Our Time on the Pyramid Stage at Glastonbury (http://blogs.arts.ac.uk/fashion/2016/06/24/dress-for-our-time-on-the-pyramid-stage-at-glastonbury) Accessed 3 August 2016

Manzini, E. (2015) Weaving People and Places (http://culturesofresilience.org/weaving-people-and-places/) Accessed 3 July 2016

Science Museum (2016) (www.sciencemuseum.org.uk/visitmuseum/Plan_your_visit/exhibitions/dress-for-our-time) Accessed 19 August 2016.

Storey, H. (2015) Dress for Our Time (www.dress4ourtime.org/) Accessed 21 June 2016

TEDx Place des Nations (www.tedxplacedesnations.ch) Accessed 3 August 2016

Till, J. Three Politics (www.jeremytill.net/read/103/three-politics) Accessed 3 August 2016

Tonkinwise, C. (2015) Is Social Design a Thing? (www.academia.edu/11623054/Is_Social_Design_a_Thing) Accessed 3 May 2016

World Bank (2014) World Development Report 2014 (http://econ.worldbank.org/WBSITE/EXTERNAL/EXTDEC/EXTRESEARCH/EXTWDRS/EXTNWDR2013/0,,contentMDK:23330018~pagePK:8258258~piPK:8258412~theSitePK:8258025,00.html) Accessed 3 August 2016

Other publications

Chapman, J. (2012) *UAL Green Week Event: TFRC Symposium* (http://newsevents.arts.ac.uk/files/2012/01/tfrc_greenweek_programme_final1-2.pdf) Central St Martins College of Art and Design 6 February 2012

Demographia (2016) *Demographia World Urban Areas 12th Annual Edition* (www.demographia.com/db-worldua.pdf)

Fashion Revolution (2016) *2016 Impact* (http://fashionrevolution.org/about/2016-impact/) Accessed 2 August 2016

JRF Joseph Rowntree Foundation (2016) *UK Poverty: Causes, Costs and Solutions* (www.jrf.org.uk/report/uk-poverty-causes-costs-and-solutions) Accessed 6 August 2016

Kessler, M. (2015) *The City and the Spectacle, Memories of Future Cites Workshop*, Institute of Modern Languages Research, School of Advanced Studies, University of London

LeGeorge, P. (2016) *Creative Climate Coalition Launch Seminar*, Kings College London, 4 May 2016

TRANSFER (2015) *Dissemination Workshop Report May 2015*, University of Sheffield, University of the Arts London, Economic & Social Research Council. (http://ualresearchonline.arts.ac.uk/8005/1/TRANSFER_Dissemination_Workshop_report%5B1%5D.pdf) Accessed 17 July 2016

Von Busch, O. and Williams, D. (2011) *Community Repair* (http://www.selfpassage.org/CoRep/Community Repair_cat-w.pdf)

22

DESIGNING INDIVIDUAL CAREERS AND WORK ENVIRONMENTS FOR SUSTAINABLE VALUE

Cynthia Scott

Design principles have long been applied to designing products, processes and built environments. Increasingly, design principles are being applied to the task of building organizations and communities. These principles can also be helpful when approaching the design of career choices. This chapter focuses on the way design principles can influence some of the ethical questions that arise in the process of creating individual careers that have an alignment between personal and organizational values. It will also point to some of the key factors that contribute to creating work environments designed for high performance and engagement. This focus brings together elements of personal hardiness and applies them to organizational resilience and agility. For the purpose of this chapter sustainability encompasses the social, cultural, economic and environmental influences that support a thriving future.

This chapter provides a structure, ideas and tools so you can be the designer of your career. There are two parts: first, the personal values and the application of these values to inform choosing and building careers that will provide meaning and fulfillment. Secondly, we will explore some broad concepts of individual resilience that can be applied to designing and managing work environments in which individuals can thrive. These two areas are brought together in applying design principles to the creation of career satisfaction.

Designing careers

Design principles can be readily applied to "design" a meaningful career in a work environment that is increasingly global, complex and fast changing. Increasingly careers come with some assembly required. The world of "secure jobs", "company loyalty", "career ladders" and "lifetime careers" is morphing into just-in-time, work-for-hire, short-term contracts which will require employees to learn new skills and potentially shift focus multiple times. Applying design principles to creating work environments and policies that support people in this navigation is a key part of social sustainability. The amount of learning and adjustment that it will take to thrive in these transitions will benefit from the principles of design thinking.

At the heart of career well-being is the design challenge of how to identify work that aligns with your values; bringing you success and satisfaction while providing value to the organization.

You spend more waking hours at work than you do on any other part of your life so it is important that you devote time to identify where you will find the best convergence between your capabilities, passion and opportunity. The focus of this chapter is on helping you – as a core asset of "human capital" – to make an investment in a career path or organization.

The nature of work is changing. At a macro level, the world is experiencing disruptions in the economic climate driven by demographics, technology and natural resource availability. On a personal level, employees are searching for meaning from work and employers are increasingly responding to this changing context by engaging their employees to ensure long-term survivability of their organization. The popular, narrow definition of sustainability (or sustainable development) is, 'meeting the needs of the present without compromising the ability of future generations to meet their own needs' (World Commission on Environment Development, 1987). This definition is frequently shortened to mean, "protecting the environment". But in recent years, sustainability has been recast as a broader concept, encompassing the social, economic, environmental and cultural systems needed to sustain any organization (Werbach, 2009; Scott and Bryson, 2012).

In the midst of all this change people still want, more than ever, a satisfying relationship with work. People want more than a salary, people want a combination of personal fulfillment and service to the community in a way that sustains the environment. The idea of "right livelihood" connects personal fulfillment with global sustainability. Good work is essential to a complete life. Albert Camus said, 'without work all life goes rotten. But when work is soulless, life stifles and dies' (Scott and Jaffe, 1997). During his trip to America, Sigmund Freud put his ideas about the difference between a healthy person and a neurotic in layman's terms. 'A healthy person must be able to work and love'. Your relationship to your work is one of the deepest, most important relationships in your life. You give a large share of your energy, intelligence, creativity and your time to work.

Understanding how your values drive the design of your career

One of the major distinguishing qualities of human beings is our ability to move beyond basic needs and drives, and to organize our lives and workplaces around a complex set of higher principles, which we call *values*. These values form the basic building block for decision-making. Understanding your basic values will give you a way to assess work opportunities and organizations.

To design a career requires identifying a personal core set of values that can then be used to align career and work with actions that build career success and satisfaction. As complex beings, we hold multiple values. The ability to reprioritize our values to fit different life stages and circumstances provides a foundation for living a coherent life. It is common to feel tension between holding a set of values and being able to apply them to making decisions. Organizing them into a framework provides a way to identify these tensions in a way that optimizes individual career choice.

Values are a set of beliefs that then influence behaviors, leading to actions that culminate in a set of behaviors or results (Figure 22.1). Careers are the outcome of this chain of values, beliefs and actions. Values provide a starting point for understanding how you make career choices.

Values as a foundation for self-awareness

Your values have developed from interaction with multiple communities – family, workplace, religions, civic groups and political groups that are defined by their values. Our lives can be

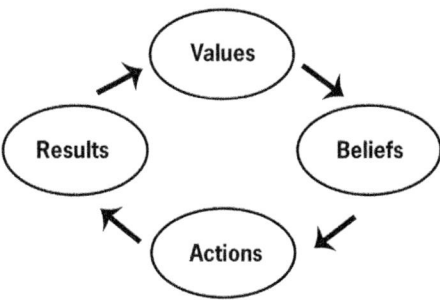

Figure 22.1 Values diagram.

viewed as a self-creation made up of numerous choices to take action, pursue opportunities, create relationships, and focus our time and energy. Every day we make small choices about what to do and over time create major commitments and projects that reflect the aspirations of our values. These choices help us organize our actions so that we can do what is most important and valuable.

They have helped us steer towards our central beliefs; we call these inner guides values, as they dictate what is important for us to do. Here are some examples of activities/behaviors that are expressions of our values.

- Becoming involved in community work
- Asking questions about the impact of choices on people who are not represented
- Taking a stand about a policy or action
- Having a conversation with someone about differences in choices
- Choosing to reduce waste and consumption
- Incorporating sustainable materials into a product

Each of these actions is connected to something we value, enabling us to choose one action over another, and often taking a leadership role in inspiring ourselves and others to act.

Values motivate us, but they are not "little computer programs" that lead us to do something. Rather, values help us make choices. As we choose behaviors/actions that match our values we feel more "coherent" – acting in a way that makes sense to our inner compass. Identifying our values helps us articulate to others and ourselves what we stand for and why we make the choices we do. These choices in turn help to further refine and give definition to our values. Values do not "cause" our actions; they are just a way we define and organize what is important to us. Your values provide a way to make choices about career and employment options.

Although some of us naturally feel that we make good choices, and feel that our values and lives are in harmony, others fret and struggle to achieve this harmony and integration. Some people feel pulled in different ways, and struggle to act in ways that line up with their values. One of the ways that we harmonize our actions is by consciously identifying a set of values and clarifying the behaviors that reflect those values. We help ourselves become *congruent*, so that what we want, what we believe, what we say and what we do all come together. To achieve this alignment, it helps to clearly identify a set of values and prioritize them so that we can organize our actions and choices.

Strengthening inner alignment

Our behavior reflects many different values. Some are "hard wired" from early experiences and others are more situational, having developed or been modified from more recent experience. As we make choices all day long, having your values top of mind will help make choices that are in line with your most basic beliefs and aspirations.

People don't easily give up or change their values. Values can shift and evolve during the life cycle, for example, what is important in your early 20s may be different in your 50s. For example, a young person may place low value on health and physical self-care and seek adventurous physical challenges, but by middle age, this same person can focus more on maintaining their daily health and lessen their pursuit of risky ventures. Over time, some of our values evolve, but others remain relatively constant. At any time of life, some values are emerging, and others becoming less important. People often experience this tension between emerging and declining values (Scott and Jaffe, 1994).

Understanding your basic values

When you ask people about their values it is common to offer a list of words (i.e. trust, integrity, peace, fairness, etc.). It is common to notice that some of the values we choose are aspirational, or not reflected in our current actions. We think of ourselves as holding that value, but when we look at our behavior, we don't do things that reflect this value as much as we think. We can avoid this lack of alignment, or we can face up to it, confront it and change our behavior, or give up that value. This is not so easy, and many of us prefer to just go through life without looking seriously at how our actual behavior is in alignment with our values. If we want to live by certain values, we have to find ways to act on them. This tension emerges in making choices about career and how to balance work and personal life commitments.

The Values Wheel model: a framework for organizing values

The Values Wheel was designed to provide a simple way for helping individuals and teams to identify what their core values are and then find areas of shared connection to provide more meaning and alignment in their work. The clusters shown in Figure 22.2 are focused on broad themes that can be applied to individuals and groups (Scott and Jaffe, 1994).

The Values Wheel model

The Values Wheel model contains six "clusters" around a central core. The individual values in each cluster and the center are expressed in one's personal life, work, and relationships. Each person has a unique pattern formed from a combination of these values. None of the values are better or worse than the others; they are just different. By looking at decisions as expressions of differences in values it is possible to have conversations about how to value and respect differences and establish common foundations for action.

These six clusters of values reflect ways that people relate to their environments, make choices about time and use their energy. People often feel most comfortable with other people who share their pattern, and feel least comfortable with those who have patterns with opposite clusters. No single pattern is preferential or better than others. A high performance

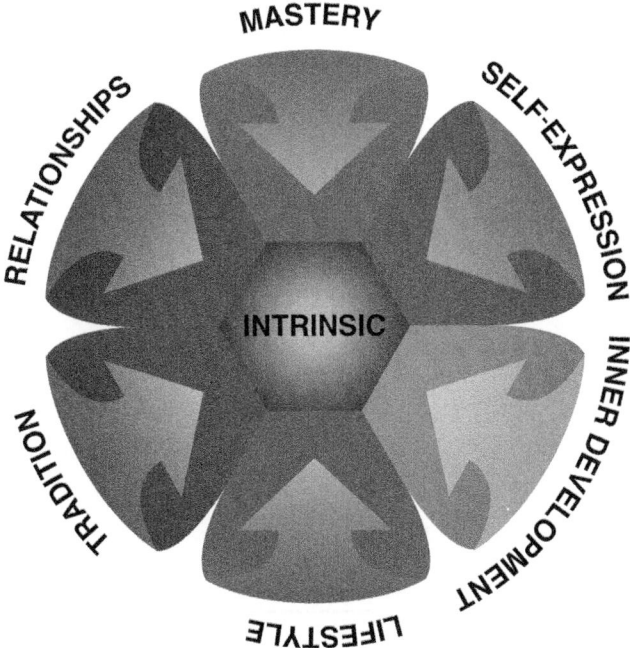

Figure 22.2 The Values Wheel model.

organization has a diversity of values patterns and makes use of them to harvest innovation and new perspectives.

Understanding the Values Wheel model

Each area of the wheel represents a different *focus*. The three clusters on the bottom half of the model (tradition, lifestyle and inner development) focus on the internal development of an individual; the top half (relationships, mastery and self-expression) focus on external relationships. The groups that are across from each other often represent areas of tension, where values "pull" at each other, for example the focus on inner development being pulled by a focus on relationships.

Intrinsic values are at the center of the Values Wheel model. They are at the center, as people often consider "good" in themselves. Values pioneer Milton Rokeach (1973) called these intrinsic values central to peoples' fundamental beliefs. These values are found in multiple ethical frameworks worldwide and tend to be foundational to creating a cohesive society. They are often selected as the most important aspirations of humanity.

We have observed an interesting pattern; some people consider these values so basic and "baked in" that they choose none or few in their initial selection. They often choose more from the values clusters, because they consider them too foundational to call out. The values in the other clusters are often chosen because they describe how they put their intrinsic values into action, and are therefore easier to articulate. The challenge is for people to actually make their actions fit these ideals, and to keep these values in focus, especially in times of stress. Intrinsic values are so broad and deep that they may be difficult to live by. You never reach them; you always striving towards them.

Table 22.1 Value Wheel Values List

• Integrity	• Excitement	• Tradition
• Peace	• Learning	• Stability
• Fairness	• Personal Freedom	• Respectfulness
• Trust	• Challenge	• Moderation
• Competence	• Forgiveness	• Loyalty
• Achievement	• Spirituality• Faith	• Conformity
• Recognition	• Inner Harmony	• Consistency
• Power	• Personal Growth	• Security
• Excellence	• Self-Respect	• Growth
• Ambition	• Open Mindedness	• Belonging
• Winning	• Self-Knowledge	• Friendship
• Tolerance	• Health	• Collaboration
• Sustainability	• Pleasure	• Resolving Conflict
• Beauty	• Appearance	• Communication
• Social Responsibility	• Community	• Teamwork
• Adventure	• Work-Life Balance	• Family
• Courage	• Play	• Helping
• Creativity	• Prosperity	
• Curiosity	• Relaxation	

Identifying your values

Because values are personal you can start with your own personal discovery before you apply them to career design. The Values Wheel Values List in Table 22.1 contains 56 values for you to choose from. To identify your values follow these four steps:

1   In the following list, place a check mark in front of values that you think describe your life/ action.
2   Now reduce the number you have chosen to 15 by circling the values that are most important to you at this time.
3   Then take the list of values you have selected and using Table 22.2 match them to the clusters in the Values Wheel Model shown in Figure 22.2,
4   Notice the pattern of where you have a larger or smaller cluster of values.

Aligning values and work

This model helps people talk about what is important to them. They also form a way to think about selecting an organization to work in. Not all of your personal values have to be reflected in your organizational values, but there needs to be enough synergy to provide enough alignment to find meaning and satisfaction.

Table 22.2 Values Wheel Model Clusters

Focus	Description	Values
Intrinsic	• Foundational belief, can be not chosen because appears to be implied. • Represent core aspirations of people worldwide.	Integrity Tolerance Peace Sustainability Fairness Beauty Trust Social Responsibility
Mastery	• Individualistic pursuits where success is defined in terms of status, power and position. • Individual desires to distinguish him or herself from others by achievement, status, results or respect. • Achievement occurs in the social world, where others can see, value and respect the outcomes of their achievements. • Support winning in competitive situations and being in charge of what is happening. • Seeking power and recognition.	Competence Achievement Recognition Power Excellence Ambition Winning
Self-expression	• Searching for personal challenge, creativity and self-development. • Seek to excel, but not by dominating other people but by doing things that are personally expressive, fostering internal growth. • Hands-on learning, seeking, innovation. Involved in challenging and meaningful projects that require new experiences and development.	Adventure Courage Creativity Curiosity Excitement Learning Personal Freedom Challenge
Inner Development	• Focus on internal states of being • interest in exploration of ways of thinking about life • Curiosity about how one's inside beliefs can affect outside experience • Personal reflection-looking inside rather than looking out. • Looking for truth and wisdom	Forgiveness Spirituality Faith Inner Harmony Personal Growth Self-Respect Open Mindedness Self-Knowledge
Lifestyle	• Focus on achieving personal satisfaction. Emphasis on individual choices about appearance, surroundings and environment. • Support differences in preferences and style seeing quality of life, and expanding one's personal experience.	Health Pleasure Appearance Community Work-Life Balance Play Prosperity Relaxation

(Continued)

Table 22.2 Continued

Tradition	• Knowing where things fit and how people will treat each other.	Tradition
	• Honoring stability, repeatability, connection to established ways.	Stability
	• Preference for continuity rather than change.	Respectfulness
	• Freedom from risk.	Moderation
	• Respecting the way things have been done.	Loyalty
	• Admiration of certainty and predictability.	Conformity
		Consistency
		Security
Relationships	• Reaching out to others.	Belonging
	• Helping and working with others.	Communication
	• Seek contact, communication and community. How others see them is important.	Friendship
		Family
	• Value people working together.	Resolving Conflict
	• Connecting people to each other.	Collaboration
		Teamwork
		Helping

Primary and shadow values

People usually have one or two clusters in the values wheel that contain most of their values. These are their primary clusters. People may find themselves in tension or conflict with people who have values in other clusters. This tension is often generated because these differences are directly opposite on the wheel from your primary clusters. We call that opposite cluster your "shadow", as it represents the values that are most different from your primary values. Because you often have the least experience with that particular cluster(s), you may have the most tension with people who have more of their values in the opposite cluster. The concept of the shadow may help you anticipate and understand potential tensions.

For example, a person with a primary value in the self-expression cluster may find it challenging to interact with a person who has the bulk of their values in the tradition cluster. In an organization, different functions or roles often map to different values clusters; for example, work in finance may have a high value on security and consistency whereas marketing work may have a focus on creativity and winning. When you can see these tensions as reflections of values it provides an opportunity to understand the source of the values tension and helps you align your values with organizational functions and roles.

Rounding out your Values Wheel

As your life changes you may find yourself neglecting several cluster of values. There is no right amount of attention to give to each cluster but you may discover that your shadow area is receiving less attention and focus. Identifying which of the clusters is receiving less attention may help to bring actions to help "round out" your values. This awareness provides the structure to explore how you might increase your attention to values in your shadow cluster. One person referred to the Values Wheel as a wok that was tipped too far to one side, allowing the contents to spill out. People who experience this kind of imbalance often benefit from putting time and attention toward connecting with the values clusters that are underexpressed.

Putting your values into action

How do values get translated into action around your career? Other people, especially those close to us, can help us look at our behavior. They may be better observers of us than we are! Getting feedback from others about how we live each of our values can offer valuable insight to areas for growth or change. Having a discussion about individual and shared values can strengthen the alignment of a team or group. Identifying several core values can help a team focus and enrich their working environment. The values wheel model enables us to think about our own values, and begin the process of identifying work that reflects those values.

Self-assessment activity

Ask someone who you interact with to give you their opinion about the values that they see your behavior expressing. Invite them to give you examples and use this feedback to explore areas of where you could bring your actions into alignment with your values.

Applying values to the workplace

Making a list of values is the first step to enhancing the resilience of the workplace. The next step is to identify more specifically what behaviors support a specific value. Often people use the same words, i.e. "trust", to represent very different actions. Many organizations/teams have values statements but have not realized the maximum benefit that comes from having a shared understanding of what actions they mean when they say they "support" a specific value. In the workplace there is often a broad range of descriptions of what behaviors indicate – for example, "trust" or "teamwork". For example, what behaviors do they consider demonstrate a commitment to "teamwork"? Taking time to identify specific actions that represent the value will help clarify when the value is being demonstrated.

Ask:

- What does it "look like" when this team/organization act in accordance with that value?
- What are the behaviors that indicate that value is being focused on?

Having a discussion with the people in the organization to understand what actions, policies and practices indicate their support of a specific value can provide welcome clarity. These discussions will help you identify a core set of values that are important for you to have in a work environment.

Values are always aspirational

In fact, just about every value is a value because it represents an ideal state. In fact, values are challenging to actually live up to. Fairness, for example, is a common value, but what does it mean for a leader to "treat people fairly"? Is that different from equally? How do you make decisions when there are differences in capability, commitment or history? Identifying actions can help to bring clarity on what actions support and detract from that value. This work of identifying actions/behaviors demonstrates a deeper commitment to values in a team or organization.

Bringing values alignment to your career

When people experience an alignment of values they feel a sense of "fit". The workplace provides a place for these discussions so a culture of clarity and respect can be established. As organizations embark on clarifying their values, it often indicates an interest in forging clarity about the behavior that represents these values. Having these deeper discussions to identify what exactly do values like "commitment", "teamwork" or "respect" mean. For example, an organization where people value teamwork can have a hard time accepting a highly competitive individual who wants to excel at the expense of everyone else.

Personal values support ethical choices

Understanding your personal values provides a strong foundation for making choices. Being able to articulate the cluster of values that make up your values code helps you articulate to others why you are supporting one set of actions over another. Engaging in values-based discussions leads to a more collaborative basis for taking action than just declaring one path or another. The process of discussing the values behind a decision enables teams to understand and reinforce their actions, which builds agility for decision making and taking action in the future.

Design principles for resilient work environments

The convergence of change in the external work environment and the increased pressure from within for satisfaction, meaning, challenge and self-fulfillment has created a set of higher expectations for work environments. This increased awareness and expectations can in some cases lead to feelings of frustration and disengagement. To stay competitive and attract motivated employees, organizations have become more focused on being "the best place to work", providing food, one-stop personal services and an array of wellness and health promotion services. These are often coupled with attention to refining and expressing an organizational set of values and mission so that employees can connect their work to a broader impact. B Corporations, a for-profit corporate structure, authorized by 30 U.S. states and the District of Columbia, enables for-profit companies to include positive impact on society, workers, the community and the environment in addition to profit as legally defined goals. The assessment provides a benchmark for organizations to assess and measure impact of various practices as a foundation for creating more attention on social and cultural factors.

This attention to creating work environments where employees experience a sense of success and satisfaction while at the same time helping the organization provide value to their customers is the emerging "sweet spot" where engagement, productivity and sustainability come together.

Balancing demand and control

There are some structural factors that can contribute to the way the work environment is designed that can provide indications of individual resilience and organizational performance. Looking at these factors is important in identifying potential environments for working and growing a career.

A key research project on Healthy Work (Karasek and Theorell, 1991) identified two key structural variables that impact the well-being of employees – the intensity of demand and the latitude of control. Some work environments seem to be more healthful even when there is considerable demand. How the work is designed and managed plays an important context for individual action. A work role is constructed with two major elements: demand (the amount, pace and complexity of work) and control (the latitude of choice available in completing the work). Karasek and Theorell's extensive research (1991) found that a high demand, low control work environment is more stressful. A person can thrive in a high demand environment if the level of control is increased. To buffer a high-demand role more choice can be given by offering more latitude of pace, sequence and timing as to when and where the work is to be accomplished. Looking at the structure of the work enables an individual to understand the context in which they are to perform. This framework provides a way to think about supporting the increased demand of a 24/7 work environment with an increased ability to structure the response time and focus on results versus hours spent. The Results Only Work Environment (ROWE) (Ressler and Thompson, 2010) focuses on measuring team members by their performance, results or output, not by their presence in the office or the hours that they work. Employees have complete autonomy over their projects, and you allow them the freedom to choose when and how they will meet their goals. This approach provided a framework for rethinking work in a high demand/high control format. The interrelationship between demand and control forms an interesting way to look at the structure of the job/role.

Self-assessment activity

Look at your job and identify the balance between demand and control. What parts of your work represent high demand, low demand? What elements of your work do you have high or low levels of control over?

- *Are their ways to adjust/renegotiate dealing with demands by having more options for where the work gets done?*
- *Are their other metrics that could be added to show the value of your work?*

Understanding the basic elements of success and satisfaction

Because work is such a contributing factor for well-being it is important to look at the markers of personal well-being (hardiness and longevity) for ways to look at finding/creating work that supports personal well-being. A number of studies have looked at how people stay resilient and thrive in challenging environments. Two large-scale studies "The Hardy Executive: Health Under Stress" (Maddi and Kobasa 1984) and "Social Networks, Host Resistance and Mortality" (Kobasa, 1979) provided foundational findings that have influenced the fields of personal well-being and organizational health.

Framework for individual hardiness

People have been curious to understand who thrives in stressful, high-demand environments so they can build design and build more successful organizations. The basis of this literature can be summarized from the literature on individual hardiness (Kobasa, 1979) and social support and health (Berkman, 1979 and 2000). These studies point to four factors – coherence, challenge, control and connection – that provide a simple model for identifying and increasing individual actions and organizational practices that support success and satisfaction. Having a framework to look at individual mindsets and organizational culture provides a way to examine work cultures and organizations (Jaffe, Scott, and Tobe, 1994; Scott and Jaffe, 1997).

The 4Cs hardiness framework

The 4Cs model identifies personal capabilities that must be activated to achieve personal hardiness. It is used here to provide a framework for self-assessment so that a person can identify an organizational environment where one can maintain hardiness.

Coherence

Coherence occurs when people have the ability to make sense of their circumstances in a way that gives them a sense of meaning and significance. Creating this understanding increases an individuals' sense of resilience and hardiness. They have a clear vision about where they are going that is largely in line with their basic values, allowing them to be involved and motivated in their work. Healthy, happy people believe that their work and actions are meaningful (Jaffe, Scott, and Tobe, 1994). They have a sense of purpose, and an awareness of what is important to them (Kobasa, 1979). With this awareness they are committed to their values, their goals and themselves. They create a personal balance, and belief in their ability to make decisions and realize their purpose. Meaning making also occurs when individuals face challenging situations. Happy, healthy people are able to appropriately recognize and manage a challenging event when one presents itself. They have personal resources available – a belief in themselves and their problem-solving skills, for example – to draw upon, and they actively use those resources (Mlonzi and Strümpfer, 1998). They are able to make sense of a challenging situation, and perceive themselves or someone they trust as being in control of the situation. In other words, they possess perceived self-efficacy and self-management resources. They see a reason to apply themselves, and they take action (Bandura, 1995).

Challenge

Challenge represents the ability to set goals and persist in achieving them. It is the ability to self-challenge and feel optimistic about achieving a desired outcome across multiple situations (Latham, 2007). People feel open to learning continually from others about how to do things better and improve their capabilities. They see change as an opportunity to develop their skills and to learn.

Members of a community begin to make progress and are encouraged by the success of others like them. As they make progress, they also share their experiences with others in the social network and influence those people to take their own steps. Finally, a community reaches a tipping point where a shared belief in the ability to truly make a difference on big issues as a group emerges. The "ripple effect" of a single individual prepared to seize on a challenge can be enormous, but it is mediated by social connections.

Control

People who feel in control are able to take action to do what needs to be done to complete their job and achieve their vision. They feel that they have latitude/choice over their how their jobs are structured and completed. Control represents the way healthy, happy people perceive having choice in situations. The concept includes three types of control (Kobasa, 1979) which are related to the concepts of self-efficacy:

- Decisional control – a person's belief that he or she can choose from multiple courses of action
- Cognitive control – being able to see challenges as part of life and anticipating the need to adjust
- Coping skills – the development and application of personal resources

People who feel control in challenging situations feel empowered, whereas those who perceive there is nothing they can do feel powerless. As determined by the concept of self-efficacy, this feeling dramatically affects the degree to which people pursue a desired outcome (Bandura, 2004). As people attempt to make change, they learn from their successes and failures (Bandura, 2006) and they can be taught by experience how to effectively manage failures and persevere. Increasing a sense of personal control frequently occurs through having experiences of mastery. Resiliency results from overcoming obstacles on a path toward change, and eventually mastery is achieved. A resilient individual knows that the effort pays off, and that they can make choices and adapt. They also have a greater ability to cope in the face of challenge, and therefore experience more control in a situation.

Connection

People who are connected feel that they could call on the help and support of other people, and that their coworkers are colleagues, not competitors. Connection represents the degree to which people can call on the help and support of others. The literature on social support demonstrates that connected individuals are more likely to believe in themselves, and to set and maintain behavioral goals (Maes and Karoly, 2005). Effective behavior change programs must stimulate and support positive connection. Through connection, individuals engaged in positive action also improve their families and communities. They make meaning by way of service to others, aspirational goal setting, and gratitude in daily life. These patterns are critical contributors to authentic happiness. Studies show that people are in fact happier with positive family and friend relationships around them (Peterson, 2006). We gain from being connected with our communities, whether through work, religious affiliations, sports teams or some other social group (Scott and Bryson, 2012).

Self-assessment activity

Use the following checklist to identify some of the elements that support personal hardiness. The more examples you check the higher level of hardiness you will have as an individual.

Commitment
- I like what I am doing and the company I work for.
- I wake up eager to start the day's work.

Challenge
- I am excited and energized by new projects.
- I seek new opportunities as an important part of my life.

Control
- I look for things that I can do something about, and I do not waste time and energy getting frustrated about what I cannot do.
- When there are demands at work, I know that trying my best is the most effective approach.

Connection
- I seek out other people when I have a problem.
- I feel that I give as much as I get from other people.

The 4 Cs are core to successful and satisfying careers

These four Cs – commitment, control, challenge, and connection – are all important factors for people who are effective at work. Although each is important in itself, when combined together they form a strong foundation for high performance. Enhancing these elements gives you a way to continually assess and make changes in how you are approaching your career. You can also use these four factors to look at work environments.

Connection between personal and organizational hardiness

To cope with the pressure of constant change, organizations must build work processes and policies that enable more control and choice into work processes and policies and management actions that provide cultures where employees have opportunities to feel connected to the mission of the work.

Because organizations are comprised of people who spend more waking hours in contact with organizational environments than they do with their families, it is possible to think about organizational hardiness as being an extended manifestation of the same components that make up individual hardiness. For example,

- Coherence – organizations that have a clear sense of meaning and vision. There are a strong set of values and agreement about what behavior and actions support their organization. Employees are clear about their role in creating success.
- Challenge – There is a healthy tension about current and aspirational performance. Clear metrics provide feedback about how the organization is doing as a way to keep track of progress.
- Control – Clear decision making is exercised closest to where the work is performed. Employees can participate and share ideas for improvement.
- Connection – Relationships are valued and attention is paid to creating community and engagement.

Self-assessment activity

Use the following checklist to identify some of the elements that support organizational hardiness. The more examples you check the higher level of hardiness will be reflected in your organization.

Commitment
- Does the organization have a clear set of values?
- Is the work of the organization connected to its overall vision?
Challenge
- Are there clear goals and metrics for measurement of success?
- Are there opportunities to develop new skills and capabilities?
Control
- Is there clarity about what each part of the organization is responsible for?
- Is there a process for employees to have input to the way their work is structured?
Connection
- Is there an emphasis on building relationships at work?
- Is there a focus on enhancing community activities at work?

The 4 Cs model of resilience provides a way to build individual capacity and a way to identify organizational environments in which individuals can thrive. These key factors can guide you towards work environments designed for high performance and engagement. Now we will use the process of design thinking to bring together these elements of personal and organizational hardiness to career navigation.

Applying design principles to career navigation

This next part of this chapter highlights how to use design principles – discover, ideate, prototype, refresh – to frame a fresh approach to finding work that is worth doing.

Imagine that you are participating in a design challenge, creating a working environment where you contribute your best. To start, put yourself in the role of the "customer" you are investing a significant amount of your waking hours in work and will bring your best productivity and contribution if you can align yourself with an organization that supports your values and creates the conditions for sustainable performance. The basic foundation of design thinking is to have empathy for yourself in the process, embrace the complexity and the journey. You are looking for deep insights about the core customer –YOU – to translate into a career role designed with your values in mind. If you do not uncover your underlying needs then you will probably repeat unsuccessful and unsatisfying patterns.

Applying what you know about your values can provide strong guidance for assessing where the purpose of the work aligns with your deeply held values. If the "why" of the work does not ignite a strong connection with how you see yourself making a contribution then it might be wise to pass on the commitment. You will probably be able to endure a disconnect with your values for a while but it will eventually wear down your engagement and your contribution will suffer. There are times when you will have to endure values tensions for the fulfillment of larger goals. Acknowledging those tensions can help you stay the course, i.e. to finish school, complete a financial milestone, etc. By casting a wide net and looking at opportunities where your values match and you can grow your capabilities might enable you to find a career that surprises you.

It is important to see there is no one enduring career or work environment. You will need to reconfigure your work several times in your lifetime. The notion that you have a passion is a destructive idea. Instead take on work that invigorates you and that will ignite your true passion. Seeing this process as a design challenge will enable you to bring a fresh look at it each time it emerges. Think of your career as an evolving canvas, shaped by many narratives that match your life stage and opportunities for contribution.

Let's follow a newly graduated MBA in her application of design principles to her career search. Anne has recently graduated with a MBA that emphasized the application of business practices through the frameworks of social, economic and environmental sustainability. She has been using her values to identify positions in social innovation in nonprofit leadership. Her education and work search can be mapped to design principles.

Discover

During her coursework she began to explore work opportunities where her capabilities could produce impact. She asked herself, if anything were possible, what kind of work would give her the most happiness? What kind of organization could make the best use of her capabilities? What were her conditions for an environment where she could be successful?

Ideate

She articulated her vision to find a role where her ability to plan and execute were effective in creating events and garnering media attention. She had a passion for technology and for women's career development. The intersection of these two areas was emerging as an area of strong social innovation and she began to look for organizations that were working on these issues. She discovered a privately held foundation started by a core of women directors thats purpose was to promote women leaders in technology. She jumped at the opportunity to work for a foundation that supported women's careers in science. Her role combined program design and development with developing a strategy for growth.

Prototype

Anne's dream work began with designing and producing a large event that showcased the work of the foundation. Her vision and her ability to plan and execute were effective in creating events and garnering media attention. She had capabilities in process improvement and stakeholder engagement and was excited to bring her skills to grow the organization.

Refresh

After a year of offering her ideas for accelerating growth and articulating impact she discovered that the leaders of the organization had goals that were not as growth-oriented as she originally believed. Her ideas for change and innovation were passed over and her role did not grow. Anne realized that it was time to create a new story; she wanted to make sure that she gathered the learning from her experience and forged some new approaches for working. She discovered that the work environment mattered as well as the mission. She did her best work on a team, with leadership that fostered collaboration. Her leaders were trained in a profession that did not foster collaboration, making it difficult for them to envision the approaches that Anne suggested. She also wanted to contribute to strategy, elevate bigger goals and measure, and was constrained in a role that was more operational than strategic.

On reflection, she found that she would now look for a new opportunity and trade flexibility for a larger amount of accountability and structure and opportunity to have broader professional exposure. She is now taking a longer view – challenging her past pattern of leapfrogging into leadership positions and not having opportunities to grow and develop. She is looking for an environment in a larger organization where she can grow capacity in improving processes, communicating between departments to improve human systems, changing her approach to career development by using design principles to help her overcome her biggest block, thinking there is only one right solution or optimal version for her life, that if you choose wrong you have blown it.

This example shows the interaction between individual values and organizational environment in a way that highlights the importance of having them be in alignment to create an environment of career success and satisfaction.

Design thinking checklist for career navigation

Discover

- Identify your values, strengths, opportunities and your passion.
- Expose yourself to conferences, meet ups, networking where you can talk with others about how they found their way to work that had value for them.
- Starting from strengths – where does you energy naturally focus?
- What kind of environment supports your success?

Ideate

- What kind of work would you do if anything were possible?
- Outline multiple fantasy jobs/careers.
- Cast a wide net to look for opportunities.
- What issue draws your attention?
- What are conditions for your success?
- What ways could you deliver impact and value?
- What would be the biggest contribution you could make to the world?

Prototyping

- Get feedback – specific, broad, deep, from lots of sources.
- What would a day in the life of this work be?
- Start small – adopt a nano-practice – one small behavior that represents your interests.
- Fail forward, get up and learn some more.
- Think of your life as as a canvas for improvisation.
- Interview someone who is doing what you think you might like to do. Ask to shadow them for a day.
- Begin to work in this new area.

Refresh and renew

- Acknowledge that it is time for a shift.
- Believe there are multiple viable options.
- Polish the story that you tell about what you have been doing and what you want to begin.
- Remind yourself of what makes you happy.
- Identify key principles to guide you in your next work.
- Assess how you could deliver value to a system.
- Refresh your understanding of your values.
- What gifts have you come to give?

Conclusion

This chapter has provided a structure, ideas and tools so you can apply design thinking to identifying and creating work and organizations that create sustainable value. You have a model of personal values and ways to apply these to identifying organizations and roles that will match your values. You have also been introduced to a model of individual resilience that can also be used to guide team and organizational development. You have followed an individual who has used design principles to navigate the identification and transition on her path of finding meaningful work. The path to individual and organizational sustainable value requires an ongoing commitment to design based on rapidly changing conditions.

References

Bandura, A. (ed). *Self-Efficacy in Changing Societies*, Cambridge: Cambridge University Press, 1995.
Bandura, A. Health Promotion by Social Cognitive Means. *Health Education and Behavior* 31, 143–64, 2004.

Bandura, A. Going global with social cognitive theory: From prospect to pay dirt, in S. Donaldson, D. Berger and K. Pezdek (eds), *Applied Psychology: New Frontiers and Rewarding Careers*, Mahwah, NJ: Lawrence Erlbaum Associates, 53–79, 2006.

Berkman L.F., Glass T., Brissette I., and Seeman T.E. From Social Integration to Health: Durkheim in the New Millennium. *Soc Sci Med.* 51(6), 843–57, September 2000.

Berkman, L.F., and Glass, T. Social Integration, Social Networks, Social Support and Health, in L. Berkman and I. Kawachi (eds), *Social Epidemiology*, Oxford, UK: Oxford University Press, 137–73, 2000.

Berkman, L.F., and Syme, L. Social Networks, Host Resistance and Mortality. *American Journal of Epidemiology* 109, 186–204, 1979.

Jaffe, D., Scott, C., and Tobe, G. *Rekindling Commitment: How to Revitalize Yourself, Your Work and Your Organization*, San Francisco: Jossey-Bass, 1994.

Karasek, R., and Theorell, T. *Healthy Work*, New York: Basic Books, 1991.

Kobasa, S.C. Stressful Life Events, Personality and Health: An Inquiry Into Hardiness. *Journal of Personality and Social Psychology* 37.I, I–II, 1979.

Latham, G.P. *Work Motivation: History, Theory, Research and Practice*, Thousand Oaks, CA: Sage, 2007.

Maddi, S., and Kobasa, S. *The Hardy Executive: Health Under Stress*, New York: Dow Jones Irwin, 1984.

Maes, S., and Karoly, P. Self Regulation Assessment and Intervention in Physical Health & Illness. *Applied Psychology* 54.2, 267–99, 2005.

Mlonzi, E.N., and Strümpfer, D.J. Antonovsky's Sense of Coherence Scale and 16 PF Second Order Factors. *Social Behavior and Personality* 26, 39–50, 1998.

Peterson, C. *A Primer in Positive Psychology*, Oxford: Oxford University Press, 2006.

Ressler, C., and Thompson, J. *Why Work Sucks and How to Fix It: The Results-Only Revolution*, Penguin USA, 2010.

Rokeach, M. *The Nature of Human Values*, New York: The Free Press, 1973.

Scott, C., and Bryson, A. Waking Up at Work: Sustainability as a Catalyst for Organisational Change. *Journal of Corporate Citizenship* 46, 139–58, June 2012.

Scott, C., and Jaffe, D. *Organizational Vision, Values and Mission: Building the Organization of Tomorrow*, Los Altos, CA: Crisp Publications, 1994.

Scott, C., and Jaffe, D. *Take This Work and Love It*, Los Altos, CA: Crisp Publications, 1997.

Werbach, A. *Strategy for Sustainability: A Business Manifesto*. Boston: Harvard Business Press, 2009.

World Commission on Environment and Development. *Our Common Future*, Oxford: Oxford University Press, 1987.

PART 4

Design for behaviour change

Part 4 of the *Handbook of Sustainable Design* probes how design influences our behaviors, habits, and actions. As previous parts have illustrated, the field of design comprises more than mere objects and products. We can make the most "eco-friendly" products, but if we do not use them as intended within its system, our efforts are futile, or worse, detrimental. Part 4 provides an in-depth look at determinants that shape human behavior. Understanding how to design with human behavior in mind has the potential for an enormous impact on environmental sustainability.

Casper Boks begins this section with *An introduction to design for sustainable behaviour* where he provides an overview of the development of Design for Sustainable Behaviour (DfSB) as a research field. This introductory chapter provides context for how the area of study has evolved over the past decade to incorporate and focus on user behavior in the design process. Boks provides case studies and methodological frameworks to apply to the process. "Addressing how and why people interact with products, services, and systems the way they do" is a vital part of understanding how we can design more sustainably.

Directly related to understanding behavior, is an understanding of habit – the many repetitive actions we do every day that add up to have a profound impact on either end of the sustainability spectrum. In *How design influences habits*, Tang Tang and Seahwa Won use psychological and sociological perspectives to explore habit in the context of sustainability. In addition to explaining the importance of behavior patterns, they also provide a number of design strategies aimed at changing habits.

Many factors influence our understanding of actions and therefore, how to design for behavior change. Emotion, rhetoric, data visualization, psychology, culture, architecture, and community design are just some of the topics that help us understand behavior on a deeper level. The remaining chapters within Part 4 explore these themes.

The temporal fallacy: design and emotional obsolescence by Jonathan Chapman and Giovanni Marmont presents a perspective on "how a deeper understanding of acts of use might be helpful in extending both the physical and emotional durability of products." Unlike other chapters, this text provides a theoretical approach to understanding emotion through our relationships with objects. Weaving together design theory and philosophy, Chapman and Marmont explore how users, products, and these person-thing relationships change over time. Subsequently, they present us with questions on how to design for these ever-changing relationships.

Our rhetoric often guides our behavior. Understanding how language influences us enriches our understanding of actions and our ability to design for positive behavior change in the future. Marilyn DeLaure's *Discourse design: the art of rhetoric and the science of persuasion* provides an overview of key concepts in rhetoric and persuasion within the context of sustainability. Case studies throughout the chapter highlight the power that word choice has over our actions.

Data visualization is a tool that helps us understand the past and project scenarios in the future. By making visual data available to people they can make more informed decisions. In *Using data visualization to shift behaviors*, Adam Nieman presents ways that designers can use data visualization to "nudge whole populations to change the way they act."

Despite knowing the vast and dire impacts of climate change on our planet, most people do little to change their behaviors to live a more sustainable lifestyle. Allison Ford and Kari Marie Norgaard present *Securing sustainability: culture and emotions as barriers to environmental change*. Using research studies from both Norway and the United States, Ford and Norgaard explain that knowledge is not enough to change behavior. Their work has uncovered that "responses to environmental danger [are] deeply connected to cultural perceptions of self in relation to social others, and the emotional response that information about environmental risk elicited." Understanding culture and one's place within it gives designers a broader understanding of contexts within sustainable design.

The design of cities and the spaces within them influence how people live and behave. In their chapter, *Nature-based design for health and well-being in cities*, Angela Reeve, Cheryl Desha, and Omniua El Baghdadi push this idea even further. They argue that urban design should not simply influence behavior, but should "directly and intentionally influence the health and well-being of people living in cities." By expanding the definition of sustainable design to include "well-being," the authors explain how nature-based design enhances personal and collective well-being to create sustainable environments.

The ideas in the chapters interweave and impact one another. Rhetoric informs how we visualize data. Emotion clarifies psychology and culture. Environmental design influences and is influenced by our emotions. An understanding of the many nuances of behavior empowers designers to inspire positive behavioral change through their work.

23

AN INTRODUCTION TO DESIGN FOR SUSTAINABLE BEHAVIOUR

Casper Boks

Introduction

Traditionally, research on design for sustainability (or sustainable product design, or eco-design, or green design) has had a very technological focus. Research groups around the world (but mainly in Northern Europe, the United States, Australia and Japan) focused in the late 1990s and early 2000s mostly on product end-of-life issues, calculating optimal disassembly sequences, making material compatibility matrices, and doing the odd life-cycle assessment to gain insight in trade-offs between designing lighter battery-powered or heavier human-powered radios – to name an example. Peculiarly enough, the user was mostly ignored, even though we now know that users can make or break a designer's good intentions. Why this omission? It is not illogical to hypothesize that this was mainly because of two reasons: legislation at this time was heavily focused on end-of-life, with production coming in second. And that is also where manufacturers of products can be and were increasingly held responsible, so no surprise that that is where most of the industrial attention was directed. Production and end-of-life is also where technology and engineering can help out. Which brings us to the second reason: this was an engineer's domain, and engineers are not particularly known for their interest and insight into the user perspective – compared to designers at least. Design strategies addressing aspects of the use phase had of course been considered from the early days of design for sustainability, in tools like the Life Cycle Design Strategy Wheel. But most of these strategies were likewise based on indirect material and end-of-life considerations; lifetime extension for example appealed to postponing the end-of-life stage, and avoiding the need for material use. Reduction of energy use focused on using technologies requiring less energy consumption. There was nothing related on behavior. This is also reflected in Figure 23.1: a simple search on Scopus, using "sustainable behaviour" (including the American spelling "sustainable behavior") as search term, illustrates the increase of attention in recent years, from almost zero publications until 2005 to well over 100 in 2015.

So, a lot has changed in the past decade. With user experience design gaining attention as a research area (which, one could argue, has occurred simultaneous with, but until 2005 mostly separate from, design for sustainability, which also originates from the early 1990s), design researchers were increasingly exposed to tools and methods to understand user behavior in relation to products and environments. This has contributed to the development of a research field that we today refer to as Design for Sustainable Behaviour (DfSB). This chapter aims to provide

Documents by year

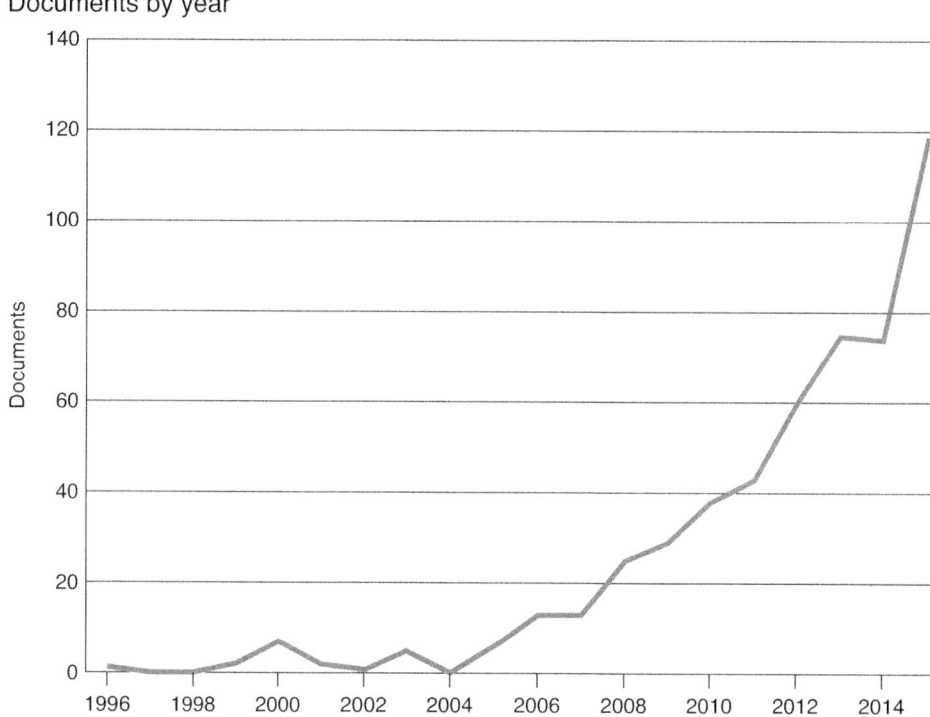

Figure 23.1 Development of scientific articles in Scopus related to "design for sustainable behaviour."

a concise overview of the development of this field, and is framed in a way that readers will be able to identify further literature on the topic that will be of interest to them.

Early inspiration

Figure 23.1 suggests that the story should begin around 2005, which is true in a sense, as around that time, sustainable behavior became a research topic in design research. But these early researchers, for example at Loughborough University in the United Kingdom and Delft University of Technology in The Netherlands, took insights from earlier work such as Jaap Jelsma, a science and technology studies scholar who in 1997 placed social scientist Madeleine Akrich's concept of 'script' within the context of attempting to reduce environmental impact through the way people interact with products (Jelsma, 1997). The idea behind a script is that the designer inscribes a kind of intuitive guide into a product that guides the user on how to use the product (Jelsma, 1997). The idea is similar to Norman's concept of affordances (Norman, 1988) and was introduced in sustainable design literature by Jelsma and Knot in 2002 (Jelsma and Knot, 2002), with applications in the white goods sector (washing machines and dryers) as well as in a service context.

Another source of inspiration for the increased focus on end-user perspectives may be found in Product-Service System (PSS research) which originates from the 1990s. This field was inspired by an understanding that in order to reach substantial sustainability improvements (in those days often referred to as 'Factor 10' improvements), a focus on final consumers and their interactions with business clients along the entire value chain would be instrumental to determine the degrees of freedom to radically design value propositions (Tukker and Tischner, 2006). These would not be limited to purchase only, but should also include use and end-of-life, opening up for solutions based on sharing and services.

Case studies in design for sustainable behaviour

As Design for Sustainable Behaviour as an academic field of interest began to gain momentum, a growing body of researchers consequently explored a broader academic landscape and incorporated insights from a much wider range of fields that had been occupied with understanding the attitudes and behaviour that people have towards the environment. Much of this literature is reviewed in Jackson (2004), Shove (2010), and Stern (2000) and includes a range of different approaches including social psychological, sociological and economic perspectives on behaviour (Eppel et al., 2013). This chapter will not address these insights in detail, but will focus on the design literature which gradually became more informed by them.

Within the Design for Sustainable Behaviour research community, Debra Lilley's doctoral dissertation from 2007 titled "Designing for Behavioural Change: Reducing the Social Impacts of Product Use Through Design" (Lilley, 2007) may be regarded as the first one within this field. Lilley continued with Jelsma's insights on how to influence user interaction with products through inscribing scripts using design, by proposing three types of design principles with varying degrees of how strongly they affected behaviour; from Ecofeedback to Behaviour Steering to using intelligent products and systems that control user behaviour towards desired patterns. This was the basis for much for future research within Design for Sustainable Behaviour, as this created a scale where, on one end, users are in complete control and can choose to read and interpret the eco-feedback, and further choose to alter their behaviour accordingly or not. On the other end of the scale, users are forced to behave the desired way by 'intelligent' products or systems. This work marked the start of an effort that focused on, as Pettersen et al. (2013) describe it, mapping the opportunities for design by screening literature from a variety of disciplines for potentially relevant design strategies. These strategies included concepts such as feedback intervention theory (Kluger and DeNisi, 1996), persuasion (e.g. Cialdini, 1993), scripts (Akrich, 1992), affordances (Gibson, 1979; Norman, 1988), critical design (Dunne, 1995) and emotional durability (Muis, 2006). They range from information provision, feedback and choices intended to make people reflect, to technological persuasion, steering and force, and eventually resulted in the control-obtrusiveness landscape (see the next section, Figure 23.2). In these years, small-scale empirical studies were done that informed the theoretical work. Daae and Boks (2015a) provide an overview of 27 DfSB case studies up to 2013. Though very few studies report an entire process, including the identification and investigation of unsustainable behavior, an evaluation of possible ways of improving it, and measuring environmental gains of changed behaviour at all, several of the case studies have had a clear impact on the field. The most cited case studies include behaviour related to choice of preferred washing machine programs (McCalley and Midden, 2002), switching off electrical appliances (Rodriguez and Boks, 2005), socially sustainable mobile phone use (Lilley, 2007), and behaviour related to leaving the door of a refrigerator open too long (Elias, 2011). These studies used a variety of user-centred research methods, such as diaries, interviews, surveys and video observation, and generally concluded with suggestions for product-oriented design interventions. These suggestions covered the entire scale referred to previously, ranging from informing and giving feedback to the user to more persuasive and steering strategies to (forcing) design interventions where the product is in complete control. For the mentioned case studies, examples of providing information and feedback included advice on how to use mobile

Table 23.1 A non-exhausive overview of DfSB case studies, sorted by everyday practice

Using various appliances	Rodriguez and Boks, 2005
	Pettersen, 2013
	Laschke et al., 2015
Using refrigerators/freezers	Elias, 2011
	Tang and Bhamra, 2012
Vacuum cleaning	Sauer et al., 2002, 2004
Using energy meters and smart grids	Wever et al., 2008
	Selvefors et al., 2013
	Kobus et al., 2015
	Geelen et al., 2012, 2013
	Van Dam et al., 2010
Laundry	McCalley and Midden, 2002
	Kobus et al., 2013
	Spencer et al., 2015a
	Spencer et al., 2015b
	Laitala et al., 2012
	McCalley et al., 2011
Wood stove use	Daae et al., 2016
Bathing	Scott et al., 2012
	Matsuhashi et al., 2009
	Pink and Mackley, 2015
	Kuijer, 2014
Cooking	de Jong and Mazé, 2010
	Oliveira et al., 2016
Thermal comfort	Kuijer and de Jong, 2012
	Pettersen, 2013
	Wilson, 2013
	Renström, 2013
	Revell and Stanton, 2016
Clothing use	Niinimäki, 2010
	Niinimäki and Hassi, 2011
	Laitala and Boks, 2012
	Laitala et al., 2012
	Laitala, 2014

phones in a socially accepted way, and real life feedback on power consumption via a TV remote control. Examples of more enabling persuasive and steering strategies included showing signs of embarrassment on the mobile phone display, and the option to set personal goal setting in relation to the right choice of washing programs. Good examples of a forcing strategy are the use of a glass refrigerator door, avoiding the need for it to be open for the purpose of looking what is in stock, or a TV shutting off when a motion sensor has detected that a user has not been around for a certain about of time. The overview by Daae and Boks referred to earlier gives many more examples of application of the various strategies.

To date, a number of substantial case studies have been published that have extensively addressed one particular type of unsustainable behavior. Table 23.1 provides a (non-exhaustive) list of case studies, mostly published in established journals, sorted by type of behavior of practices. This list provides a good starting point for designers and researchers that want to study specific practices; it is recommended to check references used in these articles, and to check which future publications refer to them. The table overlaps partly with the aforementioned overview of case studies provided by Daae and Boks (2015a), where more details can be found.

Methodological frameworks

Design with intent tool kit

Using these and other case studies both for inspiration and validation, DfSB researchers have developed methodological frameworks and tools, mostly with the aim to make designers aware of the degrees of freedom in findings solutions, and to inform them with design strategies to nudge users in a direction of preferred, sustainable behavior. Perhaps the most widely acknowledge tool, the Design with Intent Tool kit, was developed by Dan Lockton et al. (2010). He collected 101 patterns of how design may influence behaviour, distinguishing between eight different lenses of how to look at behavior change challenges:

- Architectural lens – How can physical aspects of a design guide behavior, for example by using a slanting surface to avoid that people place things on top of it?
- Error proofing lens – as in including a double-check, to avoid undesirable habitual or automatic behavior.
- Interaction lens – where interaction with a product may affect behavior, such as using feedback, progress bars and previews.
- Ludic lens – making desirable behavior tempting by making it fun
- Perceptual lens – using for example semantics and semiotics to let the product communicate with the user, giving meaning and guiding correct use
- Cognitive lens - for example using concepts of guilt, or desire for order, or authority to influence how users make decisions.
- Machiavellian lens – includes a number of rather manipulative, sometimes even unethical strategies, like manipulating the number of choices a user can make.
- Security lens – including, for example, the use of surveillance or passwords to ensure desirable behaviour.

For each lens, Lockton collected examples and presented them on a separate card, with a question pointing out the function of the pattern and an example of an application of the pattern with a short description and a picture (Lockton et al., 2010). Though not intended as a methodology but rather as an inspiration tool, the Design with Intent (DWI) card deck provides an easy to understand and use way to intuitively start to understand challenges and solutions related to sustainable behavior, as well as a low-threshold approach to apply this into practical ideation and conceptualization processes.

The design behaviour intervention model

A well-cited theoretical framework for how to design for sustainable behaviour was developed at the Loughborough University School of Design. The Design Behaviour Intervention Model (DBIM) (Tang, 2012) is the result of an iterative development at this school (Bhamra et al., 2008; Tang and Bhamra, 2008). The model suggests the type of behaviour-changing design principles that should be applied at different stages of a behaviour change process and in particular in the formation of habits, by combining a number of different theoretical models. It combines Triandis' theory of interpersonal behaviour (Triandis, 1977), Anderson's theory of development of cognitive skills (Anderson, 1982) and design strategies along the distribution of control (Lilley, 2009), and points out the level of forcefulness and points of intervention. The model was applied in a case study, demonstrating the feasibility of reducing environmental impacts by modifying consumer behaviour of using a refrigerator. Though the theoretical nature of the model may make it less suitable for application in practical design projects (Daae, 2014), Tang and Bhamra report that the "DBIM has been shown to be a useful and inspirational tool for gaining deeper understanding of consumers and making informed decisions about which strategies to apply" (Tang and Bhamra, 2012). The work has further inspired successive PhD-level research at Loughborough University on various aspects of DfSB methodology development (Hanratty, 2015; Wilson, 2013), also including DfSB application in different cultural contexts (Elizondo, 2011; Spencer, 2014).

The principles of behaviour change

The principles of behaviour change (Zachrisson and Boks, 2012) is a DfSB approach based on insights from behavioural psychology that aims at helping designers to make informed decisions about which design principles to apply when aiming to achieve a desired behaviour change for a target group. It suggest the consideration of a variety of user-centred research methods, depending on which aspects of the user may be of particular interest given the behaviour to be studied (Daae and Boks, 2015b). The core of the principles of behaviour change is to identify the most promising types of design principles that may positively influence user behavior. It makes use of a landscape that allows sorting design principles based on two parameters: the degree of control that a product allows the user to have over his or her behaviour and the degree of subtlety or obtrusiveness that is designed into the solution (Figure 23.2).

Previous research (Zachrisson and Boks, 2011, 2012) revealed these two dimensions to be important ways to distinguish between design principles, but a substantial amount of additional dimensions may assist distinguishing between and selecting design principles (Daae and Boks, 2014, 2017). The idea behind it is that some design principles likely will work better for certain users and in certain situations than for/in others. In order to appropriately select feasible design principles for different groups of users with similar characteristics, a variety of user research methods can be used. An extensive overview of tools and their suggested application is provided by Daae and Boks (2015b). The approach was applied in one of the most extensive DfSB case studies reported in literature, which is about addressing design interventions to make the use of a wood stove more sustainable. Based on the insight that the use of woodstoves for spatial heating in Norwegian homes contributes significantly to emissions, and at the same time is very behavior

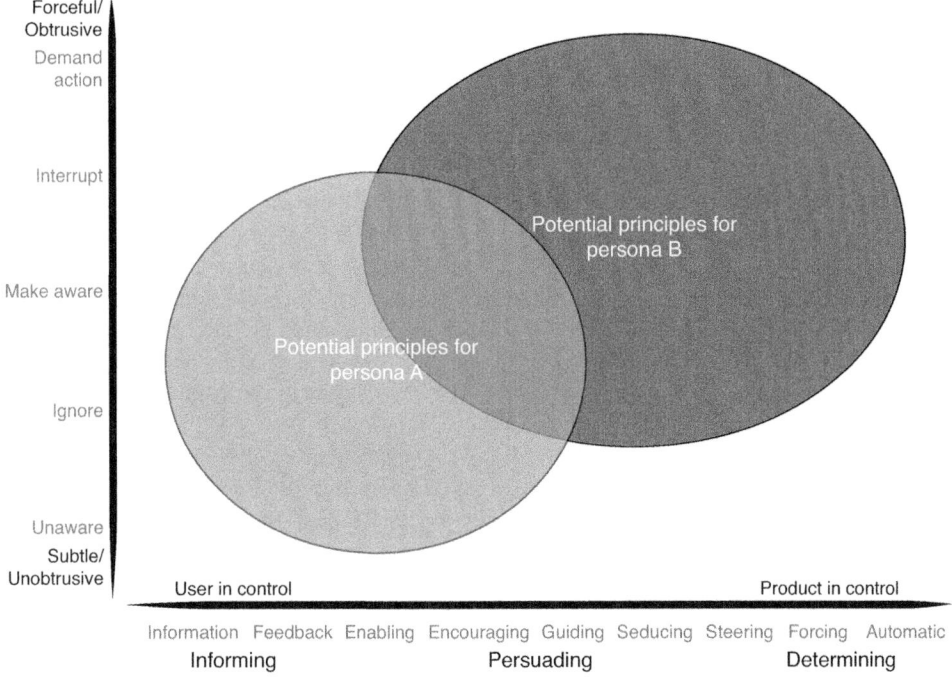

Figure 23.2 Control-obtrusiveness landscape.

dependent, the case study covered an entire DfSB process from extensive ethnographic studies, user-centred design informed behavioural psychology to a comparative testing of a prototype and a regular wood stove monitoring emissions and user behaviour. The prototype included a simple user interface, intuitively explaining the relation between temperature of the fire and the need to adjust airflow, giving the user a limited set of options to adjust ventilation. It was based on the understanding that a significant amount of wood stove users do not understand how airflow and temperature in the different stages of the burning process affect the quality of the fire and they consequently make wrong decisions in how to start and maintain a wood stove fire. The study indicated that the prototype was used more in line with the recommendations for efficient igniting and maintaining the wood burning, and that the resulting behavior resulted in less fine particles emitted compared to a conventional stove (Daae et al., 2016).

Based on a figure with two dimensions (from hidden to apparent influence, and from strong to weak influence), Tromp et al. (2011) distinguished four types of influence (decisive, coercive, seductive and persuasive) that a designer can employ when designing interventions for sustainable behaviour. Based on this framework, they proposed 11 design strategies across this landscape that may help designers to find the right 'dosage' of salience and force to influence user behavior. They also addressed social implications that these strategies may imply. Tang, Daae and Tromp are some examples of what has become discussed as the behaviour-oriented or interaction-oriented design approach for sustainable use. This type of approach typically draws from behavioural psychology to understand (un)sustainable behaviour, placing individual human beings centre stage. It contributes with concepts for understanding how behaviour is motivated by internal and external determinants, and how the desire to choose more environmentally friendly ways of behaving can be initiated and enhanced in the direct interaction with products (Daae, 2014;

Strömberg, 2015; Wilson, 2013). Researchers that favour drawing on sociology, in particular social practice theory, have criticized this approach. They advocate a broad, relational perspective, not studying individuals but practices consisting of material elements, competence and meaning (Kuijer, 2014; Pettersen, 2013; Shove et al., 2012) and how they develop in space and time following shared ideas about what is normal. It is however said to lack applicability in a guiding design processes (Kuijer, 2014), possibly making it the less popular as a topic of study in design research. However, several researchers advocate that positioning practice- and behaviour-oriented approaches against each other is counterproductive; that designers are inherently magpies, picking up whatever little bits of knowledge and theory might help to gain meaning and develop successful solutions; and that both theoretical viewpoints can be useful to achieve this, and each can inform the other (Boks et al., 2015). A third approach to guide the investigation into what people do and why has been suggested by Strömberg (2015). She states that the primary concern for the designer should be to support meaningful human activities in everyday contexts, and that neither of the two perspectives recounts behaviour change at that level, as practice theory does not acknowledge agency with the individual, and the psychological perspective tends to see the context only as constraints. She therefore proposes the use of activity theory as a framework for understanding individuals and their everyday activities in relation to the real world. Activity theory is based on work in the field of human-computer interaction, and was proposed by Norman (2005) as an improved version of user-centred design, but has so far not been explored in the context of design for sustainable behaviour, other than by Strömberg (2015).

Design for sustainable behaviour today

Today, DfSB has evolved into a research area of substantial interest which investigates, at various levels, how to influence the sustainability impact of consumers' lifestyles, through studying their behavior and the practices, developed over time and in space, that are the basis of this behaviour. Figure 23.3 visualizes and summarizes the (arguably) most relevant dissertations as well as the most cited articles in design literature, visualizing the development of DfSB as a field of academic interest. It should be noted that the figure represents a very Northern European perspective, which is here justified by the fact that the bulk of DfSB literature originates from a limited number of Northern European universities. Adjacent fields, such as sustainable human-computer interaction (HCI), critical design and persuasive technology focus on similar research questions, are perhaps more prominent in Northern America, but do not generally affiliate themselves with DfSB – perhaps the geographic distance, but also the fact that these are rooted in computer sciences rather than design sciences, contribute to that.

The previous sections highlight how, in that relatively very short time, insights have broadened from 'why didn't we think of this before' to a range of proposed tools, methods, an increasing (but still small) amount of case studies, and insights of how this field could, should, and even must develop further. The contours of the research area, and community, become rapidly more vague, as nowadays social practice theorists, behavioural psychologists, technology philosophers, persuasive technologists, nudgers, design thinkers and even design practitioners (pun intended) address the challenges of improving sustainability in society through addressing how and why people interact with products, services and systems the way they do. Many products for sale today feature elements that may nudge users in the right direction, and most probably the majority of these products have been developed without any specific awareness of the existing body of research in this area. On the other hand, the community dares to say that without this upsurge in attention for (sustainable) behavior change in design, and in design research, many of these products would not have emerged.

Dissertations related to Design for Sustainable Behaviour	2005	Rodriguez, E., & Boks, C. (2005). How design of products affects user behaviour and vice versa: the environmental implications.
	2006	Lilley, D. et al. (2005). Towards instinctive sustainable product use.
Debra Lilley (2007)	2007	
		Wever, R. et al. (2008). User-centred design for sustainable behaviour.
	2008	Lockton, D. et al. (2008). The Design with Intent Method: A design tool for influencing user behaviour.
	2009	Lilley, D. et al. (2009). Design for sustainable behaviour: strategies and perceptions.
	2010	
		Bhamra, T., et al. (2011). Design for Sustainable Behaviour: Using products to change consumer behaviour
Edward Elias (2011) Gloria Elizondo (2011)	2011	Tromp, N. et al. (2011). Design for socially responsible behavior: a classification of influence based on intended user experience.
	2012	Scott, K., Bakker, C., & Quist, J. (2012). Designing change by living change.
		2012 Special issue Journal of Design Research 10(1-2)
Ida Nilstad Pettersen (2013) Dan Lockton (2013)	2013	*2013 Special issure ACM Transactions on Computer-Human Interaction (TOCHI) 20(4)*
Johannes Zachrisson Daae (2014) Jak Spencer (2014) Lenneke Kuijer (2014) Garrath Wilson (2014) Nynke Tromp (2014)	2014	
Helena Strömberg (2015) Marcus Hanratty (2015)	2015	*Special issue International Journal of Sustainable Engineering 8(3)*
Charlotte Kobus (2016)	2016	*Key journal papers and special journal issues*

Figure 23.3   A visualization of key dissertations and journal papers on DfSB.

Many of those that regard themselves "designers for sustainable behavior", as well as those that by no means want to be associated with that term, have put forward ideas of what will be required to bring this field further, and closer to real life. From a theoretical perspective, common terminology and research protocols (Boks, 2012), more practice and less behaviour orientation (Kuijer, 2014; Pettersen, 2013), integration into life-cycle assessment or vice versa (Daae and Boks, 2015a) are just a few of such ideas. But more focus on the integration of DfSB thinking in industry is seen as the most important research priority. More case studies with testing and evaluation, industry implementation are called for, as is the exploration of cases that include multiple actors relevant to design and use of interventions (energy utilities, the public sector, NGOs, etc.) (Boks et al., 2015).

References

Akrich, M. (1992). 'The de-scription of technical objects', in Bijker, W. and Law, J. (Eds.) *Shaping Technology, Building Society: Studies in Sociotechnical Change*, MIT Press, Cambridge, MA, pp 205–224.

Anderson, J.R. (1982). 'Acquisition of cognitive skill', *Psychological Review*, vol 89 No 4, pp 369–403.

Bhamra, T., and Lilley, D. (2015). 'Editorial IJSE special issue: Design for sustainable behaviour'. *International Journal of Sustainable Engineering*, vol 8, No 3, pp 146–147.

Bhamra, T., Lilley, D., and Tang, T. (2008). 'Sustainable use: Changing consumer behaviour through product design'. Paper presented at the Changing the Change: Design Visions, Proposals and Tools, Turin, Italy, July 10–12.

Bhamra, T., Lilley, D., and Tang, T. (2011). 'Design for sustainable behaviour: Using products to change consumer behaviour'. *The Design Journal*, vol 14, No 4, pp 427–445.

Boks, C. (2012). 'Design for sustainable behaviour research challenges', in M. Matsumoto, Y. Umeda, K. Masui and S. Fukushige (Eds.) *Design for Innovative Value Towards a Sustainable Society*, Springer, Netherlands, pp 328–333.

Boks, C., and Daae, J. (2013a). 'Towards an increased user focus in life cycle engineering'. Re-engineering Manufacturing for Sustainability. Proceedings of the 20th CIRP International Conference on Life Cycle Engineering, Singapore, 17–19 April 2013.

Boks, C., and Daae, J. (2013b). 'From teaching sustainable product design toteaching sustainable behaviour design'. Proceedings of Cumulus 2013, The 2nd International Conference for Design Education Researchers, Oslo, May 14–17.

Boks, C., Lilley, D., and Pettersen, I. (2015). 'The future of design for sustainable behaviour, revisited'. Proceedings of Ecodesign2015, December 2015, Tokyo, Japan.

Boks, C., and McAloone, T.C. (2009). 'Transitions in sustainable product design research'. *International Journal of Product Development*, vol 9, No 4, pp 429–449.

Cialdini, R.B. (1993). *Influence: The Psychology of Persuasion*, William Morrow and Company, New York.

Daae, J. (2014). 'Informing design for sustainable behaviour'. Doctoral dissertation, Norwegian University of Science and Technology.

Daae, J., and Boks, C. (2014). 'Dimensions of behaviour change'. *Journal of Design Research*, vol 12, No 3, pp 145–172.

Daae, J., and Boks, C. (2015a). 'Opportunities and challenges for addressing variations in the use phase with LCA and design for sustainable behaviour'. *International Journal of Sustainable Engineering*, vol 8, No 3, pp 148–162.

Daae, J., and Boks, C. (2015b). 'A classification of user research methods for design for sustainable behaviour'. *Journal of Cleaner Production*, vol 106, pp 680–689.

Daae, J., and Boks, C. (2017). 'Tweaking the interaction – By understanding the user', in Clune, S. (Ed.) *Design for Behaviour Change*, Ashgate/Gower, to be published in 2017.

Daae, J., Goile, F., Seljeskog, M., and Boks, C. (2016). 'Burning for sustainable behaviour'. *Journal of Design Research*, vol 14, No 1, pp 42–65.

Dam, S.S. van, Bakker, C., and van Hal, J. (2010). 'Home energy monitors: Impact over the medium-term'. *Building Research & Information*, vol 38, No 5, pp 458–469.

Dunne, A. (1995). *Hertzian Tales: Electronic Products, Aesthetic Experience, and Critical Design*, MIT Press, Cambridge, MA.

Elias, E. (2011). 'User efficient design – Reducing the environmental impact of user behaviour through the design of products'. Doctoral Dissertation, University of Bath.

Elizondo, G.M. (2011). 'Designing for sustainable behaviour in cross-cultural contexts: A design framework'. Doctoral dissertation, Loughborough University, UK.

Eppel, S., Sharp, V., and Davies, L. (2013). 'A review of Defra's approach to building an evidence base for influencing sustainable behaviour'. *Resources, Conservation and Recycling*, vol 79, pp 30–42.

Geelen, D., Keyson, D., Boess, S., and Brezet, H. (2012). 'Exploring the use of a game to stimulate energy saving in households'. *Journal of Design Research*, vol 10, No 1–2, pp 102–120.

Geelen, D., Reinders, A., and Keyson, D. (2013). 'Empowering the end-user in smart grids: Recommendations for the design of products and services'. *Energy Policy*, vol 61, pp 151–161.

Gibson, J.J. (1979). *The Ecological Approach to Visual Perception*, Houghton Mifflin, Boston.

Hanratty, M. (2015). 'Design for Sustainable Behaviour: A conceptual model and intervention selection model for changing behaviour through design'. Doctoral dissertation, Loughborough University, UK.

Jackson, T. (2004). 'Motivating sustainable consumption: A review of evidence on consumer behaviour and behaviour change'. Sustainable Development Research Network, London.

Jelsma, J. (1997). 'Philosophy Meets Design'. Shortened version of a paper for presentation at the Annual Meeting of the Society for Social Studies of Science, Tucson, Arizona, USA, October 23–26.

Jelsma, J., and Knot, M. (2002). 'Designing environmentally efficient services: A "script" approach'. *The Journal of Sustainable Product Design*, vol 2, pp 119–130.

Jong, A. de, and R. Mazé. 2010. 'Cultures of sustainability: "Ways of doing" cooking'. Proceedings of the Knowledge Collaboration and Learning for Sustainable Innovation ERSCP-EMSU Conference, Delft, The Netherlands, October 25–29.

Klöckner, C., and Matthies, E. (2004). 'How habits interfere with norm-directed behaviour: A normative decision-making model for travel mode choice'. *Journal of Environmental Psychology*, vol 24, No 3, pp 319–327.

Kluger, A., and DeNisi, A. (1996). 'The effects of feedback interventions on performance: A historical review, a meta-analysis, and a preliminary feedback intervention theory'. *Psychological Bulletin*, vol 119, No 2, pp 254–284.

Kobus, C.B., Mugge, R., and Schoormans, J.P. (2013). 'Washing when the Sun is shining! How users interact with a household energy management system'. *Ergonomics*, vol 56, No 3, pp 451–462.

Kobus, C.B., Mugge, R., and Schoormans, J.P. (2015). 'Long-term influence of the design of energy management systems on lowering household energy consumption'. *International Journal of Sustainable Engineering*, vol 8, No 3, pp 173–185.

Kuijer, L., and Bakker, C. (2015). 'Of chalk and cheese: Behaviour change and practice theory in sustainable design'. *International Journal of Sustainable Engineering*, vol 8, No 3, pp 219–230.

Kuijer, L., and de Jong, A. (2012). 'Identifying design opportunities for reduced household resource consumption: Exploring practices of thermal comfort'. *Journal of Design Research*, vol 10, No 1/2, pp 67–85.

Kuijer, S.C. (2014). 'Implications of social practice theory for sustainable design'. Doctoral dissertation, TU Delft, Delft University of Technology.

Laitala, K. (2014). 'Consumers' clothing disposal behaviour – A synthesis of research results'. *International Journal of Consumer Studies*, vol 38, No 5, pp 444–457.

Laitala, K., and Boks, C. (2012). 'Sustainable clothing design: Use matters'. *Journal of Design Research*, vol 10, No 1–2, pp 121–139.

Laitala, K., Boks, C., and Klepp, I.G. (2011). 'Potential for environmental improvements in laundering'. *International Journal of Consumer Studies*, vol 35, No 2, pp 254–264.

Laitala, K., Klepp, I.G., and Boks, C. (2012). 'Changing laundry habits in Norway'. *International Journal of Consumer Studies*, vol 36, No 2, pp 228–237.

Laschke, M., Diefenbach, S., and Hassenzahl, M. (2015). 'Annoying, but in a nice way: An inquiry into the experience of frictional feedback'. *International Journal of Design*, vol 9, No 2, pp 129–140.

Lilley, D. (2007). 'Designing for behavioural change: Reducing the social impacts of product use through design'. Doctoral dissertation, Loughborough University.

Lilley, D. (2009). 'Design for sustainable behaviour: Strategies and perceptions'. *Design Studies*, vol 30, No 6, pp 704–720.

Lilley, D., and Wilson, G.T. (2013). 'Integrating ethics into design for sustainable behaviour'. *Journal of Design Research*, vol 11, No 3, pp 278–299.

Lilley, D., Lofthouse, V.A., and Bhamra, T.A. (2005). 'Towards instinctive sustainable product use'. 2nd International Conference in Sustainability, Creating the Culture, 2–4 November, Aberdeen, UK.

Lockton, D. (2013). 'Design with intent: A design pattern toolkit for environmental and social behaviour change'. Doctoral dissertation, Brunel University School of Engineering and Design.

Lockton, D., Harrison, D., and Stanton, N.A. (2010). 'The design with intent method: A design tool for influencing user behaviour'. *Applied Ergonomics*, vol 41, No 3, pp 382–392.

Lockton, D., Harrison, D., and Stanton, N.A. (2012). 'Models of the user: Designers' perspectives on influencing sustainable behaviour'. *Journal of Design Research*, vol 10, No 1–2, pp 7–27.

Matsuhashi, N., L. Kuijer, and A. de Jong. (2009). 'A culture-inspired approach to gaining insights for designing sustainable practices.' Proceedings of the EcoDesign 2009 Conference, Sapporo, Japan, December 7–9.

McCalley, L., de Vries, P.W., and Midden, C. (2011). 'Consumer response to product-integrated energy feedback: Behavior, goal level shifts, and energy conservation'. *Environment and Behavior*, vol 43, No 4, pp 525–545.

McCalley, L., and Midden, C. (2002). 'Energy conservation through product-integrated feedback: The roles of goal-setting and social orientation'. *Journal of Economic Psychology*, vol 23, No 5, pp 589–603.

Muis, H. (2006). 'Eternally yours: Some theory and practice on cultural sustainable product development', in Verbeek, P.-P. and Slob, A. (Eds.) *User Behavior and Technology Development*, Springer, Berlin, pp 277–293.

Niinimäki, K. (2010). 'Eco-clothing, consumer identity and ideology'. *Sustainable Development*, vol 18, No 3, pp 150–162.

Niinimäki, K., and Hassi, L. (2011). 'Emerging design strategies in sustainable production and consumption of textiles and clothing'. *Journal of Cleaner Production*, vol 19, No 16, pp 1876–1883.

Norman, D.A. (1988). *The Design of Everyday Things*, Doubleday/Currency, New York.

Norman, D.A. (2005). 'Human-centered design considered harmful'. *Interactions*, vol 12, No 4, pp 14–19.

Oliveira, L., Mitchell, V., and May, A. (2016). 'Reducing temporal tensions as a strategy to promote sustainable behaviours'. *Computers in Human Behavior*, vol 62, pp 303–315.

Pettersen, I.N. (2013). 'Changing practices: The role of design in supporting the sustainability of everyday life'. Doctoral dissertation, Norwegian University of Science and Technology.

Pettersen, I.N., and Boks, C. (2008). 'The ethics in balancing control and freedom when engineering solutions for sustainable behaviour'. *International Journal of Sustainable Engineering*, vol 1, No 4, pp 287–297.

Pettersen, I.N., and Boks, C. (2009). 'The future of design for sustainable behaviour'. Ecodesign 2009: Sixth International Symposium on Environmentally Conscious Design and Inverse Manufacturing, Sapporo, Japan , December 7–9, 2009.

Pettersen, I.N., Boks, C., and Tukker, A. (2013). 'Framing the role of design in transformation of consumption practices: Beyond the designer-product-user triad'. *International Journal of Technology Management*, vol 63, No 1–2, pp 70–103.

Pierce, J., Strengers, Y., Sengers, P., and Bødker, S. (2013). 'Introduction to the special issue on practice-oriented approaches to sustainable HCI'. *ACM Transactions on CHI*, vol 20, No 4, p 20.

Pink, S., and Mackley, K.L. (2015). 'Social science, design and everyday life: Refiguring showering through anthropological ethnography'. *Journal of Design Research*, vol 13, No 3, pp 278–292.

Renström, S. (2013). 'Understanding residents' use of heating and hot water'. Proceedings of the Knowledge Collaboration & Learning for Sustainable Innovation ERSCP-EMSU Conference 2013, Istanbul, Turkey, June 4–7.

Revell, K.M., and Stanton, N.A. (2016). 'Mind the gap – Deriving a compatible user mental model of the home heating system to encourage sustainable behaviour'. *Applied Ergonomics*, vol 57, pp 48–61.

Rodriguez, E., and Boks, C. (2005). 'How design of products affects user behaviour and vice versa: The environmental implications'. Proceedings of the Fourth International Symposium on Environmentally Conscious Design and Inverse Manufacturing, Eco Design 2005, pp 54–61.

Sauer, J., Wiese, B.S. and Rüttinger, B. (2002). 'Improving ecological performance of electrical consumer products: The role of design-based measures and user variables'. *Applied Ergonomics*, vol 33, No 4, pp 297–307.

Sauer, J., Wiese, B.S., and Rüttinger, B. (2004). 'Ecological performance of electrical consumer products: The influence of automation and information-based measures'. *Applied Ergonomics* vol 35, No 1, pp 37–47.

Scott, K., Bakker, C., and Quist, J. (2012). 'Designing change by living change'. *Design Studies*, vol 33, No 3, pp 279–297.

Selvefors, A., Karlsson, M., and Rahe, U. (2013). 'What's in it for the user? Effects and perceived user benefits of online interactive energy feedback'. Proceedings of World Wide Web Conference, Rio de Janeiro, Brazil, May 13–17.

Shove, E. (2003). *Comfort, Cleanliness and Convenience: The Social Organization of Normality* (Vol. 810), Berg, Oxford.

Shove, E. (2010). 'Beyond the ABC: Climate change policy and theories of social change'. *Environment and Planning A*, vol 42, No 6, pp 1273–1285.

Shove, E., Pantzar, M., and Watson, M. (2012). *The Dynamics of Social Practice: Everyday Life and How It Changes*, SAGE Publications Ltd, London.

Spencer, J. (2014). 'Exploring the implications of cultural context for design for sustainable behaviour'. Doctoral dissertation, Loughborough University.

Spencer, J., Lilley, D., and Porter, S. (2015a). 'The implications of cultural differences in laundry behaviours for design for sustainable behaviour: A case study between the UK, India and Brazil'. *International Journal of Sustainable Engineering*, vol 8, No 3, pp 196–205.

Spencer, J., Lilley, D., and Porter, S. (2015b). 'The opportunities that different cultural contexts create for sustainable design: A laundry care example'. *Journal of Cleaner Production*, vol 107, pp 279–290.

Stern, P. (2000). 'Toward a coherent theory of environmentally significant behavior'. *Journal of Social Issues*, vol 56, No 3, pp 407–424.

Strömberg, H. (2015). 'Creating space for action – supporting behaviour change by making sustainable transport opportunities available in the world and in the mind'. Doctoral dissertation, Chalmers University of Technology.

Tang, T. (2010). 'Towards sustainable use: Designing behaviour intervention to reduce household environmental impact'. Doctoral dissertation, Loughborough University.

Tang, T. and Bhamra, T.A. (2008). 'Changing energy consumption behaviour through sustainable product design, in D. Marjanovic, et al. (Eds.) *DS 48: Proceedings of DESIGN 2008, the 10th International Design Conference,* Dubrovnik, Croatia, 19–22 May, pp 1359–1366.

Tang, T., and Bhamra, T. (2012). 'Putting consumers first in design for sustainable behaviour: A case study of reducing environmental impacts of cold appliance use'. *International Journal of Sustainable Engineering*, vol 5, No 4, pp 288–303.

Triandis, H.C. (1977). *Interpersonal Behavior*, Brooks/Cole Pub. Co., Monterey, CA.

Tromp, N. (2013). 'Social design: How products and services can help us act in ways that benefit society'. Doctoral dissertation, Delft University of Technology.

Tromp, N., Hekkert, P., and Verbeek, P.P. (2011). 'Design for socially responsible behavior: A classification of influence based on intended user experience'. *Design Issues*, vol 27, No 3, pp 3–19.

Tukker, A., and Tischner, U. (2006). 'Product-services as a research field: Past, present and future. Reflections from a decade of research'. *Journal of Cleaner Production*, vol 14, No 17, pp 1552–1556.

Verplanken, B., and Wood, W. (2006). 'Interventions to break and create consumer habits'. *Journal of Public Policy and Marketing*, vol 25, pp 90–103.

Wever, R. (2012). 'Editorial: Design research for sustainable behaviour'. *Journal of Design Research*, vol 10, No 1–2, pp 1–6.

Wever, R., van Kuijk, J., and Boks, C. (2008). 'User centred design for sustainable behaviour'. *International Journal of Sustainable Engineering*, vol 1, No 1, pp 9–20.

Wilson, G.T. (2013). 'Design for sustainable behaviour: Feedback interventions to reduce domestic energy consumption'. Doctoral dissertation, Loughborough University.

Zachrisson, J., and Boks, C. (2011). 'Obtrusiveness and design for sustainable behaviour'. Proceedings of Consumer 2011, 18–20 July, 2011, Bonn.

Zachrisson, J., and Boks, C. (2012). 'Exploring behavioural psychology to support design for sustainable behaviour research'. *Journal of Design Research*, vol 10, No 1–2, pp 50–66.

Zachrisson, J., Storrø, G., and Boks, C. (2011). 'Using a guide to select design strategies for behaviour change; Theory vs. Practice'. Proceedings of EcoDesign 2011, Design for Innovative Value Towards a Sustainable Society, Kyoto, Japan, Nov. 30 – Dec. 2, 2011 pp 362–367.

24

HOW DESIGN INFLUENCES HABITS

Tang Tang and Seahwa Won

Introduction

Habit is significant in the context of approaching sustainability, as many environmentally rele-vant behaviours are habits which are recurrent, stable and persistent (Kurz et al., 2015). A better understanding of the process of habit formation and change is considered vital when designing interventions to change behaviour (Tang and Bhamra, 2008; 2012; Darnton et al., 2011; Bhamra and Lilley, 2015).

Habitual aspects of the behaviour have been approached from two different academic dis-ciplines: social psychology and sociology. From a social-psychological perspective, habits are regarded as a driver of behaviours and a barrier to more sustainable alternatives, which intercede between intentions and behaviour and determine behavioural outcomes (Jackson, 2005). From a sociological perspective, habits are regarded as routine practices which consist of several inter-connected elements enabling practices collectively shared across time and space in society. Levels of resource and energy consumption are the outcome of technical systems and routine practices arising from the ongoing interactions between individuals and the structures of the social world (Shove, 2003). Psychologists posit that the individual is central to a rational decision-making and behaviour change, while sociologists decentralise the individuals, and put the practices themselves at the centre of the enquiry (Darnton et al., 2011).

Recognising the associations between behaviours and their negative environmental impacts, several attempts have been made in design to explore the feasibility and role that designers can play to influence sustainable decision making, behaviours and lifestyles (Jelsma and Knot, 2002, Rodriguez and Boks, 2005; Ingram et al., 2007; Tang and Bhamra, 2008; Hielscher et al., 2009; Bhamra et al., 2011). Two nascent research fields of design have emerged and are concerned with the application of theories and models rooted in the social sciences to understand behaviours and habits and design products, services and systems that promote more sustainable consumption. One is Design for Sustainable Behaviour (DfSB) which draws on social-psychological theories; a range of design strategies have been developed to evoke and steer the cognitive, behavioural or unconscious reaction to sustainability in the individual (Tang, 2010; Tang and Bhamra, 2012; Zachrisson and Boks 2012; Hanratty, 2015). The other approach, resting on the social-practice theory – practice-oriented design – focuses on the social and systemic nature of consumption, the accomplishment of everyday practices and the roles of conventions and conceptions of normality in shaping interactions with technology towards more sustainable practices (Ingram et al., 2007; Hielscher, 2011; Scott et al., 2012; Kuijer, 2014; Kuijer and Bakker, 2015).

This chapter explores how design alters or interjects change in habits to encourage more sustainable consumption. It begins by introducing the role of habit in the context of approaching sustainability and two different conceptualisations of habit, coming from both social psychology and sociology. Then it outlines two subcategories of design – DfSB and practice-oriented design – which draw on the theories from psychology and sociology, respectively, for bringing about habit change resulting in environmental improvements. This is followed by a number of design opportunities, strategies and their application that elucidate the two theoretical propositions. Implications are finally drawn out for designers to address habits on multiple levels and create interventions that can bring about pro-environmental habits on multiple levels.

The importance of habit

Changing behaviour is thought to have a considerable environmental impact (IPCC, 2007; Kurz et al., 2015). For example, household energy use is responsible for 29% of the UK end-user carbon dioxide emissions (DECC, 2015) and consumer behaviours alone can affect household energy use by a factor of 2–3 in technically identical houses (Gill et al., 2010). Growing attention is paid to reducing the impact of consumer behaviours as a response to environmental problems (IPCC, 2007). Focusing on technology transfer, innovations deal with energy efficiency improvements and renewable energy technology. Focusing on individuals and attitudes, policymakers have favoured information-based campaigns to seeking the active participation of consumers in pro-environmental behaviour change. However, progress has been unsatisfactory so far. The "rebound effects", for example, offsets the beneficial effects of the technological improvements that result from the behavioural or other systemic responses (Druckman et al., 2011), and the "value-action gap" (Blake, 1999) obstructs the translation from the pro-environmental intention of individuals into actual action that requires lifestyle change (Jackson, 2005). Although information-based campaigns are successful in raising people's awareness about environmental problems as well as their intentions to act environmental friendly, their actions do not reflect their concerns (Energy Saving Trust, 2006). Few interventions have successfully created the long-term behavioural shift needed for energy consumption reduction.

These failures are not surprising. Information-based interventions informed by "rational choice model" in psychological research have increased people's knowledge and intentions to act in environmental friendly ways but the rather linear model of persuasion has some significant limitations to bridging the intention – behaviour gap. One of many reasons for such a gap is that those who have developed strong habits are less likely to attend to new information (Jackson, 2005).

Much of the recent literature relating to environmental behaviour notes that many everyday behaviours are habits and are carried out with very little conscious deliberation (Jackson, 2005; Steg and Vlek, 2009; Kurz et al., 2015). One empirical study in psychology estimates that 45% of respondents' daily behaviours are repeated at around the same time and in the same place (Wood et al., 2002). Research in neuroscience estimates that as much as 95% of our behaviours depend on deliberative and automatic thinking (Baumeister et al., 1998). Habit is significant in the context of approaching sustainability, as many environmentally relevant behaviours are habitual in nature (Kurz et al., 2015). It is frequently repeated behaviours, e.g. how people interact with technologies to heat or cool their homes, cook their meals, wash their dishes and clothes, as well as entertain themselves and communicate with others that determine the actual impact on the environment, particularly domestic energy consumption (Steg and Vlek, 2009). Such behaviours ingrained in everyday life tend to be in competition with the rational aspect of behaviour, therefore, less ruled by interventions along rational lines (i.e. reliant on the provision of information and incentives) (Jackson, 2005; Darnton et al., 2011). To influence these behaviours effectively, it requires a better understanding of habitual behaviour, the processes of habit formation and change. Furthermore, rather than to consider either single technologies or behaviours in isolation (Jelsma, 2006), a holistic vision is required to bring together diverse technical, social and behavioural elements to facilitate the environmental improvements.

Understanding habit

This section introduces two different perspectives on habit, reflecting two different academic disciplines: social psychology and sociology. The purpose of this section is to offer a brief overview of these extensive debates and draw out some important implications for understanding and influencing the habitual behaviours.

Habit as a factor in behaviour

Within social psychology, habit is studied as an individual psychological construct. Triandis (1977) proposes an integrated model of interpersonal behaviour and features habit as a factor influencing behaviour. Given the fact that it includes habitual dimension of human behaviour, Theory of Interpersonal Behaviour (TIB) (Figure 24.1) has been particularly widely applied in relation to Design for Sustainable Behaviour (discussed later in this chapter) (Tang, 2010; Tang and Bhamra, 2012; Wilson, 2013). In this model, intention is an antecedent to behaviour, which is affected by attitudes, social factors and emotions. Habits, running parallel to intentions, play an equally important role in determining end behaviour. The facilitating conditions moderate both the intention-behaviour and habit-behaviour relationships, which either enable or impede behaviour (Triandis, 1977). Although Triandis' Theory of Interpersonal Behaviour presents "dual

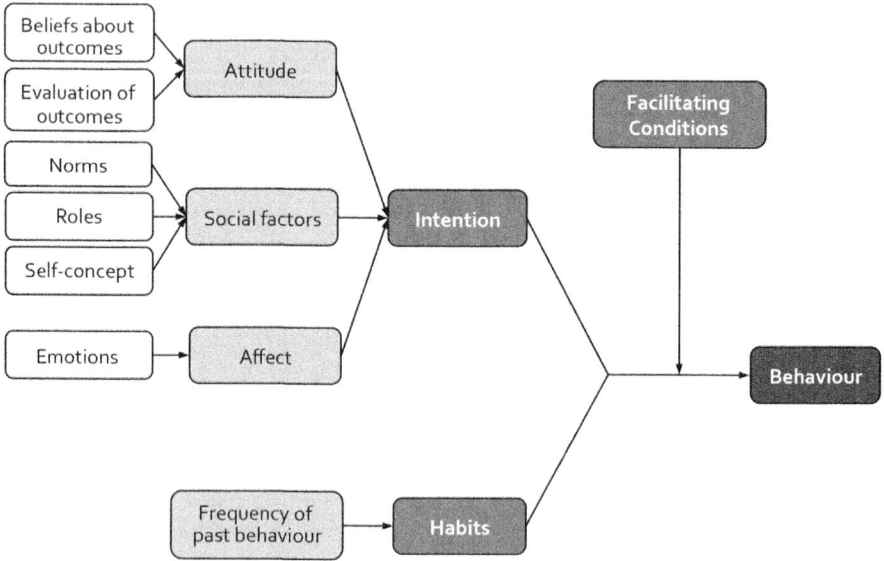

Figure 24.1   Triandis' Theory of Interpersonal Behaviour (TIB).

processes" of behaviour, i.e. that behaviour results either from intentions involving thoughtful deliberation or from habits based on the frequency of past behaviour, there has been little attention paid to the process of habit formation and change (Chatterton, 2011).

There is still no agreement upon how habits should be conceptualized and operationalized in social psychology, but there is a consensus that habits are formed through repetition (how often the action is repeated in a consistent context) and reinforcement (the strength and frequency of the positive reinforcement received) (Jackson, 2005). Firstly, a goal intention must already be in place and achieved (Gollwitzer, 1999). People must be "pre-motivated" to create habits (Darnton et al., 2011). Barbopoulos (2012) identifies why people are doing what they are doing based on the prioritisation of three goal frames (Lindenberg and Steg, 2007) and breaks the high level goals into seven related sub-goals (Barbopoulos, 2012) (Table 24.1). Lindenberg and Steg (2007) suggest that in the environmental context, normative goal frames imply acting pro-environmentally, while gain and hedonic goal frames often hinder the action in an environmentally sound manner. Therefore, pro-environmental behaviour may be stimulated by strengthening normative goals or by making gain and hedonic goals less incompatible with normative goals and behaviour change. Hanratty (2015) applies the Goal-framing Theory (GFT) as the theoretical basis for understanding behavioural motivation for reducing domestic energy use through digital media.

The satisfactory accomplishment of a goal reinforces subsequent performances of the same behaviour (Jackson, 2005; Schwanen et al., 2012). As behaviours are repeated in recurring contexts and strengthened through interval rewards, they then begin to proceed more efficiently with less thought. When people gradually learn associations between an action and a given context, the behavioural control transfers to cues in the context which triggers an automatic response: a habit (Lally et al., 2010). Once habits form, the perception of the context activates the associated response in memory (Wood and Rünger, 2016). Rewards for habit performance have, by this time, become relatively unimportant, although these may be important initially to promote the learning of context-response associations (Wood and Rünger, 2016). Habits are, therefore, measured by frequency of action (Triandis, 1977), but also by the cognitive processes that develop through frequency and association of the contextual cues and actions (Steg and Vlek, 2009; Lally et al., 2010). As defined by Orbell and Verplanken (2010), habits are built on three pillars: repetition,

Table 24.1 The three high-order goals in Goal-framing Theory (GFT) and seven related sub-goals (Barbopoulos, 2012; 2017)

Goal frame	Sub-goal	Motive
Gain	Value for money	To get value for money, pay a reasonable price, avoid wasting money
Gain	Quality	To get something of high quality and reliability, meeting one's highest expectations
Gain	Safety	To feel safe, calm and prepared for the unforeseen
Hedonic	Stimulation	To get something exciting, stimulating or unique, avoiding dullness
Hedonic	Convenience	To get something pleasant and comfortable, avoiding hassle and discomfort
Normative	Social Acceptance	To make a good impression, identifying with peers, conforming to expectations
Normative	Ethics	To act according to moral principles and obligations, avoiding guilt

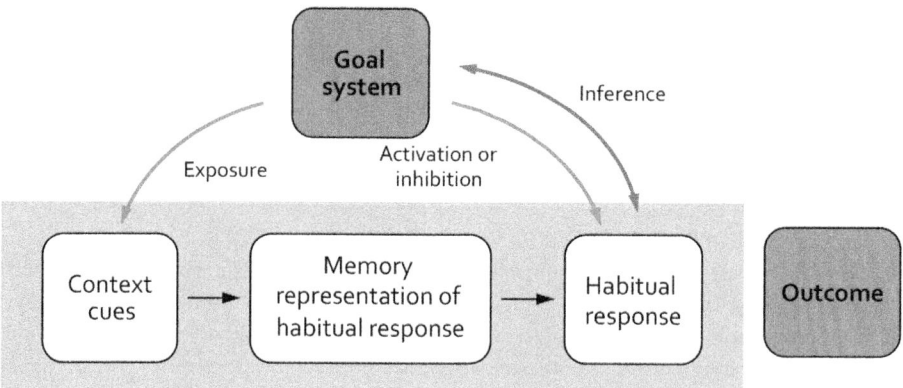

Figure 24.2 Schematic of three ways in which habits interface with deliberate goal pursuit (Wood and Rünger, 2016).

automaticity and a stable context. Given an explicit goal that is incompatible with a habit, recent work from Wood and Rünger (2016) has identified three ways in which habits interface with a goal to guide behaviour (Figure 24.2) through:

* repetition and exposure to a given context (illustrated by the arrows from goal system to context cues and habitual response),
* activation or inhibition of the habitual response, and
* inferences about the probable causes of habit responding (reflected by the double-headed arrow between habitual response and goal system).

As Jager (2003) pointed out, before the behaviour becomes habitual, it is influenced by the same factors that interact with the cognitive processes and contextual cues (Zachrisson Daae, 2014; Wood and Neal, in press). According to Prochaska et al.'s (1992) transtheoretical model (TTM), the creation of durable behaviour is assumed to go through five stages: precontemplation, contemplation, preparation, action, and maintenance. The TTM distinguishes between people who have not yet decided to change their behaviour, those who intend to, and those who are already changing and sustaining the behaviour. The rationale behind this model is that individuals at the same stage should face the same types of problems and barriers, and thus can be helped by the same type of interventions (Nisbet and Gick, 2008). Liking the stages to potential strategies, the TTM specifies ten processes how behaviour change might occur and be promoted by cognitive, affective, and behavioural strategies so that people might move through the stages (Prochaska et al., 1992). The TTM has been widely used in health intervention research, most recently in Design for Healthy Behaviour (Ludden and Hekkert, 2014) where a framework for stage-matched design interventions is proposed for healthy behaviour change, and people's water conservation behaviour (Sherrod, 1999, cited in Nisbet and Gick, 2008), where the model accurately predicts people in stages of change related to water usage. Theory of acquisition of cognitive skills developed by Anderson (1982) echoes a similar sequence of stages in TTM, which have been integrated in Tang's (2010) design behaviour intervention model (DBIM) for Design for Sustainable Behaviour.

Lindenberg and Steg's (2007) Goal-framing Theory and Wood and Rünger's (2016) framework for Habit Formation augmented with Prochaska et al.'s (1992) transtheoretical model

(TTM) will be the model of understanding taken forward within this chapter. It allows designers to give weight to the motivation to change and the habit formation and change.

Habits as routine practices

Sociologists have developed an alternative theoretical account of what psychologists term habitual behaviour. Social practice theory as a school of thought with mostly sociological roots in the writings of Bourdieu (1977) is increasingly influential in current thinking about human behaviour, particularly in the context of energy consumption, transport and waste. In this approach, habits are understood as ways of doing, routine practices, arising from the interactions between individuals and the structures of the social world. They are social and collective rather than individualised processes, organised around shared practical understanding that individuals carry. Therefore, habits are not the product of a series of factors (as it is understood in social psychology), but as routine practices, they are the emergent outcome of elements in the social world (Darnton et al., 2011). Practices are defined as 'a routinized type of behaviour which consists of several interconnected elements: "forms of bodily activities, forms of mental activities, 'things' and their use, a background knowledge in the form of understanding, know-how, states of emotion and motivational knowledge" (Reckwitz, 2002, p. 249). The role of people is to be the carriers of practices that operate social practices (Reckwitz, 2002). The purpose of this approach is to understand social change by considering behaviours in regards to their material, social and cultural contexts (Piscicelli et al., 2015).

Instead of targeting individual behaviour, practice theory takes social practice as a unit of analysis for understanding consumption but also a unit of intervention for a greater reduction in consumption (Pettersen, 2015). The focus shifts from the individual to the practice itself, such as bathing, laundering and cooking. This leads away from intervening in decisions and contextual cueing of the habit towards reflecting upon what shape actions. Taking Shove et al.'s (2008) definition of practice, the units of doing are shaped through non-linear interconnected elements of materials, meanings and competences (Figure 24.3):

Images (meanings): Socially shared conventions and interpretations associated with the practice

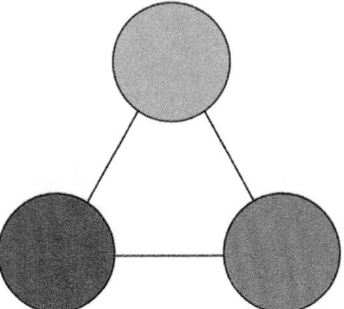

Stuff (materials): Physical objects, tools and necessary infrastructure deployed in the practice

Skills (competences): Know-how, levels of competence and ways of feeling and doing in certain ways

Figure 24.3　Shove's Three Element Model.

- Stuff (materials) – physical objects, tools and necessary infrastructure deployed in the practice
- Images (meanings) – socially shared conventions and interpretations associated with the practice
- Skills (competences) – know-how, levels of competence and ways of feeling and doing in certain ways

The elements are dynamically related to each other and the dynamic interplay of the elements is continually reproduced, maintained, stabilized, challenged and eliminated through the reiterative performance (Warde, 2005). They commingle at a particular historical moment that allows particular activities to take hold as routine practices (Kurz et al., 2015). A practice can thus not be reduced to the elements. These three elements are not factors in determining behavioural outcomes, and the individual, in turn, is not the originator of the behaviour, but the carrier of the practice (Darnton et al., 2011). Showering, for example, is more than piped hot water. Different elements must be integrated into the physical performances, and practice is considered as entity or nexus of activity, rather than as performance or the carrying out of a practice (Pettersen, 2015). To understand showering, a practice perspective would explore questions like: why daily showering has become a "necessity" for most people in the United Kingdom, whereas historically personal hygiene routines typically involved a weekly bath (meaning: the importance of daily freshness to fit in with everyday society); how showering has been co-evolved with the provision of requisite material infrastructure and technology (staff); and how it has been done and fits into the temporal organisation of daily life (skills: being able to run the boiler and get water to a desired temperature at the right times).

The Three Element Model also offers a diagnostic tool for mapping interdependency and interaction among practices. Practices may be closely related through sharing elements – e.g. meaning, stuff (Gram-Hanssen, 2011) and interact with each other in different ways: they may be complementary, or substitute other practices, or cluster together in complexes (Ropke, 2009). Networks of practices built on the connected and integrated elements can be identified at the level of "lifestyles" (Spaararen et al., 2006, in Scott et al., 2012). Intervening in habits as routines thus involves the reconfiguration of elements and links to a new configuration that works. The routinized, social, systemic but dynamic nature of practice does, however, open up new possibilities of designing behaviour change interventions, which in turn implies the need for holistic and collaborative approaches to the boundless consumption. Attempts have been made to investigate how practice theory can inform the design process to deal with sustainability issues in practice-oriented design, which is discussed later in the chapter.

Behaviour and practice

Psychology and sociology offer two distinct accounts of environmentally (un)sustainable practices and implications for bringing about change. A psychological analysis of laundry would focus on the way in which an individual washes clothes, reasons to launder, and the barriers and drivers for reducing the environmental impact of such a habit. The central challenge for changing habits as behaviours is that relapse occurs when old habits continue to be activated automatically by recurring environmental cues (Wood and Rünger, 2016). Interventions to mindfully breaking automatic engagement in laundry might alert individuals to the importance of water and detergent conservation or make it impossible to use the detergent more than necessary (e.g. designing package where only the right amount pours out). By contrast, a practice perspective would focus on a mapping of the elements that comprise laundry practices in a particular time period, and the relations between these elements and other practices (e.g. washing clothes after a workout). Instead of aiming at the motivational factors driving behaviour and contextual cues triggering habitual responses, practice-based interventions would target at rearranging the technical systems and infrastructures (e.g. a washing machine, systems of hot water provision), practical skills and symbolic elements and their integration in laundry practices.

Implications for design

This section firstly introduces design strategies aimed at changing habits drawn on social psychological models and illustrates these with examples of where they have been applied. Then it discusses the feasibility of design to foster absolute reductions by intervening in everyday practices and the conditions for the practice-based interventions.

Designing habit-based interventions

Social psychological models have been predominantly applied in promoting more sustainable behaviour through design (Tang, 2010; Coskun et al., 2015; Zachrisson Daae, 2014). Design for Sustainable Behaviour (DfSB) is a field in sustainable design concerned with the application of behavioural theory to understand users, and behaviour changing strategies to design products, services and systems that encourage more sustainable use (Bhamra and Lilley, 2015). DfSB approaches take individual behaviour as the focal unit of analysis and intervention (Shove et al., 2008; Scott et al., 2012; Kuijer and Bakker, 2015). Drawn from Wood and Rünger's (2016) Framework for Habit Formation, Lindenberg and Steg's (2007) Goal-framing Theory (GFT) and Prochaska et al.'s (1992) Transtheoretical Model (TTM), the following section presents a model for design for habit-based interventions.

As highlighted earlier, before a habit is formed, "behaviour change interventions encourage the formation of habits when people repeat an action sufficiently often in a stable context to form cognitive associations between context cues and the response" (Wood and Neal, in press, p. 5). As an evolution of Tang's (2010) work, a Design for Positive Habit Model (Figure 24.4), therefore, illustrates the factors that promote and impede habit formation and design strategies are highlighted to correspond to the stages in change for the purpose of encouraging habit change in the context of sustainable consumption. Seven categories of design strategies are outlined that change the environment around the person to disrupt the contextual cueing of the habit based on levels of motivational readiness along the process of change. Table 24.2 illustrates each design strategy with examples of where they have been applied.

Focusing on people without intention to change at the "precontemplation" stage in TTM, design strategies for goal matching respond to goal frames so as to leverage people's decision process and motivate people to expose themselves to performance contexts (Wood and Rünger, 2016). For the habits that are not necessarily promoted by goal-directed learning, five types of design strategies have been proposed with five different design aims: feedback, enabling, motivating, steering and forcing. These strategies spreading over multiple stages in TTM might help to develop the interventions that address the problems and barriers faced by individuals at the same stage and influence movement at different stages. Finally, design strategies aimed at targeting moments of change support interventions that can capitalise on the specific discontinuity or habit triggers altered through a life change – such as moving house, changing jobs, having a child or retiring from work. These life events provide windows of opportunity in which to deliver interventions that eliminate (or increase) exposure to the cues that automatically trigger unsustainable (or sustainable) habit performance. There is increasing evidence that interventions delivered at these "moments of change" can be more effective than if delivered at another time,

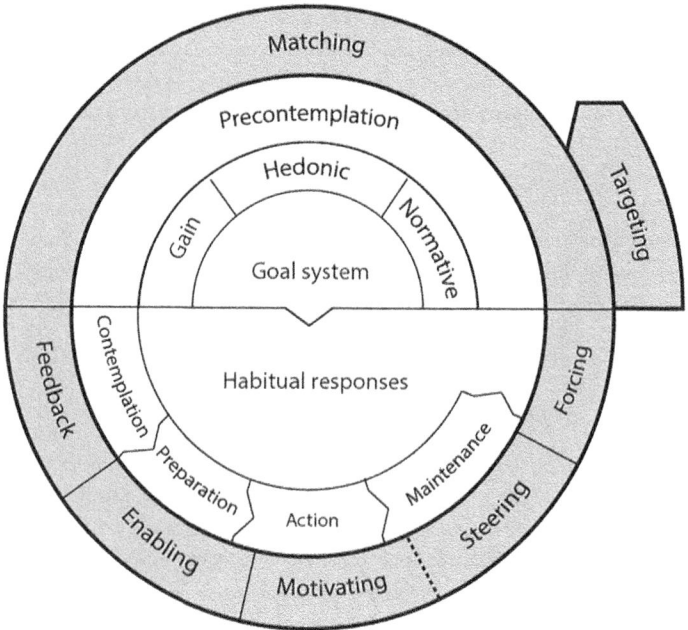

Figure 24.4 Design for Positive Habit Model.

Table 24.2 Design strategies and examples

Matching

Aim: responding to goal frames, to leverage people's decision process and encourage people to exercise a different choice in practice through reconsciousness raising or friction reducing for environmental behaviours

How it works:	*Example:*
1. Responding to normative goals that often imply pro-environmental actions, interventions make the value of action outcomes visible, understandable and accessible to provoke reflection and to act on a social or personal norm	The use of interactive online displays shows historic and current consumption data, with relevant environmental or social comparisons and facilitates a self-appraisal of energy consumption.
2. Responding to gain and hedonic goals that often hinder pro-environmental actions, interventions provide desired functionality with less impact on environment so as to remove the barriers that reduce discouragement caused by the in-built friction for environmental behaviours	Heat Me, an interactive app, persuades people to turn down the thermostat to 18°C over a period of time. By acknowledging the most prominent home heating behaviours – the desire for periodic "heat boosts", it makes it relatively easy for users to raise the temperature (i.e. 21°C) for limited periods (Hanratty, 2015).

Feedback

Aim: to inform people clearly about what they are doing and to facilitate consumers to make environmentally responsible decisions through offering real-time feedback

How it works:	*Example:*
Obtrusive feedback provides tangible aural, visual, or tactile signs as reminders to inform people of resource use	Fridge alarm detects when the door has been left open for more than 60 seconds and reacts by sounding an alarm that is impossible to ignore, and subsequently triggers the user to close the fridge door.

Table 24.2 (Continued)

Enabling

Aim: to support people in making the right choices and in taking responsibility for their actions through providing consumers with options

How it works:	**Example:**
People are empowered to make a choice and the product enables sustainable use to take place	Domestic Energy Display makes it easier for people to see what is wasting the energy without forcing the people (Design Council 2006).

Motivating

Aim: to inspire people to explore more sustainable usages through providing rewards to "prompt" good behaviour

How it works:	**Example:**
Interventions show people the consequences of actions through a variable (financial, emotional, social, physical) reward	Flower Lamp "blooms" as a reward – changing its shape when power consumption has been low for some time. To make the lamp more beautiful, a change in behaviour is needed (Interactive Institute, 2004).

Steering

Aim: to facilitate users to adopt pro-environmental habits through the prescriptions and/or constraints of use embedded in the design

How it works:	**Example:**
Interventions contain affordances and constraints which encourage people to adopt sustainable habits or reform existing unsustainable habits.	The AWARE Puzzle Switch is an on/off button that encourages people to switch off the light by playing with people's built-in desire for order (The AWARE project, 2007).

Forcing

Aim: to make it harder or impossible for people to act on undesired behaviours by introducing friction to existing context or removing cue of the habit so as to prevent relapse in the change

How it works:	**Example:**
Interventions add friction to undesired automated responses or removing cue of the habit	A speed bump forces the people to drive slowly.

Targeting Moments of Change

Aim: to improve effectiveness of the interventions by targeting events in the life course

How it works:	**Example:**
Habit-based interventions are designed to coincide with key events and other transitions in life course	TravelSmart programme delivers personalised travel planning advice (an intensive intervention) to people who have recently moved into an area (Sustrans 2008).

---

since people may be more able or willing to do things differently (Darnton et al., 2011; Wood and Neal, in press). Therefore, this type of intervention might not be dependent on individual's levels of pre-motivation.

The Design for Positive Habit Model suggests that the relative stages of habitual formation dictate the individual's motivational readiness for change and receptiveness to interventions. It provides a framework for the design of interventions based on individual differences in environmental intentions and readiness to adopt new behaviours, as well as strategies to facilitate change. For example, to encourage water conservation consumption, people contemplating this practice may need to be reminded. Eco Showerdrop (McDonough and Braungart, 2002) facilitates keeping track of the water used during a shower and sets off an alarm when more than the recommended water is used. People in the action stage may need the water company that often gives a small rebate for a reduction in water consumption on a weekly basis as rewards until they become new habits in the maintenance stage.

The behavioural theory provides heuristic frameworks for exploring and conceptualising human action, the underlying formation of habits as well as a theoretical basis for interventions. There is a growing body of work in sustainable design and an increasing number of DfSB case studies in the literature, such as, the design of the fridge in Tang and Bhamra (2008, 2012); washing machine in Lidman and Renström (2011); wood stove in Zachrisson Daae (2014), which focus solely on individual change and conceptualising habit as a factor in behaviour. A range of strategies targeting individuals and their "rational" behaviour as the result of processes of cognitive deliberation, when tested more extensively, can be effective in promoting more pro-environmental behaviour, particularly focusing on the specific product, user type and moments in time. However, the effect on behavioural change may be only feasible for the short-term (Lockton et al., 2008).

Practice-oriented design

Practice-oriented design (Shove et al., 2008) is a relatively new area of research that emerged from the "Designing and Consuming: objects, practices and processes" research program in 2005 (Kuijer, 2014). Drawing on the social practice theory as a potential way to inform the transition towards sustainable consumption, practice-oriented design takes the practice as a unit of analysis and design (Kuijer, 2014). Shove's Three Element Model has been adopted as a tool to map practice, which has been dominating the recent investigations into how design processes can be informed by practice theory, such as the work of Scott (2008) and Kuijer (2014) on bathing.

The first step towards the intervention from a social practice perspective becomes a mapping of the elements that currently circulate to allow particular practices to successfully recruit their carriers. As Shove et al. (2008, p. 5) suggest, the aim is to understand the "trajectories and careers" of practices that vary in their level of resource intensity. Kuijer (2014) visualises the activities that are necessary to undertake for the practice mapping (Figure 24.5).

Placing a practice – what is actually done, at the centre of attention could help provide a richer understanding of some hidden issues that prevent effective implementation of interventions based on single products or users, highlighting the mutual dependencies and complex interactions in systems of ideas, skills and objects that "lock-in" unsustainable behaviours (Chatterton, 2011). Using the Three Element Model as a mapping tool in the early design development process allows framing problems in a more holistic and systemic manner. This method involves convening resources and skills from different sectors around the practices in question (Darnton et al., 2011) and the identification of connection to challenges present in the technology development context, for example, related to resources and lock-in to existing manufacturing schemes (Pettersen et al., 2013).

However, as noted by Pettersen (2013, p. 55), the practice theory is strong at conceptualising "the interplay between humans and technology and system level dynamics between practices", but not equipped with the tools and approaches for defining system boundaries which is needed for the assessment of "absolute" reductions (Pettersen, 2015, p. 255). Pettersen (2015) argues that the impact would not necessarily be measured at the level of practice. Due to the systemic nature of consumption, changes in one practice may influence other relevant practices areas resulting in consumption shifting accordingly. It might, therefore, make more sense to look at changes at the

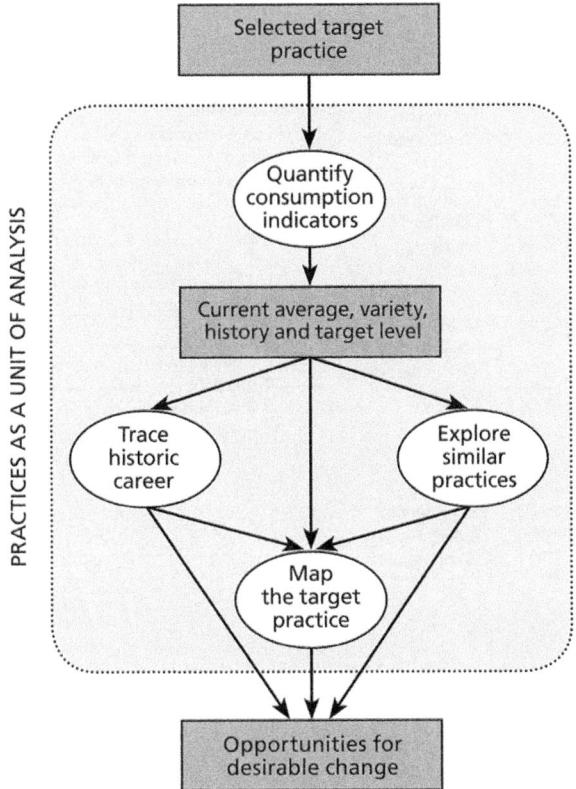

Figure 24.5 Model for practices as a unit of analysis and intervention (circles represent activities, squares intermediate results) (Kuijer, 2014).

level of households, than at the level of single practices. Drawing on practice theory and system innovation theory, Pettersen (2015) suggests using multi-level perspective (MLP) on sociotechnical change as a supplement to social practice theory that would help analyse the conditions for design activities in commercial firms to achieve actual reductions in resource consumption. The following sections briefly outline these two perspectives in relation to design.

Socio-technical system: the context for practice-oriented intervention

Socio-technical systems refer to deep-structural changes (Elzen et al., 2004), which include the wider context (e.g. firms and industries) and multiple social actors (e.g. policymakers, politicians, consumers, civil society, engineers and researchers) (Geels, 2011). Geels defines socio-technical system as "the linkages between elements necessary to fulfil societal functions" (Geels, 2004, p. 900), such as energy supply, transport or communication, and breaks them into sub-functions "production", "diffusion" and "use". The fulfilment of sub-functions requires necessary elements or resources and socio-technical systems thus consist of these elements, such as artefacts, knowledge, capital, labour and cultural meanings, etc. Figure 24.6 gives a schematic representation of social groups and their related recourses and functions, which carry and reproduce socio-technical systems.

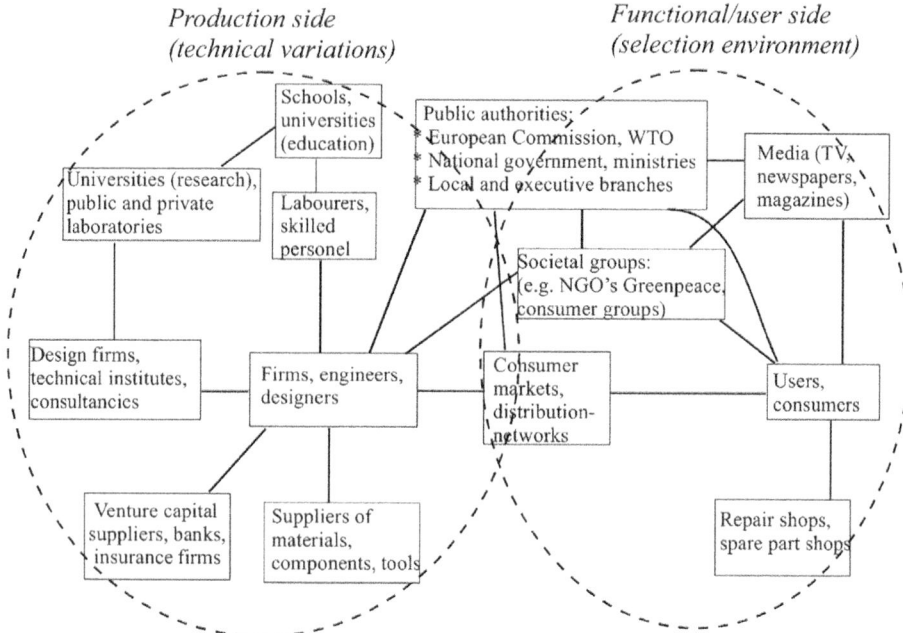

Figure 24.6 Social groups which carry and reproduce socio-technical systems (Geels, 2004, p. 901).

The ST-system presents the context that may enable and impede design actions (Pettersen, 2015). It is reconstructed and changed, as social actors work towards their goals and follow the rules that might enable, guide, organise and even constrain their activities and interactions. The rules that may be cognitive, normative and regulative are linked together and organised into rule private or social systems (Geels, 2004). Interrelated rules would form rule regimes. By recognising this, designers may produce or reproduce rules that are linked within and between regimes of policy, science, technology, user and market and sociocultural issues. This would offer designers a new perspective to understand and frame problems and identify new opportunities for creating a large scale change, which probably involves product requirements and regulations, but also the company's product portfolio management. From a systematic perspective, portfolio management covers product strategy, portfolio management process, portfolio methods and models. However, there might remain a challenge for prioritising new kinds of ideas and concepts. Pettersen (2015) suggests that the multi-level perspective (MLP) (Geels, 2004; 2011) appears to play a decisive role in helping to overcome this. MLP explains the potential effects of introducing innovation at different levels of structuration: how the innovation, established practices and society would co-evolve. The multi-level model consists of three levels: technological niches, socio-technical regime and landscape developments. Figure 24.7 presents a dynamic multi-level perspective on system innovations.

The levels of niches and landscape are defined in relation to the regime level. The niche level refers to "practices or technologies that deviate substantially from the existing regime" (Geels, 2011, pp. 26–27). Niches provide spaces for experimentation and learning in the form of small market niches where users have special demands or the form of technological niches which are often played out as experimental projects in R&D labs (Geels, 2004; 2011). Examples given of such niches include grass roots initiatives for collaborative consumption and smart city demonstration

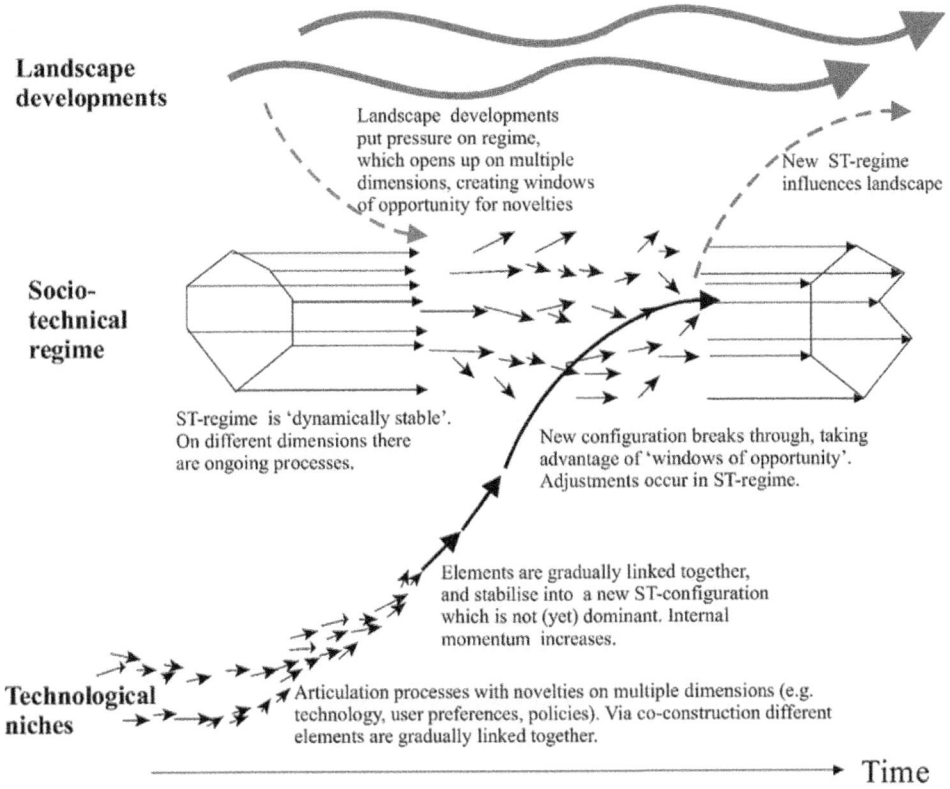

Figure 24.7 Multiple levels of a nested hierarchy (Geels, 2004, p. 915).

arenas. Niche actors hope that their novelties are used in the regime or even replace it, although this may not be easy because the existing regime is stabilised by many locked-in mechanisms.

The landscape is the most stable level. It is beyond the reach of single actors, and cannot be changed at will (Geels, 2004). The landscape refers to the wider exogenous environment that influences niches and regime dynamics, such as "demographical trends, political ideologies, societal values, and macro–economic patterns" which influences niches and regime dynamics (Geels, 2011, p. 28).

The regime level is generally stable and coordinates the activities of social groups (Geels, 2011). It includes "cognitive routines and shared beliefs, capabilities and competences, lifestyles and user practices, favourable institutional arrangements and regulations and legally binding contracts" (Geels, 2011, p. 27). Small changes accumulate, creating stable trajectories along the dimensions of technology, culture, policy, science, market, user preferences and cultural meaning. These co-evolve and have their own dynamics. The actors make moves within and between social groups, reacting to each other's actions, with changes in the sociotechnical systems as a result (Geels, 2004). Take an example of socio-technical laundering system from Pettersen et al. (2013): to reduce water consumption, washing machine manufacturers may make products more efficient, textile manufacturers may develop materials that are solid enough to tolerate frequent washing cycle, policymakers may launch gradually stricter regulations for the other actors. In the process of transition, one regime can be replaced by another (Geels, 2011), where major changes occur in the ways that societal functions are achieved (Pettersen, 2015). This may result from niche innovations, such as waterless washing machine (Xeros, n.d.) and associated infrastructures and practices that gain momentum; or from landscape changes, such as climate change that creates pressure on the regime and destabilisation of the regime to offer windows of opportunity for niche innovations (Geels, 2004).

The multi-level perspective can be particularly helpful for the understanding processes of societal co-evolution, transitional processes, and identifying hinders and opportunities for change. Although changes in habits as routine practices do not necessarily involve societal transitions and regime replacements, the space for creating such change can be constrained by reigning regimes (Hargreaves et al., 2013). The development of interventions tackling practices involves the rearrangement of the parts, the rules and resources made up the practice, which may be impeded by current systems and provisions. To capture such issues, Pettersen (2015) proposes using the strengths of practice theory and theories on system innovation and the MLP for studies of the potential role and feasibility of practice-oriented design in fostering absolute reductions. More specifically, practice theory is used to (1) understand the characteristics and development of the practice, enabler and hinders of change, and (2) identify design directions for fostering absolute reductions. The MLP is then used to (1) characterise the situation and identify resistance and inertia against and windows of opportunity for change in the direction of absolute reductions, and (2) assess the feasibility of the design directions and interventions proposed.

Feasibility of design directions for changing practices and fostering absolute reductions

Design directions for reducing the resource intensity of practices could be divided into three groups: regime compliant interventions, stretch interventions, and interventions unlikely to be implemented in the current regime (Pettersen, 2015).

Most of the regime compliant interventions are incremental innovations which do not necessarily lead to actual reductions in resource consumption. Business favours product centric interventions in pursuit of resource efficiency. It could be enhanced with traditional eco-design approaches and tools that improve the resource and energy efficiency throughout the complete life cycle of the product, e.g. low-impact material selection, product lifetime extension (van Hemel and Cramer, 2002). To make up for the limitation of eco-design (e.g. rebound effects, lack of consumer demand), practice-oriented design involves the explorations of the possible practice elements, such as, interventions (e.g. products, resources, space) may be developed to disrupt and (re)establish routines and social conventions that work, and foster collaborative action to join in the experimentation and learning (e.g. Scott et al., 2012; Kuijer et al., 2013). This would start with using the Three Element Model to map the parts, the rules and resources which make up the habit as routine practices, their relations to other practices, and finally the careers of practitioners and the trajectories of practices (Shove et al., 2012). The investigation into the practice performances in the past or other cultural contexts, and the variation between different social groups may also inspire the development of the interventions (e.g. Kuijer and de Jong, 2012).

Stretch interventions may move away from the product centric improvement and redesign into holistic approaches of function innovation in the Brezet's (1998) four stages in eco-design (Stage 1, Product improvement; Stage 2, Product redesign or eco-redesign; Stage 3, Function innovation or alternative function fulfilment; and Stage 4, Sustainable systems innovation). This would involve reconsidering firm business models, and embracing the opportunity of service-based business models building on work in the product-service systems (PSS) field (Roy, 2000). Major changes in consumer lifestyle and infrastructure are needed. The implications may go beyond individual companies or a cluster of companies, as switches to servicing to actually reduce the resource intensity of practices may require infrastructural change and initiatives from other stakeholders. This increased challenge includes investments, supplier chain, consumer acceptance or infrastructure that might not yet be in place. One possible way to do this to further develop product-service systems in practice theory (Piscicelli et al., 2015; Pettersen, 2015). Pettersen (2015) suggests the focus of the practice theory on the co-dependence of ostensibly unrelated practices opens up alternatives for service level interventions. It would redefine of service quality and establish less resource intensive conventions. Practice-oriented design could contribute with insights on sociomaterial dynamics and draws together resources and skills from different social groups around practices in which there are common interests, essentially, using practice change as a means of joining up within and across sectors (Darnton et al., 2011). Once alternative solutions have been generated, further efforts are required from distribution and sales to develop them into marketable propositions. The distribution and sales related opportunities may include transferring practical skills transfer, providing people with access to the products before the purchase, and reconfiguring the social meaning of new products and 'doings' through, for example, marketing campaign, networking and partnerships building (Pettersen, 2015).

Given that the fact an alternative solution might fall the realm of the design, business and related regime actors, some more radical interventions might be hard to achieve in the current regime. For example, manufacturers operating on commercial grounds cannot be expected to go for options that break with shared values and beliefs or to stop catering to what are taken to be desired service levels given established performance evaluation criteria.

Conclusion

This chapter has explored two different conceptualisations of habit, coming from social psychology and sociology, that offer useful intervention design insights. It has focused on design opportunities to alter or interject change in habits to facilitate the envisaged significant environmental improvements.

A social psychology approach to habit provides heuristic frameworks for exploring and conceptualising individualistic, social and psychological structures, various behavioural drivers which inform users' actions at different stages of change. Integrating different behavioural psychology models into the habit-based intervention design allows identifying and analysing the various factors influencing the interaction between users and products in given contexts. Grounded in the psychological principle of breaking habits through disruption, a range of strategies have been proposed, and they can be effective in promoting behaviour change with a potential to develop into pro-environmental habits.

In contrast, social practice theory, an emerging branch of sociology, considers practices to be connected in systems and does not focus on specific interaction at a specific product-user level. Instead of targeting individuals' motivations, practice theory calls for the rearranging of the materials, skills and meanings which hold the habit as routine together. Using practice theory and system innovation theory together provides a possibility to capture the dynamics of social practice and opportunities for design interventions that foster absolute reductions. Socio-technical systems and the multi-level perspective (MLP) have been introduced to supplement practice theory that help analyse the conditions for design activities in commercial firms to bring about systemic change in resource consumption.

The sociological critique is that the impact of the psychological approach to habit is limited to incremental environmental improvements. Practice theory from sociology gives a potential to make more fundamental changes and absolute reduction in resource use.

This is an on-going debate that approaches resulting in more radical innovations may, however, conflict with how the business currently operates. Both design for habit change and practice-oriented design are, however, still a relatively underdeveloped research area and further work needs to be carried out with a real test and generate its own materials, approaches and procedural contexts and understandings for future sustainable interactions. To solve the environmental challenges, both the improvements are needed: incremental innovations that can easily be implemented immediately, and the radical innovations that would be aided by the multi-level perspective on socio-technical change. Both psychology and sociology have relevant and interesting perspectives that can be applied into design process and contribute to the transition to sustainability. It would also be beneficial for future designers to comprehend these two dominating perspectives and the complexity in habit, and thus potentials in designing habit-based interventions.

References

Anderson, J.R., 1982. Acquisition of cognitive skill. *Psychological review*, 89(4), 369–403.

Barbopoulos, I. 2012. *The Consumer Motivation Scale: Development of a Multi-Dimensional Measure of Economical, Hedonic, and Normative Determinants of Consumption.* Licenciate Thesis, University of Gothenburg.

Barbopoulos, I. 2017. *Seven Dimensions of Consumption.* Doctoral Dissertation, Department of Psychology, University of Gothenburg.

Bargh, J.A. 1994. The four horsemen of automaticity: Awareness, intention, efficiency, and control in social cognition. In: R.S. Wyer and T.K. Srull (Eds.), *Handbook of Social Cognition* (vol. 1, pp. 1–40). Hillsdale, NJ: Erlbaum.

Bargh, J.A. and Chartrand, T.L. 1999. The unbearable automaticity of being. *American Psychologist*, 54(7), 462–479.

Baumeister, R.F., Bratslavsky, E., Muraven, M., and Tice, D.M. 1998. Ego depletion: Is the active self a limited resource? *Journal of Personality and Social Psychology*, 74, 1252–1265.

Bhamra, T. and Lilley, D. 2015. IJSE special issue: Design for sustainable behaviour. *International Journal of Sustainable Engineering*, 8, 146–147.

Bhamra, T., Lilley, D., and Tang, T. 2011. Design for sustainable behaviour: Using products to change consumer behaviour. *The Design Journal*, 14, 427–445.

Blake, J. 1999. Overcoming the 'value-action gap' in environmental policy: Tensions between national policy and local experience. *Local Environment: The International Journal of Justice and Sustainability*, 4(3), 257–278.

Bourdieu, P. 1977. *Outline of a Theory of Practice.* Cambridge: Cambridge University Press.

Brezet, J.C. 1998. *Sustainable Product Innovation.* In: Third International Conference Towards Sustainable Product Design, London, UK, October, 1998.

Chatterton, T. 2011. *An Introduction to Thinking About 'Energy Behaviour': A Multi Model Approach.* Available from: www.gov.uk/government/uploads/system/uploads/attachment data/file/48256/3887-intro-thinking-energy-behaviours.pdf [Accessed 9 June 2016].

Coskun, A., Zimmerman, J., and Erbug, C. 2015. Promoting sustainability through behavior change: A review. *Design Studies*, 41, pp. 183–204.

Darnton, A., Verplanken, B., White, P., and Whitmarsh, L. 2011. *Habits, Routines and Sustainable Lifestyles: A Summary Report to the Department for Environment.* Food and Rural Affairs Report Number 1. AD Research & Analysis, London.

DECC. 2015. *Final UK Greenhouse Gas Emissions National Statistics: 1990–2013.* Department for Business, Energy & Industrial Strategy. Available from: www.gov.uk/government/statistics/final-uk-emissions-estimates [Accessed 9 December 2015].

Design Council. 2006. *RED – Future Currents, Concepts: Votes!* Available from: www.designcouncil.info/futurecurrents/concepts.php [Accessed April 2007].

Druckman, A., Chitnis, M., Sorrell, S., and Jackson, T. 2011. Missing carbon reductions? Exploring rebound and backfire effects in UK households. *Energy Policy*, 39(6), pp. 3572–3581.

Elzen, B., Geels, F.W., and Green, K. 2004. *System Innovation and the Transition to Sustainability: Theory, Evidence and Policy.* Cheltenham: Edward Elgar.

Energy Saving Trust. 2006. *The Rise of the Machines, A Review of Energy Using Products in the Home From the 1970s to Today, Energy Saving Trust*. Available from: www.est.org.uk/uploads/documents/aboutest/Riseofthemachines.pdf [Accessed December 2006].

Geels, F.W. 2004. From sectoral systems of innovation to socio-technical systems insights about dynamics and change from sociology and institutional theory. *Research Policy*, 33, 897–920.

Geels, F.W. 2011. The multi-level perspective on sustainability transitions: Responses to seven criticisms. *Environmental Innovation and Societal Transitions*, 1, 24–40.

Gill, Z., Tierney, M.J., Pegg, I., and Allan, N.D. 2010. Low-energy dwellings: The contribution of behaviours to actual performance. *Building Research & Information*, 38(5), 491–508.

Gollwitzer, P.M. 1999. Implementation intentions: Strong effects of simple plans. *American Psychologist*, 54, 493–503.

Gram-Hanssen, K. 2011. Understanding change and continuity in residential energy consumption, *Journal of Consumer Culture*, 11, 61–78.

Hanratty, M. 2015. *Design for Sustainable Behaviour: A Conceptual Model and Intervention Selection Model for Changing Behaviour Through Design*. PhD Thesis, Loughborough Design School, Loughborough University, Loughborough, UK.

Hargreaves, T., Longhurst, N., and Seyfang, G. 2013. Up, down, round and round: Connecting regimes and practices in innovation for sustainability. *Environment and Planning A*, 45(2), 402–420.

Hemel, C. van and Cramer, J. 2002. Barriers and stimuli for ecodesign in SMEs. *Journal of Cleaner Production*, 10(5), 439–453.

Hertwich, E.G., 2005. Consumption and the rebound effect: An industrial ecology perspective. *Journal of Industrial Ecology*, 9(1/2), 85–98.

Hielscher, S. 2011. *Are You Worth It? A Practice-Oriented Approach to Everyday Hair Care to Inform Sustainable Design and Sustainable Consumption Strategies*. PhD Thesis, Nothingham Trent University.

Hielscher, S., Fisher, T., and Cooper, T. 2009. *The Return of the Beehives, Brylcreem and Botanical! An Historical Review of Hair Care Practices With a View to Opportunities for Sustainable Design*. In: Undisciplined! Design Research Society Conference 2008, 16–19 July 2008, Sheffield, UK.

Ingram, J., Shove, E., and Watson, M. 2007. Products and practices: Selected concepts from science and technology studies and from social theories of consumption and practice. *Design Issues*, 23(2), 3–16.

IPCC. 2007. *Climate Change 2007: Synthesis Report. Contribution of Working Groups I, II and III to the Fourth Assessment Report of the Intergovernmental Panel on Climate Change*. IPCC, Geneva, Switzerland.

Jackson, T. 2005. *Motivating Sustainable Consumption: A Review of Evidence on Consumer Behaviour and Behavioural Change*. A report to the Sustainable Development Research Network as part of the ESRC Sustainable Technologies Programme, Centre for Environmental Strategy, University of Surrey, Guildford.

Jager, W. 2003. Breaking 'bad habits': A dynamical perspective on habit formation and change. In: W.J.L. Hendrickx and L. Steg (Eds.), *Human Decision Making and Environmental Perception. Understanding and Assisting Human Decision Making in Real-life Settings*. University of Groningen, The Netherlands: Liber Amicorum for Charles Vlek.

Jelsma, J. 2006. Designing 'moralized' products: Theory and practice. In: P.-P. Verbeek and A. Slob (Eds.), *User Behaviour and Technology Development: Shaping Sustainable Relations Between Consumers and Technologies* (pp. 221–231). The Netherlands: Springer.

Jelsma, J., and Knot, M. 2002. Designing environmentally efficient services: A 'script' approach. *The Journal of Sustainable Product Design*, 2, 119–130.

Kuijer, L. 2014. *Implications of Social Practice Theory for Sustainable Design*. Delft University Thesis, Industrial Design, Delft University.

Kuijer, L. and Bakker, C. 2015. Of chalk and cheese: Behaviour change and practice theory in sustainable design. *International Journal of Sustainable Engineering*, 8(3), 219–230.

Kuijer, L. and De Jong, A., 2012. Identifying design opportunities for reduced household resource consumption: exploring practices of thermal comfort. *Journal of Design Research* 14, 10(1/2): 67–85.

Kuijer, L., de Jong, A., and van Eijk, D. 2013. Practices as a unit of design: An exploration of theoretical guidelines in a study on bathing. *ACM Transactions on Computer-Human Interaction*, 20(4), 1–22, Article no. 21.

Kurz, T., Gardner, B., Verplanken, B., and Abraham, C. 2015. Habitual behaviors or patterns of practice? Explaining and changing repetitive climate-relevant actions. *Climate Change*, 6, 113–128.

Lally, P., van Jaarsveld, C.H.M., Potts, H.W.W., and Wardle, J. 2010. How are habits formed: Modelling habit formation in the real world. *European Journal of Social Psychology*, 40, 998–1009.

Lidman, K. and Renström, S. 2011. *How to Design for Sustainable Behaviour?* Master Thesis, Chalmers University of Technology, Gothenburg, Sweden.

Lindenberg, S. and Steg, L. 2007. Normative, gain and hedonic goal frames guiding environmental behavior. *Journal of Social Issues*, 63(1), 117–137.

Lockton, D., Harrison, D., and Stanton, L. 2008. Making the user more efficient: Design for sustainable behaviour. *International Journal of Sustainable Engineering*, 1(1), 3–8.

Ludden, G.D.S. and Hekkert, P. 2014. *Design for Healthy Behaviour Design Interventions and Stages of Change*. In: Proceedings of the Colors of Care: The 9th International Conference on Design & Emotion.

Mcdonough, W. and Braungart, M. 2002. *Cradle to Cradle*. New York: North Point Press.

N/A. 2008. *Hughie*. Available from: www.hughie.com.au/ [Accessed March 2009].

Neal, D.T., Wood, W., Labrecque, J.S., and Lally, P. 2011. How do habits guide behavior? Perceived and actual triggers of habits in daily life. *Journal of Experimental Social Psychology*, 48, 492–498.

Nisbet, E.K.L. and Gick, M.L. 2008. Can health psychology help the planet? Applying theory and models of health behaviour to environmental actions. *Canadian Psychology*, 49, 296–303.

Orbell, S. and Verplanken, B. 2010. The automatic component of habit in health-behavior: Habit as cue-contingent automaticity. *Health Psychology*, 29, 374–383.

Pettersen, I.N., 2013. *Changing Practices: The Role of Design in Supporting the Sustainability of Everyday Life*. Doctoral thesis, Norwegian University of Science and Technology (NTNU), Trondheim, Norway, 130.

Pettersen, I.N. 2015. Fostering absolute reductions in resource use: The potential role and feasibility of practice-oriented design. *Journal of Cleaner Production*, 132, 252–265.

Pettersen, I.N., Boks, C., and Tukker, A. 2013. Framing the role of design in transformation of consumption practices: Beyond the designer-product-user triad. *International Journal of Technology Management*, 63(1/2), 70–103.

Piscicelli, L., Cooper, T., and Fisher, T. 2015. The role of values in collaborative consumption: Insights from a product-service system for lending and borrowing in the UK. *Journal of Cleaner Production*, 97, 21–29.

Prochaska, J.O., DiClemente, C.C., and Norcross, J.C. 1992. In search of how people change. *American Psychologist*, 47, 1102–1114.

Quinn, J.M., Pascoe, A., Wood, W., and Neal, D.T. 2010. Can't control yourself? Monitor those bad habits. *Personality and Social Psychology Bulletin*, 36(4), 499–511.

Reckwitz, A. 2002. Toward a theory of social practices: a development in culturalist theorizing. *Journal of Social Theory*, 5(2), 243–263.

Rodriguez, E. and Boks, C. 2005. *How Design of Products Affects User Behaviour and Vice Versa: The Environmental Implications*. In: Proceedings of EcoDesign 2005, 12–14 December 2005, Tokyo. Tokyo: Union of Ecodesigners, pp. 1–8.

Ropke, I. 2009. Theories of practice—New inspiration for ecological economic studies on consumption. *Ecological Economics*, 68, 2490–2497.

Roy, R. 2000. Sustainable product-service systems. *Futures*, 32(3–4), 289–299.

Schwanen, T., Banister, D., and Anable, J. 2012. Rethinking habits and their role in behaviour change: The case of low-carbon mobility. *Journal of Transport Geography*, 24, 522–532.

Scott, K. 2008. *Co-Designing Sustainable User Practices*. MSc Thesis, Industrial Ecology, Delft University.

Scott, K., Bakker, C., and Quist, J. 2012. Designing change by living change. *Design Studies*, 33, 279–297.

Shove, E. 2003. Converging conventions of comfort, cleanliness and convenience. *Journal of Consumer Policy*, 26, 395–418.

Shove, E., Pantzar, M., and Watson, M. 2012. *The Dynamics of Social Practice: Everyday Life and How It Changes*. London: Sage.

Shove, E., Watson, M., Hand, M., and Ingram, J. 2007. *The Design of Everyday Life*. Oxford, UK: Berg.

Shove, E., Watson, M., Ingram, J., and Hand, M. 2008. *The Design of Everyday Life*. Oxford, UK: Berg.

Steg, L. and Vlek, C. 2009. Encouraging pro-environmental behaviour: An integrative review and research agenda. *Journal of Environmental Psychology*, 29(3), 309–317.

Sustrans. 2008. *TravelSmart as Travel Behaviour Change – An Information Sheet*, May 2008.

Tang, T. 2010. *Towards Sustainable Use: Designing Behaviour Intervention to Reduce Household Environmental Impact*. PhD Thesis, Loughborough Design School, Loughborough University, Loughborough, UK.

Tang, T. and Bhamra, T.A. 2008. *Understanding Consumer Behaviour to Reduce Environmental Impacts Through Sustainable Product Design*. In: Undisciplined! Design Research Society Conference 2008, Sheffield Hallam University, Sheffield, UK, 16–19 July 2008.

Tang, T. and Bhamra, T.A. 2012. Putting consumers first in Design for Sustainable Behaviour: A case study of reducing environmental impacts of cold appliance use. *International Journal of Sustainable Engineering*, 5(4), 288–303.

Triandis, H.C. 1977. *Interpersonal Behaviour*. Monterey, CA: Brooks.

Warde, A. 2005. Consumption and theories of practice. *Journal of Consumer Culture*, 5, 131–153.

Watson, M. 2012. How theories of practice can inform transition to a decarbonised transport system. *Journal of Transport Geography*, 24, 488–496.

Wilson, G.T. 2013. *Design for Sustainable Behaviour: Feedback Interventions to Reduce Domestic Energy Consumption*. PhD Thesis, Loughborough Design School, Loughborough University, Loughborough, UK.

Wood, W. and Neal, D.T. in press. Habit-based behavior change interventions. *Behavioral Science and Policy*.

Wood, W. and Rünger, D. 2016. Psychology of habit. *Psychology*, 67, 289–314.

Wood, W., Quinn, J., and Kashy, D.A. 2002. Habits in everyday life: Thought, emotion and action. *Journal of Personality and Social Psychology*, 83, 1281–1297.

Xeros. n.d. *The Xeros Machine: A Revolution in Laundry*. Available from: www.xeroscleaning.com/the-xeros-machine [Accessed 9 October 2016].

Zachrisson Daae, J. 2014. *Informing Design for Sustainable Behaviour*. Doctoral Thesis, Norwegian University of Science and Technology.

Zachrisson, J. and Boks, C. 2012. Exploring behavioural psychology to support design for sustainable behaviour research. *Journal of Design Research*, 10(1–2), 50–66.

25

THE TEMPORAL FALLACY

Design and emotional obsolescence

Jonathan Chapman and Giovanni Marmont

In this chapter, we show how a deeper understanding of acts of use might be helpful in extending both the physical and emotional durability of products. Such attentiveness towards the actual *behavioural dimension* of person-thing encounters can enable designers to encourage longer-lasting interactions with products and services, consequently minimising the consumption of resources. Over the past decades, increasingly pressing issues of sustainability have claimed central stage within design activity. As a result, strategies like design for recycling, disassembly, service and energy efficiency, for example, have become commonplace in today's process. The prevalence of such approaches has so far overshadowed the experiential dimension of product *use*, which seemingly remains a relatively under-explored arena. This has skewed the subject area, placing uneven focus on a handful of established sustainable design methods, in neglect of less familiar yet potentially more impactful ones. The aim of this chapter, therefore, is not that of proposing instructions, standardised design research methodologies or protocols of creative action. It is instead our intention to present *a* perspective, placing under critical scrutiny a number of speculative, yet nonetheless practical, approaches to design for sustainability. Although admittedly and largely a theoretical undertaking, we hope that this investigation will also provide useful inspiration for the work of design practitioners working across a range of fields and sectors.

Introduction: one word, different agendas

First things first: the word 'sustainability', when attached to product design, has largely shown to be highly problematic. Indeed, in true umbrella-term fashion, it misleadingly suggests a commonality of intent for practitioners that instead operate with quite different agendas. A primary major distinction that needs to be made, obvious as it might sound, is whether sustainability is advocated in relation to *production* or *consumption*. This is not to say that the two are necessarily mutually exclusive by any means, but design practices that seriously engage with both aspects are few and far between.

Promoting sustainability by production can be intended as a response to the ecological impact of relentlessly wasteful manufacturing practices. The constant flood of products, interventions, experimental and conceptual work adopting strategies such as recycling or upcycling[1] is clear testament to a predominant focus on production-related concerns within design discourses. These present modes of (re)designing that encourage a do-it-yourself ethos, adhocism[2] and other forms of inventive craftsmanship through repair, reuse and re-appropriation of the already existent, thus refusing to design and, crucially, produce anew. It could be argued that the dominance of such methodologies that don't risk 'offending' existing commercial and capitalist conventions is, on some level, a compliant approach to sustainable transition. Indeed, whilst a reaction against the ruthless depletion of raw natural resources can hardly be condemned, the adequacy and efficacy of these efforts has long been put into question. One common criticism towards this approach to sustainability is its inherently 'symptom-focused' nature that, borrowing critical theorist Herbert Marcuse's words, ultimately contributes to the 'perfection of waste' (Marcuse, 1964, p. 9). That is, an exclusive emphasis on optimising material use and reuse or energy efficiency is often a limited and merely technical exercise, whereby sustainability risks being mistaken for a means rather than an end. This is notably the case for so-called greenwashing: namely, mere marketing strategies that blatantly trade on the commercial appeal of products presented as environmentally friendly. This conservative *modus operandi*, as it were, then 'liberates consumers conscience and, in doing so, generates even more waste' (Chapman, 2005, p. 10). By refusing to understand and engage the problem of sustainability 'at a level of foundational causality' (Fry, 2011, p. vii), designers thus fail again and again to grasp the deeper roots of what Tony Fry defined as 'structural unsustainability' (Fry, 2011, p. 1). In this chapter, we argue that until these roots are firmly grasped, sustainable design will always teeter around the edges of impact, but never drive the transformational changes it so passionately advocates.

A truly sustainable design discipline has to undergo a radical cultural shift that would hinge upon a concern for *immaterial* issues, prior to and as a precondition for *material* ones. It is paramount to point out here that we don't necessarily mean to align with 'post-thing' theories that strive to move designing beyond materiality *tout-court*. However, as similarly exposed by Fry, we do contend that it is the 'condition of mind and action' (Fry, 2011, p. 21) materialised within structural unsustainability that needs to be brought to the fore. By questioning the very primacy of design production itself, of acts of designing in favour of acts of use, it is then a careful attentiveness to modes, experiences and patterns of consumption that needs to be fostered. Why are people drawn to certain objects, only to then rapidly discard them while still performing their practical tasks perfectly? Deluges of manufactured objects flow through our lives providing mere glimpses of meaning along the way. From paperclips, cutlery and footwear to armchairs, kettles and cars, we engage this stuff in the hope that it will fulfil some kind of need, or lack, yet it seldom does. In this respect, sociologist Robert Bocock tells us that '[c]onsumption is founded on a lack – a desire always for something not there. Modern/postmodern consumers, therefore, will never be satisfied. The more they consume, the more they will desire to consume' (Bocock, 1993, p. 46). Bocock claims that consumer motivation, or the awakening of human need, is catalysed by a sense of imbalance or lack that steadily cultivates a restless state of being, experienced between *actual* and *desired* conditions. Though it is clear that neither designers nor consumers are solely to blame, it is evident that designers have a prominent role in regulating such a delicate balance.

How, then, does all our supposedly *meaningful stuff* transform into *meaningless rubbish* so rapidly? Why do these person-thing relationships eventually fail to be sustained, consequently titillating an insatiable cycle of desire for the new? Following such trajectory, this is the territory that we are here seeking to sift through, with a particular interest for what lies at the very heart of most discourses surrounding sustainable consumption: namely, *obsolescence*.

A wrecked relationship

What should be clarified from the outset is that our intention here is not to devise yet another critique of what has been often interchangeably called 'planned', 'in-built' or 'compulsory' obsolescence (e.g. Miles, 1998; Packard, 1960). That is, we are not specifically concerned with instances of strategic and instrumental exploitation of the phenomenon of obsolescence in and of itself. Rather, our focus will be more broadly on the nature, mechanisms and implications of obsolescence as such, specifically in its *emotional* – rather than *functional* – dimension. The distinction between functional and emotional obsolescence shall not be understated: while the former is brought about by a functional failure within the object that is encountered (e.g. its physical breakage), the latter indicates a rupture that is instead largely driven by a person's intentions and attitude. Today, it seems culturally permissible to throw away anything (Thackara, 2015) from a barely used smartphone, television, or vacuum cleaner, to an entire three-piece suite or fitted bathroom. Given the huge quantities of precious resources (including gold and other rare metals) that find their way into everyday objects, it would surely be worth us taking more care of them, repairing them when broken, and keeping them for longer. In fact, the opposite is happening: product life spans are shortening as material culture becomes increasingly disposable. Hence, we live in 'a world drowning in objects' (Sudjic, 2009, p. 5): households with a television in each room; kitchen cupboards stuffed with waffle makers, blenders and cappuccino whisks; drawers filled to bursting with pocket-sized devices powered by batteries – batteries which themselves take a thousand times more energy to make than they will ever provide.

Earlier on, we made a fleeting allusion to person-thing *relationships* that, by failing to be sustained, generate obsolescence and consequent 'novelty craving'. Thus understood, obsolescence results from a wrecked relationship between a person and an object. Or, to put it yet another way, the original conditions in which the meaningful association was formed between the user and the object have shifted, and therefore the original meaning altered – often in undesirable and unwanted ways: the crucible from which the original relationship was formed is then shattered. It is now timely to begin unpacking what constitutes this relationship in the first instance. Once understood the ground in which these relationships take root, we will hopefully be able to unravel the reason why they eventually decline. Obsolescence [whether *functional* or *psychological*] can be defined as 'the process of becoming [. . .] outdated and *no longer used*'.[3] In all its apparent triviality, this definition offers a first crucial insight in that it helps us to identify the absolute centrality of *use* within the connection established between person and object. We should now clarify that the term 'use' is here adopted in the broadest possible sense, hence not excluding less 'bodily' forms of use such as symbolic, communicative, imaginary or 'rhetorical' use (Malpass, 2012). It has been suggested that acts of use are akin to dialogues, non-verbal acts of communication and exchanges of information, not only between designers and users (e.g. see Buchanan, 1985), but also – and more critically – between persons and things encountered (cf. Crilly et al., 2008; Vardouli, 2015).[4] The idea of 'material dialogues', of exchange, is extremely valuable here because it effectively renders the intrinsic *mutuality* that characterises encounters with objects. The extent of such reciprocity between user and 'used' can be made even more evident through a brief – perhaps slightly scholastic – linguistic digression. In *The Use of Bodies* (2015), ninth and final volume in the *Homo Sacer* project, Italian philosopher Giorgio Agamben dedicates a fascinating chapter to the perplexing etymology of the Greek word *chresthai*, ordinarily rendered as 'to use'. Agamben argues that such translation, at least in its contemporary understanding, enormously oversimplifies the original richness of *chresthai*. Indeed, he claims, the Greek word was intended to express 'a relation so close between subject and object that not only is the subject intimately modified, but the boundaries between the two terms of the relationship even seem indeterminated [sic]' (Agamben, 2015 p. 26). Further, Agamben concludes that:

> use is first of all use of self: to enter into a relation of use with something, I must be affected by it [and] constitute myself as the one who makes use of it. [. . .] in the using of something, it is the very being of the one using that is first of all at stake.
>
> *(p. 30)*

Of course, this will immediately appear in glaring contrast with more common, superficial and strictly instrumentalist apprehensions of 'use' as unidirectional encounters, completely dominated by an acting subject over a passive object. Agamben's more sophisticated analysis instead brings us one step further in our undertaking by stressing the *intimacy* developed between subject and object through the process of use/*chresthai*. This is an important step in that we understand that these material dialogues, being grounded in a sort of complicity, require empathy in order to sustain a compelling 'conversation'. Such 'empathy' can be best intended as a mutual 'understanding' between user and 'used'. When this mutuality withers, dialogues of use mutate into tedious *monologues of use*.

Temporal fallacy

When and why do dialogues with artefacts become so disengaged that we decide to withdraw from them altogether? What or who is responsible for the deterioration of intimacy within these relationships? Is it us or is it 'them' – that is, the objects we live with, and through? One could obviously assume that things have simply 'changed', or, that the surrounding conditions supporting both their currency and relevance have changed. However, it is perhaps the opposite that is problematic here. Perhaps the issue is with what has in fact *not* changed, at least not as a whole: *we* have (and the world has), while our individual possessions have not.

We have, are and always will be changing, always in an incessant state of becoming. This *process* of permanent becoming, which lays bare the inherent transience, temporality and historicity of human beings, is notoriously central to the work of German philosopher Martin Heidegger. Heidegger essentially contends that human beings – or, in his terms, *Dasein*[5] – are fundamentally temporal entities that are always-already 'projected [. . .] upon [their] potentiality-for-Being' (Heidegger, 1927 p. 458). This is not the place to get too entangled in Heideggerian meanderings, but what is of particular interest to our argument here is that Heidegger's understanding of Dasein in terms of *potentiality* and of manifold 'possibilities of being' (Heidegger, 1927 p. 7), towards which we are constantly projected, can reveal the point of rupture that underpins the phenomenon of product obsolescence. That is, if the self that Agamben shows to be at stake through acts of use – the 'user' – is essentially temporal and always-already in-becoming, then it is perhaps an utterly static and ahistorical eventless-ness of the artefacts we encounter that undermines the intimate mutuality of material dialogues in the (not so) long run. Objects are thus eventually doomed to obsolescence not only when devoid of a historical *past*, not only because of the concealment of their genesis within the finished product. If this were the case, increasingly adopted design strategies hinging upon storytelling, symbolism and embedded narratives may suffice. Indeed, this type of work, often existing at the hazy intersection between design and art (and rarely intended for practical use), emerged largely as a reaction to the indistinct temporal vacuum from which mass-manufactured commodities come to us – alienated as they are from their indiscernible inception. Designers operating in such fashion frequently strive to restore artefacts' *'auratic'* qualities (Benjamin, 1936) and communicative significance by staging and indeed bringing to the fore the production process and, consequently, the historical past of the object.[6] However, we argue, this is hardly an effective antidote to obsolescence. Indeed, regardless of how compelling the story we are told by an object, we can only hear it so many times before it starts becoming stagnant. These narratives fail to evolve, or adapt as we adapt, and therefore fall into insignificance rapidly. It is instead first and foremost the very fact that these narratives, as well as the objects through which they are delivered, are *finished* that is at the root of the problem of obsolescence. Indeed, this fundamental completeness results in the object being entirely abstracted from a *relatable* conception of temporality and historicity that, crucially, would also include an ever-unfolding *future-becoming-present*.

This is to say that, while we are in a permanent state of becoming, the objects we attempt to engage with have *already become*. In this scenario, obsolescence is a somewhat inevitable outcome. The imperative significance of *change* has been a central concern across a number of fields. According to Darwinian evolutionary biology, for instance, 'it is not the most intellectual of the species that survives; it is not the strongest that survives; but the species that survives is the one that is able to best adapt and adjust to the changing environments in which it finds itself' (Megginson, 1963, p. 4). Similarly, in 'resilience thinking', the capacity to absorb disturbance, and accept change – rather than defensively resist and block it – is considered key to success. Adaptive resilience, says Robinson (2010), is 'the capacity to remain productive and true to core purpose and identity whilst absorbing disturbance and adapting with integrity in response to changing circumstances'(p. 14).

Mutual becoming

Such analysis thus brings our reasoning full-circle, back to Marcuse's words regarding the 'perfection of waste'. It might appear vaguely paradoxical to think that design practices' commitment to product life extension can in fact run the risk of nurturing obsolescence rather than countering it. We have attempted to show how this danger is not uniquely due to inattention to the unintended implications that sustainable production strategies could have on patterns of consumption and disposal. It is also the *nature* itself of such extension that is problematic. The very attempt of making objects 'immortal' – of making them simply last *longer*, rather than last *meaningfully* – in their sheer perfection and everlasting completeness, tends to cast them outside of time, hence making them somewhat unrelatable as things.

To this conclusion equally came Tonkinwise (2004), whose warning against the perilous idea of the 'design classic' – intended as an 'ahistorical, timeless product' – seeks to highlight the necessity for a 're-temporalisation of things' (pp. 188–189). His lucid analysis urges designers to:

> Design [. . .] things that can last longer by being able to *change* over time [. . .] things that are not finished, things that can keep on by keeping on being repaired and altered, things in motion.
>
> *(p. 189) [our italics]*

The fact that, in Tonkinwise's account, how such ever-changing products might be conceived is left slightly unclear is perhaps symptomatic of the overt skepticism towards this undertaking with which his investigation ends. Indeed, Tonkinwise eventually asks the compelling question of 'whether designers are capable of designing things that are not finished', being designing 'the project of pre-determin(at)ing' (pp. 190–191). Whether directly or by proximity, a concern with the finished-ness of use-objects has been a steady presence in design research and theory, particularly post turn of the Century. Several conceptualisations of this issue have attempted to grapple with its implications for both acts of designing and acts of using. 'Continuous design and redesign' (Jones, 1983), 'tactical formlessness' (Hunt, 2003), 'design after design' (Redström, 2008) or 'metadesign' (Ehn, 2008): these are but some of the better-known labels adopted to discuss the topic. What these perspectives seem to share is their intentions to question designers' absolute authorial claims, to instead promote user agency precisely by blurring the threshold between acts of design and acts of use. That is, appropriating once again Agamben's recurrent wording, to create a 'zone of indifference' (e.g. Agamben, 2005, p. 23) wherein designing extends into use, or use itself becomes a form of making. The latter formulation in particular is what Vardouli suggests in her compelling analysis of 'use-acts' (Vardouli, 2015, p. 11). Intending use as making, she argues, would encourage 'rethinking users [. . .] as active performers of open-ended, unfolding, and improvisational tasks' (p. 14). We can then see an important shift happening, whereby the object's openness, formlessness, hackability and sometimes even deliberate ambiguity are functional to a 'democratic' displacement of authorship. Which now begs the question: can these strategic authorial transferences efficiently confront the problem of obsolescence? Our answer is: partly.

Amplifying the 'voice' and agency of users through the object's open-endedness is certainly a step in the right direction in that it widens users' sphere of action. That is, in keeping with the dialogue analogy proposed before, it equips users with a broader vocabulary that permits spontaneity, improvisation and an enhanced engagement on their parts – rather than having to abide by a predetermined code of practice and simply recite a stale *script* (cf. Akrich, 1992). This can be seen as almost turning the object into a sort of *blank canvas* of use, or, at least, a space for emergent properties to manifest. However, we argue that we might still be falling slightly short of our initial theoretical intent. We have seen thus far that obsolescence (1) results from the wreckage of person-thing relationships (2) that are grounded in acts of use, (3) which entail a profound mutuality between user and used. This has eventually led us to suggest that (4) what fractures such mutuality is the out-of-time-ness of finished objects and the resulting inability for artefacts to meaningfully mutate over time – there exists, as it were, a temporal fallacy. What we are hypothesising here is that open-ended use *as such* does not entirely succeed in establishing the intimate reciprocity between subject and object that was discussed earlier on. The reason for this being that the emancipation of the subject does not automatically drag the object itself out of a condition of mere '*equipmentality*' (Heidegger, 1927, p. 97). In other words, the object – open to the user's intervention as it might be – is still reduced to somewhat of a servant to the will of a master. In its remaining 'an "in-order-to", [the object] is always inserted into a multiplicity of *instrumental* relations' (Heidegger, 1927 in: Agamben, 2015, p. 66) [our italics]. That is to say, this type of open dialogue is in fact still a monologue, dominated by a 'speaking' user and assimilated by a 'listening' artefact that nothing does but *mediating* and *facilitating* the achievement of an end – albeit now in numerous ways.

This holds true at least until objects will be provided with the ability to *respond* in their own terms, rather than being programmed to do so or forced to oblige in any possible way. To be clear, such brief is by no means meant to encourage a dystopian 'nightmare in which tyrannical things command our daily lives' (Taylor, 2011, p. 227). Rather, it speaks of things emerging in their eventfulness and asserting their own voices throughout person-thing encounters. That is, it speaks of the capacity for objects to *really* have an 'inherent process of their own' (Tonkinwise, 2004, p. 184). Of course, as we are here talking about unspoken dialogues, objects would need to find non-verbal ways to proactively contribute to 'conversations of use'. Their material conformation, their physical and structural arrangement could then be conceived as a responsive organism. Importantly, what we imagine is not some sort of science-fiction-inspired, technology-fuelled artificial intelligence. Quite the opposite, we imagine things that would rot and bloom, grow and shrink, solidify and melt, *reacting* to human interaction as if they were animated natural entities. It could be said that, this way, things *flow*.

This idea of flow draws from the famed Greek remark *panta rhei*, in English literally 'everything flows', originally attributed to pre-Socratic philosopher Heraclitus and later reported in the writings of Plato and Simplicius in particular.[7] The Heraclitean concept of *panta rhei* uses the image of the river to evoke the eternal flow of time and change – a continually moving, shifting thing in constant flux. This remark serves to remind us that, in our pursuit of permanence, we are fundamentally at odds with the most essential underlying principles of natural world – change. Indeed, Heraclitus' river itself could be described as a different river from moment to moment, since what composes it – the water flowing – is different from moment to moment. Such concept is essentially meant to stress the uniqueness of each discrete experience of the world. On an atomic level, this principle is true of all physical things, no matter how solid and stationary they may seem. For example, a child constantly changes, and we are predisposed to accept, and expect this. Importantly, like the changing Heraclitean river, the child doesn't become a different child with each change. Rather, the child has changed and adapted in some way, hence becoming a slightly 'evolved' version of what it was before.

Change is part of the basic nature of some, if not all, things. Whether we are talking about major changes in state – such as the demolition of a 40-storey block (one minute it is there, the next it is not) – or something more discreet – such as the barely noticeable growth of our finger nails – change is all around us. The latter case is reminiscent of what in psychophysics and experimental studies of perception is conventionally identified as a JND: that is, a *just-noticeable difference*. First theorised by nineteenth-century German physicist Ernst Heinrich Weber, a JND identifies 'the [smallest] amount that something must be changed for the difference to be noticeable',[8] and is a helpful concept to describe minute changes in a given object, system or experience. If we take a look around us, everything that our eyes fall on will change – from the glass in those windows to the concrete of the building you can see through them. All of this is mutating. Of course, our experience of the everyday tends to happen through a series of fleeting glimpses, which provide a fragmented, artificial portrayal of reality. These passing snapshots capture isolated moments in a far longer and more complex timeline of an object, material or building, for example. Only through sustained and attentive engagement with a given thing – be it a house, armchair, car or a pen – can we begin to understand it in the lengthier context of flow and change, over time. As if to disprove this, we fabricate the made world as though it can be fixed, set in place and frozen. Through this, we form expectations of permanence, of things that last for centuries, unchanged. In an attempt to transcend the inevitability of change, we fabricated an alien world of 'durable metals, polymers and composite materials [. . .] immune to the glare of biological decay, these materials grossly outlive our desire for them' (Chapman, 2005, p. 47), largely due to their inability to evolve – a kind of non-adaptive resilience.

Partial interruptions: looking *through* and *at* objects

In discussing his theorisation of thingness, Bill Brown (2001) refers to an excerpt from Byatt's novel *The Biographer's Tale* that might offer a useful metaphor to the present argument. Brown reports the description of one of the novel's characters delighted gazing at a dirty window, as this vision prompts him to 'relish the world at hand' (pp. 1–2). The dirt on the window causes what Brown identifies as an *interruption* 'that disclose[s] a physicality of things' (p. 4). This occurrence, he continues, is an 'interruption of habit of looking *through* windows as transparencies [that] enables the protagonist to look *at* a window itself in its opacity' (p. 4). Brown's concept of interruption bears obvious similarities with Heidegger's infamous theorisation of *presence-at-hand* (Heidegger, 1927). Crudely put, this term identifies a particular circumstance wherein an entity is stripped of its usefulness – for instance when a tool breaks – or, in the case of the window, when a specific *experience of use* gets disrupted in problematic ways. In such circumstance, the otherwise *readiness-to-hand* of an object – i.e. its 'in-order-to' serviceability and equipmentality discussed earlier – is suddenly withdrawn, enabling its user to notice its mere presence as an entity, the very fact that that thing *is* rather than purely *does* something.[9] What we then seem to be confronted with is an apparent dichotomy between presence/presenc*ing* and use, whereby artefacts must cease to *properly* function in order to be made visible in-themselves, rather than sheer in-order-to-ness.

Perhaps Brown's 'interruption of transparency' can instead offer us a less totalising polarisation. Indeed, the very idea of transparency and opacity suggests the existence of intermediate states in-between the two extremes. We can assume that a dirty window, unless entirely covered by a thick layer of grime, would have its functionality – our vision of what is behind it – *altered* rather than impeded altogether. That is to say, the interruption caused by such dirt is only a partial one. This crucially points to a type of act of use that, while not deprived of a practical dimension, is not completely exhausted in instrumental utility either. It is perhaps a peculiar capacity of looking through *and* at objects simultaneously – as they manage to alter and partly interrupt our habitual dialogues of use in meaningful ways – that can set the ground for the kind of caring, emotionally durable encounters that we have examined. That is, for an empathic mutual becoming within person-thing relationships that could do justice to the richness of the Greek *chresthai*, counter obsolescence, and thus waste. Perhaps the question to be asked, rather than solely whether designers can design for unfinishedness, could then be whether designers can endow their designs with independent potentiality for change, with an autonomous, unfolding projection upon their own possibilities of being.

Notes

1 Upcycling: a mode of production involving the reuse of discarded objects and materials in order to reduce the depletion of raw materials and energy used in manufacturing processes.
2 Adhocism: the improvisational use of materials and objects at hand. E.g. see: Jencks and Silver (1972).
3 Definition of 'obsolescence' from Oxford Dictionary. See: www.oxforddictionaries.com/definition/english/obsolescence
4 These conceptualisations have been largely inspired by Bruno Latour's work with *Actor-Network Theory* (ANT). See for example Latour (2005).
5 Dasein, literally 'being-there', is how Heidegger refers to the particular Being of human beings. The term indicates the inherent always-already 'in-the-world-ness' of human beings – also being-in-the-world – and represents the point of departure for Heideggerian ontology.
6 For further reading discussing the use of narrative and storytelling, as well as the concept of 'aura' in product design see Taylor (2011) and Williams (2009).
7 For further readings on the origins and meaning of the phrase *panta rhei* see Peters (1967, p. 178).
8 This is the rather simplified definition given by design theorist Donald Norman – see: http://jnd.org/about.html#jnd
9 What is slightly counterintuitive yet particularly important here is that, for Heidegger, encountering a thing in its presence-at-hand is how that same thing's readiness-to-hand can be theoretically perceived rather than solely experienced throughout the act of use.

References

Agamben, G., 2005. *State of Exception.* Chicago: University of Chicago Press.
Agamben, G., 2015. *The Use of Bodies, Homo Sacer.* Stanford, CA: Stanford University Press.
Akrich, M., 1992. The de-scription of technical objects, in: Bijker, W.E. and Law, J. (Eds.), *Shaping Technology/Building Society: Studies in Sociotechnical Change.* Cambridge, MA: The MIT Press, pp. 205–224.
Benjamin, W., 2008 [1936]. *The Work of Art in the Age of Mechanical Reproduction.* Penguin books great ideas. London, UK: Penguin.
Bocock, R., 2008 [1993]. *Consumption.* London, UK: Routledge.
Brown, B., 2001. Thing theory. *Critical Inquiry*, 28, 1–22.
Buchanan, R., 1985. Declaration by design: Rhetoric, argument, and demonstration in design practice. *Design Issues*, 2, 4–22. doi:10.2307/1511524
Chapman, J., 2005. *Emotionally Durable Design: Objects, Experiences, and Empathy.* London and Sterling, VA: Earthscan.
Crilly, N., Good, D., Matravers, D., and Clarkson, P.J. 2008. Design as communication: exploring the validity and utility of relating intention to interpretation. *Design Studies*, 29(5), 425–457.

Ehn, P., 2008. *Participation in Design Things*, in: Proceedings of the Tenth Anniversary Conference on Participatory Design 2008, PDC '08. Indiana University, Indianapolis, IN, USA, pp. 92–101.

Fry, T., 2011. *Design as Politics*. English ed. New York: Berg.

Heidegger, M., 2015 [1927]. *Being and Time*. 37th ed. Malden: Blackwell.

Hunt, J., 2003. Just re-do it: Tactical formlessness and everyday consumption, in: Blauvelt, A. (Ed.), *Strangely Familiar: Design and Everyday Life*. Minneapolis, MN: Walker Art Center, pp. 56–71.

Jencks, C. and Silver, N., 2013 [1972]. *Adhocism: The Case for Improvisation*. Expanded and updated ed. Cambridge, MA: MIT Press.

Jones, J.C., 1983. Continuous design and redesign. *Design Studies*, 4, 53–60.

Latour, B., 2005. *Reassembling the Social: An Introduction to Actor-Network-Theory*. Oxford, UK: Oxford University Press.

Malpass, M., 2012. *Contextualising Critical Design: Towards a Taxonomy of Critical Practice in Product Design*. PhD Thesis, Nottingham Trent University, Nottingham.

Marcuse, H., 1964. *One Dimensional Man: The Ideology of industrial Society*. London, UK: Sphere Books Ltd.

Megginson, L.C., 1963. Lessons From Europe for American businesses. *The Southwestern Social Science Quarterly*, 44(1), 3–13

Miles, S., 1998. *Consumerism – As a Way of Life*. Repr. ed. London: Sage.

Packard, V., 2011 [1960]. *The Waste Makers*. Brooklyn, NY: Ig Pub.

Peters, F.E., 1967. *Greek Philosophical Terms: A Historical Lexicon*. New York: NYU Press.

Redström, J., 2008. RE: Definitions of use. *Design Studies*, 29, 410–423. doi:10.1016/j.destud.2008.05.001

Robinson, M., 2010. Making Adaptive Resilience Real. *Arts Council England*. [Online] Available at: www.thinkingpractice.co.uk/wordpress/wp-content/uploads/2012/06/making_adaptive_resilience_real.pdf [Accessed: 25/07/2016]

Sudjic, D., 2009. *The Language of Things*. London: Penguin.

Taylor, D., 2011. *Design Art Furniture and The Boundaries of Function: Communicative Objects, Performative Things*. PhD Thesis, University of the Arts London and Falmouth University.

Thackara, J., 2015. *How to Thrive in the Next Economy: Designing Tomorrow's World Today*. London: Thames and Hudson.

Tonkinwise, C., 2004. Is design finished? Dematerialisation and changing things. *Design Philosophy Papers*, 2, 177–195. doi:10.2752/144871304X13966215068191

Vardouli, T., 2015. Making use: Attitudes to human-artifact engagements. *Design Studies*, Special Issue: Computational Making, 41, Part A, 137–161. doi:10.1016/j.destud.2015.08.002

Williams, G., 2009. *Telling Tales: Fantasy and Fear in Contemporary Design*. London: V&A Publishing.

26

DISCOURSE DESIGN

The art of rhetoric and the science of persuasion

Marilyn DeLaure

We are consumers of meaning, not matter.
Jonathan Chapman, Emotionally Durable Design (p. 36)

Sustainable designers face not only the technical and aesthetic challenges of creating environmentally conscious products, structures, and systems; they also must confront the existing attitudes and behaviors of their target user groups. Human habits are rooted in our values and structures of meaning – how we understand the world. Simply crafting a new product or space is not enough to change actions in most cases; designers also need to imbue their creations with significance, put them into compelling contexts, and ultimately help build a new sustainable paradigm for design and for living. Richard Buchanan explains that "[t]he problem for design is to put an audience of users into a frame of mind so that when they use a product they are persuaded that it is emotionally desirable and valuable in their lives. Design provides an organization of the way we feel in a direct encounter with our environment" (1989, 103). Because many people in developed, late-capitalist societies are accustomed to convenience – to the immediate gratification offered by plentiful cheap disposable consumer goods – redirecting their choices toward more sustainable options will require substantial shifts in both physical and mental environments. This chapter offers an overview of key concepts from the humanistic art of rhetoric and the social scientific study of persuasion which may serve designers as they seek to understand and appeal to audiences, precipitate behavior change, and ultimately usher in new sustainable systems.

Design and rhetoric share much in common. Both terms signify a process, a product, and a mode of inquiry; both are practical arts aiming to influence people and change the world. Designers and rhetoricians are polymaths, skilled in multiple areas and accustomed to collaborating with others. Both subjects are rooted in particular traditions, theories, and methods, but they also embrace interdisciplinarity, and have somewhat blurry, porous boundaries. As applied arts, both rhetoric and design can be used for ill or for good: the oratory of a demagogue and toxic disposable bauble, versus the unifying motivational slogan ("Si, se puede!"/"Yes we can!", "Save the Earth," "Think globally, act locally") and innovations like the solar cooker. At their best and most ethically sound, both disciplines have "similar values and goals particularly related to the possibility of changing an imperfect situation and instigating a level of social consciousness.

Furthermore, both fields work toward human advancement in both functional and moral senses" (Gallagher et al. 2011, 27).

Rhetoric

Traditionally, the province of rhetoric has been word design – crafting persuasive speeches and written arguments for public audiences. In the Western tradition, the codified teaching of rhetoric emerged in fifth-century BCE Greece to serve a civic exigence: citizens needed to acquire skills in public oratory to defend themselves in court and to participate in democratic deliberation among their peers. Aristotle's *On Rhetoric* (written circa 350 BCE) remains the most significant and influential classical treatise on the subject; in it, Aristotle defines rhetoric as "an ability, in each particular case, to see the available means of persuasion" (2007, 37). Rhetoric, then, is not merely the knack for speaking well; it is a mode of inquiry, a way of seeing. Akin to design, rhetoric is the faculty of discerning the full range of tactics available to accomplish a particular goal, and then selecting and artfully employing the best ones.

Ethos, pathos, logos

Aristotle's three artistic proofs – the modes of persuasion that originate from the speaker – have survived the ages, are commonly taught still today in college composition and public speaking courses, and remain relevant to designers of all stripes. **Ethos** refers to source credibility, whether that be a speaker, author, brand, product, or organization. For Aristotle, ethos comprises good sense, virtuous character, and good will; sustainable designers engage ethos when they highlight how their creations or clients exhibit green values, and put people and planet above profit. Indeed, as environmental concerns have moved into mainstream public awareness, many companies have sought to bolster their ethos by purporting to be eco-friendly, exhibiting good will toward the planet in some way; however, audiences are becoming increasingly savvy about recognizing greenwashing, or the disingenuous claiming of environmental credibility – such as BP's (British Petroleum) rebranding campaign, launched in 2000, featuring a new green and yellow sunburst "Helios" logo and the hypocritical slogan "Beyond Petroleum." Such logos are susceptible to guerrilla design attacks, also known as "culture jamming" (see DeLaure and Fink 2017). After the catastrophic Deepwater Horizon oil spill in 2010, Greenpeace sponsored a "Behind the Logo" competition, inviting activists to redesign BP's logo. Two winning designs are illustrated in Figures 26.1 and 26.2; other entries revised BP's tagline to read "Big Polluter," "Broken Promises," "Bird Poison," "Be Pissed," and "Bye, Planet."

Pathos, the root word of empathy and sympathy, refers to emotional appeals. The rebranded BP logos and slogans above impugn BP's brand ethos through engaging pathos: they evoke indignation, pity for the oil spill victims, and even disgust at corporate malfeasance. In Book II of *On Rhetoric*, Aristotle provides a catalog of specific emotions, from anger and fear, to calmness and confidence. Certainly, appealing to emotions and eliciting desire are central to designers of words, things, and spaces. Any kind of design that engenders joy, hope, and pleasure is more likely to be favorably received. As I discuss in more depth below, negative emotions like fear can also be powerful motivators, but only if communicators provide clear antidotes – feasible courses of action that allow people to alleviate anxiety or avoid feared outcomes.

In his book *Emotionally Durable Design*, Jonathan Chapman proposes that designers seek to cultivate lasting emotional relationships between people and objects, in order to check the common consumer habit of tossing out perfectly functional goods. He contrasts the high turnover rate of computers and electronics, in which we have little emotional investment, with blue jeans

Figure 26.1   Popular Choice winner of the Greenpeace "Behind the Logo" Best Rebranded Logo competition. Designed by Laurent Hunziker, Paris, France (used with permission of designer).

Figure 26.2   Judges' Choice winner of the Greenpeace "Behind the Logo" Best Rebranded Logo competition. Designed by Alexander Hettich, Nuremberg, Germany (used with permission of designer).

and teddy bears, to which we become more emotionally attached over time, as they're broken in, worn out, and accrue layers of meaning. Encouraging designers to think in terms of the potentially lengthy "use career" of objects, Chapman writes,

> We therefore need to design products that consumers will actually want to keep, maintain and use for longer periods of time, sustaining their value to keep users caught in the hook of consuming them. Such objects are designed for empathy and are created in an artful way, engendering powerful emotional attachments.
>
> *(2005, 183–184)*

Finally, Aristotle's third artistic proof is **logos**, or the argument proper: how a speaker or designer marshals evidence to support claims, and taps into widely held beliefs to build support for an idea. Facts and raw data can be persuasive, but only if they are contextualized and presented in appealing, comprehensible ways. Getting people to understand large and complex issues like climate change, for instance, requires the translation of scientific evidence into clear and accessible formats. Designers are already doing important work here by transforming difficult-to-grasp data (gigatons of carbon dioxide), distant and often barely visible phenomena (arctic ice melting, ocean acidification), and future projections (sea level rise by 2050 or 2100) into visually arresting forms that are easy to understand: see, for instance, the visualizations of air pollution, the ozone layer, greenhouse gas emissions, and waste streams created by Real World Visuals, which subsumed the former Carbon Visuals team (www.realworldvisuals.com). Also, in Figure 26.3, see an infographic by London-based designer David McCandless summarizing likely impacts of future carbon emissions.

Metaphor

Rhetoric attends not only to argument content, but also to style; indeed, rhetoricians see substance and style as integrated. Rhetorical tropes, or figures of speech, are stylistic devices that help shift perspective and include personification, hyperbole, and puns. Arguably the most important and pervasive trope is metaphor, which compares two unlike things: love is a rose, life is a highway. George Lakoff and Mark Johnson (1980) assert that metaphors are more than mere stylistic flourishes – indeed, they structure the ways we think and talk. For instance, the root metaphor "time is money" surfaces in many common phrases: we "spend" time, "invest" time, "save" and "waste" time. Time, of course, is literally *not* money, but this powerful root metaphor encourages many of us to worry, perhaps obsessively, about productivity and efficiency – about not "wasting" valuable time.

Metaphor is an elegant, effective trope for creating new understanding, especially for abstract, unfamiliar, or complex ideas. Conceptualizing the Earth as "mother," for example, fosters a familial, affective relationship between human cultures and the planet. Another compelling metaphor for the Earth was articulated in 1965 by Ambassador Adlai Stevenson in a speech to the United Nations:

> We travel together, passengers on a little space ship, dependent upon its vulnerable reserves of air and soil, all committed for our safety to its security and peace; preserved from annihilation only by the care, the work, and I will say, the love we give our fragile craft. We cannot maintain it half fortunate, half miserable, half confident, half despairing, half slave – to the ancient enemies of man – half free in a liberation of resources undreamed of until this day. No craft, no crew can travel safely with such vast contradictions. On their resolution depends the survival of us all.
>
> *(Stevenson 1965, 14)*[1]

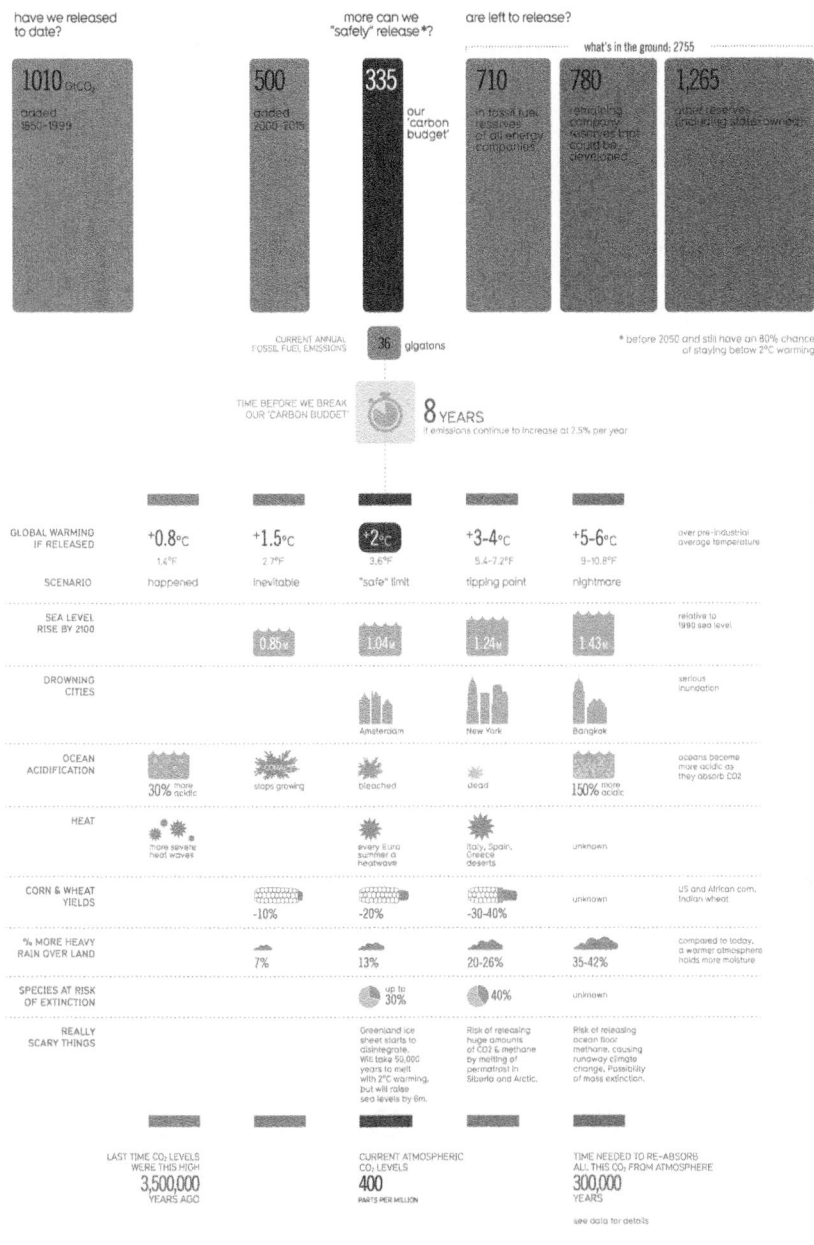

Figure 26.3 How many gigatons of carbon dioxide . . .?
Designed by David McCandless at informationisbeautiful.net (used with permission of designer).

This "spaceship Earth" metaphor renders our planet smaller and more fragile, and highlights the interdependence of all humans on each other and on other species. It evokes a pragmatic responsibility to look after the Earth, making repairs and watching our supply stores, and to care for our fellow crewmates, lest we destroy the only known vessel in the universe capable of supporting human life.

Identification

Stevenson's remarks also evoke "identification," Kenneth Burke's term for how rhetoric works to create a sense of "us" or "we" out of a state of division. Stevenson unifies all humans as passengers on the spaceship, urging us to overcome the deep political and economic divisions plaguing the world. Burke writes, "Identification is compensatory to division. If men were not apart from one another, there would be no need for the rhetorician to proclaim their unity" (1969, 22). Various symbols and rituals help forge identification among members of nations, religions, tribes, political parties, cultures and subcultures; designers seeking to appeal to audiences or change behaviors can tap into group affiliations and strategically employ identification, calling people to join a desirable "us." For example, the U.S. state of California experienced a multiyear drought that was particularly severe in the winter of 2014–15, which led to statewide mandates to reduce consumption. Since the irrigation of grassy lawns during the summer months consumes a substantial amount of water, local municipalities encouraged people to let their grass die, or convert thirsty lawns to other drought-tolerant landscaping. The San Francisco Public Utilities Commission provided free yard signs declaring "Brown is the New Green: We're doing our part to conserve water during this drought" (Figure 26.4). These signs not only excuse an unsightly patch of dead lawn with a clever play on words (being "green," or eco-friendly, now requires foregoing green grass, and instead going

Figure 26.4 "Brown is the New Green" poster.
San Francisco Public Utilities Commission (used with permission).

"brown") – they also express a positive identification with the statewide conservation effort, subtly prompting passersby to consider their own actions as well: Hmm, am I doing my part?

Narrative

Narrative is another simple but powerful rhetorical tool. People in all cultures tell stories to teach and to entertain; we also reason through narrative. According to William Lewis, "narrative is a fundamental form of human understanding that directs perception, judgment, and knowledge" (1987, 288). The story form is both engaging and familiar, and puts listeners into a receptive mood; we tend to identify and sympathize with characters struggling to achieve their goals, and yearn for resolution of the narrative tension or conflict presented in stories. The design firm Free Range, based in Oakland, California, specializes in narrative, and helped create the influential "Story of Stuff" videos by transforming Annie Leonard's research-dense, 90-minute lecture into an accessible animated format that features the villains, victims, and potential heroes (us!) in the story of consumption. In this 20-minute video, Leonard speaks in front of minimalist drawings about the extraction-production-distribution-consumption-disposal cycle: a "linear system" that is in crisis in our "finite world." Through storytelling, aided by the illustrations behind her, Leonard is able to explain complex concepts like "externalized costs" and "planned obsolescence," and show multiple points of intervention where we as citizens can act to change the system.

Narrative takes many forms, including myth and anecdote. Myths are grand stories that help explain a culture's origins and destiny, and shape our understanding of who "we" are. (Were humans granted dominion over other species when the world was created? Or are the animals and trees our cousins, and we mere humble stewards of this land that belongs to future generations?) Anecdotes, by contrast, are small, vivid stories that illustrate a particular point. (A representative anecdote exemplifying the politicization of global warming was Republican U.S. President Ronald Reagan's 1986 removal of the solar panels from the White House roof, which had been installed by his predecessor, Democratic President Jimmy Carter. The solar panels were reinstalled in 2014 at the direction of Democratic President Barack Obama.) Designers may need to tell the story of a company or organization, or of a particular object – how it's made of reclaimed materials, using green production practices, and how it will be repurposed or recycled at end-of-use. Or perhaps designers will fashion a narrative featuring target audience members as heroic characters who adopt sustainable new products and practices. In his book *Winning the Story Wars*, Free Range cofounder and CEO Jonah Sachs enumerates five qualities of effective stories:

> TANGIBLE: Stories present information that makes concepts visible and human scale. They make people feel that they can "touch" and "see" an idea.
>
> RELATABLE: Stories matter to us because their characters carry values that we want to see either rewarded or punished.
>
> IMMERSIVE: Stories allow people to feel that they have experienced things that they have only seen or heard.
>
> MEMORABLE: Stories use rich scenes and metaphors that help us to remember messages without conscious effort.
>
> EMOTIONAL: Stories elevate emotional engagement to the level of, and often beyond, intellectual understanding.
>
> *(Sachs 2012, 52–53)*

Stories crafted to accompany or contextualize a new design will be most powerful if they include these five qualities.

Framing

Another key rhetorical strategy is framing. Scholars across many disciplines – rhetoric, anthropology, sociology, psychology, linguistics – have studied frames and how they shape our knowledge and guide our actions. Frames are cognitive structures or interpretive schemas that filter what we see and influence how we make sense of the world. They allow for mental shortcuts, enabling us to reduce complex, abstract issues into simple, familiar terms. We cannot avoid framing, claims George Lakoff, nor can we simply invent new frames to replace the old; rather, any new idea, product, or proposal must make sense in terms of existing frames (2010, 72). Communicators and designers hoping to shift people to new sustainable patterns must then frame the desired actions in terms of a particular audience's values. Take, for instance, the challenge of promoting certain environmental policies in some conservative parts of the United States, where climate change has been a deeply divisive issue. Starting in the late 1990s, the politicization of climate science intensified, particularly after former Democratic Vice-President Al Gore became a prominent voice on global warming with his 2006 documentary *An Inconvenient Truth*. Many conservatives distrusted Gore and resisted progressives' calls for increased governmental regulation of greenhouse gas emissions; many Republican officials publicly dismissed climate science as a hoax. Even in this divisive context, however, some organizations have succeeded in moving politically conservative communities to reduce energy use – but it's all about the framing.

Exemplary here is work by the Climate and Energy Project (CEP), a small nonprofit based in the Midwestern U.S. state of Kansas. According to CEP founder Nancy Jackson, residents of Salina, Kansas, are deeply skeptical of climate science: "Don't mention global warming," Jackson advises, "and don't mention Al Gore. People out here just hate him" (quoted in Kaufman 2010, n.p.). Between April 2009 and March 2010, the CEP sponsored a yearlong competition among Kansas towns to see who could reduce energy use the most. Rather than framing energy conservation as a response to global warming, the "Take Charge Challenge" focused on thrift, patriotism, spiritual values, and economic prosperity. Led by local leadership teams, residents in various towns weatherized homes, switched out lightbulbs, and unplugged "vampire" appliances that suck energy even when turned off. CEP messaging for the project explicitly avoided mention of global warming, instead highlighting energy savings, cost savings, and competition; according to Jackson, "it was the contest and the community pride and community spirit that really drove this" (quoted in Fuller et al. 2010, 2). Jackson also worked with civic leaders to promote green jobs as a way of shoring up flagging communities, and spoke with local ministers about "creation care," which is the "obligation of Christians to act as stewards of the world that God gave them" (Kaufman 2010, n.p.). In the end, the winning town in CEP's contest reduced its annual energy use by over 5%.

Framing and narrative form intertwine in Kenneth Burke's discussion of dramatic frames. In *Attitudes Toward History* (1984), Burke presents several classic frames – including comedy, tragedy, satire, and melodrama – as symbolic tools we humans use to make sense of social situations and impose order on a complex and changing world (see DeLaure 2011, 453). We seek to make sense of environmental problems like oil spills, toxic pollution of air and water, and global warming by invoking dramas through which we assign blame, correct behavior or expunge guilt, and restore order. An increasingly common frame dramatizing the alarming consequences of climate change is the apocalypse: portraits of impending destruction throwing the world as we know it into chaos. As Douglas Torgerson puts it, "The leading story line in green political thought pictures the industrial cosmos as a tragic doomsday machine, a cosmos in crisis" (1999, 95). However, focusing on frightening statistics rendered in an apocalyptic frame "can actually hinder progress as they adorn the ecological crisis with a paralysing vastness that simply intimidates us as individuals," writes designer Jonathan Chapman. "Such apocalyptic data are counterproductive in most scenarios, and are often the precursor to the murmuring of 'what difference can I possibly make?'" (2005, 33).

There are different ways to spin apocalyptic framing, though: Cristina Foust and William O'Shannon Murphy, drawing on Burke, found two variants of apocalyptic rhetoric in their analysis of mainstream news coverage of climate change. The tragic apocalypse "posits the issue of global warming as extra-human, driven by cosmic forces, and, as such, Fated" (2009, 161), whereas the comic apocalypse "suggests that mistaken humans have a capacity to influence (within limits) the end of the global warming narrative" (2009, 152). Foust and Murphy argue that the tragic frame with its threatening ultimatums quashes human agency, leaving us impotent victims, whereas the comic frame allows for critical self-awareness and inspires redemptive action. It behooves sustainable designers, then, to think carefully about how they frame their projects – tapping into an audience's deeply held values, perhaps activating a familiar dramatic frame, but always heedful of maintaining a sense of empowerment.

Whereas the several rhetorical tools enumerated here are far from an exhaustive list, they can perhaps all be summed up in the simple axiom, "Know thy audience." A designer's audience might be a client, potential customers or user groups, a target demographic, the general public, or even fellow colleagues on a design team. For maximum effectiveness, then, you should seek to understand who your audience members are, what they believe and value, whom they identify with, and what they desire. Then build a bridge from that to your design vision.

Persuasion

Modern social scientific research on persuasion in the United States grew out of the practice and subsequent analysis of World War I government propaganda. The invention of new broadcast mass media (radio, and later television), the rise of social psychology as a discipline, and the development of marketing and public opinion as fields of applied research all paved the way for the systematic scientific study of persuasion. One of the most influential American scholars studying attitude change was Carl Hovland, who during World War II conducted research for the War Department measuring the measuring the effectiveness of the U.S. Army's orientation films, *Why We Fight* (Jowett and O'Donnell 1992). Hovland analyzed the motivational power of the films in terms of several independent variables, including viewer intelligence, one-sided versus balanced messages, and the importance of active participation; after the war, Hovland directed the Yale Studies on Communication and Attitudes, which published a wide range of studies on persuasion throughout the 1950s (McGuire 2009). Researchers since have conducted myriad studies in an effort to understand the factors that influence human attitudes and behavior. In many cases, these social scientific studies seek to operationalize, test, and quantify the ancient and modern rhetorical insights discussed earlier. Persuasion research has illustrated that human motivation is a complex and messy affair, and that we are not all "model rational decision-makers, looking to maximize utility in any economic decision" (Healey 2015, 79). Merely presenting clear, factual information is thus rarely sufficient to sway people.

Norms

One of the most powerful motivators is social proof – modeling our behavior on what others are doing. As Robert Cialdini explains, "we determine what is correct by finding out what other people think is correct. . . . *We view a behavior as correct in a given situation to the degree that we see others performing it*" (2001, 100, emphasis in original). Researchers have staged many experiments to test social norms, both in labs and in the field; one such study examined towel reuse messaging in a hotel. The original sign, consistent with industry standards, asked hotel guests to "HELP SAVE THE ENVIRONMENT. You can show your respect for nature and help save the environment by reusing your towels during your stay" (Goldstein et al. 2008, 473). The investigators tested several alternate messages that invoked social norms – mentioning that other people were already participating, and they should too. "JOIN YOUR FELLOW GUESTS IN HELPING TO SAVE THE ENVIRONMENT. Almost 75% of guests who are asked to participate in our new resource savings program do help by using their towels more than once . . ." (474). The standard "help save the environment" message yielded a towel reuse rate of 35%, while the "join fellow guests" message yielded a reuse rate of 44%. A second phase of the experiment explored various references to specific social groups – citizens, men and women, or "guests who stayed in this room." Curiously, this last category led to the highest reuse rate of nearly 50%. The authors suggest that "provincial norms" – when in Rome, do as the Romans do – stem from the belief that "it is typically beneficial to follow the norms that most closely match one's immediate settings, situations, and circumstances" (479). So, tapping into social norms is a way of employing identification: others like you are taking this particular green action, hence you should, too.

Subsequent studies offer further nuance to our understandings of social norms. White and Simpson (2013) explored how self-benefit appeals, descriptive norms (what others are doing), and injunctive norms (what others think you *should* be doing) interacted with messages that activated personal identity (the individual self) or social identity (the collective self). Their study examined messaging appealing to consumers to adopt a relatively unfamiliar sustainable activity, grasscycling – the leaving of grass clippings on lawns to decompose. They found that messages were most effective when there was a compatible fit between the identity appealed to (individual vs. collective) and the type of norm invoked (self-benefit, descriptive, injunctive). For instance, if the individual is hailed ("How can *you* as an individual make a difference?"), then self-benefit appeals ("Grasscycling improves lawn quality"; "you'll save time on yard work") are more effective than descriptive or injunctive norms. By contrast, if the collective self is activated ("Why should *we* grasscycle?"), then invoking descriptive ("Our neighbors are grasscycling") and injunctive ("Our neighbors want us to grasscycle") norms are most effective. Sustainable designers thus might consider ways to appeal to the collective "we," combined with social proof: Others (who are similar to us in some way) are already using this product or adopting this habit. Or, if your message design targets the individual, then be sure to highlight personal benefits.

Commitment

Another tactic of influence is commitment and consistency, which taps into the widely held belief that constancy and reliability are valuable character traits. People whose words and actions are inconsistent and unpredictable are commonly seen as confused, two-faced, or even mentally unstable, whereas consistency and predictability are associated with honesty and reason. Researchers have found that after we take an initial action – whether signing a petition, agreeing to a small request, or proclaiming a position – we become much more likely to follow up with subsequent acts that are consistent with the first one. Gerard Healey calls this "anchoring," describing the phenomenon "when our judgments are affected by an initial position, regardless of whether that initial position was set logically or arbitrarily" (2015, 82). Written commitments, like signing a pledge, seem to be more powerful than verbal ones; if people feel pressured into the commitment, however, the persuasive effect is lost.

Canada's "Turn It Off" campaign to reduce engine idling illustrates the power of commitment (McKenzie-Mohr 2011, 50–51). Two strategies were pilot tested: the first involved installing signs

For a Healthier Environment

Figure 26.5 "Turn Your Engine Off" – Natural Resources Canada, 2015.
Reproduced with the permission of the Department of Natural Resources, 2016.

in high-idle locations near schools and train parking lots that read "idle free zone/turn engine off/idling gets you nowhere." The signs alone had no measurable impact on engine idling behavior. The second strategy also included sign installation, but added personal contact and commitment: researchers approached drivers and asked them to agree to turn off their cars while parked, sign a pledge to that effect, and display a sticker in their car window stating "Turn your Engine Off/For a Healthier Environment." The second intervention reduced frequency of idling by 32% and idling duration by 73%. Because the pilot program was so effective, National Resources Canada created a free resource tool kit, which has since been adopted by over 200 Canadian communities (McKenzie-Mohr 2011, 51). Learning from this research, sustainable designers could explore ways to help their target audiences see themselves as environmentally concerned citizens, perhaps by asking for a small public commitment, as this significantly increases the likelihood of subsequent actions that are consistent with initial anchor.

Information feedback

Because sustainability often requires ongoing efforts – making repeated actions to alter habits, in contrast to a simple one-time purchase – feedback is an important feature for designers to consider. Numerous field studies have explored the impact of feedback on encouraging pro-environmental behaviors. According to McKenzie-Mohr, posting signs above recycling bins about the number of cans recycled in previous weeks increased capture rates by 65%, and giving households daily feedback on their electricity use led to their reducing energy consumption by 11%, as compared to the control group (2011, 106–107). Factors of feedback design include: (1) delay (how much time elapses between the activity and feedback), (2) aggregation (how many actions, objects, or people are covered by a measurement), (3) accumulation time (how long a time period is covered by a measurement), (4) locality (spatial proximity of the action and feedback), and (5) accessibility (how much effort is involved in accessing the feedback interface – i.e., do you need to log in to a webpage to get the information) (Gustafsson 2010, 106–107). In most cases, designing to communicate local, immediate, easy-to-access, non-aggregated and non-accumulated information is the optimal condition for persuasive feedback.

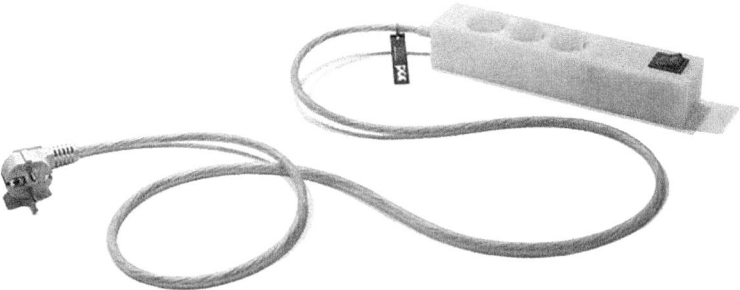

Figure 26.6 Power Aware Cord.
poweraware.com (used with permission).

Take, for instance, the challenge of tracking power consumption. Some electricity use is easy to see – we can remind ourselves and others to turn off unneeded lights. However, many of our appliances and electronics are constantly plugged in, and may be invisibly drawing power even when not in use. A Swedish design called the Power Aware Cord, or Pac, gives convenient, real-time, local, non-aggregated feedback by rendering electricity visible. A blue light is incorporated into the cord extending from the power strip to a wall socket. "[H]igh energy consumption is represented by an aggressive, flickering flow of light," Gustafsson explains, "while low consumption is portrayed by a slow graceful movement" (2010, 99). Here, Pac's design gives local, immediate, effortless, and non-aggregated feedback to consumers, reminding them of their energy consumption, and prompting them to unplug appliances when not in use.

Emotional appeal

Persuasion researchers have also investigated the effects of framing and emotional appeals. On environmental matters, scholars are especially interested in cracking the conundrum of inaction: while a majority of people surveyed seem to be aware of and concerned about climate change, few people feel the urgency to do something to combat it. Other, more immediate problems seem to take precedence. How, then, to jar people out of complacency? Is it better focus on potential gains or losses? More effective to deploy fear appeals, or to avoid negative emotional states? In general, people have a "negativity bias" – we tend to treat negative messages as more important, salient, and worthy of our attention. Behavioral economics research also suggests that people are "loss averse," meaning we perceive losses more strongly than gains (Homonoff 2015, n.p.). Given this, Joel Davis asserts that "[m]essages emphasizing losses associated with inaction are generally more persuasive than messages emphasizing gains associated with action" (1995, 286). For instance, people are more motivated by the threat of losing $350 per year by failing to use energy conservation methods than they are by the prospect of saving $350 per year (Healey 2015, 80). Tatiana Homonoff has studied the effects of offering a five cent bonus for bringing a reusable shopping bag versus charging five cents for single-use bags. Though the economic impact of both programs is identical, the bonus had very little impact, whereas the bag charge, or tax, dramatically changed consumer behavior. In Montgomery county, near Washington, DC, for instance, implementing a five-cent bag tax led to a 42% reduction in disposable bag use (Homonoff 2012, 64).

Though highlighting threats – potential losses or additional costs – may be most effective for limited, small-scale contexts like electric bills or grocery bags, it can backfire when applied to larger-scale problems. As I suggested in the preceding discussion of apocalyptic framing, it's important to pair fear appeals with proffered solutions; audiences must have some sense of agency over the threatening problem. Doug McKenzie-Mohr explains that "threatening messages are a necessary part of directing people's attention to crises. However, they are likely to be counterproductive if they are not coupled with messages that are empowering" (2011, 101). In a 2010 attitude survey, Kathleen Searles found messages appealing to positive emotions to be more effective than those invoking negative ones. Searles concluded that "enthusiasm reinforces an individual's positivity toward efforts to protect the environment and increases their overall pro-environmentalism," whereas "anxiety has a significant and negative effect on participants' views toward the environment" (2010, 180). Fear appeals, then, should be used with caution: though they may garner attention, they also risk triggering a sense of impotence and despair if they are not followed by concrete, empowering solutions.

In sum, persuasion research suggests that sustainable designers should endeavor to create active audience engagement and to accentuate the positive – but without fully eliminating the negative. Designs are more likely to be effective if they generate a sense of agency, where the user feels herself to be actively part of the solution to an environmental problem, especially if she is joining together with others in that effort. In their discussion of seven cognitive concepts for successful eco-design, Erin MacDonald and Jinjuan She highlight responsibility, recommending that designers "instill a sense of personal control over the solution, not responsibility for causing the problem, by designing products with interactive curtailing features," such as select-a-size paper towels, or switches on shower heads that allow users to turn off water while shampooing or shaving (2015, 26). The persuasion concepts explored here offer strategies for designing engaging messages, and for communicating effectively through design itself.

Conclusion

Just as designers in the past had a hand in creating a world driven by rapacious consumption and rapid disposal, sustainable designers today are remaking that world by fashioning objects, systems, and spaces that treat resources as finite, nature as wise, communities as resilient, and the planet as precious. Sustainable design is much larger than making individual green products: indeed, it encompasses a potentially radical new vision of human presence on the Earth. As Michael Braungart and William McDonough put it in their trailblazing book *Cradle to Cradle*,

> Taking an eco-effective approach to design might result in an innovation so extreme that it resembles nothing we know, or it might merely show us how to optimize a system already in place. It's not the solution itself that is necessarily radical *but the shift in perspective* with which we begin, from the old view of nature as something to be controlled to a stance of engagement.
>
> *(2002, 84, emphasis added)*

The ideas explored here, gleaned from the art of rhetoric and social science of persuasion, offer designers a range of strategies for precipitating shifts of perspective.

The ecological crises we now face are daunting, to be sure. Confronting these crises will require broad participation in making profound changes to our habits, systems, and built environments.

Designers must continue be a part of the vanguard, blazing the trail toward a new, more sustainable world. For as John Heskett writes, "considered seriously and used responsibly, design should be the crucial anvil on which the human environment, in all its detail, is shaped and constructed for the betterment of all" (2002, 1).

Note

1 This passage by Stevenson was quoted by David Brower in his "Sermon" speech, which was delivered dozens of times over the course of several decades. Brower was the first executive director of the Sierra Club (1952–69) and founder of Friends of the Earth, the League of Conservation Voters, and Earth Island Institute. Alon Tal writes that "[t]here is a surprising consensus that David Brower was probably the most effective American conservationist who ever lived" (2006, 162).

References

Aristotle (2007) *On Rhetoric: A Theory of Civic Discourse*, trans. G. A. Kennedy, Oxford University Press, Oxford

Braungart, M. and McDonough, W. (2002) *Cradle to Cradle: Remaking the Way We Make Things*, North Point Press, New York

Buchanan, R. (1989) "Declaration by Design: Rhetoric, Argument, and Demonstration in Design Practice", in Margolin, V. ed, *Design Discourse: History, Theory, Criticism*, University of Chicago Press, Chicago, 91–109

Burke, K. (1969) *A Rhetoric of Motives*, University of California Press, Berkeley, CA

Burke, K. (1984) *Attitudes Toward History* 3d ed, University of California Press, Berkeley, CA

Chapman J. (2005) *Emotionally Durable Design: Objects, Experiences and Empathy*, Earthscan/Routledge, New York, NY

Cialdini, R. (2001) *Influence: Science and Practice*, Allyn & Bacon, Needham Heights, MA

Davis, J. (1995) "The Effects of Message Framing on Response to Environmental Communications", *Journalism and Mass Communication Quarterly* 72.2, 285–299

DeLaure, M. (2011) "Environmental Comedy: No Impact Man and the Performance of Green Identity", *Environmental Communication* 5.4, 447–466

DeLaure, M. and Fink, M. eds. (2017) *Culture Jamming: Activism and the Art of Cultural Resistance*, New York University Press, New York

Foust, C. and Murphy, W. O. (2009) "Revealing and Reframing Apocalyptic Tragedy in Global Warming Discourse", *Environmental Communication* 3.2, 151–167

Fuller, M., Kunkel, C., Zimring, M., Hoffman, I., Soroye, K. L. and Goldman, C. (2010) *Driving Demand for Home Energy Improvements*, LBNL-3960E. September. Available from: http://drivingdemand.lbl.gov [18 September 2016]

Gallagher, V. J., Martin, K. N. and Ma, M. (2011) "Visual Wellbeing: Intersections of Rhetorical Theory and Design", *Design Issues* 27, 27–40

Goldstein, N. J., Cialdini, R. B. and Griskevicius, V. (2008) "A Room With a Viewpoint: Using Social Norms to Motivate Environmental Conservation in Hotels", *Journal of Consumer Research* 35, 472–482.

Gustafsson, A. (2010) *Positive Persuasion: Designing Enjoyable Energy Feedback Experiences in the Home*, PhD thesis, Interactive Institute, University of Gothenburg

Healey, G. (2015) "Winning Hearts and Minds: The Role of Emotion and Logic in the Business Case for Sustainable Building Initiatives", *Journal of Design, Business & Society* 1.1, 77–94

Heskett, J. (2002) *Design: A Very Short Introduction*, Oxford University Press, Oxford

Homonoff, T. (2012) "Can Small Incentives Have Large Effects? The Impact of Taxes Versus Bonuses on Disposable Bag Use", *Proceedings of the Annual Conference on Taxation* 105, 64–90

Homonoff, T. (2015) "Do Bag Fees Affect Consumer Behavior?", *Plastic Pollution Coalition Blog*, blog post, 23 November. Available from: www.plasticpollutioncoalition.org/pft/2015/11/23/do-bag-fees-affect-consumer-behavior [18 September 2016]

Jowett, G. S. and O'Donnell, V. (1992) *Propaganda and Persuasion*, 2nd ed, Sage Publications, Newbury Park, CA

Kaufman, L. (2010) "In Kansas, Climate Skeptics Embrace Cleaner Energy", *New York Times*, 18 October. Available from: www.nytimes.com/2010/10/19/science/earth/19fossil.html?_r=1 [19 September 2016]

Lakoff, G. (2010) "Why It Matters How We Frame the Environment", *Environmental Communication* 4.1, 70–81

Lakoff, G. and Johnson, M. (1980) *Metaphors We Live By*, University of Chicago Press, Chicago, IL

Lewis, W. F. (1987) "Telling America's Story: Narrative Form and the Reagan Presidency", *Quarterly Journal of Speech* 73, 280–302

MacDonald, E. and She, J. (2015) "Seven Cognitive Concepts for Successful Eco-design", *Journal of Cleaner Production* 92, 23–36

McGuire, W. (2009) "The Yale Communication and Attitude-Change Program in the 1950s", in Dennis, E. and Wartella, E., eds, *American Communication Research – The Remembered History*, Routledge, New York, 39–60

McKenzie-Mohr, D. (2011) *Fostering Sustainable Behavior: An Introduction to Community-Based Social Marketing*, New Society Publishers, Gabriola Island, BC, Canada

Sachs, J. (2012) *Winning the Story Wars: Why Those Who Tell – and Live – the Best Stories Will Rule the Future*, Harvard Business Review Press, Boston, MA

Searles, K. (2010) "Feeling Good and Doing Good for the Environment: The Use of Emotional Appeals in Pro-Environmental Public Service Announcements", *Applied Environmental Education and Communication* 9, 173–184

Stevenson, A. (1965) "Strengthening the International Development Institutions", *Speech Before the United Nations Economic and Social Council*, Geneva, Switzerland. 9 July. Available from: www.adlaitoday.org/articles/connect2_geneva_07-09-65.pdf [4 August 2016]

Tal, A. ed. (2006) *Speaking of Earth: Environmental Speeches That Moved the World*, Rutgers University Press, New Brunswick, NJ

Torgerson, D. (1999) *The Promise of Green Politics: Environmentalism and the Public Sphere*, Duke University Press, Durham, NC

White, K. and Simpson, B. (2013) "When Do (and Don't) Normative Appeals Influence Sustainable Consumer Behaviors?", *Journal of Marketing* 77, 7

27

USING DATA VISUALIZATION TO SHIFT BEHAVIORS

Adam Nieman

One of many technological shifts of the past decade is the ease with which we can collect, store and access data. The abundance of data brings with it opportunities that designers are only beginning to explore. There is a palpable sense among data analysts and data visualizers alike that there are wonders to be discovered – ways of using data and ways of making it available to users that no one has yet imagined. Many of these wondrous applications will involve shifting behavior – helping individuals to make more informed decisions or 'nudging' whole populations to change the way they act.

This chapter reviews some of the ways we are already using data to shift behaviors, while also serving as a guide for explorers. What do you need to be a data pioneer? What principles can support progress in this area? We will look at some specific examples – particularly around climate change – but the main emphasis is on some basic visualization theory: what do we need to know about visualization in order to apply it to behavior change? The focus is on visualizing data rather than on analyzing data. That is, we are asking: what happens when we make data available to people? rather than asking: what can we learn about people through collecting and analyzing data about them?

Pull audiences and push audiences

From a design point of view the main focus is on two audiences who each need different visualizations. The first audience is already engaged with the information presented and will 'pull' the data they need from the visualization. The second audience does not yet know they need or want the data, and the approach is to 'push' information at them. We don't have to be pushy about it though – the main barrier for this audience is that they lack a sense of connection with whatever the data represents. If we can make it real, as it already is to the first audience, we can engage them, too. In visualization for behavior change, it is mostly the push visualizations we are interested in because it is a general audience we are trying to reach – not an audience with a prior interest in the data.

The binary distinction between these two audiences is not actually as clear-cut as I have suggested. All users of data visualization are on their own 'journey of engagement'. At the outset there will be little pull from the viewer so you will need to push data at them. As the viewer gets more engaged there will be more of a pull, and even an imperative to 'drive' the visualization.

Push audiences are near the beginning of their journey of engagement, and pull audiences near the end – approaching total engagement.

A simple example of how data can affect behavior, and has done for some time, is weather forecasting. If it's going to rain, we might cancel plans for a picnic, but only if we get the forecast. Information does not change behavior by itself. To have any impact the forecast must meet its audience at the right time and place and present the information in a way they will engage with. But the most important factor affecting your engagement with the weather report is your interest. If you bring your own questions to the forecast – 'will it be raining at the time we are planning our picnic?' – then a weather forecast may change your behavior. If you don't have questions about the weather, that is much less likely. The questions audiences bring or don't bring to data are crucial. So identifying my two wholly different types of audience, and laying down two different approaches to visualization for them, begins by asking: does the audience already have questions?

Data visualization to date has mostly been by and for people who bring their own questions to the data. There is a pull from this audience – they come seeking information. Engaging a new audience is a process of 'pushing' data. The new audience won't have questions so they won't actively pull information from the visualization – we first have to convince this audience that it is in their interest to engage with the data.

For example, consider the challenge of reducing energy bills in a building – a workplace or school for instance. Can data visualization help? Energy data for the building will consist, in raw form, of meter readings. These data rightly 'belong' to building managers – they commission the meters and understand their limitations. And they have to justify the energy bills, and so they will come to the data with questions. In doing so they may recognize opportunities to reduce energy bills and improve the environmental impact of their building.

But building managers work on behalf of building users; so building users have an interest in the data also. Some of the opportunities managers identify may require users to change their behavior – shut windows or turn appliances off for instance. Some opportunities may impact on building users in other ways and will require their understanding and support, for instance lighting that switches itself off unless it detects movement in the room may annoy them unless the justification for it is clear. Energy data could have a role in the behavior change process and in seeking consent for change, but building users are a very different audience from building managers. Most significantly they don't have any reason to engage spontaneously with the meter readings. How then, can energy data for the building help? What do we have to do to the data before we can 'push' it towards building users? How can we persuade building users to 'pull' it?

The trick with data graphics is 'show, don't tell'. That is a good maxim for push audiences and pull audiences alike, but much harder to achieve with the former. If you put data in front of viewers who are not bringing questions of their own, they have to take a leap of faith. Viewers first have to trust you as an authority and accept your word that whatever you are trying to show them is important. That is why it is far preferable to present the data in a way that allows viewers to judge its significance for themselves. Making it real – not just numbers – is one way to achieve that. I will explain what that involves after a bit more discussion of the two audiences.

I am using building users and managers as an example of the two different types of audience because it is a current issue for these groups. Much of the energy we use is consumed in buildings and there is increasing pressure to improve buildings' performance and reduce their carbon footprint. There are many opportunities – minor changes in behavior can bring about dramatic savings – but there are challenges too. Modern building management systems generate a lot of useful data and are increasingly good at presenting it to building managers but not yet to building users. This is a problem my own company, Real World Visuals has been addressing. Our solution is just one way – there is wide scope for creative application of the principles we have developed. The key starting point is to understand your audience and whether they are bringing any questions to the data.

The two audiences have vastly different needs. Building managers generally need to see as much data as possible as clearly as possible so they can find answers to their questions and generate new questions. At other times they need just a few crucial metrics – they are 'driving' their building and need data in the form of a dashboard to be able to 'steer' it appropriately. The same data may be of interest to building users – they may want to see how their building is performing right now – but their interest is very different. There's no imperative to take control, and the metrics themselves may be divorced from their direct experience. A dashboard is unlikely to be a good way to share the data with users.

Building managers have learnt a 'feel' for what the units refer to (electrical energy, volumes of gas or liquid fuels, masses of solid fuels). Users probably haven't. Because the numbers seem real to managers, they can be represented abstractly without losing their relevance. A building manager can look at a plot of meter readings against time and 'see' fuel being consumed where a building user may just see a line. This is the crucial difference between the pull and the push audiences: the pull audience sees real 'stuff' in abstract graphics; the push audience sees just graphics. The not-yet-engaged push audience is not yet ready for abstraction. They lack the connection with the real world that makes abstract graphics engaging. So the first task we have in push visualization is creating that connection.

Concrete visualizations

This key requirement is easy to overlook because abstract graphics – charts, tables, etc. – are what people generally have in mind when they talk about data visualization. Regular visualization uses identical graphical elements (bars, lines, etc.) to represent very different quantities (interest rates, galaxies, hemlines, whatever). That is to say, regular visualization is a process of abstraction in which data are represented indexically (there is a correlation between the representation and the thing it represents but no resemblance of it). But there are other ways to communicate quantitative data. We can illustrate actual stuff rather than an abstract representation of it. That is to say (in the language of semiotics) we can represent quantities iconically (so the representation actually resembles the stuff) rather than indexically. I call this 'concrete visualization' to distinguish it from regular 'abstract visualization'.

Concrete visualization can be just as quantitatively accurate as abstract visualization but it also communicates a physical sense of scale. Other than my own company's work, my favorite examples of concrete visualization can be found in the work of the artist Chris Jordan who makes giant canvases that provide insight into statistics that would otherwise remain inaccessible on a personal level. For instance, one canvas depicts in the style of the pointillist artist Seurat 400,000 plastic bottle caps, which is equal to the number of plastic bottles consumed in the United States every minute; another depicts 139,000 cigarette butts – the number smoked and discarded every 15 seconds in the United States. The distinction between concrete and abstract visualization is explored in Nieman (2012). Here I focus on why it is particularly valuable in promoting behavior change.

Concrete visualization restores a sense of reality to the data. It becomes more than mere numbers. To be clear, viewers will generally understand that whatever is being represented abstractly is real. Nevertheless, 'understanding' is not enough to help a viewer see past (or through) a graph to the real stuff it represents. Viewers have to *feel* it is real in addition to knowing it is real before they will engage with it. The difference between feeling and knowing is like knowing that 139,000 cigarette butts are discarded every 15 seconds and standing in front of a canvas 5 feet high by 6 feet wide on which each of those butts is individually identifiable. The actual space the canvas takes up gives us a physical insight that is lacking if we consider the data purely numerically. It feels real because viewers can relate the number to their own bodies. In Jordan's image the butts are elements in larger image – a woodland scene – which helps us to see the number in two ways simultaneously: the whole and the parts.

Concrete visualization can make the difference between feeling and knowing very clear, and viewers can experience a shock when the way they relate to the data is suddenly transformed. I call this the 'Yeah yeah gosh effect' because, 'Yeah, yeah . . .' is the reaction you get when you try to tell somebody something they think they already know or think they have no interest in knowing, and 'Gosh!' is the reaction when someone sees something in a new way. One reaction to the shock is the spontaneous generation of questions such as, 'Is that a lot or a little?' and 'How does it compare to others?' This is the first step in persuading viewers that there is something for them in these data – encouraging them to have a look for themselves.

Concrete visualization provides the sense of reality to a push audience that a pull audience already enjoys, and which is a prerequisite for engagement with data. It has another important advantage over abstract visualization though (as well as many disadvantages). With abstract visualization we understand quantitative relationships by bringing our visual interpretive skills and experience to bear on data. However, there are other kinds of skills and experience – *embodied* experience – which abstract visualization floats free from. For instance we know what it is like to lift things and hold them and to walk around them; we know what it is like to inhabit different spaces and to move through space.

All these can be employed to make sense of data, and concrete visualization makes them available. The more it relates to viewers' embodied experience, the more powerful it is. In the case of building data, the building itself can become part of its own explanation. Building users know what it is like to move around inside and outside the building and that can be the basis of a physical sense of scale for the quantitative data.

Linking visualizations to viewers' direct experience is a powerful technique, but it also reveals one of the limitations of concrete visualization: you can't always rely on viewers having the experience you want to reference. At human scales, everyone can relate to things quantitatively with reference to their own body. At larger scales though, the experience you want to reference in the visualization may be that of standing next to particular building, or walking across a particular park, or driving between particular cities. This makes concrete visualization parochial in the sense that it works only in a limited geographical context.

There are ways to deal with this. One way is to draw on general experiences – we might not be able to rely on the audience having used a particular motorway interchange for instance, but it will be close enough to motorways they have experienced to be useful. Another way is to create an interactive visualization that can draw on map data, or reference objects and be located anywhere that is meaningful to the user – a Parisian may locate it next to the Eiffel Tower while a New Yorker locates it in Central Park. In Figure 27.1 the scale is such that just 3 versions are enough for anybody on the planet to be able to relate physically to the water. North and South Americans, Europeans and Africans, and Asians and Australasians can each relate the blue sphere to their own experience of travel. We all of us can imagine what it would be like to traverse a distance equal to the diameter of the water, and have a sense of how long it would take, and so we can for the first time 'feel' a quantity like 1,408.7 million cubic kilometers, which otherwise would be just a number.

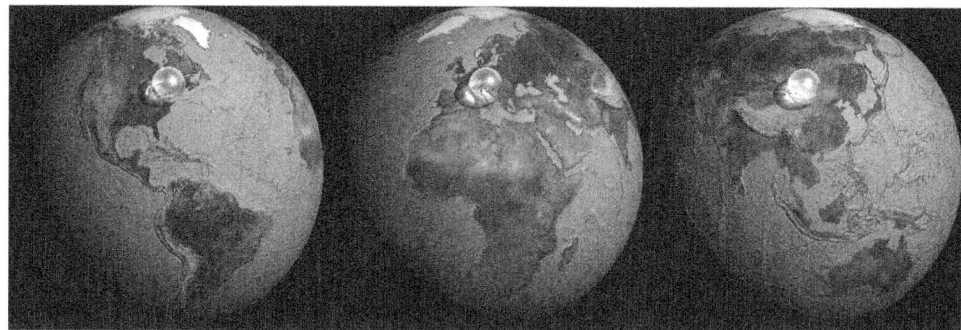

Figure 27.1 All the water in the world (including the oceans, ice, surface water, ground water and water in the atmosphere): an example of 'concrete visualization' – using the world itself in its own explanation. There is a total of 1,408.7 million cubic kilometers of water on Earth. That volume would fit into a sphere 1,391 km across (864 miles). Many people are initially surprised at the size – it seems too small – but it makes more sense when you realize that the average depth of the oceans is just 3.7 km (2.3 miles), which is tiny on a global scale.

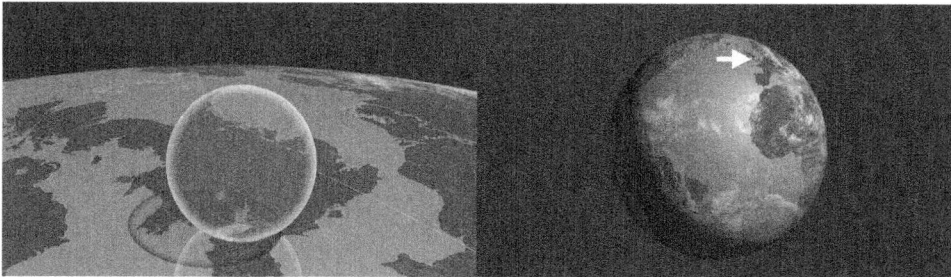

Figure 27.2 All the accessible freshwater in the world: 4.3917 million cubic kilometers in a sphere 203 km across (126 miles). Much of world's freshwater is locked up as ice or is buried deep underground. The water illustrated here is the water in rivers and lakes, in soil–moisture and shallow groundwater (up to 750 meters underground). It makes up 11.35% of all non-ocean water and just 0.31% of all water. This is an example of a 'parochial visualization': you need to know the area depicted to properly relate to the quantity. It would take many more than three versions to work for everyone on the planet.

Design tools for data graphics

When data visualization is discussed from a design point of view, the audience is assumed to be bringing their own questions to the data. As a result, principles discussed in visualization literature tend to apply mostly to pull visualizations, and not so much to push visualizations. There are many valuable insights in existing literature but they often need modification before they can be applied to the quite different design problem of pushing data towards a new audience.

Edward Tufte, for instance, introduced some valuable concepts when he developed a theory of data graphics in 1983. These include the data-ink ratio, the idea of chartjunk, data density and the data matrix, and they have influenced the development of data visualization ever since. The data-ink ratio is a way of quantifying how efficiently a graphic encodes information (Tufte 1983, 93). Tufte distinguishes the 'non-erasable core of the graphic', i.e. the ink (or pixels) that actually encodes data (the data-ink) from 'redundant' ink. The data-ink ratio is the ratio of these (data-ink/non-data-ink). Chartjunk, as conceived by Tufte, is any part of a chart that does not convey useful information. It could be any part of the chart itself that is unnecessary or distracting or any form of decoration applied to the chart (Tufte 1983, 107). Data density is a measure of the number of pieces of information encoded per square inch of a graphic (Tufte 1983, 162). The numbers that go into a graphic can be organized into a matrix of observations by variables. This is the data matrix (Tufte 1983, 162).

For Tufte, well-designed visualizations are

- inevitably comparative
- deftly multivariate
- shrunken, high-density graphics
- usually based on a large data matrix
- drawn almost entirely with data-ink
- efficient in interpretation
- often narrative in content, showing shifts in the relationship between variables as the index variable changes (thereby revealing interaction or multiplicative effects).

(Tufte 1983, 175)

Tufte's influence is such that many data visualizers today see their job as being to maximize data density by shrinking the size of their graphic, including as many data points and as many variables as possible, maximizing the data-ink ratio and eliminating chartjunk. But Tufte's principles are not helpful in all situations, so it is important to apply them intelligently – not blindly. There is evidence that graphical elements that Tufte would dismiss as chartjunk can serve a useful purpose for some audiences (Bateman et al. 2010). Our experience at Real World Visuals provides plenty of anecdotal evidence that Tufte's principles are not universally applicable. The kind of elegant, data-dense, abstract graphics that Tufte champions work well if an audience has prior questions, but bounce straight off push audiences. We see our job partly as helping people become the natural audience for elegant abstract graphics. We take our audience on a journey that starts off concrete and experiential in order that it can later be abstract and conceptual.

The water visualizations (Figure 27.1 and Figure 27.2) depart from Tufte's prescription in almost every way. The data-ink ratio and data density is as low as it could be, there is just a single number visualized in each: 1,408.7 million cubic kilometers and 4.3917 million cubic kilometers respectively. The only comparison they provide is with the entire world. There is no discernable narrative (though they take on new meaning when you learn that almost all water on Earth was delivered by comets that collided with the planet during the formation of the solar system). Nevertheless, they provide useful insight and provoke the kinds of questions that would allow someone to engage with 'proper' information-dense water-data graphics.

The goal of push visualizations is to encourage viewers to engage with the data and make it meaningful for themselves. Often we are not trying to make lots of data available, we are simply trying to bring something to people's attention. In the case of carbon dioxide emissions data for instance, a barrier to engagement is that carbon dioxide is an invisible gas. Making emissions visible is a goal in itself as it provokes the kinds of questions that will allow viewers to engage with the data on a deeper level. In push visualizations we will sometimes be visualizing a single datum (e.g. a carbon footprint). For viewers who already have questions of their own, illustrating a single number would probably not be helpful (the number itself would answer any question they had). Nevertheless, an illustration of a single number could be a valuable 'way in' to not-yet-engaged audiences.

However, there is a deeper, underlying principle that applies to both push and pull visualizations and of which the data-ink ratio heuristic can be considered a special case. I call it the principle of parsimony, and it states that visualizations should include enough detail to direct viewers' attention to the salient information, and no more. Another way to think about it is to anticipate all the ways viewers may get the wrong end of the stick and guide them away from irrelevancies. Parsimonious graphics aim to avoid any questions arising in viewers' minds other than questions about the data that are actually encoded.

For instance, every graphic has to have color of some type (even if the color is black). The principle of parsimony states that you should avoid any use of color that looks as if it may be encoding information, unless it actually is encoding information. The question: Why is it this color? Should only arise if it is relevant. It shouldn't occur to the viewer to ask the question if an arbitrary choice has been made about color. When, at Real World Visuals we visualize carbon dioxide gas, we tend to make it sky blue. We have found this provokes the fewest questions about the color and so helps viewers focus on the quantity of gas. Black or red carbon dioxide would carry negative connotations. As data visualizers we want to remove 'noise' from the data, and so we avoid baking judgment into the images (ours or any potential viewers' judgment). Blue seems to work because it looks like the sky, which is where emissions are destined to end up. Maybe that is why it causes the least diversion.

In the case of pull visualization, less is more – the best way to achieve a parsimonious visualization is usually to remove extraneous detail – but that is not always true for push visualization, especially in the case of concrete visualization. Sometimes judiciously adding detail can add clarity and close down any irrelevant questions. In concrete visualization we often need to show quantities of stuff (water, carbon dioxide, people, coal, whatever) in relation to a landmark that people can relate to physically. The principle of parsimony offers two directions. On the one hand we can strip our representation of the landmark back so nothing about it raises questions other than: 'How much stuff am I looking at?' This results in clean 3D graphics, often on an infinite plane, which provides focus by indicating clearly that everything relevant is right here before you.

The decisions we make (which we are forced to make) about lighting and color for instance should be 'un-interesting'. That is, we don't want anything in the visualization that makes viewers ask themselves: 'Is that important? Should I be paying attention to that?' We want the choices to appear as arbitrary (unmotivated) as they truly are. The choices made by the designer are not random choices – for instance, getting the lighting right helps viewers extract information from the image, so the choice is not unimportant – but they are nevertheless un-interesting details in their own right. The aim is to remove anything that may distract from the data. For example, in concrete visualization it is often important to depict people, so viewers can place themselves in the scene and relate to quantities with their own bodies, but if we add too much detail we will provoke viewers to think about the people – who they are, what they are like, whether they are attractive – rather than thinking about the scale of the quantity depicted.

On the other hand, instead of stripping the scene of detail, we can we can take the other direction and use a real scene. For example, we can place a 3D object in real footage of an area. Although there will be a lot of irrelevant detail in a visualization that places data in a real scene, it is sometimes clearer to viewers where the important information lies and easier to distinguish mere context from elements that carry information.

There is a third direction we can go, which is to use augmented reality and place our data directly in viewers' own physical contexts. That is, to depict quantities of stuff in the actual space a viewer is inhabiting, for instance by adding it to a camera view on a mobile phone. Augmented reality is usually a process of adding information to objects in our field of view. One of my favorite examples is an iPhone app called Flightradar24. When you hold your phone up to the sky Flightradar24 labels any planes in the field of view with their speed and destination. But what

I am proposing is something different. Instead of adding a layer of data to the physical world, we can turn the physical world into a device for making sense of data. This takes augmented reality and turns it on its head. It is not so much augmented reality as 'reality augmented data'. There is enormous potential for reality augmented data in push visualizations because it meets viewers in their own space – brings data to where the viewer is right now – which is half the battle with behavior change.

Having discussed some of the principles on which push visualizations are built, and outlined some techniques in general terms, let us now see these applied to a real challenge: climate change. How can data visualization help? More specifically, how can data visualization help change the behavior of building users, where much of our energy is consumed?

The core science of climate change

Much of Real World Visuals' work involves supporting behavior change to meet emissions targets. International agreements have committed countries to drastic reductions in greenhouse gas emissions. Some of the reductions will come from shifting the way people use energy. This is usually a big ask. The imperative for change may be well understood but it also seems distant. The impact we have on the environment is far from clear. Nor is it clear what impact our attempts at mitigation are having. Asking uninformed people to change their behavior is challenging, but so is informing uninterested people (a push audience rather than a pull audience).

Climate change is remarkably simple. Only the fine details are complex or contentious; the core idea is easy to understand and is built on basic science (that is, it is built on well-established, uncontroversial science that provides the foundations for, and has been tested in many fields, not just climate science). Why then does it seem to be hard to understand and easy to dismiss as a threat? One problem is that its cause is invisible. I will explain why that is a problem below, but first I want to follow up on my claim that climate change is simple by describing the mechanism in four paragraphs.

The core science of climate change can be explained in the following way. Like all things with a temperature above absolute zero, the Earth glows. It radiates energy into space. The wavelength of the radiation depends on temperature.[1] If it were really hot (about 750 °C/1,400 °F) the radiation would be in the visible part of the spectrum and we could see the planet glowing red hot. We can still be aware of the presence of a warm object even if it is not radiating in the visible part of the spectrum – we can feel the radiation coming off it because when it hits us it stimulates vibrations in the molecules that make up our skin and so causes our skin to warm up.

The average temperature on Earth is a comfortable 15 °C (59 °F) so it glows with invisible infrared 'light'. This radiation takes heat energy away from the Earth, which is how our planet cools down. Sunlight adds energy to the Earth continuously, which raises its temperature, but as its temperature rises the planet glows more brightly. Eventually it reaches an equilibrium temperature at which the energy being radiated away matches the energy coming from the sun.

Our atmosphere prevents some of the radiation from escaping into space, which is lucky because otherwise temperatures would plummet at night. Greenhouse gases are gases that are tuned to absorb infrared radiation – tuned in the sense that they vibrate at just the right frequency. When a photon of infrared light hits a greenhouse gas molecule (e.g. carbon dioxide) it transfers its energy to the vibration of the molecule. Eventually, the carbon dioxide will give up its vibrational energy creating a new photon of infrared light in the process, just like the one that got it vibrating in the first place. This new photon may carry on in the same direction away from the Earth or it may be directed back down to the surface – it could emerge from the molecule in any direction.

Enough infrared is trapped this way to keep the planet much warmer than it would have been otherwise. Without this greenhouse effect average temperatures on Earth would be well below freezing. Because we have added more greenhouse gas to the atmosphere, more infrared radiation is being trapped and less energy is escaping into space. So we are heading towards a new, higher equilibrium temperature.

That's it in a nutshell. It comes down to one thing: if we add greenhouse gases to the atmosphere they will prevent radiation escaping into space and global temperatures will increase. The details involve working out what impact the extra greenhouse gas will have. It is relatively easy to work out (with basic science) what effect it will have on the Earth's 'energy budget' (how much energy it prevents from escaping). It is then possible to work out what the new equilibrium temperature will be. It is significantly harder to model how the extra energy will be stored in the oceans and land and atmosphere, but the mathematical models of the energy flows that scientists have made to date have made good predictions so far.

The problem of invisibility

Despite its simplicity, making sense of climate change is challenging for a number of reasons that include psychological barriers such as denial and wishful thinking. These are important, but I want to consider a less familiar conceptual challenge, which is a problem with how we make sense of air itself. Air is so ubiquitous that it is easy not to notice it. Indeed it is a metaphor for nothing – we speak of things vanishing into thin air because when something enters the air, it really feels as if it has vanished. We notice wind rather than air; the movement of air takes on a sense of reality that air itself lacks. Few people notice that a half empty glass is half full of air. It is substantial enough to support large aircraft, and even fuel them as they fly (the chemical reaction that pushes jets forwards requires oxygen – supplied by the air – as well as aviation fuel). We actually know a lot about air – what it feels like, sounds like and looks like, how it nourishes us and how, when we are short of breath, it can't nourish us fast enough – and yet we still don't notice it or the way it pushes against each square centimeter of our body with a force of 10 newtons (15 pounds per square inch). The way we feel about air may be how a fish feels about water – we don't notice we are experts.

There is also a problem of scale with the atmosphere. Few people have a sense of how much air it contains or how high it extends from the surface of the Earth. Most people vastly overestimate the distance, and many have a sense of it being, from a practical point of view, infinite. In fact, when you fly in an airliner at 11 km (6.8 miles) above sea level, three quarters of the air in the atmosphere is beneath you. Nevertheless, although local changes are familiar – filling the air with smoke for instance – the idea of being able to change the constitution of the whole atmosphere is a relatively new one, and hard to come to terms with. It is common to think of pollution as only the stuff that we can see or smell. By this way of thinking, once it has mixed into the air it ceases to count as pollution.

So air is a form of 'nothing' which has the effect of transforming anything we add to it into a similar form of nothing. It is easy to see why emissions don't *feel* significant. The fact that emissions are themselves invisible just compounds the problem, but there is yet another confounding factor, which is that, as gases, they already feel insubstantial. We account for greenhouse gas emissions in units of mass: pounds or kilograms or metric tons of carbon dioxide. This makes perfect sense from an accounting point of view but creates a significant barrier for push audiences who ask, 'what does that even mean?' We tend to think of mass (the amount of stuff) in terms of weight (the force with which the Earth pulls on that stuff). The buoyancy of gases disrupts the connection between weight and mass, which makes units of mass a counterintuitive way to think of quantities of gases.

For pull audiences, none of this really matters. Carbon dioxide is already real for them. Even if they have only a vague sense of the scale of the atmosphere, they know the parameters in which they are working and they are ready to go straight to abstract representations to compare rates of emission. For push audiences though, it is asking a lot to engage with such data. The first step is to make it real. Ideally we will provoke a 'yeah yeah gosh' reaction, which in turn will generate the kinds of questions that allow viewers to engage with the data.

At Real World Visuals we have tried to make climate change real by making its cause real on a number of different scales. We have visualized all the carbon dioxide in the atmosphere and all the carbon dioxide in the air in a small room. We visualized in real-time the global rate at which we add carbon dioxide to the air (about 1,300 metric tons a second) and also the rate at which boiling a kettle adds carbon dioxide to the air (see Figure 27.3). The range of scales is important because combining different perspectives helps people make sense of the problem (we call this process triangulation). It also helps people to see themselves in the data, which brings us back to building users.

Figure 27.3 shows a system that allows consumers to see how much carbon dioxide their electric appliances create. As the appliance runs, bubbles of carbon dioxide emerge from it and build up on the table beneath it. It also allows comparison of different energy suppliers – users can switch from a normal tariff to a green tariff (which includes more renewables in the fuel mix). The principle of parsimony means we want to direct viewers to the size and rate of the spheres that emerge – not other aspects of them. For that reason it is important that they should behave as you might expect a little bubble of gas to behave. Even though no one has ever seen such a bubble we all have the experience of things falling in air. If we make the dynamics right – accounting for the size of the bubble for instance – then viewers are far less likely to be distracted. The cooling towers, trees and wind turbines serve no visualization purpose and, driven by the principle of parsimony, we would exclude them from an app we actually released.

Figure 27.3   Experimental augmented reality, or 'reality augmented data'.

Supporting behavior change in building users

So now we can bring this all together. Building managers identify behaviors in building users that they want to change. Many of these need a conversation, or some other sort of negotiation, in which both sides come to understand the imperatives of the other. In some buildings for instance, users open windows while the heating or air conditioning is on, which wastes a lot of energy and makes it harder to control the environment in the building. The strategy of asking users not to open windows won't work by itself. Managers need to understand why users are opening windows and users need to understand what impact they can have (positive or negative). If this conversation happens on a purely abstract level, the response will be: 'yeah yeah'. There may be a genuine desire to help, but without a sense of reality it will be difficult to act. Making it real – as real as it already is to building managers – can help. A 'yeah yeah gosh' experience can facilitate the conversation. It also creates a different kind of imperative – the user will be acting on something that feels real, and present and happening now.

At Real World Visuals we have built a system that takes building data for a whole campus and presents it in a physically meaningful way to help facilitate the conversation between building users and building managers. Its job is to make emissions feel as real for building users as they are for building managers tasked with reducing them. The interface is a map of the estate. When users select a building they see the actual rate at which the building is adding carbon dioxide to the atmosphere (which has been calculated from energy data). It is shown as spherical volumes of gas emerging in real-time, which makes it immediate and relevant. This system is illustrated in Figures 27.4 and 27.5.

Additional views are available showing, for instance, what a day's emissions look like. A day is a period of time that we can 'inhabit' – we can 'feel' a day. A year is a good period of time for accounting, but too long to constitute an experience. Daily emissions, then, are easier to relate

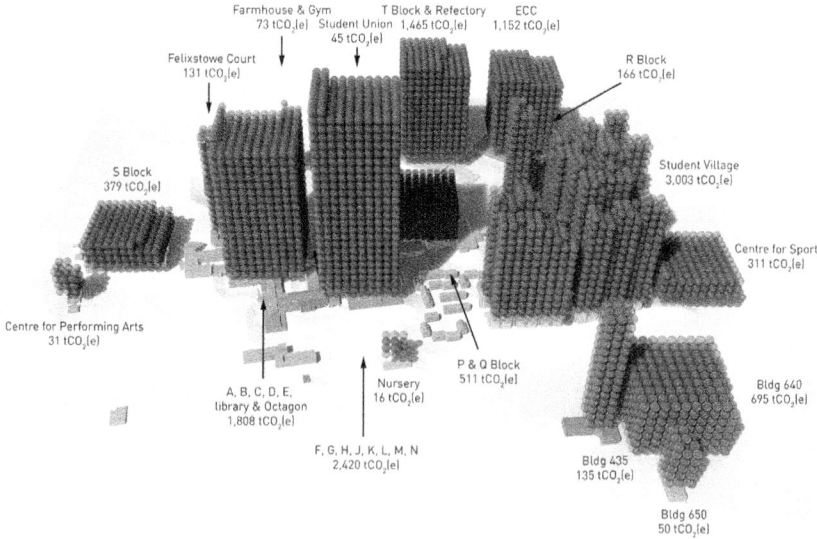

Figure 27.4 3D map of the University of the West of England, with annual emissions as 1 metric ton spheres. This is part of a prototype Estate Visualizer Tool in use at the University of the West of England, Bristol, UK. Building users can select a building on any of the university's campuses either from a map or from a drop-down list.

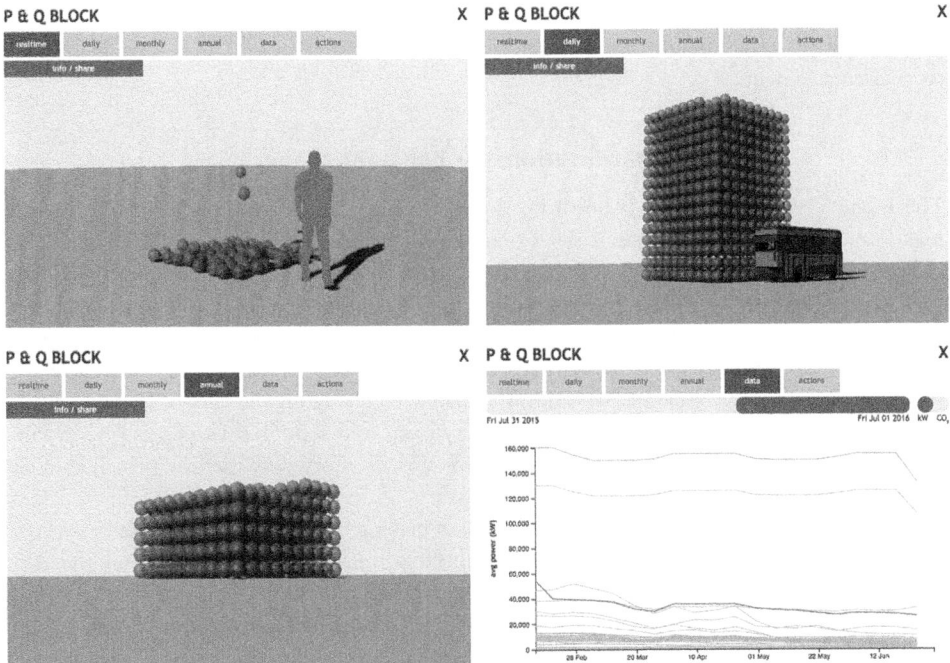

Figure 27.5 Prototype Estate Visualizer Tool. Selecting a building brings up a tabbed visualization. Top left: real-time view (animated). Users see spheres that represent the actual rate that carbon dioxide gas is entering the atmosphere. For this building, as the info box would show if selected, each sphere is 21.6 cm across (8.5 inches) and is the volume of 10 grams (0.4 ounces) of carbon dioxide gas at 15 °C (59 °F) and standard pressure. The spheres appear every 0.6 seconds. Top right: daily emissions, with a double-decker bus for scale. This time each sphere contains 1 kilogram of carbon dioxide gas. There are 1,497 of them. Bottom left: annual emissions. Each sphere contains 1 metric ton of carbon dioxide. There are 547 of them. Bottom right: this tab facilitates comparison across the whole campus. It a pull visualization ready to answer users' newly formed questions. It allows users to explore the whole time series at different levels of granularity, which helps answer questions about the base-load of the buildings, variation over seasons and the difference between term-time and vacations.

to on a personal level than annual emissions. Once viewers have a *feel* for daily emissions though, they are better able to engage with annual emissions, or any other convenient way of accounting for energy and emissions.

The 'journey of engagement' is built into the tool itself. It provokes questions such as, 'Is that a lot or a little?' and, 'How does that compare?' and provides accessible ways to answer them. Eventually users begin asking themselves the kinds of questions that building managers ask such as: 'Which buildings perform well, and which poorly?' By now viewers are ready for abstract graphics, so the tool provides visualizations that conform more closely to Tufte's prescription. It deliberately doesn't aim for the same data density you would expect from a building management system though – the Estate Visualizer has a different job to do.

The target audience, being at the beginning of their journey of engagement, will not seek out information about energy performance and emissions. For that reason the tool will not work if it is buried deep within a website or requires a download. The Estate Visualizer is a push visualization and needs to be visible to potential users. Ideally it will be running in a convenient kiosk within buildings themselves. Like a clock or a departures board, the Estate Visualizer is 'ambient media'. Alternatively, building managers can introduce the tool at the outset of an engagement process. The tool also includes ways to share visualizations, which facilitates peer-to-peer engagement.

Physicalizations for behavior change

The Estate Visualizer is not a dashboard – it does not help users 'drive' the building. It simply makes intangible impacts a little easier to think about and so supports the behavior change process. There are more direct ways to push data on unsuspecting viewers though. Concrete visualizations can have even more impact if they are taken off screens and brought right into the space the user is occupying. Augmented reality (or rather, reality augmented data) was mentioned previously, but data physicalizations – physical representations of data – can have even more impact. A simple example in relation to behavior change is the case of a company that was trying to reduce paper wastage. This is a story I was told about ten years ago. I never knew the details about the company, but as apocryphal as it is, the story illustrates the principle of data physicalization for behavior change.

Managers responsible for reducing the wastage of paper sent multiple emails to staff explaining the situation and imploring them to reduce the amount of printing and photocopying they were doing. Little changed, so they put signs on photocopiers and printers, but that had no effect. Eventually they started piling empty paper boxes in the atrium near the exit. Whenever five reams of paper had been used, the empty box was added to the pile. At the end of the day there was a large pile of these boxes, but by the next morning they had been cleared and the process would start again. It was the sheer physical scale of the pile that eventually brought about change in behavior.

The story inspired us to experiment with a number of physical interventions – some of them quite subtle and some very 'in your face'. In concrete visualization, the space a viewer is actually occupying right now is a valuable unit of measurement – one the viewer can really relate to. It can be a good way to describe rates, and bring emissions to life. As an exercise in a school we got children to measure the dimensions of each classroom and so calculate their volumes. The plan was to use the classrooms themselves as units of measurement. I had analyzed the school's energy bills and calculated its carbon footprint and built a simple application that calculated the time it would take the school to fill a classroom with carbon dioxide. The children put their measurements into the application and out popped a certificate that they could stick onto the wall explaining how long it would take for the school to fill the classroom with carbon dioxide emissions. The time varied from two or three hours in the smaller rooms to two or three days for the gym.

We are keen to try out a visual enhancement to this room-unit representation of rate. The plan is to hang several strips of lights from floor to ceiling. As the room 'fills' with carbon dioxide the lights track its level – they turn on and off in turn as the level reaches and then submerges them. This creates a virtual surface of light that makes room occupants aware of the ongoing emissions. When the room is full, the lights accelerate to the ground as if pulled by gravity and bounce a couple of times until resting on the floor. This marks a unit of emissions in dramatic fashion and also helps establish the physicality of the lights.

We designed another sculptural data visualization for a university. Problems with the building management system meant we did not get to build it in the end, but it still serves as an example. The sculpture takes live data from the building management system and from the National Grid (electricity supply system) and calculates the instantaneous rate at which the building is adding carbon dioxide to the atmosphere. The figure itself, in units of mass, would be rather uninspiring, so we wanted to show it as a volume moving through a pipe (see Figure 27.6).

Figure 27.6 Sketch for a data sculpture linked to a building management system that shows the actual rate at which the building is adding carbon dioxide to the atmosphere. Lights in bands around a clear tube turn off and on in turn. The pattern they create moves along the pipe at the speed carbon dioxide would move through the pipe at the rate it is currently being produced.

Conclusion

Behavior change is challenging in many ways. This chapter has focused on just one of the challenges, but a very important one: it is not easy to change something that is invisible – something that you know is real, but never really feels real. It is easier if you have a sense of scale for the problem and a real sense of your own agency. In short, behavior change is easier when you can see the impact you are having: good and bad.

Data visualization has an important role to play in making invisible things visible and keeping them in people's minds. I made a distinction between pull and push audiences pointing out that they have very different needs. I also noted that push and pull are not really binary categories but describe the how far someone has traveled along a 'journey of engagement'. Prescriptions such as maximize data density and eschew chartjunk, which apply to pull visualizations need modification in the case of push visualizations. The principle of parsimony states that visualizations should seek to focus viewers' questions on the data encoded and close down any ways in which viewers' attention may be misdirected.

In general, when trying to change behavior, it is push audiences we are interested in. To properly engage with data you need a sense of the reality the data refer to. You also need questions. Concrete visualization can help viewers relate to data on a physical level. The shock of seeing data brought to life this way – the 'yeah yeah gosh effect' – can provoke the kind of questions that give viewers a way in to the data.

My prescription for data visualization for behavior change is then: use the world itself in its own explanation, provoke the questions that will allow your audience to engage with the data, and keep it real.

Note

1 Note that 'radiation' here means electromagnetic radiation which includes radio waves, microwaves, infrared, visible light, ultraviolet x-rays and gamma rays. Not all radiation is ionizing radiation – the damaging radiation from radioactive materials. For anyone who wants to read more about the mechanism by which all warm objects glow, it is called black body radiation.

References

Bateman, Scott, et al. 2010, 'Useful Junk? The Effects of Visual Embellishment on Comprehension and Memorability of Charts' CHI 2010, April 10–15

Nieman, Adam 2012, 'Concrete vs Abstract Visualisation: The Real World as a Canvas for Data Visualisation' in Michael Hohl (ed.) *Proceedings of ADS-VIS2011: Making Visible the Invisible: Art, Design and Science in Data Visualisation, University of Huddersfield*

Tufte, Edward R. 1983, *The Visual Display of Quantitative Information* (Cheshire, CT: Graphics Press)

28

SECURING SUSTAINABILITY

Culture and emotions as barriers to environmental change

Allison Ford and Kari Marie Norgaard

Introduction

Scientists have long predicted the dire consequences of climate change and other ecological crises. Stories in the daily news about super-storms, record droughts, out of control fire seasons and contaminated municipal water systems confirm that these predictions are not something out of a dystopian science fiction novel, but a realistic assessment of the costs of not shifting to a more sustainable organization of society. The fossil-fueled material organization of contemporary life generates many risks. Yet the shifts in engagement that would lead to more sustainable organizations of society have been slow to come. Despite heat records, extreme weather events, and urgent warnings from the scientific community, climate change has remained a proverbial elephant in the room. Climate scientists may have identified global warming as the most important issue of our time, but for urban dwellers in rich and powerful Northern countries climate change is still mostly seen as no more than background noise.

Social scientists have puzzled over this dilemma. What are the barriers that keep people from speaking out, standing up and/or adopting more sustainable practices? Many scientists have been concerned that the public does not know about or understand complex environmental problems like climate change. Though it's true that in the United States a well-orchestrated, right-wing campaign to deny the reality of climate change has generated much confusion about the topic (Mccright and Dunlap 2013; Oreskes 2004), the majority of Americans have come to understand that climate change is real and human caused (Leiserowitz et al. 2016). In other wealthy, industrialized countries, the issue has been less contentious, and the scientific evidence for climate change has been accepted more readily. This has still not led to widespread action. Knowledge alone does not appear to be sufficient to incite action. Social science research has further examined the conditions under which people care about environmental problems, and how that care might translate to changing practices. Yet studies show that even when people *do* value the environment, they do not necessarily change their behavior to reflect this value (Blake 1999; Kennedy et al. 2009). Knowledge and values alone are not sufficient to get people to change their behavior (Norgaard 2011).

So what are the missing links between concern and public engagement? There are many ways that people potentially *could* respond to concerns about climate change. Many people around the world are actively engaged in creating collective change. In spite of widespread public apathy, organizations such as 350.org and Citizens Climate Lobby have organized citizens in protests, lobbying efforts, letter writing campaigns, and civil disobedience, engaging fellow citizens and policy makers in the fight to put a price on carbon via a carbon tax and dividend. Supported by Our Children's Trust, 21 young people from around the United States are suing the federal government for failing to protect the public trust: their future. Students on college campuses across the country are demanding that their universities divest from fossil fuel investments, and invest in renewable portfolios. Many cities have adopted climate ordinances at the urging of concerned citizens. Indigenous communities throughout North America have organized to resist the expansion of pipelines and fracking, standing down state violence to do so. And the 2015 Paris agreements of the United Nations Framework Convention on Climate Change (UNFCCC) raises the bar for governments to work even harder to mitigate emissions and decarbonize their economies with a landmark agreement to slow the increase of emissions. The agreement, however, is nonbinding, and unlikely to come to fruition without the prolonged engagement of citizens around the world.

Although these actions are heartening, they have yet to tip the scale towards a more sustainable political economy. Much more remains to be done, and it will require individuals to make major changes in the organization of society. However, many of the people who report knowing and caring about environmental problems like climate change do not appear to be actively engaging in efforts to shape a more sustainable future. Despite increasingly dire warnings that failure to act will put all of us at risk, most people living in Western democracies continue to live daily life as usual. How is this occurring?

On the sociological side, scholars have identified structural constraints that might discourage individuals from acting to curb climate change: the fossil fuel industry influence on government policy, the tactics of climate skeptic campaigns (Mccright and Dunlap 2013), corporate control of media that limits and molds available information about global warming, and even the "normal" distortion of climate science through the "balance as bias phenomenon" in journalism (Boykoff 2011). Certainly, deeply entrenched structural constraints support the fossil-fueled status quo. But none of these factors account for people who are concerned about climate change and environmental risk, but still don't act. Structures are constructed and maintained over time by the acts of individuals to support, reinforce, adapt, and repair them. They are also modified by acts of resistance, deviance, and adaptations to changing circumstances. Achieving sustainability will require individual practices that orient structures in new directions. Understanding why individuals behave in ways that support or challenge the status quo is an important aspect of seeking positive social change. When, why and how do people support, question, challenge or resist existing social orders?

To understand how people make sense of environmental risk and what shapes their pathways of response, we explore two case studies in which citizens of wealthy, Northern democracies construct different responses to environmental risk. In our first case, Norwegian villagers living in the town of Bygdaby[1] managed to collectively ignore climate change even as they outwardly acknowledged it as a concern. We examine how they participated in a process of socially constructed denial that allows many citizens of wealthy nations to acknowledge the reality of climate change without acting to mitigate it. In our second case, we look at a group of people who do not participate in the widespread implicit denial of environmental risk, American participants of self-sufficiency movements. Participants of self-sufficiency movements recognize that the political and economic organization of contemporary society comes with many risks, including environmental degradation at a global scale. Yet rather than collectively try to mitigate these risks, they focus on decreasing their dependence on the institutions that they hold accountable for putting them at risk. Americans trying to achieve self-sufficiency change their individual household practices to decrease their dependence on institutions that they deem untrustworthy (such as industrialized agricultural businesses, national electric grids and municipal utilities, and the government agencies that oversee them). Without addressing the structural cause of environmental risk, they often adopted household-level sustainability measures to ensure their own well-being in the event of political or social system collapse. In comparing these two cases, we ask, what accounts for these disparate reactions to similar threats? What ties them together? How might our understanding of these responses help us shape more productive social responses to the unsustainable organization of contemporary society?

Although the two cases we explore have some marked differences in location, and response, they share some key features. First, both take place in wealthy, Northern countries where the quality of life of its citizens is directly dependent on political-economic arrangements based on fossil fuels and trade networks ultimately responsible for climate change and other environmental risks in question. In both cases, the groups observed are relatively privileged, with high material qualities of life, access to education and cultural resources, and relative political stability. In a rapidly globalizing world, members of the global middle class share much in common. Secondly, despite differences in national culture and local social norms, Norwegians and Americans alike reported experiencing complex, uncomfortable emotions in response to what they knew about climate change and environmental risk. In both sites, people struggled to manage these emotions in accordance with macro cultural meaning structures (Alexander and Smith 1993) and local norms of attention (Zerubavel 2006), emotion (Hochschild 1983) and conversation (Eliasoph 1998). Differences in culture and social location offered each group a different set of cultural "tools" (Swidler 1986) however, allowing significantly different strategies of action to emerge.

Our research makes clear that knowledge and concern for the environment were not sufficient for people to adopt sustainable practices. Most of the people we engaged with were in fact very aware that they were living in risk. And many cared deeply. Far from being apathetic, the people we interviewed and lived amongst expressed strong emotions about environmental problems, including fear, helplessness, despair, vulnerability, and guilt. These emotions, and the culturally available channels of expression for them, were central to explaining why knowledge about environmental problems is not enough to incite action. In both Norway and the United States people's responses to environmental danger were deeply connected to cultural perceptions of self in relation to social others, and the emotional responses that information about environmental risk elicited.

Minimizing the unthinkable: socially organized denial

The ten months of 2001 that Norgaard spent in Norway were marked by unusually warm weather. Severe flooding took place in November, and the snowfall was delayed by about two months later than average. It was soon announced that that winter was Norway's second warmest in 130 years. This had noticeable effects on people's daily lives. The local ski area had to rely exclusively on artificial snow when it opened in late December. Ice fishing, a traditional winter activity, was made impossible when the local lake didn't freeze. Both changes had measurable economic impacts on the local economy; hotels, shops, taxi drivers and others in the area suffered when the usual winter features of the town failed to attract customers. Said one concerned taxi driver, "It makes a difference if we move from five months of winter tourism to only three. It affects all of us, you know, not just those up on the mountain. It affects the hotels, the shops in town, us taxi drivers, we notice it too." People clearly recognized that something was wrong.

References to "unusual weather" were linked to climate change, often with an accompanied shake of the head. Yet the social response was minimal. Why?

Even as climate change was mentioned frequently, and the unusual weather of the season was accurately associated with broader climactic trends, it was not an easy topic. Rather than focus on the overwhelming knowledge that climate change would alter their way of life within the next decades, most people remained focused on more immediate issues to avoid being overwhelmed. Vigdis, a college-age student, explained why global warming didn't enter her everyday life, even though she feared it:

> I often get afraid, like – it goes very much up and down, then, with how much I think about it. But if I sit myself down and think about it, it could actually happen, I thought about how if this here continues we could come to have no difference between winter and spring and summer, like – and lots of stuff about the ice that is melting and that there will be flooding, like, and that is depressing, the way I see it.

The lived experience of climate change could not be denied; it was making its way into everyday life. Yet the emotions this evoked generated the need for self-protection. One person expressed this need explicitly as he held his hands in front of his eyes and said, "people want to protect themselves a bit." Learning about climate change threatened Norwegian's sense of what Anthony Giddens (1984, 1991) calls *ontological security*, a sense of continuity in everyday life. To protect their sense that the world was familiar and safe, they partitioned climate change off into a form of secondary knowledge. It became something outside of the realm of everyday life that they had to "sit themselves down and think about," "but which in between is discouraging and an emotional weight."

Norwegians concerned about climate change found themselves in the uncomfortable position between strong cultural values of environmentalism and humanitarianism, and the nation's political economy, which is largely based on oil exports. The high quality of life Norwegians experience is directly linked to an industry that is responsible for climate change. Kjersti, a teacher at the local agricultural school in her early 30s, summed this up nicely: "We live in one way and we think in another. We learn to think in parallel. It's a skill, an art of living."

When information that people receive about the world does not align with their everyday experience of it, they may experience what Robert Lifton calls the *absurdity of the double life* (1982), or the experience of double reality (Norgaard 2014). This is a condition in which information that is held in cognitive awareness cannot be integrated into everyday life, without threatening its integrity. For Norwegians, one reality was made up of the collectively constructed sense of normal, everyday life, whereas in the second reality, the fundamental pieces of this life – reliance on cars, electricity, and fossil-fuel intensive supply chains bringing food, clothing, and other material objects from all over the world into local markets – posed a threat to the way of life of the future by contributing to melting ice caps, warmer winters, less snow, and predicted disasters. Adopting a double reality was cognitively difficult; it required emotional work to maintain and uphold both realities. The reward, however, was that Norwegian villagers could simultaneously acknowledge the realness and severity of climate change, while also maintaining a consistent sense of self and social order. To maintain ontological security, villagers participated in the cultivation of an implicit denial of the impact climate change was having and would have on their lives.

How do people manage the emotional weight of something like climate change that is at once voluminous and abstract? Philip Smith and Nicholas Howe point out that humans have found ways to organize their lives around many abstract, complex topics (such as religion, belief in the invisible hand of the market, etc.) (Smith and Howe 2015, 5); what makes climate change different is the failure of a coherent cultural narrative to emerge, helping people situate themselves in relationships to what is essentially a new plot. In the theater of the public arena, climate change has successfully been contested, muddling the story arch, the relationships between characters, and thus the logical conclusions that can be drawn according to deeply understood and valued cultural scripts. In the wake of incoherence in the public arena, individuals are left to incorporate disparate pieces of information into already culturally coherent lives.

In the absence of a coherent cultural narrative that helped make sense of individual's relationship to climate change, many Norwegians continued on with their daily lives. Yet the knowledge of climate change shadowed their otherwise normal activities, resulting in emotions such as guilt and fear of the future. Eirik noted in an interview,

> We go on vacation and we go shopping, and my partner drives to work every day. And I drive often up here to my office myself. We feel that we must do it to make things work on a practical level, but we have a guilty conscience, a bit of a guilty conscience.

Members of the community expressed concern over climate change; yet they had several tactics for normalizing awkward moments in which uncomfortable or socially unacceptable feelings would arise. In conversation and in action, villagers participated in collectively distancing themselves from disturbing information in a process sociologist Eviatar Zerubavel calls "socially organized denial." What people pay attention to, acknowledge or ignore is shaped by cultural norms of attention, which shape interpersonal interactions as well as political economic processes. Culturally prescribed norms of attention reinforce what to pay attention to, feel, talk and think about in different contexts (Zerubavel 1997). As Stanley Cohen notes "Without being told what to think about (or what not to think about), and without being punished for 'knowing' the wrong things, societies arrive at unwritten agreements about what can be publically remembered and acknowledged" (Cohen 2001, 10–11). For example, to avoid emotions of guilt, fear, and helplessness, people in Bygdaby changed the topic of conversations, told jokes, tried not to think about climate change, and kept the concept off the agenda of political meetings. Community members collectively held information about global warming at arm's length by following cultural norms of what to pay attention to, what to talk about, and what to feel. Feeling rules are cultural norms that shape what is appropriate to feel and how it can legitimately be expressed (Hochschild 1983). Going along with feeling rules that discouraged the expression of intimate emotions like guilt and fear allowed Norwegians to keep climate change in the background without denying the reality of it.

Norwegians readily acknowledged that climate change was real and human caused. Yet their collective response was to accept the information without following through on the implications of what climate change meant for the material and cultural organization of their lives. Individuals participated in what Cohen calls "implicatory denial," in which the implications of information are ignored. This was reinforced as a collective strategy by the silence of others in the community. Individual responses to information about climate change and other social and environmental risks take place in social contexts; how others respond to our responses further shapes their possibilities in reference to larger political economic structures. Although individual people experience the disturbing emotions of fear, guilt, and helplessness, local feeling rules shape how these emotions can legitimately be expressed. Without constructive cultural outlets for these feelings that did not threaten a valued way of life, Norwegians socially constructed a collective, implicit denial of the implications of climate change. This made it possible to maintain their sense of ontological security without having to dismiss information that their cultural identity necessitated absorbing.

Seeking self-sufficiency: individual response to collective risk

Whereas Norwegian's cultural valuation of environmental progressivism made it hard for them to ignore climate change outright, culturally specific feeling rules also made it difficult for them to apply the offending knowledge to their daily lives. How might a different political cultural context necessitate a different response to similar feelings of fear, anxiety, and concern about environmental risk? To answer this, we turn to our second case, which examines the cultural practice of self-sufficiency.

Self-sufficiency is a cultural movement in which participants seek to minimize reliance upon institutions such as the state and markets, preferring a do-it-yourself lifestyle that puts them more directly in control of their own subsistence needs. Subcultures of self-sufficiency include permaculture, homesteading, prepping, survivalism, voluntary simplicity, and transition towns. A state of self-sufficiency is defined as not relying on institutions such as the state or global markets to meet one's subsistence needs. Self-sufficiency practitioners might grow, hunt, gather and preserve their own food, seek to move off the grid and provide their own household energy needs, dig a well or build a rainwater catchment, or otherwise seek to disentangle their subsistence needs from the institutions that are responsible for them by default: globalized markets, municipal utilities, and the federal and state regulatory agencies that oversee them.

The research that Ford conducted took place in Oregon in 2014 and 2015 and focused on the practices of homesteading and prepping. While preppers were mostly preparing for future environmental disasters or societal collapses, homesteaders were actively trying to distance themselves from institutions that they did not think reflected their environmental and social concerns. Self-sufficiency practices were generally undertaken at the individual and household level, although several of the people interviewed lived in a communal unit called an "ecovillage."

Like the Norwegian villagers, Americans seeking self-sufficiency expressed strong, uncomfortable emotions about environmental risk. In a different cultural and political environment, however, culturally specific norms of attention and feeling rules contributed to a different behavioral response. Concern over climate change was experienced in combination with a broad array of other environmental problems such as nuclear radiation (especially recent disasters like Fukushima), contamination of food and water, loss of food security, and access to natural resources. Kai conceptualized interlocking environmental risks as threatening what he called his sense of "ecological security":

> We're in such a precarious state where we're vulnerable to so many different potential political economic ecological factors mainly because we're not taking responsibility for our physical security and our own ecological security. So as we've outsourced that from the family farm and the homestead to all these different levels of law enforcement agencies and all these different levels of industrial global economies, especially becoming an importer of food, and all these being leveraged so far out in our land in so many ways . . .

Security for Kai was not just a matter of national defense, but encompassed his ability to meet his subsistence needs, something that required access to environmental resources that were outsourced, under a system of globalized capitalist production. This was threatened not just by climate change, but by interlocking failures of institutions to take seriously the safety and well-being of the public, generating widespread feelings of distrust towards institutions. Don expressed his deep frustration over the distrust he felt for "the system" quite colorfully, stating, "We might as well have a chimpanzee with a ouija board making society's most important decisions for it." He went on to express concern over "the three big things: climate change, peak oil and then the economic collapse."

Unlike Norwegians who worked to ensure the maintenance of their ontological security, Americans seeking self-sufficiency saw a system collapse as inevitable, and worked to prepare themselves for it. Noah reported, "My discouragement is that there will be a great deal of chaos and destruction that comes with the inevitable transition. Things are not sustainable." Tammy said, "I do get scared sometimes about the future of the world. Sometimes my mind goes that way . . . you just don't know what's hype and what's potentially real." This sense of unease reflected the underlying belief that the very institutions that they relied upon for survival did not have their best interests at heart, and that ontological security could not be counted on. "The guiding value of economic development is one of maximizing profit," Noah reported. "It is that we have an economy based on *greed* essentially." Don's explanation of his fear for the future is infused with a sense of betrayal:

> I think some of them [political leaders] must to some degree know how utterly unsustainable things are, so therefore they're patching the world's economy together with so much chewing gum and duct tape and crazy glue that when it finally, oh and bandaids, but when it finally does fall over, it's just going to go kaboom.

The feelings of fear and uncertainty about the physical state of the world that Americans reported focused on the absence of a direct material relationship with the ecological systems that their lives depend on. Kenneth Worthy (2008) calls this "phenomenal dissociation," a lack of phenomenal, sensate engagement with the environment that results in a form of human-nature alienation. Because they felt alienated from their ecological life support system, people who seek self-sufficiency felt particularly vulnerable to the generation of environmental risk. Not only did these Americans feel alienated from the environment, but they did not trust the institutions that mediated their access to ecological goods and services. The fear of anticipated social and environmental disruption further threatened their sense of physical and ontological security.

The frustration that Americans expressed about the institutional structures they relied on left many feeling helpless and discouraged. This is an inherently political problem; yet instead of turning to collective action and political channels to address their concerns, they turned to an individual and household level practice. Why?

Although these concerned Americans were critical of the wastefulness and redundancy of the political-economic organization of society, many also questioned their efficacy to change the system. Julie, a young woman who had recently moved out to the country, aspiring to become more self-sufficient, was unsure about her self-efficacy, stating, "I don't know if it makes a big difference." However, she reported that trying to consume less, grow her own food, and reuse things made her "feel better about" the wastefulness she saw in her culture. Tammy, a single woman active in a local club for people interested in self-sufficiency, expressed many political concerns, including concern for social justice and the environment, but she downplayed politics as an avenue to express these. She framed this as a choice about how to use her limited time:

> I don't delve deep into politics. I don't have the time to do that. And I think that . . . yeah, I'm not real aware of everything that's going on, and I'm ok with that . . . there's

only so much I can pay attention to. And um, I mean I am concerned. And I do have opinions about different issues, but I . . . yeah.

Others expressed the desire to participate in political processes, but followed this with doubt about their fellow citizens' commitment to change. For example, Ellen expressed skepticism over the possibility of deep change, noting that while she theoretically saw change as possible, she didn't put a lot of faith in people's willingness to transition away from a consumer-focused lifestyle:

> You add humans into the equations and everything gets all . . . you know . . . out of whack. . . . I think that people have these really great intentions but they want to be spoon fed the information, but they also want to be consumers. Americans at least are bred from the very start and brainwashed to be consumers, you know . . . we need to find a way to make humans feel invested into it, and the only way to make humans invested into it is to put a dollar sign on it, and that is nearly impossible without actually some sort of just, massive collapse.

Ellen's frustration with her fellow Americans was echoed by others to justify the investment of their time into household-level change. Nina Eliasoph (1997) notes that citizens' decision making about where to invest change-making effort is intimately tied to their sense of personal empowerment (or powerlessness) in relation to the perceived power of social structures. Americans who seek to become self-sufficient in preparation for environmental or economic disruption channeled their frustrations with an unsustainable system into individual practices. Doing so allowed them to feel like they were *doing something*, even as this pathway arguably left the system they were dissatisfied with intact.

Whereas Norwegians sought to normalize uncomfortable information about environmental risk, these Americans became hyper-focused on it. As seen earlier, however, their distrust of political institutions limited political action as an outlet to alleviate their concerns. To relieve the distress of feeling threatened by the very institutions that were tasked with protecting them, those seeking self-sufficiency tapped into the deeply held American cultural value of individualism; in this case, the sense that individuals are capable of, and responsible for shaping their own life circumstances. This contrasts sharply with Norwegian cultural values of environmental progressivism, humanitarianism, and a sense of responsibility for others (Norgaard 2014). All of the Americans interviewed expressed a driving desire to *do something*. They also expressed the belief that their actions would have efficacy in changing their personal relationship to the environment, if not the system that structured it. The value of individualism reinforced that their primary responsibility was to safeguard themselves and their loved ones, rather than take responsibility for the collective.

Empowerment through activity was an important theme in conversations with self-sufficiency seekers. Many referenced a sense of individual responsibility, in which they were personally responsible for their own life chances, regardless of the circumstances. Some went to great lengths to frame circumstances as matters of personal choice. Samuel, a prepper, argued that although he was concerned about industrialized food production, he didn't have to rely on it to eat, because he could grow his own food:

Samuel: [referencing bowl of cherry tomatoes] I can tell you just about everything about these. Cause they came off a plant in the backyard. Now can I tell you the potting soil that we got? I mean I do my research; I know the company . . . but can I really tell you that they didn't put something in there? I have a background in agrobiz, and I know that there are certain things that [they] will certify as organic that it can have a certain amount of this or that in there, and I know that people will color it, color it very specifically to match the potting soil so it doesn't look like there's anything else in there, when there really is.

Allison: So that's a circumstance where you're doing everything you can to control what is in your food by growing your own tomatoes, but to a certain extent you still don't have a choice in what's in your tomatoes.

Samuel: Well . . . um . . . I would say that I don't choose to exercise the ultimate expression of choice. Because if I did, I could definitely get . . . you know . . . seven gallons of dirt, have it analyzed, know exactly what's in it, right? Know exactly the feed that the chicken used for my chicken manure fertilizer. Now I could go to that level. But I don't because . . .

Allison: It's extreme.

Samuel: For me that would be extreme, yeah. . . . Want one? [offers me a cherry tomato]

Samuel struggles to make sense of his own actions in conjunction with a powerful narrative that revolves around choice and control. Indeed, he goes to great rhetorical lengths to insist that he does ultimately have a choice, and thus control over his own exposure to risk, even as he must identify more and more extreme actions that would be required for him to exercise that choice, as the logic breaks down. He does not choose to exercise the ultimate expression of choice (in this case having his backyard soil tested) because it becomes extreme, but he avoids seeing this extremity as a lack of choice in the first place.

Individualism is a strong cultural narrative, shaping Americans' perceptions of self and ideal relationships between individuals and institutions (Bellah et al. 1985). O'Brien (2015) theorizes individualism as a cultural mechanism that can be employed to justify culturally relevant practices. Many social theorists see cultural values, beliefs, ideas, and objects as a sort of tool kit that individuals can pull from (Swidler 1986). In this case, a focus on individual responsibility empowered self-sufficiency seeking Americans to take matters into their own hands, but it directed their efforts inward rather than out into the public sphere.

Self-sufficiency alleviated many people's fears and concerns, however as a practice, it left the ultimate problem of an unsustainable political economy untouched. Indeed, many practitioners of self-sufficiency expressed a sense of resignation that it was simply too late to fix such an entrenched political mess. For Benjamin, self-sufficiency was a way of preparing for the inevitable collapse of society that he anticipated. He expressed his motivation for being self-sufficient as self-interested, and claimed to "not care about the environment." He then however went on to recite a litany of environmental problems and the ways in which he was prepared to respond to the consequences of them, including climate change, increasing frequency and severity of storms, drought, oil spills, ocean acidification, radioactivity from Fukushima, mercury in fish, arsenic in chicken, general toxicity of food, and the potential for a near future ice age. This did not sound like someone who "didn't care" about the environment, or the social costs of environmental collapse.

Allison: I mean, it sounds like you have done a fair amount of research about the conditions of the environment. Why would you do that if you don't care?

Benjamin: [Long pause] [sighs] I do care, but up to a point. It's just too hard. To care anymore. 'Cause I know that there's no point in fixing this. The only way to fix this is exactly what's happening.

In short, he reported, "I think that we're too late." Seeking self-sufficiency became a way to cope with the overwhelming emotions that resulted in knowledge about environmental and social conditions that felt outside of his control. He acknowledged the multidimensional emotional quality of preparing to live self-sufficiently in response to the follow question:

Allison: So preparing is stressful, but it's also kind of cathartic, in that you're working through scenarios because you feel more prepared you . . . alleviate that stress.
Benjamin: [interjecting] Right! It actually, at the end, it calms you down. Right now, I know I'm pretty [prepared for anything] . . . pretty much. Except for the zombie apocalypse.

In this case, Benjamin feels so overwhelmed with the bad news that he has given up on communal, public processes to solve these complex problems. Prepping, a form of self-sufficiency, is a solution that allows him to actively participate in alleviating his own stress, while reinforcing his sense that he must take care of himself and his family no matter what happens. Although environmental advocacy groups hope that urgent, negative messaging will spur people to action, excessive reliance on fear-inducing bad news can in fact be debilitating (Hart and Nisbet 2012), especially if it causes people to give up on collective problem solving.

Rather than minimize the perception of risk, Americans did in fact change their practices in response to it. However, it is questionable whether their individual, household level strategies did anything to challenge the institutional structures that had created the problem of inordinate risk in the first place. As sociologist Andrew Szasz (2007) points out, more and more Americans are turning towards individual, often market based solutions to respond to public environmental risks. Instead of collectively organizing to demand that industries stop polluting public water sources, or insisting that government agencies do a better job implementing the Clean Water Act, Szasz observed that Americans were buying more and more bottled water to protect themselves and their families from harm. He calls this "inverted quarantine" because rather than quarantine a small community of people to protect society at large, individuals are quarantining themselves to protect themselves from society.

Although these Americans were willing and able to face the reality of many environmental risks, they struggled to acknowledge their ultimate dependency on institutions that appeared to not have their best interests at heart. This allowed individual, household level practices to remain a logical solution to the problems they faced. Without addressing the systematic source of the problem, however, self-sufficiency potentially takes on the impossible quality of politically opting out.

Conclusion

Culture and emotions are central in organizing how people respond to environmental risk. Our combined work on how people respond to environmental threats such as climate change challenges the commonly held idea that people either don't know or don't care about shifting to sustainability. It also forces us to question rational choice models of human decision making, in which humans respond to new information logically, based on the best available information. Amongst the populations we studied, many people have access to enormous amounts of information about environmental risk. But the logic of their pathways is shaped by the emotions that information incited, rather than the knowledge itself. Further, which actions were deemed "logical" was a product of cultural worldviews in which people were immersed.

Global environmental risks such as climate change threaten our sense of normality, and thus our ontological security (Giddens 1984, 1991). This is an emotionally uncomfortable experience. Emotions serve as signals, relaying information to us via our bodies about how well we are aligning to the cultural and social expectations of others. How people respond to difficult emotions is shaped by norms of attention, as people block out certain information to maintain coherent meaning systems (Zerubavel 2006). The information we absorb or reject is also influenced by norms of emotion, the emotions it is socially acceptable to feel or express in a certain setting (Hochschild 1983). At a micro-interactional level, norms of attention and norms of emotion must also adhere to norms of conversation, shaping how we act with other individuals and small groups; these processes will necessarily be shaped by macro-cultural discourses that imbue the content of these conversations with shared meaning. These shared meanings are structured according to historical codes that transcend time and place, and allow for a consistency of cultural meaning. The citizens of Bygdaby held fast to a historical cultural narrative that frames Norwegians as human-itarian and environmentalist, even as their contemporary material dependence on the export of fossil fuels contradicts this narrative. In this case, it appears that the contradiction between cultural narrative and material organization of economic life stymied either an environmental or a human-itarian response. Americans, meanwhile, pulled from a widely accepted discourse of individualism that favors individual over collective endeavors (Bellah et al. 1985; Eliasoph and Lichterman 2003; O'Brien 2015) without reference to a shared understanding of themselves as collectively respon-sible for the well-being of anyone but themselves. Their sense of personal responsibility facilitated the acceptance of unwarranted environmental risk, but potentially stymied a more collective response that might challenge the offending institutions rather than disengaging from them.

In many cases, the cultural pathways that would allow people to move towards more sustainable organizations of material life are blocked. New ones must be constructed, but they must allow for the sense of emotional well-being that comes from an integrated, continuous social world. This, then, is the ultimate task for designers: to build bridges from old ways of being to new ones. The bridges we build must be accessible in the context of existing cultural norms, emotion norms, and they must account for the deep desire for a sense of continuity in everyday life. These bridges must, at the very least, be secure. But ideally, they are also beautiful, and pleasurable to cross.

Often the focus on sustainability is technical; what is our physical capacity to achieve a desirable outcome? Yet whether people engage with difficult information, adopt changes, and adapt well to changing circumstances is often as much a question of culture as it is rearranging material flows. Upending assumptions about human behavior as rational, and accounting for holistic, embodied, emotional humans with complex identities and ties to other individuals and institutions that cannot be severed lightly, gives us a more complicated, but also more accurate starting point for figuring out how to get from our current daily lives to an imagined future without disrupting the sense of safety that comes from the continuity of everyday life. Of course, no one designer or group of designers can singlehandedly shape something as huge and unwieldy as culture, but designers are also individuals with choices about where they choose to support, question, challenge and resist dominant narratives with their particular sets of skills and knowl-edge. Designers are especially well situated to intervene in old ways of being by designing new ones; they are more likely to succeed in doing so if they account for the emotional responses such changes are likely to trigger, and help to build bridges from the old to the new rather than designing cliffs that only the very adventurous would be willing to leap off.

Note

1 The name of the town has been changed to protect the privacy of the research participants.

References

Alexander, Jeffrey C. and Philip Smith. 1993. "The Discourse of American Civil Society: A New Proposal for Cultural Studies." *Theory and Society* 22(2):151–207.

Bellah, Robert N., Ann Swidler, Richard Madsen, Steven M. Tipton, and William M. Sullivan. 1985. *Habits of the Heart : Individualism and Commitment in American Life.* Berkeley, CA: University of California Press.

Blake, James. 1999. "Overcoming the 'Value-Action Gap' in Environmental Policy: Tensions Between National Policy and Local Experience." *Local Environment* 4(3):257–78.

Boykoff, Maxwell. 2011. *Who Speaks for the Climate? Making Sense of Media Reporting on Climate Change.* Cambridge, UK: Cambridge University Press.

Cohen, Stanley. 2001. *States of Denial: Knowing About Atrocities and Suffering.* Cambridge, MA: Polity Press.

Eliasoph, Nina. 1997. "'Close to Home': The Work of Avoiding Politics." *Theory and Society* 26(5):605–47.

Eliasoph, Nina. 1998. *Avoiding Politics: How Americans Produce Apathy in Everyday Life.* Cambridge: Cambridge University Press.

Eliasoph, Nina and Paul Lichterman. 2003. "Culture in Interaction." *American Journal of Sociology* 108(4):735–94.

Giddens, Anthony. 1984. *The Constitution of Society.* Cambridge, UK: Polity Press.

Giddens, Anthony. 1991. *Modernity and Self-Identity: Self and Society in the Late Modern Age.* Cambridge, UK: Polity Press.

Hart, P. S. and E. C. Nisbet. 2012. "Boomerang Effects in Science Communication: How Motivated Reasoning and Identity Cues Amplify Opinion Polarization About Climate Mitigation Policies." *Communication Research* 39(6):701–23.

Hochschild, Arlie Russell. 2012 [1983]. *The Managed Heart: Commercialization of Human Feeling.* Berkeley: University of California Press.

Kennedy, Emily Huddart, Thomas M. Beckley, Bonita L. McFarlane, and Solange Nadeau. 2009. "Why We Don't 'Walk the Talk': Understanding the Environmental Values/Behaviour Gap in Canada." *Human Ecology Review* 16(2): 151–60.

Leiserowitz, Anthony, Edward Maibach, Connie Roser-Renouf, Geoff Feinberg, and Seth Rosenthal. 2016. *Climate Change in the American Mind.* New Haven, CT: Yale Program on Climate Change Communication.

Lifton, Robert. 1982. *Indefensible Weapons: The Political and Psychological Case Against Nuclear Weapons.* New York: Basic Books.

Mccright, Aaron M. and Riley E. Dunlap. 2013. "Defeating Kyoto: The Conservative Movement's Impact on U. S. Climate." *Social Problems* 50(3):348–73.

Norgaard, Kari Marie. 2011. *Living in Denial: Climate Change, Emotions, and Everyday Life.* Cambridge, MA: MIT Press.

Norgaard, Kari Marie. 2014. "Normalizing the Unthinkable: Climate Denial and Everyday Life." Pp. 246–59 in *Twenty Lessons in Environmental Sociology*, edited by K. A. Gould and T. Lewis. Oxford: Oxford University Press.

O'Brien, J. 2015. "Individualism as a Discursive Strategy of Action: Autonomy, Agency, and Reflexivity Among Religious Americans." *Sociological Theory* 33(2):173–99.

Oreskes, Naomi. 2004. "The Scientific Consensus on Climate Change." *Science* 306(5702):1686.

Smith, Philip and Nicolas C. Howe. 2015. *Climate Change as Social Drama: Global Warming in the Public Sphere.* Cambridge: Cambridge University Press.

Swidler, Ann. 1986. "Culture in Action: Symbols and Strategies." *American Sociological Review* 51(2):273.

Szasz, Andrew. 2007. *Shopping Our Way to Safety: How We Changed From Protecting the Environment to Protecting Ourselves.* Minneapolis: University of Minnesota Press.

Worthy, Kenneth. 2008. "Modern Institutions, Phenomenal Dissociations, and Destructiveness Toward Humans and the Environment." *Organization & Environment* 21(2):148–70.

Zerubavel, Eviatar. 1997. *Social Mindscapes: An Invitation to Cognitive Sociology.* Cambridge, MA: Harvard University Press.

Zerubavel, Evitar. 2006. *The Elephant in the Room: Silence and Denial in Everyday Life.* New York: Oxford University Press.

29

NATURE-BASED DESIGN FOR HEALTH AND WELL-BEING IN CITIES

Angela Reeve, Cheryl Desha and Omniya El Baghdadi

Transforming the context for designing cities

We are moving into an age where, arguably, cities have become of greater significance than nations. With a rapidly increasing majority of the global population now living in cities, these are the economic engines of nations, often with distinct cultural and social milieu to which people identify with more than they do their nationality. Globally, cities now compete to attract skilled labour and capital investment, with liveability and quality of life critical factors that underpin the location choices of individuals and companies.

In the coming decades cities around the world must face the imperative to transform in the face of critical and converging challenges, to ensure urban environments are liveable and functional as the global environment, economy and society change dramatically. This includes creating conditions conducive to decoupling urban life and prosperity from fossil-fuel consumption, reducing energy needs, maintaining and restoring biodiversity, mitigating against climate change impacts and improving resource productivity (Smith et al., 2010; World Economic Forum, 2016). However in many respects this transformation is not unprecedented. Our planet contains a rich tapestry of built environments that are the result of numerous schools of thought and practices in the design and construction of cities, demonstrating how – over time – the design and development of cities has fundamentally transformed many times in response to the technologies, ideas and imperatives of the time.

In many cities today, from a high-level, macro view of cities we see patterns of urban sprawl and suburbanisation contrasted with higher-density, compact urban cores surrounded by natural spaces. From a smaller-scale, micro perspective, we see the design of individual buildings reflecting a huge cultural, geographical and temporal diversity of architectural practices, planning laws and design trends. Various artefacts in our built environment tell poignant stories of the beliefs, realities and technologies that were dominant at various points of time, and these artefacts continue to shape our cities and the way that we live within them today. Moreover, patterns of urban development that dictate the function of the city – for example, the development of low-density satellite suburbs and investment in road infrastructure that favours personal automobile usage – tend to be repeated and reinforced, as the physical infrastructure legacy, economic structures, policy settings and establishment of key development stakeholders typically favour and even lock-in these patterns as a status quo (Reeve, 2014; Matthews et al., 2015). Whilst this can be beneficial where these development patterns foster urban environments that are well suited to the current and future needs and preferences of the people who live there; too frequently these patterns produce cities that foster social inequity, environmental degradation and unsustainable behaviour and urban function.

One central idea that has underpinned much of this 'locked in' built environment design around the world relates to 'form following function' (Sullivan, 1896). Regardless of context or the time in history, designers have had a common desire to shape the built environment in ways that enable the behavioural preferences and patterns that people currently display. However, more recently we see a transformative shift to a realisation that 'function can follow form' – that our environment can actually influence and change the way that we behave and interact with a space or object (Lockton et al., 2008; Wever et al., 2008). This appreciation has led to concerted interest in the design of the built environment to influence desired behaviours and interactions (Thaler and Sunstein, 2009).

We propose that the next evolution in urban design will go beyond influencing behaviour, to directly and intentionally influencing the health and well-being of people living in cities. Whilst we know intuitively that certain design features – such as expansive views or cascading water features – are appealing and make a place 'feel good', researchers and designers have explored this phenomenon in earnest over the last half century, to better understand specifically what features promote positive emotional, neurological and physiological states – and why. Time spent in natural and green spaces has been repeatedly shown to provide manifold benefits including to (Reeve et al., 2015; Tzoulas et al., 2007; Kaplan, 1995):

- Reduced stress – Viewing nature speeds recovery from stressful experiences.
- Reduced depression and anxiety – Experiences of nature reduce depression, anxiety and anger, and increases positive feelings.
- Reduced crime – More greenery is associated with reduced crime and increased safety.
- Enhanced workplace satisfaction – Views of nature increase work and workplace satisfaction.
- Enhanced healing – Views of trees enhance recovery in hospital.
- Enhanced physical well-being – Access to green space is correlated with improved physical well-being.
- Enhanced behavioural outcomes – Access to nature improves attention, self-discipline and conduct.
- Increased attention recovery – Nature experiences restore attention-directing capacities.
- Increased community connection – Greener community areas promote connection.

Integrating nature into cities can also provide systemic environmental and economic improvements to cities, mitigating the impacts of climate change on these systems and often delaying, downsizing or negating the need for investment in conventional infrastructure (Demuzere et al., 2014; Matthews et al., 2015). This includes:

- Mitigating the urban heat island (UHI) effect and reducing risks from temperature-related illnesses
- Regulating urban hydraulic flow patterns to assist stormwater management
- Reducing electricity consumption
- Sequestering carbon and reducing greenhouse gas emissions
- Improving air quality
- Supporting biodiversity
- Increasing the likelihood of walking and cycling
- Improving road safety

Considering the range of benefits derived from urban nature, there is a significant opportunity to establish a systems-based approach to urban design that intentionally seeks to integrate nature into the built environment to promote health and well-being. Unique insights and perspectives into the design, development and/or benefits of urban nature from fields spanning the medical and human sciences, architecture, landscape architecture, ecology, horticulture, engineering and planning, all contribute to this emerging design approach.

This chapter explores how we can use this spectrum of knowledge-areas to design cities that foster happy and healthy individuals; moving beyond cities for survival, to cities for life. We explore the history, theoretical basis and supporting research for biophilic urbanism, before considering the importance of applying this design approach across multiple scales of urban design and development, including the building, street and city scales. We then introduce a whole systems approach to urban greening based on a triad of the natural, operational and economic realms of urban nature. We present examples of systemic urban greening that exemplifies this approach, demonstrating how such ideas can indeed be applied and achieved today.

Staying grounded in the rationale for urban nature

Modern explorations of human relationships with nature, and consideration of the design and development of urban areas in ways that recognise, protect and enhance the ecology and biodiversity have a basis in many fields. For example, the seminal work of Ian McHarg with his 1969 *Design with Nature* publication pioneered the concept of ecological planning as a branch of landscape architecture, and introduced methods for incorporating social and environmental values in development decision-making frameworks through spatial mapping (McHarg, 1969). His work promoted a new relationship between humans and their environment and established schools of thought and practice regarding the preservation of ecological form and function in urban development (McHarg and Steiner, 1998; Steiner, 2004). The work of Anne Spirn has similarly influenced considerations of landscape planning since the 1980s, by promoting understanding of how the natural settings of cities influence and is influenced by urbanisation (Spirn, 1984).

The field of urban ecology, which has origins in sixteenth-century work by botanists exploring vegetation growing on buildings (Sukopp, 2002), was more recently advanced in North America with the Chicago School in the 1920s, which used ecological concepts to consider the growth, metabolism, succession and mobility of cities (Park et al., 1925); and in Europe by Henry Sukopp following the Second World War, who studied the ecology of parks and the 'spontaneous vegetation' emerging in disused parts of West Berlin to find surprising diversity and richness (Marzluff et al., 2008). As a highly interdisciplinary field with roots in disciplines that include sociology, geography, urban planning, landscape architecture, engineering, economics, anthropology, climatology, public health and ecology, the pioneering efforts early researchers in this field underpin understanding and practice in urban design and development from many perspectives (Marzluff et al., 2008).

Links between human health and well-being, and explorations of evolutionary bases for a range of physiological and psychological responses to nature that have increasingly been observed in research studies, have provided additional perspectives to these fields. Two theories in particular contribute to our current understanding of how and why nature influences human neurological, physical and emotional well-being: Attention Restoration Theory (ART) and Psycho-Evolution Theory (PET). These theories both propose that natural environments have inherent qualities that promote restoration (from attention demanding tasks, and stressful events respectively) and positive emotions, and consequently that people inherently display preferences for such settings (Berto, 2005):

- ART considers how viewing, and spending time in, nature restores the ability to direct attention after periods of sustained focus and mental exertion. Kaplan and Kaplan compared the speed and extent of mental restoration achieved from viewing natural settings to urban settings, and theorised that the enhanced restoration achieved from natural environments is due to these providing four key qualities, including: (1) a sense of 'being away' – physically and cognitively – from attention demanding tasks; (2) sufficient 'extent' of detail in a landscape to be perceived as a 'whole other world' that engages the mind; (3) a sense of fascination that effortlessly captures attention; and (4) compatibility with the individual's purpose and preferences so they can relax (Kaplan 1995; Kaplan and Kaplan, 1989). A growing body of evidence supports this theory, demonstrating in laboratory and real-life contexts that natural environments are restorative to people's ability to pay attention (Berto, 2005; Hartig et al., 2003; Lee et al., 2015).

- PET seeks to explain emotional and physiological arousal responses to nature, including in particular recovery from stress. Ulrich (1991) proposed that humans have immediate and unconscious (rather than consciously controlled) emotional responses to certain natural settings to facilitate survival. Stress is a physiological state that has evolved to ensure that humans respond quickly and appropriately to threats, and actively avoid dangerous settings. However, the physiological conditions that comprise a stress response prevent other activities that are also important to survival, such as seeking food and water, reproduction and digestion. Threats (in the natural and built environments) such as a snake or a precipice, trigger fear, a sense of dislike and focused attention, stimulating appropriate movement and motivation to avoid the threat. Natural settings that provide shelter, food and safety, however – such as running water and flowering plants (precursors to fruit) – stimulate parasympathetic nervous activity and trigger a sense of pleasure and calm (Maller et al., 2006). When people view such settings after a stressful event, reduced levels of fear and negative emotions, a reduction in physiological arousal, and attention and interest in the safe setting have all been found to occur within minutes – faster than when people are viewing an alternative non-stressful but non-natural setting (Hartig et al., 2003). In other words, humans are hardwired to have reduced stress levels when viewing non-threatening natural settings to promote critical behaviours and activities, and are rewarded for seeking out such places in nature with positive emotional states.

Responding to the opportunities highlighted in these two theories, biophilic urbanism is an emergent urban design concept in which nature is intentionally integrated into the built environment as a formal design mechanism in order to provide meaningful, daily experiences of nature, whilst responding to the impacts of population pressures, climate change and resource shortages (Kellert et al., 2008; Beatley, 2011; SBEnrc, 2012).

This concept draws on the biophilia hypothesis developed by Edward Wilson and Stephen Kellert (Kellert and Wilson, 1993; Wilson, 1984), which proposes an "innately emotional affiliation of human beings to other living organisms" (Kellert and Wilson, 1993, p 31). The field of biophilic design emerged through collaboration and conversation between many theoreticians and practitioners from diverse disciplines including architecture, landscape architecture, psychology and urban ecology (Kellert et al., 2008).

Timothy Beatley expanded the initial building and infrastructure focus of biophilic design to consider how streetscapes, neighbourhoods and cities could be designed and developed to provide people with meaningful, daily experiences of nature. Beatley describes a biophilic city as one "that puts nature first in its design, planning, and management it recognizes the essential need for daily human contact with nature as well as the many environmental and economic values provided by nature and natural systems" (Beatley, 2011, p 45). Beatley (2016) proposes qualities a biophilic city should incorporate as a "tentative starting point" to what constitutes a biophilic city, including being biodiverse, abundant in nature, and offering most urbanites proximity to nature. Residents should feel an affinity with the local flora, fauna and fungi, and be able to recognise common local biodiversity so as to foster a deeper appreciation for this nature. The ecological integrity of urban nature is also important, as this provides rich, textured and multi-sensory experiences. A biophilic city should assist and inspire its residents to spend more time amongst the birds, trees and sunlight through education and celebration.

Biophilic urbanism seeks to act on the substantial body of research demonstrating the human-nature connection, and how experiences of nature can produce neurological, physiological and behavioural responses in people. It is both about the recognition, celebration and preservation of nature that already exists in cities – as well as the creation of additional nature in many forms. Within the context of increasing densification, new forms of nature are typically integrated into the built environment, such as green roofs, green walls and street trees. Given the typical land-use and financial constraints that exist, there is also a need for these to be high-value, multi-functional features.

Critically, biophilic urbanism is distinct from related fields such as water sensitive urban design, urban forestry and green infrastructure, in that the health, well-being and connection to nature of people are a central focus in the design of and argument for urban nature. "In recognizing the innate need for a connection to nature, biophilic cities tie the argument for green cities and green urbanism more directly to human well-being than to energy or environmental conservation" (Beatley, 2011, p 45).

Optimising for scales in designing for urban nature

Actually integrating nature into cities can be challenging due to competing land-use demands, financial constraints, lack of technical skills and industry experience, established planning laws and practices that do not encourage urban greening and private ownership of a large proportion of urban space (Norton et al., 2015, Matthews et al., 2015, Williams et al., 2010). A wide variety of forms of urban nature are evident (for example, Kellert et al., 2008; Klemm et al., 2015; Norton et al., 2015) and encouraging the use of these features – indeed optimising the benefits provided to cities from urban nature – requires a systemic approach that considers urban greening across multiple spatial scales, as well as considering urban nature within the broader urban system and context.

Table 29.1 summarises how nature can be included in design at multiple scales, from the mosses and lichen that inhabit crevices and cracks, through to the design of individual gardens, buildings and infrastructure, as well as the overall spatial distribution and connectivity of nature across a city as a whole, where

- Building scale elements are those that can be integrated onto, into and around a building, and are generally assumed to be limited to an individual property parcel.
- Street scale elements are those integrated into and alongside streets, roads and sidewalks, and parcel-sized blocks of land (for example vacant blocks of land within a residential suburb).
- City scale biophilic elements are larger size and likely to be fewer in number. These are not integrated into the urban fabric in the way that building or street scale elements are, and are instead large areas of vegetated space or open water within the city.

Table 29.1 Biophilic design elements at multiple scales (Adapted from Reeve, 2014)

Scale	Forms	Specific benefits	Examples of considerations for use
Building scale	**Green roofs**	– Reduce building energy demand – Increase property value – Increased roof longevity	Upfront and ongoing costs, local experience and data, species selection, building heights, resilience to storms, maintenance and plants survival, water requirements, competing roof space requirements
	Green walls	– Reduced building energy demand – Increase property value	Upfront and ongoing costs, design constraints and industry capacity, irrigation requirements, maintenance, risk of failure
	Shade trees	– Reduced building energy demand – Increase property value	Species selection, potential to increase ozone concentrations, fire risk, maintenance, water requirements
	Landscaping	– Increase property value	Net greenhouse gas emissions, water requirements, inclusion of trees in landscaping
Street scale	**Small-scale (pocket) parks and green space**	– Increase property value – Encourage physical activity – Increase social capital	Accessibility, maintenance
	Street-integrated trees and vegetation	– Reduce driving stress and incidences – Encourage active transport – Extend infrastructure longevity	Maintenance, water requirements, public safety, space requirements & competing demands, maintaining tree health, risk to infrastructure, upfront costs
City scale	**City parks and reserves**	– Catalyse economic development – Encourage physical activity	Land cost and availability, competing park uses, greater tree coverage, maintenance and management requirements, water requirements, perception of safety risks
	Linear green space	– Encourage active transport & physical activity – Catalyse economic development	Land cost and availability, competing park uses, greater tree coverage, maintenance and management requirements, water requirements, perception of safety risks
	City farms and urban agriculture	– Improve health and well-being, social capital – Retain nutrients & reduce waste – Increase food security	Lack of city support, soil contaminants, water requirements, urban climate conditions
	Urban waterways	– Increase property value	Visual amenity and waterway health, maintenance requirements, developer handover conditions, competing uses

Using a variety of forms of nature throughout a city can provide greater overall benefits. Indeed, some benefits actually require the biophilic element to be well distributed throughout the urban area. For example, optimal cooling benefits of vegetation occur when many smaller green spaces are created with sufficient intervals between, rather than an equivalent, single area of green space (Honjo and Takakura, 1991; Shashua-Bar and Hoffman, 2000). For optimal biodiversity benefits, a system of "links" and "hubs" of interconnected networks of refuge areas are needed to enable migration between refuges (Wolch et al., 2010). For optimal hydrological benefits, collections of smaller, vegetated infiltration areas distributed alongside impervious areas such as roads and roofs can achieve near pre-development hydrology conditions, even with a relatively small total footprint area (Lukes and Kloss, 2008; Cassidy et al., 2008).

Achieving such a multi-scalar urban greening, however, requires a suite of policies and approaches to address development at each of these stages and to engage stakeholders implicated across these scales. For instance, private landholders own a significant proportion of land within cities, which limits direct government investment and action in urban greening. However, the strategic development of incentives, assistance and development bylaws can encourage and enable property owners to integrate nature onto and around buildings – providing amongst the greatest opportunities to increase the overall nature within a city as it develops, and in particular to provide daily nature experiences to urbanites. In many cities, as understanding and experience of urban nature grow, market demand for buildings with integrated nature can in itself drive private investment in these features, with governments in such cases being called on to allow and regulate the development of these features in building codes and standards.

Streets (including verge areas) are generally owned by the government, facilitating direct greening efforts, however the need to consider car, bicycle and pedestrian traffic, utilities and other infrastructure, and emergency service access can complicate greening efforts. Strategic greening of these areas has, however, been shown to provide critical stormwater management benefits and to facilitate greater community connection amongst neighbourhoods. City-scale elements typically require long-term planning and land allocation, however in contrast to building and street-scale elements, generally have low technical complexity due to their larger size and limited infrastructure, and provide biodiversity refuges and opportunities for more complex and profound nature-based experiences than other scales.

In the next section of this chapter, we discuss a systems aproach to designing for urban nature that enables multi-scalar urban greening efforts through a three-pronged focus to the design, implementation and funding of natural features.

Adopting a systems approach to design for urban nature

Addressing the highly complex challenges of climate change, resource shortages and population pressures within the context of embedded socio-economic regimes that typify urban development scenarios requires a whole-systems approach to urban greening. Policy approaches and economic evaluations are needed that are capable of considering the multidimensional dynamics of urban environments as a whole (Reeve, 2014; el-Baghdadi, 2016). A systems approach to biophilic urbanism encourages multiple benefits to be captured in design outcomes. This includes considering concurrently the *natural, operational,* and *economic* realms that surround the intended biophilic element.

In the *natural realm* – as discussed in the previous section – greening across multiple scales is critical, considering many forms of integrated nature that address different property types and provide a variety of benefits to create opportunities for interconnected nature with more opportunities for human-nature contact, biodiversity, and urban system management. This includes greening at the building scale, such as greened roofs, walls and ground-level vegetation; greening at the street-scale, including street trees, roadside vegetated stormwater infrastructure and gardens, and pocket-parks; and greening at a city-scale, including city parks, extensive greenways that provide active transport and/or biodiversity corridors through a city, and urban agriculture.

Considerations within the *natural realm* also include designing with intent to optimise and promote the many potential benefits of urban nature to maximise the value gained from the space and resources dedicated to these features, including (summarised from Table 5.2 in Reeve, 2014):

- Thermal effects – Reduced heat transfer through building shell, energy demand, urban heat island effect, greenhouse gas emissions, ground level ozone production and potential increase in infrastructure life span
- Hydrologic effects –Reduced volume and speed of stormwater runoff, improved quality of runoff (due to reduced velocity of runoff), increased groundwater recharge, reduced potable water demand for irrigation (in other cases, irrigation demand may increase), improved health of receiving water bodies
- Filtering effects – Improved air quality, improved water quality (due to filtering of runoff)
- Aesthetic effects – Physical, neurological, and emotional well-being benefits; increased social capital and community connection; increased property value; increased likelihood of active transport; reduced traffic speeds and accidents
- Biodiversity effects – Increased diversity of species, provision of habitat refuges and corridors, food production
- Structural effects – Carbon sequestration, biomass production

In the *operational realm*, long-term, integrated planning is necessary to systematically protect city-scale urban nature, and consistently result in the development of building- and street-scale nature. Achieving a comprehensive approach to greening necessitates integrated planning and development approaches, both within government as well as with the community. Urban greening must be considered in concert with transport planning, long-term land-use planning and development codes, and adopt approaches inclusive of the broader community (Reeve et al., 2015). Preserving and creating the space within an urban environment for urban nature can rarely occur independently of other planning processes that shape the urban form and function. Transport and land-use planning determine the layout of a city, how the land will be used, and to a large degree, how people will move within that city. Creating space for nature can be critically enabled by policies and planning that reduces personal automobile dependence and therefore the extent of road and transport infrastructure. Similarly, land-use planning that preserves space for nature – such as nature corridors, nature reserves and parks – as well as development codes that require properties to integrate nature into and around buildings and infrastructure, are critical to ensure a city greens as it develops.

Increased coordination between levels of government and within each level of government can achieve consistency in their priorities, and alignment between entities invested with responsibilities for addressing the implications of the challenges facing the city, with those that have the responsibility for their planning and development. This can be achieved through, for example, interdepartmental taskforces for urban greening; embedding an agency for urban greening within infrastructure and/or urban planning departments; creating a high-level position within government to direct and coordinate policies and decision making across other departments with clear and consistent priorities. This may also include integrating, planning for transportation, infrastructure, environmental management and/or climate change, and ensuring the implications of these policy areas on health, productivity and liveability are clear (Reeve, 2014).

Engaging citizens in urban design and urban greening, including facilitating grassroots initiatives can foster greater ownership and appreciation of urban nature – and through connection to this nature, a sense of place and ownership over their city. It gives citizens a sense of belonging to place, which can inspire urban greening champions and advocates.

In the *economic realm*, urban nature needs to be valued across all the benefits it provides. As noted in earlier sections, urban nature has the potential to provide a wide range of benefits and services of value to people, however these benefits and services have not been quantified, let alone monetised (Hawken et al., 2010). This has led to market distortions, where urban ecosystems have been degraded at the expense of monetised goods and services (such as property development), however the loss of the benefits and services provided by this urban nature is nonetheless accruing.

Recent explorations in the field are addressing this gap by quantifying the benefits of urban nature, particularly within the broader field of ecosystem service assessment (Costanza et al., 1997). The Millennium Ecosystem Assessment and The Economics of Ecosystems and Biodiversity (TEEB) are two notable, international projects that have substantially progressed efforts to quantify the value of ecosystems and the services they provide. Building on the work of Costanza and his colleagues (1997), these assessment projects utilise a classification system for these benefits – including provisioning, regulating, supporting and cultural services. (Gómez-Baggethun et al., 2013; Millennium Ecosystem Assessment, 2005). This classification system in itself provides a more systematic perspective of the environmental, social and economic role of urban nature in the built environment, beyond the substantial investment into the quantification of the benefits (el-Baghdadi, 2016).

Quantification of ecosystem services conventionally requires biophysical measures and indicators, which are relatively easy to produce for provisioning services, and to a less extent for regulating and supporting ecosystem services (for example, tons of food produced, or tons of carbon sequestered, per hectare per year). However, cultural services in particular – such as aesthetic, inspirational and spiritual benefits of nature – are not easily measured using such biophysical measures (Gómez-Baggethun et al., 2013; Millennium Ecosystem Assessment, 2005). Recent work has adopted a range of economic valuation techniques that measure the value ascribed to these cultural services, providing common metrics across ecosystem services that can inform decision making regarding nature and ecosystems.

Research into this evolving field is still at its infancy, yet offers considerable opportunities for decision makers. The holistic economic enquiry offers a systemic approach to selecting a biophilic service that best targets the identified need in the local context. This perspective also drives the design and development of urban nature that is strategic and provides priority services to a given city. For example, throughout North America, cities are rapidly implementing green infrastructure throughout the urban environment primarily to infiltrate stormwater and mitigate combined sewer overflows and localised flooding, whereas in cities such as Singapore, greening is pursued primarily to enhance the urban aesthetic. These forms of urban nature inherently provide other services also – for example biodiversity, urban climate management, improved resident health and well-being – however the funding and development of this nature is greatly facilitated by linking this greening to a key priority for those cities.

Considering precedents of design for urban nature

There are numerous examples around the world, where design has transformed the way communities, companies and cities function. Here we highlight several examples that emulate the theoretical foundations of biophilic urbanism, the scales at which it can influence design outcomes, and the substantial benefits of holistically connecting design principles with policy and economic implications. In particular, we include several examples of building scale precedents, and also showcase the city of Singapore as a comprehensive example of greening across all scales.

What these examples point to is the growing appreciation of the significant role of design in influencing positive behaviour, health and well-being.

Building scale precedents

At a building scale, Google understands that happy employees are productive employees, and hence their approach to the design of their offices incorporates features designed to promote positive health and well-being outcomes. This includes a strong focus on integrating natural elements into the fabric of their office spaces, to promote stress reduction and attention restoration, community connection amongst employees and to facilitate greater productivity (FastCoDesign, 2014). Google is at the forefront of this revolution in office design, which focuses on enhancing productivity through creating environments conducive to creativity, well-being and interaction – in contrast to previously dominant views of increasing productivity through maximising the number of employees that can work within a given area of floor space. In recognition of the economic value of employee retention through greater workplace satisfaction, improving people's cognitive abilities and likelihood to interact with others to share ideas, Google willingly invested in these natural design features and drew on emerging knowledge to intentionally utilise these benefits of nature.

Similarly, at the building scale, the U.S.-based Clif Bar & Company, who manufacture organic food and drink, has incorporated natural elements throughout their Idaho bakery (Terrapin Bright Green, 2016). Clif Bar engaged Terrapin Bright Green, a consultancy specialised in biophilic design, to integrate biophilic design principles into the development of their Twin Falls bakery facility, going beyond LEED certification goals and becoming one of the first companies to comprehensively utilise biophilic design principles in food manufacturing.

Terrapin Bright Green aimed to create a sense of belonging and "connection to place" in the work environment through ensuring employees have access to exterior views of the surrounding farmland and natural light, and added biomorphic art in the bakery, and native stone is used throughout office areas. Walking paths and garden areas inside and around the buildings are lined with native plants that were specifically chosen for pollinator habitat restoration. In areas without exterior windows, wall-projected images of the natural outdoors that rotate daily are used to provide nature connection. The Clif Bar facility demonstrates a suite of design approaches to integrating nature, as well as images and representations of nature, into a manufacturing facility to provide not only for the health and well-being of workers, but also to provide support for surrounding ecosystems.

In a health care setting, the Lady Cilento Children's Hospital in Brisbane, Australia, provides an example of a much larger building-scale integration of nature. The incorporation of 11 healing gardens throughout the inner-city hospital, predominately as elevated, podium gardens has been achieved despite substantial space constraints, particularly at ground-level space. The gardens were designed by Conrad Gargett to provide patients, patient families and staff with a place for relaxation, contemplation and recuperation, while addressing the many design constraints including being soilless to avoid pathogen risks, highly water efficient, and to not attract bees and wasps. As such, they make use of innovative design features, such as detached vertical epiphyte columns and walls, enclosed seating areas, vine covered canopies and expansive views of the Brisbane River and Southbank Parklands to provide – even within a relatively small garden space – the sense of 'being away' from the hospital. These gardens draw on several decades of research that have demonstrated how visual access to green spaces can improve rates of healing, and reduce the experience of stress and pain (Ulrich, 1984) and promote positive mood change and a sense of renewal in patients that spent time in or observing nature (Whitehouse et al., 2001).

Comprehensive building, street and city scale precedent: Singapore

Singapore provides arguably the most advanced example of a biophilic city, with well-established policies and initiatives that drive urban greening across all scales of development, complemented by extensive programs to connect Singaporeans to the nature around them. Forty-seven per cent of the island city-state is now green cover, a remarkable achievement given that the original vegetation was nearly completely lost under the British rule and greening only commenced since Singapore gained independence in 1963 (Koh and Sodhi, 2004), and that during this time the population has also increased by over 250 per cent (Yuen, 1996).

Given Singapore's land constraints, the largest increases in green cover have been through integrating nature into the built environment, including as parks, roadside trees and shrubs, children's playgrounds, and building-integrated nature (Yuen, 1996). This is impressive by international standards, and largely reflects the leadership provided by Singapore's prime ministers, the vision and understanding of the importance of urban nature in the economic development of the city, whole-of-government collaboration, and the innovative and effective policies and programs developed (Neo et al., 2012). An overview of the history of Singapore's urban greening provides insight into how the current systemic approach to greening has been achieved, and the values that underpin this.

Following independence, rapid infrastructure construction led to the mushrooming of concrete structures throughout Singapore, and the then Prime Minister Lee Kuan Yew called for trees to be planted in Singapore to avoid the city becoming a concrete jungle (Neo et al., 2012). Lee claimed that a 'clean and green' environment would differentiate Singapore from other Asian cities, attract investment, retain talent, and ensure an ongoing high quality of life (Er and Chiew, 2013; Tan et al., 2009). Resources were scarce, and the new government had little experience in urban greening, hence urban nature was created in the most efficient means possible. Standardised park designs that were uniform and somewhat artificial (Yuen, 1996). Lee famously planted the first tree in 1963 in what was to become an annual tree planting campaign (Er and Chiew, 2013; Neo et al., 2012; Yuen, 1996), and called for 10,000 trees to be planted each year including 5,000 trees alongside new roads and in housing estates, school grounds and car parks (Neo et al., 2012). Investments in urban nature were pragmatic, focusing for example on high visibility areas such as the roads from the airport to the city which were lined with bougainvillea to ensure visitors to Singapore were given positive first impressions (Gwee, 2012). Fast growing tree species with large canopies were planted to rapidly green the urban area (Neo et al., 2012).

The Garden in a City campaign was formalised in 1968 in the Environmental Public Health Bill, which stated that "the improvement in the quality of our urban environment and the transformation of Singapore into a garden city – a clean and green city – is the declared objective of the Government" (Singapore Government, 2008; Wong et al., 2008, p 187).

From this point, the greening of Singapore began to take a more formalised and comprehensive form. In 1971, Singapore hosted the Commonwealth Prime Ministers' Conference, and Prime Minister Lee allocated $1.2 million for the planting of roadside trees and shrubs to beautify the city for this (Er and Chiew, 2013). The Garden City Action Committee was established to oversee these efforts, and it remained as a central institution directing urban greening in Singapore for many years (Auger, 2013; Yuen, 1996). The Committee comprised high-level civil servants representing all the ministries and statutory boards contributing to the greening effort, and consequently was instrumental in breaking down government silos and facilitating a whole-of-government approach to urban greening (Er and Chiew, 2013; Yuen, 1996).

The Concept Plan was finalised and accepted in 1972 as the first comprehensive plan for Singapore as an independent nation. The Plan directed the creation of parks as an essential element of a well-balanced city, marking the transition from the *ad hoc* creation of such green space in left-over spaces of the city, to strategic and intentional development of parks and recreational facilities (Yuen, 1996). Following this, the Parks and Trees Act was introduced in 1975 with statutory requirements for verge strip planting to be developed alongside new roads (Er and Chiew, 2013; Singapore Government, 2006b). This was a key legislative instrument that ensured that urban greening progressed in-line with urban development. This was enabled by the government agency with the official mandate for urban greening having been enlarged and situated within the Public Works Department, who had responsibility for infrastructure development in 1973, ensuring the alignment between urban greening and urban development (Neo et al., 2012).

Over subsequent years, a suite of programs and policies were introduced to develop green space and parks in Singapore. During the 1980s, these were focused on providing recreational opportunities and enhancing the image of Singapore as a garden city (Yuen, 1996). This included, for example, a five-year program to improve recreational opportunities at regional parks in Singapore from 1981, and the Park Connector Network, which was begun in 1989. In 1991, the Concept Plan was revised with extensive community consultation (Dale, 2008), and a new focus was evident on both economic performance and quality of life (Yuen, 2011). The growing influence of globalisation on Singapore was also evident with urban greenery used as a key strategy to help Singapore become a global city, maintain economic competitiveness and attract and retain investment, workers and tourists (Yuen, 2011). The Singapore Green Plan was subsequently introduced in 1992, providing the nation's first formal plan to balance environmental and development needs (Ministry of the Environment and Water Resources, 2013; Singapore Government, 2006a; Yuen, 1996).

The City in a Garden vision began to take hold towards the end of the century, and was formally adopted by the Garden City Action Committee in 2004 as their vision statement (Neo et al., 2012). This marked a transition in the conceptualisation of Singapore to one in which the built environment was nestled within a green, landscaped garden. The vision was accompanied by a suite of policies and programs, including the Streetscape Greenery Master Plan; the Parks and Waterbodies Plan; various skyrise greenery initiatives; continued commitment to the creation of the Park Connector Network; and the Gardens by the Bay development.

Significant efforts began in the new millennium to engage citizens in the production and maintenance of urban greenspace. In particular, the Community in Bloom programme, which was launched in 2005 formalised citizen participation in urban greenery (NParks, 2013). In 2007, the Centre for Urban Greenery and Ecology (CUGE) was established as a government-industry partnership to conduct research into new and improved forms of urban nature, and capacity building efforts to increase their use (Centre for Urban Greenery and Ecology, 2013; Er and Chiew, 2013).

Today, Singapore is host to many of the world's leading showcase biophilic developments, including the award-winning Alexandra Arch, the Khoo Teck Puat (KTP) hospital and the Gardens by the Bay development, which epitomise the new "city in a garden" paradigm for urban greening. The incorporation of urban greening into all major land use policies and strategies and prioritisation of this across government departments ensures the continued greening of the city as it develops. Several decades of greening underpin a highly supportive and engaged community that drives greening beyond compliance, and results in the community being actively involved in the maintenance of and appreciating the nature within the city.

There has been a lack of studies evaluating the impact of Singapore's urban greenery on human health and well-being, as it is generally stated that the benefits of urban nature are self-evident and widely appreciated, such that time and financial investments in evaluations (that can be complex to conduct) may have the perverse outcome of delaying actual urban greening progress (Centre for Liveable Cities, 2013). Further, the extent of greenspace coverage in Singapore is such that controlled studies within the city are virtually impossible. Indeed, one recent study that correlated the self-reported well-being of National University of Singapore students with self-reported usage of and access to green spaces (amongst other variables) found no statistically significant relationship (Le, Lim and Carrasco, 2015). This finding contradicts a substantial body of evidence of green spaces improving people's happiness and well-being (for example, White et al., 2013; van den Berg et al., 2007; Frumkin, 2001). The authors propose several reasons, including that the extent of urban greenery in Singapore is substantially higher than most cities (Singapore has 47 per cent public green space coverage, compared with New York (14 per cent), London (38.4 percent) and Hong Kong (41 per cent) (Le et al., 2015)), alongside much higher biodiversity levels, such that everyone living in Singapore is viewing nature throughout the daily course of life and receiving the benefits from doing so.

Conclusions

Cities are where an ever-increasing majority of the world's population live, and where the future of humanity and the globe will be determined. The infrastructure and cities we build now will exist for many decades and potentially hundreds of years, shaping the way that those who live there behave and how they feel – and in turn the social, environmental and economic well-being of nations globally. The long infrastructure legacy and often-irreversible spatial layout of cities is such that every decision in urban development has consequences, not only on the health, well-being and behaviour of residents now, but also into the future.

Creating urban environments that nourish the people who live there and provide a platform for building resilience to the challenges facing cities now and into the future requires new design thinking, and also new policies and economic models to enable these design principles to actually be implemented in a systemic manner. Priorities include creating urban environments that promote sustainable behaviour as well as human health and well-being through creating conditions conducive to life that are resonant with our evolved preferences and affiliations.

Drawing on theoretical and experiential learnings, we have presented a holistic urban greening design approach that considers the theoretical foundations of biophilic urbanism, the scales at which it can influence design outcomes, and the substantial benefits of systematically connecting design principles with policy and economic rationale. We have highlighted a number of examples from around the world where design has transformed the way communities, companies and cities function.

The built environment and design community globally has an unprecedented opportunity to harness rapidly emergent knowledge to create environments conducive to health and well-being. There are substantial environmental and social imperatives for this to occur, alongside increasingly strong economic rationales. As nations globally grapple to address budget deficits, with many developed nations in particular facing health care funding crises with aging populations and the rapid rise of lifestyle induced disease, there is a critical imperative to design cities today that provide for the health and well-being of citizens into the future.

References

Auger, T. (2013). *Living in a Garden: The Greening of Singapore*. Singapore: Editions Didier Millet.

Beatley, T. (2011). *Biophilic Cities: Integrating Nature Into Urban Design and Planning*. Washington, DC: Island Press.

Beatley, T. (2016). Chapter 1, Biophilic Oslo. In M. Luccarelli and P. G. Røe (Eds.), *Green Oslo: Visions, Planning and Discourse*, 2nd ed. Oxon: Routledge.

Berg, A. E. van den, Hartig, T. and Staats, H. (2007). Preference for nature in urbanized societies: Stress, restoration, and the pursuit of sustainability. *Journal of Social Issues, 63*(1), 79–96.

Berto, R. (2005). Exposure to restorative environments helps restore attentional capacity. *Journal of Environmental Psychology, 25*(3), 249–259.

Cassidy, A., Newell, J., and Wolch, J. (2008). *Transforming Alleys Into Green Infrastructure for Los Angeles*. Los Angeles, CA: Center for Sustainable Cities, University of Southern California.

Centre for Liveable Cities. (2013). *From Garden City to City in a Garden*. Centre for Liveable Cities Urban Pioneer Lecture Series. Retrieved from www.clc.gov.sg/documents/Lectures/2013/GreeningSingapore Transcript.pdf.

Centre for Urban Greenery and Ecology. (2013). *Research*. Retrieved 6 January 2014, from www.cuge.com. sg/research/.

Costanza, R., d'Arge, R., De Groot, R., Farber, S., Grasso, M., Hannon, B., Limburg, K., et al. (1997). The value of the world's ecosystem services and natural capital. *Nature, 387*, 253.

Dale, O. J. (2008). Sustainable City Centre Development: The Singapore City Centre in the Context of Sustainable Development. In T.-C. Wong, B. Yuen and C. Goldblum (Eds.), *Spatial Planning for a Sustainable Singapore*. Dordrecht: Springer.

Demuzere, M., Orru, K., Heidrich, O., Olazabal, E., Geneletti, D., Orru, H., . . . and Faehnle, M. (2014). Mitigating and adapting to climate change: Multi-functional and multi-scale assessment of green urban infrastructure. *Journal of Environmental Management, 146*, 107–115.

el-Baghdadi, O. (2016). *Exploring the Economic Business Case for Incorporating Biophilic Urbanism*. Doctor of Philosophy Thesis, Queensland University of Technology.

Er, K., and Chiew, L. C. (2013). Maintaining Identity in a Changing Landscape, Singapore's City in a Garden: 50 Years of Greening. In V. R. Savage (Ed.), *The Idea of Singapore* (Vol. 22, pp. 105–113), Singapore: The National University of Singapore.

FastCoDesign. (2014). *8 of Google's Craziest Offices*. Retrieved from www.fastcodesign.com/3028909/ 8-of-googles-craziest-offices/1.

Frumkin, H. (2001). Beyond toxicity, human health and the natural environment. *American Journal of Preventive Medicine, 20*(3), 234–240.

Gómez-Baggethun, E., and Barton, D. N. (2013). Classifying and valuing ecosystem services for urban planning. *Ecological Economics, 86*, 235–245.

Gwee, J. (2012). *Case Studies in Public Governance: Building Institutions in Singapore*. London: Routledge.

Hartig, T., Evans, G. W., Jamner, L. D., Davis, D. S., and Gärling, T. (2003). Tracking restoration in natural and urban field settings. *Journal of Environmental Psychology, 23*(2), 109–123. doi:10.1016/ s0272-4944(02)00109-3.

Hawken, P., Lovins, A. B., and Lovins, L. H. (2010). *Natural Capital: The Next Industrial Revolution*, Revised ed. New York: Routledge.

Honjo, T., and Takakura, T. (1991). Simulation of thermal effects of urban green areas on their surrounding areas. *Energy and Buildings, 15*(3), 443–446.

Kaplan, R. and Kaplan, S. (1989). *The Experience of Nature: A Psychological Perspective*. New York: Cambridge University Press.

Kaplan, S. (1995). The restorative benefits of nature: Toward an integrative framework. *Journal of Environmental Psychology, 15*(3), 169–182.

Kellert, S. R., Heerwagen, J., and Mador, M. (Eds.). (2008). *Biophilic Design: The Theory, Science and Practice of Bringing Buildings to Life*. Hoboken, NJ: John Wiley & Sons.

Kellert, S. R., and Wilson, E. O. (1993). *The Biophilia Hypothesis*. Washington, DC: Shearwater Books/Island Press.

Klemm, W., Heusinkveld, B. G., Lenzholzer, S., and van Hove, B. (2015). Street greenery and its physical and psychological impact on thermal comfort. *Landscape and Urban Planning, 138*, 87–98.

Koh, L. P., and Sodhi, N. S. (2004). Importance of reserves, fragments, and parks for butterfly conservation in a tropical urban landscape. *Ecological Applications, 14*(6), 1695–1708.

Le, E. S., Lim, F. K. S. and Carrasco, L. R. (2015). The relationship between natural park usage and happiness does not hold in a tropical city-state. *PLoS ONE, 10*(7), e0133781. doi:10.1371/journal.pone.0133781.

Lee, K. E., Williams, K. J. H., Sargent, L. D., Williams, N. S. G., and Johnson, K. A. (2015). 40-second green roof views sustain attention: The role of micro-breaks in attention restoration. *Journal of Environmental Psychology, 42*, 182–189.

Lockton, D., Harrison, D., and Stanton, N. (2008) Making the user more efficient: Design for sustainable behaviour. *International Journal of Sustainable Engineering, 1*(1), 3–8.

Lukes, R., and Kloss, C. (2008). *Managing Wet Weather With Green Infrastructure Municipal Handbook, Green Streets, Low Impact Development Centre.* US Environmental Protection Agency. Retrieved from http://water.epa.gov/infrastructure/greeninfrastructure/upload/gi_munichandbook_green_streets.pdf.

Maller, C., Townsend, M., Pryor, A., Brown, P., and St Leger, L. (2006). Healthy nature healthy people: 'Contact with nature'as an upstream health promotion intervention for populations. *Health promotion international, 21*(1), 45–54.

Marzluff, J. M., Shulenberger, E., Endlicher, W., Alberti, M., Bradley, G. A., Ryan, C., . . . Marzluff, J. (Eds.). (2008). *Urban Ecology: An International Perspective on the Interaction Between Humans and Nature.* New York: Springer.

Matthews, T., Lo, A. Y., and Byrne, J. A. (2015). Reconceptualizing green infrastructure for climate change adaptation: Barriers to adoption and drivers for uptake by spatial planners. *Landscape and Urban Planning, 138,* 155–163.

McHarg, I. L. (1969). *Design With Nature.* New York: American Museum of Natural History.

McHarg, I. L., and Steiner, F. R. (Eds.). (1998). *To Heal the Earth: Selected Writings of Ian L. McHarg.* Washington, DC: Island Press.

Millennium Ecosystem Assessment (MEA). (2005). *Ecosystems and Human Well-Being: Synthesis.* Washington, DC: Island Press.

Ministry of the Environment and Water Resources. (2013). *Grab Our Research, Singapore Green Plan.* Retrieved 5 February 2014, from Singapore Government, http://app.mewr.gov.sg/web/Contents/Contents.aspx?ContId=1342.

Neo, B. S., Gwee, J., and Mak, C. (2012). Growing a City in a Garden. In J. Gwee (Ed.), *Case Studies in Public Governance: Building Institutions in Singapore.* London: Routledge.

Norton, B. A., Coutts, A. M., Livesley, S. J., Harris, R. J., Hunter, A. M., and Williams, N. S. (2015). Planning for cooler cities: A framework to prioritise green infrastructure to mitigate high temperatures in urban landscapes. *Landscape and Urban Planning, 134,* 127–138.

NParks. (2013). *Community in Bloom.* Retrieved 03 January 2014, from Singapore Government, www.nparks.gov.sg/cms/index.php?option=com_content&view=article&id=32&Itemid=145

Park, R., McKenzie, R. D., and Burgess, E. (1925). *The City: Suggestions for the Study of Human Nature in the Urban Environment* 20(5), 577–612.

Reeve, A. C. (2014). *Mainstreaming Biophilic Urbanism in Australian Cities: A Response to Climate Change, Resource Shortages and Population Pressures.* PhD thesis, Queensland University of Technology.

Reeve, A. C., Desha, C., Hargreaves, D., and Hargroves, K. (2015). Biophilic urbanism: contributions to holistic urban greening for urban renewal. *Smart and Sustainable Built Environment, 4*(2), 215–233.

SBEnrc. (2012). *Can Biophilic Urbanism Deliver Strong Economic and Social Benefits in Cities? An Economic and Policy Investigation Into the Increased Use of Natural Elements in Urban Design.* Sustainable Built Environment National Research Centre (SBEnrc), Curtin University and Queensland University of Technology. Australia.

Shashua-Bar, L., and Hoffman, M. (2000). Vegetation as a climatic component in the design of an urban street: An empirical model for predicting the cooling effect of urban green areas with trees. *Energy and Buildings, 31*(3), 221–235.

Singapore Government. (2006a). *The Singapore Green Plan 2012 (2006 Update).* Singapore. Retrieved from http://app.mewr.gov.sg/data/imgcont/1342/sgp2012_2006edition.pdf.

Singapore Government. (2006b). *Parks and Trees Act (2006 Revised Edition).* Retrieved from www.nparks.gov.sg/cms/docs/ParksandTreesAct.pdf.

Singapore Government. (2008). *Singapore Green Plan (SGP).* Retrieved 5 April 2014, from http://app.mewr.gov.sg/data/imgcont/1342/sgp2012_2006edition.pdf.

Smith, M. H., Hargroves, K., and Desha, C. (2010). Cents and sustainability. *Securing our Common Future by Decoupling Economic Growth From Environmental Pressures.* London: Earthscan.

Spirn, A. W. (1984). *The Granite Garden: Urban Nature and Human Design.* New York: Basic Books.

Steiner, F. (2004). Commentary. *Philosophy & Geography, 7*(1), 141–149.

Sukopp, H. (2002). On the early history of urban ecology in Europe. *Preslia Praha, 74*(4), 373–394.

Sullivan, L. H. (1896). The tall office building artistically considered. *Lippincott's Magazine, 57*(3), 406.

Tan, Y. S., Lee, T. J., and Tan, K. (2009). *Clean, Green and Blue: Singapore's Journey Towards Environmental and Water Sustainability.* Singapore: Institute of Southeast Asian Studies.

Terrapin Bright Green. (2016). *Clif Bar Biophilic Design Review.* Retrieved from www.terrapinbrightgreen.com/blog/2016/09/clif-bar-biophilic-design-review/.

Thaler, R. H., and Sunstein, C. R. (2009). *Nudge: Improving Decisions About Health, Wealth, and Happiness.* New York: Penguin Books.

Tzoulas, K., Korpela, K., Venn, S., Yli-Pelkonen, V., Kaźmierczak, A., Niemela, J., and James, P. (2007). Promoting ecosystem and human health in urban areas using Green Infrastructure: A literature review. *Landscape and Urban Planning, 81*(3), 167–178.

Ulrich, R. S. (1984). View through a window may influence recovery from surgery. *Science, 224,* 42–421.

Ulrich, R. S. (1991). Stress recovery during exposure to natural and urban environments. *Journal of Environmental Psychology, 11*(3), 201–230. doi:10.1016/S0272-4944(05)80184-7.

Wever, R., van Kuijk, J. and Boks, C. (2008) User-centred design for sustainable behaviour. *International Journal of Sustainable Engineering, 1*(1), 9–20.

White, M. P., Alcock, I., Wheeler, B. W. and Depledge, M. H. (2013). Would you be happier living in a greener urban area? A fixed-effects analysis of panel data. *Psychological Science,* 24(6), 920–928.

Whitehouse, S., Varni, J. W., Seid, M., Cooper-Marcus, C., Ensberg, M. J., Jacobs, J. R., and Mehlenbeck, R. S. (2001). Evaluating a children's hospital garden environment: Utilization and consumer satisfaction. *Journal of Environmental Psychology, 21*(3), 301–314.

Williams, N. S., Rayner, J. P., and Raynor, K. J. (2010). Green roofs for a wide brown land: Opportunities and barriers for rooftop greening in Australia.*Urban Forestry & Urban Greening, 9*(3), 245–251.

Wilson, E. O. (1984). *Biophilia.* Cambridge, MA: Harvard University Press.

Wolch, J., Newell, J., Seymour, M., Huang, H. B., Reynolds, K., and Mapes, J. (2010). The forgotten and the future: Reclaiming back alleys for a sustainable city. *Environment and Planning A, 42*(12), 2874.

Wong, T., Breen, P., and Lloyd, S. (2000). *Water Sensitive Road Design – Design Options for Improving Stormwater Quality of Road Runoff.* Australia: Cooperative Research Centre for Catchment Hydrology.

Wong, T.-C., Yuen, B., and Goldblum, C. (2008). *Spatial Planning for a Sustainable Singapore.* Dordrecht: Springer.

World Economic Forum. (2016). *What Are the 10 Biggest Global Challenges?* Retrieved from www.weforum.org/agenda/2016/01/what-are-the-10-biggest-global-challenges/.

Yuen, B. (1996). Creating the garden city: The Singapore experience. *Urban Studies, 33*(6), 955–970.

Yuen, B. (2011). Urban planning in Southeast Asia: Perspective from Singapore. *The Town Planning Review, 82*(2), 145–167.

PART 5

Moving forward

The final section of the *Handbook of Sustainable Design* presents ideas and philosophies to consider as designers continue to push the field of sustainable design forward. These next steps should not be regarded individually but in the context of the other ideas presented throughout the entire handbook. As this handbook explains, sustainable design flourishes through the interconnectedness of disciplines, cultures and systems.

Fabrizio Ceschin and Idil Gaziulusoy begin the section with *How many ways to design for sustainability?* The chapter provides an "evolutionary history" of the field of design for sustainability and an overview of the key factors in its primary levels innovation. These include product design, product-service system, spatio-social, and socio-technical levels. Ceschin and Gaziulusoy propose a new framework that synthesizes the evolution of design for sustainability and presents it across three dimensions – innovation, technology/people, and insular/systemic. This chapter provides a thorough overview of the field's evolution and the impending challenges to overcome as we design for the future.

The Structure of Structural Change: Making a Habit of Being Alienated as a Designer by Cameron Tonkinwise provides a philosophical approach to structural change. This approach "requires designers to combine utopian and cynical attitudes in a constant state of creative hypocrisy." To become more sustainable, we need more than simple design solutions, but rather major structural change to both design and society. Tonkinwise looks at different structures – concrete, abstract, and belief schemata; social values and practices. Finally, the chapter explores how we might restructure within our encompassing systems of change, restructure within new environments, and agitate change.

As we think about societal and cultural change, we must also consider the relationships between sustainability, race, and class. Diamond James discusses race and resilience in *Empowering citizens through design*. Drawing on the work of Charles Kieffer, Paulo Freire, and Victor Papanek, James lays out the role of the advocate-designer as "a composite of activist, community organizer, and coalition builder with a creative mode of practice for problem solving." James provides us with a case study that demonstrates how codesign empowers citizens to reshape their communities.

Whereas the preceding chapters in Part 5 present broad ideas, the chapters that follow limit their focus to individual ideas for designing the future of sustainability. The concepts discussed in these chapters represent distinct fields, each having entire books dedicated to their study. The discussions in the following chapters serve as an introduction to each concept.

Biomimicry: nature inspiring design by Denise DeLuca provides an introduction to emulating nature's strategies to create sustainable design solutions. This chapter synthesizes Janine Benyus's pioneering work in establishing biomimicry as an approach to sustainable design. It presents the biomimicry design spiral as a process for innovating design solutions and provides case studies and examples of successful implementations of biomimicry.

The value of the sharing economy by Brhmie Balaram provides considerations for designers within sharing economy platforms and systems. Experts originally framed the sharing economy as a potential solution to sustainable consumption, though its reality has created additional challenges. Balaram's work goes beyond the sharing economy's initial popularity in the early 2010s to uncover the resulting issues, including workers' rights in the subsequent gig economy and networked monopolies. Balaram writes "its evolution has been controversial, and if the sharing economy is to become embedded in our lives it's crucial we better understand how the sector is changing as well as its impact beyond the environment."

Recognizing the need for interdisciplinary collaboration and holistic education Sara Kapadia contributes *Going from STEM to STEAM*, which demonstrates the value of science, technology, engineering, arts, and mathematics working together to create sustainable design solutions. While the discussion of STEM/STEAM education primarily originates in the United States, its story is one that relates to education both across grade levels and across the globe. Kapadia describes the evolutionary history of education, silo-ing itself into individual disciplines, and then conversely working in collaborative disciplines. The chapter presents a case for embracing artistic designs in conjunction with scientific methods to create sustainable solutions in the future. Kapadia concludes that future conversations must examine how we educate the younger generations to embrace science and art.

Finally, Ruud Balkenende, Nancy Bocken, and Conny Bakker present *Design for the circular economy*. Although discussed in a handful of other chapters throughout the book, this chapter focuses solely on the circular economy and the designer's role in it. "In a circular economy value chains and networks are closed by optimally addressing the circular design of business models, processes and products, taking simultaneously an environmental and economic perspective." Individual companies, industries, governments, and entire regions have adopted circular economy principals in their plans for their future. The authors of this chapter provide an overview of the circular economy and provide points of intervention for the design field. A case study in light fixtures gives a concrete example of both design and economic strategy.

Each chapter in this final section gives us food for thought as we attempt to sustain the design practice and our existence on a planet with finite resources. Whereas the four previous parts grapple with challenges and solutions, this last section offers hope for moving forward. Through the expanded definition of design presented in this handbook, it's evident that there is no single path, answer, or magic solution to remedy the environmental crisis upon us. An individual and collective effort of designers, scientists, policy makers, economists, and cultural representatives (and many others) is needed to create a world that sustains, replenishes, and flourishes.

30

HOW MANY WAYS TO DESIGN FOR SUSTAINABILITY?

Fabrizio Ceschin and Idil Gaziulusoy

Introduction

The discourse on sustainability has reached a point where the present common view is that there is a need for radical transformational change in how human society operates (Ryan, 2013a). This view emerged as a result of studies pointing out the fast declining of terrestrial and aquatic ecosystems with implications on biodiversity, as well as the urgent action needed to mitigate and adapt to climate change (Butchart et al., 2010; Hughes and Steffen, 2013; Rockström et al., 2009). The estimates of economic and social cost of inaction for addressing global, persistent and pressing environmental issues are alarming (MEA, 2005; Stern, 2006). In parallel with the changes taking place in socioecological contexts and increased theoretical understanding of implications of these changes, the response from the broader society in general and from business specifically has also evolved in the past decades with an increasing pace (WBCSD, 2000; 2004; 2010). Currently, studies challenging the traditionally accepted role and responsibilities of business in society and proposing new models for value creation is on the increase (e.g. Loorbach and Wijsman, 2013; Metcalf and Benn, 2012; Parrish, 2007).

Design as a primary function for innovation in business, and increasingly in government and in other social organisational units including local communities (Design Council, 2007; Gruber et al., 2015) has been engaged with different aspects of sustainability discourse and practice since the mid-twentieth century. With the beginning of active interest from industry in environmental and social issues, more systematic engagement in design has started in early 1980s.

In this chapter, we present a short evolutionary history of the Design for Sustainability (DfS) field starting from these early days of systematic engagement, and provide insights on the emerging directions in the field. The chapter is structured as follows. Firstly, we present the DfS approaches emerged in the past decades, then we propose and discuss a framework that synthesizes the evolution of the DfS field, and finally we reflect on the future research challenges of DfS.

A multiplicity of approaches to design for sustainability (DfS)

The history of Design for Sustainability (DfS) has seen, in the last decades, the development of a variegated set of design approaches. In this section we briefly present these DfS approaches following a quasi-chronological pattern. In order to simplify the understanding of this historical evolution, we have categorised these approaches in relation to their innovation focus. In particular, considering the scale of the design intervention, we have identified, in a crescent order, four main innovation levels:

- *Product design innovation level* – which includes design approaches focusing on improving existing products or developing completely new products.
- *Product-service system innovation level* – in which the focus shifts from individual products to integrated combinations of products, services and stakeholder value chains.
- *Spatio-social innovation level* – in which the innovation scope is on human settlements and the spatio-social conditions of their communities, with a focus that can range from neighbourhoods to cities.
- *Socio-technical system innovation level* – characterised by design approaches that promote and support transitions to new socio-technical systems (i.e. radical changes on how societal needs, such as nutrition and transport/mobility, are fulfilled).

Product design innovation level

Green design and eco-design

Fuller's (1969) and Papanek's (1985) teachings and work mark the earliest concerns in the design field about resource limits and the impact of our material production on the environment. Nevertheless, systematic contributions started in early 1990s as "green design" (Burall, 1991; Mackenzie, 1997). Green design focused on lowering environmental impact through redesigning individual qualities of individual products by following the waste hierarchy of reduce-reuse-recycle or using emerging technologies such as solar street lamps (Fuad-Luke, 2002). There was also a focus on efficiency improvements in product and process engineering (e.g. Fiksel, 1996). Green design developed and improved the still valid "rules of thumb" for improving environmental performance of products. However, it lacked depth and promoted green consumerism (Madge, 1997). Eco-design, instead of focusing on single components or individual qualities of products, adopted a life-cycle approach and has become the most frequently practiced approach until present. The goal of eco-design is to minimise the consumption of natural resources and energy while maintaining traditional industrial values such as profit, functionality, aesthetics, ergonomics, image and overall quality benefits for customers (Brezet and van Hamel, 1997; Tischner and Charter, 2001; Vezzoli and Manzini, 2008). However, eco-design lacks complexity with its sole focus on environmental performance and a disregard of social impacts (Bhamra et al., 2011; Gaziulusoy, 2015).

Emotionally durable design

Eco-design provides a set of design strategies to extend product lifespan from a technical point of view. However, for some product categories, a large percentage of products still function properly when discarded (Van Nes, 2003). In this cases the end of lifespan is not caused by technical issues but by psychological obsolescence (when a product is discarded for reasons such as changes in users' perceived needs, desire for social status emulation) (Cooper, 2004). For this reason, in the late 90s researchers have started to explore the user-product relationship and how design can strengthen that relationship to increase product lifetime (e.g. Van Hinte, 1997; Chapman, 2005; Mugge, 2007; Chapman, 2009). An important contribution came from Mugge (2007) who identified four main product meanings that can affect user-product attachment: *self-expression, group affiliation, memories* and *pleasure (or enjoyment)*. Various researchers have also proposed design strategies seeking at stimulating product attachment (e.g. Mugge et al., 2005; Chapman, 2005; Mugge, 2007). Examples are *designing products that 'age with dignity'* (Van Hinte, 1997), and *designing products that allow users to capture memories* (Chapman, 2005).

Design for sustainable behaviour

Even if ecodesign can help designers to reduce the environmental impact of a product throughout its whole life cycle, it must be highlighted that this approach does not devote much attention to the influence that user's behaviour can have on the overall impact. Several researches have shown that the way in which users interact with products can determine substantial environmental impacts (Environmental Change Unit, 1997; Sherwin and Bhamra, 1998). For this reason design researchers, building upon various behaviour change theories, have started to develop approaches, tools and guidelines that explicitly focus on changing user behaviour towards more sustainable outcomes: for example the *Design for Sustainable Behaviour* model developed at Loughborough University (Lilley, 2009; Bhamra et al., 2011), *Design with Intent* (Lockton et al., 2010; Lockton, 2013) and *Mindful design* (Niedderer, 2007; 2013). Applications span from product to product-service system, mobile interaction and built environment design.

Nature-inspired design: cradle-to-cradle design and biomimicry design

The two most prominent frameworks of nature-inspired design are cradle-to-cradle design and biomimicry design. Cradle-to-cradle is based on two concepts: *waste equals food* and *eco-effectiveness* (Braungart et al., 2007; McDonough and Braungart, 2002). Cradle-to-cradle design assumes that if biological and technological 'nutrients' are used in open (for biological nutrients) or closed (for technological nutrients) loops, the human society can continue production, consumption and economic growth indefinitely. By putting emphasis on regenerative processes, non-human species and future generations, cradle-to-cradle potentially enables radical innovation and mindset change in businesses, which has been acknowledged as its main value (Bakker et al., 2010). Nevertheless, cradle-to-cradle design is technically not well justified (Bjørn and Hauschild, 2013; Gaziulusoy, 2015; Reijnders, 2008). In addition, cradle-to-cradle design might shift focus from the entire life cycle of products to minimising or eliminating toxic materials, and it overlooks the impacts of energy consumption (Bakker et al., 2010; Llorach-Massana et al., 2015).

The premise of biomimicry design is using nature as model, measure and mentor (Benyus, 1997). Using nature as a model involves studying the models and processes of nature and adapting these to solve human problems. There are three levels of biomimicry (Benyus, 1997): mimicking *forms* of nature, mimicking *processes* of nature and mimicking *ecosystems*. Biomimicry design also advocates using waste as a resource and closing loops. Although mimicking nature is a well-established approach in design, it is misleading to claim that nature-mimicking leads to sustainability (Volstad and Boks, 2012) because isolating a principle, structure or process from nature and imitating it does not necessarily yield to sustainability. This is particularly true for 'reductive' biomimicry, which mimics only forms and processes (Reap et al., 2005). Biomimicry design is technologically optimistic and, although this creates opportunities for radical technological innovation, the complexity of transforming our production-consumption systems and psycho-cultural patterns are overlooked (Gaziulusoy, 2015; Mathews, 2011).

Design for the Base of the Pyramid (BoP)

In addition to environmental concerns, the last decade saw some design researchers focus their interest on social issues, with a particular emphasis on the poorest portion of the global population, the so called Base of the Pyramid (BoP). In the past decade design researchers and designers have started exploring the implications of designing for the BoP (e.g. see Gomez Castillo et al., 2012) also known as design for the other 90% (Smith, 2007). BoP people are generally characterised by a lack of income to satisfy basic needs, a lack of access to basic services, and by social, cultural and political exclusion (London, 2007). Thus, designing solutions at the BoP requires addressing specific issues that are different from those in high-income markets (Jagtap et al., 2013). In this respect a number of manuals and tools have been proposed in the past years, providing a set of complementary approaches, such as: *Design for Sustainability*, D4S (UNEP, 2006) with a focus on sustainability and business development; *Human Centred Design toolkit* (IDEO, 2009), which provides guidance and tools on user-centred design; the *BoP Protocol* (Simanis and Hart, 2008), and the *Market Creation toolbox* (Larsen and Flensborg, 2011), which focuses on business model co-creation. Recently the attention of design researchers on the BoP has moved to Product-Service System design and design for social innovation (see later sections).

Product-service system innovation level

Realising that sustainability requires a drastic reduction in resource consumption (Schmidt-Bleek, 1996), and that innovations at a product level are not sufficient to obtain such a radical improvement, several researchers have started to look at Product-Service System (PSS) innovations as a promising approach for sustainability (e.g. Stahel, 1997; Mont, 2002). PSSs can be defined as "a mix of tangible products and intangible services designed and combined so that they are jointly capable of fulfilling final customer needs" (Tukker and Tischner, 2006): value propositions that satisfy users through the delivery of functions/performances instead of products and shift the focus from a consumption based on ownership to a consumption based on access and sharing. Being complex artefacts composed of *products*, *services*, and a *network of actors*, designing a PSS requires a systemic approach considering all these elements simultaneously. Design researchers have initially focused on PSS design for eco-efficiency, looking at the economic and environmental dimensions of sustainability (e.g. Brezet et al., 2001; Manzini et al., 2001), while more recently attention has moved towards integrating also the socio-ethical dimension, referring to PSS design for sustainability (e.g. Vezzoli, 2007; Vezzoli et al., 2014).

Spatio-social innovation level

Design for social innovation

Social innovations, either refer to those innovations aiming to solve social problems (Schaltegger and Wagner, 2008) or those targeting behavioural change and social well-being (Manzini, 2007). A more broad and systemic understanding of social innovation understands it as a creative recombination of existing assets (Manzini, 2014). Social innovations usually emerge from the inventiveness and creativity of ordinary people and communities (sometimes in collaboration with grass roots technicians and entrepreneurs, local institutions and civic society organizations) (Jégou and Manzini, 2008; Meroni, 2007).

Manzini (2014) defines design for social innovation as "a constellation of design initiatives geared toward making social innovation more probable, effective, long-lasting, and apt to spread

(p. 65)". Although social innovations are often driven by citizen actors, professional designers can play a significant role in promoting and supporting them by making them more visible and tangible (e.g. to increase people awareness), more effective and attractive (e.g. to improve the experience of people involved), as well as by supporting replication (scaling-out) and connection (scaling-up) (Manzini, 2015). Currently, the focus in design for social innovation is mainly on investigating how designers can support and facilitate the process of replication and scaling-up (e.g. Manzini and Rizzo, 2011; Hillgren et al., 2011).

Nature-inspired design: systemic design

Systemic design is another nature-inspired approach that, differently from cradle-to-cradle and biomimicry, focuses on mimicking natural ecosystems. It combines elements of biomimicry, cradle-to-cradle and industrial ecology. As described by Barbero and Toso (2010),

> the Systemic Design approach seeks to create not just industrial products, but complex industrial systems. It aims to implement sustainable productive systems in which material and energy flows are designed so that waste from one productive process becomes input to other processes, preventing waste from being released into the environment.

Systemic design adopts a territorial approach, looking at local socio-economic actors, assets and resources, with the aim of creating synergistic linkages among productive processes (agricultural and industrial), natural processes and the surrounding territory (Bistagnino, 2009; 2011; Barbero and Fassio, 2011).

Socio-technical system innovation level

The 1990s saw an emerging focus in science and technology studies area on transformation of socio-technical systems for sustainability (Green and Vergragt, 2002; Quist and Vergragt, 2004; 2006; Weaver et al., 2000). Around similar times, as a means to understanding how innovation in socio-technical systems occurs, a group of scholars developed the multi-level perspective of system innovation building on evolutionary innovation theory (Geels, 2005a; 2005b; Kemp, 1994; Kemp et al., 2001). System innovation is defined as "a transition from one socio-technical system to another" (Geels, 2005a, p. 2). Building upon these insights *Strategic Niche Management* (Schot, 1992; Kemp et al., 1998) and *Transition Management* (Rotmans et al., 2001; Loorbach, 2007; 2010) theories have been developed in the past decade.

These developments in science and technology studies created a ground in the design field for cross-fertilisation. Currently the emerging field of design for system innovations and transitions is being developed by a handful of design scholars (Ceschin, 2012; 2014a; 2014b; Gaziulusoy, 2010; Gaziulusoy and Brezet, 2015; Joore, 2010; Joore and Brezet, 2015). Design for system innovations and transitions focus on transformation of socio-technical systems through technological, social, organisational and institutional innovations. In this regard, it embodies design for Product-Service Systems which aims to transform production-consumption systems through business model innovation and design for social innovation which aims to assist with social change.

A framework to understand design for sustainability

The DfS approaches described in the previous sections can be categorised looking at three dimensions:

- *Innovation level* – DfS approaches can address sustainability at different levels: product, product-service system, spatio-social and socio-technical system levels.
- *Technology/People* – Approaches that address sustainability from a technical perspective, versus approaches in which sustainability is seen as a socio-technical challenge where user and group practices and behaviours play a fundamental role.
- *Insular/Systemic* – Approaches that focus on sustainability problems in isolation (e.g. improving recyclability of a product) versus approaches that focus on making changes on the wider socio-economic systems.

If we combine these three dimensions together the result is the framework shown in Figure 30.1 (Ceschin and Gaziulusoy, 2016).

We can now map the DfS approaches onto the framework. The process of positioning the approaches onto the framework is based on (1) ordering the approaches using the Insular/

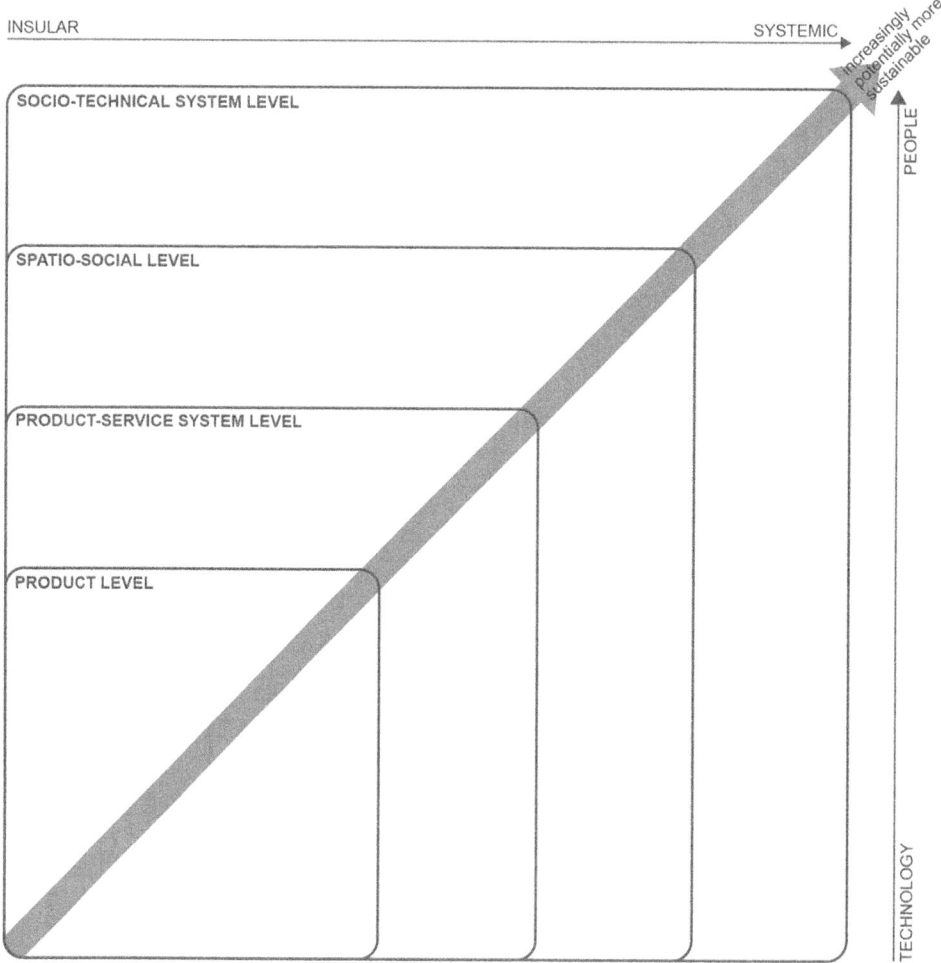

Figure 30.1 The DfS evolutionary framework (Ceschin and Gaziulusoy, 2016).

Systemic axis; (2) ordering the approaches using the Technology/People axis; (3) combining the results of the two positioning exercises onto the bi-dimensional framework by drawing, for each approach, an area corresponding to the intersection between the Insular/Systemic and Technology/People coordinates. Each DfS approach is mapped as an area because it can potentially span over different innovation levels. A colour code is used to indicate whether the approach is addressing the environmental dimension of sustainability and/or the socio-ethical one. Figure 30.2 shows the resulting framework (Ceschin and Gaziulusoy, 2016), which is meant to provide an overview of the overall evolution of DfS, as well as an understanding of how the various DfS approaches contribute to particular sustainability aspects.

Looking at the framework we can note that DfS has broadened its scope over the years, from both theoretical and operational points of view (Ceschin and Gaziulusoy, 2016). In the first half of the 90s DfS was mainly focused on the product level, with the development and subsequent consolidation of *green design* and *eco-design*. Other approaches at the product level were developed in the late 90s (see *biomimicry*), and in the first half of the past decade (see *cradle-to-cradle design, emotionally durable design, design for the base of the pyramid, design for sustainable behaviour*). Regarding the Product-Service System design approaches, the initial developments took place in the late 90s but the main acceleration came in the 2000s. In relation to the spatio-social level, *design for social innovation* was initially delineated in the first half the 2000s. The attention on the role of design at the socio-technical system level is even more recent, with the first PhD projects on the topic completed in the last few years (Ceschin, 2012; Gaziulusoy, 2010, and Joore, 2010, respectively at Politecnico di Milano, University of Auckland and Delft University of Technology).

Overall, the focus of DfS has also progressively expanded from single products to complex systems (Ceschin and Gaziulusoy, 2016). In fact earlier DfS approaches focus on insular innovations: innovations that address sustainability problems in isolation and whose solutions can be developed and implemented by an individual actor. On the other hand, DfS approaches tackling sustainability at a product-service system, spatio-social and socio-technical system levels, are increasingly much more complex. This means that their implementation might require an interwoven set of innovations and a variety of socio-economic actors (ranging from users to policymakers, local administrations, NGOs, consumer groups, industry associations, research centres, etc.). In these cases the activities of an actor (e.g. firm) need to be linked and integrated with other actors' activities.

The enlargement of the design scope has been accompanied by an increased attention to the 'human-centred' aspects of sustainability (Ceschin and Gaziulusoy, 2016). Earlier approaches have been focusing mainly on the technical aspects of sustainability (e.g. see *green design, eco-design, biomimicry*), while the following ones have recognised the crucial importance of the role of users (e.g. see *emotionally durable design, design for sustainable behaviour*), communities (e.g. see *design for social innovation*), and more in general of the various actors and dynamics in a socio-technical system (e.g. see the fourth innovation level).

The way forward: emerging synergies and new research directions

The framework we presented in the previous section is quasi-chronological. What we mean by this is that, although there is an observable evolutionary pattern of shifting focus from individual artefacts to systems, this does not mean that the earlier approaches emerged and matured in the short history of DfS are overtaken by what had come after them. Instead, these approaches find new meaning and purpose in the context of a systemic and human-centric focus. Designing at the systemic level is a strategic activity enabling us to gain insights on the required directions of design interventions that will take place in sub-systemic level and develop tactics for creating

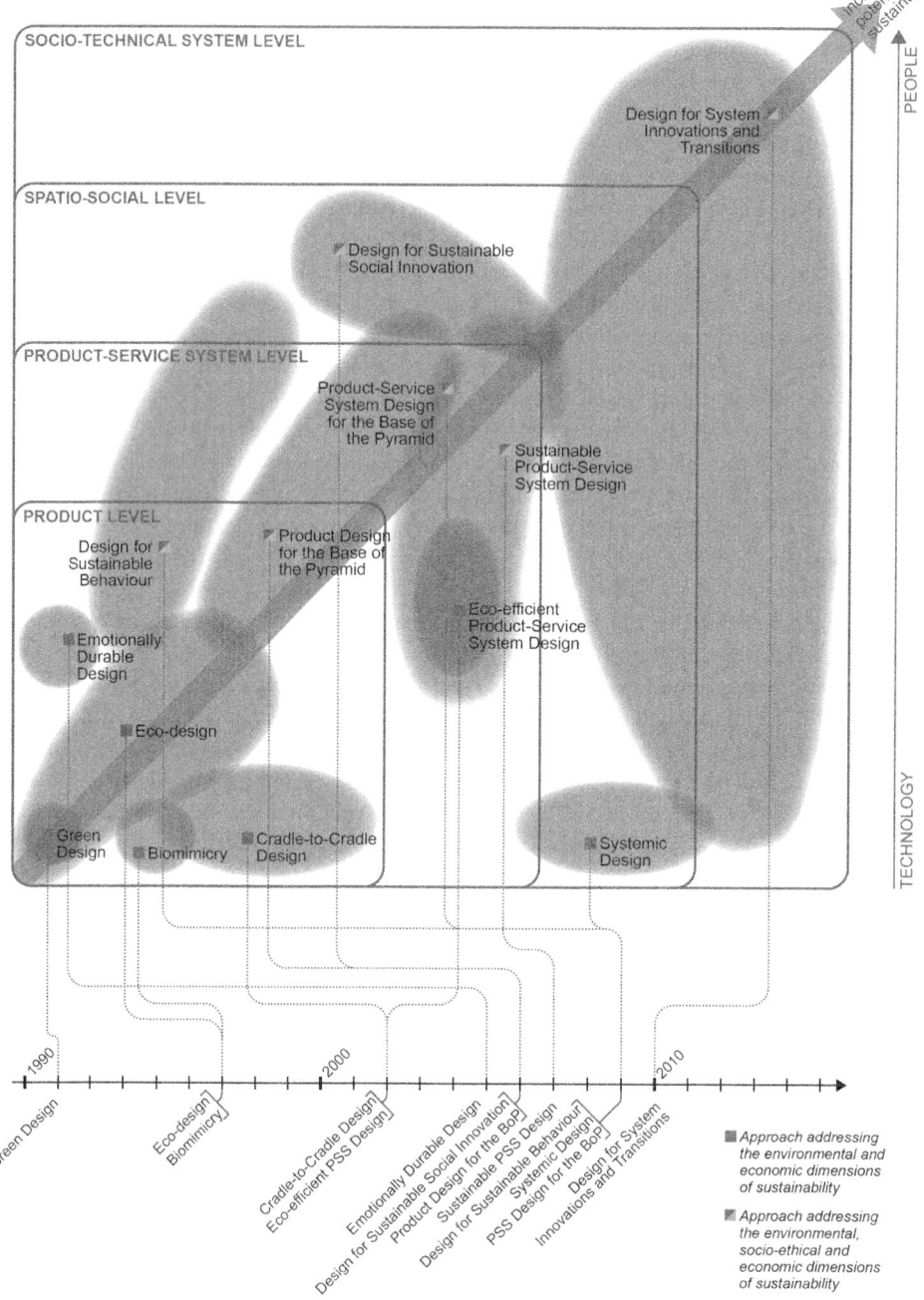

Figure 30.2 The DfS evolutionary framework with the existing DfS approaches mapped onto it. The timeline shows the year when the first key publication of each DfS approach was published (Ceschin and Gaziulusoy, 2016).

those changes. In that sense, the DfS approaches reviewed here are still valid and should be used taking into account their synergistic potential to achieve systemic level changes. Therefore in this section we highlight emerging synergies between DfS approaches and new research directions.

First and foremost, although as a specific DfS domain the emphasis on *green design* has waned, the rules-of-thumb introduced in this early phase of DfS are still strictly valid and establish a base for practices particularly aiming for product and process development. Similarly, the life-cycle approach introduced by *eco-design* forms the basis of systemic thinking in DfS and, despite its shortcomings, it is still the most sophisticated way of 'measuring' and reducing environmental impact of products, particularly when coupled with quantitative assessment methods. Therefore, with the backing legislative structure in the EU (The Framework Directive on Ecodesign of Energy Using Products) the importance and presence of *eco-design* in DfS is very likely to continue (EC, 2005).

In terms of synergies between more recent DfS approaches some observations can also be made. To begin with, *design for social innovation* and *sustainable Product-Service System (PSS) design* have shared elements: *PSS design* can in fact be combined with, and applied to, community-based innovations. Also, in addition to recent integration of socio-ethical dimension of sustainability into *PSS design*, another area where design researchers have been focusing is the application of PSS design in low-income contexts, namely *PSS design for the Bottom of the Pyramid (BoP)*. Similarly, *systemic design* shares some elements and principles with *cradle-to-cradle design* and *biomimicry*. The limitations highlighted for *cradle-to-cradle* and *biomimicry* design are also valid for *systemic design*. In addition, even if *systemic design* is helpful to design and create local material and energy networks that are more efficient and effective, it does not change consumption behaviours and habits. For this reason, *systemic design* should be combined with other design approaches (e.g. *Product-Service System design* or *design for social innovation*).

Although *Product-Service Systems (PSS)* with such synergies carry great sustainability potential, they can be difficult to design, test, implement and bring to the mainstream (Ceschin, 2013; Tukker and Tischner, 2006; Vezzoli et al., 2015). Vezzoli et al. (2015) explored the design challenges to widely implement and diffuse sustainable PSSs, highlighting the key issues for design research as (1) more in-depth studies in user behaviour to better understand what factors influence user satisfaction, as well as how to measure and evaluate this satisfaction; (2) the role that sociocultural factors play in user acceptance; (3) develop a deeper understanding of the process of introduction and diffusion of sustainable PSSs; (4) understanding the most effective strategies to transfer *PSS design* knowledge and know-how from research centres and universities to companies and designers.

In *design for social innovation* area, criticisms have been raised about the naiveté of designers proposing superficial solutions and high cost of design services (Hillgren et al., 2011). Also, a sole focus on social innovation is not likely to achieve the levels of change required in large socio-technical systems meeting society's energy, mobility or housing/infrastructure needs. For this reason, *design for social innovation* can be seen as an essential sub-component of *design for system innovations and transitions*. We can already observe emerging synergies between these two. Very recently Baek et al. (2015) proposed and tested a framework for a socio-technical approach of designing community resilience. These synergies could assist with creating insights for designers on what needs to change at the systemic level and therefore reducing the previously mentioned risk of proposing superficial solutions.

More recently, design research efforts have started to be focused on cities (e.g. Ryan, 2013a; Ryan et al., 2016), which are essentially systems of socio-technical systems. This focus on cities, as distinct from conventional sustainable urban design and planning which focuses on urban form, urban growth, liveability, walkability, energy reduction and place-making separately and sustainable architecture which focuses on individual buildings, finds its ground in theoretical framings of cities as complex adaptive systems (e.g. see Bettencourt and West, 2010; Portugali, 2012). Framing cities as complex adaptive systems requires understanding and taking into account the interrelationships between technologies, ecosystems, social and cultural practice and city governance in design decisions (Marshall, 2012). In order to achieve this, *design for system innovations and transitions* integrates different theoretical domains that might be relevant to cities as well as utilises a multiplicity of supportive design approaches such as speculative design, design futures and participatory design. Other researchers who are also integrating socio-technical change with different applications of design wrote about "synergising" or "acupunctural planning" (Meroni, 2008; Jégou, 2011) and "urban eco-acupuncture" (Ryan, 2013b) to emphasise the importance of designing a multiplicity of interconnected and diverse experiments to generate changes in large and complex systems (Manzini and Rizzo, 2011). In addition to the emerging field of *design for system innovations and transitions*, a group of scholars have developed a framework for curriculum development in undergraduate, graduate and doctoral levels on what they call as *transition design* for the first time (Irwin, 2015). Based on this framework, they also have designed a PhD course and piloted it in 2015 (Irwin et al., 2015). It is understood that this curriculum is not specifically referenced to system innovations and transitions theories but to a wider body of literature studying change in systems.

It is also worthwhile to discuss the relationship between the DfS approaches and the concept of circular economy (Lieder and Rashid, 2016; Stahel, 2016), which has acquired a dominant role in discussions regarding transitions to sustainability, particularly in the European Union. The circular economy can be defined as "an industrial economy that is restorative or regenerative by intention and design" (Ellen McArthur Foundation, 2013). At the core of the concept there are the so called 3R principles (reduction of resources, reuse and recycling), and the realization of a closed loop system of material flows (Geng and Doberstein, 2008) with the aim of reducing the material and energy resources that enter a production systems and minimising waste (Lieder and Rashid, 2016). In this sense, although branded as a new idea, the principles have been around for a long time. Strengths and weaknesses of industrial ecology, biomimicry, cradle-to-cradle are also valid for circular economy. We do see circular economy as a basic requirement of sustainable systems and not a solution on its own. There are many synergies between DfS approaches and circular economy, for example:

- *Cradle-to-cradle design* and *biomimicry design* can provide support in material and process selection.
- *Eco-design* can offer a broader approach on the whole product life cycle and can enable the integration of the 3R principles in product design, with an emphasis on both material and energy flows.
- Systemic design can be used to design products and industrial systems based on industrial ecology principles.
- *Product-Service System design* can be instrumental to design business models that enable and foster circular economy (e.g. see Tukker, 2015; Stahel, 2016).
- Finally, *design for system innovations and transitions* can propose alternative forms of circular economy – which currently can be framed as an eco-modernist idea claiming possibility of endless growth by closing loops – for new socio-technical system scenarios underlied by a variety of political-economic assumptions, thus, problematising the neoliberal foundations of circular economy and assisting in its theoretical reframing with implications on practice.

The criticisms raised for specific DfS approaches and the emerging synergies between these, as well as expansion of the DfS field to adopt a socio-technical systemic approach and embody principles of circular economy, should be discussed within the context of a broader debate about the changes needed in professional design culture and design education. As an applied discipline with highly contextual implementations, to maintain its social-relevance in a post-industrial era characterised by amplified social and environmental crises, there is a need for reform and renewal of design education to embody sociopolitical and ecological awareness as well as skills for transdisciplinary working modes. Currently, there is increased attention on 'systems thinking' in design education, primarily as a result of the influence of human-centred design becoming a norm and service design's maturation. There is also a need to expand design theory by integrating theoretical areas that deal with systems and how change happens in systems. These areas include but are not limited to evolutionary theory, theories of complex adaptive systems and chaos, and theories on how cultures emerge and transform. Similarly, there is also a need of updating and renewing professional codes of practice as well as shifting from a 'star designer' culture to 'society-serving designer' culture. In that sense, although practice-based research in design should continue to expand its horizons, there is a need for 'basic research' *into* other theoretical domains to learn from them and integrate these learnings into design theory. One of these domains is complex adaptive systems; in our understanding, for future development of Design for Sustainability field, there is a need for understanding *how, why* and *when* complex systems change using a design theoretical lens. This will enable transforming design education and practice aligned with the requirements of system innovations and transitions for sustainability: i.e. adopting a strong sustainability position, systems thinking, radicalism, long-term orientation and mindset change (Gaziulusoy, 2015).

Conclusions

In this chapter we provided an overview of the historical evolution of how sustainability has been addressed by design, and we put forward a framework that synthesises this evolution. This framework shows the multiplicity of DfS approaches developed in the last decades, and how DfS has progressively expanded from a technical and product-centric focus towards a focus on large-scale system-level changes, in which sustainability is understood as a socio-technical challenge. Reflecting on the framework, we discussed the complementarities and synergies between DfS approaches. We argued that although achieving sustainability requires changes at a socio-technical system level, DfS approaches that are less systemic are equally important. In fact, each DfS approach should be acknowledged for its associated strengths and weaknesses, and should be utilised in conjunction with complementary approaches for any given project depending on the specific challenges to be addressed.

Regarding the usefulness of the framework, we believe that it might be a valuable support for practitioners and designers to understand and navigate the complex DfS landscape and identify, in relation to specific sustainability challenges, the appropriate DfS approaches to be used. The framework might also be used as a supporting tool to help organisations in the process of integrating DfS in their culture, strategy and processes.

Some considerations can also be made about the educational value of the framework. We believe that it might be used to effectively communicate to students and complexity of the DfS field and the multiplicity of DfS approaches. Moreover, we see the framework as a potential supporting tool for educators to design courses and programmes on DfS.

In conclusion, to our knowledge this is the first time that a framework, comprehensive of all DfS approaches, has been developed. And in this respect our view is that its main value is in the ability of stimulating design academics, researchers and practitioners in the discussion on the past, present and, in particular, the future of DfS.

References

Adams, R., Jeanrenaud, S., Bessant, J., Denyer, D. and Overy, P. (2015) "Sustainability-oriented innovation: A systematic review" *International Journal of Management Reviews 18*(2), 180–205. doi:10.1111/ijmr.12068

Baek, J. S., Meroni, A. and Manzini, E. (2015) "A socio-technical approach to design for community resilience: A framework for analysis and design goal forming" *Design Studies 40*, 60–84. http://dx.doi.org/10.1016/j.destud.2015.06.004

Bakker, C. A., Wever, R., Teoh, C. and Clercq, S. D. (2010) "Designing cradle-to-cradle products: A reality check" *International Journal of Sustainable Engineering 3*(1), 2–8

Barbero, S. and Fassio, F. (2011) "Energy and food production with a systemic approach" *Environmental Quality Management 21*(2), 57–74

Barbero, S. and Toso, D. (2010) "Systemic design of a productive chain: Reusing coffee waste as an input to agricultural production" *Environmental Quality Management 19*(3), 67–77

Benyus, J. M. (1997) *Biomimicry: Innovation Inspired by Nature*. Perennial, New York

Bettencourt, L. and West, G. (2010) "A unified theory of urban living" *Nature 467*(7318), 912–913

Bhamra, T., Lilley, D. and Tang, T. (2011) "Design for sustainable behaviour: Using products to change consumer behaviour" *The Design Journal 14*(4), 427–445

Bistagnino, L. (2009) *Design sistemico: Progettare la sostenibilità produttiva e ambientale*. Slow Food Editore, Bra, Italy

Bistagnino, L. (2011) *Systemic Design: Designing the productive and environmental sustainability*. Slow Food Editore, Bra, Italy

Bjørn, A. and Hauschild, M. Z. (2013) "Absolute versus relative environmental sustainability" *Journal of Industrial Ecology 17*(2), 321–332. http://dx.doi.org/10.1111/j.1530-9290.2012.00520.x

Braungart, M., McDonough, W. and Bollinger, A. (2007) "Cradle-to-cradle design: Creating healthy emissions – A strategy for eco-effective product and system design" *Journal of Cleaner Production 15*(13–14), 1337–1348

Brezet, H., Bijma, A. S., Ehrenfeld, J. and Silvester, S. (2001) *The Design of Eco-efficient Services. Methods, Tools and Review of the Case Study Based "Designing Eco-Efficient Services" Project*. Report for Dutch Ministries of Environment (VROM), The Hague

Brezet, H. and van Hemel, C. (1997) *ECODESIGN: A Promising Approach to Sustainable Production and Consumption*. UNEP, Paris

Burall, P. (1991) *Green Design*. Design Council, London

Butchart, S. H., Walpole, M., Collen, B., van Strien, A., Scharlemann, J. P., Almond, R. E., et al. (2010) "Global biodiversity: Indicators of recent declines" *Science 328*(982), 1164–1168

Ceschin, F. (2012) *The Introduction and Scaling Up of Sustainable Product-Service Systems: A New Role for Strategic Design for Sustainability*. PhD thesis, Department of Design, Politecnico di Milano

Ceschin, F. (2013) "Critical factors for implementing and diffusing sustainable product-service systems: Insights from innovation studies and companies' experiences" *Journal of Cleaner Production 45*, 74–88

Ceschin, F. (2014a) *Sustainable Product-Service Systems: Between Strategic Design and Transition Studies*. Springer, London

Ceschin, F. (2014b) "How the design of socio-technical experiments can enable radical changes for sustainability" *International Journal of Design 8*(3), 1–21

Ceschin, F. and Gaziulusoy, I. (2016) "Evolution of design for sustainability: From product design to design for system innovations and transitions" *Design Studies 47*, 118–163, http://dx.doi.org/10.1016/j.destud.2016.09.002

Chapman, J. (2005) *Emotionally Durable Design. Objects, Experiences, and Empathy*. Earthscan, London

Chapman, J. (2009) "Design for (Emotional) durability" *Design Issues 25*(4), 29–35

Cooper, T. (2004) "Inadequate life? Evidence of consumer attitudes to product obsolescence" *Journal of Consumer Policy 27*(4), 421–449

Design Council (2007) *The Value of Design: Factfinder Report*. Design Council, UK

EC (2005) *Directive 2005/32/EC of the European Parliament and of the Council of 6 July 2005 Establishing a Framework for the Setting of Ecodesign Requirements of Energy-Using Products and Amending Council Directive 92/42/EEC and Directives 96/57/EC and 2000/55/EC of the European Parliament and of the Council*

Ellen McArthur Foundation (2013) *Towards the Circular Economy. Economic and Business Rationale for an Accelerated Transition, Vol. 1.* Ellen MacArthur Foundation. Retrieved from www.ellenmacarthurfoundation. org/assets/downloads/publications/Ellen-MacArthur-Foundation-Towards-the-Circular-Economy-vol.1.pdf. Accessed 25 April 2016

Environmental Change Unit (1997) *2MtC – DECADE: Domestic Equipment and Carbon Dioxide Emissions.* Oxford University, Oxford, UK

Fiksel, J. R. ed. (1996) *Design for Environment: Creating Eco-Efficient Products and Processes.* New York: McGraw-Hill.

Fuad-Luke, A. (2002) *Ecodesign: The Sourcebook.* Thames & Hudson, London

Fuller, R. B. (1969). *Operating Manual for Spaceship Earth.* Carbondale, IL: Southern Illinois University Press.

Gaziulusoy, A. I. (2010) *System Innovation for Sustainability: A Scenario Method and a Workshop Process for Product Development Teams.* PhD thesis, University of Auckland

Gaziulusoy, A. I. (2015) "A critical review of approaches available for design and innovation teams through the perspective of sustainability science and system innovation theories" *Journal of Cleaner Production 107,* 366–377. http://dx.doi.org/10.1016/j.jclepro.2015.01.012

Gaziulusoy, A. I. and Brezet, H. (2015) "Design for system innovations and transitions: A conceptual framework integrating insights from sustainability science and theories of system innovations and transitions" *Journal of Cleaner Production 108,* 558–568. http://dx.doi.org/10.1016/j.jclepro.2015.06.066

Geels, F. W. (2005a). *Technological Transitions and System Innovations: A Co-Evolutionary and Socio-Technical Analysis.* Edward Elgar, Cheltenham, UK

Geels, F. W. (2005b) "Processes and patterns in transitions and system innovations: Refining the co-evolutionary multi-level perspective" *Technological Forecasting and Social Change 72*(6), 681–696

Geng, Y. and Doberstein, B. (2008) "Developing the circular economy in China: Challenges and opportunities for achieving 'leapfrog development'" *International Journal of Sustainable Development & World Ecology 15*(3), 231–239

Gomez Castillo, L., Diehl, J. C. and Brezet, J. C. (2012) "Design Considerations for Base of the Pyramid (BoP) Projects", Paper presented at the Cumulus Conference, Helsinki, 24–26

Green, K. and Vergragt, P. (2002) "Towards sustainable households: A methodology for developing sustainable technological and social innovations" *Futures 34*(5), 381–400

Gruber, M., de Leon, N., George, G. and Thompson, P. (2015) "Managing by design" *Academy of Management Journal 58*(1), 1–7

Hillgren, P. A., Seravalli, A. and Emilson, A. (2011) "Prototyping and infrastructuring in design for social innovation" *CoDesign 7*(3–4), 169–183

Hughes, L. and Steffen, W. (2013) *The Critical Decade 2013: Climate Change Science, Risks and Response.* Climate Commission, Canberra

IDEO (2009) *Human Centered Design Toolkit.* Retrieved from www.ideo.com/work/human-centered-design-toolkit

Irwin, T. (2015). Transition design: A proposal for a new area of design practice, study, and research. *Design and Culture,* 7(2), 229–246. doi:10.1080/17547075.2015.1051829

Irwin, T., Tonkinwise, C. and Kossoff, G. (2015) *Transition Design Seminar Spring 2015 Course Schedule.* Pittsburg, PA: Carnegie Mellon Design School

Jagtap, S., Larsson, A. and Kandachar, P. (2013) "Design and development of products and services at the base of the pyramid: A review of issues and solutions" *International Journal of Sustainable Society 5*(3), 207–231

Jégou, F. (2011) "Social innovations and regional acupuncture towards sustainability" *Chinese Journal of Design 214,* 56–61

Jégou, F. and Manzini, E. eds. (2008) *Collaborative Services: Social Innovation and Design for Sustainability.* Edizioni POLI.design, Italy

Joore, P. (2010) *New to Improve, The Mutual Influence Between New Products and Societal Change Processes.* PhD thesis, Technical University of Delft

Joore, P. and Brezet, H. (2015) "A multilevel design model – The mutual relationship between product-service system development and societal change processes" *Journal of Cleaner Production 97,* 92–105

Kemp, R. (1994) "Technology and the transition to environmental sustainability: The problem of technological regime shifts" *Futures 26*(10), 1023–1046

Kemp, R., Rip, A. and Schot, J. (2001) "Constructing Transition Paths Thorough the Management of Niches" in Garud, R. and Karnøe, P. eds, *Path Dependence and Creation.* Lawrence Erlbaum Associates, Mahwah, NJ, 269–299

Kemp, R., Schot, J. and Hoogma, R. (1998) "Regime shifts to sustainability through processes of niche formation: The approach of strategic niche management" *Technology Analysis & Strategic Management* 10(2), 175–195

Larsen, M. L. and Flensborg, A. (2011) *Market Creation Toolbox: Your Guide to Entering Developing Markets*. DI International Business Development, Copenhagen

Lieder, M. and Rashid, A. (2016) "Towards circular economy implementation: A comprehensive review in context of manufacturing industry" *Journal of Cleaner Production* 115, 36–51

Lilley, D. (2009) "Design for sustainable behaviour: strategies and perceptions" *Design Studies* 30(6) 704–720

Llorach-Massana, P., Farreny, R. and Oliver-Sola, J. (2015) "Are cradle to cradle certified products environmentally preferable? Analysis from an LCA approach" *Journal of Cleaner Production* 93, 243–250

Lockton, D. (2013) *Design With Intent: A Design Pattern Toolkit for Environmental & Social Behaviour Change*. PhD thesis, Brunel University London

Lockton, D., Harrison, D. and Stanton, N.A. (2010) "The design with intent method: A design tool for influencing user behaviour" *Applied Ergonomics* 41(3), 382–392

London, T. (2007) *A Base-of-the-Pyramid Perspective on Poverty Alleviation*. United Nations Development Program. Growing Inclusive Markets Working Paper Series, Washington, DC

Loorbach, D. (2007) *Transition Management: New Mode of Governance for Sustainable Development*. International Books, Utrecht, Netherlands

Loorbach, D. (2010) "Transition management for sustainable development: A prescriptive, complexity-based governance framework" *Governance* 23(1), 161–183

Loorbach, D. and Wijsman, K. (2013) "Business transition management: Exploring a new role for business in sustainability transitions" *Journal of Cleaner Production* 45, 20–28

Mackenzie, D. (1997) *Green Design: Design for Environment* (2nd ed.). Laurence King, Hong Kong

Madge, P. (1997) "Ecological design: A new critique" *Design Issues* 13(2), 44–54

Manzini, E. (2007) "Design Research for Sustainable Social Innovation" in Michel, R. ed, *Design Research Now*. Birkhäuser, Basel, 233–245

Manzini, E. (2014) "Making things happen: Social innovation and design" *Design Issues* 30(1), 57–66

Manzini, E. (2015) *Design, When Everybody Designs. An Introduction to Design for Social Innovation*. MIT Press, Cambridge, MA

Manzini, E. and Rizzo, F. (2011) "Small projects/large changes: Participatory design as an open participated process" *CoDesign* 7(3–4), 169–183

Manzini, E., Vezzoli, C. and Clark, G. (2001) "Product Service Systems: Using an Existing Concept as a New Approach to Sustainability" *Journal of Design Reseearch* 1(2), 12–18

Marshall, S. (2012) "Planning, Design and the Complexity of Cities" in Portugali, J. Meyer, H., Stolk, E. and Tan, E. eds, *Complexity Theories of Cities Have Come of Age: An Overview With Implications to Urban Planning and Design*. Springer, London, 191–205

Mathews, F. (2011) "Towards a deeper philosophy of biomimicry" *Organization & Environment* 24(4), 364–387

McDonough, W. and Braungart, M. (2002) *Cradle to Cradle: Remaking the Way We Make Things*. North Point Press, New York

MEA (Millennium Ecosystem Assessment) (2005) *Ecosystems and Human Well-Being: Synthesis*. Island Press, Washington, DC

Meroni, A. (2008) "Strategic design: Where are we now? Reflection around the foundations of a recent discipline" *Strategic Design Research Journal* 1(1), 31–38

Meroni, A. ed. (2007) *Creative Communities. People Inventing Sustainable Ways of Living*. Edizioni Polidesign, Italy

Metcalf, L. and Benn, S. (2012) "The corporation is ailing social technology: Creating a 'fit for purpose' design for sustainability" *Journal of Business Ethics* 111(2), 195–210

Mont, O. (2002) "Clarifying the concept of product-service system" *Journal of Cleaner Production* 10(3), 237–245

Mugge, R. (2007) *Product Attachment*. PhD thesis, Delft University of Technology

Mugge, R., Schoormans, J. P. L. and Schifferstein, H. N. J. (2005) "Design strategies to postpone consumers' product replacement: The value of a strong person-product relationship" *The Design Journal* 8(2), 38–48

Niedderer, K. (2007) "Designing mindful interaction: The category of the performative object" *Design Issues* 23(1), 3–17

Niedderer, K. (2013) "Mindful Design as a Driver for Social Behaviour Change", Proceedings of the IASDR Conference 2013, Tokyo, Japan

Papanek, V. (1985) *Design for the Real World: Human Ecology and Social Change.* New York, Van Nostrand Reinhold

Parrish, B. D. (2007) "Designing the sustainable enterprise" *Futures 39*(7), 846–860

Portugali, J. (2012) "Complexity Theories of Cities: Implications to Urban Planning" in Portugali, J., Meyer, H., Stolk, E. and Tan, E. eds, *Complexity Theories of Cities Have Come of Age: An Overview With Implications to Urban Planning and Design.* Springer, London, 221–244

Quist, J. and Vergragt, P. J. (2006) "Past and future of backcasting: The shift to stakeholder participation and a proposal for a methodological framework" *Futures 38*(9), 1027–1045

Quist, J. and Vergragt, P. J. (2004) "Backcasting for Industrial Transformations and System Innovations Towards Sustainability: Relevance for Governance?", Paper presented at the Governance for Industrial Transformation 2003 Berlin Conference on the Human Dimensions of Global Environmental Change, Berlin

Reap. J., Baumeister, D. and Bras, B. (2005) "Holism, Biomimicry and Sustainable Engineering", ASME 2005 International Mechanical Engineering Congress and Exposition (IMECE2005) ASME, 423–431

Reijnders, L. (2008) "Are emissions or wastes consisting of biological nutrients good or healthy?" *Journal of Cleaner Production 16*(10), 1138–1141

Rockstrom, J., Steffen, W., Noone, K., Persson, A., Chapin, F. S., Lambin, E. F. et al. (2009) "A safe operating space for humanity" *Nature 7263*, 472–475

Rotmans, J., Kemp, R. and Van Asselt, M. (2001) "More evolution than revolution: Transition management in public policy" *Foresight 3*(1) 15–31

Ryan, C. (2013a) "Critical Agendas: Designing for Sustainability From Products and Systems" in Walker, S. and Giard, J. eds, *The Handbook of Design for Sustainability.* Bloomsbury, London, New York

Ryan, C. (2013b) "Eco-Acupuncture: designing and facilitating pathways for urban transformation, for a resilient low-carbon future" *Journal of Cleaner Production 50*, 189–199

Ryan, C., Gaziulusoy, I., McCormick, K. and Trudgeon, M. (2016) "Virtual City Experimentation: A Critical Role for Design Visioning" in Evans, J., Karvonen, A. and Raven, R. eds, *The Experimental City.* New York: Routledge, 61–76

Schaltegger, S. and Wagner, M. (2008) "Types of Sustainable Entrepreneurship and Conditions for Sustainability Innovation: From the Administration of a Technical Challenge to the Management of an Entrepreneurial Opportunity" in Wüstenhagen, R. Hamschmidt, J. Sharma, S. and Starik, M. eds, *Sustainable Innovation and Entrepreneurship.* MPG Books Ltd, Cornwall, 27–48

Schmidt-Bleek, F. (1996) *MIPS Book or the Fossil Makers – Factor 10 and More.* Berlin and Boston, Basel

Schot, J. W. (1992) "Constructive technology assessment and technology dynamics: The case of clean technologies" *Science, Technology and Human Values 17*, 36–56

Sherwin, C., and Bhamra, T. (September 1998). Ecodesign Innovation: Present Concepts, Current Practice and Future Directions for Design and the Environment. Design History Society Conference 1998. Huddersfield, UK: University of Huddersfield

Simanis, E. and Hart, S. (2008) *Base of the Pyramid Protocol.* Cornell University, Ithaca, NY

Smith, C. E. (2007) *Design for the Other 90%.* New York: Editions Assouline

Stahel, W. R. (1997) "The Functional Economy: Cultural and Organizational Change" in Richards, D. J. ed, *The Industrial Green Game.* National Academy Press, Washington, DC

Stahel, W. R. (2016) "The circular economy" *Nature 531*(7595), 435–438

Stern, N. (2006) *STERN REVIEW: The Economics of Climate Change,* http://www.brown.edu/Departments/Economics/Faculty/Matthew_Turner/ec1340/readings/Sternreview_full.pdf

Tischner, U. and Charter, M. (2001) "Sustainable Product Design" in Charter, M. and Tischner, U. eds, *Sustainable Solutions: Developing Products and Services for the Future.* Greenleaf, Wiltshire, UK, 118–138

Tukker, A. (2015) "Product services for a resource-efficient and circular economy – A review" *Journal of Cleaner Production 97*, 76–91

Tukker, A. and Tischner, U. (2006) *New Business for Old Europe: Product Services, Sustainability and Competitiveness.* Greenleaf Publishing, Sheffield, UK

UNEP (United Nations Environmental Programme) (2006) *Design for Sustainability: A Practical Approach for Developing Countries.* United Nations Environmental Program, Paris

Van Hinte, E. (1997) *Eternally Yours: Visions on Product Endurance.* 010 Publishers, Rotterdam

Van Nes, N. (2003) *Replacement of Durables: Influencing Product Life Time Through Product Design.* PhD Thesis, Erasmus University Rotterdam

Vezzoli, C. (2007) *System Design for Sustainability. Theory, Methods and Tools for a Sustainable "Satisfaction-System" Design.* Maggioli Editore, Rimini, Italy

Vezzoli, C., Ceschin, F., Diehl, J.C. and Kohtala, C. (2015) "New design challenges to widely implement 'sustainable product–service systems'" *Journal of Cleaner Production 97*, 1–12

Vezzoli, C., Kohtala, C., Srinivasan, A., Xin, L., Fusakul, M., Sateesh, D. and Diehl, J.C. (2014) *Product-Service System Design for Sustainability.* Greenleaf Publishing, Sheffield, UK

Vezzoli, C. and Manzini, E. (2008) *Design for Environmental Sustainability.* Springer, London, UK

Volstad, N. L. and Boks, C. (2012) "On the use of Biomimicry as a useful tool for the industrial designer" *Sustainable Development 20*(3), 189–199

WBCSD (2000) *Eco-Efficiency: Creating More Value With Less Impact.* Geneva: WBCSD

WBCSD (2004) *Running the Risk: Risk and Sustainable Development: A Business Perspective.* WBCSD

WBCSD (2010) *Vision 2050: The New Agenda for Business.* WBCSD

Weaver, P., Jansen, L., van Grootveld, G. van Spiegel, E. and Vergragt, P. (2000) *Sustainable Technology Development.* Greenleaf Publishing, Sheffield, UK

31

THE STRUCTURE OF STRUCTURAL CHANGE

Making a habit of being alienated as a designer

Cameron Tonkinwise

Redirection [of our societies toward more sustainable futures] always has to go to actor and the acted upon. It certainly cannot simply rest upon those overplayed and vague notions of 'attitudinal change' posted with individuals that are so often evoked by idealist reformers. Such a notion of change implies an inflated faith in the ability of the will of these individuals to alter the nature of cultural, economic and institutional structures. Rather, redirection requires an ontological shift in the mode of being of the actor. The value of what one knows and does may have to be fundamentally altered. . . . By implication this means that the being of professional identity and conduct [must also have to be] radically and structurally changed.

Fry (2009: 11)

Introduction: no change without change

Major change is required for our societies to become less unsustainable. For some people, and for some time, there was hope that these major changes could be effected without significant disruption to everyday lives. There were perhaps three versions of this hope.

The first was that *production-side changes* – cleaner production, eco-efficiency, circular economy – could significantly improve the environmental performance of what we were consuming without us having to change our consumption habits. New materials, new production techniques and new sources of energy could take responsibility for establishing a more sustainable way of resourcing our current ways of living and working.

The second was that if changes in how we consumed and lived and worked were needed, these could naturally evolve from small, easy actions to larger, more significant ones; and/or these changes could be reframed as pleasurable or profitable rather than painful sacrifices. 'Low hanging fruit' or 'small-steps' would 'spill-over' into structural transformations if 'everybody did their bit.'

Our societies are structurally unsustainable. Efforts at incremental or nondisruptive change have proven inadequate, with levels of unsustainability quickly rebounding. This chapter examines what structural change might entail. It explores different ideas about where structure lies: in physical infrastructures, in worldviews and social values, or in everyday habitual practices. It concludes that structural change requires designers to combine utopian and cynical attitudes in a constant state of creative hypocrisy.

If there were difficult, structural shifts needed, especially with respect to the economy, to make manufacturers undertake design for sustainability, or to make sustainable consumption less burdensome to individual households, then the third hope was that *governmental regulations* could be effected, at best backed by democratic mandates, but more likely resulting from expert advice. In either case, ways of effecting major societal changes would follow comparatively minor shifts, in the voting intentions of the electorate for instance, or as the reasoned cost-benefit analysis of clear research into current risks and preferable futures.

Three problems with these hopes for what could be cheekily called 'change without change' are now apparent.

The first was that these models of small-to-big change only ever managed to deliver small, isolated changes. There was no evidence of *domino effects* (one thing leading to many other subsequent small things) or *ratchet effects* (one small thing becoming a stable platform for a subsequent thing that is now more in reach) over time, either within households and businesses, or across neighborhoods and communities or industry sectors (Thøgersen and Crompton 2009). Where there were some concerted efforts on multiple fronts, these tended to hit plateaus (Hobson 2001). The obstacles to larger change evidenced the mismatch between individual or small-group consumer-side actions and more structural producer-side transformations, often with the blame then being put on the politicians (Hobson 2002).

The second was that what was often identified as being small, relatively easy things that every household could do to 'save the planet,' proved to be sometimes misguided. Part of the problem was that these actions frequently entailed choices between two existing options: paper or plastic bags, cloth nappies or disposable plastic diapers, local food or organic food. These either/or's concealed both/and's but also neither/nor's, third options that could exist in new, significantly changed systems. A larger part of the problem is that sustainability is a *probabilistic and wicked* phenomenon (Ravetz 2006); it has social value decisions at its heart that are not amenable to twentieth-century models of dispassionately objective, scientific expertise (in relation to Life-cycle Assessment see, for example, Heiskanen 1999). Even small steps will be complicated to identify because of the need to first determine what it is that we as societies are agreeing to sustain.

The third problem was that when actions were performed that did result in significant reductions in ecological impact, these were sometimes subsequently undermined. For instance, major efficiency gains accomplished on either the consumer or producer side tended to result in 'rebound effects,' or the Jevons Paradox (Herring and Roy 2007): the cost savings associated with such 'win–win' environmental performance boosts were respent, either directly – using heating or lighting more because the heating and lighting systems are more efficient; increasing the scale of more resource productive manufacturing – or indirectly – buying a holiday airplane ticket with the money saved from commuting with a more efficient automobile; investing in wholly new product offerings with money saved from integrating existing product lines. For instance, the shift to LCD screens involved massive energy savings compared to CRTs, not least because their reduced heat loads required less associated room cooling; but these energy savings were quickly eroded by the proliferation of screens, because of their portability, into handheld and even wearable devices, as well as the arrival of large format screens. In these cases, significant changes appear to have not been significant enough. Initiatives were overwhelmed by a reasserted business as usual.

Structure: below, above or in?

It should therefore now be apparent that we can only get the structural change needed for us to enhance the sustainability of our societies if we undertake structural change directly. But then the question is: where is structure? What are the things that we need to be acting on directly to bring about systems-level change even if they involve major cost, effort and disruption to our everyday lives?

Concrete infrastructures

A first obvious answer is that what structures our societies are our infrastructures. We are constrained by the large-scale systems that take a massive effort to construct and are then, for the most part, buried underground or concreted into place. Those systems constrain what kinds of devices are developed and therefore the kinds of everyday practices that are enabled, habits that in turn further entrench the infrastructure. For instance, consider the huge costs, financial and environmental, involved in large-scale electricity production, whether hydroelectric or coal-fired, but especially nuclear. Investments of that size are only made if investors can guarantee long-term returns. Households are therefore designed around standardized wall-plug outlets that ensure that families and businesses can make use of the electricity supplied and become dependent on such 'conveniences.' As Tony Fry (1999) has argued, the birth of industrial design in the United States (by the Streamliners Raymond Loewy, Norman Bel Geddes, Walter Dorwin Teague and Henry Dreyfuss) lay in the self-reinforcing systems of New Deal hydroelectric dam construction, household electrification, and the restyling of electrical household devices. Once outlets are in every room, designers can now contemplate powered device solutions to any possible inconvenience: in the bathroom, electric toothbrushes, electricity powered weight scales, heated toilet seats, etc. Householders relocating away from such a house now have a whole set of bathroom equipment that only works in a house that is similarly wired to such an infrastructure. (Historians of technology call this path dependency and reverse salience (MacKenzie and Wajcman 1999); Bruce Sterling (2005) refers to these as 'The Line of No Return' and 'The Line of Empire.') In such a case, to lower the energy consumption of the household, even if in 'win–win' ways, will require the significant restructuring of bathroom habits. The alternative is another huge investment in some large-scale replacement energy supply system.

However, to continue with this illustration, the barrier here is not just the subsequent cost of a new centralized, less polluting way of generating electricity, such as renewables like a wind farm. The variable nature of renewable energy generation requires a smarter grid of more distributed energy production. Such a more dynamic grid would also be aided by taking advantage of the fact that most digital devices today require lower voltage DC (direct current) rather than the infrastructure's AC (alternating current). But all this entails not just a new power supply, but new distribution systems, smart meters and even house rewiring. Further, it would also involve a series of new practices that tolerate load shifting – unplugging devices or lowering usage levels during peak load events either manually or automatically (as smart meters can do).

The point here is that resistance to structural change lies not only in the physical and financial scale of infrastructure, but in all the resulting lifestyles that then make connection to that infrastructure habitual. To put it another way, the inertial force of an infrastructure is not just material but also ideal. Scholars of socio-technical systems talk of the imaginaries associated with an infrastructure (Jasanoff and Kim 2015). Those serviced by an infrastructure come to expect particular qualities of supply. Large-scale electricity systems with centralized carbon-intense or nuclear-waste-creating forms of generation for example promise 'always-on-ness' and consistency (supplies of electricity that do not vary in quantity, such as a power surge). Households and businesses structure their everyday practices around the expectation that brown-outs or black-outs will be rare or never occur. Consequently, an increasing number of activities can be made dependent on electrical power without the need for backups or manual operability. These expectations, unless challenged, will then carry over to any alternative energy supplies (or potable water provision, food systems, transportation services, etc.), perhaps resulting in rebound effects.

Abstract infrastructures

'Structure' therefore lies not only in our societies' physical systems but also in the wider ideologies associated with them. A range of mostly unquestioned commitments, values that are normalized as pervasive or even natural, seem to structure how much of our 'modern' societies are organized, and how we each in turn organize our everyday lives within those societies. These systems-level governing values or 'logics' often interrelate but not always in noncontradictory ways.

The logic of efficiency

When we (in the colonizing global consumer class) say our societies are progressing, we generally mean that we anticipate that over time it gets possible to do more with less, that things get progressively more efficient, which translates to either things getting cheaper or more profitable, and/or easier or faster (Tierney 1993). This makes futures in which activities might prove more effortful, or take longer, appear undesirable and even unlikely. Change toward significantly more sustainable social systems therefore runs contrary to this logic, not only because the change itself might require long-term return on investment, but also because what we might need to be changing to is an existence that is, compared to now, less convenient.

The logic of individualism

Modernization presented itself as a process of detraditionalization, liberating people from communities of interdependence (Heelas et al. 1996). In capitalist societies, technological developments aimed at innovating (labor saving) devices that allowed households to progressively replace people with things: slaves, then servants, then service providers were displaced in middle-class households by appliances for self-servicing everyday needs, and these days by increasingly automated systems (Stahel and Reday-Mulvey 1981). Even extended family members were removed as households reduced in size over the twentieth century in the Global North, such that significant numbers of people living in cities in developed nations now live alone. This individualism is interpreted as increased freedom, which is why its obverse is a valorization of choice and efforts at increasing the variety to choose from (Greenfield 2001, Rosenthal 2006). Consumers seem to expect a wide range of goods to choose from, customized services and increasingly ways of earning a living that are free from the confines of a regular job. Futures that limit choice and restore interdependence seem like they will be resisted. This is then a major barrier to social systems that are Smaller and Slower, more Local (i.e., bioregionally and so seasonally specific), and more Connected (for shared resource use and resilience).

It is difficult to say where these ideologies are located, or how they get reproduced, but it is equally difficult to say they do not exist. Nevertheless one of the ways in which they have force is by appearing to be more pervasive than they probably are:

The logic of work

Despite a widespread commitment to the value of improving efficiency, there are many examples in mainstream society where value is indicated by how much effort we put into something rather than how little: sport, religion, education, avocations, etc. To put it another way, we perhaps value efficiency only to the extent that it frees up time and resources associated with some tasks that we can then put toward what we really value, projects that are enjoyable because they are effortful, where the accomplishment comes from having worked at it (see Mikko Jalas' account (2006) of practices that take time, and thus time away from direct consumerism). When the futures that sustainability advocates promote look inconvenient, they should perhaps be better understood as resisting the imperialism of convenience, the tendency to think that everything should be subject to the logic of efficiency (Maniates and Meyer 2010).

The logic of care

It is also clear that despite some individualistic tendencies, many people in most societies still also have significant communitarian aspects to their lives. Sometimes these are obligations – the need to care for our younger and older relatives, but also a wider belief in looking out for those needing care not related to us, especially if they lack their own carer-relatives. Annemarie Mol (2008) has articulated how, in health services, the logic of care in many ways opposes a logic of choice (Mol's term for what was mentioned in the logic of individualism previously): the former often entails making choices for those you care for; being taken care of means not having the burden of taking individual responsibility for yourself. And sometimes these are pleasures – not just lovers and friends, but wider forms of solidarity, whether place-based or communities of interest. Again, when more sustainable futures seem to limit individualism, they could also be opportunities for new senses of communing and belonging – what the developers of Transition Design (Irwin et al. 2015) call cosmopolitan localism (in order to lessen the risk of xenophobia at the other end of the communitarian continuum).

There are therefore ideologies that seem to both inform and emanate from our socio-technical systems, structuring the infrastructures and devices that support particular ways of living. Some of these ideologies manifest as what anthropologists call worldviews or frames that people explicitly ascribe to, while others seem to be more implicit, what sociologists describe as practices or *habitus*. Between the two are what psychologists refer to as social values.

Belief schematas

Worldviews are usually thought of as sets of explicitly stated beliefs (Kearney 1984), mapable landscapes of 'what matters' (Loewenstein and Moene 2006). These are articulatable cultural frameworks in which people locate themselves, for instance one or a combination of (even if in seeming contradiction):

- A religious faith (which may include atheism, materialism or secular humanism), which is both a theological account of the world, a guide for moral conduct and a set of ritualistic practices
- An ontology about what kinds of things are real (as opposed to imaginary) and an epistemology about how we come to know such things – for example, a scientistic worldview: that only physical things exist in ways that allow their properties to be observed through experiments; or an ecological worldview: that everything is interconnected in ways we cannot fully perceive or understand and that consequently what we currently see as discrete entities (that rock, this tree, a river) are category errors caused by our limited anthropocentric space-time perspectives; or a panpsychist worldview, or a paranoid idealist worldview such as was represented in the Matrix; etc.
- A model of how humans behave – for example: people are fundamentally competitively hedonistic, ruled by their desires; or, people strive for consistency between their self-perceptions and how they are perceived by their colleagues; or, people are mostly lazy but a

few in special circumstances are capable of heroically sacrificial acts; or people are curious or look for epiphanies, or are fearful and require stability, etc.

Sustainability advocates are aware that worldviews can obstruct promotion of sustainability [see for example, The Cultural Cognition Project at Yale Law School: www.culturalcognition.net/]. This occurs not only in obvious ways – the refusal of someone with strong religious faith to heed scientific research – but also in more complex ways – people deploying their higher levels of scientific literacy to claim climate science should be doubted in order to reinforce their other overriding worldviews. The latter points to the fact that one cannot be simply educated out of a worldview, partly because a worldview determines from who or what and how one learns. Or more precisely, a worldview concerns your identity; to change a worldview is to become a different person. As activists against racism or sexism for instance know, to shift a worldview requires an extensive 'conversion' experience, a multilevel, multistage process of change that includes varied, direct encounters with 'the other' as well as environmental change and a range of social supporters throughout the process of change.

Whilst many advocates of the idea of worldviews as forces determining what people think and do cast them as beliefs that people can articulate, the origin of the notion saw worldviews as structures embedded in languages. A worldview might manifest as a grammar – compare languages with and without tenses, or languages that commonly or rarely use reflexive verb forms – or as what George Lakoff and Mark Johnson (2008) call 'base conceptual metaphors.' The latter might derive from bodily interactions with the world – ideas and happiness are generally things associated with being up, whereas what is concrete or worrying is down – but they can also be more or less implicit cultural narratives – leadership is patriarchal whereas caring is feminine, work is about control whereas love is about losing control. Lakoff (2010) and others have advised environmentalists to be more mindful about the conceptual frames involved in how they talk about sustainability, pointing out situations where the intended content of their message run contrary to their underlying metaphors. For example, Chet Bowers (though strongly critical of Lakoff & Johnson (Bowers 2009)), draws attention to liberal educational approaches to sustainability, which advocate concern for ecosystem well-being but through discourses that contradictorily valorize universally applicable, individualistic creativity rather than forms of learning that foreground interdependence and contextual specificity of knowledge, such as should come from respecting 'the wisdom of elders' (Bowers 1995).

All this begins to indicate how complex, in critically self-reflective ways, is the task of pursuing structural change if structures are ideological and not only physical. Sustainable designers must research deeply the worldviews of others whilst maintaining a strong understanding of their own worldviews, and the ways in which both their own and others' worldviews may themselves be distinct from the worldviews that could inform more sustainable ways of being in the world (Bourdieu and Wacquant 1992).

Social values

In the late 2000s, some environmental activist organizations (initially WWF UK) noticed the short-term and mid-term ineffectiveness of many of their campaigns and so enlisted social psychologists to strategize responses (Crompton and Kasser 2010). There were three related accounts of what structural change required. There was a recognition firstly of many communications being contradictorily framed: for instance that promoting sustainability via eco-efficiency reinforced the more rationalistically consumerist frame of efficiency, explaining persistent rebound effects. Secondly, there was an acknowledgement that much talk of sustainability was being mistargeted: for example, appeals to care for charismatic megafauna were never going to work with people preoccupied by career success, but also with people preoccupied with sending a percentage of their income back to their more impoverished parents in another country. Thirdly, it was realized that even when communications were appropriately framed and targeted, there was a disconnect between the form of sustainability being valued and the applied values informing everyday activities.

The model consequently proposed to environmental organizations (see http://valuesand frames.org/) by social psychologists (e.g., Kasser 2011) was derived from the work of Shalom Schwartz (1994) amongst others. Schwartz argued people seek activities based on certain characteristics of an experience that they more or less consistently pursue. These sought-after characteristics will be a mix of intellectual, visceral, functional and/or experiential undertakings that are self-directed or other-directed, innovative or consistent with tradition, etc. The argument is that someone committed to feeling a sense of individualist accomplishment for instance, will select jobs and holidays, as well as eating-out venues and ways of commuting, that deliver that: cycling to work at a startup with evening meetings at restaurants where the menu is adventurous if not participatory and weekends spent hiking and camping. Such a person will need structural change toward more sustainable futures to be cast for them as an adventurous kind of self-reinvention. In some cases it may be possible to cast certain sustainable actions in terms of different applied values: saving energy as a competitive challenge or as a benevolent act toward those less well off or as an undertaking that makes our communities safer. In other cases, the task of the sustainability advocate is to try to shift peoples values, though with the proviso that people are unlikely to move from one life value to the opposite, but may move toward a related value: someone committed to hedonistic experiences is unlikely to become charitable, but they may be receptive to activities that are more about individual accomplishments than sheer pleasure.

These kinds of approaches to social change should be familiar to designers. Product styling and interaction aesthetics target different psychographic segments. When personas (Cooper 2004) are used in design processes, they are articulated in terms of life goals, experience goals and activity goals. However, in conventional commercial design, these applied values are precisely the ones used to compromise a supply-side commitment to sustainability. Marketing-driven design wants to normalize and expand existing consumer values, rather than shift them away from consumerism toward more sustainable lifestyles.

Practices and habitus

The perspective of social values recognizes that whilst worldviews may appear to frame what we say and believe, there are levels of everyday activity that seem to be structured by other kinds of commitments. This is why communications about the value of sustainability, as a worldview in its own right, often fail to translate to the level of everyday actions. People who are committed to a system of deep ecology for instance can do so whilst still having very carbon intense everyday travel habits, sometimes because they have to, given the nature of today's economies and urban planning, but sometimes as part of their commitment to that worldview, the food miles associated with living in more wilderness-dominated areas for instance. There are however sociological accounts that suggest that those actions also elude social values, at least as articulated in Schwartz-like frameworks. Consider that whilst many aspects of our lives are the result of deliberations and manifest as conspicuous intentions, many everyday activities are more inconspicuous and done more out of necessity than choice. We perform these chores – laundering, commuting, dining, gardening, etc. – only ever semi-consciously (Shove 2003). However, despite their mundanity, they can be some of the most ecologically harmful activities of a household.

Social Practice Theory (Shove et al. 2012) begins by noting how routinized these activities tend to be without any formal system regularizing them. It is often difficult to explain your everyday habits – who taught you how to bathe or cook or clean, for instance? – yet they remain remarkably consistent across populations and resistant to change. Pierre Bourdieu (1977) developed a specialized idea of practice to explain the expectations around gift giving. In different societies there are different senses of when it is appropriate to give a gift, and how to do so, and then in turn, when, after a certain period, to reciprocate, and how, etc. There are no explicated rules; rather, it is a sign that you are a member of that society that you have a more or less skillful sense of how to play the gift-giving game. Many everyday practices seem to follow a similar 'logic.' Each involves a certain product ecosystem and timespace (Schatzki 2010) – washing clothes takes about an hour in a plumbed laundry room equipped with detergent, etc. – a set of skills – sorting coloreds and whites, wools and synthetics, what can be tumble dried and what not, etc. – and some governing variables about when a practice has been done well – nothing was left too long between stages so it looks and smells clean and is folded or hung and returned to the wardrobe, etc. – and why that matters – the expectations our workplaces and public spaces have on presentability and healthiness, etc.

It should be acknowledged that unlike the game of gift giving, most everyday practices are tangentially subject to some formal regulations. Products that enable practices exist within legal frameworks that try to ensure safety, and in some cases, the way the practices are conducted are also restricted – practices that may impact health such as food handling, or the use of potentially harmful equipment. Our societies however tend to try to govern the practices of businesses more than households. Another kind of formality that might structure practices is economic. The purchase of goods for conducting the practices of everyday life is, for example, subject to certain contractual performance guarantees as well as more obvious issues of rivalrous affordability. However, it is important, from the perspective of Social Practice Theory to see that within minimum legal frameworks, it is the performance of practices that generates value – everyday living and working – rather than those practices being dictated by economic systems, as is the case when people are employed in formal jobs to conduct prescribed tasks.

These social practices are therefore difficult to transform because they are regular without being regulated. They are habitual and they are structured into the habitats in which we dwell, our built environments that must – to return to where we began – fit with existing infrastructures. Bourdieu uses the term *habitus* to capture both these aspects of everyday practices, but also because the term translates as 'disposition,' foregrounding the way we find ourselves thrown into practices without ever having made decisions about how they are conducted, the values they embody, or, with respect to our topic, their sustainability. From the perspective of Social Practice Theory, we practice our values before or even without considering them. Or to put it another way, Social Practice Theory explains why people can be strongly committed to the worldview of sustainability but continue to reproduce everyday practices that unsustainable.

Practices can be altered, but this is not easy. A new technology will only make a difference to an existing practice (1) if it is compatible with the other pieces of equipment, and the existing infrastructure, that make up that practice's current timespace or habitat; (2) if its introduction is accompanied by efforts to help people develop the skills involved in modifying the existing practice to take advantage of that technology (user-centered design); (3) if what that new technology accomplishes can be articulated with the existing values organizing the qualities that that practice embodies (see Roberto Verganti (2008) on 'radically innovating what things mean'). The latter would also entail that such a new product and its use conform to existing formal regulations and economies. Again, designers should already understand all this; they should already be familiar with the ways in which new product development requires paying close attention to innovation diffusion (Rogers 2010), that is, the ways in which a product can be designed to be part of a future habitual yet valuable practice. This is why designers' processes make use of participant observation, codesign, prototyping, iterative user testing, and so on.

Nevertheless, the process of getting innovation adopted into existing practice is ordinarily arduous, even without greater ambitions for structural change. Consequently, practice transformation usually needs to take advantage of other significant disruptions, openings that consumer theory refers to as 'innovation junctions.' (De Wit et al. 2002) These can be life-phase shifts that happen to particular people: moving out of home to go to college, having children, changing jobs, suffering an illness, etc. Or they can be fractures in infrastructures or imaginaries that impact whole communities: a natural disaster; the roll out of a new infrastructure; the closure of a major employer in a smaller city; new regulatory requirements on an industry sector. In all these situations, people's practices can be forced into reconsideration and built environments may consequently be reconfigured. Even if the disruptions only impact certain practices, often other contiguous practices can be more available for transformation.

The process of restructuring society's practices through multiphase and multilevel changes is currently referred to as Transition Management (Geels 2005). What is often missing from these mostly planning-derived discourses is an understanding of design's agency insofar as it facilitates how people evolve their everyday practices.

Being restructured

We have moved from finding the structure that needs to be transformed for our societies to be more sustainable in physical infrastructure, through ideological worldviews and social values, to everyday practices. However, no matter at what level such structures exist, structural change involves three related important difficulties, especially for designers.

Changing systems you are within

Throughout the twentieth century, designers tended to solve other people's problems. When clients brought creative challenges to designers it was only occasionally that those designers would directly benefit from their own solutions. For instance, male designers were often designing household devices that were intended for use by housewives. This is also why part of what is supposedly distinctive about design as a form of problem solving is its empathetic process, enabling designers to build bridges to the worlds, values and practices of their users so that they can experience situations they otherwise would not.

However, structural change toward sustainability means that designers are no longer outside of the situation in which they are intervening. As Alain Findeli (2001) notes in relation to challenge of contemporary design education:

> The designer's task is to understand the dynamic morphology of the system, its "intelligence." One cannot act **upon** a system, only **within** a system; one cannot act against the "intelligence" of a system, only encourage or discourage a system to keep going its own way; [if the current system is state A] state B of the system is, among various possibilities, the one favored by the designer and the client according to their general set of values; state B is only a transitory, more or less stable, state within a dynamic process, never a solution; the production of a material object is not the only way to transform state A into state B; and since the designer and the user also are involved in the process,

they end up being transformed, too, and this learning dimension should be considered as pertaining to the project.

(10)

Trying to restructure the systems one is within means lacking distance on the design situation, in ways that modernist design processes are ill equipped to negotiate. Because objectivity is impossible, designers must be much more reflexive, in disciplined ways, about biases in their own worldviews, social values or practices. Designers need to keep struggling to distance, in the sense of Bertholt Brecht's Alienation Effect, their own hermeneutical prejudices, and to retrieve their own everydayness from its predilection to slip back into uncritically practiced mundanity. In other words, designers need to practice – as in rehearse, repeatedly, each day building the skills needed to discern the structuring within everyday practices – if they are to become agents capable of restructuring practices sufficiently. This is in fact Findeli's recommendation:

> Moholy-Nagy used to say that design was not a profession, but an attitude. In the same vein, Pierre Hadot reminds us in his writings that ancient philosophy was not a speculative occupation like it is today, but a way of life, ("a mode of life, an act of living, a way of being"), and he describes the "spiritual exercises" which were designed to realize a transformation of one's vision of the world – that is what a paradigm shift is really about – and which involved all aspects of one's being: intellect, imagination, sensibility, and will. I suggest that we endeavor to construct our basic design in the form of a series of such "spiritual exercises," the nature and content of which would be adapted to our contemporary world and future challenges.
>
> *(Findeli 2001: 16)*

To put it glibly, it is not so much about being the change you want to see, but the ongoing effort to change the way you are in order to see structural change possibilities.

Restructuring within new systems

Shifts that are very significant, whether in how we live our lives or in how we understand the world, are shifts in which everything changes. Structural shifts should be therefore to some extent incomprehensible to us on this side of the shift, before it happens. Those experiencing the change will themselves become different kinds of people, which means that what they envisage pre-change is not what will be experienced post-change because it will be a changed person who experiences how what was merely envisaged actually unfolds.

It is a designer's job to try to foresee as richly as possible what alternative futures will look and feel like, in order to make evaluations as to which are preferable and how to anticipate future breakdowns. However, in the case of structural change, designers face limits. This does not mean that designers facilitating structural change should give up on attempting to foresight. This is in fact sometimes the conclusion of attempts at structural change coming from outside of design. Advocates of Lean processes (Ries 2011) for instance justify accelerated cycles of field testing a variety of Minimum Viable Product releases precisely because they believe that 'disruptive innovation' comes from the unanticipatable.

By contrast, to engage in structural change in a responsible manner, in the name of radically different, more sustainable futures, rather than just enhanced versions of the present, designers must engage in two distinct forms of visioning.

Firstly, because futures that result from structural change will be distinct from how they might be foreseen from existing worldviews, there is therefore the possibility that what seems improbable now may yet prove viable. There is therefore an imperative to envision even what currently appears utopian. This seeming far-fetched-ness applies not just to the quality of what needs to be visioned – that multiple interrelated systems could work equitably and sustainably – but also the quantity:

> For all of us who attempt to grasp the scale, complexity and seriousness of the problems the human race currently faces, it can seem that overcoming them is actually impossible. Yet we need to ask if we actually can, in fact, distinguish between what, at any given moment, is empirically impossible from what our limited perceptual reach tells us is impossible. . . . Not withstanding a bleak analysis and the total inadequacy of current action against the forces of defuturing unleashed by human action . . . *it has to be affirmed that the history of humanity is a history of the realization of the impossible.*
>
> *(Fry 2009: 248)*

Such structurally distinct possibilities can and should be the constant measure of our present realities, countering the inertial sense that our current everyday practices are acceptable norms.

Secondly, because structural change nevertheless contains aspects that are unanticipatable, it is also the task of the designer, in order to preserve their particular way of making decisions about futures, to imaginatively yet critically speculate on all possibilities, preferable and nonpreferable. As structural change is taking place, it is the task of a sustainable designer to try to stay ahead of the change by envisioning second-order futures, the subsequent futures that are made possible or constrained by futures that are emerging. To do this requires designers to envision not just likely near-futures that could be prototyped and perhaps enacted, but to be much more creative about all that structural change might entail. These design fictions must, despite contemplating seemingly unlikely consequences, be done in a rich manner, because we must judge whether to encourage or repulse such futures on the basis of their envisioned everyday socio-material practice. Designers familiar with Speculative Critical Design may understand what is required, though that practice has remained too sheltered in the gallery and failed to take responsibility for curating the debates its propositions are supposed to provoke (though see Noortje Marres' work [2012] on 'assembling publics').

Structural change is thus driven by a utopianism but accompanied by a cynicism, both undertaken at a level of a comprehensive detail.

Agitating

Trying to effect change to a system that cannot be fully comprehended from the system one is currently in is thus a struggle. The two previously made points aid each other in this ongoing effort:

- being utopian exposes the nature of the current system, both its inadequacies and what preserves the system despite its inadequacies (which I take to be what Soft Systems Methodology strives to reveal (Checkland and Poulter 2006))
- being cynical about our capacity to effect structural change draws attention to aspects of the current system that nevertheless already contain aspects of radically different futures (see Ezio Manzini's work (2015) which seeks to find heroic community-based innovations and amplify them into alternative ways of resourcing everyday life)

This may sound good in theory, but it involves great discomfort for the change maker trying to act responsibly. For the most part, being an advocate of structural change feels like hypocrisy. You are demanding radical change toward utopianly new ways of structuring societies; yet you are confined to the existing systems. Any action within current structures will risk replicating the inadequate small steps or vain hopes with which I began this chapter.

This hypocrisy is nevertheless an important part of being able to discern where structures lie and how they structure. Tony Fry (et al. 2015: 22), following a long tradition of left-wing activism, calls this 'creative alienation.' The obverse of hypocrisy is experimentalism. Trying to effect change to a system one is within is difficult, but does afford playing with possibilities, or trying to find the 'play' within a current system that affords other possibilities. The sustainable designer aiming at structural change must therefore be always also trying out different ways of living and working. In addition to the chance that such self-experimentation might light upon structural change pathways, the noncompliance with current structures that such a changing, experimental way of living entails will itself be an irritant to current structures. Sustainable designers should be visibly engaged in creatively critical acts, alerting others by example to the need for radical change.

References

Bourdieu, Pierre. (1977) *Outline of a Theory of Practice*. Cambridge University Press.

Bourdieu, Pierre, and Loïc JD Wacquant. (1992) *An Invitation to Reflexive Sociology*. University of Chicago Press.

Bowers, Chet A. (1995) *Educating for an Ecologically Sustainable Culture*. SUNY.

Bowers, Chet A. (2009) "Why the George Lakoff and Mark Johnson Theory of Metaphor Is Inadequate for Addressing Cultural Issues Related to the Ecological Crises." *Language & Ecology* 2.4.

Checkland, Peter, and John Poulter. (2006) *Learning for Action: A Short Definitive Account of Soft Systems Methodology and Its Use, for Practitioners, Teachers and Students*. Wiley.

Cooper, Alan. (2004) *The Inmates Are Running the Asylum: Why High-tech Products Drive Us Crazy and How to Restore the Sanity*. Sams.

Crompton, Tom, and Tim Kasser. (2010) "Human Identity: A Missing Link in Environmental Campaigning." *Environment* 52.4.

De Wit, Onno, Johannes Cornelis Maria van den Ende, Johan Schot, and Ellen van Oost. (2002) "Innovative Junctions: Office Technologies in the Netherlands, 1880–1980." *Technology and Culture* 43.1.

Findeli, Alain. (2001) "Rethinking Design Education for the 21st Century: Theoretical, Methodological, and Ethical Discussion." *Design Issues* 17.1.

Fry, Tony. (1999) *A New Design Philosophy: An Introduction to Defuturing*. UNSW Press.

Fry, Tony. (2009) *Design Futuring*. Berg.

Fry, Tony, Clive Dilnot, and Susan Stewart. (2015) *Design and the Question of History*. Bloomsbury.

Geels, Frank W. (2005) *Technological Transitions and System Innovations: A Co-evolutionary and Socio-Technical Analysis*. Edward Elgar Publishing.

Greenfield, Kent. (2001) *Myth of Choice*. Yale University Press.

Heelas, Paul, Scott Lash, and Paul Morris, Eds. (1996) *Detraditionalization: Critical Reflections on Authority and Identity*. Blackwell.

Heiskanen, Eva. (1999) "Every Product Casts a Shadow: But Can We See It, and Can We Act on It?." *Environmental Science & Policy* 2.1.

Herring, Horace, and Robin Roy. (2007) "Technological Innovation, Energy Efficient Design and the Rebound Effect." *Technovation* 27.4.

Hobson, Kersty. (2001) "Sustainable Lifestyles: Rethinking Barriers and Behaviour Change." In Cohen, Maurie, and Joseph Murray, eds. *Exploring Sustainable Consumption. Environmental Policy and the Social Sciences*. Emerald Publishing.

Hobson, Kersty. (2002) "Competing Discourses of Sustainable Consumption: Does The 'Rationalisation of Lifestyles' Make Sense?." *Environmental politics* 11.2.

Irwin, Terry, Gideon Kossoff, and Cameron Tonkinwise. (2015) "Transition Design Provocation." *Design Philosophy Papers* 13.1.

Jalas, Mikko. (2006) "Making Time: The Art of Loving Wooden Boats." *Time & Society* 15.2–3.

Jasanoff, Sheila, and Sang-Hyun Kim, Eds. (2015) *Dreamscapes of Modernity: Sociotechnical Imaginaries and the Fabrication of Power*. University of Chicago Press.

Kasser, Tim. (2011) "Ecological Challenges, Materialistic Values, and Social Change." In Robert Biswas-Diener, ed. *Positive Psychology as Social Change*. Springer.

Kearney, Michael. (1984) *Worldview*. Chandler & Sharp.

Lakoff, George. (2010) "Why It Matters How We Frame the Environment." *Environmental Communication* 4.1.

Lakoff, George, and Mark Johnson. (2008) *Metaphors We Live By*. University of Chicago Press.

Loewenstein, George, and Karl Moene. (2006) "On Mattering Maps." In Elster, Jon, Gjelsvik, Olav, and Moene, Karl, eds. *Understanding Choice, Explaining Behavior: Essays in Honour of Ole-Jorgen Skog*. Oslo: Oslo Academic Press.

MacKenzie, Donald, and Judy Wajcman. (1999) *The Social Shaping of Technology*. Open University Press.

Maniates, Michael, and John M. Meyer. (2010) *The Environmental Politics of Sacrifice*. MIT.

Manzini, Ezio. (2015) *Design, When Everybody Designs: An Introduction to Design for Social Innovation*. MIT.

Marres, Noortje. (2012) *Material Participation: Technology, the Environment and Everyday Publics*. Springer.

Mol, Annemarie. (2008) *The Logic of Care: Health and the Problem of Patient Choice*. Routledge.

Ravetz, Jerome R. (2006) "Post-Normal Science and the Complexity of Transitions Towards Sustainability." *Ecological Complexity* 3.4.

Ries, Eric. (2011) *The Lean Startup: How Today's Entrepreneurs Use Continuous Innovation to Create Radically Successful Businesses*. Crown Books.

Rogers, Everett M. (2010) *Diffusion of Innovations*. Simon and Schuster.

Rosenthal, Edward C. (2006) *The Era of Choice: The Ability to Choose and Its Transformation of Contemporary Life*. MIT Press.

Schatzki, Theodore R. (2010) *The Timespace of Human Activity: On Performance, Society, and History as Indeterminate Teleological Events*. Lexington Books.

Schwartz, Shalom H. (1994) *Beyond Individualism/Collectivism: New Cultural Dimensions of Values*. Sage Publications.

Shove, Elizabeth. (2003) *Cleanliness, Comfort, Convenience: The Social Organization of Normality*. Berg.

Shove, Elizabeth, Mika Pantzar, and Matt Watson. (2012) *The Dynamics of Social Practice: Everyday Life and How It Changes*. Berg.

Stahel, Walter R., and Genevieve Reday-Mulvey. (1981) *Jobs for Tomorrow: The Potential for Substituting Manpower for Energy*. Vantage Press.

Sterling, Bruce. (2005) *Shaping Things*. Mediaworks Pamphlets.

Thøgersen, John, and Tom Crompton. (2009) "Simple and Painless? The Limitations of Spillover in Environmental Campaigning." *Journal of Consumer Policy* 32.2.

Tierney, Thomas F. (1993) *The Value of Convenience: A Genealogy of Technical Culture*. SUNY Press.

Verganti, Roberto. (2008) "Design, Meanings, and Radical Innovation: A Metamodel and a Research Agenda." *Journal of Product Innovation Management* 25.5.

32

EMPOWERING CITIZENS THROUGH DESIGN

Diamond James

Introduction

Cities are roaring machines, powered by a series of interconnected systems including transportation, affordable housing, a robust job market, nutritional and health resources and education. Within each city's systems are intricate networks that demand symbiosis in order to give citizens fair access to clean natural resources, rights, and opportunities to thrive. However, the mechanical metaphor of an ideal city is myopic and does not consider external, spontaneous shocks to a well-running city. More importantly, it also does not address urban ecologies that malfunction because of bias or harmful designs that disproportionately affect citizens, threatening sustainability for all.

This chapter explores implications of threats to sustainability, and how designers can foster empowerment for citizen and community resilience. The chapter's case study is based in one neighborhood in Baltimore, Maryland. It is a microcosm of major American cities where sustainability is challenged by pervasive legacies of racial segregation.

Baltimore's Office of Sustainability defines the term as "meeting the environmental, social, and economic needs of Baltimore without compromising the ability of future generations to meet these needs." The most populous city in the state of Maryland, Baltimore is not alone in striving to make sustainability actionable. Although this chapter is framed in a United States context, the concept is ancient. It is an international concept that has settled into our collective, cultural lexicon in recent decades. Working in conjunction with – and sometimes in opposition to – international city governments are designers, scientists, public health professionals and activists who see the issue as immediate and much broader than compost piles and bike lanes.

As sustainability efforts grow, those who champion the global movement have expanded the conversation to address growing threats to "a lasting equilibrium." According to a 2012 *New York Times* article, "because the world is so increasingly out of balance, the sustainability regime is being quietly challenged" from those participating in the work. As a result, dialogue around "resilience" emerged. "Where sustainability aims to put the world back into balance, resilience looks for ways to manage an imbalanced world," op-ed contributor Andrew Zolli writes (Zolli 2012).

As resilience thinking has increased, the topic has been taken on by some of the world's most notable philanthropists. The Rockefeller Foundation's 100 Resilient Cities program defines urban resilience as "the capacity of individuals, communities, institutions, businesses, and systems within a city to survive, adapt, and grow no matter what kinds of chronic stressors and acute shocks they experience." Stressors contribute to a community's social determinants of health as well as the overall public health of a city. These are ongoing, impacting daily life such as "high unemployment, overtaxed or inefficient public transportation system, endemic violence or chronic food and water shortages." Shocks are unforeseen events of natural or man-made disaster. The site lists "earthquakes, floods, disease outbreaks and terrorist attacks" as examples (100 Resilient Cities 2017).

The task of equipping cities with resilience plans becomes more challenging because populations are stratified by race, class, castes, gender, sexuality and physical and intellectual ability. Furthermore, these designations often determine neighborhood and inequitable distribution of resources that exacerbate the impact of shocks and stressors. Different groups of citizens are able to rebound more or less quickly than others because of several factors.

Race and resilience

Sustainability and resilience efforts are often undercut by race and class divisions. Hurricane Katrina is an extraordinary national example of how the aftermath of massive shock is more disruptive for some because of endemic chronic stressors. The 2005 hurricane destroyed much of New Orleans, claimed lives and damaged cities in the Gulf Coast region. New Orleans' disaster is particularly significant because the storm exposed the city's design flaws and put poor black residents at greater risk.

The residents' plight was widely broadcasted in news bulletins over the course of a week. The tragedy has even been chronicled by countless media and events are solidified in our national consciousness:

> Over the course of the 20th century, the Army Corps of Engineers had built a system of levees and seawalls to keep the city from flooding. The levees along the Mississippi River were strong and sturdy, but the ones built to hold back Lake Pontchartrain, Lake Borgne and the waterlogged swamps and marshes to the city's east and west were much less reliable. Before the storm, officials worried that surge could overtop some levees and cause short-term flooding, but no one predicted levees might collapse below design height. Neighborhoods that sat below sea level, many of which housed the city's poorest and most vulnerable people, were at great risk of flooding.
>
> *(History 2015)*

Some who could not evacuate to safety because of failed traffic plans or inadequate transportation desperately waited out the storm (History 2015). Some were rescued by neighbors. Residents of wards located at lower sea levels hoped to find aid by retreating to attics and rooftops, and aerial images circulated. Food, clean water and first aid rations were frantically sought by everyone struggling to survive, but the narrative soon became racialized. Twelve years later, the governmental efficacy in handling the tragedy is still perceived as neglectful and disastrous by some. The country's Federal Emergency Management Agency's response time sparked discussions about the role race and class played in sending aid.

A 2015 *Slate* article highlights perceptions based on survey data: "In an ABC News and *Washington Post* poll taken shortly after the hurricane, 71 percent of blacks said that New Orleans would have been 'better prepared' if it were a 'wealthier city with more whites,' and 76 percent said the federal government would have 'responded faster'" (Bouie 2015). Hurricane Katrina – and its aftermath – demonstrates the need for designers to customize what sustainability looks like for different citizenry based on their perceptions of barriers, threats and pathways to resilience in the face of adversity. In order to make transformative and meaningful strides, designers must see citizen empowerment as a core part of their practices.

Empowerment defined

I present the concept of "empowerment" with a caveat. Although empowerment is a buzzword in nonprofit "do-gooder" circles, designers cannot bestow power as the literal definition of the word implies. Implicit in that definition is paternalism from elite, credentialed designers backed by the legitimacy of their academic or philanthropic institutions. It also implies that there is not already power within those citizens the design is assisting, which is incorrect. Operating within the definition, designers would be leveraging a long history of prescriptive "treatments" for the poor and traditionally marginalized groups. In order to accurately explain empowerment, let's first explore the concept of who is powerless and what ignites their inherent power.

Drawing from community psychologist Charles H. Kieffer's 1984 article "Citizen Empowerment: A Developmental Perspective", I frame my practice. Inspired by several twentieth-century theorists, Kieffer meditates on powerlessness based on the idea that certain groups are disengaged from decision making and have the perspective that they have little control over their lives. These feelings are reinforced through their environment and social institutions. Through a summation of ideas from philosophers Paulo Freire, Franz Fanon and noted others, Kieffer offers his comprehensive definition of what it means to be powerless:

> In sum the sense of powerlessness is viewed as a construction of continuous interaction between the person and his/her environment. It combines an attitude of self-blame, a sense of generalized distrust, a feeling of alienation from resources of social influence, an experience of disenfranchisement and economic vulnerability, and a sense of hopelessness in socio-political struggle.
>
> *(Kieffer 1984, 16)*

To clarify, the people experiencing powerlessness may be fluid depending on specific context, but the feeling may be attributed to those who are often left without significant political, economic and social influence within a particular place. Designations of race, ethnicity, religion, gender, sexuality, physical and intellectual ability create permutations of who is experiencing powerlessness at any given time. The term is not exclusive to one group. However, it should be acknowledged that in American context, the dominant narrative is race-based, most often around a black-white binary. The construct of race and America are inextricably linked. I pay close attention to this in my design practice, which is almost exclusively in urban settings.

Designers who want to facilitate empowerment must know that strategies will vary by individual, community and location. When working with groups, an early step designers can take is to acknowledge that the group's feelings are real and valid, based on empirically supported phenomena and lived experience. It is at that point designers can begin to create opportunities for self-realization and agency. Regardless of what designers create, keeping those opportunities as a North Star will produce a more engaged citizenry who are determined to advocate for their ideas of social justice together; coalition building to hold those with formal power accountable (elected officials, lawmakers, social or educational institutions); and capacity to better manage enduring stressors and random shocks.

To find a guide, designers can refer to Kieffer's text to help understand how empowerment works. He rejects the notion that empowerment is a singular event any designer can choreograph, and argues "the transition from powerlessness to participatory competence can best be characterized as a dynamic of long-term development" with stages of sociopolitical involvement (Kieffer 1984, 18). It is an evolutionary process where development differs for each individual within the group. Methodologies to measure individual development will need to be customized, but development is based on three tenets, which can provide a solid foundation for good design to catalyze.

The design project I chronicle in this chapter's case study was reframed based on "the centrality of a mentoring relationship, the enabling impact of supportive peer relationships within a collective organizational structure, and the cultivation of a more critical understanding of social and political relations" (Kieffer 1984, 20). I will later detail how my partner and I came to discover these tenets enhanced and helped us clarity why the work we do is meaningful.

Designers who work as social change agents, creative allies and activists will find these tenets critical to successful strategies. (Success is relative and should be defined with citizens' participation.) Designers working on complex social challenges must move with our citizen codesigners, not toward one single moment of cursory empowerment, but rather through different levels of civic engagement. Empowerment is a series of revelatory moments shaping a collective education to propel the group toward correcting purposely imbalanced social structures, and building genuine citizen power in order for all to thrive. These are very big directives, but they are essential if one considers design to be a restorative practice in service of others.

Design advocacy

The idea that designers have the ability to facilitate change in the world's complex problems can be traced to Victor Papanek's seminal text *Design for the Real World: Human Ecology and Social Change*. First released in 1971, it provides an understanding that designing goods and services that serve the greater good of humanity were no longer optional in an increasingly enlightened 1970s world. Even with that disclaimer, it is still a foundational text for designers wanting to work in the messy space that exists between social problems and sustainable social change. Papanek critiques the design discipline where each kind of designer (industrial, environmental, architectural and graphic) worked independently and left consumers and users needs unmet. At the time, the field was largely devoid of connections that might equate to production of contributions to the environment, ecological movements and ultimately, stronger communities.

"In order to work more directly for people, the whole field of design has to emphasize the role of the designer as an advocate," Papanek said (1971, 110). I believe the phrase "work more directly for people" requires clarity. The clarion call Papanek makes is about designers working for the greater good of people. To expand the sentiment, I argue that in order for the field to become service-oriented and effectively provide a better quality of life, designers must include the people we hope to serve in our creative processes.

Advocacy in design requires purposefully choosing to center strategies, processes and interventions around the citizens' ideas, perspectives and collective experiences (that are often different from what the designer has lived). Being an advocate-designer requires a consistently deliberate act regardless of project topic or funders' expectations. The act is inherent in human centered design and participatory design research, which fosters authentic collaboration. Working together, designers and communities build rapport. Rapport builds relationships. Relationships build empathy leading to compassion for the citizens the designers are serving. The steps are by no means easy, and set a course toward transformative design to disrupt social challenges that threaten sustainability.

The advocate-designer is a composite of activist, community organizer and coalition builder with a creative mode of practice for problem solving. They are mindful of their privilege and seek to diminish their own hubris. They are allies with citizens, aligned with the group's definition of success and equity.

Conversations about equity and justice are critical when thinking about sustainability. There are myriad issues for which designers position themselves as allies. Mental health, access to health care, reproductive rights, LGBTQIA rights, housing insecurity and affordable housing, police reform, inequitable schools, catalyzing prison pipelines, mass incarceration, unemployment, homelessness, spatial discrimination and disproportionate transit options, immigrant rights, minimum wage reform, clean water, and climate change are just a few umbrella topics where designers intervene for change.

Although the topics listed are broad and may appear disjointed, there is much overlap and several topics are contingent and interconnected with others. They form a system where if one piece malfunctions and hampers sustainability for some, there are ricochet effects for all communities. The advocate-designer must not frame his/her issue without considering the implications of the whole ecology. Of course it is impossible to design with all scenarios, communities and social issues in mind. However, the takeaway is that design acts are always made within the much larger context of other designs. The design act is not isolated.

As advocate-designers become particularly mindful about the impact of their work overlapping with different issues, they also should acknowledge other nondesigners that have made efforts on the same issues. In the 1970s, Papanek's then-novel wisdom that "design must become an innovative, highly creative, cross-disciplinary tool responsive to the true needs of [all]" disregards people who tirelessly work outside of the discipline (Papanek 1971). Dedicated ordinary people without formal credentials have taken up the mantle to improve their own communities by building coalitions and other grassroots efforts. For generations they have struggled to win equity and access to economic, social and political resources. Advocate-designers must not assume they are the only legitimate source of innovation. Instead, they must be committed to bring their unique skills to citizens that want change, have often been excluded from official decision-making processes.

Intervention

To avoid superficial interventions with communities, there are a set of benchmarks outlined in Sherry R. Arnstein's 1969 article *A "Ladder of Citizen Participation"*. Though the ladder concept has been reimagined a number of times, 47 years later, the basic principles are still a solid model toward authentic citizen empowerment. Never a formal designer, Arnstein's career spanned social work, public policy, medicine, housing and community development, and her seminal paper can be applied to sustainable design (AACOM 2015). Her ladder has eight rungs that outline the steps from "nonparticipation" efforts to "citizen power" as the ultimate goal (Figure 32.1).

The paper's critical message – "It is the redistribution of power that enables the have-not citizens, presently excluded from the political and economic processes, to be deliberately included in the future" – provides designers with an enduring beacon (Arnstein 1969, 1). With this mission at its core, the ladder stands firm giving designers checkpoints to be critical of themselves, processes and interventions.

Imperative to the checkpoints is the acknowledgment of privilege and power dynamics in play as designers interact with communities. Power is not exclusive to elected officials or governments that have created the conditions designers are working to change. Designers must examine how they are perceived by those they serve. Although no formal authority, designers' power is often legitimized by education, class, race, gender, technological literacy, agencies they work for juxtaposed with the participants. I am extending Arnstein's discussion of "powerholders" to include designers as well.

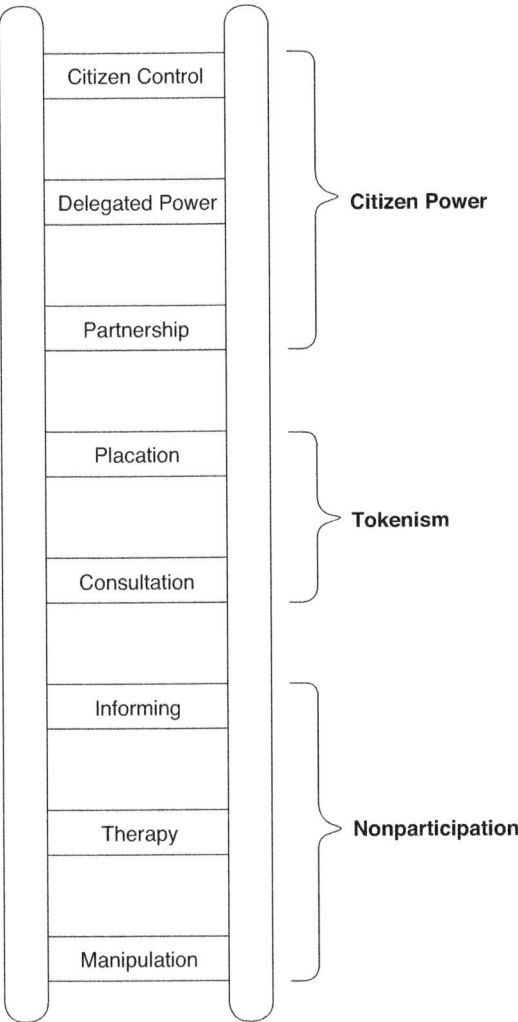

Figure 32.1 Arnstein's ladder of citizen participation.

At the bottom of the ladder, Manipulation and Therapy fall into the lowest category of Nonparticipation. Informing, Consultation and Placation are in the middle labeled Tokenism. The highest group, Citizen Power, features Partnership, Delegated Power and Citizen Control. Nonparticipation's objective "is not to enable people to participate in planning or conducting programs, but to enable powerholders to 'educate' or 'cure' the participants" (Arnstein 1969, 2). Characteristic in the Manipulation (1) and Therapy (2) rungs are advisory committees and boards that are public relations stunts, and efforts where "citizens are engaged in extensive [group] activity" which doesn't address the problems that created the stressors. The activities overlook significant factors and focus on small results such as trash-cleanups in low-income neighborhoods that divert attention from systemic issues like economic disinvestment and segregation within the same neighborhoods (Arnstein 1969, 4–5).

Tokenism "allows the have-nots to hear and have a voice," but citizens "lack power to insure that their views will be heeded by the powerful." This category is enticing because it does ask for citizen input and contribution, which is a clear move away from design that exist without community engagement. Informing and Consultation (rungs 3 and 4) give cursory facts and also ask for citizen perspective, but Placation (5) is insidious because "the ground rules allow have-nots to advise, but retain for the powerholders the continued right to decide (Arnstein 1969, 2)." Surveys, neighborhood meetings and planning committees without accountability to the citizens are characteristics of Tokenism.

Advocate-designers who want to empower citizens should not unilaterally decide what efforts the community makes. The citizens are the experts and designers are there to assist. Designers should allow citizens to inform their processes and interventions, which need to be adaptive to allow for citizen consensus. Designers who follow this philosophy begin to reach the ladder's highest rungs. Achieving Citizen Power is easier when there is Partnership (6) enabling Negotiation, Delegated Power (7) and finally, Citizen Control (8) in which "citizens obtain the majority of decision-making seats, or full managerial power" (Arnstein 1969, 3).

The ideas Arnstein presents are admittedly simplistic. Design is not linear, and there may be obstacles to achieving a complete transfer of power. Variables outside of the designer's control that can slow progress include stakeholders' competing interests, funding constraints and funder expectations, which may differ from the designer's. A city's economic, social and political climate can also complicate design initiatives and impede a transfer of power.

The ladder's rungs are not absolute. There may be finer distinctions based on specific contexts. Arnstein admits "in the real world of people and programs, there might be 150 rungs with less sharp and 'pure' distinctions among them" (Arnstein 1969, 3). However, designers should remain vigilant and critical to determine where their manner of working with citizens fits into the ladder. This directive should not make designers feel insecure if their current interventions fall within the bottom sections. It is entirely possible to increase participation by working in a scaffolded approach. It is more probable that those adjustments will come gradually as empowerment is developed over time. Evaluate early and often.

Case study: Oliver Counter Ad Youth Workshops

The following case study is an ongoing design project based on youth empowerment and civic participation in Baltimore, Maryland. The work is an official partnership of Behavioral Health System Baltimore, the Maryland State Prevention Framework, and the Center for Social Design at The Maryland Institute College of Art (MICA).

Background

Baltimore is the most populous city in Maryland, but has experienced a shrinking population since the mid-twentieth century. Peaking in 1950 at 949,708 inhabitants, the city was "the [Mid-Atlantic] region's unchallenged center of manufacturing until the 1960s." It was home to pre-war industrial giants like Bethlehem Steel and "dominated the whole state of Maryland economically, culturally and politically. The city's industry included producing war equipment and was an oasis for employment. After World War II, Baltimore's population decline can be attributed to deindustrialization, urban renewal projects that caused neighborhood instability, closure of businesses and an exodus of white residents to surrounding suburbs (Pietila 2010, 217).

Today, the city has 620,000 people. Sixty-three percent of its residents identify as black or African American, and about 30 percent are white according to U.S. Census data. Baltimore exists with a legacy of spatial discrimination based on decades of policies limiting non-white minorities from purchasing real estate freely. As a result, neighborhoods are still segregated by race, and public health issues persist disproportionately impacting the city's residents. In addition, many of Baltimore's black residents have felt the sting of limited job opportunities, disinvested neighborhoods, and aggressive law enforcement leading to protests and riots during 2015's Baltimore Uprising. The unrest was sparked by the death of 25-year-old Freddie Gray who died after suffering neck and spinal cord injuries while in police custody.

Underage drinking as a public health issue

In 2012, a community needs assessment of Baltimore high school students revealed that almost 40 percent of eleventh graders drank alcohol in the past 30 days. In addition to developmental health risks, all youth who drink alcohol are at a greater risk of experiencing negative outcomes such as dropping out of school, participating in unprotected sexual activity, getting arrested and committing suicide or homicide. It is unfortunate that while these outcomes are probable for all teens, their effects are exacerbated for African Americans.

According to reports from the Center on Alcohol Marketing and Youth (CAMY) based at Johns Hopkins' Bloomberg School of Public Health, black teens drink less than their counterparts, but "there is evidence from public health research that, as they age, African Americans suffer more from alcohol-related diseases than other groups in the population." In addition CAMY notes "alcohol use contributes to the three leading causes of death among African-American 12 to 20 year-olds: homicide, unintentional injuries (including car crashes), and suicide." CAMY also asserts that black teens are disproportionately targeted by alcohol advertisers across media (CAMY 2006). To address this public health disparity, the Oliver Counter Ad Youth Workshop was founded.

The workshops

The Oliver Counter Ad Youth Workshop was conceived with a very specific tactic to reduce underage drinking in the Oliver neighborhood. The methodology of the project, which initially began with a sample of high school students, was to educate youth on alcohol marketing strategies. Designers were also to assist them in creating media with a counter narrative to combat the alcohol industry's influence on their peer group. For a few iterations of the annual project, high school students created parodies of advertisements and fostered peer awareness through print and video media. Undergraduate and post-graduate designers from MICA facilitated weekly workshops and taught graphic design to help promote youth messaging.

When I came aboard the project in 2015, the workshops were still focused on creating counter ads, but the participants were no longer high school students. The summer before the school year, project specifics changed and we welcomed seventh and eighth graders from St. James and John Catholic Elementary/Middle School. (The K-8 school is located in the Oliver neighborhood, but all participants do not reside in the neighborhood.) This set of students eventually ushered in a new focus and new methodologies once the design team discovered our reliable framework was hardly relevant.

From October to December 2015, our team designed a series of activities to gather research on the middle schoolers' knowledge of alcohol marketing, where youth might encounter alcohol, and their ideas for reducing underage drinking. Each week our design approach was to be responsive to what we heard and observed about the students. Structured as a codesign, the workshop regards students as the experts and designers as facilitators to help frame the issue of underage drinking. The design team also strategizes local partnerships and opportunities for student opinions on the topic to be shared.

We believe our approach leads to empowerment, enabling students to assert themselves on an issue that is potentially life threatening. Supporting the very large goal of reducing underage drinking, our design team's priority is to provide a safe space for students to explore their identity as designers and critical thinkers. This priority is fundamental to any design research or activity we do. Part of our empowerment approach is guided by "anti-banking" philosophies.

"Anti-banking"

Our workshops prioritize student voices and their realities as young black students experiencing Baltimore. Their experiences are not the same, but we find shared experiences as starting points for group dialogue. The benefits of learning from students is a concept expressed in Paulo Freire's *Pedagogy of the Oppressed*. The Brazilian educator and philosopher critiques traditional teaching models which he terms "banking." Banking occurs when "education thus becomes an act of depositing, in which the students are the depositories and the teacher is the depositor. Instead of communicating, the teacher issues communiqués and makes deposits which the students patiently receive, memorize, and repeat" (Freire 1993, 72).

As designers we are not teachers. We learn what students think is important, how they interpret alcohol usage, and what they feel able to contribute to their own communities. Each week in the fall semester, our team revised workshops to account for how the students engaged with the previous week's activities.

The abridged curricula from the fall 2015 semester is as follows:

Week 1: Ad Investigator – We did a scavenger hunt for alcohol ads, and gave a worksheet to assess student ability to understand and interpret the ad's target demographic.

Week 2: Brand recognition – We did two activities assessing brand recognition through product packaging and major campaigns.

Week 3: Design for a persona – Building upon a discussion about marketers targeting specific demographics, we asked students to make an ad appealing to a particular type of person.

Week 4: Other factors – After we noticed students were not understanding media strategies, we did individual interviews, found out how else alcohol is visible in their lives, and asked them to tell us why they thought teens might drink.

Week 5: Brainstorming – Based on their reasons teens might drink, we came up with three "how might we" prompts for them to brainstorm. The prompts were: "How might we reduce underage drinking? How might we change what is considered cool? How might we reduce peer pressure?

*Pivot**

Week 6: Music & alcohol – We asked the students to read current song lyrics mentioning alcohol and prototyped quick ideas using different social media platforms.

Week 7: Final Prototype – We filmed a polished video on the student's lyric critiques and showed it to funders and stakeholders.

**The pivot*

After the fifth workshop, the design team realized there was a disconnect between our counter-ad approach and the students. The majority of the middle schoolers had little to no personal interaction with alcohol. At 12 to 14 years old, the students still had an idealized sense of morality and "right and wrong" behaviors. Although some of their adult family members drank alcohol, the students viewed drinking as a deterrent to being successful. They also likened drinking alcohol to illegal drug use. We began to question how this group could authentically participate in reducing underage drinking without resorting to scare tactics.

For two weeks, we explored their most relevant connection to alcohol: Popular music. We remembered that during the first workshop the students bobbed their heads and sang along to a playlist of songs prominently featuring drinking as tantamount party culture. We remembered how they connected with the songs even without experiencing taking shots or popping champagne bottles at a nightclub. We made a prototype with students to explore this phenomena as a peer-to-peer campaign. They also wrote anti-drinking raps and performed during the last workshop of the semester.

Designers asked students to read lyrics mentioning alcohol (in the style of the popular React Franchise in which different age groups react to songs and videos are viral). We noticed that once the melody and beat were gone, students were more critical about songs that might influence young people to drink. The critique was filmed and shared with funders and students. The video was well received but we decided the idea lacked a specific ask to inspire a change in the local teens. Without a long-term strategy, significant capital, and a celebrity to catalyze efforts it was not going to be disruptive or transformative. It would have provided awareness about the music industry's promotion of alcohol, but would not have led to a reduction in underage drinking.

After the departure from the music, we stepped back to recall what we knew about the students and Baltimore. We asked the following questions: How did the issue matter to students, and what could the students gain from being in this project based on who they desired to be? The students were not underage drinkers. Many envisioned themselves as future leaders to make their families proud. However, they live in a city that is largely segregated and is said to have "twice the per-capita number of liquor stores for other cities of the same size" according to Baltimore Health Commissioner Dr. Leana Wen who is quoted in the *Business Insider* (Owens 2015). The article – published in the wake of the Uprising – explores the role liquor stores play in exacerbating neighborhood inequity and social determinants of health. Hot-button issues such as zoning and outlet compliance have come to the forefront since the unrest.

We shifted the focus of the remainder of the workshops and activities for the school year towards empowerment. What would the students cite as barriers to success? What things in the built environment did they feel negatively about? What things did they internalize as a threat to their communities? And, what, if anything, could a middle schooler do about it?

Using Charles Kieffer's "Citizen Empowerment" article, we reimagined what the project could be to the overall development of each student. The design team saw opportunities to capitalize on the existing structure of the workshops. There was already "the centrality of a mentoring relationship" because a few of the high school participants returned to assist and were viewed as role models. We often developed activities to build rapport, group identity and to foster "supportive peer relationships within a collective organizational structure." Additionally, the funders requested a peer-to-peer approach to help reduction. The path to "cultivation of a more critical understanding of social and political relations" began as students took their first liquor store tour (Kieffer 1984, 20).

Liquor store stories

One spring afternoon, we boarded the campus shuttle with the students and rode an unconventional route to the middle school. The ride was a little more than 10 minutes, and followed a major avenue. We asked the students to count the number of liquor stores and observe the scenes around the perimeter of each. We also asked them to document the sights using social media. The students were encouraged to use Instagram and Snapchat applications to comment about how seeing more than five liquor stores made them feel. We wrote their immediate responses on sticky notes and chart paper while on the shuttle.

Commentary about the tour was the foundation for our spring design project. We partnered with a local organization that had growing momentum on the alcohol outlet regulation. The Baltimore Good Neighbors Coalition (BGNC) was one of several groups already working to improve liquor stores to meet demands for safer and healthier communities. BGNC had been working on legislation to ensure increased scrutiny and liquor store compliance, better lighting and security and property cleanliness. It was better to work with a coalition with a common goal than trying to design alone. We became allies and advocates for each other's goals.

Through the partnership, the "Liquor Store Stories" exhibit was born (Figure 32.2). We enlarged the students' social media posts and formally interviewed each to discover what is frustrating about liquor stores in their neighborhoods. Students mentioned many things, but sentiments

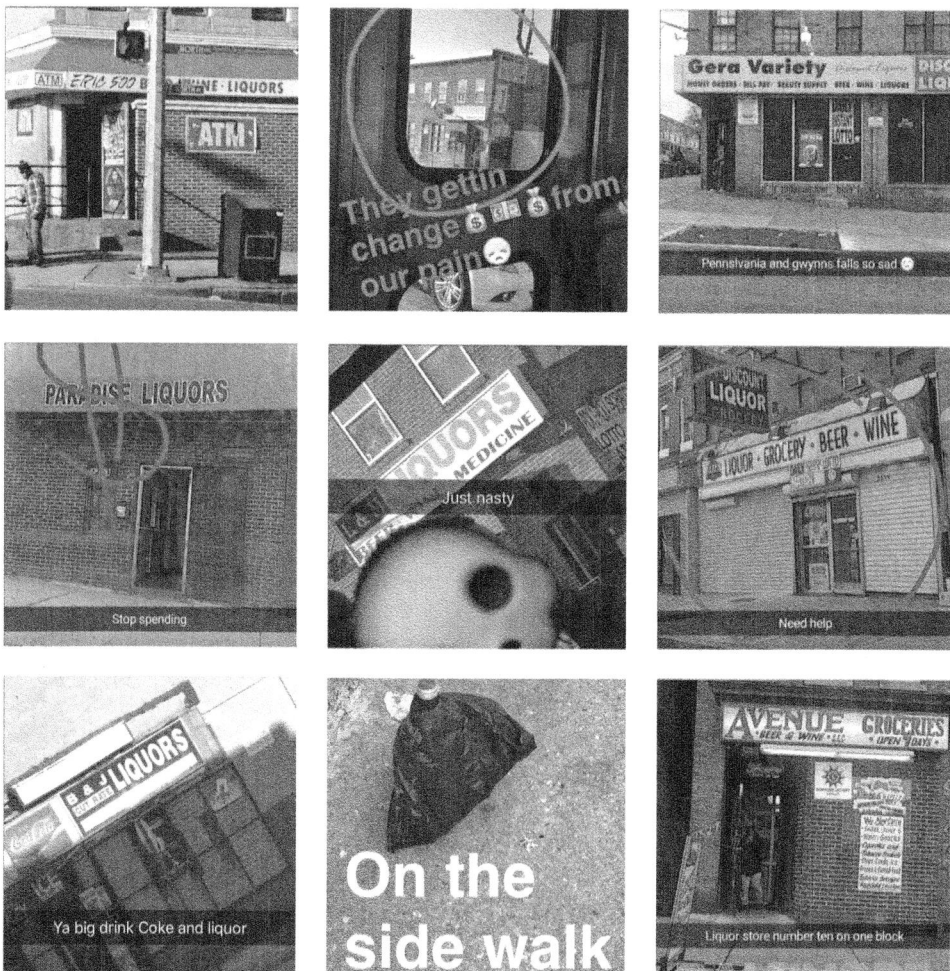

Figure 32.2 A sample of the student Snapchats featured in "Liquor Store Stories".

included disapproval in liquor stores selling treats that are enticing to youth, and the prevalence of noncustomers hanging around the perimeters. A benefit of partnering with a policy-centered coalition was that students had an audience of lawmakers and local activists who saw students' unabashed opinions about their city. Two student comments:

> It's really irritating. Every store round my way be right next to each other. It ain't right. It infects the community more than you think it do. If you see and look and pay attention it's kind of setting us up for failure.
>
> – *Amira, 14*

> What I would do is move it. I wouldn't let it stay in a child's neighborhood because a child will go in there for like chips, juice, and then, as they get older, they're gonna want liquor. Then they're going to pass it down to their children.
>
> – *Michael, 14*

The event garnered attention of some city council members aligned with BGNC's initiative. Consequently, the exhibit traveled to City Hall in September 2016. Although the majority of that year's students matriculated to high school, we rallied to keep as many active in the policy efforts. A small group of students were guests on a local radio program. A few returned to give testimony at hearings regarding the coalition's legislation. Others gave speeches and personally curated the exhibit at a public reception in City Hall's rotunda. Unfortunately, the council did not pass the plan to better manage the city's liquor outlets.

Since the "Liquor Store Stories" event, we are fully committed to use youth voice and design to promote policy change around alcohol in Baltimore. In October, we received a new group of middle schoolers from St. James and Johns. We have started this year with capacity building around environmental and structural change to impact underage drinking.

We have already done the second-annual liquor store tour. This time, we saw two liquor stores to expose how alcohol outlets vary by neighborhood. The first was in the Oliver community. According to the Baltimore Neighborhoods Indicators Alliance (BNIA) the median household income of the Greenmount East neighborhood (which includes Oliver) is $23,276. From census data compiled by BNIA, approximately 96 percent of its residents are black. Unemployment is 30 percent. Its sustainability demographics list the neighborhood's "rate of dirty streets and alleys reports per 1,000 residents" as 125.5. Eleven trees were planted (BNIA 2014). At this liquor store, students reported seeing an abundance of street litter, bullet shells, vacant houses nearby, people hanging out near the store. The exterior is completely brick without windows.

We then traveled to 1.3 miles west to the second liquor store located within BNIA's Midtown designation. This neighborhood is racially diverse with more than 50 percent white residents. Thirty-two percent are black, 7.8 percent are Asian and 3.9 percent identify as Hispanic. The median income is $38,866. Unemployment is 7.2 percent. Midtown's "rate of dirty streets and alleys reports per 1,000 residents" is significantly lower at 37.9. There were 183 trees planted (BNIA 2014). This self-proclaimed wine shop and tasting room also sells bottled liquor. Students noticed there was no presence of litter, tree-lined streets, outside tables and seating for patrons.

As a result of what they saw and how they interpreted the differences, we have done a series of related design activities. The students have role played a community meeting featuring various personalities commonly present in community development efforts. The students also proto-typed a liquor store redesign and are in the process of determining a list of youth community demands to be visualized. It is the design team's hope that the students will be allowed to distribute it to liquor store owners.

Conclusion

Our design project with Baltimore youth highlights how citizens can have a leading role in reshaping their communities. Though they may not as immediately devastating as a hurricane, chronic public health issues expose gaps in a city's ecology and leaves citizens vulnerable in the event of natural or manmade catastrophe. Consequences from chronic stressors are interconnected and cause dysfunction within communities and individual citizens. Negative outcomes such as likelihood of engaging in high-risk behaviors like underage or binge drinking, higher likelihood of fatal violence, generational trauma, food deserts, environmental pollution compound, weaken sustainability and make resilience that much harder. However, there is hope. Design is an effective tool from which communities can be strengthened to combat imbalance. Practitioners can find guidance from human centered design philosophies and a continued discourse around empathy to develop inclusive, citizen-powered interventions for change.

References

100 Resilient Cities. (2017). 'What Is Urban Resilience?,' Rockefeller Foundation, accessed 24 January 2017, www.100resilientcities.org/resilience#/-_/

American Association of Colleges of Osteopathic Medicine. (2015). 'Climbing the Ladder: A Look at Sherry R. Arnstein,' accessed 26 January 2017, www.aacom.org/news-and-events/publications/iome/2015/july-august-2015/Arnstein-bio

Arnstein, S. R. (1969). A Ladder of Citizen Participation. *Journal of the American Institute of Planners*, 35(4), 216–224. http://doi.org/10.1080/01944366908977225

Baltimore Neighborhood Indicators Alliance. (2014). 'Vital Signs for Greenmount East and Midtown, Jacob France Institute,' accessed 24 January 2017, http://bniajfi.org/community/Greenmount%20East/http://bniajfi.org/community/Midtown/

Bouie, J. (2015). 'Where Black Lives Matter Began: Hurricane Katrina Exposed Our Nation's Amazing Tolerance for Black Pain,' *Slate*, 23 August 2015, accessed 24 January 2017, www.slate.com/articles/news_and_politics/politics/2015/08/hurricane_katrina_10th_anniversary_how_the_black_lives_matter_movement_was.html

Center on Alcohol Marketing and Youth. (2006). 'African-American Youth and Alcohol Advertising,' *Johns Hopkins Bloomberg School of Public Health*, accessed 26 January 2017, www.camy.org/resources/fact-sheets/african-american-youth-and-alcohol-advertising/

Freire, P. (1993). Chapter 2. *Pedagogy of the Oppressed*, [online] p.1, accessed 22 November 2016, http://faculty.webster.edu/corbetre/philosophy/education/freire/freire-2.html

History. (2015). 'Hurricane Katrina: Before the Storm, A+E Networks Digital,' accessed 25 January 2017, www.history.com/topics/hurricane-katrina

Kieffer, C. H. (1984). Citizen Empowerment. *Prevention in Human Services*, 3(2–3), 9–36. http://doi.org/10.1300/j293v03n02_03

Owens, D. (2015). 'Baltimore Takes Aim at Liquor Stores After Freddie Gray Riots,' *Business Insider*, 15 June 2015, accessed November 2017, www.businessinsider.com/r-baltimore-takes-aim-at-liquor-stores-after-freddie-gray-riots-2015-6

Papanek, V. (1971). *Design for the Real World Human Ecology and Social Change*. Chicago, IL: Academy Chicago Publ.

Pietila, A. (2010). *Not in My Neighborhood*. 1st ed. Chicago, IL: Ivan R. Dee.

Zolli, A. (2012). Learning to Bounce Back: Forget Sustainability. It's About Resilience. *New York Times*, 2 November 2012, accessed January 2017, www.nytimes.com/2012/11/03/opinion/forget-sustainability-its-about-resilience.html

33

BIOMIMICRY
Nature inspiring design

Denise K. DeLuca

The spiraling shell of the nautilus reflects one of nature's most graceful geometries, but it also represents one of nature's many sustainable design solutions. In addition to being made from only locally available and abundant resources, using water-based earth-friendly chemistry and self-assembly, the nautilus shell is cleverly designed to allow for infinite and proportional growth. Honeycombs, made outdoors with no factories or machines or computers, are perfectly formed, optimally fit for purpose, adaptable, and completely biodegradable. Peacock feathers are not only iridescently colorful, they are lightweight, waterproof, self-repairing, and beneficial for the environment at the end of their useful life. Spider silk is so delicate you can hardly see it, yet is many times stronger, weight for weight, than steel, and to the spider, it is edible. The Namibian beetle can collect drinking water from the air in a place where it never rains. Lichens leverage synergies to create life on bare rock.

Nature has been evolving sustainable design solutions on Earth for more than 3 billion years. Over this time, the collection of organisms that make up life on Earth has expanded from just one species to the estimated 5 million different species that exist today. However, these billions of years of trial-and-error have also resulted in a 99.9 percent failure rate. Only one-tenth of 1 percent of species that have ever lived on Earth are still alive today. This suggests that nature has very high quality control standards, and that the species and ecosystems present today embed highly effective strategies for sustainability. If we can discover what these strategies are and then emulate them in our designs, the result will be sustainable design solutions. This is the goal of biomimicry.

What is biomimicry?

Biomimicry is the practice of emulating nature's strategies to create products, processes, and policies that are well adapted to life on earth over the long haul. It is the practice of learning how nature performs the functions that we want our designs to perform, and then applying what we learn to create innovative and sustainable design solutions.

There are many familiar examples of biomimicry. Corrugation, the folding pattern seen inside corrugated cardboard and in corrugated roofing, emulates the sea scallop's strategy for getting more stiffness out of a piece of material, making it more resistant to bending without adding more mass. Velcro®, the ubiquitous hook-and-loop fastener, was inspired by the common burr. After repeatedly pulling burrs out of his dog's fur, Swiss engineer George de Mestral realized that burrs represent a fantastic dry reuseable adhesive. The sharkskin swimsuit used by Michael Phelps during his 2004 Olympic victories (*Science in the News*) has a surface that is not smooth but rather covered with scales patterned after the scale-like denticles found on a shark (Smithsonian National Museum of Natural History, 2015).

Janine Benyus popularized the term "biomimicry" for her book *Biomimicry, Innovation Inspired by Nature*. Her book is a collection of stories about scientists, engineers, designers, and inventors who were discovering functional strategies in nature, and finding ways to turn those strategies into innovative products and processes. While doing research for this book, Benyus saw something far more important than a set of new and innovative technologies. She recognized that this approach to design represented an entirely new way of looking at nature, as well as the role that our technologies should play in the natural world. She realized that all of nature's design solutions are sustainable, whereas so many human-generated designs are not. She proposed that we could design "sustainable solutions to human challenges by emulating nature's time-tested patterns and strategies" (Biomimicry Institute, 2015a).

Biomimicry compared to conventional design

Conventional design practices and decisions often set off a cascade of conventional sourcing, manufacturing, distribution, use, and disposal practices that are environmentally destructive.

Conventional manufacturing, for example, tends to rely on environmentally damaging "heat, beat, and treat" processes to achieve design performance specifications. "Heat" refers to the reliance on high temperature manufacturing processes, which in turn rely on the burning of fossil fuels. "Beat" refers to the reliance on mechanical energy, such as pounding, rolling, cutting, and riveting. "Treat" refers to the use or addition of often toxic chemicals. By contrast, nature's "manufacturing" processes take place under ambient temperatures and pressures, and use self-assembly, water-based chemistry, and locally available and abundant materials.

Conventional design also tends to rely on an environmentally damaging model that Annie Leonard (creator of *The Story of Stuff*) calls "Take, Make, and Waste." "Take" refers to relying on raw materials taken from nature, even if they are limited and the taking results in environmental destruction. "Make" refers to the conventional "heat, beat, and treat" manufacturing. And "waste" refers to designing for disposal in landfills. It is a linear, one-way flow of resources, with damage to nature being done at each step. By contrast, nature uses materials that are locally available and abundant, and recycles everything in endless self-organizing systems where waste from one process becomes food for another.

In addition to relying on "heat, beat, and treat" and "take, make, and waste," human designs tend to rely on simple geometries, such as straight lines, right angles, and circles. There are obvious advantages to this approach in the design process; however, it does not always lead to the most efficient or effective design solutions. By contrast, nature creates forms to fit functions, growing products into the desired shapes, rather than relying on cutting and assembling.

Building materials

Conventional cement production is among the top industrial CO_2 emitters. That is because in conventional cement production, CO_2 is released in the burning of fossil fuels as well as in the thermal decomposition process used to transform limestone into cement. By contrast, most of life on Earth uses abundant carbon molecules (often from CO_2) to build its materials and tissues. Plants use CO_2 from the atmosphere to grow leaves, stems and other parts. Marine organisms make seashells using calcium and carbonate ions found in seawater. Inspired by nature's use of abundant carbon sources, a company called Calera uses waste CO_2 gas emitted from smokestacks and seawater to produce a calcium carbonate ($CaCO_3$) based cement, which is then made into "green concrete" and other building materials, thereby permanently sequestering the CO_2 (Calera, 2016).

Most mass-produced carpeting is made from petroleum products and manufactured into large rolls. Although efficient at the manufacturing end, carpeting is bulky to handle at waste disposal facilities and slow to decompose in landfills, yet is made from materials that are completely recyclable. Each year, about 5 billion pounds of carpet ends up in U.S. landfills, and 70 percent of that carpet is thrown out for reasons other than wear and tear. Globally, most carpeting is disposed of via incineration. A company called Interface manufactures carpet tiles (rather than large rolls) that are designed to emulate the pattern, movement, and lifecycle of leaves on a forest floor. These tiles can be installed in any direction, and reduce installation waste. When damaged, individual tiles can be removed and replaced with any tile from the same lot, rather than replacing the entire carpet. Tiles that are removed can be sent back to Interface where they are recycled into new carpet tiles. The design process Interface used to create the tiles is presented later in this chapter.

Energy

After spending years studying flow patterns in the natural world, Australian inventor Jay Harman realized that "Nature never moves in a straight line, it tends to flow in a spiraling path." Harman is not the first to discover this phenomenon; however, he is the first to design modern fluid moving devices based on nature's spiral geometry. Based on his designs, he founded a company called PAX Water Technologies (a subsidiary of PAX Scientific) to develop and market energy-efficient mixing systems for potable water storage tanks. According to PAX, their Lily Impeller (so named because of its resemblance to the Calla Lily flower), the core of the PAX Water Mixer, "replicates nature's spiral flow pattern to significantly improve the performance and energy usage of mixing water storage tanks. While the Lily is only 21 cm tall, it is capable of circulating millions of gallons of water with the same energy footprint as three 100-watt light bulbs." The energy savings in this application is substantial; however, the far greater potential of this nature-inspired design becomes clear when you consider that most of our energy-consuming designs either move fluid (liquid or gas) or move through fluid.

Water and nutrients

With over 50 percent of the world's population now concentrated in urban areas, the ability to collect and treat wastewater becomes increasingly important; however, modern wastewater infrastructure is designed based in the linear one-way "take, make, and waste" model. Nutrients are removed from farmland in the form of food, processed and transported hundreds or even thousands of miles to cities, and then, after consumption and digestion, human waste ends up in landfills and in waterways, far from the original source. In addition to the waste causing surface and ground water pollution, taking food off the land without returning any of the organic matter reflects a process called "nutrient stripping."

The Living Machine, originally created by John Todd, cleans wastewater onsite by emulating the functional principles and processes of wetland ecosystems. Nutrients are taken up by bacteria and plants, which also clean the air and provide beauty, leaving the water clean enough for onsite reuse.

Built environment

Buildings consume 20–50 percent of global energy production, and are responsible for 30–50 percent of all CO_2 emissions. With increasing population and urbanization, the need for more sustainable design in the built environment is clearly pressing. Fortunately, an increasing number of architects, engineers, and interior designers are exploring and applying biomimicry. The Bullitt Center in Seattle, Washington (USA) is considered the greenest commercial building in the world. Rather than seeking to simply "do less bad," the goal in designing the Bullitt Center was to show what was possible in sustainable building design. To do that, they looked to nature for sustainable strategies and solutions. Embedding 17 integrated sustainability strategies, most of which are bio-inspired, this building has managed to achieve net-positive energy and water. In addition to emulating nature's strategies for solar energy, rainwater collection, and composting toilets, the Bullitt Center leverages the free energy of tenants (by making stairs preferable to elevators, openable windows), myriad feedback loops (with sensor-driven HVAC and lighting systems), and the kinetic energy of the elevator.

Not all bio-inspired design is sustainable design

Nature has been inspiring design as long as design has existed; however, it should be noted not all biologically inspired design processes result in sustainable design. 'Biological engineering' is where the tools of engineering are applied to biological systems. The result is some form of biotechnology, technology made out of living tissues. The term "bionics" refers to technologies that attempt to copy or replace something biological with something technical, such as a wearable robotic arm. "Biomimetics" could also be called innovation inspired by nature; however, biomimetics does not have the explicit goal of sustainability or reconnecting people and nature. "Biomorphic designs" reflect shapes and forms found in nature, but don't necessarily function like nature. Here the goal is usually aesthetic rather than functionality or sustainability. "Biophilia" refers to our innate love of, and desire to connect with, other living things. Biophilic designs tap into and enhance our innate love of nature. The goal is a positive user experience, rather than emulating the functionality of nature. "Bio-utilization" and "bio-assisted" refer to designs that use, or are made from, something biological, such as bamboo flooring, green roofs, or fermented foods, like beer, that require the action of microorganisms.

How biomimicry can be used for sustainable design

Sustainable designers can use biomimicry in two different ways. One way is to use what are called Life's Principles as guiding design principles. The other way is to use the biomimicry design spiral to discover and emulate nature strategies.

Life's Principles

Recall that biomimicry is the practice of emulating nature's strategies to create products, processes, and policies that are well-adapted to life on earth over the long haul (The Biomimicry Institute, 2015b). These are the strategies have allowed life to exist and evolve for 4 billion years given the unique set of conditions that are present on earth. Conditions vary by location and over time; however, there are three conditions that are universal. One is that earth is in a state of dynamic nonequilibrium. Conditions on earth are constantly changing, often cyclically but not always predictably. Day follows night in a predictable fashion, but things like weather patterns, disease outbreaks, and droughts are far less predictable. On longer timescales changing conditions might be due to meteors hitting the earth, ice ages, and now human-induced climate change. Another universal condition is that earth is water based. About 71 percent of the earth's surface is covered by water. Not surprisingly, water is the most abundant molecule found in living things. The third condition is that earth is subject to limits and boundaries. With the exception of sunlight, available resources are limited to what we can access in earth's very thin crust and atmosphere. Even sunlight reaching the earth is limited. We're also bound by gravity.

Scientists have been working for years to unlock nature's secrets of sustainability – how life has sustained on Earth for 4 billion years earth given these three basic conditions Biomimicry practitioners have studied, compiled, and distilled scientific research to produce a list of nature's rules for sustainability. The first version of this list, now known as "Life's Principles," can be found in Janine Benyus's book (Benyus, 1997):

> Nature runs on sunlight.
> Nature uses only the energy it needs.
> Nature fits form to function.
> Nature recycles everything.
> Nature rewards cooperation.
> Nature banks on diversity.
> Nature demands local expertise.
> Nature curbs excesses from within.
> Nature taps the power of limits.

Since that time, "Life's Principles" has been expanded by Benyus's biomimicry consultancy, Biomimicry 3.8, and published as a set of 20 strategies organized into six main principles. For ease of understanding, however, we can discuss these strategies and ideas as they relate to two main categories: (1) life adapts and evolves and (2) life creates conditions for life.

Life adapts and evolves

Giraffes evolved over time to have long necks so that they could eat leaves that shorter animals could not reach. Polar bears evolved to have white fur so they could be camouflaged while stalking prey in the snow. Many wild and domestic animals grow thicker coats for the winter and shed them again in the spring, adapting to changing seasonal temperatures. All living things need to be able to adapt in the short term, and evolve in the long term, because conditions on earth are always changing; yet there are limits and boundaries. One way life adapts and evolves is by being locally attuned and responsive. Living things embed and participate in myriad feedback loops that allow them to constantly sense what is going on in and around them, respond and learn accordingly, and share information back to the systems in which they live. This works in real time as well as over time. Another way is by being resourceful and opportunistic. Life makes the most of whatever resources are locally available and abundant, leverages shapes and information, and relies on free energy and cyclic processes. And life builds resilience by embedding redundancies, fostering diversity, and decentralizing critical functions. Just as living things need to be able to adapt and evolve, sustainable design should be able to adapt and evolve in response to short-term and long-term changes.

Life creates conditions conducive to life

Don't foul your own nest; don't shoot holes in your own boat; don't throw stones in a glass house. These well-known words of wisdom suggest that we shouldn't do things that would threaten our own health and welfare, in other words, we should seek to create conditions conducive to living. Organisms in nature create conditions conducive to both their own life as well as the lives of others because all living things are part of interconnected and interdependent systems (ecosystems); systems that have to exist within limits and boundaries, and in a water based environment. If life did not create conditions conducive to life, the whole system would eventually collapse. Nature optimizes across systems and over time, rather than statically maximizing or minimizing individual features or functions. Nature's designs are multifunctional; each strategy contributes to more than one function, and each function is performed using more than one strategy. Nature also avoids the superfluous; nature's forms emerge to perform needed functions (form follows function). Nature synergizes and self-organizes and self-assembles. Manufacturing is done using life-friendly, water-based chemistry. Everything recycles and can be recycled. Just as life creates conditions conducive to life, sustainable designs should create conditions that allow life in nature to survive and thrive.

Example of using Life's Principles for sustainable design

The designers behind the Sahara Forest Project (SFP) set out to generate renewable energy, produce fresh water, and grow food in the desert while also reversing desertification. To achieve these ambitious goals, they used "ecosystem principles" (their version of Life's Principles) as their guiding design principles. First, SFP designers took advantage of what is locally available and abundant – sunshine and seawater. Then, they created synergies among a set of existing technologies (including salt-water-cooled greenhouses and concentrated solar power) optimized to make a whole that was more economical than the sum of its parts. Instead of damaging the local environment, the project creates conditions conducive to life, both for people (energy and food) and for nature (revegetation). SFP is also designed to be adaptable to changing demands (e.g. more food vs. more energy) and to different locations (Sahara Forest Project, n.d.).

The Biomimicry Design Spiral

Another way sustainable designers can use biomimicry is by following the Biomimicry Design Spiral – a step-by-step process for turning nature's strategies into innovative and sustainable design solutions. The Biomimicry Design Spiral was first conceived in 2005 by Carl Hastrich, an industrial designer who was one of a cluster of devoted individuals that we can thank for building the foundations for biomimicry as we know it today. Hastrich took a standard design process, added the unique steps needed for biomimicry, and then, emulating one of nature's pervasive strategies, he turned the process into a spiral. The six steps in the Biomimcry Design Spiral are identify, translate, discover, abstract, emulate, and evaluate (see Figure 33.1).

When starting with a design challenge, the first step is to **identify** the functions that the design needs to perform. These functions are then **translated** into words or terms that makes sense in the biological world. The next step is to **discover** strategies, or combinations of strategies, that nature uses to accomplish each of the functions. In the **abstract** step, the biological strategies are described in terminology appropriate to the design profession. The **emulate** step is where one or more of the abstracted design strategies are used as the basis for a design solution. The last step is to **evaluate** the design solution against Life's Principles and the initial design goals, as well as strategizing how to best proceed with the next "lap" or set of laps around the spiral.

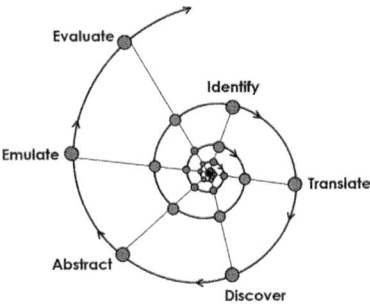

Figure 33.1 The Biomimicry Design Spiral.
Adapted from Carl Hastrich (2005) via DeLuca, Denise. "The power of the Biomimicry Design Spiral."
[weblog] Biomimicry Institute. June 14 2016, https://biomimicry.org/biomimicry-design-spiral/

Identify

A design brief provides a description of the desired solution space – *what* is to be designed. In the identify step, the designer determines the *functions* that the design needs to perform – what the design need to *do*. The deliverable for this step is a list of basic functions, which take the form of verbs or verb phrases (rather than nouns). For example, if the design brief is for a dentist chair, the designer must determine all the things that the dentist chair needs to do. This starts with the most obvious functions (e.g. provide a place to sit), then continues with more, and more basic, functions (e.g. keep patient in fixed location, allow patient to be faced different directions and positions, keep patient comfortable, resist liquids). This step can be facilitated by asking "why?" for each function (e.g. why does the patient need to be kept in fixed position?), as the answers can lead to even more and more basic functions (e.g. stay put). The identify step is required to allow the designer to proceed in the spiral process; however, it also helps the designer question and reveal hidden assumptions about the nature of the solution (e.g. is a "chair" the best way to perform these functions?) and open up thinking.

Translate

Before being able to discover nature's strategies, the list functions may need to be translated into terms that make sense in the biological world. It doesn't make sense to ask "how would nature keep a patient comfortable in a dental chair during a long appointment?"; however, it does make sense to ask "how does nature cushion" or "how does nature protect against compressive forces." The translate step can be facilitated by exploring the functional terminology presented in the Biomimicry Taxonomy, which is a classification system that categorizes the different ways that organisms and natural systems meet functional challenges (The Biomimicry Institute, 2015b).

Discover

In this step, the designer seeks to discover nature's strategies for performing the list of functions that have been identified and, if necessary, translated. This is where the designer "asks nature." The deliverable for the discover step is a list of different strategies that nature uses to perform each of the functions identified. It is helpful to focus on just one or two functions with each "lap" around the design spiral. Nature's strategies can take the form of materials, shapes, processes, and/or systems.

Note that nature usually performs a given function using a combination of strategies, and each strategy contributes to more than one function. For example, the structural support of a plant is provided by the stem, the veins, the leaf material, and by hydraulic pressure. The veins and stem also serve as the plant's resource and energy distribution system, while the leaf material also performs the functions of energy collection and transformation. When one strategy is discovered, look for others that may be contributing to or even critical to accomplishing that function. In addition, look for other functions that the strategy might be performing or contributing to. This is one way that nature can do more with less, a key to sustainable design. For non-biologists, the process of exploring and discovering nature's strategies for performing functions can begin with something as simple as going for walk outside, looking in the kitchen, or even in the mirror. Consider how a pinecone, a banana, or your own hand performs the functions that you need your design to perform.

Another way to discover strategies is by using the Biomimicry Institute's web-based portal called AskNature, found at AskNature.org (The Biomimicry Institute, 2016a). There you can type a function into the search bar provided, or explore the database using the functional terms listed in the Biomimicry Taxonomy. Following the dentist chair example, a search under "cushion" provides a dozen different strategies that organisms use for providing cushioning. One strategy comes from the spittle bug, who creates a froth of bubbles for protection, as well as for insulation. More specifically,

> The bubbles self-cushion when packed in an array and naturally leave little air amongst them. This is because nature's bubbles join according to three principles of soap bubble geometry. First, a compound bubble consists of flat or smoothly curved surfaces joined together. Second, the surfaces meet in only two ways: either three surfaces merge along a curve (edge), or six surfaces at a vertex. Third, when surfaces come together at a curve, or curves and surfaces at a point, they do so at equal angles.
>
> *(The Biomimicry Institute, 2016c)*

Other places to discover strategies include facilities such as zoos, aquariums, and botanical gardens; media such as the Discovery Channel; nature and biology books; scientific journals, including those devoted to biomimetics (e.g. *The Journal of Bionic Engineering*); and of course Internet search engines. To dig deeper, it is very helpful (and sometimes required) to consult with a biologist, especially one trained in bio-inspired design, and/or in the subject area of the discovered strategies.

To increase the number of variety of strategies, it can be helpful to look for other organisms that perform a similar function, perform the opposite function (e.g. make something very uncomfortable), that perform the function in extreme conditions (e.g. cushion in very uncomfortable places), or for whom that function is critical to existence (e.g. cushion or protect something that is very fragile).

In the discover step, the goal is to collect numerous and diverse strategies for each function (which may take several laps around the spiral). As with brainstorming processes, all strategies are considered potentially good strategies at this point. Exploring these strategies will not only provide needed information, it may give the designer entirely new ideas for how the solution could be addressed.

Abstract

It is likely that the descriptions of the biological strategies will need to be reverse engineered and then rewritten so that they are useable to other design professionals that are not familiar with biology or biomimicry. One way to do this is by simply replacing all biological terms and references in the description with technical terms, perhaps drawn from the design brief. The spittle bug strategy could be abstracted as: "The chair would include a flexible layer of frothy bubbles that can move relative to one another and in response to patient movements, following the three principles of soap bubble geometry." It also can be helpful to rewrite the strategy in different ways, focusing on different aspects of the strategy. As with most design, it is very helpful to use diagrams to visually describe the strategies.

Note that many of nature's functional strategies are not well understood; however, they can still be used metaphorically, or to spark new ideas. As with the discover step, abstracting the strategies may generate entirely new thinking around how the design or design solution might be approached.

The level of detail needed at this point depends on the nature of the design. For the first few laps around the design spiral, it is recommended to keep strategies high level and simple, only digging in deeper as needed.

Emulate

Once a variety of functional strategies have been collected, they can be used to create a design solution. If numerous and/or a diversity of strategies have been collected, it is helpful to first organize them in some way. It is likely that categories of strategy types or other patterns will emerge. For example, strategies to cushion might fall under categories described as "layer between patient and structure," "supporting structure," "eliminate source of discomfort." The designer may choose to focus on one strategy from each category, or focus on one category type. Recall that nature typically uses a combination of strategies to perform any given function, and each strategy typically performs or contributes to more than one function.

At this point, the designer proceeds using the tools, skills, and processes of their profession.

For the first few laps around the design spiral, the design solutions generated in this step are kept high level and conceptual, allowing room for new ideas in the evaluate step and likely pivoting during subsequent laps.

Evaluate

As with any design process, the design solution needs to be evaluated against the goals and specifications given in the design brief. Note, however, that the biomimicry design process can yield solutions that are radically different from what may have been originally envisioned.

In the biomimicry process, the design is also evaluated against Life's Principles. It is helpful to begin by considering the many ways that the design is reflecting Life's Principles, then explore how it is not. Evaluating against Life's Principles is not a checklist. It is important to explore and understand how the design is and is not reflecting each principle, and why that principle is important in context and under earth's operating conditions. This step will not only help provide ideas for improving the sustainability of the design, like the other steps it may provide entirely new ideas for approaching the design solution.

Before moving on to the next lap, it is wise to review all of the information and new ideas that were generated in the previous lap or set of laps, then decide how to most strategically move ahead.

Next lap(s)

A designer needs to take many laps around the design spiral, starting with very quick laps to begin to understand the range of bio-inspired design solutions that might be possible, which look most promising (or exciting or sustainable, etc.), and which might be viable given the constraints of your design process or brief.

Example of using the Biomimcry Design Spiral for sustainable design

Ray Anderson, founder of Interface carpet, recognized that his carpeting, manufacturing processes, and carpet disposal options were not sustainable, and decided he wanted to change that. Interface chose to use the Biomimicry Design Spiral to design a more sustainable product.

They began by identifying and translating the functions that the carpet needed to perform. They began with the most obvious function: cover the subfloor. Digging deeper, they identified additional functions including providing cushioning, visual pleasure, and thermal and sound insulation.

To explore potential biological strategies to perform these functions, they went for a walk in the woods. First they discovered that the forest floor was covered with a layer of leaves, and that the overall effect was beautiful, biophilic. Then they observed that there were numerous leaves and that they were randomly distributed. They also noted that all the leaves were very similar (from a distance they all looked the same), yet each one was unique. When the wind blew and redistributed the leaves, the overall look of the forest floor remained the same, even though the leaves were in different locations and positions. Digging deeper (literally) they discovered that the leaves decayed with time, which served to enrich the soil that supported the trees that grew the leaves in the first place. Looking at the bigger landscape, they noticed that other areas had different kinds of "floor coverings" (e.g. pasture grass, beach sand, and bare soil), that were beautiful on their own while also contributing to the beauty of the overall scene.

The first strategies they abstracted from these discoveries included "modularization" and "randomization." Emulating these strategies resulted in the design of individual carpet tiles (rather than large carpet rolls), each of which was unique yet very similar to others in the same lot.

When evaluating the carpet tile concept against Life's Principles, they recognized that the tiles could be placed – and replaced – in random directions in locations on the floor. This not only makes it easier and faster to carpet the floor, but it also allowed for less carpet waste during installation. It also meant that when a portion of the carpet is damaged, only individual damaged tiles need to be replaced, rather than replacing the whole carpet, again reducing waste.

Interface realized that the tiles were easily and individually replaceable, but they would still be sent to the landfill. So they decided to use subsequent laps around the Design Spiral to make the tiles easily recyclable. They went on to develop a carpet tile take-back program and specialized recycling machines so that the tiles were not only recyclable, but made with recycled materials.

Using the Biomimicry Design Spiral resulted in not only a far more sustainable carpet design solution, but their top selling product. Inspired by both sustainability and profitability, Interface took many more laps around the Biomimicry Design Spiral. Some solutions that emerged included small adhesive pads that could be placed under the tiles where four corners meet, eliminating the need for toxic floor glues and facilitating laying and replacing carpet tiles. They also used their discoveries to drive biophilic designs, so that the floor covering of a building would contribute to occupant wellness. The flexibility of tiles, combined with other discoveries, also led to new "wild" floor covering patterns and design. Interface has continued to be a leader in sustainable and innovative product design by applying the principles and practices of biomimicry.

Conclusion

Conventional design practices and decisions often lead to a cascade of sourcing, manufacturing, distribution, use, and disposal practices that are environmentally destructive. By contrast, all of nature's design solutions lead to a cascade of continuous regeneration, to conditions that are conducive to life. Biomimicry allows designers to tap into nature's infinite portfolio of sustainable, and often beautiful, strategies and solutions to create products, processes, and policies that are "well-adapted to life on earth over the long haul" (The Biomimicry Institute, 2015a).

References

2030, A. (2015). *Why the Building Sector?* Retrieved May 16, 2016, from http://architecture2030.org/buildings_problem_why/

Administration, U. E. (2016). *International Energy Outlook 2016.*

Affairs, U. N. (2014). *World Urbanization Prospects, The 2014 Revision, Highlights.* The United Nations. Retrieved May 16, 2016, from https://esa.un.org/unpd/wup/Publications/Files/WUP2014-Highlights.pdf

Benyus, J. (1997). *Biomimicry: Innovation Inspired by Nature.* New York: HarperCollins.

Biomimicry 3.8. (n.d.). *Biomimicry Case Study Entropy(R): Non-Directional Carpet Tiles.* Retrieved May 16, 2016, from www.interfaceglobal.com/pdfs/Biomimicry_InterfaceFLOR_Case_Study-2.aspx

The Biomimicry Institute. (2015a). *biomimicry.org.* Retrieved May 16, 2016, from https://biomimicry.org/what-is-biomimicry/#.VzooY5ErJhE

The Biomimicry Institute. (2015b). *Function and Strategy.* Retrieved July 26, 2016, from http://toolbox.biomimicry.org/core-concepts/function-and-strategy/

The Biomimicry Institute. (2016a). *Ask Nature.* Retrieved July 26, 2016, from www.asknature.org/

The Biomimicry Institute. (2016b). *Microstructures Create Reversible Attachment: Dragonfly.* Retrieved July 2016, 2016, from www.asknature.org/strategy/1df0f2b33d166b85b3e9064197d8e71c

The Biomimicry Institute. (2016c). *Arrangement allows self cushioning.* Retrieved July 2016, 2016, from https://asknature.org/strategy/arrangement-allows-self-cushioning/#.WUAXAxPyvdQ

Browning, W. R. (2014). *14 Patterns of Biophilic Design: Improving Health & Well-Being in the Built Environment.* New York: Terrapin Bright Green.

Bullitt Foundation. (2013). *The Bullitt Center.* Retrieved May 16, 2016, from www.bullittcenter.org/

Calera. (2016). *Calera.* Retrieved May 16, 2016, from www.calera.com/

CARE. (2013, September 25). *Carpet Recycling Worldwide.* Retrieved August 11, 2016, from https://carpetrecovery.org/carpet-recycling-worldwide/

Carpet, C. Y. (2016). *Carpet and Landfill Statistics.* Retrieved May 16, 2016, from www.coloryourcarpet.com/Environment/Landfillstats2.html

Cavalier-Smith, T. (2006). Cell evolution and earth history: Stasis and revolution. *Philosophical Transactions of the Royal Society of London. Series B, 361*(1470), 969–1006.

Costello, M. M. (2013). Can we name earth's species before they go extinct? *Science, 25,* 413–416.

Effort, C. A. (2016). *Carpet Amercia Recovery Effort.* Retrieved May 2016, 2016, from https://carpetrecovery.org/about/faqs/

Harman, J. (2013). *The Shark's Paintbrush: Biomimicry and How Nature Is Inspiring Innovation.* Ashland: White Cloud Press.

Jones, D. L.-J. (2013). Nutrient stripping: The global disparity between food security and soil nutrient stocks. *Journal of Applied Ecology, 50,* 851–862.

Living Machine. (2012). *Living Machine® Technology.* Retrieved May 16, 2016, from http://livingmachines.com/About-Living-Machine.aspx

Muzio, E. (2010). *CBS News.* Retrieved May 16, 2016, from www.cbsnews.com/videos/a-practical-approach-to-innovation

Newman, M. (1997). A model of mass extinction. *Journal of Theeoretical Biology, 189,* 235–252.

Pax Water Technologies. (2016). *paxwater.com/biomimicry.* Retrieved May 16, 2016, from www.paxwater.com/biomimicry

Priggen, E. (Producer), Leonard, A. (Writer), and Fox, L. (Director). (2007). *The Story of Stuff* [Motion Picture]. USA.

Sahara Forest Project. (n.d.). Retrieved July 20, 2016, from http://saharaforestproject.com/

Science in the News, http://www.scienceinthenews.org.uk/contents/?article=8

Smithsonian National Museum of Natural History. (2015). *Biomimicry Shark Denticles.* Retrieved July 20, 2016, from Ocean Portal: http://ocean.si.edu/ocean-photos/biomimicry-shark-denticles

University of Florida Physical Plant Division. (2015). *Carpet.* Retrieved May 16, 2016, from www.ppd.ufl.edu/departments/ref_carpet_recycle.shtml

Velcro. (2016). *History of Velcro® Brand And George De Mestral.* Retrieved July 20, 2016, from www.velcro.com/about-us/history

Wilson, E. O. (1984). *Biophilia.* Cambridge: Harvard University Press.

World Floor Covering Association. (2015). *Carpet Terms.* Retrieved August 11, 2016, from www.wfca.org/Pages/Carpet-Terms.aspx

34

THE VALUE OF THE SHARING ECONOMY

Brhmie Balaram

The potential of the sharing economy

To cope with a population of over 8 billion by 2025, it is of increasing importance that we make better use of our planet's finite resource.

The 'sharing economy' promotes access to underused assets, which is a way of prolonging the life cycle of products and materials while also undermining the need for private ownership. As we consume in a more communal fashion, the hope is that our individual carbon footprints can be reduced through making the most of our idling resources.

The idea of 'unlocking idling capacity' has been popularised by Rachel Botsman in her book with Roo Rogers on 'collaborative consumption', or the sharing economy as we know it (Botsman and Rogers 2011). To illustrate this concept, Botsman uses the example of a power drill, arguing that this tool is used only 12 to 15 minutes in its lifetime and it would thus make more sense for us to rent a power drill than to own one. For those of us who already own a power drill, we could loan or rent out our power drills rather than leave them languishing in their toolboxes. In essence, the sharing economy is a way of achieving more sustainable consumption through transforming an individual's resource into a collective good.

Professor Arun Sundarajan of New York University (NYU), recently likened the idle capacity of cars being tapped into through platforms as akin to creating an equivalent of what a national train network would have been needed for in the past (Sundarajan 2015). He noted that the BlaBlaCar (a long-distance ridesharing platform) network carries more people every day than Amtrak, a national railroad service operating across the United States. The ridesharing platform may be both more economically and environmentally friendly because it undermines the need for greater investment in concrete and steel – the infrastructure already exists to support the transport of more people. We might view this as a positive externality for governments given that they often spend billions of public resources developing and maintaining rail networks within countries.

Research from the University of California Berkeley, for example, has found that for each car shared, between nine and 13 cars are taken off the road (Martin, Shaheen and Lidicker 2010). There are uncertainties, though, about easy access (i.e. to cars) driving up overall consumption. More evidence from Berkeley suggests that consumption only increases in the first year and subsequently tails off as consumers become more open to exploring other carbon-light options (such as cycling and walking as opposed to carsharing) (Shaheen, Cohen and Chung 2009). This study dates back to 2009, however, so more recent research is needed as these platforms expand in cities globally. In London, for example, concerns have been raised about increased traffic congestion from carsharing and related consequences for air pollution and the health of passersby, such as cyclists (Transport for London 2015).

Though we do need an economic system that is less dependent on extracting value from the earth, we should be realistic about the impact that the sharing economy will have in this regard. Changes in individual consumption are helpful, but are not a substitute for collective action, such as institutional divestment from fossil fuels.

The sharing economy holds promise as a more sustainable alternative to our current economic system, but we must be mindful of how it develops. Its evolution has been controversial, and if the sharing economy is to become embedded in our lives it's crucial we better understand how the sector is changing as well as its impact beyond the environment.

Defining the sharing economy

The sharing economy eludes easy definition. The term itself has become increasingly contested in recent years, particularly in the media as boundaries blur between different concepts describing similar phenomena.

At its simplest, the sharing economy is a socio-economic system in which we make the most of our underused human and physical resources – everything from our skills to our things. It involves a spectrum of activity, or 'shades of sharing', which means it encompasses local, grass-roots-funded initiatives, such as time banks and tool libraries, as well as global, venture-backed online platforms, such as Airbnb and Uber.[1]

The term 'sharing economy' can be perplexing, especially if the focus is on the nature of the exchange between individuals or organisations. This is where some commentators seem to first stumble when trying to understand it – exchange is not always for free as the term might suggest, but can also be for a fee (Botsman 2015). Moreover, the term is most useful for referring to a new system of creating value rather than for defining individual exchanges or transactions.

As further explained by Benita Matofska, founder of The People Who Share, a global campaign promoting the sharing economy, this system implies a different set of values to most activity in the traditional economy. When we share access to our human and physical resource directly with one another we are reflecting a cultural shift in how we want to live and work, reclaiming power from the institutions and corporations that typically mediate exchange. These values are expressed to various degrees through diverse business models.

Many a term has been coined to discern between business models in the sharing economy, but they are often presented as alternative ways of describing the system or sector, further confusing commentary.

Thus, the sharing economy is conflated with the 'collaborative economy', which emphasises the role that Internet technologies play in making connections between distributed groups of people, or with the 'access economy' because of the focus on reducing the need for ownership. To some, it is synonymous with the 'circular economy', which aims to make the most of products and materials, prolonging their life cycle in part through reuse, including gifting or sharing access.

The 'gig economy' and the 'on-demand economy' are the most recent additions to our vocabulary, increasingly being favoured as stand-ins when discussing the sharing economy, especially when referring to labour of TaskRabbit or Uber's nature (Roberts 2015). The terms are trying to capture the trend of jobs fragmenting into smaller, short-term gigs, sometimes completed instantly after requested on an online platform, such as a grocery delivery via InstaCart.

Matofska challenges the need to define gig work or on-demand labour as an entirely separate sector or economy of sorts. Though the current number of gig workers in the U.S. suggests she is right, size is not why she takes issue (Harris and Krueger 2015). Rather, she is keen for activities in the sharing economy to be recognised as varied, yet all enabling lifestyles that have potential to be positive for the environment and empowering for both consumers and workers.

For instance, there is a whole movement underpinning businesses in the sharing economy that adhere to a model of local, environmentally sustainable exchange. Since 2009, Shareable, a non-profit in the U.S., has been documenting the surge of social enterprises around the world that are representative of this mode of doing business. Neal Gorenflo, a cofounder of Shareable, believes that initiatives such as time banks and tool libraries truly embody the sharing economy, relying on people power and building social capital through peer-to-peer exchange of underused assets and labour. This is a marked departure from the traditional economy which depends on resource extraction and is indifferent to whether consumers and workers interact.

Online platforms in particular have enjoyed a meteoric rise, yet there is a need to demystify their underlying business model.

To be clear, there are two ways sharing economy businesses (for profit or not) can scale – outwards and upwards. Scaling outwards is what we see when certain activities, such as coworking and bikesharing, spread through replication across cities and other localities rather than through the network of a single platform. Scaling upwards, conversely, is when a single network of activity is grown, normally under the control of a single business, and has the potential to thrive globally through the use of technology.

Although scale does not equate with impact, the fixation with growth (particularly economic) does have an undeniable impact, affecting everything from how investment decisions are made to how governments regulate. Through interrogating the sharing platform model, we can better understand how these businesses are able to scale upwards in their quest for growth.

Shared value creation

Sharing was a way of life well before Silicon Valley, but sharing on this scale has reached new heights through the proliferation of smartphones, apps for all our needs, and increasingly sophisticated algorithms for matching supply and demand.

Online platforms in particular have been instrumental in brokering the trade of spaces, skills, and commodities. What we should understand about online platforms is that they are not products. Though we cannot buy, consume, or sell them in the traditional sense, online platforms are inherently more valuable than products. As Marshall Van Alstyne of Boston University explains, online platforms are essentially conduits for third parties to connect through, enabling them to create communities that add value to the platform via the 'network effect' (Regalado 2014). The network effect is often observed in social media platforms wherein each new user of a network, such as Facebook or Twitter, increases the usefulness of the network for other users as well as its overall value.

Before the Internet era, network effects were primarily observed in telecommunications. However, there are key distinctions between telecommunication companies and online platforms. For one, the extent to which telecommunication companies are able to capitalise on the network effect to grow is restricted by costly infrastructure investments that online platforms do not have to make to the same degree. More importantly, the business of telecommunications is premised on the sale of products (i.e. phones), not on capturing value from the network of users created through the purchasing of these products.

Facebook illustrates the new business model made possible by online platforms. It is an online platform which connects over a billion users who communicate with one another through posts, photos, and event listings. Although the platform is free to use, Facebook makes its revenues through advertising and the data it collects on users so that advertisers are better able to target their messages. The more users Facebook has, the more beneficial it is as a network to other users, but also the more value the platform has for advertisers and thus as a business.

The Apple App Store is an example that Van Alstyne specifically uses to help analogise the tremendous value of online platforms, as well as to make clear that they rely on the value created by users to turn a profit. For every app that an individual develops and promotes through the App Store to sell or attract users, Apple takes a 30 percent cut even though Apple itself was not the innovator, but rather an intermediary. Online platforms do not create value themselves; they are dependent on their users doing so. When you can enable a community of users online, that community is also infinitely scalable, and thus infinitely valuable, because there needn't be a limit to numbers. For every user hosted there is little additional cost to the platform; moreover, the membership of a community is not necessarily bound by borders, depending on what is shared.

The key takeaway here should be that it is the users, whether consumers or workers, of these online platforms that share the charge of creating value. In the sharing economy, this means that users create value together through capitalising on their individual assets or resources, typically using online platforms to enable access to goods and services. This is known as shared value creation.

This is reminiscent of the concept of shared value, which Michael E. Porter and Mark R. Kramer use to communicate that there are connections between societal and economic progress (Power and Kramer 2011). However, Porter and Kramer are specifically advocating for a strategy of redefining capitalism through businesses adopting corporate social responsibility (CSR) as an integral part of their missions. Shared value creation flips this dynamic, emphasising that it is society or a community [of users] that has the power to orient the economy for the common good. The users, therefore, do not need to depend on the benevolence of businesses in order to realise social and economic benefit – they do it themselves.

When we think of the sharing economy it would be more useful to keep in mind **shared value creation** than debate the semantics of the word 'sharing'. Shared value creation helps us grasp why some ventures in the sector are estimated to be worth billions, given that value is not dependent on a finite product but on an infinite network. It also suggests that users, and in particular workers, deserve a fairer share in the distribution of the value they have created. However, at present, much of this value is still being captured by intermediaries – the platform providers.

Networked monopolies

An undeniable benefit of these platforms so far is that whereas they may be a long way off from embodying the commons, they have allowed us to experiment with alternative approaches to resource use, and in the process transition towards new ways of living, working and doing business. The technology of these platforms in particular has enabled a greater number of people to adapt to the idea of access over ownership. It is only through applying a different lens to the business model of these sharing platforms that we begin to understand how they can reach a point where it is possible for them to do us more harm than good.

Crowdsourcing monopoly power

While most start-ups may dream of one day making it big, the incentives are greater for sharing platforms. In fact, the predisposition of such platform providers is to scale up and preside over the markets they themselves create.

The legal scholar Tim Wu argues that the Internet trends towards monopolies because it is more efficient to go where everyone else is already (Ferenstein 2014). Similarly, we can say the same thing about sharing. Sharing is easier and more effective when you can access a specific marketplace – for example, accommodation or rides – through a single platform. This does not preclude other providers from existing; it simply means that one platform is likely to dominate market share by exploiting the network effect.

Harnessing the power of the network effect has become big business in our modern economy. According to Van Alstyne, traditional businesses are missing a trick by merely focusing on adding new features to products rather than imagining ways of enabling communities or network effects (Regalado 2014). This is because stand-alone products have a ceiling in terms of scale. Conversely, online platforms that draw on the crowd for their success have much more potential in terms of growth.

These platforms inherently depend on shared value creation for their success,[2] thus they may scale even at the expense of profit (as of writing, Uber is still in the red, as are other high-profile on-demand platforms including InstaCart, Postmates, and Handy); the logic being that money will follow once a mass movement is underway.

As discerned by Reid Hoffman, the cofounder of the largest online professional network, LinkedIn: "First-scaler advantage beats first-mover advantage." (Hoffman 2015) Based on his own observations as an entrepreneur, he explains: "Once a scale-up occupies the high ground in its ecosystem, the networks around it recognise its leadership, and talent and capital flood in." This strategy is self-reinforcing. Scale reassures and encourages venture capitalists to keep investing; Hoffman notes that rapidly expanding scale-ups are able to raise even more capital as a result of initial investments. In Uber's unique case, a steady flow of venture capital and its own ubiquity has enabled the platform to experiment with multiple offerings and potentially expand into other markets as well (i.e. food delivery with UberEATS, on-demand delivery for businesses with UberRUSH), despite minimal returns for investors at this stage. A final point from Hoffman drives the message home: "Most of the impact and value creation in Silicon Valley actually occurs after the start-up phase ends and the scale-up phase begins."

LinkedIn illustrates that there is a certain point when the network effect is more likely to keep on giving than to fade away. It has managed to achieve such scale that continued expansion of its user base is more probable than contraction; once users are part of a critical mass other competing platforms become less effective, and thus less attractive, as tools for connecting with your peers. This is in part because with platforms like LinkedIn, and even more so with online auction sites such as eBay, there is little point in doubling efforts for diminishing returns. QXL, eBay's U.K.-based rival, only survived for two years up until eBay expanded to the United Kingdom, giving users the option of joining a much bigger network for buyers and sellers.

What is unfolding is unprecedented. These are no ordinary monopolies that platforms are trending towards.[3] These are networked monopolies that entirely derive their value from their network of users rather than from producing a more easily replicable product or service. As with Facebook or LinkedIn, other platforms could technically compete, but it becomes difficult to offer users the same level of utility without being able to match the size of the network effect.

Unlike Facebook or LinkedIn, however, the networked monopolies of the sharing economy comprise two different kinds of users – consumers, but also largely workers of the platform as in the case of many gig and on-demand platforms. Many sharing platforms thus have a different relationship (and arguably, obligation) to their users than most other internet platforms given this interdependency based on labour.

Some may reason that these sharing platforms are *not* networked monopolies because they have viable competitors within niche stands of the overall homesharing and ridesharing markets for example. In the case of Airbnb, they are fielding competition from OneFineStay (upmarket homesharing), LoveHomeSwap (homeswapping) and HomeAway (vacation rentals), as well as facing off with the traditional hospitality industry. Uber similarly competes with Lyft ('community drivers') and BlaBlaCar (long distance ridesharing) in addition to the taxi industry and other private cars for hire.

The obvious counter to this is that given how many cities Airbnb and Uber now operate in globally, their overall market share is still higher than that of competing ridesharing companies and of some traditional industry players. Airbnb's bookings are predicted to triple in the next year, which means its current value of $25.5bn could soon surpass that of leading hotel chain, Hilton Worldwide (it is already worth more than Hyatt Hotels and Marriott International) (Mudallal 2015). Uber's impact on the taxi industry differs from city to city, but in San Francisco alone the use of taxis has dropped by 65 percent following Uber's arrival (Garber 2014).

However, market share is a narrow way of understanding and identifying monopolies. When we refer to networked monopolies we are actually stressing monopoly power.[4] As academics John Foster, Robert McChesney and R. Jamil Jonna have noted, it does not make contemporary sense to use the term 'monopoly' to only imply a market with a single seller or sole proprietorship; it is incredibly rare for monopolies to exist in the form dictated by the term's original meaning. Instead, they use monopoly to connote power in influencing the price, output and investment of an industry, as well as in limiting the entry of new competitors (Foster, McChesney and Jonna 2011). We see this with sharing platforms which wield the power of the crowd to exercise control over the market's terms and conditions (for example, barriers to entry).

It is entirely possible for networked monopolies to better serve the interests of their users, and their workers in particular. For example, we may see this in time with cooperative sharing platforms, which strive to ensure that their users capture most of the value they themselves generate. However, we should be cautious of concentrations of power even if they are in the form of useful, cooperative networks, especially since not all networked monopolies wield the power of the collective in the best interests of their users or wider society.

Considerations for designers

In this section, we interrogate the value that we create through our use of sharing platforms. This is done through highlighting trade-offs in value for consumers, workers at large, online and offline communities, and the state. Considering these trade-offs from each of these perspectives is an important starting point for anyone hoping to design for sustainable system change in the sharing economy.

Designing for consumers

Sustaining innovation has ultimately led to greater accessibility of goods and services that previously were prohibitively expensive and/or entailed the costs of private ownership. More choice is possible than ever before and control can be exercised in new ways over supply through simply posting requests for gig or on-demand workers to fulfil.

Yet, there are drawbacks to this innovation for consumers, especially in relation to the quality of products or services; in order to be hyper-affordable these are not necessarily on a par with established and leading competitors. In the sharing economy, this goes beyond quality at a superficial level to encompass safety and security. Whereas ratings and reviews are tools that platforms have introduced to reassure consumers, these are not foolproof; accidental fatalities have occurred in the absence of more rigorous mechanisms. There is no easy fix in sight given that platform providers do not want to be viewed as employers, and thus continually reinforce this by distancing themselves from the responsibilities that traditional businesses would take on in order to protect their workers or consumers.

In discussing his father's death (due to a faulty tree swing in the backyard of a home being shared), Zak Stone quoted the lawyer Jim Rosenfeld to explain how vouching for the safety of a property is not something that Airbnb and other platforms like it are necessarily prepared to do. Rosenfeld explains: "What [sharing economy start-ups] need to be in order to minimise liability is as passive a platform as possible. . . . The more they themselves are providing content and providing services the greater their risk of exposure. The more they're like a bulletin board or an old-fashioned matchmaking service the better off they are" (Stone 2015). This in turn places the burden of risk on consumers (especially as those who share, gig workers included, increasingly have options to protect their homes or cars, for example).

Agency over personal data is also an issue for users of these platforms. As more people participate in networks of sharing, and thus in scaling platforms, more data (possibly of a privacy-sensitive nature) is being generated for a small number of providers. Ownership over data is often the invisible price we pay when using these platforms.

However, some of those concerned about our data being concentrated among a few giants are experimenting with ways of supporting users to gain agency over their data. Third-party platform Traity, for example, allows more control over reputational data or capital based on ratings and reviews by enabling users to create 'reputation passports'. These passports can be used to move between multiple sharing platforms rather than locking users into the ones where they already have established a good name. This is more complicated for those who have poor ratings for various reasons, which we get into in the section on communities, and particularly for those whose ratings determine the extent to which they can participate with ease in the sharing economy as workers. In any case, the key to personal agency should not be contingent on whether we are comfortable with exploiting our own data for greater gains.

Designing for workers

The barriers for entering the sharing economy are either high or low depending on what you intend to share. The sharing economy allows us to monetise everything we own – our luxury handbags, our power tools, our cars, our homes, and so forth. The obvious point here is that we must first own assets to monetise if we are looking to share for a fee. For example, the barriers to entry to be an Airbnb host are not just high, but insurmountable for many.

The barriers to sharing skills are much lower than sharing assets. Makers selling craft products on Etsy face no additional barriers to those who are traditional skilled craft workers, and face lower barriers to entrepreneurship than they would in the offline economy. In other circumstances, the skills required are also lower than they would to be to gain employment with a traditional competitor. For instance, in London cab drivers must complete a four-year qualification to take 'The Knowledge' test, demonstrating that they intimately know their way around the city's streets; however, with the advent of GPS this test becomes less important, so there is little competitive edge in navigation over Uber drivers who have not taken the test.

Barriers to entry are in part lower because of an absence of regulation. Traditional industries argue that these newer platform businesses are not following the same rules they are subjected to, and thus that the playing field is not equal. These rules, for example, may relate to ensuring the health and safety of their workers and customers. This has knock-on consequences for workers in these industries who feel that their counterparts in newer platform businesses are cheating standards and in doing so hurting their ability to make a living.

Though risk may be better mitigated by the platforms themselves, some mediation may still be needed between consumers and workers. Price points may be satisfying consumers, but that alone is not reason enough to take an entirely hands-off approach to regulating. There are concerns from cab drivers that wages are being driven down overall by their competitors working for Uber.

For gig workers picking up low-skilled jobs, there are questions about whether they feel exploited; whereas some may place a premium on new freedoms and flexibility, we know from the filing of lawsuits that certainly some gig workers believe they are deserving of more compensation from platforms for their efforts. In an interview for *New York* magazine, Josh Felser, a venture investor at Freestyle Capital, hypothesises that the contentment of gig workers can be understood based on which category they fall into. He breaks this down as follows: "There's the control-your-hours contractor. That group seems to be very happy with where things are. There's the fulltime employee. And then there's the middle group – where they're acting like fulltime employees and being paid like contractors. That group is disenfranchised" (Roose 2014). If Felser is correct, more thought needs to be given to ways we can support full-time gig workers for platforms without penalising businesses to a point where they must close down as avenues for those looking to supplement their core incomes.

Though the solution may not be to classify these platforms as employers, another reason to explore a third way is because in the absence of assigning any legal responsibility to platforms (and in their active desire to shy away from it) there are no training and development opportunities for gig workers.[5] If we want a highly productive, high-growth economy, gig workers cannot stagnate in low-wage, insecure employment; whereas they may already be able to move laterally and try out different forms of work or learn new sets of skills they must be able to move up as well.

Designing for communities

The forging of greater trust between strangers has long been trumpeted as an achievement in the sharing economy. Trust is hailed as a cornerstone of transactions, technology being the other; the evolution of trust is thus as important to making peer-to-peer exchange at this magnitude possible.

However, there is a difference between trust and honesty. When we have two-way systems, a high rating is not necessarily indicative of whether you can trust someone; rather, it might reflect our fear of being restricted in our usage of sharing platforms. Those feeling apprehensive about this may tend to give out scores higher than deserved in the hopes of a favourable rating in return; or, they may abstain from the review process altogether to avoid the risk of retaliation.

Ratings and reviews can also be problematic when livelihoods suddenly depend on it. If scored unfairly by even a handful of consumers, that can be enough to diminish a worker's appeal on platforms or warrant dismissal from the provider. In traditional workplaces, there can be an investigation or mediation before a dismissal is ruled on, but there is not always this level of care on platforms. Moreover, when we are scored poorly under subjective criteria, how does this affect our well-being?

In another example of how the subjectivity of the system can have material (and possibly emotional) consequences for some, Benjamin Edelman and Michael Luca, two Harvard

Business School professors, found evidence of racial discrimination against black hosts on Airbnb. Their first study, based on 3,500 listings in New York City, showed that non-black hosts earned 12 percent more than black hosts for the equivalent rental (Edelman and Luca 2014). Additionally, black hosts are subjected to greater price penalties than non-black hosts for having a poor location score. In a second study by the pair and Dan Svirsky in 2015, it was revealed that requests from guests with distinctively African American names are roughly 16 percent less likely to be accepted than identical guests with distinctively white names (Edelman, Luca and Svirsky 2015).

Another recent study, this time from Harvard students, reveals that Asian hosts on average earn $90 less (or 20 percent less) per week than white hosts for similar one-bedroom rentals in Oakland and Berkeley, California (Wang, Xi and Gilheany 2015). In this study, the differential actually increases with the number of bedrooms and costs associated with upgrades.

Airbnb has previously contested Edelman and Luca's findings (although they are now in talks with the two about addressing discrimination) (Sifferlin 2014), but the overall point that the authors are making is that there can be "important unintended consequence[s] of a seemingly-routine mechanism for building trust" (Edelman and Luca 2014). There is a risk that social injustices perpetuated offline will be reproduced in online communities. After all, technology is not neutral; it is built and operated by people and therefore can be compromised by human biases.

As platforms scale, transactions can also begin to feel more commercial again as the community expands to include some who do not share in the original ethos. It can be difficult to nurture the social at scale, especially if that is not recognised by platform providers as an objective, but rather as an effect.

Moreover, there are concerns that online communities have real consequences for offline communities. Some offline communities feel adversely impacted by sharing activities in their neighbourhoods as revealed by opposition to homesharing in San Francisco. Whereas these platforms may not be the cause of crises in communities, they may feel like an aggravator, especially if not enough is being done by traditional institutions to address the real roots of anxiety.

Designing for the state

The sharing economy could be a boon for states in terms of jobs and taxes, but also in social and environmental value. There are new opportunities for workers and new revenues to draw from for the state's coffers; new communities are being created and new mindsets are being inspired by efforts to make better use of our existing resource.

Realising some of these benefits, such as more tax revenue, has been difficult, however, given that the economic activity is challenging to monitor and regulate. Taking the example of homesharing, governments have tried to strike a balance between encouraging this sort of activity and imposing limits.

Tax agents such the Internal Revenue Service (IRS) in the United States have little at their disposal to hold traders or workers on sharing platforms to account for repayment. Arguably, this is no different from their relationship with the self-employed (specifically freelancers rather than small business owners), but in part the issue with the sharing economy is that many users may not self-identify as an independent contractor or understand their tax obligations in this system, particularly if they are using these services to supplement their main income. In the early years of sharing economy growth, there may be more work required to educate users about the responsibilities that come with participating on these platforms. This is an especially dire need if transactions on sharing platforms are replacing those of a traditional nature (such as hotel bookings or taxi rides) since this implies there is actually a net loss of tax revenue.

In addition to taxes, governments oversee the protection of consumers and workers in markets. In the sharing economy, however, platforms have argued against being subjected to the same rules and regulations as traditional industries on the grounds that demanding the same level of scrutiny or obligation would drive many of them out of business. These sorts of asset-light, people-light business models that platforms assume keep their costs very low; this in turn translates into savings for customers, or from the perspective of traditional businesses allows platforms to undercut them.

Whereas it may seem unjust that sharing platforms can circumvent regulations that traditional business must adhere to, these platforms defend limited government intervention on the basis of self-regulating mechanisms that they have introduced to address concerns about safety and security. Although there are still some issues with these systems as discussed earlier, they represent a new frontier for businesses in terms of finding a new way to meet standards (of safety) that governments would typically try to account for (i.e. through monitoring or inspection bodies). The market itself is innovating so that the role of government becomes redundant in certain processes.

This level of innovation extends to support systems for workers that governments or traditional employers have thus far been expected to provide. In the United States, where there is a less robust welfare state, third-party platforms and insurers have emerged to offer benefits and coverage for gig workers. The workers themselves do not bear the full brunt of this shift; a model is being trialled where sharing economy businesses contribute to a pot that can be accessed by workers in times of need.

Others have called on the state to rethink the ways in which welfare is distributed. For example, Berkeley University professor Robert Reich has proposed a move towards offering income insurance rather than unemployment insurance (Reich 2015). He explains that if a gig worker's monthly income dips below 50 percent of the average income he or she has received from all the jobs taken over the preceding five years, income insurance would entitle the person to be in automatic receipt of half the difference in income for up to a year.

The state will continue to have an important role, but it is clear it must adapt to the changes occurring in the social and economic landscape. Third-party support frees up more government resources to spend on other essentials, such as a new system of welfare, house building, and/or assistance for traditional businesses interested in transitioning to sharing models. The speed at which sharing platforms are innovating, particularly as we move into the era of cooperative sharing platforms that operate in a decentralised manner (a few of which are originating on the Darknet) means that it will be increasingly difficult for the state to go about business as usual. They will not have the option of simply shutting down platform providers – others will simply pop up to take their place – or regulating in the same way that they have for decades.

Designing for the economy

Based on their own estimates, PwC predicts that global revenues of the sharing economy could go from $15bn [in 2014] to $330bn by 2025 (Hawksworth and Vaughan 2015). By 2025 the sharing economy will also have achieved parity with traditional industry in sectors such as holiday accommodation and ridesharing or car rental (Hawksworth and Vaughan 2015). The least developed sectors, such as P2P finance or crowdfunding and online staffing, could grow quickest of all, by 63 percent and 37 percent respectively according to PwC's 2025 projections.

There is enormous potential here for more new business models to emerge. While there will undoubtedly be more online platforms for sharing resources in new, more efficient ways, some corporates will adapt features of these platforms. Consumers and workers will also conceive of ways in which they might reap more value through building cooperative platforms that redistribute profit differently.

Though there is clearly an impetus for change, traditional industries, finance and banking included, are not yet on the brink of collapse. There is thus resistance to reform the old and there are impediments to developing the new. During this transitionary period, there may be shocks to the economy as businesses attempt to adjust and workers as well as shareholders are left vulnerable in the process.

The backdrop to all of this is growing inequality, which means that in the sharing economy some only consume while others only share. Ideally, those who share also consume and vice versa, particularly as the sector grows through maximising both supply and demand in tandem. In situations where exchange is not of a reciprocal nature there is concern that wider wealth and power imbalances are being reinforced between consumers and workers.

The deeper problem this relates to concerns the distribution of the revenues predicted by PwC. Transparency is needed about how much lines the pockets of those who oversee 'tech unicorns' in relation to the proportion shared with states globally in cities or countries of operation (i.e. through taxes), or moreover, with the users – particularly gig workers.

What the future holds for the sharing economy

If we were to analyse the direction of travel, cooperative models in the sharing economy are especially promising in terms of realising a more equitable future. However, we should also recognise that as these business models evolve we will adapt to them at different speeds, especially as we continue to experiment with what technology has made possible.

It is important to be realistic about the fact that diverse business models will likely coexist for some time. Although we cannot depend on traditional models for economic growth as environmental concerns loom, the smartphones we use to tap into our sharing networks are still products of mining the earth, mass-made in a factory. There is still a need for someone to construct or produce the assets we share or what we use to share our services with one another.

Similarly, sharing platforms, particularly as they are on the cusp of becoming mainstream, and the challenges they present, will need to be confronted rather than simply circumvented through the introduction of cooperative platforms. The former has paved the way for the latter, but is still dominant; moreover, there are issues with both (for example, tendencies to trend towards monopoly power, possible environmental repercussions). Above all, we should keep in mind that while users, both consumers and workers, of these platforms are more empowered than ever before and reap more of the value that they produce together, the ambition here should be wider than protecting their interests; participation should ultimately be encouraged based on whether these platforms are best for society.

This means that we should be taking a holistic approach to addressing issues in the sharing economy. While workers' rights are paramount as gig work in the sector becomes more prevalent, we should also be thinking about the effects on all workers, such as those in competing traditional businesses, and how we can support them in this transition. Similarly, as climate and demographic changes fundamentally alter the world we live in, there will be a stronger social and environmental imperative to design differently than might be warranted if the only stake we had in the ground was economic. We should carefully work through the impact of sharing platforms on consumers, communities, the state, the economy, and the environment as a precursor to figuring out how we as designers might make a difference.

Notes

1 Airbnb is an online platform facilitating homesharing and Uber is an online platform facilitating ridesharing.
2 Shared value creation refers to value derived from the collective of users; the more users, the more value the platform has. Because expanding their user base is how their value is created as well as how they ensure that their marketplace is the most efficient for matching supply and demand, platforms survive through scaling and doing so quickly.
3 When 'ordinary monopolies' are referred to, this means natural monopolies (i.e. public utilities such as gas, water or electricity which are costly, both economically and environmentally, to transmit through more than one network. However, this is not analogous to networked monopolies given that the network of these platforms is not a vehicle for distributing the company's products or services – it is the service). An additional consideration is other types of monopolies which arise from market failures (i.e. customer inertia, legal or technical barriers to entry), all of which can be addressed by competition law (again, not analogous to networked monopolies, which do not arise from market failures, but from the very nature of the marketplace).
4 Monopoly power is also known as market power. In some cases, we are also referring to monopsony power, which is power exercised by a dominant seller (i.e. over suppliers).
5 To offer this sort of benefit platform providers would risk being seen as akin to employers; to avoid the legal and financial ramifications of this label they thus abstain from intervening in the career progression of their users.

Full references

Botsman, R. 'The Collaborative Economy'. *Adobe Digital Marketing Symposium* [video], 27:36, 20 September. Available at: www.youtube.com/watch?v=zTd-P8M0SjA

Botsman, R. (2015) 'The Sharing Economy: Dictionary of Commonly Used Terms'. *Medium*, 19 October [online] Available at: https://medium.com/@rachelbotsman/the-sharing-economy-dictionary-of-commonly-used-terms-d1a696691d12#.uu0z11zgx

Botsman, R. and Rogers, R. (2011) *What's Mine Is Yours: The Rise of Collaborative Consumption*, HarperCollins Business, London.

Edelman, B. and Luca, M. (2014) 'Digital Discrimination: The Case of Airbnb.com'. *Harvard Business School* working paper 14–054, 10 January [online] Available at: http://papers.ssrn.com/sol3/papers.cfm?abstract_id=2377353

Edelman, B., Luca, M. and Svirsky, D. (2015) 'Racial Discrimination in the Sharing Economy: Evidence From a Field Experiment'. *Harvard Business School*, 9 December [online] Available at: http://www.benedelman.org/publications/airbnb-guest-discrimination-2015-12-09.pdf

Ferenstein, G. (2014) 'The Next Internet Monopoly: Uber, the Transportation Network'. *VentureBeat*, 20 August [online] Available at: http://venturebeat.com/2014/08/20/the-next-internet-monopoly-uber-the-transportation-network/

Foster, J.B., McChesney, R.W. and Jonna, R.J. (2011) 'Monopoly and Competition in Twenty-First Century Capitalism'. *Monthly Review* 62, no. 11, https://monthlyreview.org/2011/04/01/monopoly-and-competition-in-twenty-first-century-capitalism/

Garber, M. (2014) 'After Uber, San Francisco Has Seen a 65% Decline in Cab Use'. *The Atlantic*, 17 [online] Available at: www.theatlantic.com/technology/archive/2014/09/what-uber-is-doing-to-cabs-in-san-francisco-in-1-crazy-chart/380378/

Harris, S.D. and Krueger, A.B. (2015) *A Proposal for Modernising Labour Laws for 21st Century Work: The 'Independent Worker'*. Brookings Institute, [Paper] 8 December [online] Available at: www. brookings.edu/research/papers/2015/12/09-modernizing-labor-laws-for-the-independent-worker-krueger-harris

Hawksworth, J. and Vaughan, R. (2015) 'The sharing economy – sizing the revenue opportunity'. London: PwC, [online] Available at: *http://www.pwc.co.uk/issues/megatrends/collisions/sharingeconomy/the-sharing-economy-sizing-the-revenue-opportunity.html*

Hoffman, R. (2015) 'Expertise in Scaling Up Is the Visible Secret of Silicon Valley'. *Financial Times*, 12 September [online]. Available at: www.ft.com/cms/s/0/39001312-4836-11e5-af2f-4d6e0e5eda22.html#axzz3trdDpGtQ

Martin, E., Shaheen, S.A. and Lidicker, J. (2010) 'The Impact of Carsharing on Household Vehicle Holdings: Results From a North American Shared-use Vehicle Survey'. *University of California Berkeley Transportation Sustainability Research Center*, 1 March [online] Available at: http://tsrc.berkeley.edu/ vehicleholdings

Mudallal, Z. (2015) 'Airbnb Will Soon Be Booking More Rooms Than the World's Largest Hotel Chains'. *Quartz*, 20 January [online] Available at: http://qz.com/329735/airbnb-will-soon-be-booking-more-rooms-than-the-worlds-largest-hotel-chains/

Power, M.E. and Kramer, M.R. (2011) 'Creating Shared Value'. *Harvard Business Review*, January/ February [online] Available at: https://hbr.org/2011/01/the-big-idea-creating-shared-value#

Regalado, A. (2014) 'The Economics of the Internet of Things'. *MIT Technology Review*, 20 May 20 [online] Available at: www.technologyreview.com/news/527361/the-economics-of-the-internet-of-things/

Reich, R.B. (2015) 'Why the Sharing Economy Is Harming Workers – And What Must Be Done'. YouTube [video], 2:37, posted by Inequality Media, 27 November, Available at: www.youtube.com/ watch?v=v_Snob8–6xM

Roberts, J.J. (2015) 'As "Sharing Economy" Fades, These 2 Phrases Are Likely to Replace It'. *Fortune Magazine*, 29 July [online] Available at: http://fortune.com/2015/07/29/sharing-economy-chart/

Roose, K. (2014) 'Does Silicon Valley Have a Contract-Worker Problem?'. *New York Magazine*, 18 September [online] Available at: http://nymag.com/daily/intelligencer/2014/09/silicon-valleys-contract-worker-problem.html

Shaheen, S.A, Cohen, A.P., and Chung, M.S. (2009) 'North American Carsharing: 10-Year Retrospective', [online] Available at: http://tsrc.berkeley.edu/sites/default/files/North%20American%20Carsharing% 20-%20Shaheen.pdf

Sifferlin, A. (2014) 'Harvard Study Suggests Racial Bias Among Some Airbnb Renters'. *Time*, 27 January [online] Available at: http://time.com/2345/harvard-study-suggests-racial-bias-among-some-airbnb-renters/

Stone, Z. (2015) 'Living and Dying on Airbnb'. *Medium*, 9 November [online] Available at: https:// medium. com/matter/living-and-dying-on-airbnb-6bff8d600c04#.gegky6jjg

Sundarajan, A. (2015) 'Sharing Economy? From Crowd-based Capitalism to Blockchain Markets'. *NYU Stern School of Business* [video], 24:38, 11 November, Available at: www.youtube.com/ watch?v=h8DuaG11juo

Transport for London (2015) *Private Hire Regulations Review: Response to Consultation and Proposals.*

Wang, D., Xi, S. and Gilheany, J. (2015) 'The Model Minority? Not on Airbnb.com: A Hedonic Pricing Model to Quantify Racial Bias Against Asian Americans'. *Technology Science*, 1 September [online] Available at: http://techscience.org/downloadpdf.php?paper=2015090104

35

GOING FROM STEM TO STEAM

Sara Kapadia

Knowledge silos and sustainability

Knowledge gathering and problem solving are fundamental to how we function, survive, and progress. Humans have organized knowledge in a variety of ways, one main way has been to separate parts of knowledge into different disciplines (Turner 2000; Goodlad 1979). By transferring knowledge from one generation to the next, disciplines act as intellectual structures to document, frame, and interpret past experiences and cultivate a path for the way knowledge evolves into the future (Stehr and Weingart 2000; Reich and Reich 2006). Disciplines are also social structures and "cultural phenomena . . . embodied in collections of like-minded people, each with their own codes of conduct, sets of values, and distinctive intellectual tasks" (Becher 1981, 109). Disciplines contain individuals within the boundaries of the knowledge, expected norms, and to categorize society (Kuhn 1970; Foucault 1988; Bridges 2006).

Through a simplified and traditional view we can think of disciplines as existing in two spheres. The first sphere is the world of theory – where individuals learn the knowledge, and become socialized into one or more disciplines; this is usually within an educational context. The second sphere is the world of application – where individuals solve problems and explore ideas by utilizing the knowledge, applying the skills, and becoming experts in a discipline; this is usually within an occupational context. Disciplines are influenced by the era they exist in and in turn shape the era itself. The idea of disciplines being autonomous and discrete can be traced back to early universities in Europe that only had a few disciplines: medicine, philosophy, law and theology, since then, as greater specialization has occurred, the number of disciplines has grown.

Through a complex and current view we can think of disciplines as more porous than solid and separate. In today's era there is an acceptance of more interconnectedness, and problems are seen as multidimensional. The systems thinking approach contrasts with traditional inquiry, which studies systems by breaking them down into their separate elements. Systems thinking moves problem-solving away from silos and gets closer to the complexity of the real world by comprehending how a system's essential parts interrelate, change over time, and fit into the context of larger systems. By looking at a particular problem through systems thinking, multiple disciplines can be engaged. This interdisciplinary approach invites collaboration between experts from different disciplines, but it also nurtures individuals to become 'interdisciplinarians.' Repko (2008) highlights that being an interdisciplinarian not only about content but also about preparing the mind and building character to grapple with complex issues that exist in the world we live in.

Sustainability is one of the biggest issues of the twenty-first century. To achieve global sustainability for a planet of seven billion people, rethinking the way we manage every aspect of our planet's resources is paramount (United Nations Environment Programme (UNEP) 2012). Sustainability is not a lofty goal that policy makers and theorists can only address; it is enmeshed into our daily lives with seemingly small decisions creating knock-on effects that truly impact the entire globe. "This interconnected set of problems has an interconnected set of solutions. If humans implement these solutions, we can gradually achieve a sustainable and highly affluent set of civilizations. Working towards sustainability requires many different types of actions in different subject areas" stated the Oxford scholar James Martin in his book *The Meaning of the 21st Century: A Vital Blueprint for Ensuring Our Future* (Martin 2006, 5). Through systems thinking we can see just how much impact a designer has. Sustainable design recognizes how the actions of humans directly and indirectly influence several systems, and how these systems interact, so the effects are more expansive than at first glance. In this way the designer becomes a true interdisciplinarian with the ability to foster behaviors, policies, social justice and the very systems themselves for a more sustainable future. Sustainable design provides more than one way to examine an issue and designers have an integral role in translating how we interpret, interact with, and ultimately shape the very environment we exist in (Egenhoefer 2014).

One way in which the current era is responding to the complexity of twenty-first-century issues is to bring the arts and sciences closer together. There has been an ebb and a flow to when the arts and the sciences come closely together. Eras when science and art collide are often a result of the culture of the times (Wilson 2010). We are again entering a major shift to integrate the arts and the sciences. In order to understand the current shift we need to look back to the past.

The STEM story

STEM skills go beyond just the basic knowledge about the disciplines but as Organization for Economic Co-operation and Development (OECD) 2012 highlights STEM skills that are embedded with problem-solving have the most yield for creativity and for moving the fields forward. In the global economy where technology transcends borders and allows research, learning and work to take place beyond physical confinements, the American STEM story has led to a worldwide adoption of STEM as the acronym for both education and work. The global push for STEM excellence in education became a contest for developing nations, echoing the rise of industry, and social and economic needs. On a philosophical level the idea that the age of the enlightenment projected science and rationality was widely accepted. Science was seen as the light, and though no one says that the arts are dark, but by contrast and by default the arts were seen as less crucial. Science was seen as the way forward and the route for truth.

Science, technology, engineering, and mathematics are separate disciplines that became a part of the acronym STEM. Coined in the United States, the use of STEM continued to spread globally. Although each letter directly corresponds to a separate discipline, STEM as an acronym has become a shorthand for a multitude of different concepts, agendas, and paradigm shifts such as the quality of education, global competitiveness, and preparing the future workforce.

The Morrill Act of 1862 reshaped universities and colleges to match the needs of the industries of the time: agriculture and 'mechanic arts,' but it paved the way for science and engineering programs, eventually fueling more university research (Butz et al. 2004). By World War II the United States had produced a sufficient number of academic and industry experts and the war spawned a strong working relationship between two groups, the first being scientists, technologists, engineers, mathematicians, and the second being the military. Both groups pooled their cognitive and financial resources as they collaborated on innovative solutions. The National Science Foundation (NSF) was created at the end of World War II to document and further the research that had been achieved so far, and this strengthened the resources and importance given to the sciences (Mervis 2010). Although the war ended, a new conflict brewed as both the United States and the Soviet Union emerged as superpowers and pushed for dominance on the world's stage (Cadbury 2006). As technology improved and spaceflight became possible, venturing into space became the next frontier, and by the late 1950s, both countries were competing to be the world leader in space. Russia put the Sputnik satellite into space in 1957, which propelled the United States to deal with mounting challenges in their education system and their workforce. The United States responded in 1958 with a series of national efforts: the National Defense Education Act (P.L. 85–864) to keep pace with the Soviet school system that focused on preparing elite scientists (Passow 1957; Kelly 2012); and the establishment of the National Aeronautics and Space Administration (NASA). With the success of the Apollo mission and an American being the first on the Moon, the space race concluded (Bybee and Fuchs 2006).

Although the enthusiasm for science continued during the next decade and the number of American science graduates rose, by the 1980s the nation was once again at risk of failing schools and lagging behind in the global economy. Rutherford (1998) underlines that often it takes a crisis to bring attention to the ongoing struggles to improve education, and propel greater efforts. By the 1990s the federal efforts to unify and organize funding led the NSF to coin 'STEM' as a way to address all four disciplines (Ramaley 2009, 2011; Woodruff 2013; Sanders 2009). The acronym gained traction as the United States faced growing panic as their global educational ranking further dropped, and "grew to believe that China and India were on course to bypass America in the global economy by outSTEMming" the United States (Sanders 2009). STEM once again reinforced the notion that education was a key to ensuring American economic competitiveness (Kelly 2012; Clifton 2011; National Academy of Sciences (NAS) 1997).

As research and awareness grew, STEM was adopted as a narrative globally that often could be found in discussions about economic and educational policies worldwide. STEM helped to shape the era and fuel discussions societal needs, and opened channels for more STEM education (Drew 2014). As discussions about STEM spread internationally and nations evaluated how well their education and economic systems were performing in this new paradigm of STEM, nations were ranked in terms of STEM achievement (Katsomitros 2013; OECD 2012). Affluence, technology and globalization have caused seismic shifts in the ways knowledge is shaped, transmitted and applied, "the world is becoming flat. Several technological and political forces have converged, and that has produced a global, Web-enabled playing field that allows for multiple forms of collaboration without regard to geography or distance – or soon, even language" (Friedman 2005, para. 7). Though a current of competition still exists between different nations, there is a stronger tide that open communication and sharing knowledge would nurture an "approach that builds strength through participating in the global supply of human capital and innovation in collaboration with other nations" (Salzman 2007, 4).

The STEAM story

The big issue of sustainability stretches across the globe, beyond geopolitical lines, and beyond economic competition, at the very core the issue, is human survival within the large interwoven systems. There has been a long history of the connection or cross-fertilization of the arts and the sciences from the cave painters to Leonardo da Vinci's scientific-artistic diagrams of flying machines to photography in the 1800s (Wilson 2010) to the art-science connection in the nineteenth and twentieth centuries when the discovery of energy influenced artists and scientists to tackle the notion of what was invisible (Clarke and Henderson 2002). The reunion of art and science is again a part of the zeitgeist. Society's progression through industry over the last 150 years has evolved from farming to factory to knowledge to a new era, the 'conceptual age' that favors those individuals who can think innovatively, make meaning, and be sensitive to connections (Pink 2006).

Although there is an understanding that creative skills are crucial, there is a 'creativity crisis' (Bronson and Merryman 2010; DeGraff 2012; Dwyer 2011; Schrage 2010). The emphasis on the sciences has created nations of high performing STEM specialists who are lacking in social skills. Cornell University's president calls for a broader humanistic education: "it is through the study of art, music, literature, history and other humanities and social sciences that we gain a greater understanding of the human condition than biological or physical science alone can provide" (Skorton 2014, para. 9). Organizations are heavily investing in teaching creativity (Plucker et al. 2004), but few schools enhance creativity skills and this can even be traced to a lack of creative thinking in higher education classrooms (Jackson 2006). This is at a direct contrast to society's needs for creativity. The proficiency and aptitude needed by individuals is ever changing and in many ways demands more advanced skills earlier in life. Higher order thinking skills directly influence the reasoning needed by individuals on a daily basis (Kuhn and Weinstock 2002). In an environment that is changing faster than ever before, children born today may be entering careers that are established during their lifetime. With this in mind having fluidity between skills sets is critical to successful being adaptable. The National Academies underscore that

> interdisciplinary research can be one of the most productive and inspiring of human pursuits – one that provides a format for conversations and connections that lead to new knowledge. As a mode of discovery and education, it has delivered much already and promises more – a sustainable environment, healthier and more prosperous lives, new discoveries and technologies to inspire young minds, and a deeper understanding of our place in space and time.
>
> *(National Academies 2004, 1)*

As creative skills are becoming more vital to solving problems there is a recognition that these skills often originate in the arts. STEM alone is no longer seen as sufficient, adding the arts, the 'A' has transformed the STEM movement into a STEAM movement that represents the need for innovation in society (Maeda 2011, 2013; Beal 2013). The emerging STEM to STEAM movement is largely based in the endeavor to integrate the arts with STEM as equally significant, and not simply a complementary subject (Bequette and Bequette 2011). White (2010) cautions that STEM cannot bridge the innovation gap and underlines that a STEAM-based education will provide individuals the skills needed in economy where innovation is valued. It is the creative and innovative members of society that have the new thinking skills needed in this new economy, and the foundation for these skills can be fostered by moving from STEM to STEAM (Eger 2013, 2015). As we move to an age where creative thinking is the foundation for solving great problems and "knowledge can no longer be ascribed to, or produced within, disciplinary boundaries, but is entirely entangled" (Oxman 2016, para. 2), we are seeing projects that flow between disciplines.

STEAMing sustainability

Sustainability is the ultimate design brief (Sherwin 2012), and as disciplines are evolving to break free from siloes, design is coming onto the mainstage as a key player in solving big issues in sustainability (Shedroff 2009). Designers are widening their roles, and consumers are changing their behaviors, and the relationship between designer and consumer has great potential in bringing about progress in sustainability (Chick and Micklethwaite 2011).

> Designers now need to be equipped with the skills and knowledge that will enable them to participate in the global move towards a sustainable future. The challenges arise as Design for Sustainability deals with very complex and often contradictory issues. Collaborative learning experiences recognize that these complex issues can be addressed with the pooling of diverse knowledge, perspectives, cultures, skills and tools.
>
> *(McMahon and Bhamra 2016, 1)*

Inserting the arts into STEM provides a path for new forms of knowledge. STEAM provides alternative perspectives that STEM sometimes leaves out. Through the arts we have new ways to frame the issue, forge new methodologies, create cohesive communication, and become interdisciplinary.

Self-expression and discovery are very much foundation of the arts, and whereas STEM also explores ideas, through the arts novel ideas can be visualized and unique techniques applied. The arts feed on innovation, whereas STEM feeds on inventions that meet standards. STEM as an acronym sought to break down the simulated academic barricades created between the sciences, technology, engineering, and math disciplines that undermine student performance. With more flow between the disciplines it is easier to make connections and see relationships between ideas, and bodies of knowledge. STEAM goes further by reflecting the actual real world. Sustainability has always been a complex aspect of human life, and has become more and more urgent as humans continue to utilize the natural world's resources and systems. Learning to live in harmony with the natural world is paramount to survival of all life, not just that of the human species. The arts give new language to science by igniting curiosity, investigation, and untethered ideas. The arts, since the ancient times, have been a way to visualize the future, to map out intangible concepts in a tangible way. In today's time there is much of the arts that is used in commercial culture that results in destructive consumption, however realigning the arts to help solve sustainability issues is not only sagacious but also economically wise. Using skills in a more transdisciplinary way means that those looking to create more sustainable practices can have the full breadth of tools and skills that the STEAM approach offers. Another central aspect to sustainability is that of translating this complex concept into captivating images and messaging. Working within the realm of global sustainability means that translation needs to occur across communities, cultures, and varying values. Again, this is where a STEAM approach is more fitting. Being able to use a nuanced tactic that portrays the multilayered aspects of sustainability needs that mirrors the arts and the STEM in synergy is more authentic and can resonate with wider audiences, stakeholders, and experts across the chasms that general and more mundane approaches typically utilize. Let us review four cases studies of sustainable design that highlight how the arts and the sciences are applied through interdisciplinary STEAM approaches.

Affordable and adjustable prostheses created in FabLabs

Waag society's FabLab and the House of Natural Fiber's (Honf) FabLab

This project highlights collaboration across countries and disciplinary roles to design prostheses with locally available materials for low or almost no cost. House of Natural Fibre (Honf) is based in Yogyakarta, on the island of Java, and works as a forum to bring artists and scientists together to solve some of Indonesia's biggest technology development challenges in sectors such as health and the environment. The group facilitated the realization of innovative ideas from the creative communities, students, and researchers in Yogyakarta. Artists used traditional and novel methods in combination. The program provided facilities for creative thinkers in gathering innovative ideas into tangible processes. Honf Fablab created a broader international network through which the artists became as recognized and as appreciated as the technologists, with all exchanging knowledge, creating a mutual understanding of local and global issues, and sharing cultural differences in practical daily life. The collaboration of research and exploration of local creations and customary and progressive technologies led to problem solving for the communities involved.

Honf conceptualized bamboo leg prostheses for those who lost limbs after an earthquake hit Yogyakarta, an island of Java, in 2006. Working with the Waag Society in Amsterdam, Honf asked if it was possible to produce a sustainable, high-quality, low-cost below-knee prosthesis that could be produced in local fabrication labs using local materials, such as bamboo. An interdisciplinary effort across countries occurred as:

> the team embraced open innovation principles, like pooling knowledge from the expert users in Yakkum, the designers from Honf and FabLab Amsterdam, academic advisors such as Dr. Bert Otten (Center for Human Movement Sciences, NeuroMechanics and Prosthetics, University of Groningen) and specialized manufacturers like Orthopedie-techniek De Hoogstraat in Utrecht. Input from all the parties was used in the process of developing and designing the adjustable leg.
>
> *(Schaub 2013, 242)*

In a truly sustainable work, and where STEAM is present, the artists mind is inherent or integral to the scientific process, where both the arts and the science intermingle to realize the idea.

Edible packaging

Wikifoods

David Edwards, a bio-creator and professor at Harvard University, first had the idea for edible packaging after a discussion in one of his classes ('How to Create Things and Have Them Matter') about possible water transportation methods based around the biological cell. Edwards consulted with designer François Azambourg and biologist Don Ingbert to research this idea. Drawing inspiration from how a biological cell carries water, a vessel for food and drink was designed and WikiFoods was launched. Instead of skin cells, it makes its protective membrane out of a mix of particles from such foods as chocolate and orange, binding them with carbohydrates that are completely edible, taking plastic out of the consumer's experience. The class that fueled this project focused on generating, developing, and realizing breakthrough ideas in the arts, sciences, and engineering. Students learn basic skills of engineering design, brainstorming, prototyping, and public presentations. The course is taught in a way that design is presented as an interdisciplinary process with an emphasis on social and cultural change. These classes take place at Harvard's artscience laboratory. David Edwards states that "artscience labs provide interdisciplinary conditions and expressive environments that benefit creators while fostering productive relationships with established institutions, to bring about beneficial, sustainable change" (2010, 17).

Ecosystemic restoration: a model community at Salton Sea

IM Studio Milano/Los Angeles

This project focuses on the illustration of the model community as a case study of not only sustainable architecture but also as an example of a biomimetic approach to design inspired by natural ecosystems. The project designs a community not only composed of the housing and the public spaces around it, but that incorporates all the other elements necessary to feed, employ, and create an exchange economy with the surrounding communities. This interconnectivity does not produce waste, but creates a chain of usage. This project involved an 'ecosystemic' team that consisted of two architects, a designer, urban planner, agronomist, biologist, mechanical engineer, environmental engineer, and three architecture students. IM Studio's architect and the founder, Ilaria Mazzoleni, and her collaborator, Shauna Price, an evolutionary biologist, state that "successful nature-inspired design would need to include teams of collaborators from multiple disciplines" and that "it is not the discipline but the individual's mind-set that matters. This process happens through use of an interdisciplinary team where each specialized member keeps an open mind toward discovery and translation" (Mazzoleni and Price 2013, 5, 42).

Sea Changes

Sea Changes is an organization that aligns itself as an example of STEAM (Corser 2014). The organization believes that art strengthens communities and reaches across cultural and economic lines and uses creativity in communication and in promoting innovation for solutions. By using art along with the science, Sea Changes is committed to activities that communicate science through new media and other arts for informed civic-minded active communities.

This team is composed of artists and scientists who are concerned about the destructive changes in the oceans, including plastic pollution, dwindling fish populations, and acidification due to climate change. Each member of the team has a strong background related to environmental conservation, public policy, or education. By utilizing a transdisciplinary approach the teams of scientists and artists focus centrally on how to communicate and educate the communities surrounding each project about the environment.

One of the projects includes 'Sea Changes: ACT – Protecting Our Oceans Through Art and Science' that is a collaborative project with scientists, artists, and citizens concerned about changes destroying oceans with a focus on climate change, plastic pollution, and over fishing issues.

It began in San Diego and has since started to do work internationally. Scientists from the National Oceanic and Atmospheric Administration, Scripps Institution of Oceanography, the California Department of Fish and Wildlife, and artists in California collaborated to complete marine science and cognitive science research that has resulted in artistic and scientific installations and public outreach. The projects have shown that artists and STEM specialists can merge ideas and become interdisciplinary thinkers, for example in addressing the issue of disappearing coral reefs worldwide, a glass artist and diver were able to successfully grow baby coral onto glass art housed at an aquarium. In another instance scientists and artists designed a Virtual Undersea Experience through interactive video projections on hanging eight-foot silks.

Crystalizing STEAM as an interdisciplinary approach

STEAM has become a practical approach through which interdisciplinary thinking can be achieved. Mansilla et al. (2000) state that interdisciplinarity occurs when "disciplines are not simply juxtaposed. Rather, they are purposefully intertwined" (29). Interdisciplinary learning provides individuals with a way to recognize bias, think critically, tolerate ambiguity, and recognize ethical concerns (Repko 2009; Kavaloski 1979; Newell 1990; Field et al. 1994; Vess 2001). Interdisciplinary learning coincides with significant learning (Fink 2003) when experiences are meaningful and last. Individuals are intrinsically motivated to explore and discover more about the topic at hand, when what they learn holds value for them. How does STEAM cultivate environments that are highly interdisciplinary and where significant learning takes place?

If we imagine a group of individuals in a room each from a different discipline spanning STEAM, how do they begin to interact and work together?

Framing the issue: A centralizing prompt or issue that the entire group as a whole can focus on, can provoke a reaction from each individual and interpretations are formed as each individual responds to the issue. Disciplines have different paradigms or models that they utilize to ask questions. Individuals in an interdisciplinary team may frame the issue differently, and by doing so tease out contrasting priorities that materialize from preexisting ideas. This in itself is deeply informing as individuals can become aware of their biases by hearing how someone from another paradigm forms their questions. Interdisciplinary discussions can bring to light preconceived notions and values that individuals were not aware of until coming face to face with someone who challenges those notions. STEAM places mirrors in the room reflecting the confinements of the different disciplines. Through renewed understanding for their own disciplines and other disciplines, individuals in the group can then forge a relationship based on open communication. Although disagreements and differences may take place, an atmosphere of mutual respect can lead to conflicting views without actual conflicts.

Forging methodologies: The interdisciplinary team can discuss how they plan to obtain further knowledge, if the main prompt is a problem to be solved then a methodology or more than one methodologies need to be decided upon; if the prompt is to expand on what is known about an issue, decisions across the group about next steps are essential. Negotiating through multiple options is useful, as individuals are broken out of their disciplinary boxes and can step into an unknown, and ambiguous space where there are many more possibilities. This echoes the very exploratory nature of problem solving. By focusing on the process of knowledge gathering rather than the outcomes, an interdisciplinary team can be free to discover insights and 'play' with new ideas. Fusing disciplinary methods, or utilizing a method from one discipline in the domain of another discipline can be unfamiliar and prone to unexpected results. It is this very dynamic medium in which ideas through STEM or art alone, may not have thrived.

Cohesive communication: Working in interdisciplinary teams is much like an airport lounge, people from different places sitting across from each other, speaking in their native tongues. Whereas some terms may be shared, these simple terms become complex, as individuals may discover that the way in which they use that very term contrasts to that of their team member. The term 'model' as a verb or a noun, may mean one thing to a structural engineer, mean something else to an animator, have a different meaning to a sculptor, and have another meaning to a quantum physicist. It is important to note that terms can differ within subdisciplines as well as across disciplines. STEAM provides a platform for translation and creating shared language. By having to explain disciplinary content to those outside of the discipline forces metacognition. Individuals can ask themselves how they will explain ideas not just to a passive audience (such as in an academic conference or public art presentation), but to an active member involved with the project. Communicating across disciplines can cause an altogether new set of terms, or definitions for terms that pertain directly to the project itself. By articulated a new cohesive language to use amongst themselves, the groundwork has been laid for communicating their project to others who may span the full range of STEAM disciplines.

Becoming interdisciplinarians: Imagine each individual as bringing a bag of tools to a roundtable. The bag representing their disciplinary paradigm and the tools representing the knowledge, the methodologies, the values, and lenses through which they interact with the world. In addressing the central prompt placed on the table, each individual may look to their bag and bring out tools they deem as appropriate and explain what their tool does and how they as the expert may be able to use it for the project. Individuals in this way educate each other about their disciplinary tools, and each may bring a specific role to the project. As individuals learn about each other's tools there may be opportunities to experiment and exchange tools, and practice using the tool as it has always been used, or apply it in entirely new ways. Further still, there may be times when the bags of tools are emptied onto the table, inviting individuals to use the full range of tools.

The following STEAM examples showcase the framing of issues, the forging of methodologies, the development of cohesive communication, and how individuals become interdisciplinarians.

Professor and director of University of Delaware's DuPont Interdisciplinary Science Learning Laboratories, John Jungck is a theoretical biologist specializing in molecular evolution who favors the STEAM learning approach. "I'm interested in how life inspires design, whether it's from an engineering or artistic perspective" stated Jungck (2015, para. 4). The central focus of the laboratories is interdisciplinary 'problem based learning' instead of lectures, so that students can explore problems from the real world that highlight a contemporary issue (such as sustainability, loss of biodiversity, global warming, or production of alternative energy). The emphasis is on twenty-first-century life-long learning skills, drawn from the National Research Council (2012). One of the interdisciplinary projects is a design process practicum facilitated by faculty in plant and soil sciences, public policy and administration, and art. The practicum partnered with the Philadelphia Flower Show, one of the oldest and largest indoor shows, attracting more than 260,000 people annually. Students from multiple disciplines take part, the most recent cohort spanned art, organizational and community leadership, plant and soil sciences, landscape design, food science, engineering, and business. The students are immersed in a real world context, and are tasked with creating a hands-on display to bring awareness to the public about a specific theme, such as 'The Art of Sustainable Gardening,' and 'Forest to Pharmacy: Using Nature's Cures'. The interdisciplinary teams formulate ideas, design, and implement the final exhibition. The success of the practicum can be traced to the structure of the program itself: ample time is given for students across disciplines to meet each day, hierarchy is reduced with professors, teaching assistants and students sharing one common space, a 'preceptor' role was created so that preceptors can work with students guiding them in the interdisciplinary process. The physical spaces are equipped with technologies across the disciplines, so a student from any discipline can be found using a digital video microscope, video analysis software, a laser cutter, and 3D printer on one day.

The Broad Vision project explored the perception and interpretation of microscopic worlds, and investigated the benefits and challenges of working across disciplinary divides in a university setting (Barnett and Smith 2013). The year-long interdisciplinary project focused on microscopy and took place at the University of Westminster in London, United Kingdom. Disciplines that focused on looking, seeing and interpreting information were chosen: photographic art, life science, psychology, imaging science, illustration and computer science. Students became researchers, mentors to one another, and producers. The project was broken down into three phases. The first stage focused on disciplinary exchange, where the team shared how vision, perception, and scale were relevant in their discipline. This interchange developed into artists using scientific tools, and scientists creating visual diagrams, and eventually to a highly reflective team of individuals primed and ready for the next stage. The second stage involved interdisciplinary research with small groups that explored research ideas, and finalized on themes, such as the Art of

Microscopy (interested in the diversity of interpretation), Eye Tracking and Aesthetics (interested in how photomicrographs are scanned by the eye), Anatomy of the Eye (exploring the internal structures and mechanisms of the eye), and Growth and Form (animating cellular behaviors). The STEAM collaborations were encouraged to forge their own research methodologies and responses to the research questions that emerged. The final stage was to engage audiences, the multitude of options for representation and disciplinary norms gave rise to plethora of information displayed, shared, and conveyed in a truly interdisciplinary manner. One research member of the team, a student facilitator, described the experience:

> The project operates with a low hierarchy, assigning all students and lecturers the title of 'researchers' – a factor I believe is pivotal to successful interdisciplinary projects between scientists and artists . . . there is a loop here from science through art and back into science. I found myself looking at scientific content – a microscope slide – through scientific equipment but with an artist's mode of reasoning.
>
> *(Dinsmore 2013, 2)*

In a STEAM-inspired interdisciplinary studio course at the University of Georgia students from art education, environmental and civil engineering, and landscape architecture, with funding from the NSF, responded to design challenges. The project considered 'synergistic learning,' that is, how students made sense of the knowledge from different aspects of experience (Sochacka et al. 2013; Guyotte et al. 2015). The aim of the activities was for the individuals to transcend disciplinary boundaries and gain new understandings to their home discipline (Holley 2009). The program was sensitive to concerns that STEAM education might be conceptualized in a way that benefits the STEM fields without developing a reciprocal benefit among all the disciplines (Bequette and Bequette 2012; Sochacka et al. 2013). The design studio curriculum and pedagogy was motivated by the vision of STEAM education as a way to promote creative thinking across disciplines (Wynn and Harris 2012). The curriculum underlined the environmental sustainability as having local and global impact. The first two design challenges focused on exploring the topics of waste reduction and water ethic. Their interdisciplinary projects were visually translated into artworks displayed in the university gallery. The final design challenge was to implement an initiative focused on inspiring a water ethic in the local community and capture this community interaction. Forming a new way to document their work, the individuals created visual journals – a crossbreed between the writer's reflective journal and an artist's sketchbook or engineer's design notebook (Guyotte et al. 2015).

Challenges to STEAM

One of the major challenges is the STEM versus STEAM debate. Those in the STEM camp argue that STEM as a movement has not been fully developed and need more time, and that adding the 'A' further impedes any progress. The need for STEM workers far outweighs the need for professional artists (Dunning 2013). Forcing the arts into STEM can water down the efforts of STEM, which is still a new concept, states a dean of a college of engineering, and gives the false notion of a well-rounded education when honed STEM skills are still vitally needed (May 2015). When STEM first arose as an acronym, the separate disciplines resisted, echoing the same sentiment, that the integration would cause a dilution of the fundamental roots of each discipline, and yet integration was the very aspect that was hailed as responding to the era's needs (Sanders 2009). STEM as an acronym was not clear; for some it was a push to strengthen the disciplines represented by the letters, with greater funding and a greater number of STEM graduates. For others, STEM represents more than the separate disciplines, it is about how integration responds to the times. STEM can be found in every discipline, including the arts, states Bertram (2014), who debates that with the adding of the arts, the STEM efforts are being pushed back into only representing the sciences, when STEM is very much to do with the arts. There still remains apprehension that STEAM causes the 'watering down' of expertise not just of the STEM but also of the arts. There is a sense that STEAM does not authentically represent STEM or the arts, and has become yet another 'sticker' concept (Clapp and Jimenez 2015). STEAM programs can be difficult to implement, especially when the arts can often be seen to be an "entryway to presumably more important STEM topics" (Bequette and Bequette 2012, 43).

At the center of the STEM to STEAM debates, I see an age-old question: how does society value the arts and the sciences? The arts are seen as the proponent of creativity, the 'soft,' and the STEM seen as the 'hard' technical, one needing the other to be 'whole.' In reality the arts and sciences are far more layered, the terms 'hard' and 'soft' skills are often too simple to describe the depth found in the arts and STEM disciplines. Skills in the arts go beyond the soft, such as idea synthesis, visualization, interpretation, detailed correcting, focus and specificity to name a few (McCracken 2010). Likewise the notion that STEM specialists are devoid of creative thinking is too simplistic a judgment. Those who already excel in STEM have been found to be intensely creative, Root-Bernstein et al. (2008) found that high-performing scientists are twenty-five times more likely than the average scientist to sing, dance, or act; seventeen times more likely to be an artist; twelve times more likely to write poetry and literature; eight times more likely to do woodworking or some other craft; four times more likely to be a musician; and twice as likely to be a photographer. STEAM eliminates binary notions of hard and soft disciplines and focuses on an amalgamation of the creative potential in both the arts and STEM. There is a long history of the arts and sciences merging, and STEAM is another iteration, a new one, but another iteration and while the aspect of novelty may catch media attention and warrant the arrival of a new story. What truly matters is "how sensations are modulated by viewing a subject through a certain lens, understanding it a certain way, and how those sensations resonate with, define, and inspire a unique critique and a culture of thoughtful reflection" (Nowlin 2013, 1). The crux of STEAM is the acquiring of new lenses to view current problems in a way that adds to existing lenses, and this in turn can transform the way the separate disciplines are viewed. Ultimately various camps will sift out what they find to be useful and valuable in applying STEAM depending on their distinct motivations. Fishwick (2015) points to an imbalance in the STEM to STEAM movement, where the emphasis is on the arts serving STEM, but suggests that there should be a flow back and forth between the arts and STEM, where STEM can also serve the arts.

The philosophy that what we teach in education needs to be tied to where society is projected to be culturally and economically is outdated and should not be the focus of current efforts (Burnett 2013). If we break away from the confines of economic forces, politics, and competition, we could focus on how interdisciplinary approaches such as STEAM more closely mirror the complexities of global issues such as sustainability. Technologies that are emerging and shaping the arts, and sciences are in themselves multi-model. New advances are using components from the traditional arts arena in the sciences, and vice versa. Learning is no longer occurring in silos and confined to intangible scenarios, but rather it is entangled with current and pressing real issues. STEAM is changing the way disciplines interact. Burnett (2013) underscores that "the umbilical cord linking all of these practices and disciplines is design, which is finally receiving the attention it deserves" (para. 13). STEAM approaches to sustainable design are a natural fit for designers who are true interdisciplinarians.

Creating change for sustainable futures

STEAM moves the conversation forward by redefining how we think about the design process. Through STEAM approaches the designer has access to a more comprehensive set of tools with which to respond to issues in sustainability. Designers are truly interdisciplinary problem solvers, and STEAM perpetuates this. Through STEAM there is a greater openness to holistic strategies for achieving sustainability. Thinking about the problems and the issues can be more thoroughly navigated without having to pick between disciplines.

STEAM is a step forward, through STEAM there is new dialog about what learning can be and how we can use tools across disciplines to frame, shape, and apply new methodologies and new paradigms to solve real problems. STEAM has brought concerns to the surface about whether students are being equipped with the creative skills needed to survive in the conceptual age.

The big issues of our era are complex, and as we have progressed from one era to the next we have developed different models for how we think about thinking. That very metacognition has led us through times when problems were solved in disciplinary silos, to times when some disciplines have lived side by side, to a more integrated approach. When STEAM is formulated as a truly integrated approach there is a widening of the world, there are more possibilities for collaboration, and more pathways for interdisciplinary work. STEAM gets closer to the complexities of our era. STEAM calls for and fosters environments in which problems can be viewed through multiple lenses. Utilizing STEAM to explore major social and environmental issues nurtures divergent thinking across all disciplines. Through STEAM, sustainable design is a dynamic and collective process, where experts in the world of practice can become learners, and learners in the world of theory can become researchers. Whether the melting of disciplines occurs because disciplinary experts merge their ideas, or individuals merge ideas from different disciplines, at the very core interdisciplinary thinking is flourishing. STEAM will not be the final iteration, there is still much progress to be made, and fertile spaces need to be navigated where truly interdisciplinary work can thrive, but through STEAM the messy work of planting seeds and cross-pollination across disciplines is occurring, and approaches that solve problems are blossoming.

References

Barnett, H., and Smith, J. R. A. (2013). Broad Vision: The art and science of looking. *The STEAM Journal* 1, 1. Available at: http://scholarship.claremont.edu/steam/vol1/iss1/21

Beal, S. (2013, August 11). Turn STEM to STEAM: Why science needs the arts. *Huffington Post*. Available at: www.huffingtonpost.com/stephen-beal/turn-stem-to-steam_b_3424356.html

Becher, T. (1981). Towards a definition of disciplinary cultures. *Studies in Higher Education* 6, 2, 109–122.

Bequette, J. W., and Bequette, M. B. (2012). A place for ART and DESIGN education in the STEM conversation. *Art Education*, 65, 2, 40–47.

Bequette, M., and Bequette, J. (2011). STEM plus arts make STEAM? Effective integration of aesthetic-based problem solving across topic areas. *STEM Colloquium*. Minnesota.

Bertram, V. M. (2014). *One nation under-taught: Solving America's science, technology, engineering, and math crisis.* New York: Beaufort Books.

Biglan, A. (1973). The characteristics of subject matters in different academic areas. *Journal of Applied Psychology*, 57, 195–203.

Bridges, D. (2006). The disciplines and discipline of educational research. *Journal of Philosophy of Education*, 40, 2, 259–272.

Bronson, P., and Merryman, A. (2010). Forget brainstorming: What you think you know about fostering creativity is wrong. A look at what really works. *Newsweek*. New York: The Newsweek/Daily Beast Company LLC.

Burnett, R (2013). From STEM to STEAM. *Critical Approaches to Culture and Communications*. Available at: http://rburnett.ecuad.ca/ronburnett/2013/8/10/stem-to-steam

Butz, W. P., Kelly, T. K., Adamson, D. M., Bloom, G. A., Fossum, D., and Gross, M. E. (2004). *Will the scientific and technology workforce meet the requirements of the federal government?* Pittsburgh, PA: RAND.

Bybee, R. W., and Fuchs, B. (2006). Preparing the 21st century workforce: A new reform in science and technology education. *Journal of Research in Science Teaching*, 43, 349–352.

Cadbury, D. (2006). *Space race: The epic battle between America and the Soviet Union for dominion of space.* New York: Harper Collins Publishers.

Chick, A., and Micklethwaite, P. (2011). *Design for sustainable change: How design and designers can drive the sustainability agenda.* Switzerland: AVA Publishing SA.

Clapp, E. P., and Jimenez, R. L. (2015). STEAM not stickers, creating a meaningful role for the arts in STEM learning. *Harvard Education Letter*, 31, 2. Available at: http://hepg.org/hel-home/issues/31_2/helarticle/steam-not-stickers

Clarke, B., and Henderson, L. D. (2002). *From energy to information: Representation in science and technology, art, and literature.* Stanford, CA: Stanford University Press.

Clifton, J. (2011). *The Coming Jobs War.* New York: Gallup Press.

Corser, K. C. (2014). Does business need art and science to be innovative? *San Diego Business Journal*, STEM Supplement. Available at: www.cbjonline.com/a3sdbj/resources/supplements/PDF/20140526_STEM.pdf

DeGraff, J. (2012, March 19). MacGyvering our way out of the creativity crisis. *Huffington Post.* Retrieved at: www.huffingtonpost.com/jeff-degraff/creativity_b_1354010.html

Dinsmore, J. (2013). The unstable ground of low hierarchies. *The STEAM Journal*, 1, 1. Available at: http://scholarship.claremont.edu/steam/vol1/iss1/28/

Drew, D. E. (2011). *STEM the tide: Reforming science, technology, engineering, and math education in America.* Baltimore, MD: The Johns Hopkins University Press.

Drew, D. E. (2014). In Ossola, A. Is the U.S. focusing too much on STEM? *The Atlantic.*

Dunning, B. (2013, March 14). Can we be clear on something? It's STEM, not STEAM. *Skeptic Blog.* Available at: www.skepticblog.org/2013/03/14/stem-not-steam/

Dwyer, M. C. (2011). Reinvesting in arts education winning America's future through creative schools. *President's Committee on the Arts and the Humanities.* Available at: http://purl.fdlp.gov/GPO/gpo23762

Edwards, D. (2008). *ArtScience: Creativity in the post-Google generation.* Cambridge, MA: Harvard University Press.

Edwards, D. (2010). *The lab: Creativity and culture.* Cambridge, MA: Harvard University Press.

Egenhoefer, R. B. (2014). I am not another reusable . . . sustainable design beyond the totebag. *Sustainability Hub, Routledge.* Available at: www.routledgetextbooks.com/textbooks/sustainability/design.php

Eger, J. (2013). STEAM ... Now! *The STEAM Journal*, 1, 1, Art. 8. Available at: http://scholarship.claremont.edu/steam/vol1/iss1/8

Eger, J. (2015, November 12). STEAM Is Here—To Get into Schools Will Take a Little Longer. *Huffington Post.* Available at: http://www.huffingtonpost.com/john-m-eger/steam-is-here--to-get-it_b_8382234.html

Field, M., Lee, R., and Field, M. L. (1994). Assessing interdisciplinary learning. *New Directions in Teaching and Learning*, 58, 69–84.

Fink L. D. (2003). *Creating significant learning experiences: An integrated approach to designing college courses.* San Francisco: Jossey-Bass.

Fishwick, P. (2015, November 29). Why the STEAM argument is one-sidEd. *Creative Automata.* Available at: http://creative-automata.com/2015/11/29/why-the-steam-argument-is-one-sided/

Foucault, M. (1988). *Madness and civilization: A history of insanity in the age of reason.* New York: Vintage Books.

Friedman, T. L. (2005). *The world is flat: A brief history of the twenty-first century.* New York: Farrar, Straus and Giroux.

Goodlad, S. (1979). What is an academic discipline? in Roy Cox (Ed.), *Cooperation and choice in higher education.* London: University of London Teaching Methods Unit.

Guyotte, K. W., Sochacka, N. W., Costantino, T. E., Kellam, N., Kellam, N. N., and Walther, J. (2015). Collaborative creativity in STEAM: narratives of art education students' experiences in transdisciplinary spaces. *International Journal of Education and the Arts*, 16, 15. Retrieved at: www.ijea.org/v16n15/

Holley, K. A. (2009). Understanding interdisciplinary challenges and opportunities. *ASHE Higher Education Report, 32*(2), 1–131.

Jackson, N. (2006). *Developing creativity in higher education: An imaginative curriculum.* New York: Routledge.

Jungck, J. (2015, December 8). Adding the arts, Jungck discusses 'STEAM' approach to interdisciplinary learning. *UDaily.* University of Delaware. Available at: www.udel.edu/udaily/2016/dec/udarf-steam-120815.html

Katsomitros, A. (2013). The global race for STEM skills. *The Observatory on Borderless Higher Education.* Available at: www.obhe.ac.uk/newsletters/borderless_report_january_2013/global_race_for_stem_skills

Kavaloski, V. (1979). Interdisciplinary education and humanistic aspiration: A critical reflection, in J. Kockelmans (Ed.), *Interdisciplinarity and higher education*, 224–244. University Park, PA: Pennsylvania State University.

Kelly, B. (2012, September 10). STEM: What it is, and why we should care. *U.S. News & World Report.* Available at: http://money.usnews.com/money/careers/articles/2012/09/10/stem-what-it-is-and-why-we-should-care

Kuhn, D., and Weinstock, M. (2002). What is epistemological thinking and why does it matter? in B. K. Hofer and P. R. Pintrich (Eds.), *Personal epistemology: The psychology of beliefs about knowledge and knowing*, 121–144. Mahwah, NJ: Erlbaum.

Kuhn, T. S. (1970). *The structure of scientific revolutions.* Chicago: University of Chicago Press.

Lowell, B. L., and Salzman, H. (2007). *Into the Eye of the Storm: Assessing the Evidence on Science and Engineering Education, Quality, and Workforce Demand.* Research Report: The Urban Institute.

McCracken, S. M. (2010, September). Understanding arts training: Beyond 'soft' skills. *Academic Advising Today*, 33, 3. Available at: www.nacada.ksu.edu/Resources/Academic-Advising-Today/View-Articles/Understanding-Arts-Training-Beyond-Soft-Skills.aspx.

McMahon, M., and Bhamra, T. A. (2016). Mapping the journey: Visualising collaborative experiences for sustainable design education. *International Journal of Technology and Design Education*, 1–15.

Maeda, J. (2011, November 14). Maeda Brings STEAM to MIT. *Rhode Island School of Design Stories.* Available at: www.risd.edu/About/News/Maeda_brings_STEAM_to_MIT/?dept=4294967928

Maeda, J. (2013). STEM + Art = STEAM. *The STEAM Journal* 1, 1. Available at: http://scholarship.claremont.edu/steam/vol1/iss1/34/.

Mansilla, V., Miller, W. C., and Gardner, H. (2000). On disciplinary lenses and interdisciplinary work, in S. Wineburg and P. Grossman (Eds.), *Interdisciplinary curriculum – challenges to implementation*, 17–38. New York: Teachers College Press.

Martin, J. (2006). *The meaning of the 21st century: A vital blueprint for ensuring our future.* New York: Riverhead Books.

May, G. (2015, March 30). STEM, not STEAM. *Insider Higher Ed.*

Mazzoleni, I., and Price, S. (2013). *Architecture follows nature: Biomimetic principles for innovative design.* Boca Raton, FL: CRC Press.

Mervis, J. (2010). Innovations in STEM Education: A conversation with PCAST's Jim Gates. Science. *American Association for the Advancement of Science* (AAAS).

National Academies (2004). NAS, NAE, and IOM (National Academy of Sciences, National Academy of Engineering, and Institute of Medicine), in *Facilitating interdisciplinary research*. Washington, DC: The National Academies Press. Available at: http://www.worldcat.org/title/facilitating-interdisciplinary-research/oclc/59003279?page=citation

National Academy of Sciences (NAS) (1997). *Adviser, teacher, role model, friend: On being a mentor to students in science and engineering.* Washington, DC: National Academies Press.

National Academy of Sciences, National Academy of Engineering, and Institute of Medicine. (2007). *Rising above the gathering storm: Energizing and employing America for a brighter economic future.* Washington, DC: The National Academies Press.

National Research Council (2012). *Education for life and work: Developing transferable knowledge and skills in the 21st century.* Committee on Defining Deeper Learning and 21st Century Skills. Washington, DC: The National Academies Press.

Newell, W. (1990). Interdisciplinary curriculum development. *Issues in Integrative Studies*, 8, 69–86.

Nowlin, S. (2013). Art meets science! Get over it. *The STEAM Journal* 1, 1. Available at: http://scholarship.claremont.edu/steam/vol1/iss1/31/

Organization for Economic Co-operation and Development (OECD) (2012). *OECD science, technology and industry outlook 2012.* Paris: OECD Publishing.

Oxman, N. (2016). Age of Entanglement. *Journal of Design and Science.* Massachusetts Institute of Technology (MIT) Media Lab. MIT Press. Available at: http://jods.mitpress.mit.edu/pub/AgeOfEntanglement

Passow, A. H. (1957). Developing a science program for rapid learners. *Science Education*, 41, 104–112.

Pink, D. H. (2006). *A whole new mind: Why right-brainers will rule the future.* New York: Riverhead Books.

Plucker, J. A., Beghetto, R. A., and Dow, G. T. (2004). Why isn't creativity more important to educational psychologists? Potentials, pitfalls, and future directions in creativity research. *Educational Psychologist*, 39, 2, 83–96.

Ramaley, J. A. (2009). The national perspective: Fostering the enhancement of STEM undergraduate education. *New Directions for Teaching and Learning*, 117, 69–81.

Ramaley, J. A. (2011) in Christenson, J. (2011, November 13). Ramaley coined STEM term now used nationwide. *Winona Daily News*. Available at: www.winonadailynews.com/news/local/ramaley-coined-stem-term-now-used-nationwide/article_457afe3e-0db3-11e1-abe0-001cc4c03286.html

Reich, S., and Reich, J. (2006). Cultural competence in interdisciplinary collaborations: A method for respecting diversity in research partnerships. *American Journal of Community Psychology*, 38, 51–62.

Repko, A. F. (2008). Assessing interdisciplinary learning outcomes. *Academic Exchange Quarterly*, 12(3), 171–178.

Repko, A. F. (2009). Transforming an experimental innovation into a sustainable academic program at the University of Texas – Arlington, in T. Augsburg and S. Henry (Eds.), *The politics of interdisciplinary studies: Essays on transformations in American undergraduate programs.* Jefferson, NC: McFarland.

Root-Bernstein, R. S., Allen, L., Beach, L., Bhadula, R., Fast, J., Hosey, C., Kremkow, B., Lapp, J., Lonc, K., Pawelec, K., Podufaly, A., Russ, C., Tennant, L., Vrtis, E., and Weinlander, S. (2008). Arts foster success: Comparison of Nobel prizewinners, Royal Society, National Academy, and Sigma Xi members. *Journal of the Psychology of Science Technology*, 1, 2, 51–63.

Rutherford, F. J. (1998). Sputnik and science education. Reflecting on Sputnik: Linking the past, present, and future of educational reform. Retrieved at: www.nas.edu/sputnik/ruther1.htm

Salzman, H. (2007). Globalization of R&D and Innovation: Implications for U.S. STEM Workforce and Policy. *Statement Submitted to the Committee on Science and Technology, U.S. House of Representatives.* Available at: www.urban.org/sites/default/files/alfresco/publication-pdfs/901129-Globalization-of-R-amp-D-and-Innovation-Implications-for-U-S-STEM-Workforce-and-Policy.PDF

Sanders, M. (2009). STEM, STEM education, STEM mania. *Technology Teacher*, 68, 4, 20–26.

Schaub, A. (2013). Affordable medical prostheses created in Fablabs, in J. Walter-Herrmann and C. Büching (Eds.), *FabLab: Of machines, makers and inventors.* Bielefeld: Transcript.

Schrage, M. (2010). The Creativity Crisis? What Creativity Crisis? Response. *Harvard Business Review.* Watertown: Harvard Business School Publishing Corporation.

Shedroff, N. (2009). *Experience design 1.1. A manifesto for the design of experiences.* Indianapolis, IN: New Riders Publishing.

Sherwin, C. (2012, September 12). Sustainability is the ultimate design brief. *The Guardian.* Available at: www.theguardian.com/sustainable-business/blog/sustainability-sustainable-design-products

Skorton, D. J. (2014, January 16). Why scientists should embrace the liberal arts. *Scientific American.* Available at: www.scientificamerican.com/article/why-scientists-should-embrace-liberal-arts/

Sochacka, N. W., Guyotte, K. W., and Walther, J. (2016). Learning together: A collaborative autoethnographic exploration of STEAM (STEM + the Arts) education. *Journal of Engineering Education*, 105, 15–42.

Sochacka, N. W., Guyotte, K. W., Walther, J., and Kellam, N. N. (2013). *Faculty Reflections on a STEAM-inspired Interdisciplinary Studio Course.* Paper presented at the ASEE Annual Conference, Atlanta, GA. Retrieved at: https://peer.asee.org/19611

Stehr, N., and Weingart, P. (2000). *Practising interdisciplinarity.* Toronto: University of Toronto Press.

Turner, S. (2000). What are disciplines? And how is interdisciplinarity different? in N. Stehr and P. Weingart (Eds.), *Practising interdisciplinarity*, 46–65. Toronto: University of Toronto Press.

United Nations Environment Programme (UNEP) (2012). One planet, how many people? A review of earth's carrying capacity, a discussion paper for the year of RIO+20. *UNEP Global Environmental Alert Service (GEAS).* Available at: www.unep.org/pdf/UNEP_GEAS_June_2012.pdf

Vess, D. (2001). Navigating the interdisciplinary archipelago: The scholarship of interdisciplinary teaching and learning. In M. T. Huber and S. P. Morreale (Eds.), *Disciplinary styles in the scholarship of teaching and learning: Exploring common ground*, 87–106. Washington, DC: AAHE/Carnegie Foundation for the Advancement of Teaching.

White, H. (2010). STEAM. *White Paper: STEAM Not STEM.* Available at: http://steam-notstem.com/about/whitepaper/

Wilson, S. (2010). *Art + Science now.* New York: Thames and Hudson.

Woodruff, K. (2013). A history of STEM – Reigniting the challenge with NGSS and CCSS. *U.S. Satellite Laboratory.*

Wynn, T., and Harris, J. (2012). Toward a STEM + Arts Curriculum: Creating the teacher team. *Arts Education*, X, 42–47.

36

DESIGN FOR THE CIRCULAR ECONOMY

Ruud Balkenende, Nancy Bocken and Conny Bakker

Introduction

Sustainability describes our potential to maintain the well-being of humans and our environment now and over the long-term (WCED 1987). Until recently, the notion of sustainability was largely driven by energy efficiency during product manufacturing and in the use phase of products (Pigosso et al. 2015). We are now seeing increased concerns about materials, focusing on both physical scarcity and economic criticality. Demand of and competition for finite and critical resources continues to increase, and pressure on resources is causing greater environmental degradation and fragility. In the field of design for sustainability this primarily leads to a focus on improved recyclability of products. However, with recycling the material value is often only a small fraction of the actual product value and does not counteract the cost of collection and recycling processes. The economic perspective of recycling is therefore limited and actual recycling yields are relatively low. It makes more economic and environmental sense, therefore, to develop reuse strategies, in which value is maintained, like product reuse, remanufacturing and parts harvesting (Stahel 1981).

Circular economy offers a promising outlook. Circular economy describes an ecosystem in which resources are fully renewable, with reuse of products, components and materials, implying that natural assets are preserved. In a circular economy value chains and networks are closed by optimally addressing the circular design of business models, processes and products, taking simultaneously an environmental and economic perspective (Bocken et al. 2016; Lieder et al. 2016).

Europe and China have recently adopted circular economy principles as part of their future strategies (European Commission 2014), proposing actions that will contribute to closing the loop of product life cycles through greater recycling and reuse. Regulatory implementation still has to take place, but the European Commission defines the framework to a more circular economy with strategies such as increasing recycling, preventing loss of valuable materials, creating jobs and economic growth, and exploring new business models to Europe toward zero waste.

This requires insight in the manufacturing and recovery processes, business models, user requirements and societal needs. Value chains will need to explore new business and market models, also comprising new views on consumer behavior and acceptance. Product design and manufacturing will need to consider ways of turning waste into a resource. Here we will focus on the product design perspective. Product design for a circular economy requires new design methodologies and tools, which must be based on proper insights in dealing with products over their entire life cycle, including treatments at the end of a use cycle.

In this chapter, the circular economy will first be briefly introduced. Subsequently, business approaches that shape economically viable routes towards closing resource loops will be discussed. These provide incentives for a different approach towards design. This will first be addressed at a strategic level and subsequently design directions for technological implementation will be discussed. This will be illustrated by discussing design interventions that enable a more circular use of lighting.

Circular economy

Since the industrial revolution, our economies have developed a 'take-make-use-dispose' pattern of growth (Ellen MacArthur Foundation 2013; Bocken et al. 2016). Energy is to a large extent obtained from fossil fuels. Clear responsibilities with respect to end-of-life of a product are lacking. Usually this is left to relatively uninformed choices of the customer. Valuable materials are therefore easily lost upon disposal of a product at the end of its life cycle (Zimmermann 2016). The circular economy approach contrasts with the traditional linear economic system. The aim is to ensure that resources are renewable. This implies amongst others a different way of looking at and working with materials. From a business perspective this implies a shift in the generation of profits from one-time selling to generation of profits from the flow of materials and products over time (Bakker et al. 2014). With respect to the treatments at the end of a use cycle, the manufacturer or service provider ideally takes responsibility. The transition to a circular economy is expected to result in a more efficient use of resources.

From a product life cycle perspective circular economy aims to avoid waste by closing the materials flow. This can be done at different levels. Usually closing resource loops is associated with recycling (Stahel 1981; McDonough et al. 2002). Materials (or elements) are then recovered and can be reused in production of new products. However, recovery of materials means that all energy, effort and value put into the product during the manufacturing stage is lost. From both an economic and environmental perspective it therefore makes sense to strive for recovery while maintaining functionality and value. In addition to optimizing for recycling (materials recovery), products should therefore also be designed for reuse, repair, and refurbishment (implying recovery/harvesting at the level of the product) as well as parts harvesting (recovery at the component level) (Ellen MacArthur Foundation 2013; Bakker et al. 2014a). This is represented in the product life cycle depicted in Figure 36.1.

Stahel (Stahel 1994; Stahel 2010), referring to closed loop systems, distinguishes two different types of loops within a closed loop system: (1) reuse of goods and (2) recycling of materials. The result of the reuse of goods is a slowdown of the flow of materials from production to recycling. In earlier work, Stahel (1981) referred to this loop as the slow replacement system and to long-life products. The second loop is then related to recycling, which means closing the loop between post-use waste and production (Stahel 1981). According to Ayres (Ayres 1994) there are only two possible long-term fates for materials at the end of a life cycle: either recycling and reuse, or dissipative loss (e.g. lubricants or detergents).

Building on Stahel (Stahel 1994, pp. 178–190; Stahel 2010) and Ayres (Ayres 1994), McDonough and Braungart (McDonough et al. 2002) call for a radical change through circular approaches for the development of products and systems in their cradle-to-cradle approach. Design should already take into account the next life cycles of a product, preferably using materials at a higher level (upcycling). They differentiate between a biological and a technological cycle. Dissipative

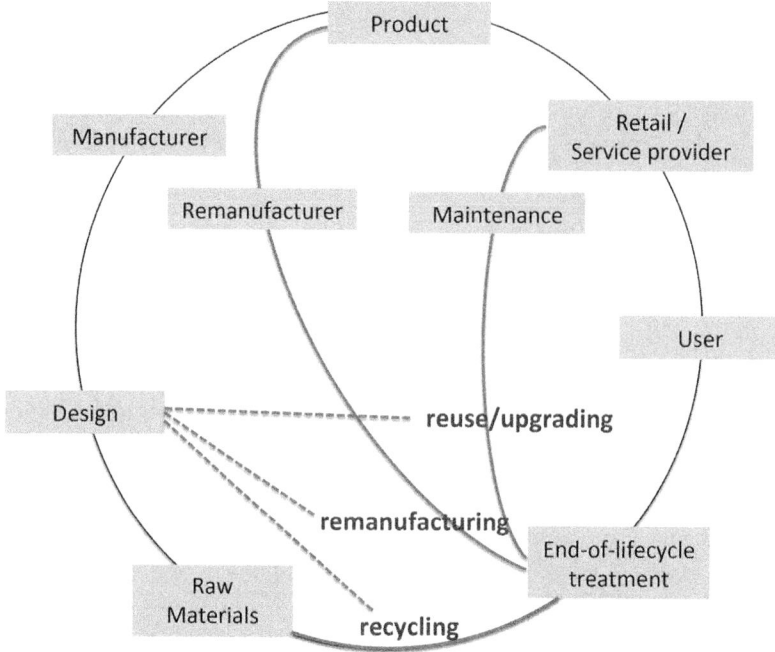

Figure 36.1 Depiction of the product life cycle in a circular economy context, emphasizing the routes toward closing the resource loop.

losses should fit in the biological cycle, in which they are finally biodegraded to start a new cycle. Other materials should be completely recycled, fitting the technological cycle. The aspiration is to close the materials loop, while working with renewable energy sources. When designing products that fit in the technological cycle, the ambition is to design products in such a way that the materials can be continuously and safely recycled into new materials (Boulding 1966). This provides a long-term vision that is inspiring to many. Circular economy is partly built upon this vision, while realizing that a practical and pragmatic approach is essential for implementation.

Business approaches

Relating these material flow strategies for slowing and closing the materials loop to business approaches, Bocken et al. (2016) distinguished between slowing resource loops and closing resource loops. Slowing resource loops is used when the utilization period of products is prolonged or intensified, resulting in a slowdown of the flow of resources. This is achieved through the design of long-life goods, product-life extension (e.g. maintenance and repair) and product-use intensification (e.g. providing services). Closing resource loops is used when the loop between the end of a product life cycle and production is closed, resulting in a circular flow of resources. At the level of materials this is achieved through recycling, at the level of products through remanufacturing (an approach that is considered slowing by Bocken et al. (2016)). These two approaches are seen as clearly distinct from a third approach toward reducing resource flows, which is narrowing resource flows. Narrowing is aimed at using fewer resources per product. This latter flow is not further discussed here, as it does not contribute to closing resource flows and is an often-applied cost reduction strategy in the linear economy. The various approaches are depicted in Figure 36.2.

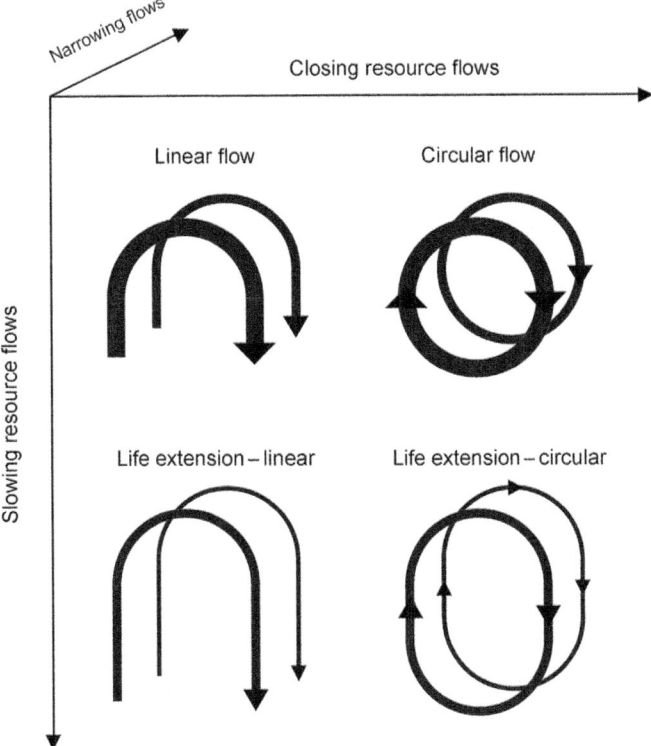

Figure 36.2 Categorization of linear and circular approaches for reducing resource use. Taken from (Bocken et al. 2016).

Summarizing business approaches for both slowing and closing of resource loops, the goal is to maintain the highest level of economic value of products, components and materials for as long as possible, while at the same time ensuring the environmental impact over time is as low as possible. A strong relation exists between product design and such business models: services lead to other incentives and requirements than sales, remanufacturing leads to other demands than recycling. A key aspect in many approaches is the direct responsibility of a manufacturing for a product over the complete life cycle, including end-of-life treatments. The collective recycling schemes for electronic products in Europe have shown that even shared responsibility does not lead to a design incentive (Atasu et al. 2012; Brouillat et al. 2012). Only if the manufacturer has a direct incentive to improve the treatments of a product at the end of a life cycle, this will be taken into account in the design of that product. In the following section business approaches will be discussed, primarily focusing on value over lifetime and incentives to take care of end-of-life treatments. This will be followed by a discussion on related design strategies.

Business approaches to slow resource loops encourage long product life (durability) and reuse of products. Three key approaches as mentioned in literature are briefly described: classic long life, access and performance, and exploiting residual product value (Bakker et al. 2014a; Bocken et al. 2014; Bocken et al. 2016).

Classic long life (Bakker et al. 2014a) is concerned with long-product life, supported by design for durability and repair. Products exhibit durable parts and materials for a high quality and a long lifetime. Although total cost of ownership can be competitive, the upfront price is usually relatively high, which might limit consumer attractivity. High levels of service regarding maintenance and repair to keep the product in a good working often accompany classic long-life products. However, as ownership is transferred to the user of the product, treatments after disposal of the product are usually less well defined. The transfer of ownership also implies that, within the current regulatory frameworks, manufacturers do not have a direct incentive to design for optimal recovery of resources after disposal.

Access and performance (Bakker et al. 2014a), also referred to as Product-Service Systems (Tukker 2015), is a combination of products and service. Examples can be found for a variety of product categories, e.g. car sharing services, document management, launderettes and phone leasing. The user does not need to own physical products to have access to a particular product or its functionality. Ownership as well as organization of service and maintenance becomes the responsibility of the manufacturer or retailer. Value is captured by pricing per unit of service (e.g. time, number of uses, performance). The advantage of the access and performance approach is that it can introduce economic incentives for slowing resource loops. Through the shift of ownership from user to manufacturer and from prolonged lease or service periods, this approach provides clear incentives to improve on durability, energy efficiency, maintenance, reusability, and repairability. Further, users only pay for the actual performance and can reduce costs when use of a particular product is not intensive. Potentially, this also reduces the total need for physical goods. Further, the shift in ownership leads to a direct incentive for the manufacturer to take responsibility for the most effective treatment at the end of a life cycle. In addition the reverse logistics stream is much better controlled than for one-time sales, which implies that the way of treatment at the end of a life cycle can be better controlled.

Exploiting residual product value is concerned with exploiting the residual value of products once they are discarded after a first use cycle, e.g. by refurbishment. The number of life cycles is increased, whereas in the classic long life the emphasis is on prolonging a single use cycle. Refurbishment basically is the process of returning a used product to a satisfactory working condition that may be inferior to the original specification (King et al. 2006; Hatcher et al. 2014). The associated business approach includes take-back systems and requires a different kind of cooperation over the value chain than business as usual in a linear context (e.g. dealing with reverse logistics companies and collection points). Refurbishment reduces the need for virgin resources and reduces material costs (while potentially increasing labor and logistics cost). Ideally, exploiting residual product value is part of business models that also incorporate classic long life or access and performance. OEMs then develop business models that support refurbishment, implying that they have a direct incentive to optimally enable this. In reality, manufacturers often neglect the opportunity of exploiting residual product value. Gap exploiters (Bakker et al. 2014) then exploit products from other companies as they see an untapped opportunity. For example, Gazelle in the United States and LEAPP in the Netherlands refurbish and sell refurbished phones and laptops. The advantage of Gap Exploiters is that value is restored and the need for new products is reduced. However, as the manufacturer is not involved, design is not optimized for this purpose.

Closing loops in business model innovation is about capturing the value from what is considered in a linear business approach as waste. These strategies may be local and dedicated in scope, for example when materials are reused in manufacturing processes within a production facility (Wells et al. 2005), or more generic when products are eventually disposed of and the content may be recycled via an entirely independent network.

Closing of resource loops can be done at different levels. Most common is recycling, in which elements (in the case of most metals) or materials (e.g. glass or particular polymers) are recovered in a series of physical separation steps and chemical recovery processes. Business models

Table 36.1 Overview of intervention options for improved recycling of products for different stakeholders. Taken from (Balkenende et al. 2014)

Business interventions
Company level design guidelines
Integrate recyclability indication into existing design software
Private scheme Producer Responsibility Organisation (PRO)
Government Regulations
100 percent recycling target with penalties for noncompliance
Standardization or specification
Suppliers are responsible for recovering their own material
Arrange intellectual property rights
EU level design guidelines
Collaboration interventions
International business cases
Kick-back fee from recyclers to producers
Designers visit recycling plant
Courses for designers (assembly, disassembly)
Societal interventions
NGOs organize consumers (increased collection)

of product manufacturers usually do not explicitly address recycling. In general, the economic incentive for recycling is low, at least for manufacturers and retailers, as they do not individually carry the cost of the recycling processes (Rahimifard et al. 2009; Atasu et al. 2012; Richter et al. 2016), nor do they benefit from the recovery yields.

Recycling is therefore currently mainly driven by regulations enforcing the recovery of materials from particular classes of products. To increase the business potential of recycling, interventions in the value network are required (Rahimifard et al. 2009). Possible interventions in the areas of business, government regulations, collaboration and society have been identified through in-depth value network analysis (Balkenende et al. 2014). This resulted in a set of potential interventions, which are listed in Table 36.1. Implementation is often strongly dependent on a specific stakeholder, though the impact affects the whole value network. As an additional complication, the benefits of particular measures do often not coincide with the required effort, thus limiting the incentive to implement actual innovations .The suitability, feasibility and acceptability throughout the network of these interventions needs further investigation. Currently, regulations remain to be the strongest driver for improving on the recyclability of products (see e.g. the directives for waste electrical and electronic equipment and for end-of-life vehicles (European Union 2000; European Union 2012)).

Recycling currently has a strong focus on recycling rates of specific products and materials categories. The 'upcycling' perspective as promoted in the cradle-to-cradle approach is lacking (McDonough et al. 2002). Linking specific obsolete materials directly to new products gives a different incentive, both regarding the design o the new product, as well as on the longer-term to the design of the original products. The collection or sourcing of otherwise wasted materials and resources to turn these into new forms of value was dubbed Renewing Resource Value (Bocken et al. 2016). A specific example is Interface Net-Works, a program that sources fishing nets from coastal areas to clean up oceans and beaches while creating financial opportunities for people in impoverished communities and serving as a source to create recycled yarn for Interface carpet (Interface 2016). The value proposition is focused on exploiting the residual value of resources, potentially making the product more appealing to certain customers (e.g. those with a 'green' interest), while reducing material costs and the overall product price. Forms of value creation and delivery include new collaborations and take-back systems to be put in place to collect source materials. Value is captured by turning otherwise wasted resources into new forms of value.

In contrast to recycling of materials, functionality and value can to a large extent be conserved in the case of remanufacturing, meaning the return of a used product or parts to at least its original performance with a warranty that is equivalent to or better than that of the newly man-ufactured product (British Standards Institution 2009). The result of remanufacturing is a new product that is assembled of components that cannot be traced back to a single previous product (Ijomah et al. 2007). In this respect remanufacturing differs fundamentally from refurbishment, where an existing product is restored. Hence, whereas refurbishment is a means to Exploiting Residual Product Value, remanufacturing leads to Renewing Product Functionality.

From a business perspective a number of reasons have been brought forward to pursue reman-ufacturing. Remanufacturing by its nature will usually be carried out by the OEM or will be certified by the OEM (another difference with refurbishment, that is often carried out by third parties). In a case study on automotive manufacturers (Seitz 2007) concluded that often-mentioned incentives like environment, legislation and profit were not considered important. More important reasons were to ensure supply of spare parts meeting customer's demands and to prevent independents from retrieving parts and potentially damaging OEM brand reputation. More generally, the economic incentive for remanufacturing will depend on competition, price and differentiation. Design should aim for a large cost difference between remanufacturing and new production (Atasu et al. 2008).

Circular product design

Circular product design aims to design products, components and materials in such a way that their environmental impact is minimized, while their economic value is optimally retained for as long as possible. This is achieved by designing for long product life and by enabling effective repair, refurbishment, remanufacture, parts harvesting and recycling in order to loop back used products, components and materials into the economic system.

It is therefore closely linked to the business approaches that implement the circular use of a particular product, while simultaneously addressing environmental requirements and user needs. Several influential nature-inspired holistic strategies, that aim for closing resource loops by opti-mizing systems (instead of improving components), have been proposed over the past decades, notably Biomimicry (Benyus 1997), Cradle-to-Cradle (McDonough et al. 2002), The Blue Economy (Pauli 2010) and Circular Economy (Ellen MacArthur Foundation 2012). Especially the Cradle-to-Cradle design philosophy describes a far reaching circular approach, in which biological materials are cascaded in a biological cycle and technological materials are part of a closed loop materials cycle. This has inspired many companies and designers to explore solutions within this framework (Bakker et al. 2010; de Pauw et al. 2013). The high level of abstraction, however, makes it difficult to directly implement these strategies, especially when complicated products like cars or electronics are considered.

Design incentives will change if a product is intended for reuse, remanufacturing or recycling after its useful life. Knowledge of the business model as such is essential, but not sufficient for cir-cular product design. In addition, knowledge of the way in which a product is treated during and at the end of a life cycle must thus be acquired and related to the design properties. If a product

Table 36.2 Overview of business strategies and design approaches with respect for slowing and closing resource flows. Building on (Bakker et al. 2014a; Bocken et al. 2016)

Resource flow	Sustainable business approach	Lifecycle design perspectives	Technological design aspects
Slowing resource flows	Classic Long Life	Durability	Material choices
	Access and Performance	Upgrading	Standardization
	Exploiting Residual Product Value	Adapting	Compatibility
		Repair	Modularity
	Gap Exploiter	Refurbishment	Accessibility
		Parts harvesting	Disassembly
Closing resource loops	Renew Resource Functionality	Remanufacturing	Reassembly
	Renew Resource Value	Recycling	

will be reused, suitability for appropriate maintenance is a prerequisite. If repair, refurbishment or remanufacturing are intended, the accessibility, disassembly and reassembly of parts or modules is important. If a product is disposed of when it is at the end of its functional life optimal recycling, i.e. complete recovery of the constituting materials should be enabled.

Discussing design strategies, we can roughly distinguish two categories. The first category focuses on enabling a particular activity with or property of the product, like reuse, maintenance, repair, recycling, refurbishment, remanufacturing or durability, usually in the context of a particular business model. The second category focuses on technologically enabling product realization and comprises aspects like modularity, disassembly and reassembly, disintegration, upgradability and adaptability, which are directly related to choices with respect to materials and their connections. In the following we will first address the strategic design goals and then zoom into the technological design aspects.

Life cycle design perspectives

The sustainable business approaches for slowing and closing resource loops intend to provide a system in which products are kept in use over prolonged periods of time, lifetimes are prolonged by maintenance and repair, the number of life cycles is increased by refurbishment or remanufacturing and materials are recovered by recycling (Bocken et al. 2016). To perform these activities in an effective way appropriate design strategies should be in place. Here we will briefly summarize a number of these strategies.

Design for durability

Durability refers to long physical durability of a product. Examples are the development of products that can take wear and tear without breaking down. Reliability, ease of maintenance, and material choices are important features for products that are intended to be durable. An example is the washing machines produced by Miele GmbH (Lofthouse et al. 2007). These exhibit a robust built, optimal service life and have an average lifetime of 18.5 years (compared to an industry average of 11.7 years (Bakker et al. 2014b)).

However, durability does not only depend on the physical and technical aspects of a product, which basically define its technical lifetime. Often it is observed that the economic lifetime of a product is considerably shorter than its technical lifetime (Bakker et al. 2014b). This might, e.g., be due to changes in fashion. An interesting design direction here is attachment to a product. Attachment is determined by multiple themes, which are difficult for designers to control. Memories, enjoyment, usability, appearance and reliability were found to have considerable impact on behavior towards product replacement (Page 2014). Self-expression and group affiliation have been identified as other important factors (Mugge 2017).

Mugge (2017) gives an overview of promising design directions to make a product irreplaceable. Design for personalization offers the opportunity to make a product more self-expressive and unique, potentially leading to a stronger emotional bond. With design employing gracefully aging materials the user might experience a shared history with the product (Mugge et al. 2008; Rognoli et al. 2013). Storytelling aims to present a narrative that is relevant to the user in the product, which can involve personal actions of the user and acts to provide memories. However, attachment will in general be difficult to control and these type of design interventions are likely to be limited to certain product categories (e.g. watches) and on people with certain personality and interests (Mugge et al. 2006).

Another reason for relatively short economic lifetimes is encountered with rapid technological developments, which can cause a product to become outdated while it is still functional. This has been evident in information and communication technology developments over the past decade where new generations of smart phones and tablets followed each other rapidly. Dependent on the pace of developments, this might at least to some extent be prevented by making products upgradable. An example is the motherboard of personal computers, that allows for upgrades in chips and memories and allows for expansion of functionality. This asks for a careful consideration of especially modularity, accessibility and interfacing (Kasarda et al. 2007; Li et al. 2008; Rashid et al. 2013).

Design for product-life extension

The second major design strategy to slow or close resource loops is to enable lifetime extension. The period of use, including reuse of the product itself, is prolonged through maintenance, repair, technical upgrading or adaption, repair or refurbishment and remanufacturing.

Design for maintenance and repair enables products to be maintained in working condition. Preventative maintenance is a regular activity performed to retain reliable functioning, e.g. replacing motor oil in a car. Repair is a corrective action to restore functional performance (Linton et al. 2005). After repair, assurances of performance are generally limited to the repaired part (British Standards Institution 2009). It is widely recognized that the repairability of consumer products has greatly decreased due to factors like increased complexity of many products, user convenience, fashion and technological obsolescence (Slade 2006). Design rules for making a product more easily repairable usually focus on the physical design and aim for component standardization and the ease of taking a piece of equipment apart (Mulder et al. 2012). Fairphone for example allows its users to easily repair and replace broken parts by a modular built and easy accessibility of the components (iFixit 2015). However, the focus on part replacement misses important factors; repair diagnostics, i.e. which part to replace, is often very difficult and time consuming and in many cases a supporting service is needed to assist in repair (Maxham 2015).

Designing for future expansion, upgrading and adaptability of products is another strategy. Upgradability is the ability of a product to continue being useful under changing conditions by improving the quality, value and effectiveness or performance (Linton et al. 2005, p. 1814). In considering possibilities for upgrading or modification, time becomes an explicit factor in design.

This implies that technological roadmaps and expected changes in user needs should be taken into account. From a technological point of view standardization of interfaces and the definition of functional modules is critical.

Although refurbishment and remanufacturing result in different product qualification, design for refurbishment and design for remanufacturing have much in common. Definitions for refurbishment and remanufacturing are not standardized and in many cases the terms are used interchangeably. Both have in common that a product gets a thorough treatment, involving physical inspection, replacement of worn parts and extensive testing. Usually these products come with warranties. Here we consider refurbished products to be restored to an acceptable level of functionality (often by third parties) (King et al. 2006; Hatcher et al. 2014). In the case of remanufacturing the product is similar or better than a new product (British Standards Institution 2009). This can only be guaranteed by the OEM. The OEM is also the only one who can take remanufacturing into account during the design stage.

Parts harvesting is the retrieval of components, modules or parts from obsolete products with the purpose of using them as spares, parts for servicing, maintenance and repair. This is quite common in in the automotive industry, for ICT equipment and professional machinery (ranging from heavy duty machinery to medical equipment). It is often closely connected to refurbishment and remanufacturing, with which it has most of the associated design principles in common.

The suitability of a product for refurbishment or remanufacturing to a large extent depends upon decisions made during product design. This implies that product design should facilitate the remanufacturing process, including component durability, disassembly and reassembly, accessibility, cleaning, reverse logistics and marketing (Shu et al. 1999; Nasr et al. 2006). Hatcher et al. (2014) compiled an overview of design concepts that are useful in design for remanufacturing: modularization, platform design, active disassembly, failure mode analysis and quality function deployment (QFD). All these concepts are familiar in traditional product design, but they get a different focus in remanufacturing. For example, modularization and platform design are usually intended to improve on manufacturing efficiency and cost, in remanufacturing the focus is on efficient disassembly and process organization. QFD, which translates user needs to quantitative engineering parameters, focuses on the remanufacturer in addition to the user of the product. Design for remanufacturing involves decisions like standardization of parts, selection of materials and fasteners.

The role of the user is especially of importance in the case of refurbishment, where user acceptance of refurbished products is of critical importance. An approach towards increasing consumer acceptance of refurbished products was proposed by (van Weelden et al. 2015). Reducing the perceived risk is an important aspect. This can be achieved through informing users as well as by increasing the benefits that are offered by refurbished products. Suggested approaches are to enable improvement of product aesthetics by easy resurfacing of vulnerable parts (Mugge 2017) or to implement information on the use history in the design (van Weelden et al. 2015).

Design for recycling

For circular use recycling must be postponed as long as possible, as recycling of materials implies loss of function and value. Nevertheless, recycling is the last option when products or parts can no longer be kept in a functional condition. This means that, in contrast to the previous activities, recyclability is a mandatory requirement for every product.

The basic requirement for improved recyclability is to establish well-defined material streams. This is achieved through disassembly (manual or mechanical) and subsequent sorting steps. A resulting material fraction should consist of materials that are compatible in the same recovery process. Even if only recyclable materials are used, the way in which different materials are connected and can be separated is crucial. An example is the screwed connection between an electronic printed circuit board (PCB), which mainly contains copper and precious metals, and the aluminum heat spreader. Both electronics and aluminum have their own dedicated recycling stream. When the connection is such that the aluminum heat spreader cannot be separated effectively from the electronics, either aluminum or copper and associated elements will be lost, while simultaneously contaminating the recycling stream in which they end up, thus potentially reducing the recovery yield of the other material (Balkenende et al. 2014).

Technological design aspects

The previously described design strategies focus on achieving particular product properties in terms of actions that can be performed on the products. Although ways in which these properties can be accomplished technologically are indicated, more concrete strategies are required for engineering design. An analysis based on product use and service requirements distinguishes a number of aspects that need specific attention when designing for circular use (van den Berg et al. 2015).

Design for standardization and compatibility

Standardization and compatibility enables exchangeability by creating products with parts or interfaces that fit other products as well (Bakker et al. 2014a). Exchangeability refers to the ease with which components or modules can be exchanged for modules with a different or improved performance. It is required for upgradeability and adaptability of products. It is usually combined with a modular approach.

Design for modularity

Modularity implies the ability to reuse (sets of) components to facilitate upgradability, repair, refurbishment or remanufacturing of a product. Modular product design is often explored to generate different products by creating combinations of modules and components providing each product with distinctive functionality, features, and performance level (Kusiak et al. 1997). Modules are defined as components whose functional, spatial, and other interface characteristics fall within the range of variations allowed by the specified standardized interfaces of a modular product (Hwang et al. 2006). Modularity is closely linked to standardization and compatibility, at least when it comes to connections and form factors within a company product portfolio. From a circular perspective it is further especially important to define the functionality of a module such that it will faclitate repairability, upgradeability and reuse opportunities. This implies that cost of the module, lifetime prognostics of its components and cost of repair are balanced in design.

Design for accessibility

Accessibility is related to the way in which parts are shaped, grouped and connected to each other. It directly affects the ease of maintenance and repair. Optimal accessibility can largely facilitate disassembly and reassembly of a product. Also cleaning of products or parts depends on accessibility.

Design for disassembly and reassembly

Disassembly and reassembly is part of every cycle. Disassembly is the first step in most actions performed to the product in order to either extend its lifetime or to give a new life to the components or materials and parts can be separated and reassembled easily (Bakker et al. 2014a).

In general, disassembly needs to be nondestructive if the product or component will be reused, implying that also reassembly has to be taken into account. Destructive disintegration is used in the recycling process and enables the reuse of materials and enables the recovery of pure materials at end-of-life to secure real resource efficiency and as the last option to recover any remaining value that a product or component has. In the case of manual disintegration, e.g. required to remove toxic materials, environmentally harmful components like batteries, or valuable materials like high-end electronic circuit boards, disintegration is similar to manual disassembly. If products are mechanically disintegrated, e.g. in a shredder, design should take the shredding process into account.

Design approaches illustrated: case studies in lighting

Closing the materials loop: design for recycling

Lamps have been redesigned taking into account design guidelines for recycling as described earlier (Aerts et al. 2014). Application of these design guidelines led to widely varying solutions that can significantly improve the recyclability and environmental performance of the lamps, while costs remain competitive. This has been validated in small-scale recycling runs.

A 'standard' LED spot (MR16) has a relatively large aluminum heat spreader. The PCB containing the driver electronics as well as the PCB with the LEDs are fixed to the heat spreader by screws, to guarantee a reliable thermal connection. For recycling it is necessary to separate heat spreader and PCBs, because the materials are not compatible in recycling. However, in mechanical disintegration the PCBs are hardly separated from the heat spreader. This has been largely improved by introducing fracture lines in the aluminum heat spreader along the screw holes. This controls fracturing of the heat spreader in such a way that the screws are released and the PCBs are detached (Figure 36.3). Except for some slight differences in the mold for manufacturing the heat spreader, the processing of the lamp does not need to be adapted. This is shown in Figure 36.3.

Figure 36.3 MR16 spot light, fragmentation resulting from shredding, and fragmentation resulting from shredding with fracture lines.

Prolonged use through service: design for performance

Delivering performance as a service is potentially an attractive offer to users, who only pay for what they need and don't need to bother with maintenance, repairs and upgrades. Simultaneously, the shift in ownership and responsibility for operation and end-of-life treatments poses a clear incentive to the manufacturer to increase lifetime, improve maintenance and optimize the value at the end of a life cycle (Tukker 2015).

As an example we discuss the Light-as-a-Service (LaaS) concept. Shifting from sales to 'light as a service' requires changes in every part of the value chain. It starts with the product design. Products for one-time sale are optimized to have the highest value for the lowest price at the moment of sale. Products for LaaS require optimization for serviceability and total lifetime. Technological advancements and changes in consumer demand should be foreseen through roadmaps that incorporate expected technological developments as well as consumer behavior. A shift will occur from reliance on ownership to optimal service of space and quality of light.

Handling of a product during its lifetime requires an integrated service organization that manages the servicing needs of the product, whilst taking care of the reverse logistics to get the product or part back to the right place in the company (production, parts storage, etc.). Predictable whole life performance of building assets, including performance systems and maintaining a high standard of efficiency will be crucial. The marketing will be different and the products need to be financed upfront.

Setting up LaaS as a business requires the right products, business logistics that fit the model, partners that service parts of the ecosystem, marketing concepts and an organization that can and will set the right targets and propositions. A concrete example is provided by the performance lighting contract between Philips and Schiphol Amsterdam Airport regarding the lighting in a departure hall (Philips 2015). As a third partner in the contract Cofely will monitor and maintain the system during the life of the contract. Parts of its system that must be replaced will be reclaimed and recycled. Lighting fixtures have been adapted to increase the lifetime by 75 percent (at a somewhat higher cost). Real-time lighting management is provided as part of the contract to optimize user experience as well as energy consumption. At the end of the contract period the light fixtures can be upgraded and reused.

Conclusion and outlook

The transition to a circular economy implies that resource loops need to be slowed down and closed to maintain products, components and materials at the highest possible economic value, while simultaneously minimizing the environmental impact. Business approaches that support this aim at products that are durable. A shift from selling products to services that provide access to products or guarantee a particular performance is considered an important step. Such a shift provides manufacturers with the incentive to create products that are durable, easy to maintain and repair and can be exploited at the end of a use cycle through refurbishment, remanufacturing, harvesting of modules and components and effective recycling of materials.

Circular product design supports this development by designing products in such a way that their environmental impact is minimal, while their economic value is optimally retained for as long as possible. This implies that design takes a life-cycle perspective, including the resources used for production and the processes at the end of a use cycle, taking into account the environmental impact associated with manufacturing, use and recovery processes.

The technological design aspects that are involved, like material choices, standardization, compatibility, modularity, accessibility, disassembly, and reassembly are to a large extent common to product design in general, but require specific attention in the case of designing for a circular economy. This is needed to enable optimal accomplishment of the treatments at the end of a life cycle in order to retain product value.

To realize the transformation of a linear to a circular economy, developments in design strategies should not only focus on resource efficiency, but also take into account behavioral and social aspects. Further, the complexity of value chains, with the various stakeholders involved, should be dealt with. Finally, understanding the design process also involves assessing environmental impact, which in a circular context is still relatively unexplored.

References

Aerts, M., Felix, J., Huisman, J. and Balkenende, A.R. (2014) "Lamp Redesign: Shredding Before Selling". In B. Kopacek, ed. *Proceedings of Going Green – CARE Innovation 2014: Towards a Resource Efficient Economy*. International CARE Electronics Office, Vienna, 4–7.

Atasu, A., Sarvary, M. and Van Wassenhove, L.N. (2008) "Remanufacturing as a Marketing Strategy". *Management Science 54*, 1731–1746.

Atasu, A. and Subramanian, R. (2012) "Extended Producer Responsibility for E-waste: Individual or Collective Producer Responsibility?". *Production and Operations Management 21*, 1042–1059.

Ayres, U.R. (1994) "Industrial Metabolism: Theory and Policy". In B.R. Allenby and D.J. Richards, eds. *Greening of Industrial Ecosystems*. National Academy Press, Washington, DC, 23–37.

Bakker, C.A., Den Hollander, M., Van Hinte, E. and Zijlstra, Y. (2014a) *Product That Last: Product Design for Circular Business Models*. TU Delft Library, Delft.

Bakker, C.A., Wang, F., Huisman, J. and Den Hollander, M. (2014b) "Products That Go Round: Exploring Product Life Extension Through Design". *Journal of Cleaner Production 69*, 10–16.

Bakker, C.A., Wever, R., Teoh, C. and Clercq de, S. (2010) "Designing Cradle-to-Cradle Products: A Reality Check". *International Journal of Sustainable Engineering 3*, 2–8.

Balkenende, A.R., Occhionorelli, V., Meensel, W. Van, Felix, J., Sjölin, S., Aerts, M., Huisman, J., Becker, J., Schaik, A. Van and Reuter, M. (2014) "Greenelec: Product Design Linked to Recycling". In B. Kopacek, ed. *Proceedings of Going Green – CARE Innovation 2014: Towards a Resource Efficient Economy*, International CARE Electronics Office, Vienna.

Benyus, J.M. (1997) *Biomimicry: Innovation Inspired by Nature*. Morrow, New York.

Berg, M.R. van den and Bakker, C.A. (2015) "A Product Design Framework for a Circular Economy". In T. Cooper, N. Braithwaite, M. Moreno, and G. Salvia, Eds. *Product Lifetimes and the Environment*. Nottingham Trent University, Nottingham, 324.

Bocken, N.M.P., Farracho, M., Bosworth, R. and Kemp, R. (2014) "The Front-End of Eco-Innovation for Eco-Innovative Small and Medium Sized Companies". *Journal of Engineering and Technology Management – JET-M 31*, 43–57.

Bocken, N.M.P., Pauw, I. de, Bakker, C.A. and Grinten, B. van der (2016) "Product Design and Business Model Strategies for a Circular Economy". *Journal of Industrial and Production Engineering 1015*, 1–12.

Boulding, K.E. (1966) "The Economics of the Coming Spaceship Earth". In H. Jarrett, ed. *Environmental Quality in a Growing Economy: Essays From the Sixth RFF Forum*. John Hopkins University Press, Baltimore, 3–14.

British Standards Institution (2009) *British Standard BS 8887–2. Design for Manufacture, Assembly, Disassembly and End-of-life Processing (MADE). Part 2: Terms and Definitions*, https://www.standardsuk.com/download-british-standards.

Brouillat, E. and Oltra, V. (2012) "Extended Producer Responsibility Instruments and Innovation in Eco-design: An Exploration Through a Simulation Model". *Ecological Economics 83*, 236–245.

Ellen MacArthur Foundation (2012) "Circular Economy – UK, USA, Europe, Asia & South America". www.ellenmacarthurfoundation.org/ [Accessed December 11, 2016].

Ellen MacArthur Foundation (2013) *Towards the Circular Economy: Opportunities for the Consumer Goods Sector*. Ellen MacArthur Foundation, Cowes, UK.

European Commission (2014) "Circular Economy Strategy – Environment – European Commission". http://ec.europa.eu/environment/circular-economy/index_en.htm [Accessed December 11, 2016].

European Union (2000) "Directive 2000/53/EC – End-of-Life Vehicles". *Official Journal of the European Communities 6*, 34–42.

European Union (2012) "Directive 2012/19/EU of the European Parliament and of the Council on Waste Electrical and Electronic Equipment (WEEE)". *Official Journal of the European Union 13*, 1–24.

Hatcher, G.D., Ijomah, W.L. and Windmill, J.F.C. (2014) "Design for Remanufacture: A Literature Review and Future Research Needs". *Journal of Cleaner Production 19*, 2004–2014.

Hwang, J.Y., Huang, X. and Xu, Z. (2006) "Recovery of Metals From Aluminum Dross and Saltcake". *Journal of Minerals and Materials Characterization and Engineering 5*, 47–62.

iFixit (2015) "Fairphone 2 Teardown". https://nl.ifixit.com/Teardown/Fairphone+2+Teardown/52523 [Accessed December 13, 2016].

Ijomah, W.L., Mcmahon, C.A., Hammond, G.P. and Newman, S.T. (2007) "Development of Robust Design-for-Remanufacturing Guidelines to Further the Aims of Sustainable Development". *International Journal of Production Research 45*, 4513–4536.

Interface (2016) "Interface' Products, Brands & Services". www.interfaceglobal.com/Products/Net-Works. aspx [Accessed December 11, 2016].

Kasarda, M.E., Terpenny, J.P., Inman, D., Precoda, K.R., Jelesko, J., Sahin, A. and Park, J. (2007) "Design for Adaptability (DFAD) – A New Concept for Achieving Sustainable Design". *Robotics and Computer-Integrated Manufacturing 23*, 727–734.

King, A.M., Burgess, S.C., Ijomah, W. and Mcmahon, C.A. (2006) "Remanufacture or Recycle?". *Sustainable Development 14*, 257–267.

Kusiak, A. and Huang, C. (1997) "Design of Modular Digital Circuits for Testability". *Ieee Transactions on Components, Packaging, and Manufacturing Technology – Part C 20*, 48–57.

Li, Y., Xue, D. and Gu, P. (2008) "Design for Product Adaptability". *Concurrent Engineering 16*, 221–232.

Lieder, M. and Rashid, A. (2016) "Towards Circular Economy Implementation: A Comprehensive Review in Context of Manufacturing Industry". *Journal of Cleaner Production 115*, 36–51.

Linton, J.D. and Jayaraman, V. (2005) "A Framework for Identifying Differences and Similarities in the Managerial Competencies Associated With Different Modes of Product Life Extension". *International Journal of Production Research 43*, 1807–1829.

Lofthouse, V. and Bhamra, T. (2007) *Design for Sustainability: A Practical Approach.* Gower Publishing Ltd., Hampshire, UK.

McDonough, W. and Braungart, M. (2002) *Cradle to Cradle: Remaking the Way We Make Things.* North Point Press, New York.

Maxham, J. (2015) *The Art of Troubleshooting.* Self-published via CreateSpace Independent Publishing Platform, Charleston.

Mugge, R. (2017) "A Consumer's Perspective on the Circular Economy". In J. Chapman, ed. *Routledge Handbook of Sustainable Product Design.* Routledge, London.

Mugge, R., Schifferstein, H.N.J. and Schoormans, J.P.L. (2006) "Product Attachment and Product Lifetime: The Role of Personality Congruity and Fashion". *European Advances in Consumer Research 7*, 460–467.

Mugge, R., Schoormans, J.P.L. and Schifferstein, H.N.J. (2008) "Product Attachment: Design Strategies to Stimulate the Emotional Bonding to Products". In N. J. Hendrik, H.N.J. Schifferstein, P. Hekkert, eds. *Product Experience.* Elsevier Ltd, London, 425–440.

Mulder, W., Blok, J., Hoekstra, S. and Kokkeler, F. (2012) *Design for Maintenance.* University of Twente, Enschede.

Nasr, N. and Thurston, M. (2006) "Remanufacturing : A Key Enabler to Sustainable Product Systems". In J. R. Duflou, LCE2006, *Proceedings of the 13th CIRP International Conference on Life Cycle Engineering.* Katholieke Universiteit Leuven, Leuven, 15–18.

Page, T. (2014) "Product Attachment and Replacement: Implications for Sustainable Design". *International Journal of Sustainable Design 2*, 265–282.

Pauli, G. (2010) *The Blue Economy: 10 Years – 100 Innovations – 100 Million Jobs.* Paradigm Publications, Taos.

Pauw, I. de, Karana, E. and Kandachar, P. (2013) "Cradle to Cradle in Product Development: A Case Study of Closed-Loop Design". In A.Y.C. Nee, B. Song, S.-K. Ong, eds. *Re-engineering Manufacturing for Sustainability, Proceedings of the 20th CIRP International Conference on Life Cycle Engineering.* Springer Singapore, Singapore, 47–52.

Philips (2015) "Philips Provides Light as a Service to Schiphol Airport". www.philips.com/a-w/about/news/archive/standard/news/press/2015/20150416-Philips-provides-Light-as-a-Service-to-Schiphol-Airport.html [Accessed December 13, 2016].

Pigosso, D.C.A., McAloone, T.C. and Rozenfeld, H. (2015) "Characterization of the State-of-the-Art and Identification of Main Trends for Ecodesign Tools and Methods: Classifying Three Decades of Research and Implementation". *Journal of the Indian Institute of Science 95*, 405–427.

Rahimifard, S., Coates, G., Staikos, T., Edwards, C. and Abu-Bakar, M. (2009) "Barriers, Drivers and Challenges for Sustainable Product Recovery and Recycling". *International Journal of Sustainable Engineering* 2, 80–90.

Rashid, A., Asif, F.M.A., Krajnik, P. and Nicolescu, C.M. (2013) "Resource Conservative Manufacturing: An Essential Change in Business and Technology Paradigm for Sustainable Manufacturing". *Journal of Cleaner Production 57*, 166–177.

Richter, J.L. and Koppejan, R. (2016) "Extended Producer Responsibility for Lamps in Nordic Countries: Best Practices and Challenges in Closing Material Loops". *Journal of Cleaner Production 123*, 167–179.

Rognoli, V. and Karana, E. (2013) "Toward a New Materials Aesthetic Based on Imperfection and Graceful Aging". In E. Karana, O. Pedgley and V. Rognoli, eds. *Materials Experience: Fundamentals of Materials and Design*. Elsevier, Amsterdam, 145–154.

Seitz, M.A. (2007) "A Critical Assessment of Motives for Product Recovery: The Case of Engine Remanufacturing". *Journal of Cleaner Production 15*, 1147–1157.

Shu, L.H. and Flowers, W.C. (1999) "Application of a Design-for-Remanufacture Framework to the Selection of Product Life-cycle Fastening and Joining Methods". *Robotics and Computer-Integrated Manufacturing 15*, 179–190.

Slade, G. (2006) *Made to Break: Technology and Obsolescence in America*. Harvard University Press, Cambridge, MA.

Stahel, W.R. (1981) "The Product-life Factor". In S. G. Orr, ed. *An Inquiry Into the Nature of Sustainable Societies: The Role of the Private Sector*. The Mitchell Prizes 1982, HARC, Houston, 72–96.

Stahel, W.R. (1994) *The Utilization-focused Service Economy: Resource Efficiency and Product-life Extension*. B.R. Allenby and D.J. Richards, eds. National Academy Press, Washington, DC.

Stahel, W.R. (2010) *The Performance Economy*. Palgrave Macmillan, London, UK.

Tukker, A. (2015) "Product Services for a Resource-efficient and Circular Economy – a Review". *Journal of Cleaner Production 97*, 76–91.

Weelden, E. van, Mugge, R. and Bakker, C.A. (2015) "Paving the Way Towards Circular Consumption: Exploring Consumer Acceptance of Refurbished Mobile Phones in the Dutch Market". *Journal of Cleaner Production 113*, 743–754.

Wells, P. and Seitz, M. (2005) "Business Models and Closed-loop Supply Chains: A Typology". *Supply Chain Management – An International Journal 10*, 249–251.

World Commission on Environment and Development (1987) *Our Common Future ('Brundtland Report')*. United Nations, Oxford University Press, Oxford.

Zimmermann, T. (2016) "Uncovering the Fate of Critical Metals: Tracking Dissipative Losses Along the Product Life Cycle". *Journal of Industrial Ecology*, available online. doi:10.1111/jiec.12492

INDEX

Note: figures and tables are denoted with italicized page numbers; end note information is denoted with an n following the page number.

ABCD planning method 45–6
activity-centered design (ACD) 203–4
activity theory 322
Actor-Network Theory (ANT) 254
adaptability *see* change and adaptability
addictions: impactful design strategies for breaking 35; political economy of design feeding 4, 5; *see also* substance use/abuse
Addiction by Design, Natasha Schüll, 5
advertising: citizen empowerment via counter advertising project 453–5; global brand promotion via 104; global economic growth fueled by 126; information-based campaigns in 329; online platforms for 473; political economy of design driven by 3, 4, 5; tourism-related 259–60
advocate-designers 449–50, 452
agriculture: biomimicry design related to 461, 464; Dujiangyan irrigation system in 206–7; greenhouses for 129; localized economy approaches to 129, 132–3; nature-based urban design use of 405; organic certifications in 59, 69; scale and considerations related to 57, 58, 59, 68, 69; self-sufficiency movements on 392; systems thinking on 22, 24
AirBnB 235, 471, 475, 476, 478, 481n1
Anderson, Ray 468
anecdotes, rhetoric and persuasion via 363
Anthropocene 86, 187
Apple 4, 473
applied sustainability: ABCD planning method or backcasting for 45–6; cultural considerations for 47; for digital media 48, 50–2; industry uses of 48–52; life-cycle assessment of 41–3, 48; Living

Principles for Design framework for 46–7, *47*; The Natural Step™ framework for 44–5, 46; overview of 11, 40, 48–52; for packaging and print design 41, 43, 49–50; for product design 48–9; systems thinking on 40, 43–9, *44*; Triple Bottom Line approach to 46, 51–2; Whole Systems and Lifecycle Thinking method on 48–9
Arnstein, Sherry R. 450–2, *451*
Artisan Economy Initiative 133
Attention Restoration Theory (ART) 401–2

backcasting 45–6
Bacon, Francis 87, 88, 215
Baltimore: citizen empowerment in 446, 452–8; Uprising 453, 455
Base of the Pyramid (BoP) design 420, 425
behavior: belief schematas for 437–8; consumer, with electronics 160–4, *162*; designing for changes of (*see* behavior change); feedback loops of 17–19, *17–19*; habitual (*see* habits); problematic system behaviors 19–21; structure creating behavior possibilities 17–19, *17–19*; sustainable behavior design (*see* Design for Sustainable Behaviour); systems thinking on 17–21; values translated into 303–4
behavior change: culture and emotions as barriers to 314, 387–98; data visualization for 314, 372–86; Design for Sustainable Behaviour leading to 313, 315–23, 328, 332, 335, 418–19; habits and 313, 328–44; nature-based urban design influencing 314, 399–411; overview of 313–14; person-thing relationships influencing 313, 348–55, 418–19; rhetoric and persuasion influencing 314, 357–70

bio-assisted designs 462
biological engineering 462
biomimetics 462, 489
biomimicry: adaptability and evolution in 463;
    bio-inspired designs other than 462; Biomimicry
    Design Spiral 464–8, *465*; identify step in 464,
    465; translate step in 464, 465; discover step
    in 464, 465–6; abstract step in 464, 466–7;
    emulate step in 464, 467; evaluate step in 464,
    467; next lap in 464, 467; building materials in
    460–1; built environment using 462; conditions
    conducive to life in 464; conventional design
    vs. 460–2; definition and description of 459–60;
    energy approaches in 460–1, 462, 464; in
    evolution of sustainable design 419, 425, 426;
    Life's Principles as design principles in 462–4,
    467; nature's patterns as building blocks of 94;
    overview of 416, 459, 468; as sustainable design
    462–8; water and nutrients approaches in 461
Biomimicry Institute, AskNature portal 466
biomorphic designs 462
bionics 462
biophilia 462
biophilic urbanism: building scale 403, *404*, 408;
    city scale 403–5, *404*, 409–11; economic
    realm of 405, 407; natural realm of 405–6; as
    nature-based urban design 402–11; operational
    realm of 406; overview of 411; policies, laws,
    and regulations affecting 405, 406, 409–10;
    precedents for 407–11; scales in 403–5, *404*,
    407–11; street scale 403, *404*, 409–11; systems
    approach to 405–7
biopiracy 92
bio-utilization 462
boundaries: fashion designer creating 286; of
    identity, impactful design strategies stretching
    36, 37, 38; of systems 16, 20
Braungart, Michael 24, 274, 338, 369, 419, 499
Broad Vision project 491–2
Brower, David 370n1
Brundtland *see* United Nations: Brundtland
    Commission Report
Buddhism: compassion in 211–12, 216;
    consciousness in 214; interrelatedness in 215;
    mindfulness in 220, 221–2, 223–4, 226–7;
    wisdom in 213, 216
buildings: conventional *vs.* biomimicry design for
    462; nature-based urban design of 403, *404*,
    408; political economy of design of 3, 7; smart
    design of 115, 120–2; systems thinking on 16,
    18, 22
burden shifting, scale and consideration of 63, 67

capacity building, in humanitarian design 235, 237
carbon emissions *see* greenhouse gas emissions
careers and work environments: alignment of
    values with 298, 300, 303–4; applying values to

303; challenge in 306, 308; child labor in *151*;
    coherence in 306, 308; connection in 307, 308;
    control in 304–5, 306–7, 308; demand-control
    balance in 304–5; designing of 295–6; discovery
    of opportunities for 309, *310*; ethical choices in
    304; hardiness framework for 305–8; ideation
    of ideal 309–10, *311*; Internet effects in attitude
    toward *271, 272*; nature-based urban design
    in 408; navigation of, design principles for
    309–10, *310–11*; overview of 295, 311; primary
    and shadow values influencing 302; prototype
    of 310, *311*; refreshment and renewal of 310,
    311; resilience in 303, 304–8; self-awareness for
    296–7; success and satisfaction in 305–8; values
    reflected in 192, 295–311; Values Wheel model
    for 298–300, *299–302*, 302
carpet design and recycling 461, 468, 504
Carson, Rachel 212–13
cellular phones: applied sustainability issues related
    to 48; data visualization via 378; Design for
    Sustainable Behaviour case studies of 317, 319;
    digital media environmental impacts related to
    174; electronics global lifecycle of *156*, 156–7,
    158, *159*, 161–2, *162*; Fairphone as *156*, 156–7,
    506; humanitarian innovations involving 233–4;
    Light Phone as *34*, 34–6; mobile-first strategies
    using 51; scale challenges in design of 61, 62
Centre for Sustainable Fashion 283, 288, 291
change and adaptability: behavior change as (*see*
    behavior change); biomimicry following Life's
    Principles on 463; Internet-based design for
    274–6; in person-thing relationships 352–4;
    service design in education addressing 81;
    structural change as 415, 433–44; systems
    thinking on 22
Chetna Coalition 68
Chicago School 401
child labor, electronics global lifecycle involving
    151
circular economy: accessibility goals in 508;
    business approaches in 500–4, *501, 503, 505*;
    case studies of *509*, 509–10; circular product
    design for 504–5; cradle-to-cradle thinking
    in 74, 504; definition and description of
    12, 74, 426, 499–500, *500*; disassembly and
    reassembly goals in 509; durability goals in
    505–6; electronics global lifecycle role in
    154, 158; evolution of sustainable design and
    426–7; life-cycle thinking on 74, 499, *500*, 502,
    505, 505–8; modularity goals in 508; outlook
    for 511; overview of 416, 498–9, 510–11;
    political economy supporting 7–8; product-
    life extension goals in 506–7; recycling in 498,
    499–500, *500*, 502–5, *503*, 507–8, 509, *509*;
    remanufacturing in 504, 505, 506–7; reuse,
    repair, refurbishment in 498, 499, *500, 501*, 502,
    505, 506–7, 508–9; service design and 74, 502,

510; standardization and compatability goals in 508; technological design perspectives on *505,* 508–9; upgradability goals in 506–7, 508

cities *see* urban areas

citizen empowerment: in Baltimore 446, 452–8; codesigning as tool for 448, 453–7; definition of empowerment 448–9; designer as advocate for 449–50, 452; interventions to build 450–2, *451,* overview of 415, 446–7; race and 446, 447–8, 452–4, 457; resilience and 446–8

citizen participation *see* civic participation

Citizens Climate Lobby 388

civic participation: in climate change response initiatives 388; GIS as tool for 181, 186–7, 188; in nature-based urban design 406; political economy of design in relation to 4, 7; self-sufficiency movements and 393–4

Clean Development Mechanism (CDM) 116

Climate and Energy Project (CEP) 364

climate change: cultural and emotional barriers to behavior change addressing 314, 387–92; data visualization related to 379–80; double reality adoption related to 390; ecological theory on evidence of 86, 95, 96; empathy and compassion for Earth in response to 211–12; fashion as statement on 288; greenhouse gas emissions leading to 58, 96, 115, 116, 379–80; nature-based urban design consideration of 399, 400; People's Climate March on 212; political economy of design and 4, 7; political incentives for addressing 115, 116; rhetoric and persuasion on 360, *361,* 364, 365, 368; socially organized denial of 389–92

clothing or apparel: competence to make 7; Design for Sustainable Behaviour case studies of *318*; fashion and identity with 192, 281–91; globalization of design and production of 109; localized economy approaches to 133; scale and design of 65, 66, 68, 69; systems thinking on 22; zero waste lines of 69

Club of Rome 14

codesigning for development: case studies of 250, 252–3, 254, 255–60; citizen empowerment via 448, 453–7; contacts for 252; core concepts of 253–5; decolonial theory and methodology in 250, 251–3, 257–8; in fashion industry 286–7, 289–90; for Lol-Balché honey cooperative 250, 254, 255–8; nature-based urban design involving 406; negotiating in 254, 257, 260; overview of 192, 250, 260–1; parachuting *vs.* 256, 257; relationality in 253–4, 257, 259; representing in 255, 260; sharing in 254; for Xyaat community ecotourism cooperative 250, 255, 258–60

collective action, systems thinking on 25

colonialism: codesigning based on decolonial theory and methodology 250, 251–3, 257–8; economic impacts of 117, 251; indigenous

sovereignty *vs.* 227; postcolonialism following 105–6, 109

commitment, persuasion via 366–7, *367*

communities: GIS as tool for participation of 181, 186–7, 188; globalization response and impacts in 104–5; logic of care in 437; mindfulness and unlearning for work with 224–5; political economy of design supporting 7; resilience of 446–8; self-organization of 22; sharing economy designing for 477–8; social human centered design focus on *200,* 201; Transition Town movement for 203; urban (*see* urban areas)

competence: ecological design supporting 6–7; intercultural 136–7, 139

complexity, scale and reduction of 67

concrete design and manufacturing 460–1

conflict minerals 150, 156

conjunction, impactful design strategy goal of 29

connection: in careers and work environments 307, 308; empathy and connectedness 212–13; fashion production-consumption disconnection *vs.* 284, 288–9; *see also* interrelatedness

consumers *see* users

Cooper-Hewitt Design Museum *Design for the Other 90%* exhibition 251

cosmopolitanism: cosmopolitan localism 437; global perspective framework on 107, 109–10

costs: human centered design cost effectiveness 203; humanitarian design funding challenges for 236; life-cycle costing assessing 42–3

cradle-to-cradle design 41, 74, 419, 425, 426, 504

cradle-to-grave design 41

critical regionalism 105

Cultural Cognition Project 438

culture: applied sustainability adaptation to 47; behavior change inhibited by 314, 387–98; climate change responses influenced by 314, 387–92; codesigning for development reflecting 192, 250–61; colonialism impacting (*see* colonialism); disposable 350; fashion reflecting 192, 281–91; globalization impacts on 103–5, 106; gratitude practices in 213; intercultural design collaborations in education 99–100, 135–46; Internet use and applications in context of 276; localized economies reflecting 125, 130, 132; ontological security tied to 390, 392–3, 396; postcolonial 105–6, 109; practices restricted within 440; race-related (*see* race and racism); self-sufficiency movements influenced by 388–9, 392–6

Cultures-Based Innovation initiative 251

data visualization: for behavior change 314, 372–86; in carbon dioxide emissions visualizations 377, 378, 379–84, *381–3, 385*; chartjunk with 376–7; in climate change visualizations 379–80; color in 378; as concrete visualizations 374–5,

376, 384; data density with 377; data-ink ratio with 376, 377–8; data matrix for 377; data physicalizations as 384, *385;* design tools for 376–9; in energy reduction projects 373–4; Estate Visualizer tool for *382–3,* 383–4; invisibility barriers addressed with 377, 380–1, *381,* 385; lighting in 378; parsimony in 378, 381; pull and push audiences for 372–4, 385; reality augmented data in 378–9, *381;* real scene presentation of 378; scale conveyed via 374–5, *376,* 380–1, 384; user engagement via *382–3,* 382–4; in water visualizations 375, *376,* 377; in weather forecasting 373

death and mortality, experiential learning about 27–9, *28,* 32–4, *37,* 37–8

decolonial theory and methodology 250, 251–3, 257–8

dematerialization: digital media design and 67, 176; scale and applications of 67; service design and 73

Descartes, Rene 87

design behaviour intervention model (DBIM) 320, 332

Design for Development (D4D) 192, 250–61

design for efficiency (DfE) 274–5

Design for Positive Habit Model 335–8, *336–7*

design for sufficiency (DfS) 274, 275

Design for Sustainable Behaviour (DfSB): activity theory on 322; affordances in 316, 317; case studies in 317–19, *318;* critical design in 317; data and literature on 316, *316,* 322, *323;* design behaviour intervention model for 320, 332; design with intent tool kit for 319–20; early inspiration for 316–17, 418–19; for electronics global lifecycle 161, *162;* emotional durability in 317, 418–19; evolution of modern 322–3; feedback intervention theory in 317, 319; habits addressed in 328, 332, 335; methodological frameworks for 319–22; overview of 313, 315–16; persuasion in 317; principles of behaviour change approach to 320–2, *321;* scripts incorporation in 316, 317

design with intent tool kit 319–20

DESIS Network (Design for Social Innovation and Sustainability) 251

Digital Aid 233–4

Digital Food Aid 233–4

digital media: applied sustainability issues related to 48, 50–2; citizen empowerment via use of 456, *457;* the cloud in 171–3, 175–8; data visualization and 314, 372–86; dematerialization and use of 67, 176; economy-wide impacts of 176–7; efficiency impacts of 175; energy use and requirements for 50–1, 67, 170, 171–4, 175, 177, 273; environmental impacts of 4, 50–1, 58, 60, 67, 100, 170–8; e-waste from 4, 50, 58, 60, 153–5, 159–60; fashion and 285, 288;

Geographic Information Systems using 100, 179–88; globalization and communication via 102, 104; human centered design interaction with 195; humanitarian design involving 233–4, 235; indirect impacts of, design interventions for 174–7; intercultural design collaborations via 137, 139; life-cycle impacts of 173–4; materials for 170, 174; mobile-first strategies for 51; rebound impacts of 176; scale and limits related to 58, 59, 60, 61; smart design applications with 175; substitution impacts of 175–6; sustainability promotion via 177–8; systematic transformation impacts of 177; systems thinking on 170, 171–3; Triple Bottom Line approach to 51–2; *see also* cellular phones; electronics global lifecycle; Internet use and applications

dignity, in humanitarian design 231–2, 239

Doctors without Borders (MSF) 231, 234

Dress 4 Our Time (D4OT) 288

Dujiangyan irrigation system 206–7

Eames, Charles and Ray 30

EcoGrader 51

ecological design: basic rules for 6; designer-user interaction in 120; as design for efficiency 274–5; ecological theory underlying 12, 86–97; economic development goals undermining 119–20; electronics global lifecycle thinking on 165; evolution of sustainable design including 418, 423, 425, 426; goals of 6–7; political economy of 6–8, 96; practice-oriented design *vs.* 342; rhetoric and persuasion on 369

ecological theory: alternative epistemologies in 91–2; characteristics of 88–92; definition of 86; ecological entanglement and 88, 95–7; ecological epistemology in 90–1; ecological ethics in 89; ecological literacy on 92–5; ecological ontology in 89–90, *90;* ecological rationality in 89; epistemic selectivities in 92; historical attitudes toward nature and 87–8; nature's patterns and processes in 94; origins of 88; overview of 12, 86–7, 97; participant designers engaging with 86, 88, 93–4, 97; political economy of design and 94–5, 96; traditional ecological knowledge in 92

Economics of Ecosystem and Biodiversity project 407

economy: circular economy 7–8, 12, 74, 154, 158, 416, 426–7, 498–511; codesigning for development consideration of 260; colonialism and 117, 251; debt financing in 117; digital media impacts on 176–7; ecological theory on 90, *90,* 94; economic externalities, ecological impacts of 94; economies of scale 56; electronics global lifecycle impacts on 150; energy tied to 115, 117–20, 126–31; fashion industry effects on 283; gig economy 471–2, 475, 477, 479; global

economy (*see* global impact); green economy 115, 118–19; humanitarian design and self-reliance in 238–9, 243; Internet-based 263–5, 268–70, *269, 273–4, 276*; localized economies 99, 125–33; nature-based urban design benefits for 400, 405, 407; neo-liberal theory on 106, 108; on-demand economy 471–2, 475; political economy 3–8, 94–5, 96; practices restricted within 440; rebound effect on 115, 152, 176, 329, 434; sharing economy 416, 470–80
eco-services 73, 74–5, *75, 76, 77–8, 78; see also* service design
education: dialogue and critical reflection on globalization encouraged in 110–11; ecological literacy as 92–5; electronics global lifecycle improvements via 165; humanitarian design and access to 238, 243; intercultural design collaborations in 99–100, 135–46; interdisciplinary approaches in 82, 165, 181, 183, 186–7, 188, 401, 402, 483–4, 486, 487, 488–92, 494; knowledge silos in 483; service design in 76, 80–1; STEAM education evolution 416, 483–94; STEM focus in 70, 484–5, 492–3; unlearning 221, 222, 224–5; *see also* knowledge; learning
electricity: digital media use of 50–1, 171–4, 175, 177; electronics global lifecycle use of 151–3; humanitarian design to provide 235; scale and limits related to 61; structural change to infrastructure for 435
electronic media *see* digital media
Electronic Product Environmental Assessment Tool (EPEAT) 157
electronics global lifecycle: component and product manufacturing in *149,* 151–2, 158; consumer trends and behavior influencing 160–4, *162*; convergent and multifunctional device design for 161–2; design solutions for sustainability improvements for 155–60; enabling systems for improving 164–5; end of life processes in *149,* 153–5, *155,* 159–60; energy use in 151–3, 158, 161, *162*; e-waste management systems in 153–5, *155,* 159–60; formal 153–4; informal 154–5, *155,* 159; health impacts of 150, 152, 154–5, 163–4, *164*; life span extension for 158, *159*; multidisciplinary educational focus on 165; overview of 100, 148, *149,* 165; product use in *149,* 152–3, 158; recycling and recyclable products in *149,* 150, 153–5, 159–60, 164; resources extraction and refinement in *149,* 149–51; reuse options in 154; sustainable behavior design for 161, *162*; sustainable materials selection strategies for 155–7, *156–7*; systems-level sustainability in 162–4, *163–4*; 3D printing and digital fabrication in 163, *163*
Ellen MacArthur Foundation, 12, 74, 153–4, 499, 504

embodiment: concrete data visualization relation to 375; experiential or embodied learning as 27–9, 30, 31, 32–4, 36–8
emotions: behavior change inhibited by 314, 387–98; climate change responses influenced by 314, 387–92; DfSB emotional durability incorporation 317, 418–19; evolution of sustainable design in relation to 418–19; happiness as 29–30, *30,* 125, 133; human centered design consideration of 195; impactful design strategies eliciting 29–30, 33–4; nature-based urban design influence on 402; pathos as appeals to 358, 360; person-thing relationships and emotional obsolescence 313, 349–52, 353, 418–19; recognition and awareness of 211; rhetoric and persuasion via appeals to 358, 360, 368–9; self-sufficiency movements influenced by 388–9, 392–6; technology interactions generating 195; *see also* empathy
empathy: apathy dulling 209–11; compassion and 211–12, 216; connectedness and 212–13; Dujiangyan irrigation system approach reflecting 206–7; expanding notion of 209–12; human centered design focus on 191, 193–204, 207; integrity of people and places with 212–14; interrelatedness in living system and 214–17; people-environment relationship redefined in terms of 207–9; in person-thing relationships 351; practice and cultivation of 191, 206–17; reciprocity and symbiotic relationships with 213; similarity bidirectional relationship with 209; Three Gorges Dam approach lacking 206–8
empowerment *see* citizen empowerment; power
emptiness, and mindfulness 221, 222, 226–7
E-Nable 163, *163*
End of Life (Bruce & Wojtasik) 28, *28,* 32–4, *37,* 37–8
energy: applied sustainability issues related to 47, 50–1; biomimicry design approach to 460–1, 462, 464; cultural and emotional barriers to alternatives for 387–92; data visualization for reduction of 373–4; digital media use of 50–1, 67, 170, 171–4, 175, 177, 273; e-commerce use of 273; economic ties to 115, 117–20, 126–31; electrical (*see* electricity); electronics global lifecycle use of 151–3, 158, 161, *162*; fossil fuel-driven (*see* fossil fuels); habits in relation to 329; humanitarian design to provide 231, 235, 236, 240–5, *242, 244*; localized economy approaches to 128–30, 131, 132, 133; nature-based urban design consideration of 399, 406; political economy and 4, 5–6; political incentives for policy changes for 115, 116–20; renewable (*see* renewable energy); rhetoric and persuasion related to 363, 364, 366–8, *367, 368*; scale and limits related to 55, 58–9, 61; smart design

optimizing use of 115, 120–2; structural change to infrastructure for 435

environmental impacts: apocalyptic rhetoric on 364–5; of climate change (*see* climate change); of digital media 4, 50–1, 58, 60, 67, 100, 170–8; ecological theory incorporation to minimize 12, 86–97 (*see also* ecological design); electronics global lifecycle creating 150–1, 152, 154–5; energy-related (*see* energy; fossil fuels; renewable energy); feedback loops on 17–18, *18*, 20–1; global economy creating 126; habits affecting 329; Internet use and considerations of 265, 273–4; life-cycle assessment of (*see* life-cycle assessment; life-cycle thinking); of pollution (*see* pollution); recycling lessening (*see* recycling and recyclable products); rhetoric and persuasion related to 358–70; self-sufficiency movement preparation for 388–9, 392–6; service design reduction of 73, 74–5, *75*, 77–80, *78*, *79*, 82; stewardship mitigating 36, 40, 68–9, 125, 126

Environmental Performance Index (EPI) 69

environmental stewardship: applied sustainability and awareness of 40; environmental laws and regulations supporting 68–9, 125, 126; impactful design strategies consideration of 36

escalation, systems thinking on 20

Estate Visualizer tool *382–3*, 383–4

ethical standards: ecological ethics as 89; humanitarian design in relation to 192, 231–45; integrity orientation to 212–14, 219–20, 222–3; intimacy orientation to 220–1, 222–3; mindfulness of 36, 191, 219–28; overview of chapters on 191–2; political economy of design and adherence to 6; scale of practice of 216; spirituality as 226–7; values supporting ethical choices and 304; *see also* morality; values

Ethiopian Gaia Association 241

ethnography, human centered design incorporation of 197, 198

ethos, rhetoric and persuasion via 358, *359*

evolution of sustainable design: Base of the Pyramid design in 420, 425; biomimicry in 419, 425, 426; circular economy and 426–7; cradle-to-cradle design in 419, 425, 426; Design for Sustainable Behavior in 418–19; eco-design in 418, 423, 425, 426; emerging synergies in 423, 425–6; emotionally durable design in 418–19; framework for sustainable design in 421–3, *422, 424,* 427–8; green design in 418, 423, 425; multiple approaches to sustainable design in 417–21; nature-inspired design in 419, 421, 425, 426; new research directions in 425–7; overview of 415, 417, 427–8; product design innovation level of 418–20, *422, 423, 424;* Product Service System innovation level in 420, *422, 423, 424,* 425, 426; socio-technical system innovation level in 421, *422, 423, 424,* 425–7; spatio-social

innovation level in 420–1, *422, 423, 424,* 425; systemic design in 421, *422, 423, 424,* 425–7

exhaustion of resources, scale and limits of 55–6, 57–8

experiential learning, impactful design strategies involving 27–9, 30, 31, 32–4, 36–8

ExxonMobil 4

fabric or textiles: competence to use 7; scale and considerations related to 58, 59, 65, 68, 69; service design in industry of 77–8, *78*; systems thinking on 22; *see also* clothing or apparel

Fair Labor Organization 69

Fairphone *156,* 156–7, 506

fair trade movement 108, 127

farming *see* agriculture

fashion: Avetisyan's 'In loving memory of Spring Summer 2014' collection in 288; case studies of 287–91; codesigning approach to 286–7, 289–90; designer's role in 285–7, *286,* 288–91; digital media and 285, 288; Dress 4 Our Time in 288; economic impacts of 283; Fashion Design for Sustainability 282, 285, 286–7, 290; Fashion Revolution in 288–9; Fletcher's Craft of Use project in 288; Habit(AT) research project in 290; habitus and 282–3; identity constructs associated with 192, 281–91; individualism and 284, 285; McQueen's Highland Rape collection in 287–8; modernity and changes in 283; Nike Making in 291; overview of 192, 281–2, 291; production-consumption disconnection in 284, 288–9; TRANSFER research in 289; von Bush's Do-It-Together in 289

feedback loops: balancing loops as 18–19, *19,* 22; Design for Sustainable Behaviour use of 317, 319; electronics life span extension creating 158; information flow affecting 19; in intercultural design collaborations 139; reinforcing loops as 17–18, *18*; rhetoric and persuasion via 367–8, *368*; systems thinking on 17–19, *17–19,* 20–1, 22

feminist theory, ecological theory intersection with 91–2

fixes that fail, systems thinking on 20

Fletcher, Kate, Craft of Use project 288

flow: feedback loop information flow 19; in person-thing relationships 353–4; process flow limits 59; stock-and-flow structures, in systems *15,* 15–16, 17, 20

food and beverage: biomimicry design related to 461, 464; codesigning with honey cooperative for 250, 254, 255–8; edible packaging for 488; humanitarian design related to 233–4, 235, 237; impactful design strategies related to 36–7; intercultural design collaboration activity tracking interactions with 139–41, 143; localized economy approaches to 129, 132–3;

self-sufficiency movements on 392, 394–5; systems thinking on 24; *see also* agriculture; water

footprint assessments, scales and use of 65–6

forests and trees: market-based approaches to protection of 127; reinforcing loops with 17–18, *18*; Sahara Forest Project using 464

Forrester, Jay 14

fossil fuels: conventional *vs.* biomimicry design approach to 460–1; cultural and emotional barriers to alternatives to 387–92; digital media energy via 171; double reality adoption related to 390; electronics global lifecycle use of 151–2; extraction patterns for 55; greenhouse gas emissions from (*see* greenhouse gas emissions); nature-based urban design on consumption of 399; political economy and use of 4, 6; renewable energy *vs.* (*see* renewable energy); scale and limits related to 55, 58, 61; subsidies for 131

framing: goal-framing theory using 331, *331*, 335; rhetoric and persuasion via 364–5; STEAM approach to 490; structural change and use of 436–7

General Motors 4

General Systems Theory 215

Geographic Information Systems (GIS): bases and procedures for urban applications of 181–2; community participation and engagement via 181, 186–7, 188; data and metadata in 180–1, 182, 183, 184, 186; deployment of 184, 186–7; geographic scale in 180, 184, 186; GRID (RASTER) model of 182; Information Matrix Plan with 184, *185*; interdisciplinary approach to using 181, 183, 186–7, 188; overview of implications of urban use of 100, 179–80, 187–8; Resende, Brazil experience using 182–7, 188; smart design using 187; 3D perspective in 181; urban sustainability uses for 100, 179–88; urban voids identified in 184, 186, *186*; vector model of 181–2

geography: data visualization in context of 375; electronics global lifecycle perspective related to 150–1; geographic differences at scale 61; Geographic Information Systems identifying 100, 179–88; geographic scale 57, 68–9, 180, 184, 186

gig economy 471–2, 475, 477, 479

global citizenship 107, 109, 135, 137

global impact: digital media environmental impacts as 100, 170–8; electronics global lifecycle as 100, 148–65; Geographic Information Systems for urban sustainability as 100, 179–88; global perspective framework for 99, 101–13; intercultural design collaborations for 99–100, 135–46; localized economies and 99, 125–33; overview of 99–100; politics for 99, 115–22

Global Organic Textile Standard (GOTS) 69

global perspective framework: complex identities in 103–4; cosmopolitanism in 107, 109–10; cultural changes and complexities in 103–5, 106; debates on globalization in 102; description of 106–7; dialogue and critical reflection importance in 110–11; future developments in 112–13; global brands and homogeneity in 104; global citizenship in 107, 109; globalism in 106; globalization in 101–13; global outlook in 107–8; inequality of wealth and power in 108–9; knowledge importance in 106, 107, 112; neo-liberalism in 106, 108; overview of 99, 101–2; plurality of responses to globalization in 104–5, 110; postcolonialism in 105–6, 109; production of goods in 103; social imaginery in 108; social justice in 109–10; sustainable development perspectives in 111–12; themes of 107–11

Global Positioning System (GPS) 175, 177

goals: of circular economy 505–9; of ecological design 6–7; economic development 119–20; goal-framing theory on habits and 331, *331*, 335; of life-cycle assessments 41; in systems 16, 20, 24; UN Sustainable Development Goals 101, 112, 136, 148; in work environment 306

Google: Google Search Console 51; nature-based urban design of building for 408; Project Ara 158, *159*

Gorenflo, Neal 472

gratitude, and connectedness 213

green building revolution 5

green design 418, 423, 425

green economy 115, 118–19

Green Guides 69

greenhouse gas emissions: climate change ties to 58, 96, 115, 116, 379–80; conventional *vs.* biomimicry design approach to 460–1; data visualization of 377, 378, 379–84, *381–3, 385*; ecological theory on impacts of 96; habits responsible for release of 329; market-based approaches for reduction of 127; nature-based urban design consideration of 400, 406; political incentives for reduction of 115, 116–18, 119–20; rhetoric and persuasion on 360, *361*, 364; scale and saturation limits of 58

Greenpeace "Behind the Logo" competition 358, *359*

green policy approaches 115, 118–19

greenwashing 48, 132, 349, 358

Habit(AT) research project 290

habits: changing, and fostering absolute reductions 342–3; Design for Positive Habit Model of 335–8, *336–7*; Design for Sustainable Behaviour addressing 328, 332, 335; design influencing 313, 328–44; as factor in behavior *330–2*, 330–3, 334–5; framework for habit formation 332,

332, 335; goal-framing theory on 331, *331,* 335; habit-based interventions on 335–8, *336–7;* importance of 329–30; overview of 313, 328–9, 343–4; practice-oriented design focus on 328–9, 338–43, *339–41;* as routine practices *333,* 333–5; social practice theory on *333,* 333–4, 338–9, 343, 440; social psychological perspective on 328, 329, *330–2,* 330–3, 334–8, *336–7,* 343–4; sociological perspective on 328–9, *333,* 333–5, 343–4, 439; socio-technical systems and 339–42, *340–1;* structural changes to 439–41; theory of interpersonal behaviour on *330,* 330–1; Three Elements Model of *333,* 333–4, 338, 342; transthoretical model of 332–3, 335

habitus: fashion and 282–3; structural change to 439–41

Haeckel, Ernst 88

happiness: economics of 125, 133; HappoDammo Ratio on 29–30, *30*

HappoDammo Ratio 29–30, *30*

'The Hardy Executive: Health Under Stress' study 305

health: citizen empowerment addressing issues affecting 453–7, 458; ecological design supporting 6; electronics global lifecycle impacts on 150, 152, 154–5, 163–4, *164;* humanitarian design related to 234; Internet use and applications affects on 266–7; logic of care related to 437; nature-based urban design for 314, 399–411; substance use/abuse affecting 263–4, 453–7

heating and cooling systems: Design for Sustainable Behaviour case studies of *318,* 320–1; digital media and data center needs for 172–3; localized economy approaches to 128–30; smart design for 115, 120–2

hierarchy, systems thinking on 21

HIGG Index 66

high-leverage design 23–5

holistic approach to design: circular economy in 504; global interactions in (*see* global impact); habits in 330, 334, 338, 342; human centered design as 195, 196, 197; humanitarian design paradoxes for 231, 234, 245; nature-based urban design in 407, 411; overview of 1–2; political economy and goals of 6; sharing economy in 480; STEAM education in 416, 494; systems thinking as (*see* systems thinking)

holon theory 29, 36

homogeneity, globalization leading to 104

HTTP Archive 51

human centered design (HCD): activity-centered design and 203–4; cost effectiveness of 203; definition of 195–6; emotions considered in 195; empathy focus in 191, 193–204, 207; ethnographic methods in 197, 198; fundamental human needs satisfaction via 202; history and

focus of 194–7; human-computer interactions and 195; human factors work in 194, 195, 196; individual applications of *200,* 200–1; make tools in 198; methodology of 197–8; nested context for 199, *199;* overview of 191, 193–4, 203–4; participatory action research applications for 201–2; participatory design in 193–4, 196–7, 198; practice applications of *200,* 201–2; service design as 75, 199, *199,* 201; social applications of *200,* 201; for sustainable design 197–204; systems applications of *200,* 202–3; technology innovation and 194, 195; terminology for 204; transition design in *199,* 202–3; user experience in 195, 196

Human Factors and Ergonomics Society (HFES) 194

humanitarian design: business and economic considerations with 236, 238–9, 243; capacity building in 235, 237; complexity of issues for 245; dignity and human rights mandates for 231–2, 239; environmental paradox of 231, 236–7; example of 240–5, *241, 242, 244;* funding challenges for 236; hands-on experience importance to 245; idea generation for 243; identification of real needs in 242; innovation in 233–5, 239; listening and observation informing 241–2; multiple-agenda paradox in 239–40; overview of 192, 231–3; paradoxes of 192, 236–40; prototypes of 244, *244;* scalability of 234–5, 240; self-reliance paradox in 238–9; service design as 234–5, 237, 243; short- *vs.* long-term solutions in 231, 232–3, 235, 237–8; stakeholder analysis for 242–3; systems thinking on 234–5, *244*

Hurricane Katrina, aftermath of 210, 447–8

hydroelectric power 206–8, 435

iameco personal computer 157, *157*

identity: empathy as expression of (*see* empathy); fashion constructing 192, 281–91; globalization and complex identities 103–4; impactful design strategies stretching boundaries of 36, 37, 38; overview of chapters on 191–2; rhetoric and persuasion influencing *362,* 362–3, 366

IKEA 234, 240

imagination *see* social imaginery

impactful design strategies: anthropological insights in 32; conjunction as goal for 29; definition of impact for 29; emergence in 32; for end of life film project 27–9, *28,* 32–4, *37,* 37–8; experiential learning and 27–9, 30, 31, 32–4, 36–8; holon theory on 29, 36; identity boundaries stretched in 36, 37, 38; leverage points in 29, 36; for Light Phone *34,* 34–6; measurement of impact for 29–30; overview of 11, 27–9, 38; personas in 31; probes and prototypes in 32–6; productivity of being uncomfortable and 36–8; reductive design in 34–5; reverberation in 30–1, 32; scale in 29, 30–2

incentives, systems thinking on rules and 24

indigenous peoples: biopiracy against 92; colonialism *vs.* sovereignty of 227; TEK (traditional ecological knowledge) of 92

individualism: fashion and 284, 285; self-sufficiency movements and culture of 395, 397; structural change to abstract infrastructure for 436

inequality: empathy lack and perpetuation of 209; global perspective framework on 108–9; urban area experience of 183

information and communication technology *see* digital media

integrity of people and places: empathy and 212–14; mindfulness and 219–20, 222–3

intercultural design collaborations: activities in 139–40, 142–6; colocated peer support in 140–1; communication in 138–9; digital or virtual tools for 137, 139; feedback in 139; global citizenship supported via 135, 137; global perspective development via 139–42; intercultural competencies for 136–7, 139; language choice in 138; overview of 99–100, 135; photography exchange as 142–3; poster pairs as 143–4; structural overview of 137–8; sustainability defined for 135–6; sustainability safari as 144–5; sustainable city visual narrative as 145–6; time differences in 138, 139

Interface 461, 468, 503–4

Interface Net-Works 503–4

International Red Cross (ICRC) 231, 237

Internet use and applications: agricultural 24; the cloud connection via 171–3, 175–8; consumption effects of 268–70, *269*, 273, 275; cultural context for 276; design for change in 274–6; design for efficiency adoption of 274–5; design for sufficiency adoption of 274, 275; e-commerce via 263–5, 268–70, *269*, 273–4, 276; economic growth and spending via 263–5, 268–70, *269*, 273–4, 276; energy consumption and 273; environmental considerations with 265, 273–4; feedback loops with 20–1; globalization via 102; health effects of 266–7; individual and family effects of *271, 272*, 273; intercultural design collaborations via 137, 139; Internet of Things (IoT) 161, 192, 265–70, *266–9*, 277; lifestyles and sustainable values with 192, 263–77; millennials" interaction with 265–74, *266–9, 271–2*; nature/environment relationship effects of *271, 272*; sharing economy interaction with 471–80; social life and interactions effects of 267, *267–8, 271, 272*, 273; successful examples of 263–4; sustainable development consequences of 273–6; time/space orientation effects of *271, 272*;

values and value orientation with 192, 270–3, *271–2*; work attitude effects of *271, 272*; *see also* cellular phones; digital media

interpersonal behaviour, theory of, on habits *330, 330–1*

interrelatedness: codesigning for development relationality concept on 253–4, 257, 259; empathy and 214–17; mindfulness and 219, 221, 222, 223, 226, 228; *see also* connection

intimacy orientation: mindfulness and 220–1, *222–3*; of person-thing relationships 351, 353

invisibility: data visualization overcoming 377, 380–1, *381*, 385; scale and challenges of 62–3, 69–70

Jobs, Steve 4

Jordan, Chris 374, 375

Kasulis, Thomas 219–22, 226, 228

Kieffer, Charles H. 448–9, 455

knowledge: cultural and emotional responses to 314, 387–98; epistemology as study of nature of 90–2; experiential learning and 27–9, 30, 31, 32–4, 36–8; global perspective framework on 106, 107, 112; knowledge scale 57, 69–70; knowledge silos in education 483; *see also* education; learning

Ladakh Ecological Development Group (LEDeG) 99, 129–30

Landsat 182, 188n1

laws and regulations: circular economy affected by 503, *503*; citizen empowerment in conjunction with 456, 457; electronics-related 156, 159; energy-related 119; environmental 68–9, 125, 126; incentives for behavior from 23–4; localized economies supported via 131–2; nature-based urban design affected by 405, 406, 409–10; practices restricted within 440; scale of design affected by 61, 68–9; sharing economy issues with 478–9; structural change backed by 434; tax (*see* taxation); urban master plan as 187; *see also* policies

LEAPP 502

learning: experiential 27–9, 30, 31, 32–4, 36–8; fashion designer role in 287; unlearning 221, 222, 224–5; *see also* education; knowledge

leverage points: definition of 64; high-leverage design including 23–5; impactful design strategies including 29, 36; at scale 64–5

life-cycle assessment (LCA): alternatives to 65; appropriate use of 43; challenges with 43; of circular economy 74; cradle-to-cradle 41, 74, 419, 425, 426, 504; cradle-to-gate 41; cradle-to-grave 41; definition 41–3; ecologically-based 41; goals and scope of 41; interpretation of 42; life-cycle costing in 42–3; life-cycle impact assessment in

41–2; life-cycle inventory in 41; scale and use of 65; of service design 74; steps of 41–2
life-cycle thinking: circular economy in 74, 499, *500, 502, 505,* 505–8; digital media life-cycle impacts as 173–4; electronics global lifecycle as 100, 148–65; life-cycle assessment for (*see* life-cycle assessment); politics and sustainability in terms of 119
Life's Principles 462–4, 467
lifestyle: health and 266–7 (*see also* health); Internet use influences on 192, 263–77; millennials" 265–74, *266–9, 271–2*; people-centric lifestyle research on 275–6, *276*; self-sufficient 388–9, 392–6; singleton 263, *264,* 273; social life and interactions in 267, *267–8, 271, 272,* 273; substance use in 263–4, 453–7
Light Phone *34,* 34–6
Lilley, Debra 317
Limits to Growth (Meadows et al.) 14
Living Principles for Design framework 46–7, *47,* 251
Local Futures 128
localized economies: cultural reflection in 125, 130, 132; current global economy *vs.* 125–8, 130–1; decentralization via 131, 132–3; designing for 132–3; financial policies supporting 131; Ladakh solar energy project lessons for 99, 128–30; overview of 99, 125; renewable energy support in 99, 128–30, 131, 132, 133; scale of 125, 128, 131, 133; taxation effects on 131–2; transition to 130–2, 133
logos, rhetoric and persuasion via 360, *361*

McDonough, William 5, 24, 338, 369, 419, 499, 503–4
Macy, Joanna 207, 210–11
Maryland Institute College of Art, Center for Social Design 452
materials: conventional *vs.* biomimicry design approach to 460–1; dematerialization and reduction of 67, 73, 176; for digital media 170, 174; for electronics, selection of sustainable 155–7, *156*–7; fabric or textiles as (*see* fabric or textiles); globalization impacts on 103; plastic as (*see* plastic); recycling of (*see* recycling and recyclable products); scale and limits of 55, 58; supply chains of (*see* supply chain)
Mazzoleni, Ilaria 489
Meadows, Donella 11, 13, 14, 15, 23–5, 29
media: advertising via (*see* advertising); digital (*see* digital media); fashion portrayal via 285; global brand promotion via 104; persuasion via 365
Menara Meisiniaga Tower 105
metaphors: in rhetoric and persuasion 360, 362; worldview or belief schematas manifesting via 438

Middle of the Pyramid (MoP) strategy 275
millennials, Internet use and lifestyles of 265–74, *266–9, 271–2*
Millennium Ecosystem Assessment project 407
mimicry: biomimicry 94, 416, 419, 425, 426, 459–68; impactful design going beyond 31
mindfulness: being and becoming with 223, 228; definition and description of 223–4; in designing 36, 191, 219–28; differences understood and respected with 222–3; emptiness and 221, 222, 226–7; fluidity of cyclical motion with 221–3; impactful design strategies focus on 36; integrity orientation to 219–20, 222–3; interrelatedness and 219, 221, 222, 223, 226, 228; intimacy orientation to 220–1, 222–3; practicing of 227–8; seawater analogies with 220, 226, 228; surrender and 221, 222, 226–7; unlearning and 221, 222, 224–5
mindsets: global 107–8; systems thinking on 24
MODIS 182, 188n1
modularity: circular economy design for 508; electronics life span extension via 158, *159*
morality, political economy urging lack of 3–5; *see also* ethical standards; values
Morrill Act (1862) 484
Motorola Project Ara 158, *159*
myths, rhetoric and persuasion via 363

narratives, rhetoric and persuasion via 363
National Aeronautics and Space Administration (NASA) 485
National Defense Education Act (1958) 485
nationalism, as globalization response 104
National Science Foundation 485
The Natural Step™ (TNS) 44–5, 46
nature-based urban design: Attention Restoration Theory on 401–2; behavior change influenced by 314, 399–411; benefits of 400–1; biophilic urbanism as 402–11; building scale 403, *404, 408;* city scale 403–5, *404,* 409–11; economic realm of 400, 405, 407; emotional responses to 402; interdisciplinary perspective in 401, 402; natural realm of 405–6; operational realm of 406; overview of 411; policies, laws, and regulations affecting 405, 406, 409–10; precedents for 407–11; Psycho-Evolution Theory on 401–2; rationale for 401–3; scales in 403–5, *404,* 407–11; in Singapore 409–11; street scale 403, *404,* 409–11; systems approach to 400–1, 405–7; transforming context for urban design to 399–401
nature-inspired design: biomimicry as 94, 416, 419, 425, 426, 459–68; cradle-to-cradle design as 41, 74, 419, 425, 426, 504; in evolution of sustainable design 419, 421, 425, 426; nature-based urban design as 314, 399–411; STEAM project development using 488–9; systemic design as 421

negotiation, in codesigning for development 254, 257, 260

neo-liberalism, global perspective framework on 106, 108

nesting: ecological ontology on 89–90, *90*; human centered design nested context 199, *199*; systems thinking on 21

networked monopolies 473–5, 481nn3–4

network effects 472–3, *474*

Newton, Isaac 87

norms: climate change responses influenced by 389, 391; persuasion via 365–6

Norwegian Refugee Council (NRC) 231

obsolescence: definition of 350; emotional, in person-thing relationships 313, 349–52, 353, 418–19

on-demand economy 471–2, 475

online communication *see* digital media; Internet use and applications

Orr, David 92–3

package design 49–50, 334

packaging: applied sustainability issues related to 41, 43, 49–50; e-commerce use of 273; edible, STEAM-based development of 488; life-cycle assessment of 41, 43; scale and design of 60, 62, 67, 70; service design in refillable packaging systems 78–80, *79*

Papanek, Victor 5, 449, 450

parachuting, codesigning *vs.* 256, 257

pathos, rhetoric and persuasion via 358, 360

Patterson, Jacqui 214

personas: impactful design strategies use of 31; structural change framed for 439

person-thing relationships: behavioral dimension of 313, 348–55, 418–19; change and adaptive resilience in 352–4; consumption- *vs.* production-focused sustainability and 348–9; emotional obsolescence in 313, 349–52, 353, 418–19; flow in 353–4; intimacy of 351, 353; looking through and at objects in 354–5; mutual becoming in 352–4; novelty craving in 350; open-endedness of design in 352–3; overview of 313, 348; reciprocity and mutuality in 350–1, 353; temporal fallacy in 351–2; use/*chresthai* understanding for 350–1

persuasion: behavior change influenced via 314, 357–70; commitment and consistency in 366–7, *367*; Design for Sustainable Behaviour incorporation of 317; emotional appeal in 368–9; feedback in 367–8, *368*; norms in 365–6

Pinchot, Gifford, III 29–30

Pinchot, Libba 29

plastic: applied sustainability issues related to 42, 45, 46–7, 48; electronics global lifecycle handling of 149–50; recyclability of 42, 45, 67; rhetoric

and persuasion related to use of 368–9; scale challenges related to 63–4, 67

policies: citizen empowerment in conjunction with 457; electronics-related 164–5; financial policies supporting localized economies 131; fixes that fail in response to 20; green policy approaches 115, 118–19; nature-based urban design affected by 405, 406, 409–10; tax (*see* taxation); *see also* laws and regulations; politics and sustainability

political economy of design 3–8; addictions fed in 4, 5; advertising driving 3, 4, 5; circular economy supported by 7–8; civic participation in 4, 7; climate change and 4, 7; community support in 7; ecological design in 6–8, 96; ecological literacy and 94–5; energy use and development in 4, 5–6; ethical standards in 6; holistic approach support in 6; morality challenges in 3–5; systems thinking in 8; *see also* politics and sustainability

politics and sustainability: carbon emission reduction in 115, 116–18, 119–20; ecological modernization in 118–19; energy policy changes in 115, 116–20; fashion as political statement 287–8; green policy approaches in 115, 118–19; overview of 99, 115; smart design reinvention in 115, 120–2; *see also* laws and regulations; policies; political economy of design

pollution: burden shifting of 63; ecological theory on impacts of 95, 96; fashion industry 281; rhetoric and persuasion on 360, *361*; scale and saturation limits of 58

postcolonialism, global perspective framework on 105–6, 109

power: citizen empowerment for 415, 446–58; global perspective framework on inequalities of 109; *see also* energy

Powers of Ten (Eames & Eames) 30

practice-oriented design 328–9, 338–43, *339–41*

practices: of empathy 191, 206–17; gratitude practices as 213; habits as routine *333*, 333–5 (*see also* habits); practice-oriented design on 328–9, 338–43, *339–41*; social practice theory on *333*, 333–4, 338–9, 343, 440; structural change to 439–41

predictability, scale and limits of 60

probes, impactful design strategies including 32–6

process: electronics global lifecycle end of life processes *149*, 153–5, *155*, 159–60; nature's patterns and processes in ecological theory 94; processes and tactics for addressing scale 66–70; scale and process flow limits for 59

product design 48–9, 118–19, 155–65, 235, 245, 274, 315, 348, 418–26, 468, 498–510

Product Service Systems (PSS): in circular economy 74, 502; Design for Sustainable Behavior and 316–17; in evolution of sustainable design 420, *422*, 423, *424*, 425, 426; habits and 342–3;

sustainable, in service design 73, 74–5, *76*, 77–8, *78*, 80, 81–2

prototypes: of careers and work opportunities 310, *311*; citizen empowerment projects building 454, 455, 457; codesigning for development using 257; design prototypes 32–5; of humanitarian design 244, *244*; impactful design strategies including 32–6; participatory prototyping cycle in HCD 198; scale decisions informed by 69

Psycho-Evolution Theory (PET) 401–2

QXL 474

race and racism: citizen empowerment in relation to 446, 447–8, 452–4, 457; ecological thought underlying 88; sharing economy affected by 478

Real World Visuals 360, 374, 377, 378, 379, 381

rebound effect 115, 152, 176, 329, 434

recycling and recyclable products: applied sustainability issues related to 42, 43, 45; biomimicry-design products goals for 461, 464, 468; circular economy and 498, 499–500, *500*, 502–5, *503*, 507–8, 509, *509*; electronics global lifecycle including *149*, 150, 153–5, 159–60, 164; life-cycle assessment of 42, 43; scale and consideration of 58, 59, 67

regulations *see* laws and regulations

relationality *see* interrelatedness

renewable energy: applied sustainability related to 47; biomimicry design approach to 464; circular economy use of 500; digital media energy via 171; humanitarian design using 240; hydroelectric power as 206–8, 435; localized economy approaches to 99, 128–30, 131, 132, 133; market-based approaches to 127–8; political economy and development of 5–6; reinforcing loops with 18; scale and technology limits for 58–9; solar technologies for (*see* solar technologies); structural change to infrastructure for 435; wind technologies for 5, 128, 129, 171

representation, codesigning for development involving 255, 260

Resende, Brazil, GIS use in 182–7, 188

resilience: in careers and work environments 303, 304–8; citizen empowerment and 446–8; in person-thing relationships 352–4; systems thinking on 22; urban 446–8

Responsive Web Design 51–2

reverberation, impactful design strategies consideration of 30–1, 32

rhetoric and persuasion: apocalyptic rhetoric 364–5; audience for, knowing and engaging 365, 369; behavior change influenced via 314, 357–70; commitment and consistency in 366–7, *367*; definitions of 358; emotional appeal in 358, 360, 368–9; ethos in 358, *359*; feedback in 367–8, *368*; framing in 364–5; identification in *362*, 362–3; logos in 360, *361*; metaphors in 360, 362; narratives in 363; norms in 365–6; overview of 357–8, 369–70; pathos in 358, 360; persuasion, specifically 365–9; rhetoric, specifically 358–65

Sahara Forest Project (SFP) 464

saturation, scale and limits of 58

scale: challenges of designing at 60–3; complexity reduction and 67; cross-sector collaboration on 66, 70; data visualizations conveying sense of 374–5, *376*, 380–1, 384; definition and description of 56–7; economies of scale 56; of ethical principles practice 216; exhaustion limits with 55–6, 57–8; extreme examples informing decisions at 69; on a finite planet 55–6; footprint assessments for design at 65–6; geographic differences at 61; geographic scale 57, 68–9, 180, 184, 186; humanitarian design scalability 234–5, 240; impactful design strategies consideration of 29, 30–2; importance of 57–60; invisibility challenges at 62–3, 69–70; knowledge scale 57, 69–70; laws and regulations affecting design at 61, 68–9; leverage points with 64–5; life-cycle assessment and alternatives for design at 65; limits affecting 55–6, 57–60; localized economies shifting 125, 128, 131, 133; materials and material property limits with 55, 58; in nature-based urban design 403–5, *404*, 407–11; overview of 11–12, 70; physical scale 56, 66–7; processes and tactics for addressing 66–70; process flow limits with 59; production variances at 61; product multiplication or diversification at 60–1; product take back and refurbishment at 68; recyclability considerations at 58, 59, 67; saturation limits with 58; sharing economy scaling 472, 474; shifting scale paradigms 57; stakeholder mapping of impacts at 64; supply chain management at 68–9; sustainable attribute selection at 69; sustainable design for 11–12, 55–70; systems mapping for design at 64; systems thinking for 63–6; technology limits with 58–9; temporal scale 56–7, 67–8; three Rs of design at 70; time limits with 59; tragedy of the commons with 62; understandability and predictability limits with 60; virtual products considered in design at 65–6; volume use for 66

Sea Changes 489

search engine optimization 52

Sears, Paul 86, 87

self-organization, systems thinking on 22

self-sufficiency movements 388–9, 392–6

service design: case studies of 76–81; circular economy and 74, 502, 510; continuum of products and services in 73; cross-disciplinary approach to 82; definition and description of

75–6; dematerialization and 73; eco-services in 73, 74–5, *75, 76,* 77–8, *78;* in education 76, 80–1; habit changes and 342–3; human centered 75, 199, *199,* 201; humanitarian design as 234–5, 237, 243; implications of 81–2; in leather industry 77–8, *78;* overview of 12, 73–4, 82; Product Service Systems in 73, 74–5, *76,* 77–8, *78,* 80, 81–2, 316–17, 342–3, 420, *422, 423, 424,* 425, 426, 502; in refillable packaging systems 78–80, *79*

sharing: codesigning for development involving 254; sharing economy based on 416, 470–80

sharing economy: barriers to entry in 476–7; as collaborative consumption 470; community design issues in 477–8; consumer design issues in 475–6; definition and description of 471–2; design considerations in 475–80; economy-related design issues in 479–80; future of 480; gig economy and 471–2, 475, 477, 479; global revenues of 479; Internet use and online platforms in 471–80; networked monopolies in 473–5, 481nn3–4; on-demand economy and 471–2, 475; overview of 416; potential of 470–1; ratings and reviews in 476, 477; safety and security issues in 476, 479; scale of 472, 474; shared value creation in 472–3, 474, 481n2; state design issues in 478–9; unlocking idling capacity via 470; worker design issues in 476–7

Shinto, interrelatedness in 226

Singapore, nature-based urban design in 409–11

smart design: Design for Sustainable Behaviour using 317, *318;* digital media design as 175; electronics design as 161–2; GIS in urban planning for 187; Internet of Things using 161; political incentives for reinvention of 115, 120–2; structural change involving 435

social imaginery: global perspective framework on 108; structural change affecting 435

social innovation: human centered design for 199, *199;* spatio-social innovation level, in evolution of sustainable design 420–1, *422,* 423, *424,* 425

social justice: global perspective framework on 109–10; urban area lack of 183

'Social Networks, Host Resistance and Mortality' study 305

social practice theory, on habits *333,* 333–4, 338–9, 343, 440

social psychology: on Design for Sustainable Behaviour 317; on habits 328, 329, *330–2,* 330–3, 334–8, *336–7,* 343–4; on persuasion 365; on structural change 438–9

sociology: on cultural and emotional barriers to environmental change 388; on Design for Sustainable Behaviour 317, 322; on habits 328–9, *333,* 333–5, 343–4, 439; nature-based urban design roots in 401

socio-technical systems: evolution of sustainable design including 421, *422,* 423, *424,* 425–7; habits and 339–42, *340–1*

soil quality, feedback loops with 17–18, *18,* 20–1

solar technologies: applied sustainability related to 47; digital media energy via 171; humanitarian design using 240; localized economy inclusion of 99, 128–30; narrative on need for, at White House 363; political economy and development of 5; reinforcing loops with 18; Trombe wall using 128–9

spatio-social innovation, in evolution of sustainable design 420–1, *422,* 423, *424,* 425

spirituality: belief schematas for 437, 438; Buddhist 211–12, 213, 214, 215, 216, 220, 221–2, 223–4, 226–7; as ethical perspective 226–7

stability of system structures 17, 19

stakeholder mapping 64

STEAM (Science, Technology, Engineering, Arts and Math): challenges to 492–3; cohesive communication in 490; disciplinary knowledge exchange in 491; ecosystem restoration project via 489; edible packaging development via 488; framing the issue in 490; interdisciplinary approach in 483–4, 486, 487, 488–92, 494; knowledge silos *vs.* 483; methodology development in 490; overview of 416; prostheses development via 487–8; Sea Changes alignment with 489; STEM *vs.* 484–5, 492–3; story and evolution of 485–6; sustainable design and 484, 486–9, 494

Stella McCartney 69

STEM (Science, Technology, Engineering and Math): scale and integration of 70; STEAM *vs.* 484–5, 492–3; story and evolution of 484–5

stock-and-flow structures, in systems *15,* 15–16, 17, 20

Storey, Helen 288

structural change: to abstract infrastructures 436–7; agitation or discomfort from 443–4; to belief schematas 437–8; to concrete infrastructures 435; creative alienation with 444; within existing systems 441–2; historical attempts of 433–4; hypocrisy concerns with 444; within new systems 442–3; overview of 415, 433–4; to practices and habitus 439–41; to social values 436–7, 438–9; visioning of 442–3

substance use/abuse: citizen empowerment to address 453–7; Internet-based availability of 263–4

supply chain: electronics 149–51, 155–7; fashion industry 285; globalization impacts on 103; scale and management of 68–9

surrender, and mindfulness 221, 222, 226–7

Sustainability Insights tool 65

Sustainable Apparel Coalition 66

sustainable behavior *see* Design for Sustainable Behaviour

sustainable design: applied sustainability in 11, 40–52; behavior change with (*see* behavior change); biomimicry and 94, 416, 419, 425, 426, 459–68; careers and work environments for *151, 192, 271, 272, 295–311*, 408; circular economy and 7–8, 12, 74, 154, 158, 416, 426–7, 498–511; citizen empowerment via 415, 446–58; codesigning for development of 192, 250–61, 286–7, 289–90, 406, 448, 453–7; cultural influences on (*see* culture); data visualization as tool in 314, 372–86; Design for Sustainable Behaviour as 161, *162*, 313, 315–23, 328, 332, 335, 418–19; digital media issues in (*see* digital media; Internet use and applications); ecological theory in 12, 86–97 (*see also* ecological design); electronics global lifecycle and 100, 148–65; emotional influences on (*see* emotions); empathy expression via 191, 193–204, 206–17, 351; evolution of 415, 417–28; fashion and 192, 281–91 (*see also* clothing or apparel); Geographic Information Systems use in 100, 179–88; global impact of (*see* global impact); global perspective framework for 99, 101–13; habits and 313, 328–44, 439–41; holistic approach to (*see* holistic approach to design); human centered design in 75, 191, 193–204, 207; humanitarian design in 192, 231–45; identity alignment with (*see* identity); impactful design strategies for 11, 27–38; intercultural design collaborations for 99–100, 135–46; localized economies and 99, 125–33; mindfulness in 36, 191, 219–28; nature-based urban design as 314, 399–411; overview of 1–2; person-thing relationships influencing 313, 348–55, 418–19; political economy of 3–8, 94–5, 96; politics and sustainability influencing 99, 115–22, 287–8; rhetoric and persuasion in context of 314, 357–70; scale in (*see* scale); service design as (*see* service design); sharing economy and 416, 470–80; STEAM education evolution and 416, 483–94; structural change and 415, 433–44; systems thinking for (*see* systems thinking); users of (*see* users); values and ethics in (*see* ethical standards; morality; values)

Sylvan, John 24

systems thinking: ABCD planning method or backcasting for 45–6; applied sustainability in 11, 40–52; basics of 15–21; boundaries in 16, 20; characteristics of systems in 21–2; collective action in 25; conditions of sustainability in 13; designers as thinkers and leaders in 25; digital media environmental impacts in 170, 171–3; ecological theory in 12, 86–97; electronics design for systems-level sustainability as 162–4, *163–4*; escalation in 20; evolution of sustainable design including 421, *422*, 423, *424*, 425–7; feedback loops in 17–19, *17–19*, 20–1, 22; fixes that fail in 20; General Systems Theory on 215; goals in 16, 20, 24; hierarchy or nesting in 21; high-leverage design in 23–5; human centered design in *200*, 202–3; humanitarian design reflecting 234–5, *244*; impactful design strategies in 11, 27–38; intercultural design collaborations encouraging 139; intervention points in systems 23 (*see also* leverage points); Living Principles for Design framework for 46–7, *47*; The Natural Step™ framework for 44–5, 46; nature-based urban design in 400–1, 405–7; overview of 11–12; political economy of design addressing 8; problematic system behaviors in 19–21; resilience in 22; scale in (*see* scale); self-organization in 22; service design in 12, 73–82; socio-technical systems in 339–42, *340–1*, 421, *422*, 423, *424*, 425–7; STEAM education evolution using 483–4; stock-and-flow structures in *15*, 15–16, 17, 20; structural change and 415, 433–44; structure creating behavior possibilities in 17–19, *17–19*; sustainability as question in 13–15; in system dynamics 14; system engagement through design in 23–5; systems mapping analysis of 48–9, 64 (*see also* life-cycle assessment); tragedy of the commons in 20–1; unsustainability in 14, 24–5; urban planning and management using 179; Whole Systems and Lifecycle Thinking method analysis of 48–9

take-back and refurbishment programs 68

taxation: localized economies affected by 131–2; sharing economy effects on 478

technologies: cellular (*see* cellular phones); data visualization 314, 372–86; dependence on 6–7; design for efficiency adoption of 274–5; design for sufficiency adoption of 274, 275; digital (*see* digital media); electronics (*see* electronics global lifecycle); emotions generated by interactions with 195; human centered design ties to innovation in 194, 195; Internet-based (*see* Internet use and applications); political economy of design and use of 5–7, 8; renewable energy (*see* hydroelectric power; renewable energy; solar technologies; wind technologies); scale and limits of 58–9; smart technologies 115, 120–2, 161–2, 175, 187, 317, *318*, 435; socio-technical systems and 339–42, *340–1*, 421, *422*, 423, *424*, 425–7; STEAM education including 416, 483–94; STEM education including 70, 484–5, 492–3; technological design perspectives on circular economy *505*, 508–9

TEK (traditional ecological knowledge) 92

telework, digital media and 176

The Natural Step™(TNS) 44–5, 46

three-dimensional (3D) printing 163, *163*

Three Elements Model of habits *333*, 333–4, 338, 342

Three Gorges Dam 206–8
350.org 388
time: Internet effects on time/space orientation *271, 272*; metaphors on 360; scale and limits of 59; short- *vs.* long-term humanitarian design solutions 231, 232–3, 235, 237–8; temporal fallacy in person-thing relationships 351–2; temporal scale over 56–7, 67–8; time differences in intercultural design collaborations 138, 139
toxic shell game 63–4
Toyoda, Eiji 70
trade: fair trade movement in 108, 127; global economy based on 126, 131
tragedy of the commons 20–1, 62
Traity 476
TRANSFER research 289
Transition Management 441
Transition Town movement 203
transportation: applied sustainability of 42–3; capacity building related to 235; digital media applications for 175, 176, 177; electronics global lifecycle including *149*; fixes that fail in 20; global economy reliance on 126, 131; light-rail systems 3–4; nature-based urban design consideration of 399, 405, 406; political economy of design of 3–4; scale challenges related to 63; sharing economy affecting 470–1, 474, 475, 476, 477, 481n1; stock-and-flow related to *15*, 15–16, 17, 20; systems thinking on *15*, 15–16, 17, 20, 63
transthoretical model (TTM) of habits 332–3, 335
Triple Bottom Line approach: applied sustainability using principles of 46, 51–2; Living Principles for Design framework based on 46
Trombe wall 128–9
Tufte, Edward 376–7
'Turn It Off' campaign 366–7, *367*

uncomfortableness: impactful design strategies creating 36–8; structural change creating 443–4
understandability, scale and limits of 60
United Nations: Brundtland Commission Report 13, 94; COP 21 Climate Conference 288; Development Program 234; Environment Programme 55, 56, 237; Framework Convention on Climate Change 388; High Commissionaire for Refugees 234, 237, 239, 241; humanitarian aid from 231; Human Rights Council 288; Sustainable Development Goals 101, 112, 136, 148
unlearning, and mindfulness 221, 222, 224–5
unsustainability, systems view of 14, 24–5
urban areas: biogenic *vs.* biocidic 283; citizen empowerment in 415, 446–58; energy and resource use in 126–7; evolution of sustainable design in 425–6; fashion in 281, 282–5, 291; GIS use for sustainability of 100, 179–88; modernity

and changes in 283; nature-based urban design for 314, 399–411; resilience of 446–8; smart design of 115, 120–2, 187; sustainable city visual narrative of 145–6
users: behavior of (*see* behavior; behavior change); civic participation of 4, 7, 181, 186–7, 188, 388, 393–4, 406; codesigning with 192, 250–61, 286–7, 289–90, 406, 448, 453–7; data visualization engagement of *382–3, 382–4*; ecological design designer-user interaction 120; electronics global lifecycle influenced by trends and behavior of 160–4, *162*; empowerment of 415, 446–58; human centered design user experience 195, 196; lifestyles of (*see* lifestyle); person-thing relationships of 313, 348–55, 418–19; sharing economy among 416, 470–80

values: abstract infrastructures for 436–7; alignment of, with work environment 298, 300, 303–4; aspirational aspect of 303; of care 437; careers and work environments reflecting 192, 295–311; codesigning for development reflecting 192, 250–61; of efficiency 436; empathy as expression of (*see* empathy); fashion reflecting 281–2, 283, 284–5; human centered design focus on 191, 193–204; identification of personal 300, *300–2*; of individualism 436; inner alignment of 298; Internet use influences on 192, 270–3, *271–2*; mindfulness of 36, 191, 219–28; overview of chapters on 191–2; primary and shadow 302; self-awareness foundation in 296–7; structural changes to 436–7, 438–9; value-action gap 329; value-action translation 303–4; Values Wheel model of 298–300, *299–302*, 302; of work or effort 436–7; *see also* ethical standards; morality
virtual products, scale consideration of 65–6; *see also* digital media
volume, scale utilizing 66
von Bertalanffy, Ludwig 215
von Bush's Do-It-Together 289

Waag Society 488
water: applied sustainability issues related to 41, 42; biomimicry design related to 461, 464; data visualization related to 375, *376*, 377; edible packaging for 488; habits related to 337–8; humanitarian design related to 235, 236, 237; hydroelectric power from 206–8, 435; intercultural design collaboration activity tracking interactions with 139–40, 143; localized economy projects for access to 129; mindfulness-related analogies with 220, 226, 228; nature-based urban design consideration of 405, 406; quality of 20–1, 150; rhetoric and persuasion related to *362*, 362–3; scale and limits related to 57, 58, 61; self-sufficiency movements on 392, 396

water quality: electronics global lifecycle impacts on 150; feedback loops with 20–1
weapons, political economy of design of 5
weather forecasting, data visualization in 373
Web Bloat Score 51
Web Design 50–1, 175, 201, 383
Web Index 52
Whole Systems and Lifecycle Thinking method 48–9
wind technologies: digital media energy via 171; localized economy inclusion of 129; market-based approaches to 128; political economy and development of 5
work environments *see* careers and work environments
worldviews: belief schematas for 437–8; global perspective framework for different 105–6
Wright, Frank Lloyd 4

xenophobia, as globalization response 104
Xyaat community ecotourism cooperative 250, 255, 258–60